Politics in Western Europe

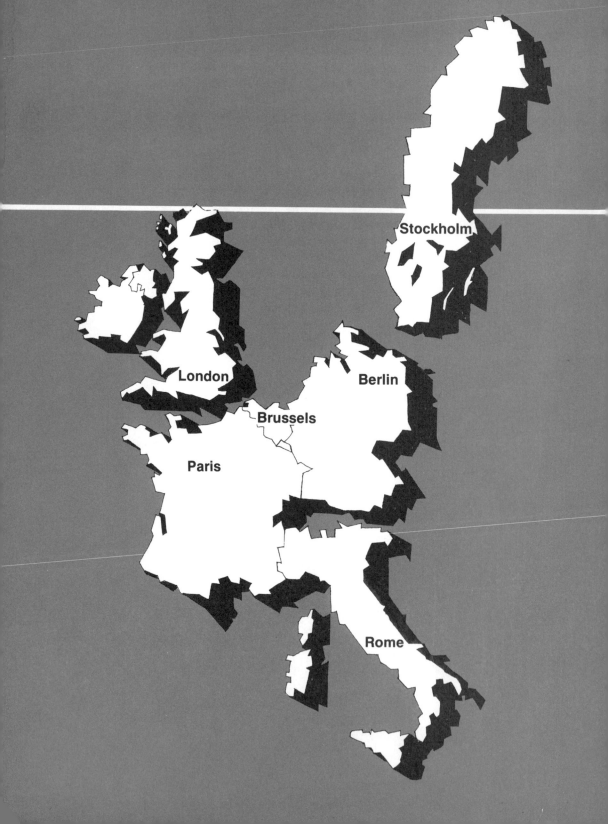

Politics in Western Europe

An Introduction to the Politics of the United
Kingdom, France, Germany, Italy, Sweden,
and the European Community

M. Donald Hancock
Vanderbilt University

David P. Conradt
East Carolina University

B. Guy Peters
University of Pittsburgh

William Safran
University of Colorado, Boulder

Raphael Zariski
University of Nebraska, Lincoln

Chatham House Publishers, Inc.
Chatham, New Jersey

Politics in Western Europe

Chatham House Publishers, Inc.
Post Office Box One
Chatham, New Jersey 07928

Publisher: Edward Artinian
Production editor: Chris Kelaher
Interior design: Quentin Fiore
Cover design: Lawrence Ratzkin
Composition: Bang, Motley, Olufsen
Printing and binding: R.R. Donnelley and Sons Company

Library of Congress Cataloging in Publication Data

Politics in western Europe / M. Donald Hancock ... [et al.].
      p.   cm.
   Includes bibliographical references and index.
   ISBN 0-934540-30-6
   1. Europe—Politics and government—1945–
I. Hancock, M. Donald.
JN94.A91P65 1993
940.55—dc20
                                             92-25189
                                             CIP

Manufactured in the United States of America
10 9 8 7 6 5 4 3 2

Contents

Part Four: Italy   Raphael Zariski

Part Five: Sweden   M. Donald Hancock

Part Six: The European Community
M. Donald Hancock and B. Guy Peters

List of Tables

List of Figures

Preface

In a rapidly changing political and economic world, Western Europe continues to command the attention of students, informed citizens, scholars, and other professionals. Democratic principles and the postwar economic performance of the West European nations helped inspire the dramatic events during the late 1980s and early 1990s that transformed the countries of Central and Eastern Europe and the former Soviet Union into fledgling market economies and pluralist political systems. Continued movement toward economic and political union among the members of the European Community underscores the EC's importance as an increasingly powerful actor in regional and global affairs. Domestically, national politics have assumed new and, in some cases, unsettling dimensions in response to internationalization, increased electoral volatility, and an ever-evolving political agenda.

The emergent "new Europe" encompasses both continuity and change. Democratic constitutional principles and institutional arrangements—well-established on the basis of historical experience in the United Kingdom, France, and Sweden and the product of postwar consensus in countries such as West Germany and Italy—remain firmly entrenched as the basis of parliamentary government throughout Western Europe. Traditional political parties and organized interest groups continue to occupy center political stage. At the same time, new movements—ranging from the Greens on the non-Marxist left to Sweden's populist New Democracy and the rightist *Republikaner* in Germany —have emerged in recent years to challenge the established order. Familiar conflicts over economic management and social welfare dominate national electoral campaigns, yet new issues have arisen concerning immigrants and the rights of women and various social minorities. While the North Atlantic Treaty Organization still provides the basis for West European national security, the 1991 Treaty on European Union signed by the twelve members of the EC points toward the potential establishment of a new regional security system. Germany's unification in 1990 constitutes another important change in Europe's political and economic landscape. The Federal Republic confronts formidable financial and social costs in westernizing former East Germany, but unification has significantly enhanced Germany's status and influence within Europe.

Contributors to this book address these disparate themes of contemporary West European politics with an empirical focus on the United Kingdom, France, Germany, Italy, Sweden, and the European Community. The volume is organized to facilitate both single-country analysis and cross-national comparison of key political variables: the historical and cultural context of national politics, important institutional and political actors, the exercise of power, and prospective political change. Twenty-five figures dispersed throughout the text display cross-national comparisons among the five West European nations and the United States at given points in time. Their purpose is to present visually useful "snapshots" of salient demographic, political, economic, and social characteristics of each country. In addition, detailed statistical tables on postwar elections, executive leadership, and socioeconomic performance are included in the appendix to make possible systematic comparisons among the various countries over time. The data in these tables also serve as a basis for generating hypotheses and conducting preliminary research.

This volume is dedicated to students of comparative politics who seek enhanced knowledge of the new Europe at a time when all Western democracies confront the challenge of adaptive economic, social, and political response to changing international conditions. We would like to thank our students, colleagues, and others who have contributed to our own understanding of European affairs. A special note of appreciation is due Joe Adams, Larry Romans, and Stacy McMillen at Vanderbilt University for their assistance in compiling the statistical data contained in the figures and the tables in the appendix.

— M. Donald Hancock
Vanderbilt University

Introduction

The study of comparative politics serves multiple purposes. These include acquiring greater knowledge about similarities and differences among nations and their subsystems, testing various scientific propositions, and deriving political lessons from the experience of others that might usefully be applied or studiously avoided in one's own place and time.[1] Throughout the evolution of comparative politics as a core field within political science, this endeavor has involved varying degrees of empirical, normative, and theoretical analysis.[2] Traditionally, Western scholars concentrated on constitutional norms and institutional arrangements in the established democratic systems of the United Kingdom, the United States, France, and, for a time, Weimar Germany. After World War II, many of the most creative comparative scholars turned their attention to problems of modernization, leadership, and revolution in the Third World countries of Asia, Latin America, the Middle East, and Africa in an effort to devise more rigorous concepts and methods of comparative political analysis.[3] More recently, scholars have reincorporated West European politics into the mainstream of comparative politics as they have sought to extend and refine basic concepts of the field.[4] This volume of country surveys is testimony to the renewed relevance of the West European political experience for comparative purposes.

A compelling justification for the comparative analysis of West European politics lies in the historical contributions of nations such as Britain, France, Germany, and Italy to basic philosophical, cultural, and institutional tenets of Western civilization. Immigrants from throughout Europe have helped create new nations in the United States, Canada,

Israel, and elsewhere. Many of their descendants understandably look to Europe to comprehend the significance of their national origins and the European roots of their own country's constitutional and political development.

From a historical perspective, Western Europe also offers important insights for the comparative study of different "paths to modernity." The striking contrast between the success of Britain and Scandinavia in sustaining an evolutionary pattern of political change and the far more tumultuous experience of France, Germany, and Italy during the nineteenth and twentieth centuries provides crucial knowledge about underlying factors of system stability (versus instability) and political effectiveness.[5] In the contemporary world of nations, Europe's postwar political and economic achievements—including its democratic convergence and unprecedented material growth—comprise a series of "most similar cases" broadly comparable to other advanced industrial democracies in North America, Asia, and parts of the British Commonwealth. As such, Western Europe provides a rich laboratory for the comparative study of political parties and organized interest groups, political culture, institutional arrangements, economic management, social services, and public policy.[6]

A Common Analytical Framework

Consistent with these multiple purposes of comparative political inquiry, this volume addresses fundamental features of modern European politics on the basis of a common analytical framework designed to facilitate both single-country and cross-national analysis. Various country specialists address five important European nations according to the following criteria: (1) the context of national politics (including basic geographic and demographic factors, history, and political culture); (2) formal decision-making and implementation structures; (3) political parties, organized interest groups, and electoral behavior; (4) the uses of political power; and (5) the future of politics under changing domestic and international conditions.[7] Accompanying the country sections are tables, graphs, and a set of statistical appendices containing empirical comparative data.

The choice of country studies is based on a variety of considerations. One is the traditional inclusion of the United Kingdom and France in most comparative courses on European politics. Both countries have provided major contributions to the emergence of Western democracy and continue to play important political and economic roles in regional and world affairs. A second consideration is the significance of Germany as a compelling instance of fundamental system change. Theoretically and empirically, the German case offers crucial insights into processes of socioeconomic and political development under successive historical conditions of regime discontinuity, postwar stability in the West, the failure of Communism in the East, and the recent unification of the Federal Republic and the German Democratic Republic. Third, the inclusion of Italy and Sweden provides important systemic contrasts to more familiar case studies with respect to their distinctive patterns of postwar political dominance—Christian Democratic versus Social Democratic, respectively—and the central role of civil servants and organized interest groups in the policy-making process. Moreover, Sweden's status as one of the world's most comprehensive welfare states and its innovative experiments in the area of workplace reform raise challenging questions about future directions of social and economic change in advanced industrial democracies.

The sixth section of this volume deals with the European Community (EC). Since the early 1950s, institutionalized economic cooperation among principal West European nations has resulted in the emergence of the EC as an increasingly powerful regional political system. The completion of an integrated market for both goods and services by the end of 1992 and the projected attainment of economic, monetary, and political union among the EC's twelve member states by the middle of the decade underscore the Community's importance as a key economic and political actor in its own right.[8] The distinctive features of the EC as a regional political system compel the authors to depart from the analytical framework that is used in the country studies elsewhere in the volume. Instead, they concentrate on institutional actors, decision-making processes, and policy outcomes.

Contrasting System Types

While each author concentrates on a single case, their analyses illuminate contrasting features of three basic types of democratic polities that transcend national boundaries: (1) *pluralist* (the United Kingdom and the EC), (2) *étatist* (France and Italy, albeit for different reasons), and (3) *democratic corporatist* (Sweden and to a lesser extent Germany).[9] The first of these types—pluralist systems—is characterized by dispersed political authority and a multiplicity of autonomous organized interest groups representing employers, farmers, labor, and other special interests vis-à-vis the state. In such systems competitive economic and electoral relations dominate intergroup relations, with most groups oriented more toward short-term material and social gains than intermediate or long-term goals of system transformation. A dominant feature of pluralist systems is group reliance on coalition formation—often with respect to specific policy issues—as a means to maximize a group's economic and/or political influence. Policy making in pluralist systems tends to be incremental and tentative, with successful outcomes dependent on the strength (or fragility) of winning coalitions. These decision-making features characterize both the United Kingdom and the European Community as well as non-European polities such as the United States and Canada.

In contrast, étatist systems are political regimes that embody more centralized authority structures and policy-making processes. A chief feature of étatist regimes is the concentration of bureaucratic power at the apex of the political system, as is the case in Italy. If accompanied by a parallel concentration of executive power (as in the Fifth Republic of France), the likely result is a high degree of institutional efficacy in the political process. Thus, forceful policies can be more efficiently decided and implemented than is typically the case in pluralist systems, but for that very reason they can also be more readily reversed by an incumbent or successor government.

Democratic corporatist systems, finally, encompass institutionalized arrangements whereby government officials, business groups, and organized labor jointly participate on a sustained basis in making (and in some cases implementing) economic and social policies. Such decisions are subsequently enacted through executive decrees and/or legislative endorsement.[10] Democratic corporatism is more highly developed in Sweden, the other Scandinavian countries, and Austria than in other West European countries; yet, primarily in the sphere of national economic policy making, corporatist linkages exist in the Federal Republic of Germany as well.[11] By facilitating institutionalized participation by organized interest groups in the political process, democratic corporatism encourages majoritarian government and a consensual style of politics. Critics, however, fault corporatist arrangements because they tend to bypass legislative channels of representation, impede leadership accountability, and discourage democratic participation on the part of rank-and-file members of trade unions and other mass organizations.[12] These different system types are relevant for explaining contrasting patterns of socioeconomic and political performance on the part of modern democracies. Without question, many aspects of system performance —including those measured by basic indicators such as annual rates of economic growth, inflation, and unemployment levels—are influenced by external economic and other factors beyond the direct control of national policy actors. Nonetheless, national policy-making structures and processes mediate the domestic economic and social consequences of exogenous trends and events. As Hugh Heclo has observed, in commenting on different national responses to the international crisis of stagflation during the 1970s and early 1980s: "Each nation has embarked on a search for innovations in economic policy making, although each has done so in its own way. This recent agitation for economic policy innovation in the midst of constraints provides a good example of what [has been] termed 'structured variation' in public policy."[13] As contemporary European politics demonstrates, "structured variations" among nations with respect to policy choices and their effects on socioeconomic performance are products of contrasting patterns of institutionalized power, different ideological preferences on the part of governing political parties, and varying degrees of access by the principal organized interest groups to national policy counsels.

The central questions of comparative political analysis remain, in short, who governs, on behalf of what values, with the collaboration of what groups, and with what socioeconomic and political consequences. The experience of the five European democracies included in this volume and the European Community reveals illuminating answers.

Notes

1. This definition of comparative politics is based on Robert Dahl, *Modern Political Analysis,* 4th ed. (Englewood Cliffs, N.J.: Prentice-Hall, 1984); and Lawrence C. Mayer, *Comparative Political Inquiry: A Methodological Survey* (Homewood, Ill.: Dorsey, 1972).

2. Dahl, *Modern Political Analysis.*

3. For a summary overview of innovation in postwar approaches to comparative political analysis, see Ronald H. Chilcote, *Theories of Comparative Politics: The Search for a Paradigm* (Boulder, Colo.: Westview, 1981). A critical assessment of the failure of the behavioral revolution to live up to many of its promises can be found in Lawrence C. Mayer, *Redefining Comparative Politics: Promise Versus Performance* (Newbury Park, Calif.: Sage Library of Social Research, 1989). Standard sources on the methodology of comparative research include Mattei Dogan and Dominique Pelassy, *How to Compare Nations: Strategies in Comparative Politics* (Chatham, N.J.: Chatham House, 1984); Adam Przeworski and Henry

Teune, *The Logic of Comparative Social Inquiry* (New York: Wiley-Interscience, 1970), and *The Methodology of Comparative Research,* ed. Robert Holt and John Turner (New York: Free Press, 1970).

4. Note in particular the increased relevance of West European politics for the comparative study of public policy. See Arnold J. Heidenheimer, Hugh Heclo, and Carolyn Teich Adams, *Comparative Public Policy: The Politics of Social Choice in America, Europe, and Japan,* 3d ed. (New York: St. Martin's Press, 1990).

5. See Barrington Moore, Jr., *Social Origins of Dictatorship and Democracy* (Boston: Beacon Press, 1966); and *The Formation of National States in Western Europe,* ed. Charles Tilly (Princeton, N.J.: Princeton University Press, 1975).

6. Important examples of comparative studies of groups, institutions, culture, and public policy incorporating European data include Francis Castles, *The Impact of Parties: Politics and Policies in Democratic Capitalist Society* (Beverly Hills, Calif.: Sage, 1982); Giovanni Sartori, *Parties and Party Systems: A Framework for Analysis* (New York: Cambridge University Press, 1976); Russell Dalton, et al., *Electoral Change in Advanced Industrial Democracies: Alignment or Realignment?* (Princeton, N.J.: Princeton University Press, 1984); *West European Party Systems,* ed. Peter H. Merkl (New York: Free Press, 1979); Kay Lawson, *Comparative Study of Political Parties* (New York: St. Martin's Press, 1976); *Organizing Interests in Western Europe: Pluralism, Corporatism, and the Transformation of Politics,* ed. Suzanne Berger (New York: Cambridge University Press, 1981); Gabriel Almond and Sidney Verba, *The Civic Culture: Political Attitudes and Democracy in Five Nations* (Boston: Little, Brown, 1963, 1988); *The Civic Culture Revisited,* ed. Gabriel Almond and Sidney Verba (Newbury Park, Calif.: Sage, 1990); Ronald Inglehart, *The Silent Revolution: Changing Values and Political Styles Among Western Publics* (Princeton, N.J.: Princeton University Press, 1977); Inglehart, *Culture Shift in Advanced Industrial Democracies* (Princeton, N.J.: Princeton University Press, 1990); Robert Dahl, *Dilemmas of Pluralist Democracy: Autonomy vs. Control* (New Haven, Conn: Yale University Press, 1982); Arend Lijphart, *Democracy in Plural Societies: A Comparative Exploration* (New Haven, Conn: Yale University Press, 1977); Theda Skocpol, *States and Social Revolutions: A Comparative Analysis of France, Russia, and China* (New York: Cambridge University Press, 1979); Peter Hall, *Governing the Economy: The Politics of State Intervention in Britain and France* (New York: Oxford University Press, 1986); Douglas A. Hibbs, Jr., *The Political Economy of Industrial Democracies* (Cambridge, Mass.: Harvard University Press, 1987); and Gøsta Esping-Andersen, *The Three Worlds of Welfare Capitalism* (Princeton, N.J.: Princeton University Press, 1990).

7. The same conceptual framework is utilized in the companion Chatham House volume to this one entitled *Comparative Politics: An Introduc-*

tion to the Politics of the United Kingdom, France, Germany, and the Soviet Union (Chatham, N.J.: Chatham House, 1983).

8. The original signatories of treaties establishing the European Coal and Steel Community in 1951 and the European Economic Community in 1957 included France, West Germany, Italy, Belgium, the Netherlands, and Luxembourg. The United Kingdom, Denmark, and Ireland joined the Community in 1972 and were followed by Greece in 1981 and Spain and Portugal in 1987.

9. The distinction between étatist, pluralist, and democratic corporatist regimes is utilized to help explain contrasting patterns of economic policy management in *Managing Modern Capitalism: Industrial Renewal and Workplace Democracy in the United States and Western Europe*, ed. M. Donald Hancock, John Logue, and Bernt Schiller (Westport, Conn.: Greenwood, 1991).

10. Excellent compilations of reprinted articles and original research on varieties of democratic corporatism can be found in Philippe Schmitter and Gerhard Lehmbruch, eds., *Trends toward Corporatist Intermediation* (Beverly Hills: Sage, 1979) and in Lehmbruch and Schmitter, eds., *Patterns of Corporatist Policy-Making* (Beverly Hills: Sage, 1982). Also see Reginald J. Harrison, *Pluralism and Corporatism: The Political Evolution of Modern Democracies* (Boston: Allen and Unwin, 1980).

11. Democratic corporatism was most fully institutionalized in former West Germany in the form of "concerted action," which involved high-level consultations focusing on economic policy among government officials and representatives of employer associations and trade unions during the years from 1967 to 1977. Since then formal trilateral policy sessions have been replaced by much more informal policy discussions among key economic actors that are periodically convened at the behest of the federal chancellor. See M. Donald Hancock, *West Germany: The Politics of Democratic Corporatism* (Chatham, N.J.: Chatham House, 1989).

12. From a critical ideological perspective, Leo Panitch argues that corporatism in liberal democracies promotes the "cooptation" of workers into the capitalist economic order and thus impedes efforts to achieve greater industrial and economic democracy. Panitch, "The Development of Corporatism in Liberal Democracies," *Comparative Political Studies* 10 (1977): 61-90.

13. Heidenheimer, Heclo, and Adams, *Comparative Public Policy,* 136.

Politics in Western Europe

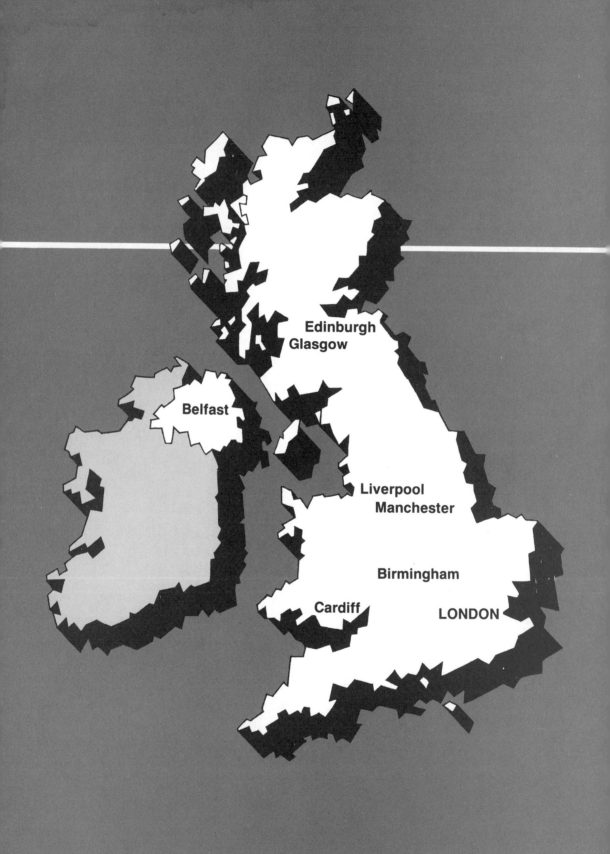

Edinburgh
Glasgow

Belfast

Liverpool
Manchester

Birmingham

Cardiff

LONDON

Part One

The United Kingdom

B. Guy Peters

1

The Context of British Politics

British society and British politics are often discussed in terms of homogeneity and integration. Authors have written of the absence of significant social cleavages other than social class and of the presence of a uniform set of political and social values. Consensus is said to exist on the nature of the political system and the general policies of government. The impression commonly given is one of homogeneity, stability, and indeed of a rather boring locale in which to study politics, an impression reinforced by the ability of one political leader—Margaret Thatcher —to stay in power for over a decade.

In reality, the social and political systems of the United Kingdom are substantially more diverse than they are frequently portrayed, and many of the factors that divide other democracies politically also divide the citizens of the United Kingdom. Not only is there diversity, but the setting of British politics has a number of seemingly contradictory elements that make the management of government much more of a balancing act than might be thought at first glance. In fact, the genius of British politics in maintaining a stable political system over several centuries is not the good fortune of operating in a homogeneous society but the development of a set of institutions, values, and customs that permit the pragmatic acceptance of diversity and an accommodation to gradual change. This chapter explores some of the contradictory elements in the environment of British politics and their relationship to the functioning of the political system.

A United Kingdom of Four Countries

Perhaps the fundamental point of diversity in British politics is that the United Kingdom is a multinational state composed of four parts. To begin, therefore, let us introduce some nomenclature with real political importance. The proper name of the nation usually referred to as Great Britain is the United Kingdom of Great Britain and Northern Ireland. Great Britain, in turn, is composed of England, Wales, and Scotland. All are constituent parts of the United Kingdom, albeit rather unequal partners in terms of population and economic productivity. Over 83 percent of the total population of the United Kingdom lives in England, 9 percent in Scotland, 5 percent in Wales, and 3 percent in Northern Ireland. Over 90 percent of total wages and salaries are paid in England, with only 1 percent going to residents of Northern Ireland.

The three non-English components of the United Kingdom—or the Celtic Fringe, as it is sometimes called—joined with England at a number of times and in a number of ways.[1] Wales was added first, by conquest, in 1301. The English and Scottish crowns were united in 1603 when the Scottish James I became the first Stuart king of England, and the parliaments of the two countries were joined by the Act of Union in 1707. This did not, however, terminate the conflict between the northern and southern portions of Great Britain. Scottish uprisings in 1715 and again in 1745 resulted in English (or British) occupation of Scotland and the outlawing of a number of Scottish customs, such as the kilt and bagpipes. These restrictions were removed, at least informally, by 1822, and manifestations of Scottish nationalism have been substantially less violent since that time.

The involvement of the British government in Ireland has had a long and tortuous history. English armies began invading Ireland in 1170; the island was finally conquered in 1603 and was joined with Great Britain to form the United Kingdom in 1800. The unity was more legal than actual, and Irish Home Rule was a persistent political issue during the second half of the nineteenth century. Political arguments were accompanied by increasing violence and then by armed uprisings against British rule. Following a long period of negotiation, the twenty-six southern counties of Ireland were granted independence in 1922 as the Irish Free State (later the Republic of Ireland), while six northern counties in Ulster remained a part of the United Kingdom. This partition did not solve "the Irish Question." Continuing violence between Catholics seeking to join with the rest of Ireland and Protestants desiring to maintain their unity with the United Kingdom is a persistent problem for any British government. The Anglo-Irish Agreement, signed in 1985 by the United Kingdom and the Irish Republic and meant to foster a spirit of compromise, has not put an end to "the troubles" in Northern Ireland.

The unity of the United Kingdom does not prevent the expression of a number of differences among its constituent parts, and to some degree those differences are enshrined in law and the political structure. Each of the three non-English components of the United Kingdom has a cabinet department that is responsible for its affairs. Laws are commonly passed in Parliament with separate acts for England and Wales, for Scotland, and for Northern Ireland; Scottish and Welsh legislation is treated somewhat differently in Parliament. Prior to the imposition of direct rule in Northern Ireland in 1972, Stormont, which was the parliament of Northern Ireland, had a major role in policy making for that province, and there is still a separate Northern Ireland Civil Service, which is responsible for implementing the policies of the government in London.

Law, language, and religion also differ in the four parts of the United Kingdom. Scottish law is derived in part from French and Roman law as well as from common law, and various legal procedures and offices differ between English and Scottish practice. Language is also different in various parts of the United Kingdom. Welsh is accepted as a second language for Wales, although only about 20 percent of the population can speak it and only about 1 percent speak it as their only language. Some people in Scotland and Northern Ireland speak forms of the Gaelic language, but it has not been accorded formal legal status, perhaps because only just over 1 percent of the population speak Gaelic. Finally, the established religions of the parts of the nation are different: The Church of England (Anglican) is established in England, the Church of Scotland (Presbyterian) in Scotland; Wales and Northern Ireland do not have established churches because of their religious diversity. The diversity in Wales between Anglicans and various "chapel religions" (Methodism in particular) has not had the dire consequences of the differences between Protestants and Catholics in Northern Ireland, but it has been a source of political diversity.

Finally, the four components of the United Kingdom differ economically. This is less true of their economic structures than of their economic success. Differences in the proportion of the working population employed in manual jobs, or even in the proportion employed in agriculture, are relatively slight between England and the Celtic Fringe. The major differences in patterns of employment are the much higher rates of public employment in the Celtic Fringe. Measures of economic success do differ, with levels of unemployment much higher in the non-English parts of the United Kingdom than in England. In discussing the economy, however, the divide in the United Kingdom is as much between the south of England and the rest of the country as it is between England and the non-English countries. Unemployment rates in some parts of northern England are as high as or higher than in Scotland or Wales, while London and the southeast have at times had shortages of workers (see table 1.1). Average personal income in all three parts of the Celtic Fringe is also lower than in England, and by a large margin in the case of Northern Ireland. These economic differences have political importance, for they create a sense of deprivation among non-English groups within the United Kingdom, as well as among some residents of northern England.

TABLE I.I

UNEMPLOYMENT LEVELS BY REGION,

JUNE 1991

England		Northern Ireland	13.8%
North	10.3%	Scotland	9.0
Northwest	9.5	Wales	8.6
Yorkshire	8.7		
W. Midlands	8.5		
E. Midlands	7.4		
Southwest	7.4		
Greater London	7.9		
Southeast	6.9		
East Anglia	5.8		

SOURCE: Department of Employment

The differences among the four countries of the United Kingdom are manifested politically, although fortunately infrequently with the violence of Ulster politics. Scottish nationalism never really died following the Act of Union, but it has experienced a number of cyclical declines. Votes for the Scottish National party (SNP) had an upsurge from 1959 to 1974. The SNP at least doubled its vote in every election from 1959 to 1974, and received more than 36 percent of the Scottish vote in the October 1974 election but only 14 percent in 1987. Welsh nationalism has been less successful as a political force, but Plaid Cymru, the Welsh National party, won over 13 percent of the Welsh vote in the October 1974 election. Since 1974, nationalist voting has declined, but it remains a significant factor in these "Celtic" portions of the United

Kingdom. Party politics in Northern Ireland, which has been based on cleavages of the seventeenth century as much as the twentieth century, bears little resemblance to politics in the rest of the United Kingdom.

The first thing, therefore, that we must understand about the United Kingdom is that it is a single state composed of separate parts. Unlike the states of the United States, these elements of the union have no reserved powers, but only powers delegated to them by the central government. The political system remains unitary while still allowing a certain degree of latitude for the Scottish, Welsh, and Northern Ireland offices in the administration of policies. Only rarely has the unity of the United Kingdom been questioned by its constituent parts, at least since the Scottish uprising of 1745. One such challenge was at least partially successful, however, and most of Ireland did receive its independence. The failure of referenda on the devolution of additional powers to Scotland and Wales in 1979 appears to make the unity of the nation even more secure, but this is but one more event in a long history of regional and national politics within the United Kingdom.

Stability and Change

A second feature of the context of contemporary politics in the United Kingdom is the continuity of social and political institutions combined with a significant degree of change. If a subject of Queen Victoria were to return during the reign of Elizabeth II, he or she would find very little changed—at least on the surface. Most of the same political institutions would be operational, including the monarchy, which has vanished in a number of other European nations. Laws would still be made by the House of Commons and the House of Lords, and there would still be a prime minister linking Crown and Parliament. There would be a new political party commanding one of the more important positions in partisan politics—the Labour party—but party politics would still be primarily *two*-party politics. Finally, the majority of the subjects of the queen would be loyal and supportive of the basic structures and policies of the government.

At the same time that there has been this great continuity, there has also been great change. The political system has been greatly democratized since Victorian times. When Queen Victoria came to the throne, only about 3 percent of the adult population were eligible to vote; that despite the "Great Reform Act" of 1832. In the reign of Elizabeth II, almost all adults are entitled to vote. Before 1911, the House of Lords was almost an equal partner in making legislation; since that date, the

House of Lords has exercised only minor influence over policy. A Victorian prime minister was definitely *primus inter pares* ("first among equals"), while in the twentieth century collegial patterns of decision making have changed to create something approaching a presidential role for the prime minister. And the monarchy, which in Victoria's day still had substantial influence over policy, has today been constitutionally reduced to virtual impotence. Finally, but not least in importance, the United Kingdom has changed from perhaps the strongest nation on earth and the imperial master of a far-flung empire to a second-class power in a nuclear age.

Social and economic trends have paralleled political trends. Just as the monarchy has been preserved, so too has a relatively stratified social system that includes hereditary (as well as life) peerages. In contrast, the growth of working-class organizations such as trade unions has tended to lessen the domination of the upper classes and to generate some democratization of the society as well as the political system. The economic structure of the United Kingdom is still primarily based on free enterprise, but government ownership and regulation have had a significant impact. Compared with other industrialized nations, the British economy is no longer the great engine of production it once was. The relative poverty of the United Kingdom, compared to its European and North American counterparts, has severely restricted the policy choices that are open to government but has not significantly affected governmental stability. Whether governmental stability can continue, with high levels of unemployment among minority populations (especially the young), will be a major question in British politics.

The evolutionary change so characteristic of British political life has been facilitated by the absence of a written constitution. It would be more accurate to say the absence of a single written document serving as a constitution, for a number of documents (Magna Carta, the Bill of Rights, the Petition of Right, the Statute of Westminster) have constitutional status. In addition, the Parliament of the day, expressing the political will of the British people, is competent to do virtually anything it deems necessary, without the limitations of judicial review, as in the United States. Such constitutionally unlimited powers have the potential for great tyranny, inasmuch as governments are restrained only by other politicians, the threat of elections, and their own good sense.

The same political system has persisted for a number of years in the United Kingdom, except that it is greatly changed. Like American constitutional principles, British constitutional principles are undergoing constant change and adjustment in the face of changing conditions. Perhaps the major difference is that formal change is less necessary in the United Kingdom because change in practice is sufficient to produce a change in principle.

The Political Culture of the United Kingdom

Much of the ability to accommodate to political change while maintaining older political institutions in Britain may be explained by the political culture of the United Kingdom. That is to say, it may be explained by the values and beliefs that citizens have about politics and government. One way of describing this culture has been "traditionally modern."[2] A number of traditional views are combined with a number of modern elements to produce a blend that, if apparently internally contradictory, appears to function well and produce effective government. This culture has not been static but has permitted relatively gradual change based on pragmatic acceptance of changing national needs. The traditional elements of the political culture are best known, with deference, trust, and pragmatism the most important for an understanding of how the British political system functions. As with any statement about national cultures or patterns of values, these statements may appear to be a stereotype; taken with a grain of salt, these observations on political culture can help us understand not only how British politicians and citizens function politically but also how they think about politics.

In the first place, the British population is generally said to be deferential to authority. Authority implies the lack of opposition by citizens to the actions of their government, or perhaps even the positive acceptance of those actions. The British government has, by all accounts, a large reservoir of authority, for few citizens question the correctness of the current political arrangements or the right of the government to make and enforce laws. The diffuse support the populace gives the political system and its willingness to obey laws and accept the authoritative decrees of government make the United Kingdom a much easier nation to govern than most.

There have been only a few major challenges to the authority of elected governments in the United Kingdom—aside from the peculiar politics of Ulster. One is the trade unions' attempts to bring down Conservative governments and their economic and industrial policies. This succeeded against the Heath government in 1973–74 but not against Mrs. Thatcher in the mid-1980s. In both cases the miners were the central union involved. The miners were able to bring about the changes they desired with the fall of Heath, but a year-long strike against mine closings and conditions of work under Mrs. Thatcher resulted merely in a reassertion of the power of government to make law. Another major challenge to the authority of government—riots in the inner cities—occurred during the Thatcher government.[3] Although the authority of government was again asserted, such disturbances have produced some policy responses to aid these severely depressed areas. Finally, during the early 1990s, the Thatcher government's attempt to change the system of local government finance from property taxes (rates) to a per capita community charge (poll tax) provoked political violence and significant tax evasion. The Major government quickly reversed the decision and is implementing a complex mixture of property and household taxes.

Deference is a special case in the United Kingdom. Even in a modern, secularized political system, a number of citizens still feel obliged to defer to the upper classes as the appropriate rulers of the society. In political terms, this gives the Conservative party an advantage and prevents it from being the permanent minority that it would be if people voted strictly on class lines. This traditional attitude is being transformed, however, as many "working-class Tories" have adopted a more pragmatic conception of the upper classes as being better educated and trained to govern, as opposed to merely accepting their position from deference. In addition, a number of working-class voters have started voting for the Tory party because it has benefited them through lower taxes, opportunities to buy cheap council houses, and other changes brought in by Mrs. Thatcher. For the working class who are working, the Conservative era from 1979 onward has been one of growing prosperity and increasing acceptance of the Conservative party. Also, an increasing number of Tory politicians (including John Major) have come from modest backgrounds, have worked their way up socially and economically, and believe that others should be able to do the same.

Associated with deference toward authority and political leaders is a high degree of trust in the political system as a whole and in its leadership. Survey evidence for the United Kingdom indicates an extremely high level of trust, higher than in almost any other political system, in the fairness and general benevolence of government.[4] This high level of trust, though declining in the face of more abrasive political campaigns, permits a form of political democracy to flourish in the United Kingdom that would fail in almost any other industrial society. In this form of democracy the decision-making process is closed to scrutiny or participation by citizens, or even by politicians who are not members of the cabinet. The United Kingdom is a democracy, but it is a system of democracy "by consent and not by delegation, of government of the people, for the people, with, but not by, the people."[5]

Citizens expect to participate in politics at election times; most have been content to settle back, watch the government work, and pass judgment at the next election. Breaks in official secrecy have given citizens and academics a better view of the internal workings of government, but much of this still remains hidden to outsiders. To run a government on such a basis requires an extraordinary level of trust on the part of citizens. The increasingly participative nature of British citizens, however, is making them increasingly resentful of their lack of involvement in government, and there is now a need to reexamine the secrecy and limited democracy of British government.[6]

The obverse of the public's trust is the responsible behavior of elected leaders. Government has generally conducted itself responsibly, even benevolently, and has not violated existing political norms. When those norms have been violated, as when elections were suspended during the two world wars, it has been by broad agreement among the political parties. Responsibility has also meant that parties and governments are expected to deliver more of what they promised in election campaigns than would be expected of American parties. Although there is continuing agitation for increased openness in government, the responsibleness of the great majority of British politicians has helped prevent these demands from gaining wide popular acceptance. The credulity of the population was strained by a number of scandals during the Thatcher decade, but even those did not have so great an impact as they might have had in other democratic nations.[7]

The acceptance of a rather secretive government in exchange for responsible performance—assuming these two traits are connected—points up another feature of the political culture of the United Kingdom: its pragmatism. Although ideologies are frequently spouted during campaigns or in speeches delivered for mass consumption, British politics is extremely practical. An empirical, pragmatic mode of political thought has so dominated British political life that the preservation of traditional political institutions such as the monarchy is justified not on grounds that they are right and just but on grounds only that they have worked. Even in the more ideological Thatcher government, there were enough turnarounds and changes in policy to illustrate the pragmatic mode of thinking about government at work. Obviously such a political epistemology will be associated with gradual change and a continuous adjustment to changing conditions, a factor that has assisted the system in altering in all but its essential features to accommodate a modern world. It could be argued, in fact, that it was rigidity over several issues (the poll tax and Europe) that led to her replacement by John Major in November 1990.

The traditional values of deference, trust, and pragmatism exist in the context of a modern, or even postindustrial, political system. The policies pursued, the presence of mass democracy and mass political parties, a very large level of public revenues and expenditures, and some neocorporatist linkages between state and society are evidence of the modernity of the political system. Yet with all that, political leaders are allowed the latitude to discuss and decide political issues without directly involving the public or press. This is a modern democracy, but a democracy permitting an elite to govern and exercising latent democratic power only at agreed upon times.

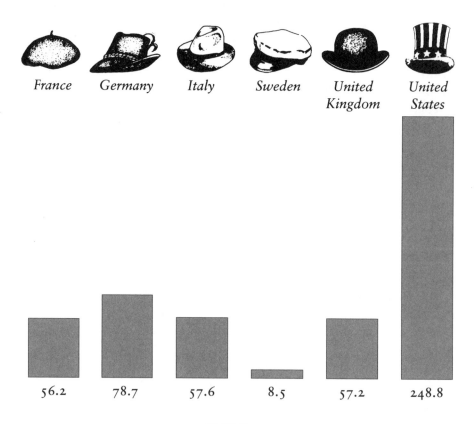

France	Germany	Italy	Sweden	United Kingdom	United States
56.2	78.7	57.6	8.5	57.2	248.8

FIGURE 1.1
POPULATION (IN MILLIONS)

Class Politics, but ...

The characteristic most commonly identified with politics and political conflicts in the United Kingdom is social class. The principal basis of social differentiation and political mobilization is social class, meaning primarily levels and sources of income. The major partisan alignments in politics are along class lines, with the Labour party representing the interests of the working classes and the Conservative party (and to a lesser extent Liberals and Democrats) reflecting the interests of the middle and upper classes. We have already seen that the correspondence between class and party is less than perfect, but the generalization remains a useful one.

Social class is both an objective and a subjective phenomenon. Objectively, the United Kingdom has significant inequalities of income, even after the redistributional effects of taxes and governmental expenditures are taken into account. But despite the prominence given to class politics in Britain, the inequalities are in general less than in many other industrialized democracies. The bottom one-tenth of income earners in the United Kingdom earns 2.1 percent of the total income in the nation, while in the United States the same proportion of income earners receive only 1.2 percent of total income.[8] The highest decile in the United Kingdom earns 25 percent of total income, compared with 28 percent in the United States and 31 percent in Germany. Britain is more class based, however, in that a larger proportion of income earners in Britain is still employed in industrial working-class occupations, meaning primarily manual labor, whereas the largest single category of employment in most other European and North American nations is now service jobs.

Access to other goods and services is also affected by class considerations, although again perhaps not as much as in other European nations. In particular, education is class related, both in the small elite private sector and in the larger state sector that until very recently tracked or streamed all children at an early age. Access to secondary and post-secondary education retains a pronounced upper-class bias, although again less so than in many European nations. And, in part because of the class basis of education, social mobility is rather low in Britain, although it is still apparently higher than in much of continental Europe.

Subjectively, people in the United Kingdom are generally more willing to identify themselves as members of a particular social class than are Americans, who overwhelmingly identify themselves as members of the economic middle class. Issues of all kinds may become polarized on a class basis. Any policy that preserves or extends the privileges and power of the more affluent is immediately held suspect by the Labour party and the trade unions, even when (as with selling council houses to their current tenants) the policy may have a number of positive benefits for working-class families as well as the government.

Several caveats must be raised about a simple class model of British politics. The first is that recently there has been some change, and the *embourgeoisement* of the working classes, so obvious in many European nations, is occurring to some degree in Britain also. Manual labor is a declining share of the labor force, even though it remains a larger share in the United Kingdom than in most other European countries. Also, the wages paid to manual workers now often approach or even surpass wages and salaries paid to many nonmanual workers, and manual workers find some of their economic interests served by the Conservatives. Changes are occurring within the occupational and economic structure, then, that may mitigate the impact of class on politics.

Numerous other issues also lessen the dominance of class. We have already mentioned the existence of ethnic and regional cleavages based on the national constituent elements of the United Kingdom. Scottish and Welsh nationalism has tended to cut broadly across class lines and to be concerned with national rather than class consciousness. A "new ethnicity" recently entered British politics, as the formation of the anti-immigrant National Front indicates. Such groups have declined in size in the last few years, but they are still active in many places. In 1988 an estimated 2.8 million people of "New Commonwealth and Pakistani" origin (i.e., "coloured") lived in Great Britain. These ethnic minorities now dominate many older industrial towns, and in some inner-city schools English is taught as a second language. As these groups are also multiplying more rapidly than white Britons, the specter of nonwhite domination and the loss of jobs by whites are powerful weapons for some political groups. Pressure by the minorities for representation has already begun to affect the local and national political systems.

Religion is also a factor in British politics. The monarch is required to be a Protestant, which in practice has meant a member of the Church of England. This Anglican monarch (Presbyterian while in Scotland) rules a population that is only approximately three-quarters Anglican and that contains a significant Roman Catholic minority. This issue has surfaced most obviously in Northern Ireland, but cities such as Liverpool and Glasgow also have large and politically relevant Roman Catholic populations.

Politics in Britain is not entirely about class, but it is very much about class. The importance of other cleavages varies with the region of the nation (with the Celtic Fringe being the most influenced by nonclass cleavages) and by the time and circumstances of the controversy. Nevertheless, to attempt to understand British politics through only class divisions is to miss a good deal of the complexity of politics and the political system.

Finally, politics in Britain may also be about substantive issues. For example, the Green Party received 14.9 percent of the votes in the 1989 European election and had some success at the local level, although it has not fared as well since then. The nature of the electoral system prevents new parties or social movements from gaining representation in Parliament rapidly, but there does appear to be a real interest in issues that go beyond simple class politics.[9]

Conservatively Liberal Policy Ideas

Another apparent paradox about British political life is the conservatively liberal nature of many of the policies and policy ideas of the nation. Members of the Labour party speak of socialism and sing the "Red Flag" at their party congresses. Members of the Conservative party speak about the restoration of laissez-faire economics and dismantling a good deal of the welfare state. In practice, however, most of the policies adopted by most governments have borne a remarkable resemblance during the postwar period. The Labour party accepted that most of the British economy was privately owned, and at the same time pressed nationalization of certain industries and the extension of social services to the disadvantaged. The Conservative party while in office has tended to accept the virtual entirety of the welfare state, as well as government ownership of such industries as coal, steel, and the railways. The major deviation from this pattern in recent memory was Margaret Thatcher's Conservative government. This government began to sell off government stock in nationalized industries such as British Gas, British Telecom, British Steel, and British Airways, as well as to encourage local authorities to sell off their council (public) housing to tenants. There was talk of ending the Post Office monopoly over the delivery of mail. These policies represent something more of an ideological style of policy making than has been true for most recent governments. The public water supply system has been sold off to the private sector, and a number of local government services (garbage collection, for example) have been contracted out to the private sector. These changes are continuing, albeit less energetically, under the Major government.

Despite the intrusions of ideology, there does appear to be broad support for a mixed-economy welfare state. All major political parties favor the major programs of the welfare state such as pensions, other social insurance programs such as unemployment protection, and the National Health Service. The fate of the National Health Service played a significant role in the 1992 general election. At the same time the majority of the population accepts private ownership and management as the major form of economic organization, despite the presence of a (declining) number of nationalized industries. What the parties and politicians appear to disagree about is just what is the proper mix of the mixed economy and just how much welfare there should be in the welfare state.

Isolated but European

One of the standard points made about Britain's history is that its insular position relative to the European continent has isolated Britain from a number of influences and has allowed it to develop its own particular political institutions and political culture. The mental separation from Europe was to some degree greater than the geographical separation, so Britain may have looked European from North America; but Britons did not always feel European on their islands. The separation of Britain from the Continent and from the world can be overstated. Britain has not been successfully invaded since 1066, but it has been deeply involved in European politics and warfare. Also, Britain was by no means insular when dealing with the rest of the world, managing a far-flung empire and even more far-flung trade routes, from its little islands. And, unlike that other great island nation, Japan, Britain was never isolationist but was always involved in world politics and trade.

One of the major changes in the political environment of the United Kingdom has been its entry into the European Community (EC, or Common Market). After two denials of admittance, largely at the instigation of France and Charles de Gaulle, Britain joined the EC in 1973, followed by the first advisory referendum in its history. This obviously has brought Britain closer to its continental counterparts, and it has had important internal effects as well. Joining the EC introduced a whole new level of government to the United Kingdom; some of the previous rights of Parliament to legislate for British subjects now actually reside in Brussels. The importance of Europe for Britain is increasing, and pressures toward full integration of the European market in

1992 put even more economic decision-making power in Brussels. Mrs. Thatcher was virtually alone among European leaders in expressing skepticism about the future of the EC. Further, the British people, more than those of any other nation in Europe, express reluctance toward greater economic and political unification. Britain may be a part of Europe, but it maintains some distance (psychological as well as geographic) from the Continent. The issue of Britain's involvement with Europe came to a head in the summer of 1991 with a debate over the possibility of a "federal Europe." Mrs. Thatcher had lost office primarily as a result of her European policies, but she continued to oppose deeper involvement from the back benches. Prime Minister Major sought to follow the more moderate path of a greater political role for European institutions but without full union. The issue of European unification remains divisive in Britain, as well as within the Conservative party, but Britain does not appear able to accept isolation from Europe any longer and may have to accept an ever increasing involvement with the European Community.

Joining the EC has also required something of a retreat from long-standing British commitment to its Commonwealth countries, whose special economic privileges are gradually being phased out as Britain slowly aligns its trade policies with European policies. The political commitment to the former colonies remains, and the queen and prime minister both make a point of attending Commonwealth meetings and dealing with Commonwealth business.

The context of British politics is not a neatly ordered class politics among an otherwise homogeneous population isolated from the currents of European politics. British society is actually rather heterogeneous, divided among four separate countries within the confines of the United Kingdom, and made more complex by millions of immigrants who have flocked there. Class politics are certainly important, even dominant, but a variety of other issues also influence British politics. In addition, the consensus that is sometimes said to exist on the policies of government is less universal than it once was, and the economic problems of the nation may encourage more drastic actions by either Labour or Conservative governments or both.

Just as the environment of politics is not uniform, so too the institutions that make policy in Britain are a mixture of traditional and modern elements. They frequently represent compromises between what Walter Bagehot, a nineteenth-century commentator on the British constitution, called the "dignified" and the "efficient" parts of government.

Many of the dignified, ceremonial aspects of government and society remain unchanged, while their actual operations may have adapted to changing demands and circumstances. We next turn to a description of those governing institutions as institutions and return somewhat later to look at them in action as they make policy.

Notes

1. Richard Rose, *The Territorial Dimension in Government: Understanding the United Kingdom* (Chatham, N.J.: Chatham House, 1982).

2. Richard Rose, "England: A Traditionally Modern Political Culture," in *Political Culture and Political Development,* ed. Lucian Pye and Sidney Verba (Princeton, N.J.: Princeton University Press, 1965); see also Dennis Kavanagh, "Political Culture in Britain: The Decline of the Civic Culture," in *The Civic Culture Revisited,* ed. Gabriel Almond and Sidney Verba (Boston: Little, Brown, 1980).

3. Zig Layton-Henry, *The Politics of Race in Britain* (London: Allen & Unwin, 1984).

4. Gabriel A. Almond and Sidney Verba, *The Civic Culture* (Princeton, N.J.: Princeton University Press, 1963), 142–43.

5. L.S. Amery, *Thoughts on the Constitution* (London: Oxford University Press, 1947), 20.

6. Lord Crowther-Hunt and Alan T. Peacock, *Memorandum of Dissent,* Royal Commission on the Constitution, Cmnd. 5460–1 (London: HMSO, 1973).

7. These scandals included the procurement of helicopters from Westland Company, the firing of the civil servant Clive Ponting for giving sensitive information to Parliament, and even the sinking of the Argentine battleship *General Belgrano* during the Falklands War.

8. Organization for Economic Cooperation and Development, *Public Expenditure on Income Maintenance Programs* (Paris: OECD, 1976), 108.

9. This fits with the argument of Ronald Inglehart and others that as some of the basic issues of economics and class are addressed there is latitude to cope with other issues such as the environment. Britain has been less capable of dealing with class issues than its wealthier Continental counterparts, and the growth of environmentalism may represent the real degradation of the environment in most industrialized nations.

2

Where Is the Power?

The fundamental difference between the constitutional and institutional structures of American government and those of British government is in the relationship of the executive and legislative branches. The United States is accustomed to a presidential form of government with a separation of powers between the legislature (Congress) and the executive (the president). Each branch is legitimated by election, and each can claim equally to represent the people. Each has powers that can be used, and are used, to block actions by the other branch; and each is further checked by the powers of the judicial system. This system of government was designed to limit executive power, indeed to limit the power of government in general.

Parliamentary government, in contrast, links executive powers directly to legislative powers. The executive of a parliamentary government such as that of the United Kingdom is elected not directly and independently of the legislature but by the legislature. With modern political parties, voters know that when they vote for a certain political party, if they are in the majority, they will have a certain person as the next executive (prime minister in the case of the United Kingdom); but becoming prime minister still requires action by the Parliament. Margaret Thatcher was not elected prime minister by the British people in 1979; they voted for a majority of Conservative party members of Parliament, who in turn had previously voted to have their party leader as prime minister.

If at any time a majority of the members of Parliament decide they no longer want the current government to continue in office, they can vote that government out by a vote of no confidence or by defeating a major government legislative proposal. As there are now a majority of Conservatives in Parliament, removing the prime minister would require the defection of members of Mr. Major's own party, an uncommon but not unheard-of occurrence. Also, as the Conservatives did when they elected Mr. Major in November 1990, a majority party can change its leader and thereby change prime ministers.

Remaining the "queen's first minister" requires the continual support of Parliament; if that support is lost, the prime minister and the other ministers must by convention either reorganize themselves or go to the people for a new election.[1] And not only the prime minister must go. The doctrine of collective responsibility makes the government as a whole responsible for its actions and in consequence requires that the government as a whole resign. Individual ministers may be forced out of office for their own particular failures, but when a government falls, all ministers must leave.

Presidential and parliamentary forms of government have their respective advantages and disadvantages. Presidential government is commonly valued because checks and balances restrain a single individual or group and allow more viewpoints to influence policies. The presidential system also provides a clearer focus for national political leadership. Having a president in office for a fixed term provides a predictability to policies that is not necessarily found in parliamentary regimes, which may have frequent changes in executives. Such instability has not plagued British government, but the possibility is there, especially as the established two-party system threatens to dissolve.

The parliamentary form of government allows an executive, once in office, to govern. While presidential governments frequently have conflicts between the legislative and executive branches over which should control a policy issue, this rarely occurs so overtly in a parliamentary regime. A political executive that cannot command the acquiescence of the legislature will soon cease to be the executive. On the one hand, the parliamentary system allows voters to make more clearly defined policy choices; on the other hand, the greater policy stability of presidential regimes may permit citizens to feel more secure.

British Parliamentary Government

While a number of political systems practice parliamentary government, each practices it differently. Several features of parliamentary government as practiced in the United Kingdom should be described before we describe each of the major institutions. The first is the principle of government and opposition. Bipartisanship has little place in this form of parliamentary government; instead, it is the job of the Opposition to oppose the government. Even if the Opposition should agree with the basic tenets of the government's policy, it still must present constructive alternatives to that policy. It is assumed that through this adversarial process better policies will emerge, and the voters will be given alternative conceptions of the common good from which to choose at the next election.

British parliamentary government is also party government. While there are certainly barriers to the effective implementation of party government, the idea that political parties are a major instrument for governing pervades the system. Parliament is now conceived of, to some degree, not as an institution in itself but as an arena in which political parties clash. Parties are expected to be responsible, to stand for certain policies and programs, and to attempt to carry out those programs if elected. There are always necessary compromises once in office, but parties are expected to attempt to implement their programs.

Finally, British parliamentary government is sovereign. There are, strictly speaking, no legal limitations on the powers of Parliament. There are no means by which a citizen can challenge an act of Parliament as unconstitutional, although some actions may be found to go beyond the powers of a particular minister. There are, of course, very real political limitations on the activities of a Parliament, but its actions, once taken, are law until Parliament acts again.

With these considerations in mind, let us now proceed to a brief description and discussion of the six major institutions of British national government: the monarch, the prime minister, the cabinet and government, Parliament, the courts, and the civil service. We will describe the features most salient for an understanding of the manner in which the British system converts proposals into law.

The Monarch

The United Kingdom is a constitutional monarchy; even though there is grumbling about the cost of maintaining the royal household and about the wealth of the queen and the royal family, there is little serious question about the continuation of the monarchy. The powers of the monarchy, however, are very circumscribed; although many acts are performed by the queen or in her name, the actual decisions are made by the prime minister or the cabinet. Declarations of war, making treaties, granting peerages, and granting clemency to prisoners are all royal prerogatives, but all are exercised only on the advice of the prime minister and other ministers. Similarly, the royal assent is necessary for legislation to become law, but this has not been refused since Queen Anne in 1703.

One major point at which the monarch could possibly influence policy and politics substantively is in the selection of the prime minister. There is little or no possibility for the exercise of independent judgment by the monarch if one major party wins a clear majority. The British party system is tending to fragment, however, and the probability of a clear majority in every election appears to be lessening. If there were no clear winner, the monarch might be able to exercise some independent judgment, albeit with the advice of the outgoing prime minister. The conventions governing such an eventuality have only been clearly articulated in the early 1990s.[2]

The monarch must also dissolve a sitting Parliament, and the decision to do so could be made independently if the government did not resign and call for elections after a vote of no confidence or if it lost on a major issue. As governments in the 1970s and 1980s seemed unwilling to resign in the face of defeats, this power of the monarch to force a government to go to the people may become important in making policy choices. It would, however, be exercised at some peril for the monarch, as such a direct intervention into the fray of politics might threaten the legitimacy of the institution of the monarchy.

The great commentator on British politics, Walter Bagehot, described the monarch as a real part of the policy-making system in Britain, concealed in a cloak of dignity and ceremony. Much of the impact of a monarch on policy and politics remains hidden and is very subtle. The monarch's influence is exercised through frequent meetings and consultations and requires her to be as well briefed as her ministers. The power of the monarch, then, may be as personal as the power of any other political actor, even more so. It would be easy for a monarch not to have influence, given the dominant partisan mold of the policy-making system. For the monarch to be effective, she must not only perform the extensive ceremonial functions of the office but also be a real politician in her own right. The most important function of the monarch, however, is to be a symbol of the nation as a whole and to be above partisan strife. She must be a unifying force when much else in the political system tends to be centrifugal and adversarial.

The Prime Minister

The monarch is head of state; that is, she is the representative of the nation as a whole. The prime minister is head of government and its chief executive officer. Of course, in the United States, the two roles are merged in the president, who is both head of state and head of government. Separating the two roles in Britain means that a citizen or a politician can criticize the prime minister without being seen to be attacking the legitimacy of government.

The office of prime minister has evolved slowly since the beginning of the eighteenth century. The prime minister is at once just another minister of the Crown and above the other ministers. There is increasing discussion of the role of the prime minister becoming presidential. This alleged "presidentialization" of the prime minister derives from several factors. The first is that parliamentary campaigns have become increasingly directed toward electing a particular prime minister rather than toward the selection of a political party to govern. The personalization of British politics increased substantially while Mrs. Thatcher was prime minister, but even before that time campaigns were oriented toward the appeal and personality of individuals. Party remains important in the voting decision, but so too do the prospective leaders of the nation.

Another aspect of the presidentialization of the office of prime minister is the staffing of the office. The staff of the prime minister has begun to evolve much as the Executive Office of the President has, although on a much smaller scale. And there has been a tendency for the prime minister, both through control of the Cabinet Office and through the hiring of personal assistants, to attempt to gain greater personal involvement in policy. Mrs. Thatcher's placement of several special assistants in departments indicates the extent to which the prime minister may seek a role expanded beyond *primus inter pares* ("first among equals").

Certain characteristics, powers, and limitations on the prime minister are important for understanding the office. First, the prime minister is the leader of the majority party in the House of Commons. Until 1902, prime ministers frequently came from the House of Lords, but by convention, the prime minister now is a member of Commons. For example, Lord Home renounced his hereditary title in order to sit in the House of Commons and eventually become prime minister. The selection of a potential prime minister is first made by the political party; whoever would be prime minister must first win an election within the party. Even sitting prime ministers may have to be reelected by their party; sometimes they lose the confidence of their party, as Mrs. Thatcher did in 1990, and with it their office. This is but one of many ways in which the customs and conventions of the British political system reinforce the cohesiveness and integration of political parties. The prime minister, therefore, must be able to command the apparatus both of a political party and of government.

In addition to being the leader of a political party, the prime minister must be the leader of the House of Commons. Becoming prime minister indeed may say more about one's abilities in Parliament than about the skills necessary to run a government. The prime minister is expected to lead parliamentary debates. The ability to win in verbal jousts in the House of Commons frequently seems to be more important to success as prime minister than winning policy and administrative battles. The skills usually associated with the rise to office of prime minister thus are by no means those we might identify as being crucial to running the government of a large industrialized nation.

Although technically only *primus inter pares,* the powers of the prime minister are actually more substantial. First, the prime minister is the formal link between the Crown and the rest of government. The queen invites a prospective prime minister to form a new government, and relationships between the monarch and Parliament are channeled through the prime minister. In like manner, the prime minister serves as chief political adviser to the queen, especially on major issues such as the dissolution of Parliament. The prime minister also dispenses office. Once the queen has invited a prospective prime minister to form a government, it is the prime minister who assembles a team. Certainly members of that team will have political followings of their own, and may have to be included to placate certain segments of the party, but the office held by each cabinet member will be a decision of the prime minister. The power to dispense office also extends to a number of other offices, including life peerages, which are nominally appointed by the Crown but in actuality are in the gift of the prime minister.

Once in office, the prime minister has considerable personal power over policy and the activities of the cabinet. We have already mentioned the growth of the prime minister's staff and the alleged presidentialization of the office. As the organizer, leader, and summarizer of the business of the cabinet, the prime minister is also in a position to enforce views over his or her nominal equals. As the head of the government, the prime minister has substantial visibility and influence. Finally, in time of emergency, the powers of a prime minister are not limited by a constitution, as are those of an American president.

We should also mention the role of the leader of the Opposition who, as leader of the largest minority party in the House of Commons, would probably be prime minister if the sitting government were defeated in an election. Although lacking the official powers of office, the role of the leader of the Opposition is not dissimilar to that of the prime minister. He is expected to be the leader of a political party, a leader in Parliament, and the leader of a cabinet, albeit one out of office (the "shadow cabinet"). The adversarial style of British politics obliges the leader of the Opposition to oppose the program of the government and to propose "searching alternatives" to all government programs, in preparation for the day when the Opposition becomes the government and must make its own policy proposals. As the alternative prime minister, the leader of the Opposition is paid a special salary and is kept briefed on important policy issues because he or she must be ready to become prime minister on very short notice.

Cabinet and Government

Working beneath, or with, the prime minister are the cabinet and the government. Although these terms are often used interchangeably, they actually designate different things. The cabinet is composed of the individuals—in the 1992 Major government the twenty men and two women—who meet with the prime minister as a collectivity called the cabinet. The term "government" is more embracing, including all ministers regardless of their seniority or degree of responsibility. The cabinet is technically a committee of the government selected by the prime minister to provide advice in private meetings and to share in the responsibility for policy. Although the prime minister is certainly primarily responsible for government policies, the cabinet is also collectively responsible, and all cabinet members tend to rise and fall as a unit rather than as individuals.

There are several varieties of ministers: secretaries of state, ministers, and junior ministers; to a degree, parliamentary private secretaries are also ministers. The distinction between secretaries of state and ministers is rather vague. Each tends to head a department of government (e.g., the Department of Health, Department of Employment, or the Department of the Environment), although secretaries of state tend to head larger or more prestigious departments. Some may carry titles other than minister (e.g., chancellor of the exchequer). Also included in the government, and in some instances the cabinet, are a number of posts without departmental responsibilities, either ministers without portfolio or holders of such titles as Lord Privy Seal, included in the government as general or political advisers or as the leadership of the House of Commons, or the House of Lords, that is, the managers of government business in that house. Junior ministers are attached to a department minister to provide political and policy assistance in the management of the department, and these positions serve as steppingstones for persons on the way up in government. Ministers of state are in a position somewhere between junior ministers and ministers, and are commonly members of the House of Lords. Finally, parliamentary private secretaries, unpaid (aside from their normal salaries as members of Parliament) assistants to ministers, are responsible primarily for liaison with Parliament. There are, then, in any government, some eighty to ninety positions to be filled in the political executive, most coming from the House of Commons.

The job of a minister is a demanding one. A British minister remains a member of the legislature and an active legislator for a constituency; consequently, he or she must fulfill a number of positions and responsibilities simultaneously. The first of these multiple tasks is to run the department. The minister must be able to run the department in two ways. First, he is responsible for the day-to-day management of the large, bureaucratic organization of which he is the head. Few politicians have experience with the management of such large organizations, so they are at some disadvantage in making the department run effectively. The minister must also manage department policies. That is, he must develop policies appropriate to the department's responsibilities, policies that will be in keeping with the overall priorities of the government. In this task, ministers are generally hindered by their lack of expertise. Ministers are seldom chosen for their expertise in a policy area; more often, they are appointed for their general political skill and voter following. It is estimated that only five of fifty-one ministerial appointments in the Wilson government of 1964–70 had any prior experience in the area of their department's responsibilities.[3] The consequences of their lack of expertise are exacerbated by the tendency to shift ministers from one department to another, even during the lifetime of a government. Furthermore, in their departments ministers are faced with experienced and relatively expert civil servants, who tend to have views of their own on proper departmental policies. An inexperienced and inexpert minister must then fight very hard just to manage his own department.

If the minister is also a member of the cabinet, there will be additional demands on his or her time. On average, the cabinet meets five to six hours per week, but preparation for those meetings requires even more time. Membership in the cabinet requires that each minister be at least briefed on all current political issues. And there are the cabinet committees necessary to coordinate policies and deal with issues requiring consideration prior to determination by the cabinet.[4] A minister cannot afford to take cabinet work lightly, even though he may be only a part of a collectivity dominated by the prime minister, for it is in cabinet as well as Commons where political reputations are made and where the interests of one's department must be protected.

The minister remains an active member of Parliament and as such is required to appear in Parliament for a substantial amount of time each day, especially when the government has only a small majority. The minister must also be prepared to speak in Parliament on the policies of his department or for the government as a whole. A minister must also be prepared to respond to questions in the four question hours per week and may have to spend hours being briefed and coached on the answers to anticipated questions. The responsibility of the executive to the legislature places a great burden on ministers in a parliamentary government.

As a member of Parliament, the minister also retains constituents in the district from which he was elected, and these must be served. This involves spending weekends in the "surgery" (i.e., their constituency office) in the district and receiving delegations from local organizations. And, since there is no fixed term for a Parliament (other than that an election must occur within five years), British politicians, even more than American politicians, must always be preparing for the next election.

Finally, the minister must be a general-purpose politician and a representative of the government. This role may involve a number of honorific functions as well as a number of more demanding appearances. As one former minister put it, a minister is at the beck and call of every Tom, Dick, and Harry. The combination of all these duties amounts to an extremely demanding task for any individual; it is even more demanding given that ministers lack a personal staff of the sort that American political executives enjoy. To the extent that they do have staff, most are civil servants rather than personal friends and advisers. The considerable demands of constituents on the time and energy of ministers also make it difficult for a political party, as it comes into office, to place its stamp on the public policies of the United Kingdom rapidly or effectively. The resistance within any political system to change, combined with the likely brevity of ministers' terms, means that policy changes resulting from changes in governments will, on average, take place slowly.

Despite the rigors of ministerial office, any number of people seek to become ministers. Most of these are in the so-called shadow cabinet, which is the leadership of the Opposition party. Just as the leader of the Opposition is the alternative prime minister, so too does every member of the government have a shadow minister in office who is prepared to be the Opposition's spokesman on that policy area. He or she is briefed on policy issues, leads debates for the Opposition in Parliament, and prepares for the time when the Opposition may become the government.

The cabinet does not work entirely alone, and one of the important developments in British politics has been the development and expansion of the Cabinet Office. The Cabinet Office, or secretariat, grew out of the Committee of Imperial Defense in World War I. Currently, a very senior civil servant, along with a small number of associates, serves the cabinet. The secretary to the cabinet is himself influential in shaping cabinet decisions, although not by obvious means. The cabinet agenda is set by the secretary, and he distributes cabinet papers to the appropriate individuals. By so doing, he determines which ministers will be heard quickly and which will have to wait for their day in cabinet. Although the prime minister summarizes cabinet meetings orally, it is the secretary to the cabinet who as a result of the meetings drafts written communications to the departments for action and prepares the formal written records of the meetings. These records are not subject to change, even by the prime minister. While there is little or no evidence of these powers being abused, the position of secretary to the cabinet is extremely influential.

There is also a small prime minister's staff of political and personal advisers. This is far from approaching the magnitude of the White House staff in the United States, but it has been growing and is seen as one more bit of evidence of the concentration of policy-making powers in the cabinet rather than in Parliament as a whole. Each minister also is increasingly likely to have some personal policy advisers. The difficulties that cabinet ministers encounter in trying to make policy have also produced suggestions that each should be given a group of advisers, similar to the *cabinet du ministre* in France. The Thatcher government, more than previous governments, sought more partisan and ideological policy advice than it was likely to receive from civil servants, and it may be difficult to return to the policy dominance of permanent officials.

Parliament

The government of the United Kingdom has already been described as parliamentary, implying a significant role for Parliament in government.

Despite the nominally strong position of Parliament in the constitutional arrangements of the United Kingdom, there are serious questions as to the real, effective powers of Parliament. With the growing strength of the political executive and the increased discipline of political parties, Parliament as an institution is less capable of exercising control over policies than it once was. Parliament has been attempting to reassert its position in the political process, but the evidence is not yet in on how successful those efforts will be.

Members of Parliament

The first thing that must be understood about a legislative body such as Parliament is the nature of the individuals involved and the incentives offered to them to participate. Parliament has 650 members, elected from a like number of constituencies, meaning that the average member of Parliament (MP) represents fewer than than 90,000 people (compared to approximately 550,000 represented by members of the U.S. House of Representatives). Compared with members of other legislative bodies, MPs have few advantages. Their pay, even with continuing raises, is a modest £26,701 (roughly $50,000 at 1992 rates of exchange), compared to over $100,000 for U.S. congressmen. MPs receive a limited travel allowance for parliamentary business, which they commonly use to travel back to their district on weekends when Parliament is in session, and some limited housing expenses (approximately £10,000) for maintaining a second residence. Some members may have sponsoring organizations that will either help with their expenses or provide some direct remuneration. For Labour politicians, these are commonly trade unions; for Conservatives and some Liberals, they are industrial groups or large corporations.

In return for these modest rewards, MPs work long hours and receive relatively little staff support. While American legislators are accustomed to having several dozen staff members working for them, the average MP has funding only for a part-time assistant or secretary unless the member is paying personally for the assistance or is receiving assistance from a sponsor. MPs often lack even a private office, and unless they are in the government or the shadow cabinet, they may share a small office with other MPs in or near the Palace of Westminster (the Houses of Parliament). The job of member of Parliament was designed for a gentleman of independent means, and the rewards of office have not changed to match the apparent demands of a modern legislative bodies.

Organization

Parliament is composed of the House of Commons and the House of Lords. As the House of Lords has become relatively unimportant in the policy-making process, let us first describe it briefly and then proceed to a more extended discussion of the House of Commons.

The House of Lords is composed of the lords spiritual (representing the hierarchy of the Church of England) and the lords temporal. The lords temporal comprise hereditary and life peers. The right of the hereditary peers to sit in the House of Lords is based on inherited titles, while life lords are appointed by the queen (on the advice of the government) only for their lifetime. The development of the concept of life peerages (in 1958) was in part to rectify the partisan and ideological balance in Lords against the Labour party. Currently there are only about 360 life peers out of a total body of 1,300, and the majority of the hereditary peers are Conservative; thus there remains a strong majority against Labour in Lords.

The major impetus for limiting the powers of the House of Lords was Lloyd George's "people's budget" of 1909. This budget introduced a progressive income tax (the first since the Napoleonic wars) and a rudimentary public health insurance program. The Conservative Lords balked at this Liberal proposal and refused to pass the budget. Parliament was then dissolved; but when the Liberals were returned with a (reduced) majority, the House of Lords accepted the budget. And after a second election in 1910, in which the Liberals were again successful, the House of Lords accepted the Parliament Bill of 1911, which greatly limited its powers.

Lords now cannot delay money bills longer than one month—and cannot vote them down and prevent their implementation—and any legislation passed by two successive sessions of Parliament, provided one calendar year has passed, goes into effect without approval by Lords. Lords does still occasionally delay legislation; mainly, however, it serves as a debating society, and as a locus at which the government can accept amendments to its proposals that it would be less willing to accept in the more politicized House of Commons. The House of Lords actually serves a useful function in British policy making despite its diminished role, as many useful modifications to legislation result from the attention of the Lords.

The structure and functions of the House of Commons have evolved over centuries and to some degree still reflect their medieval roots. Much of the ceremony and procedure derives from the past, but despite complaints about the vestigial aspects of the procedures, these do not appear to inhibit in any significant way the functioning of a modern legislative body. To the extent that the House is seriously overshadowed by other institutions of British government, the fault resides more with other characteristics of British government than with the trappings of power and antiquity within the House of Commons.

British politics is conducted in an adversarial style, and even the design of the House of Commons emphasizes that fact. Most legislatures sit in semicircles, and the individual members sit at desks and go to a central rostrum to address the body. The House of Commons is ar-

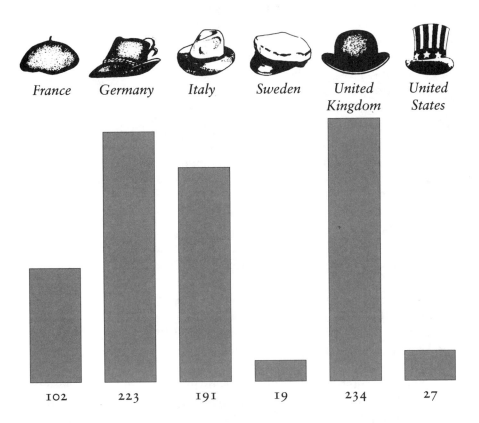

France	Germany	Italy	Sweden	United Kingdom	United States
102	223	191	19	234	27

FIGURE 2.1
POPULATION DENSITY (PERSONS PER SQUARE KILOMETER)

ranged as two opposing ranks of benches, placed very close together in a small chamber. Speakers generally face their political opponents, and although the form of address is to the Speaker, the words are clearly intended for the opponents. The proceedings of the House of Commons are now broadcast, and statements by members therefore are also directed at the voting public. The front benches on the two sides of the aisle are populated by leaders of the government and the Opposition. From these two front-row trenches, the two major belligerents conduct the verbal warfare that is parliamentary debate. Behind the front benches are arrayed the foot soldiers of the "backbenches," ready to vote to their party's call, and perhaps to do little else. The style of debate in the House of Commons, as well as being contentious and rather witty, is very informal, and for the MP addressing the House there are few protections against heckling.

As well as being a partisan body, the House of Commons is a national institution. Ideas of cabinet government and collective responsibility are closely allied to ideas of party government, and there is a strong sense that political parties should present clear and consistent positions on policy issues either in or out of government. They can then be judged by the electorate at the next election on the basis of those policies. In addition to responsibility for policy, the dependence of the executive on the ability to command a majority of the House requires that parties vote together. Political parties in the House of Commons are organized in order to deliver votes when required. Members know that voting against their party on an important issue is tantamount to political suicide, and each party has a whip whose job it is to ensure that the needed votes are present. The British system of government does not allow much latitude for individual MPs to have policy ideas of their own, although the parties do allow their members free votes on issues of a moral nature, such as abortion or capital punishment.

From the partisan organization and behavior of the House it follows that it is a national institution. The U.S. House of Representatives is usually conceptualized as a group of ambassadors from the constituencies. The British generally acknowledge that MPs are more responsible to the party and its national goals and priorities than to the individual interests of their constituency. This is signaled by the fact that MPs are not required to live in their constituencies, and many do not. Of course, the MP tries to satisfy the constituency whenever possible, but it is generally assumed that the member owes the office to the party and the national policies advanced in the election campaign rather than to any geographically narrow interests of the constituency. Nevertheless, as with free votes on moral issues, MPs are often allowed to abstain from voting for, and in rare cases to vote against, party proposals when they would clearly be inimical to the interests of the MP's constituency.

Amid this adversarial and partisan politics, the Speaker of the House is an impartial figure. The Speaker is seated between the two front benches, on his or her "throne," and is dressed in the style of the eighteenth century. The otherworldliness of her dress is perhaps to accentuate the complete impartiality assumed to reside in the office. Although an MP and elected from the House, the Speaker is selected for not having been a vociferous partisan; the aim is to find someone who can be elected unanimously rather than as a result of a partisan confrontation. Once elected, the conventions are that a Speaker may remain in the office as long as she wishes, with her seat rarely if ever contested (only four times since 1714). Although still an MP, her constituency duties are discharged by another member, and the Speaker will vote only in case of a tie. Then, by convention, the Speaker's vote is cast to preserve the status quo. As an impartial figure, the Speaker can discharge her role as a moderator and, to some degree, be the embodiment of the dignity of the House. The Speaker is not without real influence over decisions, however; for example, her use of the "kangaroo" decides which amendments to legislation will be debated and which not, and her acceptance of a motion of closure ends debate.

One important question a student of national legislatures would ask concerning the House of Commons would be: What is the nature of its committee system? While the House of Commons does have committees, they are by no means as central to the legislative process as the committees in the U.S. Congress or the German Bundestag. Eight standing committees in the House of Commons are composed of from sixteen to fifty members. Unlike American committees, only the core of the committee is permanent; other members are added to the committee depending on the nature of the bill being considered. Any one committee may consider a variety of bills during a session of Parliament, with the composition of the committee changing to match the nature of the bills. The composition of the committees, as well as reflecting the expertise of its members, reflects the partisan composition of the House as a whole, and a small majority in the House may result in a more substantial majority in committee. Also unlike American committees, the standing committees of the House of Commons are not really independent of the whole House but tend to reflect the whole House. Their role is not expert and transformative, as is that of U.S. committees; instead, they are miniature legislatures where bills may be discussed and improved and before which the government can accept amendments without jeopardizing its political stature in Commons. As an indication of this more limited capacity, the committee stage for legislation in the United Kingdom is *after* the principal political debate on the bill rather than before its primary consideration. As such, the major battles over the legislation have already transpired before the committee sees the legislation. Its purpose is to refine and amend the bill rather than significantly to influence its basic nature.

The preceding description of the committee system in the House of Commons holds true for legislation in England and to some extent Wales. Because most legislation is passed with a separate Scottish bill, in part a result of special features of Scots law, there is a separate committee system for Scottish bills. If a bill is meant primarily for Scotland, a special standing committee will be composed of approximately thirty MPs from Scottish seats and twenty others chosen for their interest in the legislation and to provide a proper partisan balance. For Scottish affairs there is also the Scottish Grand Committee, composed of all seventy-two MPs for Scottish seats along with such other MPs as are necessary to provide a partisan balance. The Scottish Grand Committee has rather broad responsibility for legislation intended for Scotland and reviews expenditures for Scottish concerns and any matters of particular interest to Scotland. There is an analogous set of Welsh committees, but these generally have not been as influential as the Scottish committees. This is in part because much Welsh legislation is joined with English and in part because of the significantly fewer (thirty-eight) Welsh MPs.

In addition to the standing committees, there are several select committees in the House of Commons. The most important of these are the Statutory Instruments Committee, the Public Accounts Committee, and the Expenditure Committee. The first of these committees monitors the issuing of statutory instruments, or delegated legislation, by government departments. Like all governments of industrialized societies, the workload of British government has increased to the point that Parliament cannot make all the needed laws. Instead, it delegates the authority to decide many legislative matters to the executive with the provision that this delegated legislation be subject to review by the Statutory Instruments Committee and potentially by the entire House of Commons. In contrast, the Public Accounts Committee is a manifestation of the traditional parliamentary function of oversight of expenditures; it monitors the government's expenditure plans, especially through the postaudit of the final expenditures. The Expenditure Committee is concerned more with prior examination of expenditure plans by the government. While not as effective as some might wish, these financial committees provide places to ventilate views on public expenditures and provide some parliamentary scrutiny of the massive volume of government expenditures.

One of the most interesting developments in the committee structure of Parliament has been the creation of twelve (now fourteen) select committees to follow the activities of government departments. This has been an attempt to establish the legislative oversight by committee so familiar to American political executives, although a similar suggestion was made by Richard Crossman in 1963, and even earlier by the Haldane Commission on the structure of government (1918).[5] Each of the twelve select committees monitors a functional area of government policy and holds hearings on and independent investigations into policy. Although their success has varied, they have provided Parliament with more institutionalized mechanisms for investigation; some of them, such as the Treasury and Civil Service Select Committee, have had a substantial impact on the direction of policy. This Select Committee, for example, has been active in monitoring and evaluating the administrative reforms of the Conservative government such as "Next Steps" (see below).

As indicated by the activities of the select committees, an important function of Parliament is the scrutiny of the political executive and its policies. Perhaps the most famous mechanism through which this takes place is the question hour. On four out of five sitting days during the week, the House of Commons opens its legislative day with an hour of questions for the government from members of the House. These questions have been submitted at least forty-eight hours previously in writing, so a minister has some opportunity to prepare an answer. In recent years, however, the practice has been to ask a very vague question in writing and then follow it with more probing supplemental questions orally. Thus a seemingly innocuous question as to whether the prime minister intends to visit Finland during the year may be an introduction to more important questions about foreign policy. All members of the government may be subjected to the question hour, and the prime minister answers questions on two of the four days. The question hour places an additional burden on already overburdened ministers; but in a political system where secrecy is the norm, this institution serves as one mechanism for the Parliament, and the people as a whole, to find out what is happening in government and exercise some control through the ventilation of possible malfeasance.

As an institution, Parliament is threatened. It has had difficulty maintaining its independent powers in the face of the growing powers of the prime minister and cabinet. Most of the important weapons in the struggle are in the hands of the executive. These include information, access to staff, and, more important, party discipline. Parliament now rarely exercises free and thorough scrutiny of the activities of a government; the outcomes of votes are known in advance, and it is the rare politician who will risk his political career on the basis of a principle. There are instances in which the Parliament does have a more open and influential debate on policy, as they did over European policy in the summer of 1991, but parliamentary government has, in effect, become cabinet or party government. Even these venerable institutions have been thought to be threatened by the power of the actor in the political process next to be discussed, the civil service.

The Civil Service

The traditional domination of the policy process by the British civil service—the "mandarins"—has been one of the great mysteries of British government. On the face of it, the British civil service is unprepared to perform the expert role it now performs in policy making. The recruitment of civil servants is less on the basis of expert knowledge in a substantive policy area than on the basis of general intellectual abilities. Also, for a large proportion of their careers, civil servants are moved from job to job and from department to department, gaining a permanent appointment only rather late in their careers. The cult of the "talented amateur" and the generalist dominates thinking about selection and training of civil servants, despite attempts at reform following the Fulton Committee, which expressed concern about the absence of specialized education of persons selected for the civil service.[6] Two decades after Fulton the pattern of recruitment has changed relatively little, and there are still more humanities graduates than scientists or social scientists entering the civil service.[7]

How can civil servants who themselves are hardly expert in the policy areas they administer have the influence over policy described by commentators and participants in policy making? Several factors seem to be related to this influence. The first is that although it may lack formal training in a policy area, the senior civil service is a talented group of individuals and thus has the intellectual ability to grasp readily the subject matter it must administer. Second, despite their relative lack of specialized training compared with civil servants in other countries,

British civil servants are generally more knowledgeable than their political masters about the relevant subject matter of departmental policy. They learn a great deal on the job, while their ministers are not on the job very long themselves. Finally, civil servants have a much longer time perspective than politicians and so are able to wait out and delay any particular minister with whom they disagree. Further, their ministries have an even longer collective memory than any single civil servant, so the accumulation of expertise and experience can easily counteract the legitimacy of the political master.

The relationship between civil servants and their political masters is important for defining and understanding the role of the civil service in policy making. The prevailing ethos of the civil service is that it can serve any political master it may be called upon to serve. But this "service" may be an attempt to impose the "departmental view," or the particular policy ideas of the department, on the minister. Any number of reasons can be advanced to explain why the ideas of the minister are not feasible and why only the proposals made by the department itself will ever work. Only the exceptional minister is able to counter such views.

The minister's task of countering a departmental view is made more difficult because the department may appear to speak with one voice. American executive departments tend to be fragmented, with a number of independent bureaus advancing their policy ideas. Executive departments in Britain have few such independent organizations; and policy ideas arising in departments are channeled upward through a hierarchical structure, with a permanent secretary being the primary link between the political world and the civil service. The permanent secretary is the senior civil servant in a department (though several departments now have two or more civil servants of this rank) and serves as the personal adviser to the minister. Because the minister lacks any substantial personal staff, he must rely heavily on the permanent secretary both for policy advice and for management of the department. This in turn gives the civil service, through the permanent secretary, a significant influence over policy. We would not argue that the civil service abuses this position, and in general the evidence is that it is responsible and scrupulous in the exercise of its office. Nevertheless, the structural position in which it is placed as the repository of information and of a departmental perspective, and the lack of alternative views coming to most ministers places the civil service in a powerful position.

The cozy world of the civil service is now under considerable challenge. We have already pointed out that the Thatcher government was unwilling to accept the advice that might be offered by civil servants and sought to bring its own advisers into government. The present Conservative government also appears to many to have sought to make the civil service more political, so that neutrality of the civil service may no longer be either possible or valued.[8]

Some observers of the British civil service, whether correctly or not, believed that Mrs. Thatcher played a more important role in the selection of senior officials than had previous prime ministers and that it would be difficult for some civil servants who were made permanent secretaries during her government to serve any subsequent Labour government. The reason for her appointment may not have been partisan, but there was involvement by the Prime Minister.

A second major challenge to the traditional role and functions of the civil service is that many individual civil servants question whether they have obligations to Parliament and to the public that transcend their loyalty to ministers. Several civil servants who knew of malfeasance in government have chosen to "blow the whistle," and in some cases they have been supported by the courts. Actions of this sort are uncomfortable and difficult in a system built on secrecy and ministerial responsibility, and the need for greater openness in government has become a political question.

Finally, the Thatcher and Major governments have been implementing a number of reforms in the civil service designed to minimize its policy advice role and to emphasize its managerial role. The most important of these reforms is "Next Steps," which will create several hundred semiautonomous "agencies" to implement most policies of government.[9] The policy and planning functions would be retained within relatively small ministries that would also be responsible for supervising the operations of the agencies. This administrative change also means that ministers may be less responsible for activities seemingly under their supervision and that some of the traditional mechanisms for accountability in the system of government will be less viable. Few things about the role and status of the civil service in the United Kingdom can now be taken for granted, as the internal machinery of government undergoes some very fundamental changes.

The Judiciary

By this time, the student of Western political systems would have wondered what has happened to the court systems. There are courts in the United Kingdom, but they are by no means as central to the political process as courts in the United States. In large part this is the result of the doctrine of parliamentary supremacy and the consequent inability of the courts to exercise judicial review of legislation. There is simply no way that British courts can declare an act of Parliament unconstitutional. As Dicey put it many years ago: "If Parliament decided that all blue-eyed babies should be murdered, the preservation of blue-eyed babies would be illegal."[10]

Little has changed to expand the power of the judiciary in Britain. The most significant change in the role of the courts results from Britain's membership in the European Community, with the European Court of Justice declaring some activities of the British government to be out of conformity with the Treaty of Rome or the European Convention on Human Rights.

The courts do have some role to play in the policy-making system. Although they lack the ability to declare actions unconstitutional, the courts can issue a number of writs, including *ultra vires* (literally, "beyond the powers"), inquiring as to the statutory authority of specific actions; and *habeas corpus,* requesting to know under what authority a citizen is detained by the authorities. Each case is each case, however; the courts cannot make sweeping statements about the legality of actions, and even the issuing of these writs may be suspended by the government, as it has been in Northern Ireland.

In recent years, the courts have become more aggressive in declaring the actions of a government to be *ultra vires*. This is in part a function of Britain's joining the European Community and the necessity of monitoring government implementation of Community law and in part because of the perceived need for independent checks on government. In particular, there has been some revival of interest in the role of administrative law as a check on government.[11] The courts do follow the election returns, however, and there are serious questions by some as to the extent to which there can truly be a government of laws when there is little independent ability to adjudicate the laws. This difficulty is further exacerbated by the attorney general's being a political official who in several instances in the late 1970s was charged with allowing his political affiliations to interfere with his legal duties. The courts have also had to deal with several major incidents of police misconduct that have shaken public confidence in the judicial system.

The Rest of Government

This final section on government institutions, which discusses the remaining activities and structures of government, is composed primarily of two parts: local government and public corporations. British government is unitary, but local governments have a substantial impact on the ultimate shape of public policies in the United Kingdom. In like manner, many public activities are carried out through public corporations rather than directly by a government department. This choice has consequences for the ability of government to control these functions.

First, local government is not an independent set of institutions with its own constitutional base of authority; instead, it is the creation of central government. Local government is divided into a two-tier system. The larger tier, the county (region in Scotland), covers a large population or large land area or both. For example, some English counties have several million inhabitants, while the Highlands Region of Scotland has an area of over six million acres. Beneath the regional level are districts, corresponding to cities or territories roughly equivalent to American counties. The numerous functions of subnational governments are divided among these two tiers of local government in a manner roughly related to the size of the area and population necessary for efficient service delivery. In fact, the local government reorganization that created the current system of local government has been the subject of a number of criticisms, both of the efficiency of the arrangements created and the loss of political influence in such large units as the regions.

Unlike American state and local governments, local governments in the United Kingdom are closely supervised by the central government. In England, the Department of the Environment supervises local governments; the Scottish, Welsh, and Northern Ireland Offices supervise local governments in their respective portions of the United Kingdom. A much larger proportion of the expenditures of local governments in the United Kingdom are funded through grants from the central government than is true in the United States (49 as opposed to 18 percent in 1986), making British local authorities more dependent on the center. These factors do not preclude conflict between central government and local authorities, especially when the two happen to be governed by different political parties. The conflicts between Conservative central governments and Labour local councilors in Clay Cross (1974), Lambeth (1979–80), and Liverpool (1985 onward) are indicative of such conflicts. In the early 1990s there have been major conflicts between central government and local governments over finance, especially the implementation of the poll tax.

The Thatcher government sought to increase control over local authorities from the center. This was in part for financial reasons, to ensure that the activities of local authorities did not counteract central government financial policies—especially reducing public expenditures. It was also for policy reasons and sought to ensure that local authorities were not able to manage their own affairs very differently from the desired policies of the center. Finally it was for political reasons, with a desire to reduce major power bases for the Labour party. In concrete terms, this meant that (among other things) the large metropolitan governments of large cities (e.g., the Greater London Council), were abolished. In addition, the basis of local government finance is being changed from a property tax (the rates) to a flat-rate "community charge," or poll tax. The latter change greatly reduces the capacity of local authorities to raise local revenues and thereby reduces their capacity to make local expenditures. From 1993 onward this will be replaced by a new council tax.

Public corporations have been an important part of the total governmental sector in the United Kingdom even though they are, at least in theory, distinct from the government itself. The central government has the right to appoint members to the boards of the nationalized industries and to make broad policy decisions—including which corporations will become or will remain nationalized—but the day-to-day decisions of these industries are made independently. This independence is constrained by their reliance on government funds both to cover operating deficits and especially to provide capital for new ventures. Also, decisions by a nationalized industry may produce political discontent with a government, as when the decision by the National Coal Board in 1979 to close several less productive Welsh pits prompted a strong outcry. This outcry increased in the mid-1980s, leading to a bitter year-long strike when more pit closings were announced.

The Thatcher government was willing to give up its role in the economy in order to privatize a number of nationalized industries, including gas, telecommunications, and British Airways. The government also sold off much of a major local "industry"—public housing—to the occupying tenants. These sales helped balance the budget and helped fulfill ideological dreams and campaign promises on behalf of free enterprise. There are ongoing plans to sell off other public assets and water, and British government is becoming much less of a direct economic actor. It has not been able to get out of the economy entirely, however, and almost every privatization has required increased regulatory authority to control the new industries.

The preceding has been a discussion of the major institutions of British government. While the functions performed by these institutions are similar to many performed in the U.S. presidential system, the manner in which they are performed is quite different. Perhaps even more important, the assumptions underlying the activities are frequently quite different. Most fundamental here is the lack of a formal limitation on the powers of a government and a Parliament. In addition, the traditional American doctrine of the separation of powers has no place in British politics, and an executive (prime minister) must have the support of the legislature (Parliament) in order to govern. Likewise, federalism has no place in British government, and local authorities are (and are increasingly) creatures of central government. Although it is, at times, popular to speak of "Anglo-American democracies," and although the United States and the United Kingdom share a number of common political precepts, there may be as much separating the two systems as uniting them.

Notes

1. Ivor Jennings, *Cabinet Government,* 3d ed. (Cambridge: Cambridge University Press, 1969), 277–89.

2. Anthony Bevins, "Unwritten Doctrine of Hung Parliament," *The Independent,* 21 June 1991.

3. Bruce Headey, *British Cabinet Ministers* (London: George Allen and Unwin, 1975).

4. Brian W. Hogwood and Thomas T. Mackie, "The United Kingdom: Decision Sifting in a Secret Garden," in *Unlocking the Cabinet: Cabinet Structures in Comparative Perspective,* ed. Mackie and Hogwood (London: Sage, 1985).

5. See Gavin Drewry, ed., *The New Select Committees* (Oxford: Clarendon Press, 1985).

6. Peter Kellner and Lord Crowther-Hunt, *The Civil Servants: An Inquiry into Britain's Ruling Class* (London: Macdonald, 1980), 209–19; and John Garrett, *Managing the Civil Service* (London: Heinemann, 1980).

7. Gavin Drewry and Tony Butcher, *The Civil Service Today* (Oxford: Basil Blackwell, 1988), 166ff.

8. Clive Ponting, *The Right to Know* (London: Sphere, 1986).

9. Kate Jenkins, Karen Caines, and Andrew Jackson, *Improving Management in Government: The Next Steps* (Ibbs Report) (London: HMSO, 1988).

10. A.V. Dicey, *Introduction to the Study of the Law of the Constitution,* 10th ed. (New York: St. Martin's, 1959), 74.

11. JUSTICE-All Souls, *Administrative Law: Some Necessary Reforms* (Oxford: Oxford University Press, 1988).

3

Who Has the Power and How Did They Get It?

A democratic political system requires a means for the public to influence the decisions of political leaders. This influence may be exercised only intermittently, as during elections, but in most democratic systems it is exercised almost constantly through mechanisms such as political parties and, increasingly, through interest groups. The government of the United Kingdom is no different. While some pundits have said that the United Kingdom is a democracy only once every five years (the statutory maximum term for a sitting Parliament), in fact the day-to-day decisions of British government are influenced by popular demands and pressures. The popular pressures are in part transmitted through partisan institutions, but the influence of pressure groups also requires careful scrutiny. This chapter is an investigation of the impact of popular demands on British government and the linkage between organizations such as political parties and interest groups and decision-making institutions.

Political Parties

To an American reader accustomed to political parties that are little more than electoral aggregations and mean little or nothing in organizational or policy terms, British political parties may come as a surprise. British political parties have discernible policy stances, even if sometimes these are designed merely to oppose the policies of the other party. Although they do have policy stances, British parties are primarily "catchall" parties and include a relatively wide range of opinion within any one party. This is true despite the ideological bent of the Conservatives during the 1980s and the attempts of the Labour party to purge its more confrontational elements on the left. Perhaps the major differences between British and American parties is that the parliamentary system in Britain requires greater party responsibility; and the absence of federalism requires the parties to act as national organizations. Thus, although a single British party may contain a variety of opinions on issues, it is expected that once the party *as a party* has spoken, the members of the party will attempt to implement those ideas if in office or will continue to espouse them if out of office. Further, the party is expected to say about the same thing in the north of Scotland as it says in the south of England. Parties do this less than perfectly, but they are much clearer about policy than American parties.

The Party System

The British party system has been described variously as a two-party system and as a two-and-one-half-party system. Election results during the 1970s and party realignments in the 1980s indicate that a more complex multiparty system may be evolving. The parties that constitute the addition to the two-party system have had some difficulty in organizing themselves and in presenting real alternatives to the two parties, but there has been some real change in the system.

The two major parties in Great Britain are the Labour party and the Conservative (Tory) party. They are national parties in every sense of the word and almost always run candidates in every Parliamentary constituency in Great Britain. The "half party" that has at times been mentioned was the SDP/Liberal Alliance. This was formed out of two parties, with an agreement not to oppose each other in a constituency. The Alliance ran candidates in every constituency in Great Britain in the 1987 election and won twenty-two seats scattered from the Shetlands to Cornwall, although mostly in Scotland and Wales. After that election, the party divided again into two parties. The larger portion went into the Liberal Democrats, while a splinter led by Dr. David Owen retained for a while the name of the Social Democrats. This split has eliminated, at least in the short run, any real potential this centrist grouping had of presenting an electoral alternative to the free-market neoliberalism of the Conservatives and the collectivism of the Labour party. This is especially true since the bitterness created by the split has prevented the two parties from working together effectively. In the 1992 election the Liberal Democrats lost two of the seats won in 1987. Even with their own internal problems, these centrist elements do appeal to voters disenchanted with both major parties.

Two other political parties regularly win Parliamentary seats in

Great Britain. These are the Scottish National party in Scotland, and Plaid Cymru, the Welsh National party, in Wales. These parties experienced a marked decline in their electoral fortunes in 1979, following defeat of devolution referenda in 1978. They made a minor comeback in the 1987 election, increasing their total from four to six seats, and have been doing well in by-elections since that time. Their vote as a percentage of the vote in their regions also increased very slightly, to almost 14 percent for the SNP in Scotland and 8 percent for Plaid Cymru in Wales. There is also substantial variation in their vote within their own regions, with Plaid Cymru receiving a high of 57 percent and a low of less than 1 percent in Welsh constituencies. The SNP vote ranged between 43 percent and 4 percent in Scottish constituencies.

Finally, the partisan politics of Northern Ireland reflect the troubled history of that province and the religious and nationalist cleavages that divide the population. In 1987, five political parties elected members of Parliament from Northern Ireland. Three of these—the Official Unionists, the Democratic Unionists, and the Popular Unionists—are Protestant and are dedicated to the continuing union of Northern Ireland and the United Kingdom. Two of the parties winning seats in Northern Ireland are primarily Roman Catholic and would like to unite Northern Ireland with the Republic of Ireland to its south. The Social Democratic Labour party is overwhelmingly Catholic and would like to unite all of Ireland as a single, socialist society; despite its sectarian appeal, it is a secular organization. The other Catholic party is Provisional Sinn Féin, generally regarded as the political arm of the Irish Republican Army. It is committed to the unification of Ireland by almost any means and has not completely disavowed violence. Unable to win any seats in the 1987 election was the Alliance party (not to be confused with the former Alliance in Great Britain), which is an attempt to be a "catchall" party cutting across religious lines as well as across class lines.

Before discussing political parties any further, we should add several points on the British electoral system. The system is a single-member district, plurality system. Each constituency elects a single representative (member of Parliament), and all that is required for election is a plurality (i.e., the individual with the most votes wins whether receiving a majority or not). Such a system has the advantage of producing majorities for Parliament, and although Britain has not had majority victories in terms of popular votes since 1935, there have been Parliamentary majorities. As a consequence, the smaller parties are severely disadvantaged; the Liberal Democrats have advocated proportional representation as a more equitable means of selecting members of Parliament.

As long as the electoral system continues to benefit the party in power, however, it is unlikely to be changed.

One aspect of the British electoral system unlike that of the United States is that the legal principle of "one-person, one vote, one value" is not honored. Scotland and Wales are overrepresented, while Northern Ireland has been significantly underrepresented (see table 3.1). The justification for this maldistribution of seats is that Scotland and Wales, because of their national identity and history, were deemed to have special interests requiring greater representation. In contrast, Northern Ireland has been underrepresented because, until 1974, it had substantially greater self-government, with its own Parliament sitting at Stormont, than did other parts of the United Kingdom. With the imposition of direct rule from Westminster, that justification is no longer valid, and subsequent changes in the distribution of seats have made representation more like that in Great Britain, albeit still lower than in the other parts.

TABLE 3.1

CITIZENS PER PARLIAMENTARY SEAT

	England	Wales	Scotland	Northern Ireland
Seats	523	38	72	17
Citizens per seat	89,600	73,900	71,500	92,900

Another feature of the British electoral system that differentiates it from the American is the importance of by-elections. If a seat becomes vacant during the life of a Parliament, an interim election (by-election) is held to fill the seat. As well as ensuring full membership of the House of Commons, by-elections serve as something of an ongoing vote of confidence by the people, and poor performance can be quite embarrassing for a government. For example, by-elections in the winter of 1986–87 were used as gauges of Mrs. Thatcher's electoral strength, as well as that of the SDP/Liberal Alliance, and became one part of the evidence used in deciding when to call the 1987 election. Elections to the European Parliament now serve as a similar barometer of public opinion, and the poor showing of the Conservatives in the 1989 European election was taken as a rebuke of Mrs. Thatcher's negative policy toward the European Community.

Those electoral losses and troubles in by-elections in 1990 helped set the stage for the revolt within the Conservative party that pushed Mrs. Thatcher out of office as prime minister.

The Two Major Parties

Although many voters may choose other parties, only two parties—Labour and Conservative—can be expected to form a government. These governments may depend on the explicit or implicit support of smaller parties, as did the Labour government for a short period in the late 1970s. During this period, the Labour party had a narrow majority from the beginning of the session and frequently depended on Liberal votes as well as the tacit support of the Scottish National party and portions of the Northern Ireland delegation to prevent a significant defeat in Parliament. There was not a formal coalition government, however, and the Liberals had no positions in the cabinet. There is a great deal that divides the two major parties in Britain, but in many ways they are similar. They are both "elite" or "caucus" parties, having a relatively small mass membership compared to their electoral strength. The parties are also aggregative, with both covering a range of social and political opinion and consequently having internal ideological divisions as well as disagreements with the other party. Both are relatively centralized and disciplined parties compared with decentralized American parties. Finally, both are national parties, drawing strength from all parts of the country, and they are generally the two top vote getters in each constituency.

The Conservative Party

The Conservative, or Tory, party has its roots in the political conflicts of the eighteenth century, and to some degree those roots produce conflicts within the emerging character of the Conservative party today. In the late 1980s, the majority of adherents to the Conservative party would feel akin to Conservative parties in Europe and North America, resisting encroachments into the affairs of individuals by government. Traditionally, however, the Conservative party has advocated strong central government, in part because of the perception that the poor and less educated cannot be counted on to make decisions on their own and need guidance by their "betters." "Old Tories" thus want significant governmental control over the private sector, albeit control used to preserve the interests of the upper classes. "New Tories," or "Thatcherite Conservatives," tend to advocate greater freedom for private-sector action and consequently a diminished role for government in economic and social life. The programs of Margaret Thatcher's decade in office would clearly correspond to this newer conception of Conservatives.

The Conservative party is an elite party, both in terms of the socio-economic characteristics of its adherents and in terms of the relationship between party members and the voting strength of the party. The voting strength of the Conservative party is at least four times greater than its membership, and although the party has over one million members, it remains a relatively small mass organization compared to its ability to organize voters and campaigns.

The Conservative party outside Parliament has two major components. One is a mass organization headed by the National Union of Conservative and Unionist Associations in England and Wales; there are similar bodies in Scotland and Northern Ireland. The governing body of the National Union is its Central Council, composed of representatives from the constituencies, Conservative members of Parliament and prospective candidates for that position, representatives of the Conservative Central Office, and other leaders of the party. The total membership of the Central Council is some 3,000 individuals. In practice, however, the National Union is run by a president and an Executive Committee of some 150 members elected by the Central Council. Power further tends to concentrate in the General Purpose Subcommittee of the Executive Committee, composed of only 50 members.

The territorial organization of the Conservative party is similar to the national organization. There are twelve provincial area councils; within each council the party is organized by constituencies, each with a leadership structure similar to that of the national party. The constituencies are also served by agents responsible for the administrative functions of the party. The constituency parties are important because it is at this level that most funds are raised and the majority of campaigning is managed. Also, the constituency must decide to accept candidates offered to them by the national party, or to develop candidates of their own who will be acceptable to the national party. Thus, although the Conservative party is centralized for many functions, such as the writing of the party platform (manifesto), in many important ways the party is decentralized to its constituency parties.

Assisting the local and national officers is the second major arm of the Conservative party outside Parliament: the Central Office. This office is directed by the chairman of the party organization and employs a number of professional workers, including those in the Conservative Research Department. The major officials in the Central Office are appointed by the party leader, and it is from this direct connection with party leadership that the Central Office derives most of its authority. The latter points to the overriding fact that the Conservative party is largely a party based on Parliament. Certainly the annual conference of the party has become much more assertive than it once was, and a leader must pay attention to the mass members of the party, but the real control over a leader comes from the party in Parliament, not from the mass membership.

The basis of Conservative party organization in the House of Commons is the 1922 Committee, composed of all Conservative members of the House of Commons, other than ministers, when the party is in government. The 1922 Committee has exercised considerable power over Conservative leaders, and that power had appeared to be increasing prior to Mrs. Thatcher. The leader of the Conservative party does not have to stand for annual election but can be challenged every year. Five of the ten leaders of the party since 1902 have been forced out of the leadership by backbenchers, either by direct vote or by the obvious disapproval of the leader by the led. Even sitting as prime minister for a decade and having molded her party in her own image did not prevent Mrs. Thatcher from being removed from office.

In addition to exercising control over the leadership of the party, another function of the party in Parliament is to maintain the voting discipline of the party members. The Conservative party has not "denied the Whip" (expelled) any of its members since 1945, although a number of members have refused the Whip during that period. In general, the Conservative party has not been beset with the deep internal splits that have plagued the Labour party and therefore the Conservatives have found it less necessary to employ the available sanctions. Also important for conflict management within the party are certain genteel traditions, such as not taking votes in the 1922 Committee but instead reading the "sense of the meeting" and the withdrawal of minority candidates for leader of the party after the first vote.

The selection of party leader is left almost entirely to the Parliamentary party, although there are provisions for constituency parties and other concerned groups to make their views known. To select a leader, a ballot is held of all Conservative MPs. In order for a candidate to be elected on the first ballot, he or she must receive not only an absolute majority but at least 15 percent more votes than the nearest competitor. If there is no successful candidate on the first ballot, a second ballot is held with only a simple majority required for election. If the second ballot fails to produce a winning candidate, a third ballot is held among the three top contenders with MPs indicating their second choices. If no candidate receives a majority of first-place votes, the second choices of those voting for the weakest candidate are distributed and a new leader is elected. As noted, however, it is now conventional for less successful candidates to resign after the first ballot to prevent deepening any divisions within the party.

The Conservative party in the 1980s offered a clear choice, a choice made even clearer by the first two years of Mrs. Thatcher's rule. Although purporting to accept many tenets of the welfare state, the Conservative government moved vigorously to reduce government expenditures and the role of government in industry and society. The party, to some people surprisingly, actually has done what it said it would do in its election campaigns. At first this created some dismay. But a combination of factors kept the Conservatives in power in two subsequent elections: disarray in the other parties, a strong showing in the Falklands War, and the creation of new Thatcherite voters through the generally increasing affluence of the employed throughout the nation. In his first few months in office, John Major has softened some of Mrs. Thatcher's policies, but not significantly. There is still a clear idea of what Conservative policy is and what the party intends to do in its next five years in office.

The Labour Party

The roots of the British Labour party are in the industrial revolution. The Labour party is the principal representative of the "working class" in British politics, although its support is broader than industrial labor. The Labour party professes socialism as a major portion of its program, but at the same time is an aggregative party that includes a variety of definitions of socialism and many who do not accept socialism as the goal of the party or society. Ideological cleavages within the Labour party are both more pronounced and more intense than those found in the Conservative party. Factionalism in the party prevented it from being a viable competitor to the Conservatives for much of the 1980s, but Neil Kinnock as leader of the party has sought to create a more moderate image and heal some of the strife within the party. For example, the Labour party has dropped its campaign pledge of unilateral nuclear disarmament in an attempt to appear stronger in foreign affairs and has moderated some stances on the re-nationalization of privatized industries, as well as its criticism of the European Community. Thus, it has behaved like a party in a two-party system should— seeking the electoral center—but has found that center farther to the right than it had been.

To comprehend the organization of the Labour party outside Parliament, one must first understand the role that labor unions play in the party. The British Labour party originally was an alliance of trade unions and socialist organizations, with unions the dominant element in that coalition. Currently, both the majority of the party membership (over five million of six million members) and the majority of the party's financial base come from the labor movement. Thus, when one speaks of the membership of the Labour party, one is really speaking of the unions, although members, through socialist organizations and constituency parties, have influence that is much greater than their numerical strength. This power was increased by a change in the party's constitution, electing the leader of the party through an electoral college that has a large share of constituency party members, albeit still dominated by the Parliamentary party.

As with the Conservative party, the Labour party has a National Executive Committee (NEC) that supervises party operations outside Parliament and, to an increasing extent, manages the whole party. Of the twenty-eight members of this committee, twelve are direct representatives of labor unions; only seven are representatives of constituency parties. The remaining members are the leader and deputy leader of the party (from the House of Commons), five women members, and a treasurer elected by the annual conference of the party. Major voices in the NEC and the annual conference other than elective politicians make their actions less predictable and manageable than those of the Conservative party's Executive Committee. This is especially true when the Labour party is the opposition party and the leader lacks the power of office. The bureaucratic arm of the party—equivalent to the Conservative Central Office—is the Labour party secretary and his staff. As noted, the party bureaucracy is rather closely controlled by the National Executive Committee. This control extends to having subcommittees of the NEC supervise various sections of the party organization such as research, press and publicity, and finance.

As with the Conservative party, the Labour party has regional organizations, but these organizations do not have the degree of importance of their equivalents in the Conservative party. Also, there are constituency parties that, until the 1980 changes in the party's structure, lacked even the autonomy granted to their equivalents in the Conservative party. These constituency parties now have the right to reselect their candidates before each election, removing that power from the central party. This power has led to the selection of some extreme left-wing candidates and some further division within the party. For example, in a Liverpool by-election, the moderate Labour candidate was opposed by a "Real Labour" candidate from Militant Tendency, the extreme left of the party.

The power of the unions in the Labour party is especially evident at the Labour party's annual conference. Of the approximately 4,000 participants in these autumnal affairs, there will be more representatives of constituency parties than unions. Voting is not based on the number of delegates present, however, but on the number of dues-paying party members represented by those present. Unions therefore hold the balance of power, with approximately five-sixths of all votes. In fact, the votes of the six largest unions constitute a majority in the conference.

The relationship between the Labour party's annual conference and the party in Parliament is not so clearly defined as in the Conservative party, and, at times, the annual conference has attempted to force its views on the Parliamentary Labour party (PLP). The formal statements of the party do in fact indicate that the annual conference has the right to make binding policy decisions for the PLP, but party leaders from the inception of the party have been unwilling to be controlled by policy pronouncements of those out of office, especially when there is a Labour government. The tension arises from the fact that "Labour began as a movement which created a Parliamentary party to serve its interests," so there is a greater tradition of mass party control than in the Conservative party, which began as a faction in Parliament.

Some tensions between segments of the Labour party—both institutional and ideological—have been illustrated by the conflict over the Commission of Inquiry mandated by the 1979 annual conference. This commission was charged with investigating the structure and constitution of the Labour party, especially questions of the authorship of the party manifesto, the reselection of Parliamentary candidates in each constituency prior to each general election, and the election of the party leader by a more broadly constituted body than the PLP. All these issues pitted the ideological left of the party, based in constituency organizations, against the ideological right in the PLP, especially the leadership of the PLP (then most prominently James Callaghan and Denis Healey). These issues came to a head after the annual conference accepted the report of the commission favoring the stand of the left, whereupon Callaghan resigned as party leader. The provisions of the new constitutional arrangement for electing a party leader were now finally decided, and Michael Foot—a representative of the left, although a less divisive one than most—was elected leader. These changes in the Labour party led to the defection of what became the Social Democrats from the party, and seemed to be pushing the Labour party farther left than has been true in the past. Several disastrous electoral defeats gave the right and center the opportunity to reassert their case for a more centrist party dedicated to winning elections, not ideological wrangles. Even the "modernized" Labour party could not, however, win the 1992 election, and Neil Kinnock resigned and was replaced by John Smith.

The Parliamentary Labour party (PLP) is composed of all Labour MPs, including ministers or shadow ministers. As this group is not strictly a backbench group (such as the 1922 Committee), there is a greater emphasis on its role as a liaison committee to keep the leadership informed of the opinion in the party; when in Opposition, the annual election of a Parliamentary Committee serves as a mechanism for linking the average Labour MP with his or her leadership.

When there is a conflict, it is clear that the PLP is the dominant element in decision making for the party. This is changing, however. It is also clear that there are already more opportunities for the mass membership to challenge the leadership than exist for members of the Conservative party. And the PLP itself is frequently not united. Neil Kinnock managed to paper over most of these divisions, but they still lurk beneath the surface and threaten the electoral viability of the Labour party.

Voting and Elections

Elections are a crucial driving force for democratic politics. Or are they? Certainly all conventional analyses of British politics assume that the policies of government are decided by the clash of political parties over issues. In like manner, voters are assumed to be both interested in politics and to make their choices among parties on the basis of issues. These may be assumptions largely unsubstantiated by evidence. Let us look at the evidence about the turnout of voters and reasons for their voting choices, and then ask a few pertinent questions about the role of elections in policy choice in the United Kingdom.

Before we do that, however, we should point to several salient features of British elections. British elections are national elections, but they are national elections conducted in constituencies. Although it is clear who will be prime minister should one party or the other win, only two constituencies actually vote for prospective prime ministers. Also, these constituencies are quite small compared with electoral districts in most Western countries. The average English MP represents 90,000 people, and the average Scottish MP 73,000 people. By way of contrast, the average member of the National Assembly in France represents over 100,000 people and the average congressman in the United States over 500,000 people. Also, the expenses of constituency campaigning in Britain are regulated so that a candidate cannot spend more than £2,700, plus 2.3 pence (about 4 cents) per voter in urban districts and 3.4 pence per voter in rural districts. This combined with the short campaign period (six weeks or less) and the difficulty of purchasing electronic media time other than for specified "party political broadcasts" make British campaigns very different from the extended electronic contests familiar to Americans.

Also, the parties control the selection of candidates more centrally than American parties do. The concept of a primary is unheard of, although the constituency parties do have an active voice in the initial selection of their candidates. A prospective candidate must be accepted by the constituency party, with the Central Office exercising a largely advisory role. This holds true for the acceptance of a new candidate, although candidates already sitting for a seat in Parliament, or having stood for a seat in the constituency in the previous election, do not have to be reselected in the Conservative party but now do in the Labour party.

Turnout

British citizens tend to vote more readily than American citizens do, although not so readily as citizens in other Western democracies. Turnout is also relatively evenly distributed across the country. As is true for most other countries, the abstainers are concentrated in the working class, a factor that goes a long way to explain the ability of the Conservative party to win as many elections as it does, given that approximately half the populace are generally classified as working class, and perhaps even a higher percentage identify themselves as working class. The British government is active in registering citizens to vote with the local government having a positive obligation every October to bring the electoral rolls up to date and to register all possible electors, so that approximately 95 percent of all eligible electors are registered.

Partisan Choice by Voters

As well as deciding whether to vote, a voter must decide for whom to vote (see table 3.2). There has been a great deal of research on the determinants of the partisan choices of voters. Three factors are usually discussed as the principal determinants of partisan choice in Britain: social class, region of the country, and issues. These three factors obvi-

TABLE 3.2

CHANGES IN PERCENTAGES OF PARTISAN VOTING[a]

Party	1970	Feb. 1974	Oct. 1974	1979	1983	1987	1992
Conservative	46.4	38.2	35.8	43.9	42.4	42.3	42.8
Labour	43.0	37.2	39.3	36.9	27.6	30.8	35.2
Liberal[b]	7.5	19.3	18.3	13.8	25.4	22.6	18.3
Scottish National	1.1	2.0	2.9	1.6	1.1	1.3	1.7
Plaid Cymru	0.6	0.5	0.6	0.4	0.4	0.4	0.5
Other	1.4	2.8	3.1	3.4	3.1	3.2	1.5
Totals	100.0	100.0	100.0	100.0	100.0	100.0	100.0
Two-party	89.4	75.4	75.1	80.8	70.0	73.1	78.0

a. Percentages of votes cast for each party at each election.

b. In 1983–87 the Liberals were part of the Alliance; Liberal Democrats in 1992.

ously interact. Members of social classes are not evenly spread across the country, with more working-class voters living in Scotland, Wales, and the industrial North and Midlands of England and more middle- and upper-class voters living in the southeast or southwest of England. The issues to which citizens are assumed to respond also have different impacts on members of different social classes and on residents of different regions. Consequently it is hard to disaggregate the effects of these different influences, but let us at least describe some apparent effects.

Social Class. Social class is generally considered to be the dominant factor in explaining voting in Britain. As noted, much of British politics has been conceptualized in class terms. While there is strong evidence that class remains an important factor in the voting decisions, there is also some evidence that it is not so overwhelming as often believed. For example, in the 1987 election approximately 40 percent of the electorate did not vote for the party (between the two major parties) usually associated with its class interests. This statement may be taken to say either that over half the voters seem to vote along class lines or that almost half do not, and over one-third cross class lines rather explicitly when voting.[1] The rate of defection was especially high among working-class voters.

Several factors reinforce class voting among citizens, especially members of the working class. Three factors of importance are membership in certain organizations, patterns of residence, and patterns of communication. In general, members of labor unions are substantially more likely to vote Labour than are members of the working class as a whole. For example, in 1987, 60 percent of union members voted Labour, while 44 percent of working-class voters who were not members of unions voted Labour. This was true even though many of those not voting for Labour were in objectively worse socioeconomic conditions

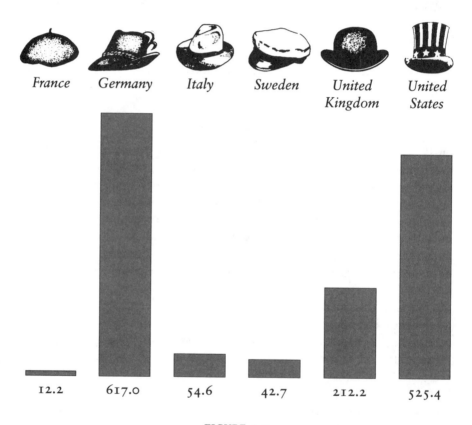

FIGURE 3.1
ANNUAL IMMIGRATION
(IN THOUSANDS)

SOURCE: *U.N. Demographic Yearbook, 1989.*

than the union members. Nevertheless, the impact of union membership on voting has been declining, in part because union members who have jobs have begun to make middle-class incomes and have begun to behave politically more like the middle class.

Membership in religious organizations also tends to affect the class dimension of voting. On the one hand, adherents of the Church of England tend to vote Conservative more than do members of other churches. To characterize the Church of England as the "Tory party at prayer" may be to overstate the identity of church and party, but there is an influence of church membership. On the other hand, Catholic members of the working class tend to vote Labour more consistently than do workers as a whole. Even leaving aside the influence of Northern Irish politics on voting, Catholic voters in cities such as Glasgow and Liverpool are among the most consistent Labour supporters.

Finally, certain "life-style" characteristics are important in explaining why members of the working or middle classes tend to vote for or against the nominal interests of their class. Working-class voters living in council (public) housing are much more likely to vote Labour than members of the working class living in other accommodations. Similarly, members of the middle class who enjoy such middle-class amenities as automobiles and telephones (not so widely distributed in the United Kingdom as in the United States) are more likely to vote Conservative than their more deprived colleagues. Finally, the receipt of social benefits appears to have some influence on voting, with individuals receiving benefits more likely to vote Labour. At least until the recession of 1990–91, working-class voters with jobs often had good incomes, and the Labour party appeared to be becoming the party of the unemployed and intellectuals. Some analysts have argued that these life-style factors have become more important in explaining patterns of voting behavior than simple membership in a social class.[2]

Patterns of Residence. Where people live seems to affect their voting behavior. First, living in the Celtic Fringe may affect voting. Leaving aside opportunities and motivations to vote for third-party candidates, the division of votes between the two major parties also differs in different parts of the country. Wales is the most heavily Labour portion of the United Kingdom, followed closely by Scotland. Were it not for Wales and Scotland, the Conservatives would have a permanent majority in the House of Commons because of their strength in England. The north of England has become more similar to the Celtic Fringe, with the partisan divide (as well as the economic divide) in Britain now appearing to lie on a line from the Wash to Bristol Channel. The tendency of Labour to pile up huge majorities in its safe constituencies also means that it generally must receive more votes to win an election than would Conservatives: votes are important, but winning parliamentary seats wins elections.

Second, rural voters tend to vote Conservative in greater proportions than do urban voters. This is in part a function of the concentration of workers in urban industrial areas, but there also appears to be some direct effect of residence. This may reflect the traditional deference of rural residents. Finally, the constituency within which a voter lives influences voting. This is especially true of prospective Labour voters who vote Labour in much greater proportions in safe Labour seats than in competitive, or safe Conservative, seats. This is a function of the reinforcing effects of interactions with other Labour voters and of union efforts to mobilize the vote.

Issues. Voters are assumed to respond to candidates on the basis of the issues. British parties are at once centrifugal and centripetal. They express class differences more clearly than do American parties, but they are also sufficiently centrist to attempt to disguise some of their potential differences in order to gain votes. Although some issues divide voters, the majority of voters of both parties tend to be on the same side of most major political issues in Britain, with conflicts often being over how best to reach the common goals. Labour and Conservative majorities were on the same side of seven of ten issues in 1979, with the issues on which they were more divided having to do primarily with the powers of labor unions.[3] In 1986, majorities of the two parties agreed on ten of sixteen issues.[4] The parties have polarized somewhat since that time, but their voters still share many common goals. Also, it should be noted that there was substantial disagreement within the parties on the issues, especially within Labour, and that the level of agreement *within* parties was not always higher than the level of agreement *across* parties.

In addition, there is evidence that the parties are increasingly perceived by British voters as "much of a muchness," rather than parties that present distinct policy alternatives. During the 1950s, at least two-thirds of the citizens polled perceived important differences between the two major parties; by 1987, only half recognized any important differences. The more ideological Thatcher government has tended to accentuate the differences between the parties, and later polls have shown greater perceived party differences by voters. This is, in part, because

Mrs. Thatcher herself has become an issue, of substantive content of policies as well as of the style with which she manages government.

Despite the pressures toward greater ideological thinking by the Conservatives and Labour's attempts to call its faithful back to the fold, partisan identification has been declining in Britain. Strong identifiers with parties have decreased by over 50 percent since the 1960s.[5] This dealignment is also found in most other Western countries. It appears that voters are indeed more willing to think for themselves and to make decisions in each election based on issues, candidates, or whatever. This makes the task of political leaders that much more difficult, because they cannot count on a solid base of party identifiers when they begin their election campaigns.

There is no neat means of summarizing voting behavior in Britain. The class model does not seem to fit the increasing complexity of the situation as well as is often assumed. Yet no other model can adequately describe the complexity of the situation either. As important as elections and parties are for the choice of governments in the United Kingdom, a number of interacting factors enter into party choice. More important, there is some question whether elections and the choice of parties really have much consequence for the policies of government. Richard Rose has done a detailed analysis of whether parties in Britain make a difference in policy terms, with the conclusion that such differences as do result are more matters of emphasis and the timing of policies than absolute differences in the content of policies.[6] Clearly parties do make a difference, but the differences are subtle and not much based on a simple class model of politics.

Part of the reason for the consensual nature of the policies between the two major parties is the nature of the individuals recruited by the two parties to their leadership. If we look at the social and educational origins of Conservative and Labour politicians, we find more similarity than difference. The Labour party began as a party of the workingman, with the majority of the leadership coming from the ranks of manual workers. The party in 1980 had few in leadership positions with this background—the majority were Oxford or Cambridge graduates, many with private school secondary education. And some leaders of the Conservative party (e.g., Margaret Thatcher, Edward Heath, and John Major) come from less elegant social backgrounds than the usual caricature of the Tory party.

British politics is built on an adversarial model. In recent years much of the controversy generated has been over great issues of policy and the direction of government. The two major parties do have different basic goals, but with John Major replacing Mrs. Thatcher the differences may moderate.

Pressure Groups and Corporatism

One factor that has pushed toward the homogenization of policies between the two parties is the growing influence of interest groups in British politics. As with most industrialized countries, there has been a movement toward "corporatism" in British politics, with a number of interest groups granted something approaching an official status as generators of demands and implementers of policies once adopted.[7] The role of groups is rarely acknowledged officially—the doctrine of Parliamentary supremacy is still invoked—but in practice much public policy is influenced or even determined by interest groups. So, no matter which party is in office, there are pressures for continuity of policies rather than change from one government to the next. Also, the policies made in conjunction with pressure groups tend to be made through stable patterns of interaction between civil servants and pressure-group leaders, and through institutionalized processes of advice. Changes in government, therefore, would have little opportunity to affect the basic content of the policies.

Major Groups

A number of different groups affect policy. They range from small "attitude" groups with narrow and largely noneconomic concerns (e.g., ecological groups, peace activists) to large, influential "interest" groups that seek to have their economic interests magnified through the policy process. The most notable example of the economic groups are labor unions, although business and agriculture are also highly organized and effective politically.

Labor Unions. The largest and most influential of the interest groups are the unions, with a total membership of 11.5 million workers, or about 45 percent of the total labor force. These unions are organized into one national federation, the Trades Union Congress (TUC), linked to the Labour party. The unions are a major counterforce to the power of government, and British elections have been fought over whether the unions or the government actually ran the country, with ambiguous results. The political power of the unions, combined with the threat of industrial action by their members, makes them a formidable political influence indeed. This influence is perhaps best exercised when Labour is out of government, for the close ties between the Labour party and the unions tend to restrain the unions' political activities; restrain, but by no means stifle. Despite its size, the TUC has been losing some of its power. In the first place, a declining proportion of the labor force belongs to unions, and there is a shift from blue-collar to white-collar union membership. Although some white-collar unions have shown a willingness to use the strike weapon (e.g., in the public sector), most are less militant than blue-collar workers. Further, the TUC has not been able to enforce any discipline on its own members. When the miners struck in 1985–86, after some negotiations with the government, the TUC urged them to return to work, but the miners refused. The failure of the miners to win concessions from the government weakened the trade union movement. Union militancy can still produce widespread and disruptive strikes (e.g., the transportation strikes of the summer of 1989), but a good deal of the power appears to be gone.

Management. Although there is a single large labor movement, management groups are divided into several groups. The Confederation of British Industries (CBI) is the major management organization, but a number of other general and specialized industrial groups also speak for management. The linkage between management groups and the Conservative party is not so close as that between the unions and the Labour party, although it certainly does exist. They have relatively less direct influence on party policies and programs than the unions do in Labour. The Institute of Directors, for example, was increasingly important during the 1980s and has emerged as another important group speaking for business. Although not really management per se, financial interests in the City of London ("the City") also have a substantial influence over economic policy and over the Conservative party. This has become especially apparent as financial deregulation during the Thatcher government has helped the London Stock Exchange and other financial markets to prosper.

Agriculture. Relatively few workers are employed in agriculture in the United Kingdom, but farmers and their colleagues in fishing are well organized and very effective. The most important organization is the National Farmers Union (NFU), but commodity groups ranging from beekeepers to dairymen are actively engaged in lobbying and other political activity. Agricultural groups have traditionally been successful in obtaining subsidies for their crops and have been especially advantaged by Britain's entry into the European Community and the access to the subsidies of the Common Agricultural Policy of the EC. They have shifted a good deal of their lobbying focus to the European level, but still are effective in extracting subsidies and benefits from the Ministry of Agriculture, Fisheries and Food in London, and the Scottish Agricultural Department in Edinburgh.

Professional Organizations. A large number of professional organizations exist in the United Kingdom, such as the British Medical Association, the Royal College of Nursing, and the British Association of Social Workers. These groups tend to be politically unaffiliated and as much concerned with the maintenance of professional standards of practice as the protection of the political and economic interests of their members. In the former role, professional groups frequently serve in a public capacity as the source and implementers of standards and as accrediting agencies for practitioners. Nevertheless, given that the major employer of health care professionals and social service professionals is government, these associations do press their own political interests. These have to do with economic issues such as pay and working conditions, as well as social concerns such as the overall level of funding and service in the National Health Service.

Education is another service area dominated by the public sector. The major education associations in the United Kingdom are at once professional associations and unions. The National Union of Teachers (NUT) and the Association of University Teachers (AUT) are both affiliated with the TUC, and both have struck or have threatened striking. They are also vitally concerned with professional issues such as academic freedom and tenure. The AUT has been especially active during the Thatcher and Major years attempting to ward off the resource starvation that has been imposed on universities in Britain.

Attitude Groups. In addition to the economic interest groups described above, a number of attitude groups are important in British politics. There are a huge number of such groups, covering almost the gamut of social issues. Three sets of groups have been particularly important. One of these sets are peace movement groups. The Campaign for Nuclear Disarmament (CND) has been the longest-lived of these, beginning its protests against British nuclear weapons and American weapons on British soil in the 1950s and continuing until the present. CND has been joined by a number of other peace and antinuclear groups, such as the Greenham Common women protesting the location of American cruise missiles in Britain. Nature and environmental groups have been a second of these sets. With the Royal Society for the Prevention of Cruelty to Animals on one end of a spectrum of tactics and radical antivivisection groups on the other, this movement has sought to protect wildlife in Britain and increasingly has been involved with similar issues throughout the European Community. The third of these sets have been those stressing human rights rather than animal rights: Amnesty International, Oxfam, Save the Children, Shelter, and a host of other social service and international aid organizations.

Patterns of Influence

As in virtually all democratic systems, there are a number of means through which pressure groups in the United Kingdom can attempt to influence the policies of government. Given that government in the United Kingdom is less receptive to interest groups than many other governments, the routes of influence may be somewhat more circuitous. The four major methods for pressure-group influence in the United Kingdom are lobbying, direct sponsorship of MPs, direct representation on government bodies, and consultation with ministries.[8]

Lobbying. Lobbying is perhaps less common in the United Kingdom than in the United States, in part because party discipline makes it less likely to influence an MP's vote. Lobbying does occur, with the purpose being to get a voice in Parliament, more than a vote. MPs receive delegations from their constituencies or from nationally based organizations. Such delegations are particularly influential when a constituency has a single major economic interest, as with automobile manufacturing in Coventry or coal mining in some Welsh constituencies. Some pressure groups are sufficiently well organized to hire "Parliamentary agents" or "correspondents" to maintain contact with MPs, attempting to influence the few potential crossover MPs and feeding friendly MPs ideas and information. In turn they receive attention for their interests at those opportunities that even backbench MPs have to introduce business (e.g., the question hour or adjournment debates).

Direct Sponsorship of MPs. In the United Kingdom it is permissible for interest groups to "sponsor" prospective MPs, that is, to pay the majority of their electoral and other expenses. A group may even keep an MP on a retainer as long as that relationship is registered with the leadership of the House. Naturally, sponsorship involves some degree of control by the sponsor, although in cases such as those of unions and working-class MPs, it is unlikely that the sponsor would ask the MP to do anything he or she would not otherwise have done.

Direct Representation. Interest groups have direct and official links with government in several ways. In some instances, interest groups are directly represented in advisory committees attached to ministries. In other cases, pressure groups may actually compose the majority of public organizations, such as the National Economic Development Council ("Neddy"), established to promote economic growth through the cooperation of business, labor, and government. Finally, interest groups may actually administer programs for government, as the Law Society does with Legal Aid. In all these cases, it is clear, first, that governments cannot readily ignore interest groups so closely tied to the public sector, and second, that many of the traditional ideas about the separation of state and society in Western democracies make relatively little sense in the light of the increasing use of private organizations for public purposes.

Consultation. Less formally, government organizations frequently consult with interest groups. Interest groups have expert knowledge of their particular areas, and they are able to predict the reactions of their members to proposed policy changes. A government agency can gain not only in the technical quality of its proposals but also in their legitimacy by full consultation prior to the enactment. In an era in which delegated legislation is increasingly important, this means that a substantial amount of policy will be determined by consultations between civil servants and interest-group members. And interest groups are having an increasing impact on policies of all kinds, with a consequent decline in the relative influence of political parties and elective politicians.

This chapter has sought to outline the basic features of the party and pressure-group universe in the United Kingdom. In so doing, it has also raised some questions about the manner in which public policy is made, and the impact of elections on policy. The purpose was not to put the efficacy of elections and mass democracy into doubt, but to point to the immense difficulties of making mass democracy an effective influence on policy in contemporary political systems such as that of the United Kingdom. In addition, with the increasing influence of interest groups on policy—in Britain as well as other industrialized democracies—a citizen may question whether parties or interest groups are, in fact, the more effective route of political organization. The next chapter discusses in more detail how the institutions of government arrive at decisions and how they put those decisions into effect.

Notes

1. David Butler and Dennis Kavanagh, *The British General Election of 1979* (London: Macmillan, 1980), 350.

2. Richard Rose, "Britain: Simple Abstractions and Complex Realities," in *Electoral Behavior,* ed. Richard Rose (New York: Free Press, 1974).

3. Richard Rose, *Do Parties Make a Difference?* (Chatham, N.J.: Chatham House, 1980), 39.

4. Richard Rose, *Politics in England,* 5th ed. (Glenview, Ill.: Scott, Foresman, 1989), 262.

5. Ivor Crewe, "The Electorate: Partisan Dealignment Ten Years On," *West European Politics* 6 (1983): 213–45.

6. Russell J. Dalton, Scott C. Flanagan, and Paul Allen Beck, eds., *Electoral Change in Advanced Industrial Democracies* (Princeton, N.J.: Princeton University Press, 1984).

7. Rose, *Do Parties Make a Difference,* 43.

8. J.J. Richardson and A.G. Jordan, *Governing Under Pressure* (London: Martin Robertson, 1979).

4

How Is Power Used?

To this point we have described the institutions of British government, but have done so in rather a static fashion. This chapter attempts to bring these structures to life and show how actors and institutions produce policies. We also show how the distinctive character of British governmental institutions affects the policies produced so that they may be different from those emanating from other political systems, even those faced with similar policy-making problems.

It is helpful in this discussion to consider two broad kinds of policy making that must go on in any government. The first is making *new* policies, as when the institutions of government decide to engage in new activities or to undertake their current activities in different ways. This type of policy making is typically a legislative process, although administrative actors are certainly involved in the initiation of new policy ideas and in their implementation. Also, the making of new policies tends to be more overtly politicized, with parties and interest groups directly involved in the process.

The second major form of policy making is simply maintaining the existing policies and programs of government. This is frequently less political in a partisan sense; instead, it involves the bargaining of existing program managers with their financial overseers (in Britain, the Treasury) as well as overt or covert competition between existing programs. Thus the majority of this kind of policy making is not legislative but involves executive and administrative actors. Further, there will be very little discretion in much of this category of policy making because of the existing commitments of government to citizens and organizations. We now look at the British political system as it processes both kinds of policy decisions.

The Parliamentary Process and New Policies

To understand how new policies are made and then put into operation, it is convenient to follow a "typical" piece of legislation through the process of lawmaking, from an issue being placed on the agenda for consideration through its implementation. Of course, no piece of legislation is typical; some bills are passed in a matter of days the first time they are proposed, while others wait for years before being passed. Some policy ideas may never be made into law, or they may have their intentions almost totally altered through implementation. Despite these differences, an underlying policy-making process is common to all.

Agenda Setting and Policy Formulation

The first thing that must be done if a piece of legislation is to be adopted is to place it on the policy-making agenda. This is true in an informal sense in that the policy must be considered important for the government to act on, and is true in the more formal sense of being placed before Parliament for consideration and possible adoption.

Deciding what issues are public and require the consideration of government is a very diffuse and uncertain process in Britain, as it is in almost all countries. Political parties and the governments they form are principal agents in placing issues on the agenda, but other actors are also involved. These others include individual members of Parliament who may have special interests and strive—sometimes for years—to have an issue considered. Interest groups are also involved in agenda setting and attempt to dramatize the needs and desires of their members. Increasingly the media is placing issues into the consciousness of citizens and that of governing institutions. Finally, Britain's membership in the European Community has meant that a number of issues arising in Brussels have to be dealt with by the government in London.

In the formal sense, the easiest way for an issue to come before Parliament is for it to become a part of the government's legislative program. Parliament's legislative time is limited, and the government must select those issues and bills it believes are most important. This requires difficult choices by the government because it introduces relatively few bills in any year. For example, during the Thatcher years, governments introduced an average of just under fifty bills per session. Since several of them involved annual budget and finance considerations, and a large number of others involved consolidation and clarification of existing legislation, few significant policy bills were introduced during each parliamentary session.[1] In almost all cases, the policy bills that were passed were a part of the government program, and the government can, if it wishes (and it usually does), control the agenda of Parliament.

Bills and issues may also come before Parliament without acceptance by the government. Backbenchers can introduce legislation, although it has little chance of being passed. First, a backbencher must win a lottery to have the opportunity to introduce a bill and then there are generally only twelve or sixteen Fridays—the day on which private members' bills are debated—during a session in which a bill may be considered. Bills may also be introduced under the ten-minute rule, which allows for ten minutes of debate, pro and con, followed immediately by the vote. Both kinds of legislation allow for a consideration of issues the government may as soon forget, or issues of a moral nature on which the government does not wish to take a stance, and some private members' bills are really submitted as a favor to the government. Backbenchers cannot, however, introduce legislation involving the expenditure of public funds.

It is easier to have issues discussed in Parliament than to pass legislation. The question hour is an obvious example. Adjournment debates and motions by private members also allow individual MPs to air grievances. On average, backbenchers receive approximately 15 percent of parliamentary time, an allocation made by the government, and much of that time is spent discussing specific constituency grievances. This allows the average member relatively little opportunity to have an impact on major policy issues.[2] The Opposition is also given a substantial amount of parliamentary time to present its alternatives to the government program, the major opportunities being the debate on the Queen's Speech (actually written for her by the government), which opens each session of Parliament, and the twenty-six supply days scattered throughout the session.

In addition to controlling the agenda and timetable, the government must be heavily involved in formulating legislation. This is generally done by the cabinet prior to the legislation's being proposed to Parliament. Much of the impetus for policy formulation comes from the party's election manifesto. Nevertheless, parties are not the only source of policy intentions and policy formulation, and many policy ideas come up from the departments themselves. And, as with many industrialized democracies, the balance of power between elective and nonelective officials may have swung in favor of the unelected. In any case, the process of formulating policy is complex, involving the interaction of ministers with their civil servants and, in turn, consultation with the affected interests in society. Further, within the cabinet, legislation typically is considered by a cabinet committee composed of interested ministers (usually with some Treasury representation) before consideration by the entire cabinet.

Policy Legitimation

Once the cabinet has agreed on a policy proposal, it is introduced into Parliament as a bill, with all politically controversial legislation by convention first going to the House of Commons. For a bill to become law, it must pass the House of Commons, pass the House of Lords (unless it is passed by three successive Houses of Commons), and gain royal assent. There are ways of shortcutting this process, and a significant amount of lawmaking in Britain is done by the government itself, using "orders in council" that do not require the approval of Parliament.

When a bill is introduced into the House of Commons, it is given a formal first reading and then printed for distribution. After two or three weeks, the second reading takes place, which is the major political debate on the principles of the legislation. For noncontroversial legislation, however, the second reading may occur in committee. After the second reading, a bill typically goes to committee for detailed consideration and possible amendment. Note that the committee stage occurs *after* Commons has agreed to the legislation in principle. Although committees are organized to mirror the partisan composition of Parliament, the government is much more willing to accept amendments in committee than on the floor of the House where this might be taken as an admission of defeat. Finally, the bill is reported out of committee with any amendments, a third reading is given, and the legislation is passed. The bill then goes to the House of Lords for consideration and possible amendment. Any amendments made in Lords must be considered by Commons. And although deadlocks are possible, they are infrequent. After agreement is reached, the bill is given to the queen for royal assent, which is virtually automatic.

Of course, legislation does not necessarily move so easily through the policy-making system, and so there must be some means of regulating the flow, particularly preventing the delay of important legislation. At the report stage, a number of amendments may be reported out of committee, and the Speaker is given the power to decide which amendments should be debated and which would be repetitious of debates in committee. The government can also attempt to impose closure and the "guillotine" (allocation of time order). Closure is a motion to end debate made by a hundred or more MPs, but it will be accepted only if the Speaker believes all relevant positions have been heard. When there are a number of different points of dissent and closure is ineffective, the guillotine is employed. An allocation of time order is voted by the House of Commons, and the government makes a determination of how much time will be spent on each section of the bill. Once that time is exhausted, the Speaker must move the section to a vote. The use of the guillotine is often cited as contradictory to the interests of the House as a deliberative body, especially when it is imposed on major constitutional issues, such as the devolution debates during the Callaghan government in the 1970s. But the guillotine may be necessary if Parliament is to process the amount of legislation a contemporary democracy requires.

With party discipline, much of the legislative activity of Parliament appears foreordained, but it is still important. First, the legal and constitutional requirements for the passage of legislation must be fulfilled. Second, amendments can be accepted and the amended legislation must be approved, both in the committee stage in Commons and in Lords. Finally, some legislation that seems perfectly reasonable to the majority of the cabinet may not appear so reasonable to backbenchers in the party, and the legislation may never be passed. On average about 10 percent of all government bills introduced into Parliament do not become law; few are defeated, but others may be withdrawn. Thus, although the presence of disciplined majorities in the House of Commons is certainly important, legislative action is never certain.

British democracy has long been representative democracy, but there were several interesting occurrences of direct democracy as a means of legitimating policies during the 1970s. Of particular significance were two referenda on policy issues—in 1975 on whether Britain should enter the Common Market, and in 1979 on the devolution proposals in Scotland and Wales. The latter proposals were voted on in Scotland and Wales only, but the principle was the same: The government and Parliament to some degree abdicated their decision-making powers to the people in an election. Although these referenda were not legally binding, they were declared binding by the major parties. Referenda represent a major departure from the traditional means of decision making in British government and have potential importance for major policy decisions.

Policy Implementation

After a bill is passed by Parliament, perhaps the most difficult portion of the process of changing society through government action occurs: the implementation process. This is the process of taking the bare bones of parliamentary legislation and putting some meat on them. This meat consists of both substantive policy declarations and organizational structure to carry out the intent of Parliament, or at times, to thwart that intent. Most legislation passed by Parliament is passed in a broad form, allowing a great deal of room for interpretation as the laws are put into effect.

Public policies may be implemented in a number of ways. Probably the most common is through departments of the central government. Most legislation coming from Parliament contains a broad mandate of power, with the ministry then having the power and the requirement to make the necessary regulations and engage in the activities for the intent of the legislation to come into being. A principal means for the departments' doing this is through statutory instruments developed pursuant to acts of Parliament. Statutory instruments contain more detailed regulations than acts do, and allow the executive to have a major impact on the nature of the policy actually implemented. Parliament exercises scrutiny over these instruments, but cannot hope to master completely the volume or technical content of all such regulations. Even when the issuance of a statutory instrument is not required, the departments are heavily involved in shaping the meaning of policy and in making it work. The departments may also be barriers to effective implementation, especially when the policy enacted by Parliament appears to run counter to their usual practices. In like manner, the existence of regional and local offices of the ministry is frequently associated with varying patterns of implementation and, at times, great variations from the original intentions of Parliament in some parts of the country.[3]

Policies of the central government are also implemented through local authorities. Unlike a federal system, local authorities in Britain are creatures of the central government, and there is less differentiation between national and local policy than in the United States.[4] While the major policy decisions in areas such as education, health, social services, and the police are made by the central government, these services are actually delivered by local authorities. These public services are not delivered uniformly; local authorities provide different quantities and qualities of service, albeit within centrally determined parameters and subject to inspection and control by central government. This relationship between central policy making and local administration does not work without friction, especially when local and central governments are controlled by different parties. Recent examples of conflicts include Conservative local authorities delaying implementation of Labour policies for comprehensive education, and Labour local authorities refusing to implement Conservative cash limits on expenditures for health care and housing. Thus, while it may at times be impossible to do so, the central government needs to "bring along" the local authorities when it is considering a new policy if it hopes to have that policy implemented effectively.

In return for the administration of national policies, the local authorities receive the majority of their revenues from the central government. Some of the grants to local authorities are tied to the provision of

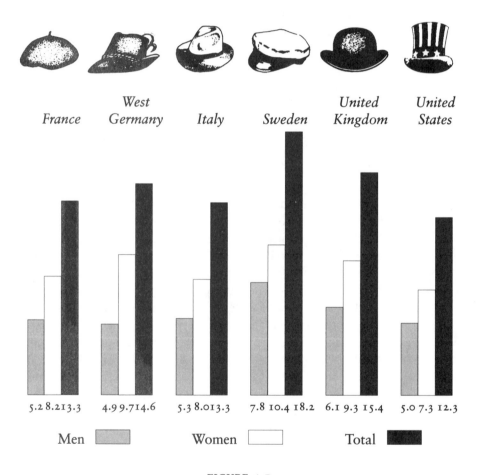

FIGURE 4.1

PERCENTAGE OF POPULATION AGED 65 AND OVER

SOURCE: *U.N. Demographic Yearbook,* 1990.

specific services (e.g., the police), while the largest single grant—the rate support grant—is a general grant. (The formula for computing the rate support grant does, however, include weightings for the levels of service provided by a local authority.) If a local authority *wishes* to provide services not funded directly by the rate support grant or the categorical grants from central government, then it must be willing to raise funds from local revenues, generally "the rates" (property tax). The Thatcher government, by shifting local revenues from rates to a "community charge," or poll tax, made it more difficult for local authorities to undertake their own activities and therefore keeps them under greater central control. Local authorities that spent more than the central government wanted might be punished by the central government by losing some of their central government grant support. The composite local government tax to go into effect in 1993 will again loosen these constraints.

Finally, policies may be implemented by private organizations. Interest groups are frequently regarded as barriers to effective implementation, but such groups may have an increasingly important positive role to play in implementation. Minimally, the interest group can function as a watchdog on the implementation of a policy, substituting for the army of public inspectors that might otherwise be required. Environmental groups have been particularly active in this monitoring role. A more important involvement of groups in implementation involves the group actually implementing a policy for government. This occurs frequently in agriculture when the National Farmer's Union applies general policies to individual cases, for example, in compensation for crop or livestock damage. These activities would otherwise require huge amounts of time and public money, and might not be performed as well. Further, at times government subsidizes an organization to provide a service that government supports as a matter of policy and that would have to be provided at public expense if the private organization were not willing to provide it. One example of this is the Law Society's providing legal assistance to the indigent.

Policy Evaluation

The last stage of making a policy occurs some time after the policy has been adopted or even implemented. This is the evaluation of the policy. Here we are discussing the formal evaluation of the policy, whereas informal evaluation begins almost at the time of passage. Policy evaluation is also closely related to policy making for continuing policy, which is our next major topic, for the annual decisions to continue policies and programs made in the budgetary process to some degree involve evaluation of the effectiveness and efficiency of those policies.

Parliament is assumed to conduct ongoing scrutiny of the policies of government, and a number of instruments for policy evaluation are housed within the government itself. The now defunct Programme Analysis and Review (PAR) and the diminished Public Expenditure Survey Committee linked program evaluation directly with financial management. The Select Committees of the House of Commons are increasingly active in evaluating existing programs, and the few committees in the House of Lords also are engaged in limited oversight. A growing staff in the Prime Minister's Office also monitors policies on behalf of the executive. Through the parliamentary commissioner, or ombudsman, Parliament maintains additional evaluative control over the administration of policy.[5] Finally, the comptroller and auditor general and the National Audit Office have become increasingly important watchdogs. Like auditing organizations in other industrialized nations, these offices have added policy evaluation to their former duties as financial auditors. These offices monitor policy developments in both the central government and the local authorities.

A number of mechanisms for policy evaluation exists independent of the government. One of the most commonly used devices is the appointment of parliamentary or royal commissions to investigate particular policy concerns that are more fundamental than any government may want to become involved in without advice. These commissions and their reports often constitute milestones in the evolution of policy and program management. Such was the case of the Fulton Report on the civil service, the Plowden report on public expenditure control, and the Kilbrandon report on devolution. The commissions have no formal powers, however, and even excellent reports often go unheeded. In part because of her reliance on her own advisers and on a more ideological style of government, there were almost no royal commissions during the Thatcher years. A number of public inquiries into specific policy questions have taken place, some with substantial policy and political relevance (e.g., into nuclear power and into the fire in the London Underground).

Finally, there are a number of less official mechanisms for policy evaluation. The news media constitute one such mechanism, although they remain severely hampered by the Official Secrets Act and the lack of access to important information. The number of policy "think tanks" continues to increase; some of them represent clearly defined ideological positions, while others strive toward greater objectivity. Finally, research units of political parties and pressure groups also produce evaluations of existing policies. A great deal of official and unofficial policy evaluation occurs, although tight control by the government over the parliamentary agenda makes consideration of many policy changes unlikely.

Although policy evaluation ends one cycle of policy making, it often begins the next. Governments rarely make perfect policies the first time they try, but often they know so little about the dynamics of the problem area into which they intervene that trial-and-error learning may be the only means available for improving conditions. Therefore, governments often have to modify existing policies based on their experiences with those policies. That experience is often reflected in the evaluation process. Further, the social and economic conditions that are the objects of a particular policy may also change, and government will have to modify its programs to meet those changing conditions. Thus, although we have depicted policy making as beginning at the beginning and going through to the end, this may be just the start of another cycle. At times the messages from the consumers of policies are very clear signals for change, as they were for the poll tax in 1991.

Policy Continuation: Budgeting

Most policy making is not making new policies; it is reaffirming old policies or making marginal adjustments in those policies. In many ways this form of policy making is politically more sensitive than making new policies, for existing programs have existing employees, clients, and organizations, while new policies have no inertia pushing existing commitments forward. Although there may be some modifications or even threatened terminations, in most years the most important decisions for continuing policies are made in the budgetary process in which the huge number of existing policy commitments are financed, their relative priorities determined in pounds and pence. (Here we are speaking of the budgetary process in an American sense; in Britain the term *budget* refers to the government's revenue, not expenditure, proposals.)

The control of the public purse has been central to the powers of the British Parliament historically, but the existence of disciplined partisan majorities, and the general uncertainty about economic growth, has transformed substantially the locus of effective budgetary powers. Budgeting can be best thought of as taking place in two stages. One is an administrative stage during which the spending ministries negotiate with the Treasury and with the cabinet over expenditure commitments. The second stage is the parliamentary stage during which these decisions are legitimated and occasionally changed.

The Executive Stage

The Treasury is the central actor at the executive stage of budgeting. The Treasury is charged not only with making recommendations on macroeconomic policy but also with formulating detailed expenditure plans that fall within those economic constraints. The Treasury has traditionally been the most prestigious appointment for a civil servant, and those in the Treasury have adopted the "Treasury view" concerning the proper amount of public spending and who should spend the money. Since at least the days of Gladstone, that view has been skeptical about expenditures and concerned with saving "candle ends" as well as billions of pounds. This view does not always prevail, but it must always be considered.

The first round of bargaining over expenditures is typically at the level of civil servants—those from spending departments and those from the Treasury. This bargaining takes place with the knowledge of the relevant ministers, but can be conducted more easily by officials who know both one another and the facts of the programs. Both elements are important. Interpersonal trust and respect are important components of the success of any bargainer, especially when the spending departments must have their requests reviewed annually.[6] The same Treasury civil servants may see the same departmental civil servants year after year, and any attempts to manipulate or deceive may gain in the short run but will surely lose in the long run. Also, civil servants tend to understand the technical aspects of their programs better than ministers do. In addition to their annual (or at times more frequent) bargaining for expenditures, departments must also bargain for deviations from expenditure plans during the year, allowing the Treasury a number of opportunities to monitor and intervene in departmental policies.

The second stage of executive bargaining occurs among the spending ministers, the Treasury, and the cabinet as a whole. Budget decisions are manifestly political, and if nothing else, they reflect the relative political powers and skills of the ministers involved. The task of the spending ministers is to fight for their programs and to try to get as much as they can. The Treasury ministers (the chancellor of the exchequer and the chief secretary of the Treasury) are the guardians of the public purse and play the role of skeptic. The prime minister must moderate any conflicts, but knows that he or she can rarely go against her Treasury ministers if the government is to function smoothly. Also, in today's more conservative period, there is some political advantage to opposing expenditure increases. The fight over the budget occurs on a one-to-one basis between spending and Treasury ministers, in cabinet committees, and finally in full cabinet meetings. Under the Thatcher government, a special cabinet committee (referred to as "Star Chamber") was formed in most years to review disputes between the Treasury and spending departments, usually siding with the Treasury.

The Treasury is in a powerful position politically and enjoys the right of making the first presentation of expenditure figures in cabinet meetings, but after that there is a tendency for the spending ministers to gang up against the Treasury. As this is a political process, a coalition can usually be formed to increase expenditures that enables all spending ministers to make their constituents happy, and to make themselves look good in the eyes of their departments. It takes a very strong chancellor, backed by an equally strong prime minister, to oppose that type of coalition. Opposition to spending in government was very successful while Mrs. Thatcher was prime minister, but it appears less cohesive under the less assertive and somewhat less conservative John Major.

British government has made a great deal of effort to control the costs of government through analytic programs such as PESC (Public Expenditure Survey Committee) and PAR (Programme Analysis and Review). The major input of PESC into the decision process is a projection of the expenditure implications of existing programs, showing what the expenditure level would be if programs were to provide the same level of services in the year being budgeted as in previous years. PAR was intended as a comprehensive evaluation of specific programs, with the intention of making those programs more efficient or perhaps eliminating them. PAR obviously ran counter to the established norms of government and budgeting, and was quietly phased out of existence by the Thatcher government. In addition to rationalist methods of expenditure control, the British government also uses blunter instruments, such as cash limits. This program assigns a maximum expenditure level for a program, and the program is not allowed—regardless of inflation, changes in demand, or whatever—to spend any more money.

The Parliamentary Phase

After the civil servants and the cabinet prepare their expenditure plans (estimates), these are presented to Parliament for adoption. Although the emphasis on control and on techniques for budgeting such as PESC have produced significant modernization, much of the terminology and procedure used by Parliament when considering public expenditures dates from earlier periods in which the monarch and Parliament were engaged in more intense conflicts over power. The major debates on expenditures occur during the twenty-six "supply days" each session, although the topics selected by the Opposition for debate on these days range far beyond expenditures. The civil estimates are introduced into Parliament by the chief secretary of the treasury in February, with the minister of defense introducing defense estimates at about the same time. Parliament then has until July or early August to pass the Consolidated Fund (Appropriations) Bill authorizing the expenditure of funds. Given the difficulties in forecasting expenditures, especially in uncertain economic circumstances, the government usually must also introduce supplemental estimates in December and March.

The budget is an important locus for parliamentary control over the executive. By standing order, Parliament cannot increase expenditures on its own; any increases must be recommended by a minister. Parliament can, however, recommend decreases. One means of expressing displeasure with the management of a ministry is to move the reduction of the salary of the minister, frequently by a trivial amount such as £100. This signals a debate not so much on the £100 as on the policy of the ministry. Members of Parliament may move less trivial changes in expenditure plans as well, but all these are likely to be defeated by the majority party, lest they be seen to be losing confidence in the House.

Parliament as a whole is perhaps too large and disorganized to scrutinize expenditure programs effectively, and so it has developed a pair of committees to more closely examine the government estimates. One is the Treasury and Civil Service Select Committee, the successor to the Expenditure Committee. This rather small committee is composed of members of the House of Commons who are well versed in issues of public spending but still cannot cover the total range of the budget each year. It therefore concentrates on particularly important spending issues. Still, this committee has played an important role in the development of policy in Britain and has ventilated a number of important issues, sometimes to the discomfort of the government.

The second important parliamentary committee for controlling public expenditures is the Public Accounts Committee (PAC). Unlike most committees in Parliament, PAC is headed by a member of the Opposition; it has the task of monitoring public expenditures after they have been made and after they have been audited (by the National Audit Office). Out of the mass of public expenditures, PAC selects certain topics for consideration each year, and has the power to call civil servants before it to account for their actions. Other than calling attention to mismanagement or outright deception, however, PAC has few powers to improve the expenditure of funds.

In addition to the two principal committees examining expenditures, the select committees monitoring the activities of ministers may be a useful device for parliamentary control of expenditures. It appears that these committees have been more successful than had been anticipated. They have attracted the interest of MPs, and have demonstrated their ability to keep track of the huge volume of work produced by the ministries. Their powers are primarily to publicize any failures in the executive, but even that can be a useful check on the power of ministers and civil servants.

To this point we have been discussing the expenditure side of budgeting. On the revenue side, there is the same balance of power in favor of the cabinet and the Treasury. If anything, the balance of power is more in the hands of the executive, as Parliament has yet to develop a committee structure for monitoring revenue proposals. A small subcommittee of the Treasury and Civil Service Select Committee does look at revenue issues, but this is a minor role compared to the scrutiny of public expenditures. And, within the executive, the balance appears to favor the officials, as there are no ministers pushing for increased taxation as they do for increased expenditures. This is not to say that there are no political influences on taxation, as the shift from direct taxation (income taxes) to indirect taxation (VAT) in the first Thatcher budget, and the launching of the poll tax in her third term, indicate.

Revenue recommendations are introduced around the first of April each year in the chancellor's budget message. Immediately, Commons will pass the necessary budget resolutions, allowing for the immediate collection of some portions of the proposed taxes. This is done to prevent the legal avoidance of taxes by purchasing large quantities of alcoholic beverages, selling assets, paying off debts, and so on, under the prior tax laws. There follows a period of debate leading to the formal introduction of the Finance Bill, which is to be passed sometime before Parliament takes its summer recess in August.

One of the common criticisms about the British budgetary process, which is also true of the budgetary process in many other nations, is that there is little or no integration of revenue and expenditure decisions. Citizens and politicians both tend to like expenditures and loathe taxation, and this commonly results in government's failure to collect adequate revenues to meet expenditures and the creation of a deficit budget. Changes to coordinate taxation and expenditures would involve changes in many historic procedures, but might well produce an improvement in the management of public-sector finances. Despite these institutional problems, the British government did not run substantial deficits during the 1980s (unlike the United States), apparently because of the political will of the prime minister and her fiscal advisers.

Policy making in Britain involves the interactions of cabinet, Parliament, and the civil service—to mention only the primary actors. In this interaction the formal location of power and the actual location of decision may be markedly different. The formal powers of decision reside in Parliament, but the effect of strong party discipline has been to make the cabinet the primary decision-making institution. Given a government majority, once the cabinet decides on a policy, the dutiful members of the party will almost certainly ratify it on the floor of the House of Commons. There are, of course, instances in which the backbenchers overtly or covertly oppose government policy, and the cabinet rarely tries to run roughshod over its own party members, but if it must push, the cabinet does have the ability to get most of what it wants passed into law.

The powers of the cabinet are restrained in other ways. The ministers must contend with skillful and permanent civil servants. Especially in the budgetary process, the Treasury and its "mandarins" dominate the decision making. Even in nonfinancial decisions, the expert knowledge of the civil servants, when compared with the relative dearth of expertise held by their nominal political masters, places the permanent civil service in a powerful position to influence outcomes.

Finally, a number of interests and organizations other than these three major actors influence policy decisions. Interest groups not only attempt to influence policy as it is being formulated but also may directly implement policies for the government. Local governments administer and implement a significant share of the programs of central government, and the central government must try to coopt and encourage local governments to implement the policy as it was intended.

Making policy in Britain, as elsewhere, is difficult and complicated. Many good intentions are rendered ineffective by the need to gain agreement from a number of actors. British policy making is especially complicated by the many vestigial procedures and offices, although to abandon these may threaten the legitimacy of the system of government.

Notes

1. Derived from Ivor Burton and Gavin Drewry, "Public Legislation," *Parliamentary Affairs,* various years.

2. See Peter G. Richards, *The Backbenchers* (London: Faber and Faber, 1972), 89–113.

3. This is perhaps especially pronounced for programs that are administered through the Scottish Office, the Welsh Office, and the Northern Ireland Office. For a general view, see R.A.W. Rhodes, *Beyond Westminster and Whitehall: The Sub-Central Governments of Britain* (London: Unwin & Hyman, 1988).

4. See Rhodes, *Beyond Westminster and Whitehall.*

5. Frank Stacey, *The British Ombudsman* (Oxford: Clarendon Press, 1972); and William B. Gwynn, "The Ombudsman in Britain: A Qualified Success of a Government Reform," *Public Administration* 60 (1982): 177–95.

6. Hugh Heclo and Aaron Wildavsky, *The Private Government of Public Money* (Berkeley: University of California Press, 1974), 76–128.

5

What Is the Future of British Politics?

Governments constantly face challenges. Even in the most prosperous and well-managed political system, there are always crises and decisions. Because Britain is neither the most prosperous nor the best-managed nation on earth, it must sustain itself in the face of a significant number of challenges to its political and economic systems. Many of these challenges arise from the international economic and political environment within which Britain operates, but some challenges arise from the characteristics of the political system itself.

The Economy

Perhaps the overriding problem of any British government is the state of the British economy. Even with the bonanza of North Sea oil and a decade of Thatcherite policies extolling the virtues of free enterprise, the British economy remains weak and slow growing compared with those of its European neighbors. This poor economic performance may be beyond the realm of political control; it may be the product of decades of neglect and mismanagement of the private as well as the public sector. Government, however, may be blamed for any poor performance in the short term, and for the resulting unemployment and inflation. This is especially true because the effects of poor economic performance are highly concentrated in Scotland, Wales, and the north of England.

The two potential governing parties have approached the problem of slow economic growth differently, but apparently with equal success or lack of it. The Labour party was more interventionist and stimulative in its approach, seeking to accelerate the growth of the economy by public expenditure and reduce inflation by voluntary or mandatory wage and price controls. If Labour returns to power, it may return to this approach to economic management. The Conservative party has been more reluctant to become involved in the economy and has sought to encourage growth by deregulating industries and encouraging entrepreneurship. Severe economic downturns, however, have prompted direct intervention by the Tories, albeit with less intrusive instruments than those of Labour. The underlying economic philosophy of many leaders of the Conservative party is indicated by the approach of Margaret Thatcher in reducing industrial subsidies and denationalizing some previously nationalized industries (e.g., British Airways, British Telecom, British Gas, and now water). Mrs. Thatcher and her supporters such as Douglas Hurd and her last chancellor of the exchequer (now prime minister) John Major sought to restore British industry through the application of the "chill wind of free enterprise," but the report on the success of their efforts remains mixed. The Major government appears set to continue most of those policies, and the economic future appears more uncertain than for most other European countries.

The uncertainty about the economic future of Britain has been increased by the accelerated movement toward greater economic (and political) integration in the European Community. If all the plans of the Single European Act are implemented, the twelve-member nations of the EC will constitute a single free trade area by 1992. This increased international openness may place British industries into very direct competition with continental industries usually considered more efficient. The British government has been reluctant to support all the moves toward economic integration, especially the proposal for a common currency, but the nation may not be able to avoid the competitiveness problems posed by 1992.

The Public Sector

Associated with the slow growth of the economy is the question of the size and shape of the public sector. Despite the efforts of the Thatcher government to reduce the size of government, tax revenues in the late 1980s averaged over 35 percent of gross national product. The amount of public borrowing has been gotten under control, but Britain still spends a great deal of money through the public sector. In fact, during the early years of the Thatcher government, public expenditures increased as a proportion of gross national product, in large part because GNP was stable or declining. While the Labour party might well consider higher public expenditures a positive feature, many Conservatives do not, and believe Britain could be more competitive with the continental countries if government were less intrusive. We already have discussed some of the sophisticated machinery Britain has developed for analyzing public expenditures, but these devices appear to have been ineffective when faced with the political pressures to spend more.

Running parallel to the attempt to reduce the size of public expenditures has been an attempt to reduce government ownership of industry in Britain. As noted, the Thatcher government privatized a number of nationalized industries and sold off council (public) housing to the tenants. These moves have produced a good deal of income for the government and have helped to balance the budget. And they may have made some industries more efficient. Privatization may also have created a "property owning democracy," which Mrs. Thatcher said was one of her ideals. The distribution of ownership of shares and other assets is not as widespread as some in the Conservative party would like to believe, but it is more widespread than in most other countries. What privatization has done, above all, is to make the public sector even more a central issue in British politics. The postwar consensus on the mixed-economy welfare state has been broken, perhaps for good, and any future government will have to make very clear choices about the social and economic future of the nation. Choices such as these run the risk of dividing the nation and of raising the political stakes in any policy discussion.

Who Rules Britain?

We have mentioned the power of interest groups, especially unions, in Britain several times. One prospective difficulty for British government is maintaining the locus of authority in the political institutions of the nation rather than in other segments of society, be they unions or the CBI. Unions have presented the major challenge to government, possessing as they do a large number of members, the potential to curtail essential services, and direct ties to a political party. The miners have attempted several times to exert their control over government policy —with mixed results—and in the summer of 1989 the railway workers tried their hand. The role of the unions appears to be a persisting, and fundamental, question for government.

The style by which trade unions attempt to influence government policies varies depending upon which major party is in office. When the Labour party is in office, unions have direct access to government, although there were numerous instances during the last Wilson government and the Callaghan government when the government was clear in asserting its mandate to rule against the unions over economic policy. When the Conservatives are in office, the style is more confrontational, as indicated by the miners' strikes during the Heath government and later during the Thatcher government. Equally important is the extent to which public-service unions joined in the opposition to government policies during the 1980s. Over issues of their own pay and privileges, as well as over broader public policy issues, unions in the public sector chose to oppose the Conservative government overtly.

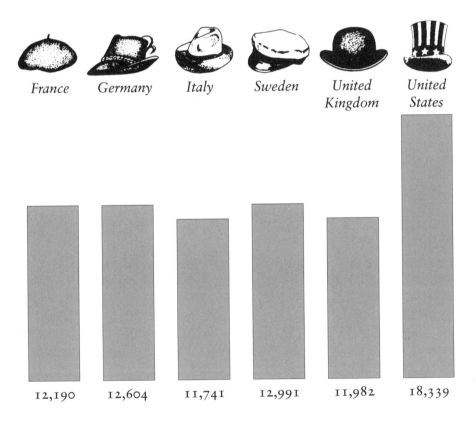

FIGURE 5.1
GROSS DOMESTIC PRODUCT (GDP) PER CAPITA
(IN 1980 CONSTANT DOLLARS)

SOURCE: Summer and Heston, 1991.

This was true of unions representing the very top of the white-collar civil service in ministries as well as poorly paid clerical and janitorial workers.

Any group in a liberal democratic political system has the right to attempt to influence public policy. The question that arises is, To what extent may that influence be extended before the nature of the democratic regime is fundamentally altered? This question is even more pertinent when the groups attempting to exert influence represent the workers in government itself. A strong prime minister, such as Margaret Thatcher, may be able to resist any assaults on their prerogatives from outside government, but less capable and determined leaders may find that this question of governance is a very vexing one.

Who Rules in Government?

Even if we could say with certainty that the government runs Britain, we would still need to know which institution(s) were most influential. The problem here is also one of democratic governance. Voters in the United Kingdom go to the polls every few years and make choices about the party they wish to govern them for a period of up to five years. And the Parliament to which the members of that victorious party are elected (along with the opposition parties) nominally has the power to govern. As we have been emphasizing, however, the cabinet within partisan institutions of government and the civil service within government as a whole are increasingly important in policy making. This means that the voting choices of millions of citizens may be negated, or perhaps only ignored, in the policy-making process. This is a serious problem for all democratic political systems, as citizens believe that the institutions of government are no longer responsive to their wishes and are overly bureaucratic and technocratic, rather than democratic. This alienation is apparently less evident in Britain than in several other industrialized countries, but it is still an important threat to the legitimacy of the system of government.

The Conservative government in the 1980s addressed at least one part of this problem of democratic governance. Rightly or wrongly, that government did not consider many members of the civil service sufficiently committed to the party program to implement it faithfully. Therefore, the Conservatives (and perhaps especially Mrs. Thatcher) sought to reduce the influence of the civil service over policy. They brought more personal policy advisers into government and therefore were able to ignore advice from senior civil servants. Also, through a series of structural reforms, they sought to make the civil service more managerial and less a source of policy advice. Some analysts have argued that the government has even interfered in the appointments of senior civil servants, although the evidence on this point is far from clear. In short, the structure of government was changed, perhaps permanently, to provide the party in power even greater control over policy. This may make the system more "democratic," but perhaps at the price of reducing the overall quality of policy making by government. Further, it means that any future governments will want to exercise the same control over policy, with more pronounced changes in policy when there is a change in governments. Beyond the question of which institution within British government is dominant is the question of government from Brussels—the governmental seat of the European Community. The ideas of parliamentary sovereignty and cabinet government are being challenged from abroad just as they are at home. The nature of British government within an expanded Europe is not yet known, but it is likely to be different from that existing today.

Devolution, Breakup, or What?

Will there continue to be a United Kingdom? Indications are strongly that this question can be answered in the affirmative, at least for the time being. The referendum of Scottish and Welsh devolution in 1979 indicated that there is certainly substantial support for a more independent Scotland (less support in Wales) but that this support was not overwhelming. Support for greater powers for a Scottish government has, by 1992, grown to a majority in Scotland. In the nation as a whole, there has been relatively little sympathy for devolution or other substantial changes from the current constitutional arrangements. If anything, the Conservative governments in the 1980s centralized control over policies. Still, the demand for the accommodation of long-standing cultural, social, and economic interests for the nation is unlikely to disappear.

Related to the question of Scotland and Wales, although certainly much more serious, is the problem of Northern Ireland. That country continues to be an open sore in the side of the United Kingdom, with little or no hope for quick healing. Any number of attempts have been made to find institutional mechanisms for accommodating the interests of both religious groups, but all have ultimately failed and the violence continues. An agreement with the Republic of Ireland over the future of Northern Ireland holds some promise for resolving the conflict; but little concrete has yet happened as a result of these negotiations, and talks broke down in 1991. This is an intractable problem that will continue to plague British policy makers and to threaten the legitimacy of the system of government. This threat is direct in that forces in Northern Ireland renounce the rule of London; it is indirect in that the use of extreme measures in Northern Ireland to suppress terrorism may place the benevolence of the government, and the rights of citizens, in question.

British policy makers are much like other policy makers, although they have their own particular problems and potential. The conduct of contemporary democratic government requires British government to balance traditional norms and procedures that legitimate decisions with the more modern techniques for analysis and control. Older institutions for policy making are challenged by more technically sophisticated and professionally qualified officials. And the underlying social divisions in society refuse to be homogenized, despite the pressures of mass media, industrialization, and urbanization. Whether in the United Kingdom or elsewhere, modern government is a balancing act between the new and the old—those things that unite and those that divide.

For Further Reading

ASHFORD, DOUGLAS E. *Policy and Politics in Britain: The Limits of Consensus.* Philadelphia: Temple University Press, 1981.

BUTLER, DAVID, AND KAVANAGH, DENNIS. *The British General Election of 1987.* London: Macmillan, 1988. This is the latest of an ongoing series of analyses of British elections, commonly referred to as the Nuffield series.

BUTLER, DAVID, AND STOKES, DONALD E. *Political Change in Britain.* 2d ed. London: Macmillan, 1975.

CROSSMAN, RICHARD. *The Diaries of a Cabinet Minister.* 3 vols. London: Hamish Hamilton and Jonathan Cape, 1974–77.

CROUCH, COLIN, AND DORE, RONALD. *Corporatism and Accountability: Organized Interests in British Public Life.* New York: Oxford University Press, 1987.

FRANKLIN, MARK N. *The Decline of Class Voting in Britain.* Oxford: Clarendon Press, 1985.

GOLDTHORPE, JOHN. *Social Mobility and Class Structure in Modern Britain.* 2d ed. New York: Oxford University Press, 1987.

HEATH, ANTHONY; CURTICE, J.; JOWELL, R.; EVANS, G.; FIELD, J.; AND WITHERSPOON, S. *Understanding Political Change: Britain Votes, 1964–1987.* Oxford: Pergamon, 1988.

HECLO, HUGH, AND WILDAVSKY, AARON. *The Private Government of Public Money.* Berkeley: University of California Press, 1974.

HENNESSY, PETER. *Cabinet.* Oxford: Basil Blackwell, 1987.

————. *Whitehall.* Rev. ed. London: Fontana, 1990.

HOGWOOD, BRIAN. *From Crisis to Complacency? Shaping Public Policy in Britain.* Oxford: Clarendon Press, 1987.

JOHNSON, NEVIL. *In Search of the Constitution: Reflections on State and Society in Britain.* Oxford: Pergamon, 1977.

KAVANAGH, DENNIS. *Thatcherism and British Politics: The End of Consensus?* Oxford: Oxford University Press, 1990.

KELLAS, JAMES G. *The Scottish Political System.* 4th ed. New York: Cambridge University Press, 1989.

KELLNER, PETER, AND CROWTHER-HUNT, LORD. *The Civil Servants: An Inquiry into Britain's Ruling Class.* London: Macdonald, 1980.

MARSHALL, GEOFFREY. *Ministerial Responsibility.* New York: Oxford University Press, 1989.

NORTON, PHILIP. *Parliament in the 1980s.* Oxford: Basil Blackwell, 1985.

RHODES, R.A.W. *Beyond Westminster and Whitehall: The Sub-Central Governments of Britain.* London: Unwin & Hyman, 1988.

RICHARDSON, J.J., AND JORDAN, A.G. *Government and Pressure Groups in Britain.* New York: Oxford University Press, 1987.

ROSE, RICHARD. *The Problem of Party Government.* London: Macmillan, 1974.

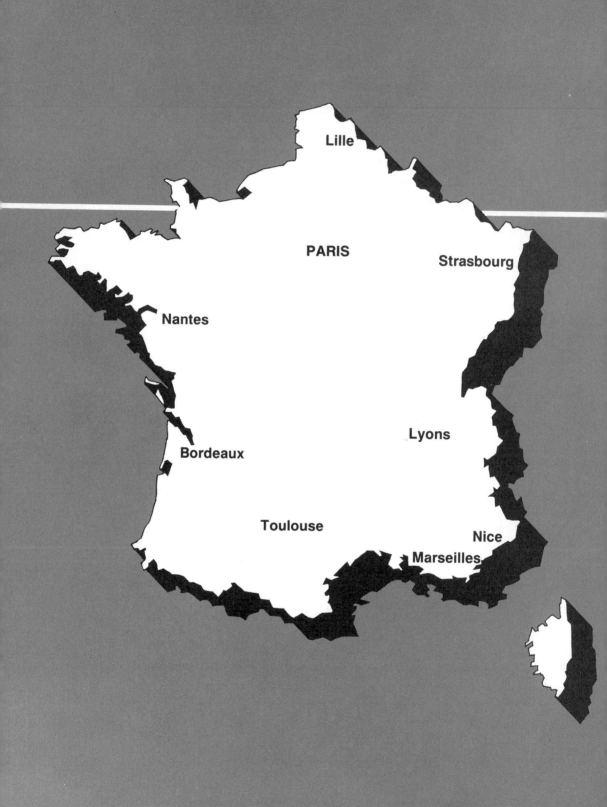

Lille

PARIS

Strasbourg

Nantes

Bordeaux

Lyons

Toulouse

Nice

Marseilles

Part Two

France

William Safran

6

The Context of French Politics

France has been one of the important countries in the world. Its culture, architecture, and cuisine have been much admired and copied; its language has served as the chief medium of diplomacy; and its political philosophies and institutional patterns have exerted influences far beyond the country's borders. Until the end of World War II, France was the second-greatest colonial empire, with possessions in Southeast Asia, South America, the Caribbean, and North and West Africa.

The third-largest country in Europe (after Russia and the Ukraine), France is more than twice the size of Britain, 60 percent larger than Germany, and four-fifths the size of Texas. Except in the north and northeast, France has natural frontiers: the Atlantic Ocean on the west, the Pyrenees in the south, and the Alps and Jura mountains in the east. Wide variations in landscape—the northern flatlands of Flanders, the forests of Normandy, the mountainous east and center, the beaches of the Vendée in the west, and the subtropical Riviera coast in the south—are accompanied by regional variations in cuisine, dress, speech, and attitude.

It cannot be said that the French are of a single stock; the mixture of Celts, Latins, and Germanic elements, and the descendants of more recent Slavic, North African, and other immigrants, have made the population of the country truly multiethnic. Living in one of the first large European countries to have its boundaries more or less permanently fixed, the French have a highly developed sense of national identity. At the same time, it should be pointed out that the Alsatians, Bretons, Corsicans, and other minority ethnic groups—and more recently the Jewish community—have not been content with being merely French and have demanded that their cultural uniqueness be recognized.

Ever since the country's early efforts at unification under centralized auspices, Paris has been the locus of national political power. Unchallenged by other cities, the political capital is also France's cultural and economic center. Paris contains the biggest university complex, three-fourths of the nation's theaters, and the majority of its museums and art galleries; and it is the hub from which most railroad lines radiate. The Paris region constitutes about 2 percent of the nation's land area, but by the early 1980s it included 20 percent of its total population, boasted its largest factories, and accounted for a third of its industrial production.

For many years, the impression was widespread, among foreigners as well as natives, that apart from Paris, France was essentially a peasant country. That perception resulted from a number of factors. The Industrial Revolution did not proceed so early and so thoroughly in France as it did in Britain and Germany; by the end of World War II, an estimated one-third of the French labor force was still employed in agriculture. Most of the farms were and still are small; the consolidation of landholdings was impeded by the traditional division of a family's acreage among several descendants, and industrial development was long delayed by the lack of private investment capital and the limited need for industrial manpower in the cities. In the past thirty years, however, there has been impressive progress in agricultural modernization. As a consequence, employment in agriculture has declined: from more than 30 percent of the active population in 1946 to less than 7 percent. In 1946, 21.5 out of 40.5 million people lived in cities; today, 43 million out of nearly 57 million do. While the number of farms and rural villages declined steadily, the number of urban agglomerations continued to grow, and so the French began to speak of the "terminal peasantry." In a parallel development, rapid modernization of highways, mass rail transport, and telecommunications tied the provinces more closely to Paris, and the sense of separation between the small towns and the capital diminished.

Despite this urbanization, many French people continue to share the belief that life in the country is more satisfying than an urban existence. In recent years, this myth has been reflected in the tendency of middle-class big-city dwellers to acquire second homes in the country.

For many years, a "peasant romanticism" was fortified by the patterns of family loyalty, parsimony, and conservative moral values carefully nurtured by the Catholic church; today, this romanticism has been rediscovered as an ideal by those disenchanted with the economic insecurities, overcrowding, unemployment, and growing social disorganization and crime in the cities and has become a component of the ideology of extreme-right movements. There is no doubt that urbanization has contributed to a rapid increase in criminality. In 1989, the crime rate (counting nearly 3.3 million crimes) was 58.3 per thousand, compared with 39.2 in 1977, 32.3 in 1972, and 13.6 in 1963.

Religion and Social Class

For a long time, most of the population embraced Roman Catholicism; France was considered the "most Catholic" of countries. To be sure, the Reformation spread to France; in the sixteenth century, the country was riven by bitter struggles between Catholics, who were supported by the ruling elite, and Protestant Huguenots (mainly Calvinists), many of whom were massacred. After a period of toleration, the privileges of the Protestants (e.g., the right to live in certain fortified towns) were revoked in the seventeenth century, and many Protestants left the country. With the consolidation of absolute rule under the Bourbon kings, the position of Catholicism as the state religion was firmly established. Dissatisfaction with monarchism meant a questioning of the church and its privileges, and revolutionary sentiments were accompanied by anticlerical attitudes.

The hold of Catholicism gradually weakened as a consequence of industrialization, the rise of a new working class, the nineteenth-century development of a unified school system, and finally, demographic and social changes. In the first decade of the twentieth century the Catholic church was formally "disestablished." France became, like the United States, a secular country, at least constitutionally (except in the province of Alsace where, for historical reasons, the clergy is supported by public funds). Today about 90 percent of the population is Roman Catholic, but little more than a third of the Catholics are "practicing." A large proportion of inhabitants of the larger cities and the great majority of industrial workers are "de-Christianized" except in the most formal sense.

Yet Catholicism cannot be divorced from French culture and political consciousness. The cathedral remains the heart of small towns, most legal holidays are Catholic ones, and many political movements and interest groups are still influenced by Catholic teachings. Furthermore, public policy attitudes have often been inspired by Catholic social doctrine: aid to large families, the notion of class collaboration (instead of conflict) and the "association" of employers and workers in factories, the long-held opposition to the legalization of birth control and abortion, and the legal dominance, until well into the 1960s, of the male head of the family. Today, between 15 and 20 percent of parents opt to send their children to Catholic parochial schools, which benefit from governmental financial support.

There are about a million French Protestants, many of them prominent in business, the free professions, and, more recently, politics and administration. There have been Jews in France since before the Middle Ages; today they number about seven hundred thousand. During the Dreyfus Affair in the 1890s, antirepublican feelings were accompanied by a campaign to vilify Jews and eliminate them from public life. With the Nazi occupation of France (1940–44) and the resulting persecutions and deportations, the Jewish community was ravaged and reduced by a third. Catholic Frenchmen were ambivalent about those events. Since the early 1960s, the number of Jews has been augmented by repatriates from North Africa. Much like Protestants, Jews have tended to support republican regimes and have decidedly preferred left-of-center parties identified with anticlericalism. Since the mid-1960s, there has also been a significant influx, primarily from North Africa, of Muslims, many of whom perform the most menial work in industrial cities. Today, the Muslim population is estimated at 2.5 to 3 million. The growth of this population has provoked a reaction on the part of many ordinary French people (especially the lower-middle and working classes), who feel that the presence of these "exotic" immigrants has contributed heavily to the rise in unemployment and criminality and will ultimately disfigure the very nature of French society.

Superficially, the French social system is typical of that found in other European countries. The medieval divisions of society into nobility, clergy, townsmen, and peasants gradually gave way to a more complex social structure. The traditional, land-based aristocracy declined as a result of the use of the guillotine and the diminishing economic value of agriculture, and today the aristocracy has a certain vestigial importance only in the military officer corps and the diplomatic service.

The modern upper class, or *haute bourgeoisie* — a status derived from graduation from a prestigious university or the inheritance of wealth or both — comprises the higher echelons of the civil service, the directors of large business firms, and bankers. The next social group is the *grande bourgeoisie,* which includes university professors, high school teachers, engineers, members of the so-called free professions (such as lawyers, physicians, and architects), middle-echelon government functionaries, and the proprietors of medium-sized family firms. The middle and lower-middle class, today the largest social category, comprises elementary school teachers, white-collar employees, petty shopkeepers, and lower-echelon civil servants. The lower classes (*classes populaires*) include most of the industrial workers, small farmers, and possibly artisans.

These class divisions have been important insofar as they have tended to influence a person's political ideology, general expectations from the system, lifestyle, place of residence, and choice of political party. Thus, as we see below, a typical member of the free professions has tended to adhere to a liberal party, a businessman to a conservative (or moderate) one, and an industrial worker to a socialist party. The class system and interclass relationships have been constantly changing, however; these changes have taken place with particular rapidity since the dramatic events of May-June 1968, when masses of students and workers joined in a general strike and almost brought down the government. Nor is there a precise correlation between class membership and adherence to a specific political party. In recent years there has been a growing underclass of uprooted farmers and artisans, redundant industrial workers, and immigrants who cannot be precisely categorized and whose relationship to the political system is fluid, if not marginal. Moreover, distinctions between classes have been partially obscured by the redistributive impact of a highly developed system of social legislation and the progressive democratization of the educational system. Table 6.1 gives an idea of some of the changes that have taken place in the past generation.

Education

Since the last century, a centralized national school system has existed, based on uniform curricula stressing national, secular, and republican values and theoretically creating opportunities for upward mobility on the basis of talent, not wealth. Traditionally, the Ministry of Education controlled the educational curricula, from public elementary school in small villages to lycées in large cities, and had the major voice in the administration of universities. In practice, the system (at least until the late 1950s) fortified existing social inequalities because most children of the working and peasant classes were not steered toward the lycées, the academic secondary schools whose diplomas were required for admission to university, and thus were condemned to perpetual lower-class status. Since the early 1960s, there has been a spate of reform legislation aimed at the "comprehensivization" of schooling, at least up to the age of sixteen. Curriculum design has been made more practical, more techno-

TABLE 6.1

FRANCE: SOME CHANGES IN FORTY-FIVE YEARS

	1946	*1975*	*1985*	*1990*
Total population (in millions)	40.5	52.6	55.0	56.56
Number of adolescents over 14 enrolled in schools (in thousands)	650	4,000	4,200	
Average annual duration of full-time work (hours)	2,100	1,875	1,763[a]	
Infant mortality per 1,000 live births	84.4	13.8	10.1	7.5[c]
Standard of living (growth of net per capita income: 1938 = 100)	87	320	—	
Number of private cars in circulation (in thousands)	1,000	15,300	20,800	22,750[c]
Longevity of males (in years)	61.9	69.1	71[b]	
Longevity of females (in years)	67.4	77.0	79[b]	

SOURCE: Based on Jean Fourastié, *Les trente glorieuses ou la révolution invisible* (Paris: Fayard, 1979), 36; *Quid, 1988* and *1992*. (Paris: Robert Laffont, 1987), 121, 1210, 1381, 1603; and Dominique Borne, *Histoire de la Société française depuis 1945* (Paris: Armand Colin, 1988), 95.

a. 1986   b. 1982   c. 1989

logical, and less classical-humanistic. Laws have been passed to permit universities to become more flexible and less hierarchical and to allow students to participate in decision making (but there are complaints that the pace of implementation has occasionally been slowed down because of insufficient funds and the resistance of the academic establishment). In recent years, there has been a veritable explosion of university enrollments, which reached a million in 1985 and 1.2 million in 1990. But the inability of many university graduates to find jobs has acted as a brake against further significant increases. A large proportion of students drop out after one or two years at the university; many others, coming from families in straitened circumstances, complain that state scholarship aid is insufficient.

The attitudes of the French toward politics have been shaped by their education and by their social condition. Scholars have suggested that the French are more critical of their regime than are Americans or Englishmen of theirs. French citizens have frequently participated in uprisings and revolutions; they have exhibited "anticivic" behavior patterns such as tax evasion, draft-dodging, and alcoholism. They have often shown contempt for law (and the police), and large segments of the lower classes in particular have been convinced that the legal-penal system favors the "established" classes. Finally, for many years, a large segment adhered to political ideologies and political parties oriented to the replacement of the existing political order.

The insufficient acceptance of the existing regime—a phenomenon called "crisis of legitimacy"—was produced by, and in turn reflected in, the apparent inability of the French to create a political formula that would resolve satisfactorily the conflict between state and individual, centralism and localism, the executive and the legislature, or representative and "direct" democracy. Since the abolition of the Old Regime of royal absolutism, there has been a dizzying succession of governments —republics, monarchies, empires, and republics again—most of them embodying drastically different conceptions of the proper division of governmental authority (see table 6.2).

TABLE 6.2
POLITICAL CYCLES AND REGIMES

Moderate Monarchy	*Liberalization*	*Conservative Reaction*
Constitutional monarchy of 1791	Republic of 1792	Dictatorial government of 1795
Restoration of 1815	"July Monarchy" of 1830	Second Empire 1852
Early Third Republic (1870–79)	Later Third Republic (1879–1940)	Vichy regime (1940–44)
	Fourth Republic (1946–58)	Early Fifth Republic (1958–81)
	Fifth Republic (since 1981)	

SOURCE: Adapted from Dorothy Pickles, *The Fifth French Republic,* 3d ed. (New York: Praeger, 1965), 3–5.

Revolutions, Regime Changes, and Legitimacy Crises

Many regimes created institutional solutions that were too extreme and therefore could not last. The Revolution of 1789 led to the abdication of King Louis XVI in 1792 and was followed by a series of experiments

that, collectively, has been termed the First Republic. It was characterized by the abolition of the old provinces and the restructuring of administrative divisions, the reduction of the power of the church and the
inauguration of a "rule of reason," the proclamation of universal human rights, and the passing of power from the landed aristocracy to the
bourgeoisie. It was also marked by assassinations and mass executions
("the Reign of Terror"), which were ended when order was established
under Napoleon Bonaparte. At first the leader of a dictatorial Consulate
(1799), then president (1802) of what was still, formally, a "republic,"
Napoleon had himself proclaimed emperor in 1804. Napoleon's empire

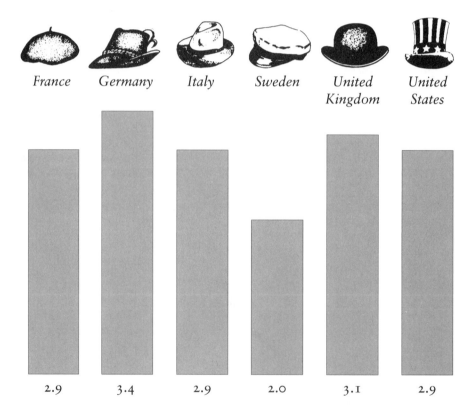

France	Germany	Italy	Sweden	United Kingdom	United States
2.9	3.4	2.9	2.0	3.1	2.9

FIGURE 6.1

AVERAGE ANNUAL GROWTH RATE OF GROSS
DOMESTIC PRODUCT (IN PERCENT)

SOURCE: OECD, 1991.

collapsed after ten years, but the emperor left behind a great heritage of reforms: an efficient system of tax collection, a body of codified laws, the notion of a merit-based professional bureaucracy (much of it trained in specialized national schools), and a system of relationships (or rather, a theory about such relationships) under which the chief executive derived his legitimacy directly from the people (through popular elections or referenda). The chief executive's rule was unimpeded by a strong Parliament, subnational government units, or other "intermediary" institutions or groups. At once heroic and popular, the "Bonapartist" approach to politics had a strong impact on segments of the French nation; much of what came to characterize Gaullism was heavily influenced by that approach.

The power of the clergy and nobility was revived in 1814 when the Bourbon monarchy was restored, but that was to be a constitutional regime patterned on the English model and guaranteeing certain individual liberties and a limited participation of Parliament. In 1830 the Bourbon dynasty, having become arbitrary and corrupt, was in turn replaced by another regime, that of Louis-Philippe of the House of Orleans. In 1848 the French rebelled once more and inaugurated what came to be known as the Second Republic. They elected Louis Napoleon (a nephew of Napoleon I) president for a ten-year term, but he soon (in 1852) proclaimed himself emperor. The "Second Empire" was a "republican" empire insofar as a weak legislative chamber continued to exist and, more important, because Louis Napoleon derived his power from the people rather than from God.

The Second Empire was noted for many achievements: industrial progress, a stable currency, and the rebuilding and modernization of Paris. But popular disenchantment with what had become a dictatorial regime, boredom, and France's military defeat at the hands of the Prussians in 1870 brought it down.

The Third Republic, the regime that followed, was inaugurated in bloodshed: the Paris Commune of 1871, in which thousands of "proletarians" rebelled and were brutally suppressed by bourgeois leaders. Most of these leaders did not, in fact, want a republic. The assembly elected to make peace with the Prussians was dominated by monarchists, but the latter disagreed on which of the competing pretenders—Bourbon, Orleans, or Bonaparte—should be given the throne. Consequently, the assembly adopted a skeletal constitution that provided, on a temporary basis, for an executive and legislative branch and outlined the relationship between them. This constitution, which contained no bill of rights, was to last nearly seventy years and set the pattern for subsequent republican regimes. In the beginning, the president (elected by Parliament for seven years) tried to govern while ignoring Parliament, and to dissolve the Assembly, whose political composition he did not like.

In 1877, Parliament rebelled and forced the president to resign. Henceforth, presidents became figureheads; prime ministers and their cabinets were transformed into obedient tools of powerful Parliaments and were replaced or reshuffled about once every eight months. This instability, which was viewed by many as endemic to republican systems as such, encouraged romantic monarchists in attempts to subvert the republic. Yet this republic had many achievements to its credit, not the least of which was that it survived from World War I; it might have lasted even longer had France not been invaded and occupied by the Germans in 1940.

Following the German defeat of France, the "unoccupied" southern half of the country was transformed into the "French State," an authoritarian puppet regime led from Vichy, a provincial resort town, by Marshal Philippe Pétain, an aging hero of World War I. The behavior of the French during this period, both in the Vichy state and in the occupied part of the country, was complex and ambivalent, and the question of who collaborated and who resisted continued to be debated for many years.

The Fourth Republic, which was instituted in January 1947, two years after Liberation, essentially followed the pattern established during the Third. Although its highly detailed and democratic constitution included an impressive bill of rights, it made for a system even less stable than that of the Third Republic. There were twenty governments (and seventeen prime ministers) in a twelve-year period; the Assembly, though theoretically supreme, could not provide effective leadership. Ambitious deputies, seeking a chance to assume ministerial office, easily managed to topple cabinets, and a large proportion of the legislators —notably the Communists on the left and the Gaullists on the right— were not interested in the maintenance of the regime.

The Fourth Republic was not without accomplishments. It inaugurated a system of long-term capitalist planning under which France rebuilt and modernized its industrial and transport structures. It put in place an extensive network of welfare state provisions including comprehensive statutory medical insurance. It took the first steps in the direction of decolonization—relinquishing control of Indochina, Morocco, and Tunisia—and paved the way for intra-European collaboration in the context of the Coal and Steel Community and, later, the

Common Market. Some of the failures of the Fourth Republic—for example, its inability to institute meaningful local democracy and its foot-dragging on tax reform—were to be failures, equally, of the political system that replaced it.

It is likely that the Fourth Republic would have continued if it had not been for separatist pressures within Algeria and the convenient presence of a war hero, General Charles de Gaulle. Algeria could not be easily decolonized, or granted independence, because more than 2 million French men and women—many of them tracing their roots in that territory several generations back—considered it their home and regarded it as an integral component of France. A succession of Fourth Republic politicians lacked the will or the stature to impose a solution of the problem; the war that had broken out in the mid-1950s in Algeria threatened to spill over into mainland France and helped discredit the regime.

Under the pressure of the Algerian events (and the threat of a military coup in continental France and North Africa), the Fourth Republic leadership decided, in mid-1958, to call upon de Gaulle. De Gaulle had been a professional soldier, a member of the general staff, and several months after the outbreak of World War II, deputy minister of war. After France's capitulation in June 1940, de Gaulle refused to accept the permanence of surrender or the legitimacy of the Pétain regime. Instead, de Gaulle fled to London. There he established a "government in exile" and organized the "Free French" forces, which were joined by numerous Frenchmen who had escaped from the Continent. In 1944 de Gaulle became the provisional civilian leader of liberated France, presiding over a government coalition composed of Christian Democrats, Socialists, and Communists. In 1946 he retired from the political scene, having failed to prevent the ratification of the Fourth Republic constitution (a document he opposed because it granted excessive powers to Parliament). In retirement de Gaulle continued to be a political force: more precisely, a force of inspiration to a political movement, the RPF, the Rassemblement du Peuple Français (the Gathering of the French People). These original "Gaullists" wanted to replace the Fourth Republic with a new regime that would be led by a strong executive.

The Fifth Republic, established in 1958, is an institutional mixture of a very powerful executive and a weak legislature. The institutional relationships are discussed later; for the moment, it is useful to make some remarks about French "political culture" (i.e., political attitudes that are widely held and behavior patterns that cut across specific social classes and party ideologies).

Aspects of French Political Culture

Except for parts of the industrial working class, most French people have shared the universal ambitions of French civilization and have not seemed to consider the (often exaggerated) chauvinism of their intellectual elite to be inconsistent with such ambitions. They have taken pride in France's international prestige, cultural patrimony, and intellectual accomplishments, although these may have borne little relationship to objective reality, may not have benefited all citizens equally, and may not have compensated for the more immediate economic needs of the underprivileged. The French have had a tendency to hero worship that has led them, on several occasions, to accept "men on horseback": the two Napoleons, Marshal MacMahon (in the 1870s), Marshal Pétain, and General de Gaulle. This has been balanced by an equal tendency to rebellion against authority. Moreover, the French have often opted for leftist or revolutionary ideologies and politicians; at the same time, such leftist thinking and speaking has sometimes been a meaningless exercise because there was little expectation that it would (or ought to) translate itself into leftist governmental policies. Public opinion polls conducted from the 1950s to the 1980s have shown, typically, that the proportion of French voters preferring Socialist party candidates was consistently higher than the proportion of those who favored the nationalization of enterprises or the equalization of incomes—both traditional components of Socialist ideology.

The French have often held their politicians in contempt but have allowed them greater leeway than do Americans with respect to tax evasion, collusion with business, or (personal) behaviorial departures from bourgeois moral norms. At the same time, there is a widely disseminated desire to enter the public service, and much prestige is attached to it. Traditionally, the French have been sharply critical of the regime, but they have had a highly developed sense of belonging to the nation, and great expectations of the "state" regarding what it should do for them. But there have been important changes, especially in the past two decades. There is now little question about the legitimacy of the political system. More than 90 percent of the French people accept the institutions of the Fifth Republic, a consensus reflected in a gradual convergence between parties of the right and left and, indeed, in a growing impatience with ideological labels. Conversely, the state has been desanctified in the eyes of many French citizens. While the French still have an "instrumental" view of the state—in the sense that it is expected to continue to play an important role in economic, social, and cultural affairs—their expectations have become somewhat more realistic. This development is reflected in the fact that the French, in recent years, have been attaching a greater value to liberty than to equality. A recent poll revealed that, for 63 percent of the respondents, French national identity is essentially symbolized by a commitment to human rights— roughly the same percentage for whom that identity is symbolized by French cuisine.[1] While the French have become more ego oriented, they have also come to attach increasing importance to "civil society" and its component parts. There has been a greater reliance on the market; at the same time, there has been a rapid growth of voluntary associations on national and local levels. These developments have served to reduce the social distrust, to lessen the "fear of face-to-face relations" that was once considered a major aspect of French political culture,[2] and to foster a greater openness to "out-groups," both within France and outside it.

Notes

1. Passages/CSA poll of October 1987, cited in Gérard Mermet, *Francoscopie 1989* (Paris: Larousse, 1988), 82.
2. See Michael Crozier, *The Bureaucratic Phenomenon* (Chicago: University of Chicago Press, 1969), 220 ff.

7

Where Is the Power?

The Fifth Republic constitution was drawn up several weeks after de Gaulle was invested as the (last) prime minister of the Fourth Republic. The new constitution, which was adopted by an 80 percent affirmative vote in a popular referendum (September 1958), was tailor-made for de Gaulle. It contains many features found in previous French republics: president, prime minister, and a Parliament composed of two chambers—a National Assembly and a Senate. Institutional relationships were rearranged, however, so as to reflect the political ideas that the famous general and his advisers had often articulated, that is, the ideology of Gaullism.

The President and the Government

De Gaulle and his advisers—foremost among them Michel Debré, the principal draftsman of the constitution, who was to become the Fifth Republic's first prime minister—wanted to have a strong government. It would be capable of making decisions and conducting an assertive foreign policy without having to worry about excessive parliamentary interference or premature ouster.

The president is clearly the central feature of the Fifth Republic system. He is elected independently of Parliament. The constitution had originally provided for his election by an electoral college composed of some 80,000 national, regional, and local legislators; but since the approval, by referendum, of a constitutional amendment in 1962, presidents have been elected by popular vote for seven-year terms.

The president is invested with nearly monarchical powers, and these have been expanded through interpretation by at least the first three of the four incumbents of the office so far: Charles de Gaulle (1958–69), Georges Pompidou (1969–74), Valéry Giscard d'Estaing (1974–81), and François Mitterrand (since 1981). According to the constitution, the president appoints the prime minister, who thereupon supposedly selects the rest of the cabinet. But de Gaulle and Pompidou took an interest in many of these appointments, and Giscard decided the composition of the entire cabinet on a rather personal basis. The composition of these cabinets was endorsed by the Assembly, which was controlled by politicians more or less in the same (conservative) ideological camp as the president.

Under President Mitterrand, a Socialist, the situation has been more complex. For five years following his election in 1981, and the election immediately thereafter of a Socialist-controlled Assembly, the composition of governments reflected the president's wishes to a large extent. But after the legislative elections of 1986 and 1993, when the Gaullists and their allies recaptured control of the Assembly, the president was forced to appoint a prime minister and cabinet to the Assembly's liking rather than his own. The "cohabitation" of a Socialist president with a Gaullist government—a situation not clearly envisaged by the writers of the Fifth Republic constitution—led to a restructuring of the relationship between the two: a delicate form of power sharing in which the prime minister took responsibility for most domestic policies, while the president retained a measure of authority in foreign affairs and national defense, as well as a vaguely defined influence in internal affairs.

After the reelection of Mitterrand as president in 1988, and the recapture of control of the Assembly by the Socialists immediately thereafter, the situation returned to "normal," that is, the president's preeminence was reestablished. But Mitterrand decided not to exercise his restored powers fully but to share it with his prime minister, Michel Rocard, and, to a lesser extent, with Parliament—not only because the "cohabitation" experience had chastened him but also because he had, in a sense, become an elder statesman and transcended politics.

The president has a variety of appointive powers, which he has continued to exercise without interruption: over military officers, political advisers, and some of the members of several judicial organs (on the advice, to be sure, of the prime minister). In addition, he retains the powers traditionally associated with chiefs of state: the appointment of ambassadors and other high civilian personnel, the receiving of foreign dignitaries, the signing of bills and the promulgation of laws and decrees, the issuing of pardons, and the right to preside over cabinet sessions and to send messages to Parliament. The president cannot veto bills; however, he may ask Parliament to reexamine all or part of a bill he does not like. Furthermore, the president has the right to dissolve the Assembly before the expiration of its maximum term of five years and thus to call for new elections. The only two constraints are rather mild: the requirement that he "consult" with the prime minister and the Speakers of the two chambers; and the stipulation that the Assembly not be dissolved less than a year after its election. Thus far, presidents have made use of the dissolution power on four occasions: in 1962, 1968, 1981, and 1988.

The president may submit to the Constitutional Council (see below) an act of Parliament or a treaty of doubtful constitutionality; and he may submit to a popular referendum any organic bill (i.e., one relating to the organization of public powers) or any treaty requiring ratification. The constitution stipulates that he may resort to a referendum only on the proposal of the government (while Parliament is in session) or following a joint motion by the two parliamentary chambers; but President de Gaulle ignored this stipulation when he called for a referendum in 1962. Since the founding of the Fifth Republic, there have been six referenda (after the popular ratification of the constitution itself): in January 1961, on self-determination for Algeria; in April 1962, on the Evian agreement on independence for Algeria; in October 1962, on the method of electing the president; in April 1969, on the reform of the Senate; in April 1972, on approving Britain's entry into the European Common Market; and in November 1988, on proposals of autonomy for New Caledonia.

It is the president who "directs" the nation's diplomacy. He negotiates and signs (or "ratifies") treaties, and he must be alerted to the progress of all international negotiations conducted in the name of France.

One of the most interesting—and awesome—provisions relating to presidential power is Article 16, which reads (in part) as follows:

> When the institutions of the Republic, the independence of the nation, the integrity of its territory or the fulfillment of its international commitments are threatened in a grave and immediate manner and when the regular functioning of the constitutional governmental authorities is interrupted, the president of the Republic shall take the measures commanded by these circumstances, after official consultation with the prime minister, the [Speakers] of the assemblies, and the Constitutional Council.

Such emergency powers, which can be found in a number of Western democracies, are intended for use during civil wars, general strikes, and similar public disorders that presumably cannot be dealt with through normal, and often time-consuming, parliamentary deliberative processes. De Gaulle invoked the provisions once, during a failed plot organized in 1961 by generals opposing his Algerian policy. Although Article 16 is not likely to be used again soon, and though there is a stipulation that Parliament must be in session when this emergency power is exercised, its very existence has been a source of disquiet to many who fear that a future president might use it for dictatorial purposes. Others view Article 16 more liberally, that is, as a weapon of the president in his role as a constitutional watchdog, mediator, and umpire.

The constitution makes a clear distinction in its wording between the chief of state and the government. Thus it is the prime minister, not the president, who "directs the action of the government," who "ensures the execution of the laws," who "exercises regulatory powers," and who "proposes constitutional amendments to the president." There is, unfortunately, some doubt whether the prime minister and the government can be functionally separated from any president who wishes to be more than a figurehead. Indeed, the constitutional text is not without ambiguity. Thus, while one article provides that the prime minister is in charge of national defense, another makes the president commander-in-chief of the armed forces; similarly, the prime minister's power to "determine the policy of the nation" may conflict with, and be subordinated to, the president's responsibility for "guaranteeing national independence."

Except during the two "cohabitation" periods, prime ministers have in fact had little independence and little discretion vis-à-vis the president in all areas in which the latter has taken a personal interest. Furthermore—here again, except under "abnormal" conditions when the Assembly and the president are on different sides of the political divide—the prime minister may be dismissed not only by Parliament but also (though the constitution does not stipulate this) by the president. Thus far, nine of the twelve prime ministers preceding Pierre Bérégovoy were replaced while still enjoying the confidence of the Assembly. Prime ministers have come and gone for a variety of reasons. Their appointment does not need to be officially approved by Parliament—though most prime ministers have in fact gone before the Assembly to be "invested" (that is, formally voted into office) and to ask for that chamber's approval of the government's general policy directions. Prime ministers do not, in principle, have to reflect the party composition of the Assembly, and they do not have to belong to any party at all—though it is clear that, in practice, they cannot function, or even remain in office, without the support of a majority of deputies.

Michel Debré (1958–62) had been a loyal Gaullist even during the Fourth Republic; but he was eventually replaced by Pompidou (1962–68), who had been a lycée professor and banker (and not a party politician) but had once worked intimately with de Gaulle and had been the leader of his presidential staff. Pompidou was in turn replaced by Maurice Couve de Murville (1968–69), a professional diplomat, because blame for the mishandling of problems that had given rise to the mass rebellions of May-June 1968 had to be deflected from the president.

Jacques Chaban-Delmas (1969–72), a former Radical-Socialist and hero of the wartime Resistance, was chosen by Pompidou on the election of the latter to the presidency because of the president's desire to cultivate a more progressive image and thus entice centrist parties to join the government majority forces in Parliament. Subsequently, Chaban-Delmas was ousted in part because his popularity threatened to eclipse the president's own, and he was replaced by Pierre Messmer, a Gaullist (1972–74).

Jacques Chirac (1974–76) was chosen prime minister of the first government under Giscard's presidency as a reward for having bolted the Gaullist party—temporarily, as it turned out—and having supported Giscard's presidential candidacy; but he was later replaced by Raymond Barre (1976–81), a "nonpolitical" professor of economics, because of disagreements over economic policy as well as over Chirac's insistence on playing a more significant decision-making role.

Pierre Mauroy (1981–84), the first Socialist prime minister of the Fifth Republic, was selected by Mitterrand because of his nearly ideal background: Originating in a working-class family and trained as a teacher, he served as the mayor of a large industrial city. He had been prominent in the old Socialist party of the Fourth Republic and managed to get along well with the leaders of the party factions.

Mauroy was succeeded by Laurent Fabius (1984–86) when Mitterrand decided to change direction from a progressive, redistributive policy to a program of austerity and economic restraint. Chirac was reappointed as prime minister (1986–88) because the president had little choice—because, as pointed out above, the Gaullist party that Chirac led had gained dominance of the Assembly. Michel Rocard was chosen to head the government in 1988, in part because he had an important following within the ranks of the Socialist party and among the population at large. An ambitious politician, a nondogmatic and technocratic Socialist, he had (in late 1980) been a rival of Mitterrand for nomination as a candidate for the presidency and had served in a number of ministerial posts under Mauroy.

In May 1991 Rocard was in turn replaced by Edith Cresson. It is unclear whether this change constituted an abrupt firing or an "amicable divorce" of two politicians whose political marriage had been one of convenience; in any case, it had become necessary because the public image of the government—and, by derivation, that of Mitterrand himself—had been tarnished by continued unemployment, growing delinquency, riots of immigrants, and scandals involving campaign funding of Socialist politicians. Madame Cresson, the first woman prime minister in French history, had headed a succession of ministries. She had a reputation both as a loyal follower of Mitterrand and his brand of socialism (which was to the left of that of Rocard) and as a proponent of government policies favoring business and industry.[1]

In April 1992, Mitterrand asked Mme. Cresson to resign as prime minister. This decision followed upon the regional and cantonal elections in March, in which the Socialist party had incurred heavy losses. Mme. Cresson's successor, Pierre Bérégovoy, had served as Mitterrand's presidential chief of staff, as minister of social affairs, and (before and after the first "cohabitation" period) as minister of finance. In that last position, Bérégovoy developed a reputation for fiscal responsibility.

The most recent change of prime ministers occurred just after the parliamentary elections of March 1993. Since the RPR and the UDF won overwhelming control of the National Assembly, Mitterrand had to appoint Edouard Balladur to head a new government. Balladur had been minister of finance during the cohabitation government led by Chirac.

Cabinet stability has been much greater under the Fifth Republic than under the Fourth—with only thirteen prime ministers (one of whom, Chirac, served on two separate occasions) in a thirty-five year period (1958–93) (see tables 7.1 and 7.2). But there have been two dozen important cabinet changes during that time. Such "rearrangements" have been made for a variety of reasons: deaths, changes in policy orientations, voluntary resignations (often prompted by disagreement over government policy), and changes in the political party composition of the Assembly.[2]

The constitution provides that the chief of state preside over cabinet sessions. Similar provisions had existed in previous regimes, but (especially in the Third and Fourth republics) had meant little, since *working* sessions of the cabinet were in effect led by the prime minister. In the Fifth Republic, the president—except, again, during the "cohabitation" interlude—has effectively led most cabinet meetings and determined their agenda. Moreover, he has had a major voice in determining the size of the government (which has ranged from 24 to 49 "full" and

TABLE 7.1

POLITICAL COMPOSITION OF SELECTED FIFTH REPUBLIC GOVERNMENTS BEFORE 1979

President:	de Gaulle				Pompidou		Giscard d'Estaing		
Prime minister:	Debré	Pompidou		Couve de Murville	Chaban-Delmas	Messmer	Chirac	Barre	
Political party	January 1959	April 1962	April 1967	July 1968	June 1969	July 1972	June 1974	August 1976	July 1979
Gaullists	6	9	21	26	29	22	12	9	12
Republicans	–	3	3	4	7	5	8	10	11[a]
Centrists	3[b]	5[b]	–	–	3[c]	3[c]	2	2[d]	4[d]
Radicals	1	1	–	–	–	–	6[e]	5	1[f]
Left Radicals	–	–	–	–	–	–	–	–	–
Socialists	–	–	–	–	–	–	–	–	–
Communists	–	–	–	–	–	–	–	–	–
Miscellaneous	7[g]	–	–	–	–	–	–	–	3[h]
Nonparty	10	11	5	1	–	–	8	10[i]	10[i]
Totals (including prime minister)	27	29	29	31	39	30	36	36	41

a. Known until 1977 as Independent Republicans
b. MRP
c. Center for Democracy and Progress (CDP)
d. Center of Social Democrats (CDS)
e. Reformers
f. "Democratic Left"
g. Includes 5 Independents
h. Includes one "Social-Democrat," one member of CNIP, and the prime minister, attached to the UDF
i. Collectively designated as "presidential majority"

TABLE 7.2

POLITICAL COMPOSITION OF SELECTED FIFTH REPUBLIC GOVERNMENTS SINCE 1981

President:	Mitterrand								
Prime minister:	Mauroy		Fabius[a]	Chirac[b]	Rocard		Cresson[c]	Bérégovoy[c]	Balladur
Political party	May 1981	June 1981	July 1984	March 1986	May 1988[d]	June 1988[e]	May 1991	April 1992	March 1993
Gaullists	–	–	–	20	–	–	–	–	14
Republicans	–	–	–	7	–	1	–	–	7
Centrists	–	–	–	7f	–	1	2g	–	5f
Radicals	–	–	–	2	1	1	–	–	1
Left Radicals	3	2	3	–	2	3	2h	2	–
Socialists	39	37	36	–	26	25	32	31	–
Communists	–	4	–	–	–	–	–	–	–
Miscellaneous	1i	1i	1j	–	2k	3k	1l	–	2m
Nonparty	–	–	3	6	11	15	9	9	1n
Totals (including prime minister)	43	44	43	42	42	49	46	42o	30p

a. Cabinet: 18 ministers (incl. 14 Socialists)
b. Cabinet: 15 ministers (incl. 7 Gaullists, 5 various UDF, 3 nonparty)
c. Cabinet: 20 ministers (incl. 16 Socialists, 1 Centrist [France Unie], 1 Ecologist, 2 nonparty). The government included 6 women, 2 in the cabinet. Madame Cresson was replaced by Pierre Bérégovoy in April 1992.
d. Cabinet: 19 ministers (incl. 14 Socialists)

e. Cabinet: 22 ministers (incl. 14 Socialists, 1 Left Socialist, 1 nonparty)
f. Center of Social Democrats (CDS)
g. France Unie—a coalition formed in the Assembly in 1990 of Left Radicals and Centrists to enlarge the presidential majority toward the center and support Michel Rocard
h. MRG—These 2 ministers also belonged to France Unie.

i. Movement of Democrats, an ex-Gaullist group supporting Mitterand in the presidential elections of 1981
j. Parti Socialiste Unifié (PSU)
k. Direct (nondifferentiated) members of UDF
l. Ecologist movement
m. Two "direct" adherents of UDF.
n. Madame Simone Veil, a centrist close to Giscard d'Estaing.
o. In cabinet: 21 ministers.
p. In cabinet: 24 ministers.

"junior" ministers) and in deciding which of the full ministers (usually between 16 and 20) are "cabinet" ministers, that is, participate in the weekly cabinet sessions.

That does not mean that the prime minister's role has been negligible. Most prime ministers have been political personalities in their own right and have accepted the prime ministership for reasons of ambition, more than half viewing it as a steppingstone to the presidency. The prime ministers' leadership of the government has meant that they have presided over important interministerial committees, counseled the president on policy, and promoted and defended legislation in Parliament and before public opinion. Nevertheless, the association between president and prime minister does not necessarily constitute a genuine policy-making partnership; in fact, all presidents thus far have clearly rejected the notion that there is a "bicephalous" or "dyarchical" executive and have affirmed presidential supremacy, except when, between 1986–88, the executive was temporarily "depresidentialized."

The Parliament

In terms of its bicameral structure and internal organization, the Fifth Republic's legislature clearly resembles that of earlier republics. The National Assembly is composed of 577 deputies—555 from metropolitan France and 22 from overseas *départements* and territories. All are elected for a five-year term by direct popular vote on a single-member constituency basis. Members of the Senate are chosen for nine-year terms by an electoral college composed of National Assembly deputies, *département* councilors, and delegates of city councils. One-third of the membership is renewed every three years. In 1979 the Senate contained 295 members; in 1981, 305, and in 1991, 321. In theory, the two chambers have equal powers, with the following exceptions: Budget bills must always be submitted to the Assembly first, and only the Assembly may oust the government on a vote of censure (see below).

The organization of Parliament follows traditional patterns. Each chamber is chaired by a president (Speaker)—elected in the Assembly for five years, in the Senate for three—who is assisted by vice-presidents (or deputy speakers): six in the Assembly and four in the Senate, reflecting roughly the number of major party groupings in each chamber. These officers, which collectively constitute the "conference of presidents" in each chamber, formally determine the allocation of committee seats and the organization of parliamentary debates.

In order for deputies to participate meaningfully in legislative affairs, they must belong to a "parliamentary party" (*groupe parlementaire*). In the Fourth Republic, 14 deputies sufficed for a parliamentary party. With the establishment of the Fifth Republic, the required number was raised to 30; this change has forced small contingents of deputies to align (*s'apparenter*) with larger ones, thus reducing the number of parties in the legislature. After the parliamentary elections of 1988, the number was reduced to 20 in order to reward the 27 Communist deputies for their selective support of the government and, in particular, for having supported the election of Laurent Fabius, the former Socialist prime minister, as Speaker of the Assembly.

The decision-making role of Parliament is limited, particularly in comparison with earlier French republics and with other Western Euro-

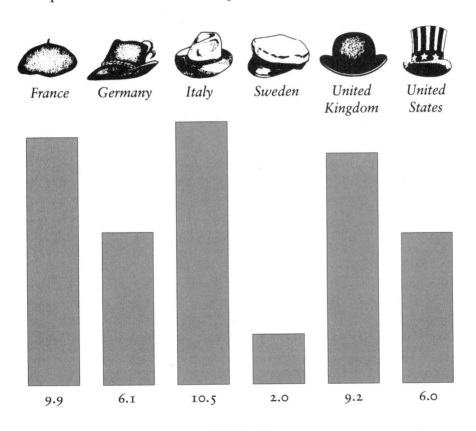

FIGURE 7.1

UNEMPLOYMENT RATES

NOTE: Five-year averages: 1985–90.

pean democracies. The maximum duration of ordinary sessions of Parliament is five and a half months per year: eighty days in the fall (from early October) and ninety days in the spring (from early April). Special sessions may be convened at the request of the prime minister or a majority of the deputies, but such sessions must have a clearly defined agenda. There have been many special sessions in recent years, convoked in most cases to deal with budgetary matters.[3]

The areas in which Parliament may pass legislation are clearly enumerated in the constitution (Article 34). They include, notably, budget and tax matters; civil liberties; penal and personal-status laws; the organization of judicial bodies; education; social security; the jurisdiction of local communities; the establishment of public institutions, including nationalized industries; and rules governing elections (where not spelled out in the constitutional text). Matters not stipulated fall in the domain of decrees, ordinances, or regulations, which are promulgated by the government directly. The distinction between "laws" and "decrees" is not a clear-cut one. In some areas—for example, local government, education, or labor and social policy—the Parliament often does little more than establish "general principles" and leaves it to the government to fill in the details by decree. In addition, the Parliament may be asked (under Article 38) to delegate to the government the power to issue decrees in areas normally under parliamentary jurisdiction, a procedure resorted to on many occasions under de Gaulle's presidency.

As is the custom in all parliamentary democracies, a distinction is made between a government bill (*projet de loi*) and a private member's bill (*proposition de loi*). The former has priority; in fact, since the founding of the Fifth Republic, less than 15 percent of all bills passed by Parliament originated with private members (or "backbenchers"), and most of these passed because the government raised no objections or because it encouraged such bills. Finance bills can be introduced only by the government, and backbenchers' amendments to such bills are permissible only if these do not reduce revenues or increase expenditures. Furthermore, if Parliament fails to vote on (in practice, to approve) a budget bill within a period of seventy days after submission, the government may enact the budget by decree.

The government has a deciding voice on what bills are to be discussed and how much time is to be allocated to debate on parts of a bill. It can also make amendments to a bill virtually impossible by resorting to the "blocked-vote" procedure (i.e., demanding that the text of the bill as a whole be voted on). Thus far, this procedure has been used well over 140 times in the Assembly, with more than 90 percent of such bills passing. In the Senate, about a third of the bills introduced in the blocked-vote fashion have been rejected.

Enactment of a bill requires its passage in both the Assembly and the Senate. Should there be disagreement between the two chambers, a variety of procedures may be used. The bill in question may be shuttled between the chambers until a common text is agreed upon; alternatively, the government may call for the appointment of a conference committee, or it may ask each chamber for a "second reading." If disagreement persists, the Assembly may be asked to pronounce itself definitively by simple majority vote, thereby enacting the bill in question.

Constitutional amendments are subject to a special procedure. The initiative belongs both to the president (after he consults with the prime minister) and to Parliament. An amendment bill, having passed in both chambers in identical form, is then submitted to the people for ratification. A referendum may be avoided if the amendment is ratified by Parliament in joint session—convoked for this purpose by the president—by a three-fifths majority.

Although the constitution grants the legislature jurisdiction in areas broad enough to embrace, in principle, the most important domestic policy matters, the Fifth Republic Parliament has been in a poor position to exercise this power. In the Fourth Republic, more than two dozen Assembly standing committees contributed much legislative input. These committees, because of the expertise of their members, became quasi-independent centers of power. Though they produced high-quality legislative proposals, they sometimes offered "counterproposals" to government bills, designed to embarrass the government and bring it down. In contrast, in the Fifth Republic only six standing committees, consisting of 61 to 121 deputies each, are provided for. They do their work within carefully limited time periods and are forbidden to produce "counterbills."

In theory, the Parliament can do much more than just register and ratify what has been proposed to it by the government. During the first decade of the Fifth Republic, Parliament, and above all the Assembly, was relatively docile; but (especially since the mid-1970s) Parliament has become increasingly assertive. This can be seen in the growth of the number of amendments to government bills introduced and passed.[4]

In weekly question periods, questions (in written or oral form) are addressed to individual ministers. Answers, not always immediately forthcoming, may be provided by a minister or by a person such as a higher civil servant deputized by him. Such question-and-answer sessions are sometimes followed by a very brief debate, sometimes by no debate at all. They cannot be followed by a vote of censure, which would cause the resignation of the government.

Motions of censure in the Assembly must be introduced by a unique and specific procedure and separately from the Assembly's routine business. These motions require the signatures of at least one-tenth of all the deputies—who may co-sponsor only one such motion during each parliamentary session (i.e., fall and spring)—and can be voted on only after a "cooling-off" period of forty-eight hours; and the motion carries only if a majority of the entire membership of the Assembly supports the censure. The government may also "dare" or provoke the Assembly into a motion of censure, simply by making a specific bill or a general policy declaration a matter of confidence. If no successful censure motion is forthcoming, the bill in question is considered to have passed —and the government, of course, remains in place. In thirty-three years, more than forty motions of censure have been introduced, but only one (in October 1962) obtained the requisite majority vote. In that instance, President de Gaulle was required to accept the parliamentary dismissal of his prime minister (then Pompidou). But de Gaulle nullified the effect of the censure by dissolving Parliament and, after the elections that followed, simply reappointed Pompidou to head a "new" government.

Another weapon that Parliament can use against the executive is the Constitutional Council. This body consists of nine members—one-third each chosen by the president, the Speaker of the Assembly, and the Speaker of the Senate—appointed for nine-year terms (with a one-third renewal every three years). Its function was originally viewed as largely advisory. The constitution provides that the council must be consulted on the constitutionality of an organic bill before it becomes law and of treaties before they are considered "ratified." It also pronounces on the legality of parliamentary regulations and the propriety of referendum procedures; it watches over presidential and legislative elections and confirms the results; and it must, of course, be consulted if the president invokes the emergency clause (Article 16) of the constitution. In addition, any bills may, before they become law, be submitted to the council for a judgment of their constitutionality by the president, the prime minister, the speaker of either chamber, and (since the passage of a constitutional amendment in 1974) by sixty deputies or sixty senators.

Under the Fourth Republic, deputies were often too willing to unseat a government in the hope that there would be a ministerial portfolio for them in a subsequent cabinet; if they should in turn be ousted from the cabinet, they would still retain their parliamentary seats. But the Fifth Republic constitution purposely changed all that. Under Article 23, a position in the cabinet is "incompatible" with simultaneous occupancy of a seat in Parliament. Consequently, any deputy (or senator) who ascends to the cabinet must resign his parliamentary seat —which is immediately filled, without special election, by his "alternate" (*suppléant*), whose name was listed on the ballot alongside that of the deputy during the preceding Assembly elections. (If the alternate, too, resigns, there must be a by-election.)

The spirit of the incompatibility clause has been violated repeatedly. Cabinet ministers have run for parliamentary seats they do not intend to occupy; presidents have encouraged that practice because in this way popular support for the government can be tested; and constituents have voted for such candidates because it is much better, for securing "pork-barrel" appropriations, for local voters to have their representative sit in cabinet rather than in Parliament. Furthermore, deputies appointed by the government for special tasks (as *chargés de mission*) may retain their parliamentary seats if the appointment is for less than six months.

The incompatibility rule has not affected the "accumulation of elected offices" (*cumul des mandats*). For many years, most deputies were concurrently mayors as well as members of regional, departmental, and municipal councils, and a sizable number were also serving as members of the European Parliament. All these activities cut deeply into the time available to deputies or senators to devote themselves to parliamentary work, let alone to oppose the government. In 1982, 82 percent of the deputies (and 93 percent of the senators) were members of municipal councils. A (perhaps extreme) example of multiple office-holding was that of Jean Lecanuet, who (in addition to holding the leadership of the UDF) concurrently served as senator, mayor of a sizable town (Rouen), president of a general council, member of a regional council, and member of the European Parliament. In order to rectify such a situation—and perhaps increase the attention span of parliamentarians—an act was passed in 1985 to limit the accumulation of elective offices to no more than two.[5] Since the enactment of this reform, about half of the deputies have opted to retain their positions as mayors.[6]

The limitations on the power of the deputy have not served to improve his or her public image or, indeed, self-image. Still, there is no proof that individual legislators in France are substantially less powerful or less rewarded than their counterparts in Britain. The gross annual salary of deputies is about $75,000 (roughly corresponding to that of higher civil servants and senior university professors), a sum that includes base pay plus rental subsidy. In addition, the typical deputy receives about $60,000 a year for administrative assistance (partly paid for by the Assembly), as well as travel allowances and tax concessions. For many deputies, such compensation is insufficient to cover the cost of maintaining two apartments and traveling to and from their constituencies. Hence they may be forced to pursue, as best they can, their "normal" professions.

Most deputies are not rich; in fact, in terms of social background, age, and occupation they are reasonably representative of the population. Statistics reveal that National Assemblies produced in the past four elections (i.e., since 1978) have included a large number of national government officials, educators (especially among the Socialists), and white-collar employees, and a fair number of physicians. The number of blue-collar workers and farmers has been insignificant.

The Administrative State

One of the features of the French polity that has been subjected to relatively little change and that is not likely to alter drastically in the near future is the administrative system. Since the time of the Old Regime and Napoleon, that system has been highly centralized; the various echelons below the national government—*départements,* districts (*arrondissements*), and communes—have remained administrative rather than decision-making entities, whose responsibilities can be defined, expanded, or contracted at will by the national government. (For recent decentralization policies, see pages 125–27).

At the pinnacle of the system is the permanent civil service. Defined in its broadest sense, it is the corpus of about 3 million government employees and constitutes about 15 percent of France's total labor force. In addition to the ordinary national civil servants, it includes military officers, teachers from the public elementary schools through the university, employees of local bodies, and the staff employed by the railroads, civil aviation, electric power companies, and other nationalized sectors.

The French civil service proper (*la fonction publique*) numbers about 1 million. It is subdivided into a number of categories ranging from custodial and manual workers to high administrative functionaries who are directly responsible to cabinet ministers. The civil service is functionally divided into "sectoral" categories. The most prestigious of these are the General Inspectorate of Finance, the Court of Accounts, the Foreign Ministry, and the Council of State (the pinnacle of the national administrative court system)—collectively labeled the *grand corps*. This body also includes the prefectoral corps, whose members, the prefects, are the chief agents of the government on departmental and regional levels and are under the authority of the minister of the interior.

Since the time of Napoleon, recruitment to the higher civil service has been tied to the educational system. A variety of national schools, the likes of which are not found in other countries, train specialized civil servants. These schools, the *grandes écoles,* are maintained alongside the regular universities and have highly competitive entry and graduation requirements. The best known are the Ecole Polytechnique, for training civil engineers and scientists, the Ecole Normale Supérieure, whose graduates become professors in prestigious lycées and universities, and the Ecole Nationale d'Administration (ENA). The last-named, which opened its doors only in 1946, has trained the majority of higher administrative personnel for the *grand corps* and the prefectoral corps. It numbers among its graduates a former president (Giscard), three prime ministers (Chirac, Rocard, and Balladur), and many cabinet ministers.

The French have often criticized the important position of the higher civil service. They have argued that while it makes for stability, it tends to undermine democracy. This criticism has been based on the upper- and upper-middle-class origins of most of the higher functionaries, on the fact that they are subject neither to popular elections nor adequate controls, and on the belief that they have tended to serve not the citizen but an abstraction called "the state."

Nevertheless, the higher civil service has not been monolithic or dictatorial, nor has it been immune to internal conflicts and external pressures. Although the ENA has recruited only a minuscule portion of its student body from the working class and the peasantry—despite a number of halfhearted attempts to broaden the method of recruitment[7] —its graduates, the *Enarques,* have been as likely to be identified as progressives, or even leftists, as conservatives or reactionaries. There is sometimes a conflict between civil servants who work for the Ministries of Finance and Industry, who often have close personal and ideological ties with big-business managers, and those who work in the Ministries of Health and Education, who tend to have affinities with their clientele and therefore to have a "social reform" outlook. There is also a certain tension between the traditional bureaucrats who serve in the standard ministries and have a legalistic orientation and the technocrats who have been trained in economics, statistics, and management methods and are found in the National Economic Planning Commission.

Public Corporations

A component of the administrative system that is difficult to categorize, yet is of great importance, is the nationalized sector. In France, about 15 percent of the economy is in government hands, including (but not limited to) the following: mass transport, gas, electricity, nuclear energy, the postal service, civil aviation, the procurement and distribution of fuel, a large proportion of banking and insurance, and one automobile manufacturing firm (Renault). The reasons behind nationalization—the influence of socialist ideology, the limits of the private capital market, the monopolistic nature of certain enterprises, the need to consolidate production or services in order to make them more efficient, and so on—need not detain us here. Suffice it to say that the state's involvement in the management of economic matters has resulted in special approaches to recruitment, job classification, and political control. Sometimes positions of responsibility in nationalized, or "public," enterprises are given to individuals coopted from the private sector or are handed over as political plums to politicians who have proved their loyalty to the president. Because of the complexity of the management problems, nationalized enterprises are difficult to subject to parliamentary surveillance; at the same time, their very existence can be a useful weapon in the hands of a government interested in long-term economic planning or at least in influencing the behavior of the private economic sector in its production and pricing policies.

In 1981–82, the Socialist government (in conformity with its preelection platform) introduced bills to bring additional sectors under public control, among them a dozen industrial conglomerates (manufacturing, metals, chemicals, electronics, and machine tools) and most of the remaining private banks. Such a policy proved to be ill advised, and soon after coming to power in 1986, the Gaullist government of Chirac proceeded to denationalize most of these sectors, as well as most of the hitherto governmentally owned television networks.

Control and Redress

One of the institutions that has played a significant role as a watchdog over administrative activities is the Council of State (*Conseil d'Etat*). Originally created by Napoleon (in 1799) for resolving intrabureaucratic disputes, it has gradually assumed additional functions. It advises the government on the language of draft bills; it passes on the legality of decrees and regulations issuing from the executive; and most important, it acts as a court of appeal for suits brought by citizens against the administration. Such suits, involving charges of bureaucratic arbitrariness, illegalities, or abuse of power, are initiated in departmental (prefectoral) administrative tribunals. Unfortunately, several years may elapse before such cases are dealt with by the Council of State.

A relatively recent (1973) innovation is the "mediator," the French equivalent of the ombudsman, or citizens' "complaint" commissioner. This official, appointed by the president for a six-year term on the recommendation of Parliament, may take upon himself the examination of a variety of complaints involving, for example, social security agencies, prisons, nationalized industries, and administrative and judicial malfunctions. He may request from any public agency information he considers pertinent, initiate judicial proceedings against misbehaving bureaucrats, and suggest to the government improvements in the laws. Appeal to the mediator (which is free of charge) cannot be direct; it must be made via a deputy or senator.

Subnational Government and Administration

The extent to which national decisions can be, or should be, influenced or deflected on local levels has been a matter of intense debate in France for the past two decades. There has been some question whether the existing subdivisions are of the proper size, whether they are adequately financed, and whether they provide a meaningful arena for the political participation of citizens.

Metropolitan France consists of ninety-six *départements,* which are the basic subnational administrative units into which the country was divided during the Revolution of 1789. In addition, there are five overseas *départements.* Each *département* is both self-administering *and* an administrative subunit of the national government. Whatever autonomy the *département* possesses is reflected by its General Council, which votes a budget, decides on local taxes and loans, and passes laws on housing, roads, welfare services, cultural programs, and educational services (supplementary to those made mandatory by the national government). The General Council, which is elected by popular vote (by single-member constituencies—the cantons) for a six-year term (with half of the membership renewable every three years), in turn elects a president, or chairperson. Traditionally the latter, however, was not properly speaking the executive officer of the *département.* That role was filled by the prefect, an agent of the *national* government who used to be charged with administering the *département* in behalf of the Ministry of the Interior and other national ministries. Thus the prefect (together with the mayor of a town) would be involved in the maintenance of public order; but the (local) police force was itself an instrument of national administration and, as such, was directly under the authority of the Ministry of the Interior in Paris.

In 1982 the office of prefect was abolished and replaced by that of commissioner of the republic (which meant, in effect, that the prefects were renamed commissioners). The commissioners still functioned as agents of the national government, but they left budgetary and many other policy decisions to the General Council (except for services and expenditures mandated by national legislation). In 1987, the title of commissioner was changed back to that of prefect.

The prefect is assisted by a cabinet composed of specialists in public works, agriculture, housing, and other services. On the next lower level are the 325 *arrondissements,* the basic (single-member) constituencies for parliamentary elections. (Some heavily populated *arrondissements* are subdivided into two or more constituencies.) A further subdivision is the canton, which contains a number of agencies such as units of the national gendarmerie, tax offices, and highway services.

Since 1972, the *départements* have been grouped into twenty-two regions. These have their own assemblies, elected by popular vote (on the basis of proportional representation) for six-year terms. The regional assemblies, their presiding officers, and the regional commissioners of the republic all serve to coordinate the activities of several *départements.*

The lowest, but most significant, administrative unit is the commune. Communes, of which there are more than 36,000, may range in size from villages of fewer than a hundred inhabitants to the national capital. Some communes have become too small to maintain a full range of services; they have been either administratively merged with neighboring communes or compelled to associate with them functionally. Under provisions put into effect in the early 1970s, certain services may be performed jointly by several communes, such as water supply and fire protection. Conversely, some communes are so large that special regimes have been invented for them. For instance, Paris and Lyon are themselves subdivided into *arrondissements.*

Paris has always been a special case. Between 1871 and 1977, Paris did not have a mayor but was ruled by two prefects directly on behalf of the national government: a prefect of the Seine (the former name of the *département* in which the capital is located) and a prefect of police. Each of the twenty *arrondissements* had its own mayor, whose functions were generally limited to such matters as the maintenance of civil registers, the performance of marriages, the changing of street names, and the like. Since the reinstitution of the mayor for all of Paris, the twenty district mayors have been replaced by "civil administrators." The prefect of the Paris *département* and the prefect of police, however, remain in place.

The relationship between the national government and subnational units has been rendered confusing by the existence of functional units that overlap geographical boundaries. Thus in addition to the *départements* and regions there are twenty-five educational districts (*académies*), which administer educational programs from elementary school through universities; sixteen social security regions; and six military districts. All of these have been, in the final analysis, administrative conveniences put in place by the national government; for many years, they provided little in the way of local decision-making opportunities. Nevertheless, the situation improved considerably after the election of Mitterrand when (under the decentralization laws enacted between 1981 and 1983) municipal and general councils were given greater authority to collect revenues.

A major purpose of subnational units is to serve as arenas of citizen involvement in politics and the recruitment of politicians for both national and subnational echelons. This is particularly true of communes: The outcome of municipal elections, which occur every six years and produce nearly 500,000 councilors, ultimately affects the composition of the Senate, since the councils are part of the electoral college that chooses senators. Municipal elections also enable the citizenry to express "midterm" attitudes regarding the performance of the national government and, more specifically, that of the party in power. Thus, the outcome of the municipal elections of March 1983, in which many Socialist and Communist councilors (and, indirectly, mayors) were replaced by Gaullist or Giscardo-centrist ones, was viewed as an expression of voters' impatience with the record of the Mitterrand presidency and the Socialist government after two years in office; conversely, the outcome of the municipal elections of March 1989, in which many Gaullists were in turn ousted, was interpreted as a reflection of a relative satisfaction with the performance of the Socialist government led by Rocard.

Notes

1. Madame Cresson developed a reputation for outspokenness and lack of tact, and within a few weeks of her assumption of office, the popularity of her government plummeted, as did that of Mitterrand.

2. For example, in early 1991 Jean-Pierre Chevènement was forced to resign as minister of defense because he disagreed with Mitterrand's decision to support the United States in its policy of military intervention in the Persian Gulf.

3. There were seventeen special sessions between 1981 and 1986, four between 1986 and 1988, and four in 1989.

4. In 1968, 1,431 amendments to bills were introduced in the Assembly, of which 606 passed; in 1975, 4,036 (1,605 passed); in 1981, 5,060 (1,370 passed); and during the "cohabitation" period 1986–88, 9,268 (2,237 passed).

5. See Albert Mabileau, "Le cumul des mandats," *Regards sur l'Actualité* 169 (March 1991): 17–29.

6. An exception to this development was the decision of Alain Carignon in 1988 to resign his position as deputy while retaining that of mayor of Grenoble and member of the general council of his *département*.

7. In 1983, the Socialist government attempted to diminish the existing bias in favor of Parisians, graduates of the better universities, and children of higher civil servants by providing for an alternative entry into ENA (by means of special examinations) to local politicians and middle-echelon officials of public agencies, but the Chirac government subsequently suspended that method. The present Socialist government, however, has committed itself to reinstating it.

8

Who Has the Power, and How Did They Get It?

France has a complex political party system, which many view as symptomatic of disorder and confusion. At any given time—especially during elections—it is possible to distinguish more than a dozen parties. Some of these can be traced back several generations and have been of national importance; others are of passing interest because of their ephemeral or purely local nature or weak organization; and still others are mere political clubs, composed of small clusters of intellectuals more anxious to have a forum for expressing their political views than to achieve power.

From the point of view of national politics, one may identify six major "ideological families" within which political parties have been arranged—at least from the post-World War II period until recently: Communists and Socialists; Radical-Socialists and Catholics; and Conservatives and Gaullists. For the sake of analytic convenience, these may in turn be grouped into the left, the center, and the right. Each of the "families" has tried to represent different social classes and/or different views regarding economic policy, executive-legislative relations, and the place of religion in politics. Before looking at specific parties, one should be warned that their positions have not always been consistent; that the traditional ideologies often failed to be adjusted in terms of changing socioeconomic realities, including the structure of the electorate; that politicians elected under the label of one party have sometimes shifted to another; and that tactical considerations have often forced parliamentary deputies to vote on issues in such a way as to ignore their party platforms.

The Old Right

Historically, the political right was characterized by its identification with the status quo. It had favored monarchism and had deplored the revolutions of 1789 and 1848. Inclined toward authoritarian rule, the right evolved from support of Bourbon kings to support of Napoleon and other "heroic" leaders, and still later to support of de Gaulle. It favored an elitist social structure; defined society in "organic" (i.e., hereditary) and hierarchical terms; had contempt for the masses, who were considered too irrational and selfish to be entrusted with political participation; and invested the "state" with an aura of sanctity. Originally, the support of the right was derived from the established classes: the aristocracy, the landed gentry, the clergy, and, later, the military and big business.

The importance of the political right was gradually reduced with the transformation of the French economy and society, specifically the decline of the sectors that had been its main electoral base. Furthermore, by the beginning of the Fourth Republic, much of the political right had become discredited because many of its adherents had been collaborators of the Germans during the war, while the "respectable" right had become converted to republicanism. The main political expression of the postwar right was the CNIP, the Centre National des Indépendants et Paysans (National Center of Independents and Peasants), a group of politicians sometimes also known as "Moderates." The CNIP (later known simply as CNI) was feebly represented in the Assembly, however, in part because it reflected two conflicting positions: a "liberal" one (i.e., a belief in laissez-faire economics) and a "conservative" one (i.e., a continued commitment to the values of elitism, religion, authority, and family). Another reason for the weakness of the traditional right was that it had to compete with the "center" parties for voters. A third, and most important, reason was the rise of Gaullism, a political movement that drained off many of the right's old supporters, notably the nationalist and populist-authoritarian elements.

Gaullism is a unique phenomenon. Many of the French had shared General de Gaulle's dislike of the Fourth Republic. They objected to its central feature: a Parliament that was, in theory, all-powerful but in practice was immobilized because it was faction ridden. They favored a regime with a strong leader who would not be hampered by political parties and interest groups; these were considered particularistic and destructive interpositions between the national leadership and the citizenry. Above all, Gaullists wanted France to reassert its global role and rediscover its grandeur. Many of their early supporters had been identified with the general as members of his Free French entourage in London or had been active in the Resistance. Others had worked with him when he headed the first provisional government after the Liberation; still others saw in him the embodiment of the "hero-savior." Gaullism can thus be described as nationalistic as well as Caesaristic, or "Bonapartist," in the sense that the legitimacy of the national leader was to be based on popular appeal.

Gaullism never contained a clear or consistent domestic policy program, however, and, at least in the beginning, did not seem to show great interest in economic reform or social justice and therefore failed to get significant support from the working-class electorate. Yet Gaullists would vehemently reject the label of "rightist" because, they argued, nationalism is not incompatible with social reform, and because the first Gaullist party, the Rassemblement du Peuple Français (RPF), established in 1947, was intended to be a movement that would appeal to all social classes. The RPF, however, was not to become a mass party until the collapse of the Fourth Republic.

The Old Left

Leftism and socialism have been particularly important in modern French political history because they have stood for progress, equality, rationalism, and democratic government—precisely the aims with which the Revolution of 1789 was associated. In response to the gradual democratization of the suffrage and the growing electoral importance of the working class, many parties appropriated the label "socialist." Socialist parties have been inspired by different traditions, some of them dating to the eighteenth century—utopian, revolutionary, and reformist—but these parties shared a preoccupation with the systematic explanation of social phenomena: an emphasis on the importance (and the claims) of society as a whole; and a belief that economic, political, and social structures were intimately related.

The major party of the left is the PS, the Parti socialiste (Socialist party). Originally formed in 1905 out of small and disparate leftist groups, and known until 1969 as the SFIO (Section Française de l'Internationale Ouvrière), it was inspired by revolutionary Marxism and appealed to the industrial working class. Increased parliamentary representation, participation in bourgeois governments, and the takeover of leadership positions by intellectuals and other middle-class elements caused the Socialist party to lose its revolutionary dynamism and commit itself to the idea of gradual, nonviolent reform. The party came to attach as much value to the maintenance of democratic processes as to socioeconomic redistributive policies. In 1936, Léon Blum, the party leader, headed a government that (with the support of some of the other leftist parties) instituted far-reaching social reforms. When the party was reconstituted in the Fourth Republic, it continued to promote progressive legislation. But the Socialist party was hampered in its growth by competition from the Communist party.

Established in 1920, the PC, the Parti communiste (Communist party) had taken much of the Socialists' working-class electorate from them. The two parties of the left collaborated on many bills in the legislature; but whereas the Communists wanted to bring down the Fourth Republic, the Socialists were committed to maintaining it. In 1958, most Socialists voted in favor of the investiture of de Gaulle as prime minister; the Communists opposed it. Later that year, while a large number of Socialist leaders endorsed the Fifth Republic constitution, the Communists expressed opposition to it. In the 1960s, the Socialists lost much of their membership, whereas the Communists were able to retain most of their hard-core adherents. Both leftist parties were consigned to an opposition status from which they emerged only in 1981.

The Old Center

For at least a century, there has been an ideological family that has represented the broad interests of the *petite bourgeoisie*—the shopkeepers, artisans, and certain farmers—as well as portions of the intellectual and professional classes. It has occupied the "center" position in French politics insofar as it rejected both the elitism and static orientation of the Conservatives and the loudly articulated egalitarianism of the left. It favored selective social reforms but rejected collectivism. It was committed to republicanism and to a progressive democratization of political institutions, which meant, among other things, the extension of the suffrage and the increased power of Parliament. The political center has always been difficult to pin down with precision, because many centrists pretended to adhere to a more fashionable "leftism" and provided themselves with misleading labels, and because the center has been fragmented. It is necessary to distinguish between two basic kinds of centrism: Catholic and Radical-Socialist.

The Radical-Socialist party is the oldest existing party in France.

Officially founded in 1901, its origins must be traced to the beginning of the Third Republic and, as some would insist, to the French Revolution. The party backed a strongly centralized republic but has been consistently led by local notables. It was "radical" in the sense that it favored—and helped achieve—the elimination of the role of the Catholic church in politics and the promotion of a secular school system. It viewed the state as the enemy, and hence it argued strongly for civil rights (especially property rights). But this did not prevent the Radicals from asking the state to give protection to that segment of their electorate that felt its livelihood to be threatened by economic consolidation at home and competition from abroad. Such attitudes were "leftist" enough as long as the *petite bourgeoisie* constituted the bulk of the politically underprivileged masses. With industrialization, a new class became important: that of factory workers. The ideology of Socialist parties—the belief in the class struggle and opposition to private productive property—that this new class embraced made the Radicals' leftism increasingly illusory and pushed them into a defensive posture. Nevertheless, the tactical position of the Radical party often made it an indispensable partner in government coalitions and allowed it to play a dominant role in the Third and Fourth republics and to provide both regimes with numerous prime ministers.

Another orientation that must be classified as centrist is that of Christian democracy. Originally, Catholicism could not be equated easily either with republicanism or with social progress; the Popular party founded toward the end of the Third Republic, which fully supported the parliamentary system, was relatively insignificant. But political Catholicism gained a new respectability during World War II; after Liberation, devout Catholics who had been active in the Resistance established the Mouvement Républicain Populaire (MRP), which, although communalist in orientation and clericalist, was committed to civil liberties and social reform in a republican context. In the beginning of the Fourth Republic, the MRP's position was leftist enough, and its parliamentary representation strong enough, to make it a coalition partner with the Socialists and Communists. Moreover, the party competed with the Radicals in its adaptability. Toward the end of the Fourth Republic, the MRP was weakened for the same reason as the Radicals. Some of the party's leftist adherents turned with interest to the Socialists, while its conservative ones, who were far more numerous, embraced Gaullism. In 1958, a large proportion of the MRP politicians joined the Gaullist bandwagon. (The pitiful remnant of the MRP dissolved in 1966.)

Elections and Political Parties in the Fifth Republic

The return of de Gaulle to power produced a temporary eclipse of all political parties that the public mind associated with the discredited Fourth Republic. Under that republic, an electoral system based on proportional representation had made it possible for many parties to gain parliamentary seats. The "game of politics" had been such that most parties could easily turn rightward or leftward, or switch from support of the government to opposition status. The system of Assembly elections instituted in 1958, however, forced parties to make the kind of clear choice they were often unprepared to make. That system is based on the single-member district. A candidate for the Assembly is required to obtain a majority of all votes cast in his constituency. If no candidate obtains such a majority, a second, or "runoff," balloting must be held one week later, in which a candidate needs only a *plurality* of the votes. (Only the candidates who receive at least 12.5 percent of the first-round votes may run in the second.) The system of presidential elections is similar: If a majority is not obtained on the first ballot, a "face-off" contest occurs two weeks later between the two candidates who had received the largest number of first-round votes.

The French are fond of saying that "on the first ballot one votes, and on the second, one eliminates." Electoral realism has required that a political party, in order to maximize its chances, think in terms of combining forces with another party by means of preelectoral deals and second-ballot withdrawal, or mutual-support, agreements. Such activities have produced polarizing tendencies: the reduction of the number of political parties and their rearrangement into two opposing camps, much in the manner of the United States and Great Britain (see tables 8.1 and 8.2, pages 136–38).

The Gaullist party emerged as the major beneficiary of the new system. Relabeled the Union pour la Nouvelle République (UNR), subsequently renamed as Union Démocratique pour la République (UDR), and obtaining a dominant position in the Assembly, it became relatively institutionalized; in many localities, Gaullist machines were set up and many local notables, drawn by the magnet of power, associated with them. Most of the old centrist formations remained in the opposition (though a large proportion of centrist *voters* had flocked to the banner of de Gaulle while not necessarily embracing Gaullist ideology). One of the collecting points of centrist anti-Gaullism was the Democratic Center, which included some of the old MRP politicians who distrusted or detested the general.

Both major parties of the left were reduced to impotence. The

Communist party could count on the support of about 20 percent of the electorate but could not win without allies. Clearly, the only possible ally was the Socialist party. The Socialists had, theoretically, two options: an alliance with either the Communists or the opposition centrists. In the presidential elections of 1965, a "united left" tactic was preferred, but one that implied the cooptation of part of the center. Both major parties of the left agreed on a single presidential candidate, François Mitterrand. Mitterrand's hand had been considerably strengthened when he succeeded in forming the FGDS, the Fédération de la Gauche Démocratique et Socialiste (Democratic and Socialist Left), which grouped around the Socialist party a variety of small leftist clubs as well as the Radical-Socialist party (which had begun its decline into insignificance). But after various electoral failures, and because of the continued disunity between Socialists and Communists, this alliance disintegrated, and in 1969 each of the two parties fielded its own presidential candidate.

The Socialists then decided to restructure their organization, rejuvenate their leadership, alter their platform, and project an image of dynamism. One idea the Socialists were (later) to advocate for a number of years was *autogestion*, a form of self-management of industrial firms by workers. At the same time, the party enrolled many members of the bourgeoisie: shopkeepers, artisans, white-collar employees, technicians, and even devout Catholics. Its new position of strength encouraged the Socialist party to rebuild its alliance with the Communists. In 1972, the two parties signed a joint platform (the "Common Program of the Left") and agreed to support one another in subsequent national elections.

The centrists, meanwhile, remained weak. The election of Pompidou in 1969 had been the excuse for some politicians of the Democratic Center, already starved for power, to join the conservative majority; they reasoned, somewhat disingenuously, that the new president, although a Gaullist, was much more inclined to accommodate himself to centrist thinking than de Gaulle had been. Specifically, they hoped that Pompidou would support the policies most dear to them: European unification, more power for Parliament, and meaningful decentralization within France. The centrists who were still disinclined to make peace with Gaullism embraced another option, an electoral alignment with the Radical-Socialists known as the Reformers' Movement. The creation of that movement marked a turning point in French politics because it implied that the Catholic-anticlerical discord had been reduced to a manageable scale. But the movement rested from the start on too narrow an electoral base. Moreover, the left wing of the Radical party was

TABLE 8.1

PARLIAMENTARY AND PRESIDENTIAL ELECTIONS, 1958–93 (IN PERCENTAGE OF TOTAL VOTES CAST)

Elections — Parliamentary	Elections — Presidential	Communists	Socialists	Radicals & Left-Radical	MRP	Democratic Center	Independents & Moderates	Gaullists	National Front	Others
1958 (1)		18.9	15.5	11.5	11.6		19.9	17.6		5.0
(2)		20.7	13.7	7.7	7.5		23.6	26.4		0.4
1962 (1)		21.7	12.6	7.5	8.9	9.6	4.4[f]	31.9		0.4
(2)		21.3	15.2	7.0	5.3	7.8	1.6[f]	40.5		1.3
	1965 (1)	→	32.2[a]	→		15.8	→	43.7		8.3
	(2)	→	45.5[b]	→			→	54.5		—
1967 (1)		22.5	18.8[b]			17.9		37.8		3.0
(2)		21.4	24.1[b]			10.8		42.6		1.1
1968 (1)		20.0	16.5[b]			10.3		43.7		9.5
(2)		20.1	21.3[b]			7.8		46.4		4.4
	1969 (1)	21.5	5.1			23.4[c]		43.9		6.1
	(2)	→	→			42.4[c]		57.6		—
1973 (1)		21.5	21.2		13.1[d]			36.4		7.8
(2)		20.6	25.1		6.1[d]			46.2		2.0
	1974 (1)	→	43.2[a]	→		32.6[e]		15.1		10.1
	(2)	→	49.2[a]	→		50.8[e]				—
1978 (1)		20.5	22.5	2.3[b]		23.9[g]		22.6		8.2
(2)		18.6	28.3	2.3[b]		24.8[g]		26.1		—

Parliamentary	Presidential	Communists	Socialists	Radicals & Left-Radical	MRP	Democratic Center	Independents & Moderates	Gaullists	National Front	Others
	1981 (1)	15.3[i]	25.8[a]	2.2[j]	←		28.3[e]	17.9[k]		10.3[l]
	(2)		51.8[a]		←		42.2[e]			
1981 (1)		16.2	37.5[m] →			19.2[g]		20.8		6.3
(2)		6.9	49.3[m] →			18.6[g]		22.4		2.7
1986		9.8	31.0	0.4[b]		8.3[g]	21.5[n]	11.2	9.7	7.8
	1988 (1)	6.7	34.1[a]			16.5[o]		19.9[k]	14.4	8.2[p]
	(2)		54.0[a]					47.0[k]		
1988 (1)		11.3	37.5[q]				44.4[r]		9.8[s]	0.9
(2)		3.4	48.7[q]				46.8[r]		1.1	2.6
1993 (1)		9.2	19.2[q]				39.7[t]		12.4	19.5[u]
(2)		4.6	31.3[v]				55.0[w]		5.7	3.3[x]

NOTE: (1) = first ballot; (2) = second ballot; ←, ——→ = extent of support

a. Mitterrand
b. Federation of Democratic and Socialist Left (FGDS)
c. Alain Poher, Christian-Democratic Centrist
d. "Reformers"
e. Giscard d'Estaing
f. Independent Republicans
g. UDF and "presidential majority"
h. Left Radicals (MRG)
i. Georges Marchais
j. Michel Crépeau, a left Radical
k. Jacques Chirac

l. Including 3.9 for Brice Lalonde, the Environmentalist candidate
m. Including Left Radicals
n. Gaullist-UDF combined list
o. Raymond Barre, UDF
p. Including Ecologists (Greens) 3.8, and miscellaneous left, 4.4
q. Including left Radicals and other allies
r. Union du Rassemblement et du Centre (URC), an electoral alliance of RPR and UDF
s. Le Pen

t. Union pour la France (UPF), an alliance of RPR (19.83), UDF (18.64), and smaller groups.
u. Of these, three environmentalist parties, 10.7 (subdivided among Verts [Greens] 4.02, Génération Ecologie 3.61, and Nouveaux Ecologistes 2.5).
v. Socialist party 29.79, Left Radicals and other allies 1.54.
w. UPF, of which RPR 27.84, UDF 25.11.
x. Ecologist groups 0.18, miscellaneous right-wing parties 2.85.

TABLE 8.2

COMPOSITION OF THE NATIONAL ASSEMBLY SINCE 1956

Parliamentary elections	Communists	Socialists and allies	Radicals and allies	MRP and Center	Conservatives, Moderates, Independents	Gaullist	Miscellaneous and unaffiliated	Total seats
1956	150	99	94	84	97	22	50	596
1958	10	47	40	56	129	206	64	552
1962	41	66	43	55	268[a]		9	482
1967	73	121[b]		41[c]	242[a]		10	487
1968	34	57[b]		34[c]	344[d]		18	487
1973	73	100[e]	34[f]		270[d]		13	490
1978	86	105	10[g]		9[i] 123[h]	153	5	491
1981	44	286[e]			62[k]	88	11	491
1986	35	214[e]			132[k]	158	38[l]	577
1988	27	277[e]			130[k]	129	14[m]	577
1993	23	70[e]			213[k]	247	24[n]	577

a. Gaullists and Independent Republicans
b. Socialist and Radical alliance
c. Progress and Modern Democracy
d. Gaullists, Independent Republicans, and progovernment Centrists
e. Socialist and Left Radicals
f. Reformers (Moderate Radicals and Opposition Centrists)
g. Left Radicals (MRG)
h. UDF
i. Independents and Peasants (CNIP)
j. Identified only (and directly) with UDF rather than one of its components
k. UDF (Republican, CDS, and Moderate Radical-Socialists)
l. Including 32 National Front and 6 unaffiliated
m. Including 13 miscellaneous right and 1 National Front deputy (who has since left the party)
n. CNIP and others affiliated with the center-right coalition.

offended by this open collaboration with "clericalist" forces and wanted no part of the Reformers' experiment; instead, it reorganized into a distinct party, the MRG, the Mouvement des Radicaux de Gauche (Movement of Left Radicals), which became the third partner of the Common-Program alliance.

Bipolarization and Fragmentation

By the early 1970s, the French party system appeared to have become permanently bipolarized into a right-wing majority and a left-wing opposition. But the presidential elections of May 1974, into which France was propelled by the sudden death of Pompidou, began as a three-way race. Mitterrand was again the candidate of a united left. The Gaullist party's candidate was Jacques Chaban-Delmas, whose background as a faithful adherent of the late general *and* as a former Radical-Socialist could appeal to a good portion of the (heretofore oppositionist) centrist electorate. Giscard d'Estaing's candidacy complicated the presidential race. Giscard had been a prominent politician since the beginning of the Fifth Republic, had supported de Gaulle's presidency, and had served as minister of finance for several years while never, formally, joining any Gaullist party. He had been originally associated with the conservative CNIP, which had remained a component of the majority. But in the early 1960s, he had formed his own political organization with the help of a number of other CNIP Parliamentarians.

This group, the Independent Republicans, articulated a technocratic, problem-solving approach to a policy of industrial modernization and a more serious reorientation to free-market economics, as distinct from the Gaullist emphasis on the directing hand of the state. Giscard had differed from the Gaullists also in taking a stronger stand in favor of civil liberties and an enlarged role for Parliament, political parties, and interest groups. Finally, he had opposed the Gaullist-sponsored referendum of 1969 for the restructuring of the Senate and was instrumental in its defeat, and thus in bringing about the resignation of de Gaulle. In any case, Giscard's background, his youthful image (he was born in 1926), his selective non-Gaullist policy positions, his promises of social reform, and his apparent sympathy for close intra-European cooperation—all these secured for him the support of most of the Democratic Centrists and most Radicals. They were persuaded that Giscard was essentially a centrist himself and that he would pursue policies that would be neither Gaullist nor collectivist.

Giscard's accession to the presidency (with the support of the Gaullists on the second ballot) raised the question whether the old polarization of French politics was ending and whether France was in process of
becoming "post-Gaullist." A year before the parliamentary elections of
1978, it still appeared that bipolar confrontation would continue. The
parties adhering to the Common Program of the left pledged to support
one another electorally, as did the various components of what had
come to be known as "the presidential majority": the Gaullists, the Independent Republicans (now known as the Parti Républicain), the Radicals, and the Democratic Center (restructured since 1976 and renamed
the Centre des Démocrates Sociaux—CDS).

Unfortunately, the internal cohesion in both camps was more apparent than real. Within the left, a bitter quarrel had broken out between the
Communists and the Socialists over the meaning of the Common Program, particularly the extent of the nationalization of industries, the
equalization of wages, and the distribution of cabinet seats in the event of
a victory of the left. The Communist party accused the Socialist party of
not wanting a genuine restructuring of the economy and of merely trying
to "use" the Communists to gain power. The Socialists, now the senior
partner of the left alliance, in turn accused the Communists of not having
"de-Stalinized" themselves sufficiently and of hoping to destroy democratic institutions. In the end, the left failed, by a few percentage points,
to gain a parliamentary majority, a result widely attributed to the refusal of the left-wing parties in many constituencies to support one another on the second ballot.

Within the majority, there were similar problems. Upon assuming
the presidency, Giscard had, so it seemed, managed to coopt the Gaullists—who had no place else to go—by giving them a few cabinet posts
and by retaining the essentials of Gaullist foreign policy: hostility to
NATO, the development of an independent nuclear strike force, and a
show of independence vis-à-vis the United States. Giscard's first prime
minister, Chirac, was a Gaullist, but he resigned from the prime ministership in 1976 in the wake of disagreements with Giscard. Subsequently, Chirac became the leader of the Gaullist party—by then renamed Rassemblement pour la République (RPR)—as well as mayor of
Paris, and he made no secret of his ambition to run for the presidency
in 1981. Giscard, who had every intention to run for a second term, still
needed the support of the Gaullists, the largest party in the Assembly,
but he wanted to reduce this dependence. Shortly before the 1978 legislative elections, he encouraged the establishment of the Union pour
la Démocratie Française (UDF), an electoral federation of all non-

Gaullist elements of the presidential majority: the Republicans, the CDS, the Radicals, and a few smaller groups. The UDF had decided to put up single first-ballot candidates in many districts and to support Gaullist candidates only if necessary on the second ballot. One of the results of this tactic had been a realignment *within* the majority: an impressive expansion of the number of "Giscardist" deputies at the expense of the Gaullist parliamentary party.

The Elections of 1981

Early in 1981, as the presidential elections approached, the Common Program had been shelved, the unity of the left appeared to be near collapse, and the Socialist and Communist party each ran its own candidate, Mitterrand and Georges Marchais, respectively. Before the first round of balloting in April, Marchais had been almost as critical of Mitterrand as of Giscard; but after obtaining only 15 percent of the popular vote (the lowest for the party since the end of World War II) as against over 26 percent obtained by Mitterrand, Marchais endorsed Mitterrand on the second ballot without qualification—thereby permitting himself to claim the victory of the Socialist candidate as that of his own supporters. Similarly, the mutual-support agreement between Socialist and Communist candidates was effective for the second round of the parliamentary elections that followed in the wake of Mitterrand's accession to the presidency, and Socialist parliamentary candidates were the principal beneficiaries.

After these elections, it was clear that although the PS had emerged with an absolute majority of all Assembly seats (for the first time since 1936), the PC, with barely 9 percent of the seats, had been reduced to a marginal status. Several reasons may be cited for this decline: the excessive Stalinism of its leadership; the deteriorated public image of its secretary general, Marchais; the party's refusal to condemn Soviet aggression in Afghanistan and elsewhere; a widespread attribution to the party of the blame for the defeat of the left in 1978; and the lack of internal democracy. In any case, the PC had become a supplicant; in exchange for several unimportant ministerial posts, the party accepted the conditions imposed on it by Mitterrand: a condemnation of Soviet actions in Afghanistan and Poland, a commitment to the Western alliance, a respect for public liberties, and an adherence to a policy of transforming the economy (including selective nationalization) on the basis of gradual and democratic methods.

Within the camp of the Gaullist and centrist-conservative alliance there were far greater complications. On the first round of presidential balloting, both Giscard and Chirac were candidates competing for the same (bourgeois and right-of-center) electorate. While continuing to be critical of each other's personalities and policy preferences, both candidates stressed the disastrous consequences for France of a victory of the left. During the runoff between Giscard and Mitterrand, Chirac gave only a halfhearted endorsement of Giscard. Chirac's refusal to issue a clear call to his Gaullist supporters to vote for the incumbent was considered by Giscard to have effectively sabotaged his reelection.

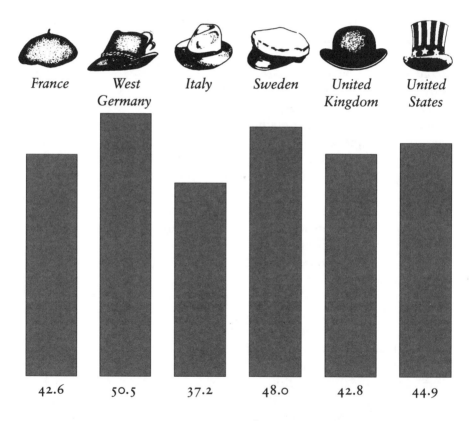

France	West Germany	Italy	Sweden	United Kingdom	United States
42.6	50.5	37.2	48.0	42.8	44.9

FIGURE 8.1

PERCENTAGE OF FEMALES IN WORKFORCE

SOURCE: ILO, 1991.

During the parliamentary elections, the erstwhile majority of Gaullists (RPR) and Giscardists (UDF) reestablished an uneasy electoral alliance. The optimistically named UNM, the Union pour la Nouvelle Majorité (Union for the New Majority) decided to support common first-round candidates in more than 300 constituencies and made the usual mutual-support agreements for the second round. The alliance was virtually buried by the Socialist landslide, which significantly altered the complexion of Parliament and, indeed, of the whole political party system for the first time since the founding of the Fifth Republic.

There were a number of reasons for the defeat of the Gaullist-Giscardist forces. The first was the lack of unity: the incessant infighting between Giscard's friends and the "Chiraquists" had sapped the strength of both. Second, there were the growing inflation and unemployment and the widespread conviction that Giscard's policies were inadequate for dealing with these problems. Third, there were several scandals involving a number of ministers and, in fact, Giscard himself. The feeling that Giscard had been corrupted by power was exacerbated by his increasingly "monarchical" behavior: his contempt for Parliament, his unsatisfactory press conferences (which, in terms of their stage-managed nature, came to resemble those of de Gaulle), the tightening of presidential control over the news media, and what many considered to be an unscrupulous use of presidential patronage—the appointment of many of Giscard's friends and relatives to important positions.

Many French voters had been uneasy over the prospect of having Giscard as president for fourteen years, a longer term than had ever been served by a president in France, and they thought that in a democracy there must be an occasional transfer of power from one group to another. But, for several years, the Gaullists and Giscardists had argued that a transfer of power to the left would be too dangerous, since the Socialists would be "hostages" to the Communists. Such an argument proved less convincing as the PS strengthened its position vis-à-vis the PC, and it lost most of its "scare value" after the first round of the presidential elections in which, as we have seen, the PS received nearly twice the support that the PC got.

After the parliamentary elections of 1981, the now leaderless UDF was reduced to a demoralized vestige of some sixty deputies (i.e, about half its previous strength). Some of the UDF politicians were hoping that, at some time in the future, Giscard would come out of his retirement, as de Gaulle had once done, and revive their party. Several leaders of the CDS, the Christian Democratic component of the UDF, were examining the possibility of autonomous behavior including, perhaps, a rapprochement with the new majority; the Radical party, however, had been so weakened that it seemed to have no credible options left. Chirac now prepared to assume the leadership of the combined centrist-conservative (or Giscardist and Gaullist) opposition forces. He appeared finally to have achieved his ambition of eclipsing Giscard—but it was a hollow victory because the Gaullist contingent in the Assembly had itself been reduced from 153 to 83 deputies.

The Socialist majority in the 1981 Assembly was so overwhelming that Mitterrand and his government could use it to put into effect an ambitious program of reforms. Among the most important of these were the enhancement of civil liberties, an expanded budget for education, the liberalization of the penal code, cultural programs for ethnic minorities, and an ambitious program of administrative decentralization. Bills were enacted providing for the nationalization of a number of industries and the redistribution of income—by means of more steeply progressive taxation, higher minimum wages, and expanded social benefits. These redistributive policies reflected elements of the Common Program and were, by and large, supported by the Communists. But such support was hardly necessary. By 1983, Socialist reforming zeal had begun to cool; as the budget deficit grew, the cost of nationalizing proved too high and its benefits doubtful; production slumped and unemployment—which stood at over 10 percent—was not reduced. In response to these developments, the government changed course abruptly and embraced an austerity program aimed at rationalizing industry, keeping wages under control, and encouraging economic growth.

The changed strategy had the effect of alienating the Communist party, whose ministers opted out of the government. A more serious consequence was the Socialists' slippage in public support—a result of the government's failure to solve the problems of unemployment, increased crimes of violence, and the presence of masses of North African immigrants—all widely believed to be interrelated phenomena. One symptom of the growing public concern with these problems was the sudden rise of the National Front, an extreme-right party led by Jean-Marie Le Pen. Founded in 1972, that party is a conglomerate of fascists, Pétainists, right-wing Catholics, ultranationalists, erstwhile supporters of Algérie Française, antiparliamentarists, former Poujadists,[1] anti-Semites, racists, and xenophobes. It burst upon the French political scene in the municipal elections of 1983, when it captured 17 percent of the vote in an industrial town near Paris heavily settled by immigrants, and in the elections to the European Parliament a year later, when it won 10.5 percent of the popular vote.

At the same time, the popularity of the RPR and UDF was rising, and public opinion polls predicted that in the next parliamentary elections, the Socialists would lose their majority. In order to limit the damage, the government reintroduced a variant of the old (Fourth Republic) system of proportional representation. It was thought that under the new system, the National Front would get enough votes to gain representation in the Assembly, but in so doing would take so much electoral support away from the Gaullists as to make the victory of the latter less certain and less crushing.

The "Cohabitation" Interlude

The results of the legislative elections of March 1986 proved the wisdom of Mitterrand's electoral stratagem. The RPR and UDF together obtained a bare majority (290 out of 577 seats) in the Assembly, not enough to enable them fearlessly to undertake policy changes without the support of the National Front, which managed to seat 32 deputies. But it was enough to enable them to insist upon the appointment of a politically compatible (i.e., a Gaullist-Giscardist) government. The new government embarked on an unprecedented experiment in power sharing (see above). Its head, Gaullist leader Chirac, was forced to "cohabit" with a Socialist president. During the early phases of cohabitation, France appeared to undergo a process of "depresidentialization" as Chirac asserted his (and the government's) leadership in the formulation and execution of internal policies, particularly in regard to privatizing public enterprises, fighting terrorism, and controlling the movements of resident aliens. Mitterrand confined himself largely to foreign policy pronouncements and, intermittently, to selective criticism of Chirac's domestic measures.

Chirac's power to govern turned out to be less than absolute. It was limited by the need of the Gaullists to "cohabit" with the Giscardists, who were not always in a cooperative mood; they were unhappy over some of Chirac's policy choices as well as over an inadequate sharing of political patronage. Furthermore, there were rivalries between the leaders of the RPR and UDF, as well as disagreements between them—and within the RPR itself—about the posture to be adopted vis-à-vis the National Front. The "liberals" wanted to have nothing to do with Le Pen (whom they regarded as a danger to democracy), while the "hardliners" (notably among the Gaullists) advocated a selective embrace of the National Front's positions, especially on immigrants, in order to strengthen their support base within the Assembly and, more important, to retrieve the support of former Gaullist voters who had "crossed over" to the National Front and prevent further attrition. Because of these conflicts, Chirac's leadership suffered and he became the major target of popular discontent; Mitterrand, in contrast, appeared increasingly like a conciliatory and unifying statesman.

Consensus and Convergence: The Elections of 1988

The presidential elections of April and May 1988 pitted Mitterrand against three major rivals on the right: Chirac (RPR), Raymond Barre (UDF), and Le Pen (National Front). Several months before the elections, "cohabitation"—at first welcomed by most French citizens—had already become a dubious pattern as the president and the prime minister each sought to draw electoral advantage by discrediting the other.

The reelection of Mitterrand suggested that he had succeeded better than his rival. But his impressive margin of victory must also be attributed to the disunity among the right. The outcome of the first round reflected that disunity, as Barre and Chirac publicly criticized one another. In addition, Le Pen, the leader of the National Front, drew votes from the "respectable" right (especially from the RPR) and made a surprisingly strong showing.

Mitterrand's decision to dissolve the Assembly and call for new elections was made in hopes that the delicate power-sharing pattern of the previous two years would be replaced by a more "normal" relationship between president and Parliament. The result, however, of the two-round Assembly elections—the Gaullists had restored the single-member constituency system a year earlier—was ambiguous. Although the RPR and UDF (putting up joint candidates in most constituencies under the label Union du Rassemblement et du Centre—URC) lost control of the Assembly, the Socialists failed to get the absolute majority the pollsters had predicted. There are several explanations for the outcome of that election, in which the abstention rate (over 34 percent) was the highest since 1962. Some traditional Socialist voters had abstained because Mitterrand, running as a statesman above parties rather than as a Socialist, had not made great efforts to appeal to them or even to mobilize the party activists. Others had been so sure of a Socialist victory that they believed their votes to be unnecessary; and still others were tired of voting so often. In addition, there were those who had supported Mitterrand but did not want a clearly Socialist regime, hoping instead that Michel Rocard, the new prime minister, would construct a pragmatic center-left government.

Rocard did not disappoint them; his government (as reconstituted after the legislative elections) included twenty-five Socialists and twenty-four non-Socialists, among them six centrists (of the UDF). Moreover, in an attempt to show that he paid as much attention to "civil society" as to the political establishment, he also included fourteen nonparty people.

Rocard's "opening up" (*ouverture*) toward the political center was a reflection, however imperfect, of the changes in France's party system, changes in which some parties had lost their traditional electoral supporters, others their credibility, still others their ideological coherence, and all of them much of their dues-paying membership.[2] Just as the victory of Mitterrand was not quite a victory for the PS, the reestablished dominance of the latter in the political arena and in the Assembly was not quite a victory for socialism. Under the pressures of electoral reality and, later, of governmental responsibility, the PS had given up most of its Marxism and had transformed itself into a social-democratic party not unlike the social-democratic parties of Scandinavia or Germany. During the 1988 election campaigns, it presented a minimum platform whose ingredients—social justice, productivity, solidarity among various segments of French society, and European unity—did not differ sharply from the equally vague generalities of the RPR/UDF—about liberty, security, economic progress, and patriotism. This platform was designed to paper over continuing disagreements among the major party personalities, including Mitterrand and former Prime Ministers Mauroy, Fabius, and Rocard. These disagreements were not only matters of personal ambition but related also to the tactical and long-term orientations of the PS. Thus, while Rocard wanted to distance himself as much as possible from the PC, Mitterrand continued to express the need to keep the left as united as possible and to keep the door open to traditional Communist voters.

These disagreements were echoed at the PS congress in Rennes in 1990. There the nationalists were pitted against the Europeanists, the Jacobins—the believers in a France "one and indivisible"—against the pluralists, the statists against the "liberals," and the growth-oriented productivists against those favoring redistribution and socioeconomic equality. This "war of party factions" (*guerre des courants*) was hardly resolved by a document that aimed at a "synthesis" of these diverse positions.[3] The internal divisions were aggravated during the Persian Gulf crisis, which set Mitterrand and his loyalists, who supported the American war effort, against a faction led by Chevènement, which favored a foreign policy that was a combination of Gaullist independence-mindedness and hysterical anti-Americanism. These divisions and the conflict between tactical and programmatic orientations were reflected in the government of Edith Cresson, who was accused of "conducting a policy of the right while positioning herself on the left."[4] Specifically, she prepared a rapprochement with the Communists and alienated the Centrists while abandoning the Socialists' traditional infatuation with the Third World, continuing the denationalization policies of Rocard, and even appearing to adopt the kind of hard-nosed stance toward immigrants that had previously been associated with the right. Nevertheless, the various factions decided to suspend their disputes until the Assembly elections anticipated for 1993.

The Communist party, too, was divided. Already in 1987, Communists who rejected the rigid Stalinism of the party and held that outlook—and its leader, Marchais—responsible for its steep electoral decline set up a rival party of "Renovators" and put up their own presidential candidate in 1988. After the elections, the PC alternated between a desire to remain in opposition and a readiness to support the government on specific issues. How much the PC leadership would be influenced by *perestroika* and *glasnost* in the Soviet Union remained to be seen. The twenty-seventh congress of the PC in September 1990 saw an expression of interest in a "pluralistic" communism instead of a bureaucratic or authoritarian one, a more open discussion than had been known previously, and even the submission of a minority report.[5] Yet the autocratic leadership of Georges Marchais was reconfirmed.

The RPR was torn between the nationalism and populist statism of the disciples of de Gaulle on the one hand and a pro-European "neoliberalism" on the other. Moreover, though some Gaullist politicians were still thinking of a rapprochement with the National Front, most of the Gaullist leadership had come to reject collaboration with that party on any level. The UDF (from which the RPR had copied much of its neoliberalism) was divided between the probusiness elitism of the Republican party, its largest component, and the moderate progressivism of a number of Christian-Democratic (CDS) and Radical politicians. There was also a confusion of strategies. Some "Giscardists" wanted to align themselves closely with the RPR and harden their opposition to the new government; others (including Giscard himself, who had become the official leader of the UDF) wanted to signal their centrist views by a "constructive opposition"; and still others (including Barre) even held out the possibility of an eventual "cohabitation" with the Socialist-led government. Meanwhile the CDS (which had increased its Assembly representation from thirty-five to fifty) reconstituted itself as a separate parliamentary party while still formally remaining a component of the UDF! Finally, as the RPR and UDF were preparing their list of candidates for the elections to the European Parliament (in the spring of 1989), there were (abortive) attempts by younger politicians in both parties to oust Giscard and other veterans from leadership positions.

In June 1990, in order to maintain the integrity and effectiveness of their respective organizations yet to achieve a measure of unity—and, incidentally, to be better equipped to face Le Pen and his National Front—the RPR and UDF founded a "confederation" entitled Union pour la France (UPF). The UPF began by issuing joint communiqués and adopting a system of "primaries" for designating a common candidate for the presidential election of 1995. This common approach would, it was hoped, be used for future legislative elections as well.

The National Front, which was responsible for some of the problems of the RPR and UDF, was itself torn; it alternated between the bourgeois, respectable behavior of some of its politicians and the provocative pronouncements of others—the one reflected in an emphasis on the neoliberal segments of the party's platform (e.g., the free market and individual rights), the other in a stress on nationalist and racist themes. Some have regarded the National Front as a genuine alternative to the "gang of four" (the PC, PS, UDF, and RPR), but many more voters have been turned off from the party by Le Pen's irrepressible penchant for demagogy and have come to consider him a danger to democracy.

As the National Front's credibility as a democratic alternative party weakened, that of another party, the Greens (ecologists), assumed increased importance. Formed in the early 1980s out of a number of environmental associations, the Greens opposed the construction of nuclear reactors. Although officially aligned neither with the right nor the left, the Greens advocated a number of policies often associated with the left, such as the reduction of the workweek, the strengthening of local government, and a foreign policy more sympathetic to the Third World. The Greens did surprisingly well on the first ballot of the presidential elections, but achieved insignificant scores in the parliamentary elections (apart from a number of constituencies in Alsace).

A note of caution is in order. The bipolarization of the party system and the overwhelming dominance of the Socialist party (until 1993) applied to the Assembly but not necessarily to other elective bodies in France. As tables 8.3 and 8.4 indicate, multipolarity—specifically a meaningful representation of the left, the center, the Gaullists, and the traditional right—can still be observed in the general (departmental) councils and the Senate.[6]

TABLE 8.3

RECENT CANTONAL ELECTIONS: NUMBER
OF GENERAL COUNCILORS ELECTED
(RESULTS AFTER SECOND ROUND)

	1982	1985	1988	1992
Extreme Left	4	1	6	—
Communists	199	149	175	135
Socialists	515	424	592	440[c]
Left Radicals	59	57	44	—
Miscellaneous Left	39	59	68	—
Ecologists	—	2	1	213
Regionalists	—	—	1	—
UDF	555	525	441	—
Gaullists	348	400	365	763[d]
Miscellaneous Right	295[a]	425	328	—
Extreme Right	—	2	2[b]	241[e]
Other	—	—	—	88[f]

SOURCE: *Regards sur l'Actualité* and *Le Monde*. Figures for each party include affiliated (*apparentés*) councilors.

a. Moderates and CNIP
b. Includes 1 National Front
c. "Presidential majority": Socialists and allies."
d. Union pour la France ([UPF] common

list of RPR and UDF) and allies.
e. Essentially the National Front.
f. Including a new party, "Hunting, Fishing, Nature, and Traditions" (Chasse, pêche, nature, et traditions).

Interest Groups

A French citizen who becomes disillusioned with political parties, finding them confusing or doubting their effectiveness, has the opportunity to voice demands more directly through interest groups. Originally, political thinkers with "revolutionary" and centralizing perspectives were as suspicious of economic and professional associations as of political parties. Consequently, after the Revolution of 1789, organized groups were banned for nearly a century. Today, numerous freely organized interest groups play significant roles in France's political life. There are groups representing, on a national level, every conceivable sector and interest: labor, business, agriculture, self-employed professionals, teach-

TABLE 8.4
COMPOSITION OF THE SENATE, 1959–92
(SELECTED YEARS)

	Communists	Socialists	Democratic Left[a]	MRP/ Democratic Center	Independents	Gaullists	Unaffiliated	Total
1959	14	51	64	34	92	41	11	307
1965	14	52	50	38	79	30	11	274
1968	17	54	50	40	80	29	13	283
1981	23	63	38[b]	67[c]	51[d]	41	15	305
1989	16	66	23[e]	68[c]	52[d]	91	5	321
1992	15	70	23	66[c]	47[d]	90	10	321

SOURCE: *L'Année politique, 1959–1989; Le Monde,* and *Regards sur l'Actualité.* Figures for each party include affiliated (*apparentés*) senators.

a. Mainly Radical Socialists
b. Incudes Left Radicals (MRG)
c. Center Union
d. Republicans and Independents
e. *Rassemblement démocratique et européen*

ers, and proponents of such diverse outlooks or policies as laicism, Catholicism, elitism, racism, antiracism, birth control, women's rights, and environmental protection.

Interest groups in France participate in the political process in much the same way as they do in the United States. They lobby with legislators, help elect candidates to political office, engage in collective bargaining, and seek to influence the higher civil service and the leadership of political parties.

Two of the more important characteristics of French interest groups are their ideological fragmentation and their linkage to political parties. These characteristics can be clearly seen in the case of labor, which is represented by several competing organizations. The oldest, and once the largest, is the CGT, the Confédération Générale du Travail (General Confederation of Labor). Essentially a federation of constituent unions (such as the automobile, chemical, metal, and transport workers' unions), it has had a revolutionary ideology, that is, the conviction that the interests of the working class can best be promoted through direct political action. In its belief in the class struggle and its opposition to the capitalist system, the CGT has shown a clear affinity to the Communist party. Many of the CGT's members (numbering today about 900,000) have in the past voted Communist, and a significant proportion of its leaders has been prominent in the PC hierarchy. In fact, the relationship between the CGT and the PC has sometimes been so close that the union has been described as a "transmission belt" of the party. The CGT has frequently engaged in strikes and other political action for the Communists' political purposes, such as opposition to NATO, to French policy in Algeria, to German rearmament, and (more recently) to the Socialist government's overall socioeconomic policies.

Another labor union is the CFDT, the Confédération Française Démocratique de Travail (French Confederation of Democratic Labor), with about 800,000 members. Originally inspired by Catholicism, it split, in the mid-1960s, from the CFTC, the Confédération Française des Travailleurs Chrétiens (French Confederation of Christian Workers), which continues to exist, and "deconfessionalized" itself. One of the most dynamic trade unions, it is closely related to, though not formally affiliated with, the Socialist party. An important idea of the CFDT, the promotion of self-management (*autogestion*), was incorporated into the PS platform in the 1970s.

The FO, the Force Ouvrière (Workers' Force), and the CGC, the Confédération Générale des Cadres (General Confederation of Cadres), are two other unions of some importance. The FO (with about 1.1 million members) is an industrial workers' federation noted for its preference for union autonomy vis-à-vis political parties, for its staunch anticommunism, and for its emphasis on American-style collective bargaining. The CGC (with about 450,000 members) is not very ideological in orientation; it represents supervisory, middle-echelon technical, and other white-collar employees.

This fragmentation, coupled with a relatively feeble extent of unionization—fewer than 20 percent of French workers are unionized—has added to the predicament of organized labor. Until recently, unions had been at a disadvantage because their "patron" parties, notably the Communists and Socialists, were in the opposition. In order to overcome that disadvantage, unions learned to cooperate in practical matters. They often present common demands to employers and the government, and often join in demonstrations and strikes. During the Socialist government of 1981–86, trade unions gained important concessions under legislation (the Auroux laws) that strengthened their right to organize and bargain collectively at plant levels. But these concessions have been in part nullified by developments that have weakened the position of unions: the "scab" effect of immigrant workers; the growth of the tertiary sector, in which unionization has been weak; and the decline of traditional, "smokestack," industries and the concomitant reduction of total union membership. For many years, trade unions were able to use the existence of nationalized industries to their advantage—in the sense that the wage contracts negotiated there often served as pacesetters for privately owned firms. The privatization of many industries, especially under the Chirac government of 1986–88, reduced the power of unions and forced them to moderate their wage demands.[7] Nevertheless, French workers continue to enjoy much better working conditions and social protections than do their American counterparts.

Organized business is much more unified than organized labor. The major business association is the CNPF, the Conseil National du Patronat Français (National Council of French Employers), the "umbrella" organization of more than eighty manufacturing, banking, and commercial associations that represent more than 800,000 firms. In its lobbying efforts, the CNPF has been fairly effective. Many of its leaders have old-school ties with the government's administrative elite; it is well heeled financially; it provided ideas and other kinds of assistance to the Gaullist and Giscardist (notably the Republican) parties that ruled France from 1958 to 1981 and again from 1986 to 1988; and it has been an important partner of the government in the push toward economic modernization.

Small and medium-sized manufacturing firms, shopkeepers, and artisans have their own organizations. These have lobbied separately against economic consolidation policies that have been a threat to them, but their success has been mixed.

The greatest organizational complexity is found in agriculture, where associations reflect different kinds of farms, product specialization, ideology, and even relationships to the government. Thus there are associations of beet growers, wine producers, cattle raisers, young farmers, Catholic farmers, agricultural laborers, and so on. Farmers' interests were in the past well represented by the centrist and conservative parties; the decline of these parties has been associated with the decline in the number of farmers and the reduced importance of agriculture in the French economy. Yet the farmers cannot be totally neglected, if only for social reasons; and they often find a receptive ear in the government. In recent years, farmers' associations have collaborated with the government in the shaping of policies that encourage land consolidation, mechanization, the retraining of redundant farmers, and the promotion of agricultural exports, especially in the context of the European Community and its "supranational" Common Agricultural Policy.

Patterns and Problems of Interest-Group Access

One of the important features of French interest-group politics is the fact that most groups have a fairly institutionalized relationship to government authorities. Several hundred advisory councils are attached to ministries; these councils, composed largely of representatives of interest groups, furnish data that may influence policy suggestions and regulations that emanate from ministries. Similar councils are attached to nationalized industries in which one finds spokespersons for consumers and trade unions. One of the most important entities is the Economic and Social Council, a body of 230 delegates of trade unions, business associations, civil servants, and other groups (and "qualified" individuals appointed by the government), which must be consulted on all pending socioeconomic legislation. In addition, a network of regional economic development committees, composed in part of interest-group spokespersons, provides input for the four-year economic plans. Similarly composed councils are attached to the highly differentiated national and regional social security organisms that administer statutory health care, unemployment insurance, pension schemes, and family subsidy programs. The implementation of pricing policies takes place with the participation of farmers' groups; the application of rules on apprenticeships involves employers' associations; and the adjudication of labor disputes takes place in specialized tribunals (*conseils de prud'-hommes*), which include trade union representatives. Interest-group delegates to these bodies and to regional professional, agricultural, and commercial chambers, factory councils, and similar institutions are elected by the groups' rank-and-file members without the mediation of political parties. On occasion, interest groups "colonize" Parliament in the sense of having their officials put up (via a sympathetic party) as candidates for elections to the Assembly. Finally, interest-group leaders may be coopted into official positions in a ministry with which they have "clientelistic" relations.

It is a matter of controversy whether the institutionalization of relations enhances or reduces the power of groups. In the first place, not all interests are sufficiently important or well enough organized to benefit from reliable patterns of relationship with the government—for example, foreign workers, ethnic minorities, domestics, and certain categories of small businessmen. Second, while a formalized network of involvement—sometimes labeled "neocorporatism" or, more recently, an aspect of the "new institutionalism"—guarantees group access to public authorities, such access does not by itself ensure that the views of a particular group will prevail. Furthermore, highly formalized relationships with the government may weaken the will of a group to bargain collectively or resort to more traditional means of pressure, such as strikes.

To many observers, the events of May-June 1968 suggested clearly that the access of interest groups to the authorities was either too underdeveloped or too insecure to influence political decisions. It is not necessary to recount the complexities of these events. Suffice it to recall that students and workers, in a rare display of unity, engaged in a massive general strike that, for two weeks, paralyzed the country and threatened to bring down the government and endanger the republic itself. These events had several causes: for the workers, dissatisfaction with de Gaulle's economic and social policy that seemed to favor big business and permitted wages to lag woefully behind prices; for the students, disgruntlement over the failure to modernize, with sufficient speed and thoroughness, a university system whose curriculum was antiquated and not relevant to the labor market, whose physical facilities were cramped, and whose administration was too rigid. The general strike—as an example of anomic political behavior—achieved certain reforms that formalized interest-group relations with the government had failed to achieve: the partial democratization of university governance, enormous wage increases for workers, improved trade union rights, and a loosening of relations between social classes. In the process, however, de Gaulle's leadership was discredited and his image severely tarnished.

The preceding discussion must be supplemented by a reference to a variety of noneconomic interests or sectors, such as women, ethnic minorities, and environmentalists. France has several national women's associations. These may not be so large or so well organized as their U.S. counterparts, yet they have successfully pressured the authorities, since the middle and late 1960s, to abolish legal disabilities based on sex (e.g., inheritance, adoption, and property ownership), to legalize birth control and abortion, and to make the initiation of divorce easier for women. Environmental groups grew rapidly during the same period; in all parliamentary elections since 1978, and in the presidential elections of 1981 and 1988, ecologists (under various labels) fielded their own candidates. Antiracist groups, such as SOS-Racisme, have developed rapidly since the early 1980s to fight for the rights of ethnic minorities, in particular immigrants. At the same time, the government legalized (and sometimes even encouraged) immigrants to form their own associations.

Notes

1. The Poujadists were supporters of the Union for the Defense of Shopkeepers and Artisans, an interest group established during the Fourth Republic to protect elements of the *petite bourgeoisie* against the vicissitudes of rapid economic modernization. Led by Pierre Poujade, it ran in the parliamentary elections of 1956 under the label of Union et Fraternité Française, combining hostility to industrialism with antiparliamentarism and anti-Semitism.

2. The membership of the various parties was estimated as follows: RPR, 800,000; PC, 600,000 according to some sources, 100,000 (dues-paying members) according to others; PS, 200,000–250,000; MRG, 22,000; National Front, 70,000; UDF, 300,000 (of which Republican party 60,000; Radical-Socialists, 60,000; and CDS, 50,000). These figures are approximate and are based on a number of (often conflicting) sources. Typical annual membership dues are about $30.

3. On these cleavages, see Pascal Perrineau, "Les cadres du Parti socialiste," in *SOFRES, L'Etat de l'Opinion 1991*, ed. Olivier Duhamel and Jérôme Jaffré (Paris: Seuil, 1991).

4. Jean-Pierre Soisson, "Les grands mots," *Le Point*, 13 July 1991, 16.

5. Alain Rollat, "M. Leroy se refère au communisme ... balsacien!" *Le Monde,* 25 September 1990.

6. Moreover, the bipolar lineup is not replicated in the European Parliament. The French results of the June 1989 elections to that body were as follows: Joint RPR-UDF, 28.9 percent (and 26 seats); PS, 23.6 percent (22); National Front, 11.7 percent (10); Greens, 8.4 percent (7); Centrists, 8.4 percent (7); and Communists, 7.7 percent (7).

7. See René Mouriaux, "Trade Unions, Unemployment, and Regulation: 1962–1989," in *Searching for the New France* ed. J.A. Hollifield and G. Ross (London: Routledge, 1991), 173–92.

9

How Is Power Used?

The mere outline of the powers of the principal institutions—the executive, the legislature, and the civil service—found in the constitution and the laws cannot adequately convey how policies in France are decided and implemented. The distinction between what the French have called "the legal country" and "the real country" can be seen, first, in the tendency of Fifth Republic presidents to interpret the constitution in such a way as to increase their power at the expense of that of the prime minister. This has applied not only to cabinet appointments, in which most presidents have had an almost free hand. Most important, it has also applied to the content of policy decisions. De Gaulle (who took little interest in economics) and Pompidou did give their prime ministers a great deal of discretion, except, of course, in the areas of foreign and defense policies; but Giscard (an *Enarque* specialized in economic matters) took an active lead in almost all aspects of domestic policy (even while his government was headed by Barre, a professor of economics) and even "meddled" in the drafting of the language of government bills.

In short, the president's domain, as distinct from that of the government, has been stretched almost at will. Under de Gaulle, presidential decisions included the blackballing of Britain's entry into the Common Market, the raising of the minimum wage of industrial workers, and the vetoing of an appointment to the prestigious Académie Française; under Pompidou, the devaluation of the franc, the lowering of value-added taxes on foodstuffs, and the modification of rules on the maximum height of buildings in Paris. Under Giscard, there were hundreds of "intrusions" in matters affecting taxes, wages, social security, and interest rates. Mitterrand (before and after the first "cohabitation" interlude) personally decided on the construction of a series of grandiose public buildings and even interfered in the appointment of the director of an opera house.

In promoting his policies, the president is helped by the prime minister and the cabinet, and he "uses" his ministers to transform his ideas into concrete legislative proposals, to defend them in Parliament, and to take the blame for them when they prove unpopular or unsuccessful. The distance the president thereby establishes in the public mind between himself and his ministers is a political convenience. To provide one example: Although the austerity policies adopted between 1976 and 1980 were largely of Giscard's inspiration, public opinion surveys showed that the president was less unpopular than Prime Minister Barre. Much of the above did not, of course, apply during the exceptional period of 1986–88; even then, however, Mitterrand was able to veto Prime Minister Chirac's original choices for several cabinet posts (including that of foreign minister); moreover, although Mitterrand could not interfere effectively in the government's domestic policy decisions, he was able to prevent a number of measures from being enacted by decree. Yet the president was sufficiently removed from the daily operations of government so that his popularity rose while that of Prime Minister Chirac declined.

The president does not rely on the cabinet alone. He appoints, and presides over, "restricted" committees composed of selected ministers, higher civil servants, and whatever additional personalities he may co-opt. Furthermore, there is a growing staff of presidential experts who, like the White House staff in the United States, often function as a supplementary cabinet.

Deputies and Decisions

In a formal sense, Parliament has been weakened by the constitution as well as by the legislature's own standing orders. Nevertheless, that institution is not *intrinsically* so weak as to be dismissed. Although in most cases—and certainly in all budget matters—the initiative belongs to the government, deputies have succeeded in significantly modifying government bills through amendments: for instance, on abortion, unemployment, farm credits, education, the reorganization of the television networks, and the reform of local fiscal administration.

Sometimes the government virtually abandons a legislative project to which it is ostensibly committed if it becomes apparent that there is insufficient support for the project among deputies belonging to the majority, as happened in 1976 with capital gains taxation. In other cases, the government permits, or encourages, leaders of a parliamentary group belonging to the majority to introduce legislation. This is what occurred in 1980 with a Gaullist-sponsored bill on "participation" —the distribution of industrial shares to the workers in given firms. The government itself lacked enthusiasm for the policy but did not wish needlessly to antagonize the Gaullist party, whose support would be required for other matters. In still other cases, public opposition to the project may be strong enough to entail political risks for its supporters, lead deputies to abandon their endorsement of it, and, finally, cause

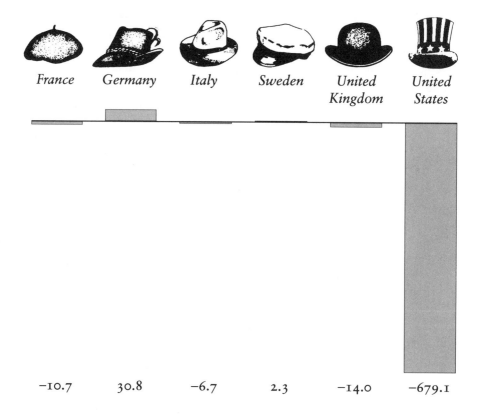

France	Germany	Italy	Sweden	United Kingdom	United States
−10.7	30.8	−6.7	2.3	−14.0	−679.1

FIGURE 9.1

AVERAGE BALANCE OF TRADE

(IN BILLIONS OF DOLLARS)

SOURCE: World Bank, 1984–87.

the government to abandon it. This happened in 1983 in the case of a bill to bring private schools under greater control of the Ministry of National Education, and in 1986 in the case of a bill to reform the citizenship and naturalization laws.

If there is little evidence of open conflict over policy between majority deputies and the government, this does not necessarily mean that deputies have resigned themselves to inaction. Instead, it may indicate that deputies have made their influence felt during the bill-drafting phase through "backstage" negotiations with ministers or higher civil servants. Frequently, too, a government bill reflects the pressures exerted by interest groups. The watering down of tax bills, the softening of price controls, and the government's failure to institute genuine participation of workers in industrial decisions within firms—all these have been due largely to the successful lobbying of the National Council of French Employers. It must be understood that this is not U.S.-style lobbying by means of appearances before legislative committees; instead, lobbying is done through frequent contacts between leaders of big business and higher civil servants. In this respect, trade unions continue to be at a disadvantage (even under Socialist governments) because the personal links of their leaders to upper-echelon bureaucrats are weak. In the past, unions compensated for this weakness by threatening strikes and unrest and succeeded in pushing the government into making periodic wage adjustments in their favor, particularly during election years. But with the continuing moderation and the increasingly "centrist" orientation of the Socialist leadership, such methods are less likely to bear fruit.

Parliamentarians who are unhappy with government bills have a juridical weapon at their disposal. They may try to block the passage of bills by resorting to the Constitutional Council. That body is not a "judicial review" organ in the sense of the U.S. Supreme Court; it is not a court of appeals to which citizens' complaints about constitutional violations may be brought; and it has not been in the habit of nullifying laws already in effect. Its major legislative function used to be the examination of "organic" bills (which may also include the budget) *before* their complete parliamentary passage and before they are signed into law. In recent years, the council has widened its scope considerably—beginning with a ruling in 1971 by which it forced the government to withdraw a bill that would have given prefects the power to forbid or cancel public meetings. In this case, the council acted on the grounds that the bill violated freedom of association.[1] In 1977, the council nullified a bill that would have allowed the police, without a warrant, to search parked cars, because the bill violated a constitutional provision (Article 66) on judicial safeguards of individual liberties. In 1980 the council nullified a bill aimed at special surveillance of foreign workers on the grounds that it violated the principle of equality before the law. In 1982, he council voided parts of the Socialist government's nationalization legislation dealing with the compensation to private shareholders on the grounds that it amounted to an unconstitutional deprivation of property. During the earlier period of the Fifth Republic (i.e., under Presidents de Gaulle and Pompidou), the council, being heavily Gaullist in composition, tended not to take issue with decisions by the executive; since then—in large part because it has been increasingly called on by opposition deputies—it has taken a very independent position.[2]

If contributions of Parliament to the legislative process have amounted to less than many had hoped, that has been the result not only of the "rationalized" legislative process but also of the condition and the behavior of the deputies themselves. Parliamentarians have often lacked the expertise of the administrative professionals who draft government bills. Furthermore, the deputies' absenteeism has made it difficult for them to acquire mastery over a subject or to participate in parliamentary debates with consistency. Absenteeism has continued to be a problem despite the recent limitation of the number of additional elective offices a deputy might hold.

Even if such problems were completely overcome, deputies would still be unable to make their wills prevail as individuals. Under Gaullist presidents and under Giscard, the deputies belonging to parties of the left lacked unity and voting strength; and the Gaullist or Giscardo-centrist deputies hesitated to confront the government in open parliamentary sessions, for they, too, were divided between enthusiastic and reluctant supporters of the government. After the elections of 1981, the tables were turned. The right-of-center parties were too small and fragmented to fight the executive, whereas the Socialist deputies became part of an obedient machine for endorsing presidential wishes.

There is the factor of party discipline; there is also the fact that majority deputies do not wish to endanger their prospects for political advancement (i.e., appointment to ministerial posts) or pork-barrel favors to their constituents. Moreover, the lack of seriousness with which deputies have often viewed their own efforts could be attributed in part to the realization that much of the work done in Parliament does not necessarily have permanent value: The decisions that count are made elsewhere.

Bureaucratic Politics

In theory, civil servants do not make policy but only do the research and prepare the groundwork for policy and then implement it at various levels. But administrators have been in effect co-decision makers. During the Fourth Republic, the political executive had been subject to such frequent change, and hence had been so unstable and weak, that the permanent, professional civil service was depended on for decisional continuity and even initiative. In the Fifth Republic, the distinction between the political decision-making elite and the higher bureaucracy has been obscured by the tendency of presidents to recruit a large proportion of the cabinet from the administrative corps. In addition, civil servants have frequently dominated interministerial committees as well as the *cabinets ministériels,* the staffs of intimate collaborators appointed by each minister. In principle, the members of these *cabinets* are responsible to the minister whom they serve; but since they tend to understand the technicalities of a dossier better than the minister, they often act according to their own discretion, sometimes in concert with the staffs of other ministries.[3]

There has been a steady growth of the size of such staffs, from an average of about 10 per minister and about 300 for the ministries collectively during the 1960s and 1970s to 12.5 per minister and a total of 580 under Chirac (1987), and more than 600 in the Rocard government. This growth of what has been called a "parallel administration"[4] in part reflects the growth in the number of ministries. It is also, however, a manifestation of a spoils system in which jobs are given to more people, but money is saved at the same time because a smaller proportion of the appointees (i.e., 22 percent under Rocard versus 36 percent under Chirac) are professional civil servants who graduated from the Ecole Nationale d'Administration.

There are also the "study commissions," whose establishment is from time to time encouraged by the president, the prime minister, individual ministers, or the commissioner of economic planning. These commissions (which are roughly comparable to the Royal Commissions in Britain) may include academics, managers of public enterprises, and politicians, but civil servants have tended to dominate them. There have been many such commissions: for example, the Toutée Commission on wage negotiations in nationalized industries (1967); the Sudreau Commission on workers' participation in industrial management (1974); the Nora Commission on the impact of computer technology (1978); the Giraudet Commission on the reduction of the workweek (1980); and the Long Commission on the reform of citizenship and naturalization laws (1987). The commissions' reports to the government, which reflect the input of interest-group leaders and miscellaneous experts, may be used by the government as a basis for legislative proposals, or, if the government does not agree with the reports' conclusions, they may be ignored. There have been several reasons for the proliferation of such committees: the need to circumvent a Parliament that might make proposals that would be unwelcome to the government or, conversely, to supplant a Parliament that has been unwilling to make decisions (and failed to use the power to set up its own special study or investigation committees); the desire of the government to "pass the buck" for politically risky policies; and—on a more positive note—the quest for a policy based on a broad consensus.

Once the parliamentarians have passed a bill, it gains substance only when it is enforced. But governments (and higher civil servants) may show their reservations regarding a bill by failing to produce the necessary implementing regulations or ordinances. Thus the government has "denatured" acts of Parliament by delaying, or omitting, follow-up regulations on bills dealing with educational reforms, birth control, prison reform, and the financing of local government. Occasionally the administrative bureaucracy may, at the behest of a minister, produce regulations that contravene the intent of the law passed by Parliament. For example, after Parliament had passed a bill requiring equal treatment of immigrant workers, administrative regulations subjected them to special disabilities; similarly, an act of Parliament forbidding discrimination on the basis of religion or race aimed at firms engaged in international trade was followed by a government regulation permitting such discrimination. The Council of State may nullify such regulations after a legal challenge; however, litigation is selective and may take several years.

The Delegation of Responsibility

In order to weaken the effects of long-established legislation, the executive and its administrators may resort to various forms of buck-passing. Thus, to avoid using public moneys to keep the governmentally controlled health insurance funds solvent, the funds were permitted to raise the social security contributions of the insured. Similarly, the autonomous public corporation that runs the Paris subway system contracted with private firms to obtain workers to clean the subway stations, instead of employing its own workers and having to pay them the minimum wage generally granted by legislation to public employees. Finally, although all subnational administrative activities remain ultimately subject to the "guardianship" (*tutelle*) of the national government, the latter has saved itself trouble and money by permitting considerable local variations in the implementation of elementary school curricula and vacation policies, public health standards, and social services for the aged. The decentralization measures of 1982–83 institutionalized that approach and at the same time provided for greater local autonomy and grass-roots participation.

Since the early days of the Fourth Republic, governments have been committed to a form of capitalist national planning. The four-year economic modernization plans were prepared through complex procedures involving the cabinet (notably the Ministry of Finance), governmental statistical offices, several hundred technocrats working in a National Planning Commission, and numerous interest-group spokespersons who were consulted regularly in the Economic and Social Council and the regional modernization committees. This "concertation" of conflicting class interests was supposed to result in a fair plan that represented a fine balance between a "productivity" orientation and a "social" one. Hence the plan was invested with a certain moral authority; it led the government and Parliament to process specific pieces of legislation that were consistent with the plan: for instance, bills on public-works investments, social welfare, wages, employment, housing, and so on. For both de Gaulle and Pompidou, the plan was an "ardent obligation"; under Giscard and his prime ministers, the planning institutions were retained, but planners did little more than prepare position papers and statistical forecasts, while many of their policy recommendations were ignored by the government.

After the election of Mitterrand (and the appointment of Rocard as minister of planning), the economic plan was not only to be revived, geared to the production of social goods, and made more redistributive in orientation, but was to be given extra weaponry with an enlarged number of nationalized industries and a plethora of economic regulations. But the ninth development plan, theoretically in effect in 1983, became in practice a dead letter, as it was "displaced" by an interim plan conforming to the austerity policy to which the government committed itself. Part of the plan, moreover, was replaced by piecemeal economic policy contracts with individual regions (*contrats Etat-région*). Under the Chirac government, not much remained of the plan except its name and its institutions; whatever economic policy there was to be was confided to the cabinet as a whole and, more specifically, to the Ministry of Finance.

Indeed, given its program of reprivatizing a variety of industries and banks, its commitment to deregulation and "degovernmentalization," and its reliance on market forces, the government would have little if any room for planning. Under the Rocard government, a plan (the Tenth Development Plan, 1989–92) was adopted; but there was only a junior minister in charge of it, and planning in a meaningful sense was not revived.

Conflicts within the System

It should not be inferred that governmental attitudes are monolithic. Occasionally, the national administration is hampered by internal conflicts as well as conflicts with parliamentary and local politicians. For instance, the ministers in charge of labor (especially unskilled labor) and social affairs have been interested in raising minimum wages and upgrading working conditions, but ministers of finance have interfered with such policies in the interest of saving money both for the treasury and for the influential business sector, whose profits are maximized by cheap labor. While the minister of solidarity has been concerned with protecting the rights of immigrants, the minister of the interior has attempted (in the name of "law and order") to control their movements.

Some of these conflicts are resolved in response to political (i.e., electoral) considerations rather than merely administrative ones. It is true that the cabinet, the Parliament, and other political institutions have been bureaucratized; it is also true that administrative institutions have remained politicized. Deputies may serve on the boards of nationalized industries, on regional bodies, and in agencies involved in economic policy making. These deputies may be trained technocrats or civil servants and hence professionally concerned with "objective" approaches to problem solving; at the same time (and perhaps primarily), they are politicians responsive to local electorates.

The conflict between administration and politics is seen most clearly in the relationship between the mayor and prefect. The latter is legally responsible to the national government; he still (even after the passage of the decentralization laws) has the power to nullify acts of a city council, to veto the budget adopted by the general council, and even, under certain circumstances, to depose a mayor. He takes such action rarely, however, for a mayor may be more powerful than a prefect, especially if the former heads a large city and is, simultaneously, a member of Parliament or, better, a cabinet minister. Here it should be noted that a large number of ministers (including Prime Ministers Chaban-

Delmas, Barre, Mauroy, Chirac, Rocard, and Cresson) continued to function as mayors of towns while exercising their national functions.

Sometimes a mayor may be too political and too powerful to suit the taste of the national government. In 1978 Chirac, the mayor of Paris, was "punished" for his presidential ambitions and his unreliable support of the president: the mayor (at the president's instigation) failed to get a national financial supplement for the maintenance of the municipal police force—a development that forced the mayor to increase local tax assessments and threatened to reduce his popularity.

The preceding was not intended to suggest that France has a "mixed" political system in which various institutions and individuals filling a variety of different political positions play equally significant roles. Still, the fact that the constitution has given the chief of state vast powers to make decisions and that he has added to these powers by one-sided interpretation does not mean that he always makes use of these powers. Under Giscard, for instance, the distinction between president and prime minister was made more obscure than before. Giscard did not, in reality, freely decide all policies. He sometimes avoided tough decisions for electoral reasons, contenting himself with making a good impression on television and otherwise "playing at being president." During the election campaign of 1988 Mitterrand, in a "Letter to all the French,"[5] outlined his ideas about the constitution, economic policy, education and research, social security, citizenship, and foreign and defense policies, but after he retrieved his presidential powers he gave only general direction to Prime Minister Rocard. The latter, in turn, produced his own "circular" in which he articulated his ideas of government.[6]

Notes

1. The actual provisions of the 1958 constitution do not include a "bill of rights." But the preamble of that document includes references to the Declaration of the Rights of Man and the Citizen of 1789 and to the preamble of the Fourth Republic constitution, both of which have extensive listings of rights and liberties, among them freedom of association. In its decisions, the Constitutional Council has "inserted" these references into the constitution by according them operative validity.

2. Between 1949 and 1987, the Constitutional Council rendered decisions on 187 pending bills; only 29 between 1949 and 1974; 65 between 1974 and 1981; 74 between 1981 and 1986; and 19 in 1986–87. Of these,

70 (or 41 percent) voided the bills in question. See Louis Favoreu, "Conseil constitutionnel: mythes et réalités," *Regards sur l'Actualité,* no. 132 (June 1987): 18.

3. The "old-boy network" consisting of *Enarques*—graduates of the Ecole Nationale d'Administration—facilitates this relationship, for (as "insiders" have observed) "there is less difference between an *Enarque* of the left and an *Enarque* of the right than between an *Enarque* and a non-*Enarque.*" See Philippe Roqueplo, "Regards sur la complexité du pouvoir: Enquête dans les cabinets ministériels," *Annales des Mines,* June 1990, 4–30. On decentralization see Vivien A. Schmidt, *Democratizing France: The Political and Administrative History of Decentralization* (Cambridge: Cambridge University Press, 1990).

4. Jean-François Doumic, "L'administration parallèle," *Le Monde,* 2 February 1989.

5. "Lettre à tous les Français," *Le Monde,* 8 and 9 April 1988.

6. "Gouverner autrement," dated 25 May 1988, in *Regards sur l'Actualité,* no. 143 (July-August 1988): 15–18.

10

What Is the Future of French Politics?

If institutional stability and economic progress are used as the principal criteria for judging a political system, the Fifth Republic must be considered a success. Over three decades after its inauguration, the regime has amply reflected the themes of "change within continuity" articulated by Presidents Pompidou and Giscard d'Estaing. A remarkable balance has been achieved between French traditionalism and the spirit of innovation; the old institutions have been retained, but their functional relationships have been rationalized. The executive has sufficient unity and power to make decisions, and it has used this power fairly effectively.

Modernization and Democracy

The political party system has been simplified and political conflicts have been reduced—in part as a consequence of the manipulation of the system of elections, but, more important, as a consequence of socioeconomic changes and a clear popular consensus about the legitimacy of the constitutional system. Subnational administration has been adapted to respond to new realities, and local communities have been given significantly greater powers of decision and revenue gathering. The voting age has been lowered to eighteen; great progress has been made toward legal equality for women, minorities, homosexuals, and illegitimate offspring. Institutions have been created to make the bureaucracy more accountable; prison conditions have been improved, and the rights of those detained for criminal investigation have been enlarged. Apart from occasional lapses, freedom of association, including the right of workers to organize in factories, has been made more secure. There has been continuing experimentation aimed at modernizing and democratizing the educational system and at adapting it to the requirements of the job market, despite budgetary constraints and the opposition of part of the traditional academic establishment. Decolonization was achieved without undue bloodshed (except for Indochina and, later, Algeria) and without tearing French society apart, and the North African "repatriates" have been more or less successfully integrated. The French economy has adapted with remarkable success to the challenges of the European Common Market, and France has reached the status of the world's fifth-largest industrial power and fourth-largest exporter. The national and urban mass transport networks have been modernized and are among the finest in existence. The social security system has responded fairly well to the needs of the majority. France has become a prosperous country oriented to mass consumption; its currency is stable, and the living standard of its people corresponds to that of Americans. Having lost its position as a world power more than two generations ago, France has regained a part of its earlier prestige and has constructed a privileged relationship with African and Arab countries. Its nuclear strike force has been sufficiently enlarged to convey the impression (or illusion) that the country possesses the capacity to defend itself.

Administration and Justice: Developments and Reforms

To many of the French, especially Gaullists, the "administrative state" has been preferable to the "regime of parties" because civil servants have been viewed as more professional, less ideology ridden, and less particularistic than party politicians. Being less influenced by electoral pressures, the administrative bureaucracy is supposed to be much better able to make long-term policy in the public interest.

It is true that most upper-echelon civil servants are highly cultivated and public spirited; moreover, the social esteem and excellent pay they receive have made them, by and large, immune to corruption. But given their bourgeois or upper-class origins, they have also tended to be elitist and paternalistic. They are often too far removed from the people, and their actions are not subjected to adequate parliamentary surveillance. The citizens' means of redress against bureaucratic misbehavior are unreliable, despite such institutions as the administrative courts, topped by the Council of State and such newer institutions as the "mediator." In order to lighten the load of the Council of State, five new regional administrative courts were added to the thirty-one in existence; yet 22,000 cases were still pending before the council in 1989.

The judicial system, too, whose essential features date to Napoleon's rule, is in need of liberalization. The network of courts is large; the appeals echelons are well distributed geographically; and most Western-type due process criteria are followed. Although Anglo-American-style habeas corpus provisions are omitted in the constitution, they have been introduced gradually by means of ordinary legislation. Yet elements of class justice persist; preventive (pretrial) detention is often still too long, especially for suspects belonging to the working class and the peasantry. The police, the prosecuting attorneys, and the courts have dealt particularly harshly with immigrants from the Third World. For many years, the government hesitated to liberalize the penal code, a hesitancy attributed in part to continued fear (shared by large segments of the population) of disorder and violence. This fear had (until 1981) prevented governments from sponsoring legislation to abolish the death penalty; it also explained the retention of the State Security Court, which dealt with cases of sedition. That court had been set up in 1963 in the wake of a series of violent acts by opponents of de Gaulle and his policies. Under Mitterrand, the State Security Court was abolished.

In the spring of 1980, the government introduced (and the Assembly passed) a bill to reform the penal code. This bill, labeled "Security and Liberty," aimed at making the punishment for crimes of violence more severe and at reducing the discretion of judges in the imposition of sentences. At the same time, the bill provided for a reduction of the maximum period of pretrial detention. During the first term of Mitterrand's presidency, the government, in particular the minister of justice, Robert Badinter, initiated numerous measures aimed at reforming the legal system. The illiberal features of the "Security and Liberty" law were rescinded; prison conditions were improved; the indigent were guaranteed the right to counsel; the rights of immigrant aliens were more or less aligned with those of citizens, and the former were given greater protection against harassment by public officials; and the power of the police was curbed—not without opposition from the minister of the interior.[1]

The process of reforming the judicial system is continuing. Yet much remains to be done to deal with the problems of understaffed courts, underpaid police officers, overcrowded prisons, and the (still) inadequate protection of the rights of citizens against the state. Finally, in order to protect such rights better, Mitterrand came out in favor of a constitutional amendment that would permit the Constitutional Council to examine bills at its own initiative and that would grant ordinary citizens involved in a trial the right to bring the issue of the constitutionality of a law before the council. Although in 1990 the Assembly passed an appropriate amendment bill in first reading, there is insufficient support among the conservative parties (especially in the Senate) to secure the passage of the amendment in the near future.

On occasion, governments have intervened in judicial matters, thus degrading political democracy. Such intervention was sometimes inspired by foreign policy considerations: for example, in 1977, the release without trial of an Arab suspected of terrorist action; in 1980, the physical interference by the (nationally controlled) Paris police in a

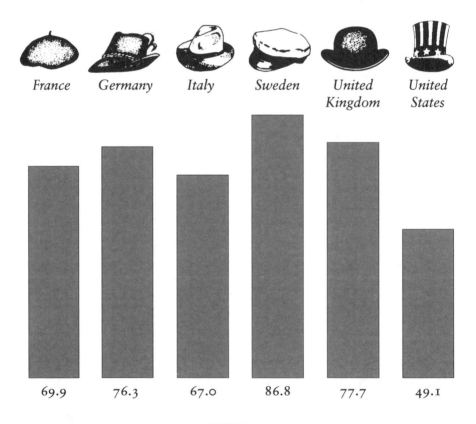

FIGURE 10.1
VOTER TURNOUT (PERCENT OF ELIGIBLE VOTERS)

NOTE: Most recent general election (U.S.: 1988 presidential election).

peaceful demonstration in front of the Soviet embassy; and in 1987, the (unsuccessful) attempt by the Chirac government to interfere in the trial of another Arab implicated in the assassination of diplomats in Paris.

Under the presidencies of de Gaulle, Pompidou, and Giscard, there were a number of constraints to the expression of opinion in the mass media. The television networks and most radio stations were public monopolies, and they were often used by the government to distort the news. The press was free and pluralistic, but governments would occasionally confiscate issues of periodicals that had published articles critical of the president, and in one case (under Giscard) even instituted legal proceedings against a newspaper. Under Mitterrand, such practices have ceased; moreover, the setting up of private radio stations was permitted, and the television networks were put under autonomous management and, in most cases, privatized.

Problems and Prospects

The Economic Challenge: Welfare Statism

For many years, most French citizens accepted their country's version of the "mixed economy" under which a large and pluralistic private sector coexisted with a significant array of nationalized industries. In addition, France has had a highly developed welfare state, reflected in a complex of redistributive policies that had been gradually evolving from the end of the Third Republic through the first years of the Mitterrand presidency. These policies include a progressive income tax; income supplements to families with several children; low- and moderate-rent housing; state-subsidized (and virtually tuition-free) higher education; and (compared with the United States) generous retirement, unemployment, maternity, and medical benefits and paid vacations (of five weeks)— financed in large part by employers. In addition, there are governmentally imposed minimum wages (which are higher than in the United States), complemented, until recently, by a system of semiautomatic wage increases, indexed to changes in the cost of living.

Although most citizens accepted these features as almost inalienable rights, these were not regarded as solutions to a number of persistent problems, among them the inequality of incomes, housing shortages, unemployment, and large-scale tax fraud (compensated only in part by the more or less automatic—but regressive—system of value-added taxes now required for all members of the European Community). Moreover, the heavy governmental involvement in social and economic matters was thought to have a stifling effect on private initiative in general and industrial (and employment-creating) investment in particular; and the existence of a large nationalized sector was held responsible for impeding productivity and competition. Responding to the pressures of the international and the European market, and inspired to some extent by the (presumably) successful examples of the United States and Germany, French governments—especially under the prime ministerships of Barre, Fabius, and Chirac—discovered the virtues of the marketplace and promoted policies of selective denationalization and deregulation. These policies were continued by Rocard and Madame Cresson and (despite protests from left-wing Socialists) by Bérégovoy as well.

Foreign Policy

Under de Gaulle, France's foreign policy was inspired by aspirations to grandeur. But, given the limitations of the country's economic and military power, these aspirations could not be realized. Unable to play a decisive role in the international system, de Gaulle pursued a policy of symbolism and rhetoric that expressed itself in hostility to the two superpowers, in opposition to the institutional development of a supranational Europe, in futile attempts to interfere in regional disputes (e.g., the Middle East), and in efforts to mediate relationships between industrialized Europe and the developing countries (notably in Africa). An important element of de Gaulle's policy was his resentment of the "Anglo-Americans," a resentment reflected in his hostility to NATO. Such attitudes were in part determined by fears of U.S. economic domination and of "Anglo-Saxon" cultural hegemony, by doubts about the reliability of the U.S. commitment to defend Europe in case of Soviet aggression, and, more recently, by doubts about the adequacy of U.S. power.

Responding to the pressures of the Gaullist party, and reflecting the outlook of much of the French intellectual elite, Pompidou and (to a lesser extent) Giscard adhered to the main lines of de Gaulle's foreign policy, but they were considerably less hostile to the United States and to the development of European unity. Under Mitterrand, France continued to develop its national nuclear deterrent and, on the cultural level, to foster as much as was still possible the cultivation of the French language abroad; at the same time, it abandoned the Gaullist illusions about France's international power and became more favorably inclined toward NATO and more pro-American. This has been the case particularly since the reunification of Germany, a development that has weakened the relative position of France in Europe. Henceforth, France's foreign policy came increasingly to reflect a concern with its economic aspect, that is, European and global competitiveness.

Societal and Systemic Issues

The problems that preoccupy the majority of the residents of France are domestic in nature. Chief among them is the presence of several million immigrants and their impact on French society. Progressive elements, led by Mitterrand, have attempted to fight racism and to speed the process of legal integration and cultural assimilation of immigrants, and to that end have promoted a liberal approach to naturalization. But opponents have expressed the fear that easy acquisition of French citizenship would actually hamper the assimilation process and that, ultimately, French society would be changed beyond recognition. A related problem has been the existence of regional and nonterritorial French ethnic minorities (e.g., Bretons, Alsatians, Basques). A growing sensitivity to these minorities has been evinced in the Socialists' decentralization policies, a greater tolerance to cultural diversity, and the grant of autonomy to Corsica and a number of overseas territories (including New Caledonia). Nevertheless, there are those who fear that excessive attention to the claims of minorities might weaken France's cultural and political unity and put in question its "national identity."[2]

There are other problems, among them overcrowded (and often unsafe) secondary schools and an insufficient number of teachers; the pollution of the environment; and the persistence of unemployment and its corollary, the risk of depleted social-security funds. Finally, there is a widespread recognition of the need for strong steps to curb delinquency, urban violence, and terrorism, and to protect society from the spread of AIDS, but there is an equal interest that in the process there should be no infringement on civil liberties.

In recent years, there has been some concern about citizens' loss of interest in traditional forms of political participation. There has been a growing electoral abstentionism (it was 30.80 percent in the first round of the 1993 Assembly elections and 32.44 in the second round); and there has been a steady decline of identification with political parties, as reflected in a loss of dues-paying members in all the major parties. This situation is only partly compensated by growing membership in interest groups, especially on the local level.

The decline of partisan identification affected especially the major parties. This was manifest in the regional and cantonal elections of March 1992, in which less than 20 percent of the electorate voted for the Socialist party (PS). The PS was held responsible for a number of problems and failures: the persistent unemployment; crime and urban violence; financial scandals involving Socialist politicians and the PS as a whole; the revelation that the government allowed the use of blood products contaminated with the AIDS virus; and the Habbash affair, in which a Palestinian terrorist leader was secretly flown to France for medical treatment and (after a public outcry) spirited out of the country.

However, the other major parties did not fare much better, with the RPR and UDF together gaining only 33 percent of the votes. The two right-wing parties suffered from internal divisions and a lack of credibility. The major gainers were the National Front (FN) and the environmentalist parties, which made significant inroads into regional councils. However, the FN, with 13.9 percent, did not improve its previously obtained national score; and the environmentalists, with a slightly higher combined score, were hurt by a division of this movement into two parties, the Greens and Génération Ecologie, whose leaders sniped at one another while proclaiming a desire for unity.

The results signaled above all a disenchantment with the "political class."[3] This disenchantment was reflected in a steeply falling approval rating not only of Prime Ministers Cresson and Bérégovoy (and their governments) but of President Mitterrand as well. The public's disenchantment with the government was finally reflected in the results of the 1993 parliamentary elections, which decimated the Socialist party representation in the Assembly, threatened to fragment, if not destroy, the party as a whole, and reduced the role of Mitterrand, already a lame-duck president, to a marginal and essentially symbolic one.

The new government of Edouard Balladur began with high popular opinion ratings and an enormous parliamentary majority (more than 80 percent—the largest majority enjoyed by any group in more than a century). However, it remained doubtful whether this government would be able to solve France's economic problems. The very intractability of these problems may undermine the public trust in the new government, shatter the cohesion between the RPR and the UDF, and bring the rivalries between their leaders, Chirac and Giscard, out in the open again as they jockey for position in preparation for the presidential elections that are scheduled to take place in 1995.

Despite the growing public distrust of politicians, there is a widespread consensus about the regime itself. There continue to be disagreements about specific institutional questions: whether the term of the president should be shortened from seven to five years in order to "align" the executive more closely to the legislature; whether there should be a return to proportional representation for Assembly elections; whether the referendum should be resorted to more or less frequently; and whether citizens should be able to appeal directly to the Constitutional Council. But there is little doubt that the constitutional system as a whole is sound and well enough designed to meet France's challenges in the future.

Notes

1. See William Safran, "Rights and Liberties under the Mitterrand Presidency: Socialist Innovations and Post-Socialist Revisions," *Contemporary French Civilization* 12, no. 1 (Winter/Spring 1988): 1–35.

2. See William Safran, "State, Nation, National Identity, and Citizenship: France as a Test Case," *International Political Science Review* 12, no. 3 (1991): 220–39.

3. Denis Jeambar, "Ce que les Français ne veulent plus," *Le Point*, March 1992, 44–49.

For Further Reading

ALDRICH, ROBERT, AND CONNELL, JOHN, eds. *France in World Politics*. London and New York: Routledge, 1989.

ANDREWS, WILLIAM G. *Presidential Government in Gaullist France*. Albany: State University of New York Press, 1982.

ANDREWS, WILLIAM G., AND HOFFMANN, STANLEY, eds. *The Fifth Republic at Twenty*. Albany: State University of New York Press, 1980.

ARDAGH, JOHN. *France Today*. New York: Penguin, 1987.

BAUMGARTNER, FRANK R. *Conflict and Rhetoric in French Policymaking*. Pittsburgh: University of Pittsburgh Press, 1989.

BERGER, SUZANNE. *Peasants against Politics: Rural Organization in Brittany, 1911–1967*. Cambridge, Mass.: Harvard University Press, 1972

CHARLOT, JEAN. *The Gaullist Phenomenon*. New York: Praeger, 1971.

CHRISTOFFERSON, THOMAS R. *The French Socialists in Power, 1981–1986*. Newark: University of Delaware Press, 1991.

CODDING, GEORGE A., AND SAFRAN, WILLIAM. *Ideology and Politics: The Socialist Party of France*. Boulder, Colo.: Westview Press, 1979.

CONVERSE, PHILIP E., AND PIERCE, ROY. *Political Representation in France.* Cambridge, Mass.: Harvard University Press, 1986.

CROZIER, MICHEL. *Strategies of Change: The Future of French Society.* Cambridge, Mass.: MIT Press, 1982.

FRIEND, JULIUS W. *Seven Years in France: François Mitterrand and the Unintended Revolution, 1981–1988.* Boulder, Colo.: Westview Press, 1989.

GAFFNEY, JOHN. *The French Left and the Republic: The Discourses of Communism and Socialism in Contemporary France.* New York: St. Martin's Press, 1989.

GAULLE, CHARLES DE. *The Compete War Memoirs.* 3 vols. New York: Simon and Schuster, 1972.

GODT, PAUL, ed. *Policy-Making in France from de Gaulle to Mitterrand.* London: Pinter, 1989.

GOUREVITCH, PETER A. *Paris and the Provinces.* Berkeley: University of California Press, 1980.

HALL, PETER; HAYWARD, JACK; AND MACHIN, HOWARD, eds. *Developments in French Politics.* New York: St. Martin's Press, 1990.

HAUSS, CHARLES. *Politics in Gaullist France: Coping with Chaos.* New York: Praeger, 1991.

HAYWARD, JACK. *The State and the Market Economy.* New York: New York University Press, 1986.

HOFFMANN, STANLEY. *Decline or Renewal? France since the 1930s.* New York: Viking, 1974.

HOLLIFIELD, JAMES F., AND ROSS, GEORGE, eds. *Searching for the New France.* New York and London: Routledge, 1991.

KEELER, JOHN T.S. *The Politics of Neocorporatism in France.* New York: Oxford University Press.

KOLODZIEJ, EDWARD A. *French International Policy under de Gaulle and Pompidou.* Ithaca, N.Y.: Cornell University Press, 1974.

LORD, GUY. *The French Budgetary Process.* Berkeley: University of California Press, 1973.

MACHIN, HOWARD, AND WRIGHT, VINCENT, eds. *Economic Policy and Policy-Making under the Mitterrand Presidency, 1981–84.* New York: St. Martin's Press, 1985.

MITTERRAND, FRANÇOIS. *The Wheat and the Chaff.* New York: Seaver Books, 1982.

PENNIMAN, HOWARD, ed. *France at the Polls, 1981 and 1986: The National Elections.* Durham, N.C.: Duke University Press, 1988.

ROSS, GEORGE; HOFFMANN, STANLEY; AND MALZACHER, SYLVIA, eds. *The Mitterrand Experiment.* New York: Oxford University Press, 1987.

SAFRAN, WILLIAM. *The French Polity,* 3d ed. New York: Longman, 1991.

SULEIMAN, EZRA. *Elites in French Society: The Politics of Survival.* Princeton, N.J.: Princeton University Press, 1978.

TIERSKY, RONALD. *French Communism, 1920–1972.* New York: Columbia University Press, 1974.

WEBER, EUGEN. *Peasants into Frenchmen: The Modernization of Rural France, 1870–1914.* Stanford: Stanford University Press, 1976.

WILSON, FRANK L. *French Political Parties under the Fifth Republic.* New York: Praeger, 1982.

———. *Interest-Group Politics in France.* Cambridge: Cambridge University Press, 1988.

Kiel

Rostock

Hamburg

Bremen

BERLIN

Hanover   Potsdam

Leipzig

Duesseldorf   Dresden

Cologne

Bonn

Frankfurt

Nuremburg

Stuttgart

Munich

Part Three

Germany

David P. Conradt

11

The Context of German Politics

In any study of modern Western European politics an examination of Germany must occupy a prominent place. Germans are the most numerous people in Western and Central Europe. From 1945 to 1990 Germany was divided into two states: the Federal Republic of Germany (FRG) or West Germany and the German Democratic Republic (GDR) or East Germany. The unified Federal Republic, which was formed in 1989–1990, unlike France, Britain, Italy or Sweden, must now integrate 16 million new citizens into its economy, society and polity. The vast majority of these former East Germans have had little or no experience in democratic citizenship.

The collapse of the GDR in 1989–90 and its incorporation into the Federal Republic is another example of the frequent and sudden changes that have characterized Germany history. Indeed, the study of modern German politics offers an exceptional opportunity to examine the problems associated with political change and development. Few societies have experienced such drastic changes in their political system as has Germany. In little more than a century Germany has had an empire (1871–18), an unstable democratic republic (1919–33), a totalitarian dictatorship (1933–45), military occupation (1945–49), two separate states (1949–90): a federal republic in the West and a one-party communist state in the East and since 1990 a single federal state. Thus Germany and the Germans have experienced most of the major political and ideological movements in modern history. The development of the West German Republic during the past forty-three years, however, illustrates the extent to which a country can largely overcome its political heritage and change its political culture. Few modern democracies have been as stable, effective, and legitimate as the Federal Republic that we examine in the following chapters. The success of West Germany and its attraction to East Germans was an important factor in the deterioration of the communist regime. How can all these changes be explained?

Not only is the Federal Republic a stable democracy; in recent years it has emerged out of the shadows of the Third Reich to become an increasingly important and assertive actor in European and international politics. It is one of the world's largest trading nations and has Europe's strongest and most dynamic economy. Its army is the largest national contingent in the North Atlantic Treaty Organization (NATO). Germany has also supplanted Great Britain as the chief European ally of the United States. Yet the Federal Republic remains keenly interested in improving its relations with Russia and other republics of the former Soviet Union and Eastern Europe and has become the leading advocate in the West of a new era of East-West cooperation. West German support of the reform policies of Soviet leader Mikhail Gorbachev was an important factor in the unification process. No nation, apart from the former Soviet Union itself, invested as much political (and economic) capital in *perestroika* as did Germany. The collapse of communism in Eastern Europe and the Soviet Union together with the breakup of the Soviet empire means that the Federal Republic will assume a greater leadership role in Central and Eastern Europe. Clearly, much is to be gained from an examination of this country in the last decade of the twentieth century.

Historical

Europe has known German-speaking people and German political units for almost a thousand years. Nevertheless, the Federal Republic of Germany is one of Europe's and the world's newest states. In May 1989, it observed only its fortieth anniversary—a time span hardly comparable to that of most of its European neighbors. Although a relatively young state, the Federal Republic claims to be the legitimate successor to the Third Reich (1933–45) and the Bismarckian Second Reich (1871–1918). This claim also makes the Republic the heir to the German political tradition, a tradition characterized by national division and frequent change. Before there were "Germans," Europe was populated by numerous Germanic tribes: Saxons, Franks, Bavarians, Swabians, Silesians, and Thuringians, to name a few. No single state has ever united all of Europe's ethnic Germans. The 1945–90 division between West Germany, East Germany, and the "Eastern territories," now part of Poland and the former Soviet Union, was thus only one more variation on a constant theme in German and European history. The political division of the German nation has been the rule rather than the exception.

The Empire (1871–1918)

Until 1871, Europe's German-speaking people were divided into many small principalities, a few moderate-sized kingdoms, and two large yet divided major powers: Austria in the southeast and Prussia in the north. The German Reich, or Empire, proclaimed in 1871 was a Prussian-dominated structure that did not include Austria. Nonetheless, it was by far the most successful unification effort in German history. This empire was largely the work of the Prussian prime minister and first imperial chancellor, or head of government, Otto von Bismarck, and was brought about through classical European power politics. Prussia, under Bismarck, fought successful wars against Denmark (1864), Austria (1866), and France (1870) to become the dominant power in northern and western Germany.

National unification did not, however, represent any success for German liberalism. Nationalism, which historically has been closely associated with liberalism in countries such as France and the United States, has been an illiberal force in the German political experience. The empire was established through the fabled "blood and iron" policies of Bismarck and not by Germany's parliamentary liberals. After 1871, they in fact deferred to the "Iron Chancellor" and became more national than liberal.

During the imperial period, Germany became one of the world's great powers. Industrialization and urbanization advanced rapidly, as did the Reich's military power. Yet the industrialists and other members of the expanding middle class did not challenge the political authority of the traditional Prussian ruling elites: the military, the bureaucracy, and the landed nobility. Germany had become a modern society ruled by a premodern, traditional elite. The empire was an authoritarian political structure with some democratic features. While the chancellor and his government were appointed by the kaiser, a freely elected parliament held the power of appropriations and could exert some influence and control over the executive. The upper house, however, which represented the states and could block most lower-house initiatives, was effectively dominated by Prussia. And in Prussia the voting system still gave a disproportionate influence to the upper-middle and upper classes. Military and foreign policy as well as internal security remained very much the province of the Prussian elite. Parliament could not prevent, for example, Bismarck's campaigns of suppression against Catholics and socialists.

None of Bismarck's successors could maintain the delicate foreign and domestic equilibrium that characterized Germany from 1871 to 1890. In creating the Reich, Bismarck and the Prussians made many enemies in Europe, especially France, which lost the provinces of Alsace and Lorraine after the 1870 Prussian War. To the east, Russia feared German power. Bismarck was able to avoid a Franco-Russian alliance, but his successors were not. With a romantic nationalist, Kaiser Wilhelm, on the throne, Germany after Bismarck sought to acquire overseas colonies, and through the expansion of the fleet to challenge British naval superiority. By the turn of the century, post-Bismarckian foreign policy had managed to provoke Britain, France, and Russia to ally against the Reich.

Internally, the paradox or contradiction of a rapidly modernizing society controlled by premodern political elites continued to produce socioeconomic and political tensions. The expanding working class provided a solid electoral base for the Social Democratic party, which, however, was unable to achieve political influence commensurate with its growing numerical strength. The middle-class parties that also grew throughout the empire were unable and probably unwilling to oppose the militarist and imperialist policies of the kaiser and his chancellor.

Indeed, in many cases, the middle-class parties deferred to the traditional Prussian elites and supported measures such as the naval arms race with Great Britain. Unlike their counterparts in Britain and France, the German middle classes did not exert a moderating influence on policy. Militant nationalism was one means by which the traditional elite could unify a divided society and maintain its power position.

The empire so carefully constructed by Bismarck did not survive World War I. While the war dragged on after the failure of the initial German offensive, the many tensions and contradictions in the socioeconomic and political structures of the empire became apparent. Socialists, liberals, and Catholics began to question a conflict that pitted Germany against countries such as Britain and the United States, whose democratic values and constitution they hoped someday to achieve in Germany. A victory on the battlefield would strengthen a regime they had opposed in peacetime.

Severe rationing caused by the Allied blockade, mounting casualty lists, and the pressures of wartime production began to take their toll on civilian morale, especially among factory workers. When the army's spring offensive in 1918 failed, the military, which in the final years of the war actually made most key economic and political decisions, advised the kaiser to abdicate and the parliamentary leadership to proclaim a republic and negotiate a peace with the Western powers.

The Weimar Republic (1919–33)

In January 1919 Germans elected delegates to a constituent assembly that met in the city of Weimar to formulate a new constitution for the postwar republic. The delegates, many of whom were distinguished legal scholars, produced a model democratic constitution, one of the most advanced in the world. It contained an extensive catalog of human rights and provided numerous opportunities for popular participation through referenda, petition, and the direct election of a strong president.

The republic, however, began under very unfavorable circumstances. Following the departure of the kaiser, some German Marxists attempted to duplicate the Bolsheviks' success in Russia. Workers' and soldiers' councils were established in several cities, and Bavaria experienced a short-lived socialist republic. A coalition of moderate social democrats, liberals, and conservative nationalists crushed these abortive efforts at a communist revolution. As a consequence, the working class remained divided throughout the Weimar Republic between the Social Democratic party, which supported the parliamentary system, and the Communist party, which sought its overthrow. These events also established a pattern of political violence that was to continue throughout the period. In addition, the republic was identified from the beginning with defeat, national humiliation, and ineffectiveness.

The conservative nationalists, urged on by the military, propagated the myth that Germany had not really lost World War I but had been "stabbed in the back" by the "November criminals," identified as socialists, communists, liberals, and Jews. Large segments of the bureaucracy and the judiciary also were more attached to the authoritarian values of the empire than to those of the republic, and they acted accordingly.

The republic's brief history was characterized by a steady polarization of politics between left and right. In the early elections of the 1920s, pro-Republican parties—Social Democrats, the Center (Catholic) party, and the Democratic party (Liberals)—had a solid majority of seats. By the early 1930s, the pro-Republican share of the vote had dropped from about 65 percent to only 30 percent. The Nazis on the right and the Communists on the left together held over half of the parliamentary delegates. With most voters supporting parties opposed to the republic, it became impossible to build a stable governing coalition. Policy making became increasingly the responsibility of the president, who made extensive use of his power to issue executive decrees without regard to the wishes of the fragmented parliament.

The worldwide depression of 1929 dealt the republic a blow from which it could not recover. By 1932, over a third of the work force was unemployed, and the Nazis became the largest party in the parliament. The German public wanted an effective government that would "do something." The democratic parties and their leaders could not meet this demand.

The Third Reich and World War II (1933–45)

The only party that thrived on this crisis was the Nazi party, under its leader Adolf Hitler. The Nazis, or National Socialist German Workers party (NSDAP), was one of many nationalist and *völkisch* (racialist) movements that had emerged after World War I. Hitler's leadership ability set it apart from the others. A powerful orator, Hitler was able to appeal to a wide variety of voters and interests. He denounced the Versailles treaty, which had imposed harsh terms on Germany after World War I, and the "criminals" who signed it for Germany. To the unemployed, he promised jobs in the rebuilding of the nation (rearmament and public works). To business interests, he represented a bulwark against communism. To farmers and small businessmen, caught between big labor and business, he promised a recognition of their proper position in German society and protection against Marxist labor and "Jewish plutocrats."

In January 1933, Hitler was asked by President von Hindenburg to form a government. The conservatives around the president believed they could easily control and "handle" Hitler once he had responsibility. Two months later the Nazis pushed an Enabling Act through the parliament that essentially gave Hitler total power; the parliament, constitution, and civil liberties were suspended. The will of the Führer (leader) became the supreme law and authority. By 1934, almost all areas of life had become "synchronized" (*gleichgeschaltet*) to the Nazi pattern.

There is little doubt that most Germans until at least the start of World War II supported Hitler. A survey conducted in 1951, six years after the war, found that a majority under forty-five years of age still stated that the prewar years of the Third Reich (1933–39) were the "best" that Germany had experienced in this century.[1] They were years of economic growth and at least a surface prosperity. Unemployment was virtually eliminated; inflation was checked; and the economy, fueled by expenditures for rearmament and public works, boomed. That during these "good years" thousands of Germans were imprisoned, tortured, and murdered in concentration camps, and hundreds of thousands of German Jews were systematically persecuted, was apparently of minor importance to most citizens in comparison with the economic and policy successes of the regime. Most Germans, at least between 1933 and 1939, were willing to give up the democratic political order and the liberal society and accept the regime's racism and persecution of political opponents in exchange for economic prosperity, social stability, and a resurgence of national pride.

World War II in Europe was, in the words of a former chancellor of the Federal Republic, Helmut Schmidt, "totally started, led, and lost by Adolf Hitler acting in the name of the German people."[2] The world paid for this war with a total of fifty-five million dead including eight million Jews and other political and racial victims murdered in concentration camps. The most ruthless and inhuman Nazi actions were directed against European Jewry. From the beginning of the Nazi movement, the Jews were regarded as the prime cause of all the misfortune, unhappiness, and disappointments endured by the German people. Hitler in his autobiography, *Mein Kampf,* written in the early 1920s, repeated in print his oft-spoken conviction that Jews were not humans, nor even subhumans, but rather "disease-causing bacilli" in the body of the nation that must be exterminated. Unfortunately, at the time, few took his rantings seriously, yet Hitler and the Nazis remained firm to this policy after they came to power. From 1933 on, first in Germany and then throughout the conquered lands of Europe, the Nazis systematically began a process that denied the Jews their dignity, economic livelihood, humanity, and finally, by the early 1940s, their right physically to exist. The "final solution" to the "Jewish problem" meant the deportation of millions of Jewish men, women, and children to extermination camps especially constructed for this purpose in isolated sections of Europe.

Only the total military defeat of the Third Reich by the United States, Britain, France, the Soviet Union, and forces from other allied nations in May 1945 prevented the Nazis from exterminating European Jewry. The remnant that remained amounted to less than 10 percent of the prewar Jewish population of Europe. The Federal Republic has accepted legal and moral responsibility for the crimes of the Nazi era. It is, of course, impossible to atone for the Holocaust. Nevertheless, since the early 1950s the Federal Republic has paid almost $65 billion in reparations to the state of Israel and Jewish victims of Nazism. In 1990 the first and last freely elected government in the German Democratic Republic acknowledged East Germany's responsibility for the Holocaust and apologized to the world Jewish community and the state of Israel for the refusal of the Communist regime to deal with this issue.

For many Germans, the real distress began after the war. During the war, the Nazis, mindful of the effects of Allied blockades during World War I, had gone to extensive lengths to ensure a relatively well-fed, housed, and clothed population. That this meant the ruthless exploitation of regions conquered by Hitler's armies was a matter of minor concern to the Nazi leadership. Military defeat ended this supply of foodstuffs, raw materials, and labor from the occupied territories. Germans after 1945 were put in the same position as the populations in other European countries. In 1945 and 1946, the average caloric intake was set at only a third of the daily requirement. In large cities, such as Berlin and Düsseldorf, 80 to 90 percent of all houses and apartments were uninhabitable; in Cologne, a city with a population of 750,000 before the war, only 40,000 people remained during the winter of 1945–46. Heating fuel was also in critically short supply. Before the war, the coal mines of the Ruhr had an average daily production of 400,000 tons; in 1945–46, this dropped to only 25,000 tons per day.

The end of World War II meant the end of Germany as a political entity. The victorious Allies returned some of the territory conquered by the Nazis to its prewar rulers (Czechoslovakia, Poland, Austria, France) and divided the remainder into zones of military occupation. But by the late 1940s, the onset of the Cold War dashed any hopes that the wartime coalition could agree on a single postwar German state. In 1949 the American, British, and French zones of occupation became the Federal Republic of Germany, or West Germany, with its capital in the small city of Bonn on the Rhine river. In the same year the Soviet zone of occupation became the German Democratic Republic, or East Germany, with East Berlin as its capital.

The Federal Republic

Since its inception in 1949, the Federal Republic has developed into a strong, dynamic democracy. Unlike the Weimar Republic, the Bonn Republic has from the beginning been identified with economic prosperity and foreign and domestic policy successes. There is also considerable evidence that a consensus on democratic values and norms has developed during this period. The vast majority of the West German population supports this system and believes in its fundamental norms: individual freedom, the rule of law, civil liberties, free political competition, and representative institutions. In this sense, Germany and the Germans have changed.

The history of the Federal Republic can be divided into five rather distinct phases. The first, from 1949 to 1961, was characterized by an emphasis on economic reconstruction and the stabilization of the new political system both internally and externally through German participation in the European Community and the Atlantic Alliance (NATO). This stabilization occurred within the context of the Cold War. Politics during this period was dominated by the Christian Democratic Union (CDU) and the republic's first chancellor, Konrad Adenauer. The construction of the Berlin Wall in 1961 marked the end of this period. The Cold War foreign policy of "strength" had failed to reunify the country or "roll back" communism in Eastern Europe. The search for alternatives to confrontation had begun.

The second phase encompassed most of the 1960s and ended with the election of 1969 when, for the first time in the Federal Republic's history, the Christian Democratic Union was put into the opposition and was replaced by a government led by the Social Democratic party (SPD). This phase was marked by a search for new domestic and foreign policy directions. Many domestic areas, such as education, urban development, economic planning, and social welfare programs, relatively neglected during the hectic years of reconstruction, now moved up on the political agenda. The 1960s also witnessed the beginning of the increase in mass political participation that continued throughout the 1970s. The student protest movement; the "extraparliamentary opposition," spawned by dissatisfaction with the 1966 "Grand Coalition" between the CDU/CSU and the SPD; and the beginnings of a grass-roots citizens' action group movement (Bürgerinitiativen) were all expressions of this growing politicization.

The third phase began with the social-liberal coalition of 1969. The politics of "internal reform," the modernization and expansion of the republic's social security and welfare system, liberalized divorce and abortion legislation, criminal law reform, and worker codetermination in industry were major domestic developments in this period. Although Germany, like her Western neighbors, experienced an economic recession following the first oil price shock in 1973, the levels of unemployment and inflation remained well below those of other industrial societies. More important, the 1974–76 recession did not produce any significant antisystem political movements. In foreign policy, reconciliation and normalization with Germany's Eastern neighbors were continued and extended through treaties with the Soviet Union and Poland (1970), East Germany (1972), Czechoslovakia (1973), and an additional agreement with Poland (1976). The second oil price shock in 1979 sent the Federal Republic into another economic recession, the worst since the Great Depression of the 1930s. High unemployment, inflation, and rising state deficits took their toll on the social-liberal coalition, which collapsed in 1982.

The fourth phase in the republic's history began with the return to power of the Christian Democrats in 1982 and lasted until the unification with East Germany in 1990. Together with their Free Democratic partners, they promised a *Wende,* or fundamental change, especially in the republic's domestic policies. Social programs were cut, incentives to business were increased, and government budget deficits declined. This was a modest German version of the "supply-side" economics practiced by Prime Minister Thatcher in Great Britain or the Reagan administration in the United States. But the new government also attempted to turn Germany away from what it regarded as the excessive permissiveness and liberalism of the social-liberal era. Traditional values of family, country, thrift, work, and duty were emphasized, at least by the new chancellor, Helmut Kohl. Yet the trends toward increased politicization and mass protest evident since the late 1960s continued. In 1983 the first new political party in almost thirty years, the Greens, entered the national parliament. Their success was due above all to the "new politics" of environmental protection, women's rights, and disarmament. This phase saw the Federal Republic assume a higher profile in international relations. In 1989 it strongly opposed the policies of the United States over the question of the modernization and deployment of new short-range missiles in West Germany.

The fifth and present phase in the Federal Republic's development began, of course, with the collapse of the East German communist regime in 1989–90 and the admission of the five East German states into the federation in 1990. These dramatic changes were part of the larger disintegration of Communism throughout Eastern Europe and the Soviet Union and are closely connected with the reform policies of then–Soviet President Mikhail Gorbachev. No Eastern European communist regime was more opposed to democratic reform than East Germany, because unlike Poland, Czechoslovakia or Hungary, East Germany was not a nation. Indeed, its only source of identity and legitimacy was its claim to be the only "socialist" German state. East German leaders believed that if this commitment to the ideology of Marxism-Leninism were to be diluted or abandoned, as Gorbachev seemed to be propos-

TABLE 11.1

GERMAN UNITY, 1989–90: A CHRONOLOGY

Summer–Fall 1989	East Germans flee through Hungary, Czechoslovakia, and Poland to the West
October 1989	Mass demonstrations in Leipzig and other cities
9 November 1989	Opening of the Berlin wall
13 November 1989	Hans Modrow becomes prime minister of East Germany
24 November 1989	Communist party gives up its monopoly of power
28 November 1989	Kohl announces 10-point plan for unity
3 December 1989	Communist party leadership resigns
12 December 1989	Round table talks (Communists and democratic opposition) in East Germany
19 December 1989	Kohl and Modrow agree on a "community of treaties."
1 January 1990	Demonstrations in Leipzig demand German unity
2 January 1990	Modrow announces plan for unity
18 March 1990	First free elections in East Germany; Kohl-led "Alliance for Germany" is the strongest party.
12 April 1990	Lothar de Maizière (CDU) becomes East German prime minister
5 May 1990	Beginning of talks between the four World War II powers and the two German states over unification and the status of Berlin.
1 July 1990	Currency union between the two German states; the West German DM becomes the sole currency.
14–18 July 1990	Kohl-Gorbachev summit in the Soviet Union
23 August 1990	GDR parliament agrees to join the Federal Republic on 3 October 1990
12 September 1990	Conclusion of "2 + 4" talks; World War II allies agree to give up all rights in Germany and Berlin
3 October 1990	GDR joins the Federal Republic; Day of Unity a national holiday
2 December 1990	First all-German election. Kohl-led governing coalition is returned with an increased majority

ing it would eventually lead to demands for unification and the end of the East German state. They were right.

In the summer and fall of 1989 East Germans on "vacation" used the newly opened border between Hungary and Austria to escape to the West. Later, the "Great Escape" would also take place via Czechoslovakia and even Poland. Between May and September, 1989 over 90,000 East Germans had fled, the largest number since the construction of the Berlin Wall in 1961. Meanwhile, those who stayed behind began to demonstrate and organize new, but illegal, opposition political parties. By October, 1989 when Gorbachev arrived in East Berlin to commemorate the fortieth anniversary of the regime, an additional 60,000 East Germans had departed. Gorbachev told the aging and ailing East German leader Erich Honecker that the time for reform had come and that "life punishes those who arrive too late." His warning fell on deaf ears.

The demonstrations continued as hundreds of thousands took to the streets in Leipzig, East Berlin and other cities chanting *"Wir sind das Volk!"* ("We are the people!") and demanding reforms. For the first time in German history, a grass-roots democratic revolution was under way. By mid-October, Honecker was forced to resign. On 9 November 1989 in a desperate attempt to acquire some popular support, the new Communist leadership opened the country's borders to West Germany including the Berlin Wall. As the world watched, millions of East Germans flooded into Berlin and West Germany. But the vast majority returned and now called for a unified Germany—*"Wir sind ein Volk!"* ("We are one people!") was added to their demands.

By the end of 1989 the East German state was on the verge of collapse. The country's first (and last) free elections were set for March, 1990. West German parties moved quickly to organize the East German electorate. At the election, about 80 percent of the voters supported parties advocating a speedy unification. In May, 1990 the two German states concluded a treaty which unified their monetary, economic, and social security systems. On 1 July 1990, the West German Mark (DM) became the sole legal currency for all of Germany. On 3 October 1990, less than a year after the fall of the Berlin Wall, East Germany ceased to exist, and, reconstituted as five states, joined the Federal Republic. Europe's almost eighty million Germans were once again united in a single state. But unlike the Bismarckian Reich or Hitler's Third Reich, German unity in 1990 was achieved without violence and with the full support of its neighbors in East and Western Europe.

The focus of German politics now is on the economic, social, and political integration of these new East German states into the Federal

Republic. In the present phase Germany must also adapt to a new role as Western and Central Europe's strongest power. While the Federal Republic remains committed to the Western Alliance and is firmly embedded in the European Community, it must accept more responsibility in the international arena, especially in its relationships with the newer democracies of Eastern Europe and the former Soviet Union. The days when the Federal Republic was content to be an "economic giant, but a political dwarf" are past.

In the enlarged Federal Republic there are also more citizens who question the necessity of Germany's membership in NATO and especially the continued presence of large numbers of foreign troops and nuclear weapons on German soil. Sentiments favoring a more neutral foreign policy and large-scale reductions in defense programs have clearly increased through the unification process.

Social and Economic Structure

Throughout its history West Germany has enjoyed a relatively continuous pattern of increased economic growth and prosperity. While not immune to the ups and downs of the business cycle and the world economy, West Germany's economic record cannot be matched by any other large, advanced, industrial society, with the possible exception of Japan. The country's three postwar recessions in 1966–67, 1974–76, and 1981–82 were mild by prewar German and international standards. The last recession, which followed the 1979 oil price shock, was the most severe: unemployment doubled to over two million, and the economy failed to grow in 1981 and 1982. By 1991, however, unemployment in West Germany had dropped from over 10 percent at the height of the 1981–82 recession to about 6 percent, and the economy has grown each year since 1982.

What has this economic performance meant for the average German in the past forty years? Table 11.2 shows the average net yearly wage for employees, blue and white collar, from 1949 to 1989. In 1949 the net annual wage, after taxes and social security deductions, for a German employee was about $1,400. By 1969 this had increased to about $4,750, and in 1989 the net annual wage of a worker was about $13,400. Thus there has been an increase of about 950 per cent in net wages. In terms of buying power (i.e., net wages adjusted for inflation), the increase has been about 375 percent. This is the highest real increase in wages and salaries among the world's ten major industrialized countries.

TABLE 11.2

AVERAGE YEARLY NET WAGES OF EMPLOYEES

(MANUAL AND WHITE COLLAR)

1949–89

	1949	*1969*	*1989*
Nominal, net after taxes	$1,385	$4,750	$13,390
Corrected for inflation	1,385	3,372	4,545

SOURCE: Federal Bank Statistics cited in *Das Parlament*, no. 17 (21 April 1989): 16. 2 DM = $1.00

Federalism

Germany, unlike Britain or France, is a federal state in which certain governmental functions are reserved to the constituent states. Each of the sixteen has its own constitution and parliament. The states have fundamental responsibility for education, the mass media, and internal security and order (police power). In addition, most laws passed at the national level are administered by the bureaucracies of the states. As table 11.3 shows, the states vary widely in area, population, and socioeconomic structure. The three "city states" of Hamburg, Berlin, and Bremen are largely Protestant and industrial commercial areas. They have generally been strongholds of the Social Democrats throughout the postwar period. The two other northern Protestant states are Schleswig-Holstein, which is relatively rural and small town, and Lower Saxony, which is more balanced between urban-industrial and rural-agrarian activity. Politically, Schleswig-Holstein's politics have been generally in the hands of the Christian Democrats. In 1988, however, following a major Watergate-style "dirty tricks" scandal, the Social Democrats won an absolute majority for the first time in the state's history. Lower Saxony has had a more competitive style of party politics with relatively frequent alternations between SPD and Christian Democratic-led governments.

The most populous state is North-Rhine Westphalia, which contains over 20 percent of the Federal Republic's 79.7 million inhabitants. A heavily industrialized and urbanized state, North Rhine Westphalia has a relative balance between Catholics and Protestants. Its politics have been largely controlled by the Social Democrats during the past fifteen years. Another very industrialized, religiously balanced, western

TABLE 11.3

THE STATES OF THE FEDERAL REPUBLIC

I. Area and population

	Capital	1991 population (millions)	Area (thousands of sq. km.)	Population per sq. km.
North-Rhine Westphalia	Düsseldorf	17.3	34.1	507
Bavaria	Munich	11.4	70.6	161
Baden-Württemberg	Stuttgart	9.8	35.8	274
Lower Saxony	Hanover	7.4	47.4	156
Hesse	Wiesbaden	5.8	21.1	275
Saxony	Dresden	4.8	17.7	271
Rhineland-Palatinate	Mainz	3.8	19.8	192
Berlin	—	3.4	.9	3,778
Saxony-Anhalt	Magdeburg	2.9	20.3	143
Schleswig-Holstein	Kiel	2.6	15.7	166
Brandenburg	Potsdam	2.6	29.0	90
Thuringia	Erfurt	2.6	15.2	171
Mecklenburg–West Pomerania	Schwerin	1.9	26.7	71
Hamburg	—	1.6	.7	2,286
Saar	Saarbrücken	1.1	2.6	423
Bremen	Bremen	.7	.4	1,750
Total or average		79.7	358.0	223

Continued ...

state is Hesse, which has been ruled by Social Democrats for most of the postwar period.

The remaining Western states—the Rhineland-Palatinate and the Saarland—are heavily Catholic. The Rhineland is less industrialized than the much smaller Saarland, which has had an extensive, but now declining, steel industry. In the Saar, the Social Democrats were in the minority until 1985, when they won their first state election since 1945. The Rhineland-Palatinate until 1991 had been governed continuously by Christian Democratic led coalitions. The Social Democratic–Free Democratic coalition formed in 1991 is the first in the state's history.

TABLE II.3 — *Continued.*

THE STATES OF THE FEDERAL REPUBLIC

II. Gross national product

	Total ($ billions)	Percentage of total	Per capita ($)
North-Rhine Westphalia	335.9	24.0	19,416
Bavaria	235.1	16.7	20,627
Baden-Württemberg	219.6	15.6	22,412
Lower Saxony	116.3	8.3	15,714
Hesse	116.3	8.3	20,048
Saxony	37.1	2.6	7,729
Rhineland-Palatinate	64.6	4.6	17,000
Berlin	57.1	4.0	16,794
Saxony-Anhalt	19.2	1.4	6,616
Schleswig-Holstein	51.7	3.7	19,877
Brandenburg	17.3	1.2	6,635
Thuringia	17.2	1.2	6,610
Mecklenburg–West Pomerania	12.7	1.0	6,694
Hamburg	64.6	4.6	40,375
Saar	19.4	1.8	17,618
Bremen	13.9	1.0	18,457
Total or average	1,398.0	100.0	16,414

Continued ...

West Germany's "sunbelt" is composed of the two states of Bavaria and Baden-Württemberg. Bavaria is strongly Catholic. It is the only large state whose borders were restored intact following the war. It terms itself a "free state" with its own strong historical traditions. Separatism in various forms has at times been a significant force in Bavarian politics. It has been governed without interruption since 1946 by the Christian Social Union (CSU), the sister party of the Christian Democratic Union (CDU), that is, the CDU does not contest elections in Bavaria. Historically rural and small town in character, Bavaria has become an increasingly industrialized and urbanized state in the postwar period. It is the center of the country's aerospace industry.

TABLE 11.3 — *Continued.*
THE STATES OF THE FEDERAL REPUBLIC

III. Work force, religion, politics

	Foreign residents %	Work force in agriculture (1987) %	Roman Catholic %	Governing party or coalition
North-Rhine Westphalia	8	2	51	SPD
Bavaria	6	7	69	CSU
Baden-Württemberg	10	5	46	CDU-SDP
Lower Saxony	4	7	19	SPD-Green
Hesse	9	3	33	SPD-Green
Saxony	1	7	5	CDU
Rhineland-Palatinate	5	6	55	SPD-FDP
Berlin	12	–	11	CDU-SPD
Saxony-Anhalt	1	12	8	CDU-FDP
Schleswig-Holstein	3	5	6	SPD
Brandenburg	1	15	5	SPD-FDP-Alliance 90/Green
Thuringia	1	10	9	CDU-FDP
Mecklenburg-West Pomerania	1	20	5	CDU-FDP
Hamburg	10	–	8	SPD
Saar	5	–	73	SPD
Bremen	8	–	10	SPD-FDP-Green
Weighted average	6	5	36	

Baden-Württemberg in the past fifteen years has had the most dynamic economy of any state. It is the location for many of Germany's computer, robotics, and other high tech industries and the home of Daimler-Benz and Porsche. Its high rate of economic growth contrasts with the more sluggish economies of many northern areas. The Christian Democrats have been the dominant party in this state.

The New Eastern States

The five new states which joined the Federal Republic in 1990 are all relatively small. The largest state, Saxony, with about five million residents, is only the sixth largest of the sixteen states. Saxony is also the major industrial center of the former East Germany, accounting for about 35 percent of the area's gross national product. Before 1933 Saxony was a stronghold of the Social Democrats, but the Christian Democrats won an absolute majority at the state's first free election in 1990. The strip-mining of lignite, an outmoded chemical industry, and decades of neglect have left the state with massive environmental problems.

The remaining four states are all less industrialized than Saxony. Its neighbor, Saxony-Anhalt, has the shortest history as an independent political entity. The state, which contains some of Germany's most fertile farm land, is currently governed by a coalition of Christian Democrats and Free Democrats. Thuringia, with 2.6 million inhabitants has a more mixed economy than Saxony or Saxony-Anhalt. It was the center of the former East Germany's high-tech microelectronics industry. The Christian Democrats and Free Democrats won Thuringia's first state election in 1990. Brandenburg, which was once the core province of Prussia, is a sparsely populated state in the northeast. Until 1920 Berlin was a province of Brandenburg; the city lies within its borders and the two states may merge into a single state in the near future. It is the only state where the Social Democrats are the dominant party. The SPD governs in coalition with the FDP and the Greens. The smallest of the new states in population with less than two million residents is the coastal state of Mecklenburg–West Pomerania. This region is primarily agricultural, but it has a shipping industry which could become competitive in the international market place. The Christian Democrats and the Free Democrats formed this state's first freely elected government in 1990.

Geographical

The newly unified Germany comprises about three-fourths of the pre–World War II territory of the German Reich. The remainder is now part of Poland or Russia. With a total area of about 138,000 square miles, the Federal Republic is roughly half the size of Texas. Its population of almost eighty million, however, makes Germany one of Europe's largest and most densely populated states. Since 1945 the population has grown through (1) the influx between 1945 and 1961 of fourteen million refugees and expellees from Germany's former eastern territories and East Germany; (2) the migration of foreign workers, which began in the late 1950s and reached a high point of about three million workers in 1973; and (3) the addition of sixteen million East Germans by unification. Since the late 1980s almost one million ethnic Germans, largely from Poland, the Soviet Union, and other areas in Eastern Europe, have resettled in West Germany.

During the past two decades, however, the Federal Republic has had one of Europe's and the world's lowest birthrates. Indeed, deaths have out numbered births in most of these years, and whatever growth in population West Germany has experienced has been due to foreign workers and their much higher birthrates. Between 1970 and 1987, the native population actually declined by 1.3 million, while the number of foreign residents increased by 1.7 million. If these trends continue, the native German population will decline to seventy million by the year 2000.

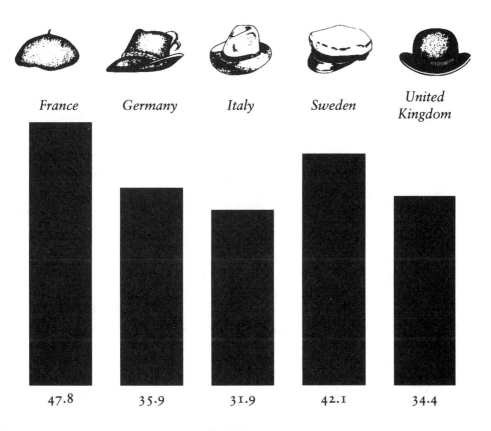

FIGURE 11.1
VOTE FOR SOCIALIST AND COMMUNIST PARTIES (IN PERCENT)

NOTE: Most recent election.

The effects of World War II are still noticeable in the age and sex distribution of the population. The low wartime birthrate and casualty losses have left some age groups (35–45, 50–55, and 60–65) under-represented in the population relative to other groups. Because of the war, women are still in the majority (52 percent), and almost 60 percent of persons over sixty-five are females.

Religion

Most West Germans are "born" into one of two churches: the Roman Catholic or the Evangelical Protestant (Lutheran).[3] Since the Reformation, Protestants and Catholics have been divided along regional lines. The east and north are predominantly Protestant; in the south and west adherents of Roman Catholicism are in the majority. Historically the respective secular rulers (princes) in these areas acted as "protectors" of the faith in their kingdoms, thus making the churches dependent on state authority for their survival. The close, dependent relationship with the state meant that both churches, but especially the Protestant, which has no international ties comparable to those of the Roman Catholics, were conservative, status quo oriented institutions. The separation of church and state, fundamental in the political tradition of the United States, is thus alien to the German political tradition; both churches occupy a privileged position in society and politics.

The Lutheran and Catholic churches are largely financed through a church tax, a surcharge of about 7 to 10 percent on the individual income tax. The tax is collected by the state via withholding and is transferred free of charge to the churches' treasuries. This tax ensures them of a generous and inflation-proof income. The Cologne archdiocese of the Roman Catholic church, for example, is the richest in the world. An individual can escape the church tax only by formally leaving the church, a procedure that most people have declined to follow. Yet between 1970 and 1987, the proportion of citizens electing to contract out of the church tax increased from 8 percent to 15 percent. Religious instruction in public schools by teachers acceptable to the churches is paid from public funds, and the state also pays the salaries of some church officials.

Although formal affiliation with the established churches is generally automatic and hence high, most West Germans and especially Protestants are religiously not very active. Only about 15 percent of Protestants and 35 percent of Catholics report "regular" attendance at church services. Church attendance is strongly related to gender and age, with older females being especially active.

In spite of this at best moderate level of religiosity in postwar Germany, the political position and influence of the churches have been strong. The postwar occupation authorities viewed the churches as relatively untainted by Nazism and gave them preferential treatment. In addition, the Christian Democratic Union (CDU), the dominant political party from 1949 to 1969, was generally successful in projecting an image as a political movement that would govern with some regard to Christian principles. Cynics and political opponents strongly disputed this CDU claim to be more concerned with religion and morality than other parties, but the CDU has definitely enjoyed the favor of, especially, the Catholic church. While in power, the CDU reciprocated by being particularly sensitive to the issues such as state support of church schools and strict divorce and abortion laws stressed by the church. This close CDU–Catholic church relationship also compelled the Social Democrats by the late 1950s to seek at least a normalized, less conflictual relationship with the church.

Religion in East Germany

Historically, the regions that comprised East Germany were predominantly (about 90 percent) Protestant. The Communist regime imposed after 1945 at first tried to eliminate the churches as independent social institutions. Funds for the upkeep of Church buildings, seminaries, publications as well as the salaries of pastors were steadily reduced. Religious instruction was banned from the schools and replaced by courses on "scientific atheism." As a substitute for the traditional confirmation, the communist party instituted a *Jugendweihe* ceremony in which young people pledged fidelity to socialism and eternal friendship with the Soviet Union. Failure to participate usually meant that the young person would be denied admission to a university-track secondary school program. This antireligious policy of the regime had some success. Only 21 percent of East Germans as compared to 61 percent of West Germans, believe "there is a God" and belief in a life after death is held by 14 percent in the East and 51 percent in the West.[4] About 55 percent of East Germans in 1990 reported no religious affiliation as compared to 15 percent in West Germany. About 40 percent of East Germans remain affiliated with the Protestant church, which throughout all of the turmoil of the past forty years still maintained close ties with its West German counterpart; about 7 percent are practicing Catholics.

The addition of East Germany to the Federal Republic in 1990 has made it a more secular society. The proportion of all Germans with no ties to the churches has increased to about 22 percent. Whether East Germans who left the churches because of political pressures will now return is an open question.

Socioeconomic

The Federal Republic is an urban, industrial, and economically prosperous society. But it also has a stratified social structure with considerable degrees of inequality between different socioeconomic classes.

Most Germans live in towns and cities with populations greater than 20,000; over half of the 79.7 million inhabitants live on less than 10 percent of the land. There are nine major urban areas whose population exceeds one million: the Rhine-Ruhr region between the cities of Düsseldorf and Dortmund, the Rhine-Main, or Frankfurt, area, Berlin, Stuttgart, Hamburg, Munich, the Rhine-Neckar region, and in the East the Leipzig and Dresden regions.

Germany is one of the world's major economic powers. Its per capita income, industrial production, and currency reserves are among the world's highest. It consistently ranks, along with the United States and Japan, as one of the world's largest trading nations. The economic system is "mixed" with private property and free enterprise coexisting with substantial state involvement. It is also a "social" market economy in which an elaborate social welfare system is supported by both management and labor, as well as by all significant political parties.

Industrial production is the largest single contributor to the country's gross national product. A look at table 11.4 shows that the dominant industrial enterprises are concentrated in the electronics, automobile, chemical, and energy fields. White-collar, technical, and service employees now constitute the largest occupational group. Between 1950 and 1989, the proportion of the work force in these occupations increased from 23 percent to 48 percent. Industrial workers, once the largest group, now constitute 38 percent of the work force. The remainder is composed of those in independent nonmanual occupations (small businessmen, shopkeepers), independent professionals (physicians, lawyers), and farmers.

The fruits of the economic system have enabled the great majority of citizens to achieve a high standard of living. In spite of inflation, the disposable income of all occupational groups, including industrial workers, has steadily risen during the past forty years. Foreign vaca-

TABLE 11.4

THE TEN LARGEST FIRMS IN THE FEDERAL REPUBLIC
(BY GROSS SALES)

Enterprise	in DM bill.
Daimler-Benz (motor vehicles, electronics)	86
Volkswagen[a] (motor vehicles)	68
Siemens (electronics)	63
VEBA[a] (energy)	55
BASF (chemicals)	47
Hoechst (chemicals)	45
RWE[a] (energy)	44
Bayer (chemicals)	42
Thyssen (steel)	36
Bosch (electronics)	35

SOURCE: *Die Zeit,* 31 (26 July 1991): 20.

a. Partially under state ownership.

tions, automobiles, television sets, and modern appliances and gadgets are now commonplace in most families.

Nonetheless, inequality is very much a characteristic of German society. The same manual worker who is satiated with consumer goods is much less likely in his lifetime to own a home or apartment. His children in all likelihood will not receive a university education. The inequality is greatest in the areas of income and capital resources. Table 11.5 presents the average monthly income in 1988 for independents (professionals, owners, and directors of enterprises), white-collar employees (including civil servants), and manual workers. Independents enjoyed an average monthly income that was 153 percent greater than the monthly income of manual workers. White-collar workers and civil servants had a 31 percent greater income than manual workers.

When one examines the ownership of *capital resources* (land, stocks, bonds, securities, savings, life insurance) the differences are even greater (see table 11.6). Independents and farmers, comprising only 10 percent of all households, held over 44 percent of the nation's capital. On a per capita basis they had resources averaging about $190,000. For manual workers, the average amount of capital (mainly savings accounts and life insurance) was only about $4,600, and for white-collar employees about $8,400. Civil servants, although far below the level of

TABLE II.5

MONTHLY INCOME BY OCCUPATION, 1988

Occupational group	Average monthly income[a]
Independents (owners, directors of enterprises, free professionals, farmers)	$6,020
White collar, civil servant	2,380
Manual worker	1,820

SOURCE: Federal Statistical Office, Wiesbaden.

a. 2.00 DM equals $1.00.

TABLE II.6

CAPITAL RESOURCES, BY OCCUPATION

Occupation	Percent of households	Percent of capital resources	Capital resources per capita[a]
Independents (owners, directors of enterprises, free professionals) and farmers	10.2	44.1	$190,000
Civil servants	6.3	4.4	25,500
White-collar employees	20.1	14.8	8,400
Manual workers	28.2	15.8	4,600
Nonemployed (retired, housewives, students, etc.)	35.2	20.9	3,900

SOURCE: Horst Mierheim and Lutz Wicke, *Die personelle Vermögensverteilung in der Bundesrepublik Deutschland* (Tübingen: J.C.B. Mohr Verlag, 1978), cited in M. Jungblut, "Die heimlichen Reichen," *Die Zeit,* no. 46 (10 November 1978): 25.

NOTE: Capital resources include land, stocks, bonds, securities, savings, life insurance.

a. 2.00 DM equals $1.00.

independents, still held capital resources that were on the average worth over five times more than the capital of manual workers.

These data show that beneath the surface prosperity of the Federal Republic are substantial differences in personal wealth. This distribution of capital reflects in part the postwar decision of German and Allied occupation elites to take the free-market route to economic recovery. West German political leaders of all major parties, even the Social Democrats, have generally sought to create a favorable climate for investment capital through low tax rates on profits and dividends, as well as subsidies and tax benefits for new plants and equipment. The currency reform of 1948, for example, clearly favored capital-holding groups. Citizens with savings accounts or cash in old Reichsmarks received only about 1 new mark (DM) for every 14 old marks. Thus millions of lower- and lower-middle-class Germans saw their savings largely wiped out. Those with stocks, securities, and land lost nothing.

Education

The German educational system has generally reflected and reinforced this socioeconomic inequality. Traditionally this system was designed to give a basic, general education to all and advanced academic training to only a few. Most education is still structured along three tracks. At about the age of six, all children enter a four-year primary school. But in most states, after the fourth year, with most children at about the age of ten, the tracking process begins.

1. About 35 percent of all children will attend a general secondary school for an additional six years. After this, at about the age of sixteen or seventeen, they will enter the work force, in most cases as apprentices, and attend vocational school part-time for about three years.
2. A second group, comprising about 30 percent of a given age group, will attend an intermediate school (*Realschule*) for six to eight years. The *Realschule* combines academic and job-oriented training. Medium-level careers in business and administration usually require a middle-school educational background.
3. The remaining 35 percent of school-age children will pursue an academic or university-level educational program. Attendance at an academic high school (*Gymnasium*) for up to nine years culminates in the *Abitur* (a degree roughly comparable to an American junior college diploma) and the right to attend a university.

It is possible for children to change tracks, especially during the first two or three years, which are considered an orientation period. Most students, however, do not switch, and the decision made by their parents and teachers after four to six years of school is usually decisive for their educational and occupational future.

The entire system has a class bias. *Gymnasium* and the university are still largely preserves of the middle and upper-middle classes, and the majority of children in the general vocational track come from working-class backgrounds. One study, conducted in 1980, found that the children of government officials were twenty times more likely to attend a *Gymnasium* than were the children of manual workers; the children of self-employed and white-collar employees also were much more likely to be in the academic track than were the offspring of manual workers.[5]

But the trend since the 1950s has been toward a reduction of this bias. Between 1955 and 1985, for example, the proportion of children from working-class families enrolled at universities increased from 4 percent to 20 percent. This is in part the result of a large enrollment increase in the *Gymnasia*. In the past twenty years, attendance in the university preparatory track has tripled.

German education also has no lack of critics. There has been no more controversial policy area in the last twenty years than education. Critics and reformers emphasize, in addition to the class bias, the system's inflexibility: the difficulty children have in changing tracks as their interests and values change. The key element in plans for reforming and restructuring education is the merger of the three-tracked secondary system into a single comprehensive school (*Gesamtschule*). Instead of tracking after the fourth grade, all children would remain in the same school for an additional six years, or until about the age of sixteen. At that point, the tracking process would begin. The purpose of the comprehensive school plan is to provide more equality of educational opportunity and social mobility. Since 1969, comprehensive schools have been introduced in all states, but more extensively in those governed by social democratic or liberal political parties. Conservatives have generally opposed comprehensive schools, citing their concerns about a decline in educational standards and their support for the traditional *Gymnasium*.

Education in East Germany

The East German states are currently restructuring their educational systems to the West German pattern. This is a massive task involving the establishment of new schools, curricula, textbooks, and teacher retraining. The communist system, in addition to the standard academic subjects, included extensive programs designed to indoctrinate young people with Marxist-Leninist ideology and thus produce the "new Socialist person." The influence of the communist party was pervasive. Many teachers and almost all school administrators were in the party. Communist youth organizations, modeled on their counterparts in the Soviet Union, were present in all schools.

Most teachers are now on probationary status and are being given the opportunity to demonstrate that they can adapt to the demands of education in a free society. Many administrators—principals and assistant principals—have been dismissed or demoted. It is expected that about 30,000 of the 185,000 teachers and administrators in the old GDR will be replaced after the probationary period.[6]

Political Attitudes

In 1949, few if any observers in Germany or elsewhere gave the Federal Republic much of a chance to survive, much less prosper. The decision to establish a West German state was made by neither the German political leadership nor the German electorate in any referendum; it was the decision of the three victorious Western powers in World War II—the United States, Britain, and France. The Federal Republic was a product of the foreign policies of these countries, which sought to counter what they perceived as a growing Soviet threat in Central and Western Europe. The Germans living in the American, British, and French occupation zones thus had imposed on them by their conquerors a new political system, which they were to regard as their own. Moreover, the new state was to be a liberal parliamentary democracy, a form of government that Germany had tried between 1918 and 1933 with disastrous consequences. Even the committed democrats in postwar Germany had few fond memories of that first democratic experience—the Weimar Republic. In addition, this establishment of a West German state was seen by some citizens as a move that would result in the permanent division of the country. Hence the regional and state leaders in the Western zones, who were requested to begin the process of drafting a constitution for the new state, were very reluctant to make the republic appear as a permanent entity. The constitution that was drafted was not even called such, but rather a Basic Law.

But while the Germans were not consulted about their new state, many of them in 1949 did not really care. The great majority of the population had had enough of "politics," "parties," and "ideals." Following the mobilization of the Nazi years, the incessant propaganda, the endless calls for sacrifice, and the demands of total war, they wanted above all to put their private lives back together again. They had been badly burned by politics and were quite willing to let someone else, even foreigners, make political decisions for them as long as they were more or less left alone to pursue their private concerns—the family, making a living, catching up for all that was missed during the war years. This privatized character of postwar attitudes meant that both Allied and German political elites had considerable freedom to develop and initiate policies. The Germans, in short, were willing to follow the orders of their occupiers that they now be citizens in a democracy, even though most inhabitants had little if any experience with a successful, functioning democratic political order. Thus the institutions of democracy preceded the development of an attitudinal consensus on democracy. The need to educate the postwar population and change political attitudes was, however, strongly perceived by Western and especially American occupation authorities and by some Germans.

But one did not have to be an enthusiastic supporter of political democracy to oppose any sort of return to a Nazi-style dictatorship after 1945. Apart from any personal predilection for a one-party state, the *performance* of the Third Reich made it distinctly unattractive as an alternative for most citizens in the postwar period. While there has been a consistent relationship between a positive attitude toward the Third Reich and opposition to the key values and institutions of the Bonn Republic after 1945, it should not be overlooked that a sizable proportion of respondents with little sympathy for liberal democracy still rejected a return to some form of dictatorship. These non- or antidemocrats were nonetheless not willing to support a restoration. This was hardly a firm foundation on which to build a stable and effective political democracy, yet it did provide postwar elites and the consciously democratic segments of the larger population with a breathing space in which the republic was given an opportunity to perform and socialize postwar generations to its values and norms.

The early years of the republic were characterized by an ambivalence on the part of many citizens about political democracy. Surveys revealed that significant proportions of the population retained the traditional authoritarian if not antidemocratic attitudes acquired during earlier regimes. In 1949, for example, about half of the population still agreed with the statement that "National Socialism was a good idea, which was only badly carried out." When asked to choose between a hypothetical government that guaranteed economic success and security and one that guaranteed political freedom, Germans in the late 1940s preferred the former by a two-to-one margin.[7]

In the early 1950s, about a fourth of the adult population still preferred a one-party state; almost half of the electorate in 1951 stated they would be "indifferent" to an attempt by a new Nazi party to take power; and one of every three adults had positive attitudes toward a restoration of the monarchy. Moreover, although the turnout at elections was high, most voters went to the polls out of a sense of duty and not because they believed they were participating in the making of important political decisions. Only about a fourth of the population in the early 1950s expressed any interest in political questions, and most citizens reported that they rarely talked about politics with family or friends. They had, in short, largely withdrawn from political involvement beyond the simple act of going to the polls.

This pattern of mass political attitudes and behavior was not conducive to the long-run viability of the Bonn Republic should it have encountered a major economic or social crisis. Most citizens in the 1950s, even those with fascist or authoritarian dispositions, were quite willing to support political democracy as embodied in the Federal Republic as long as it "worked," but they could not be counted on if the system encountered major problems. The Germans were "fair-weather" and not "rain or shine" democrats, but they were willing to give democracy a chance.

As the Federal Republic entered its fifth decade, this pattern of political attitudes changed.[8] There was now a solid consensus on the basic values, institutions, and processes of parliamentary democracy. Support for such key values as political competition, freedom of speech, civil liberties, and the rule of law ranged from a minimum of about 75 percent to over 95 percent for a principle such as political competition. Similar proportions of citizens by the 1980s had a positive orientation toward the parliament, the constitution itself, and the federal structure of the state. Consistent with this consensus on the present political system is the high level of satisfaction with the way democracy is functioning. As table 11.7 shows, Germans are the most satisfied of the major European countries in which this question was asked.

Political Attitudes in East Germany

The 16 million people who joined the Federal Republic in 1990 lived for forty years in a different political, economic, social and cultural

TABLE 11.7

SATISFACTION WITH DEMOCRACY

(GERMANY, BRITAIN, FRANCE, ITALY)

Q. *On the whole, are you very satisfied, fairly satisfied, not very satisfied, or not at all satisfied with the way democracy works in [name of country]?*

	Germany[a]	Britain	France	Italy	European Community[b]
Satisfied[c]	75%	50%	42%	21%	52%
Not satisfied[d]	22	44	50	76	43
Undecided or no response	3	6	8	3	5

SOURCE: Commission of the European Communities, *Euro-Barometer, Trends, 1974–1990* (Brussels: March 1991), 21, 24, 26, 30, 31.

a. German percentages include the former East Germany.
b. Twelve-nation average.
c. Percentage "very satisfied" and "fairly satisfied."
d. Percentage "not very satisfied" and "not at all satisfied."

setting than West Germans. What effects will unification have on the overall pattern of political attitudes discussed above? Will the postwar consensus on liberal democratic values, institutions and processes change? Will the Federal Republic move to the left as East Germans demand the types of social and economic programs—a guaranteed job, low rents, subsidized food, low-cost day care—that some in the old German Democratic Republic consider the successes of the former communist regime?

It is too early to give definitive answers to these questions. Only since the opening of the Berlin Wall in 1989 have social scientists had free access to East Germany. The rapid pace of events since 1989—the opening of the borders, the currency union, unification, the collapse of the economy—also make it difficult to determine how well-defined East German political attitudes have become. Tossed and turned by unprecedented developments, it could be argued that few East Germans have any stable political attitudes.

The evidence thus far is mixed. On the one hand, there is little doubt about the commitment to democratic values among the East German revolutionaries who brought down the communist regime. The great majority of voters in a series of free elections in 1990 also supported democratic parties. On the other hand, there is also evidence that forty years of authoritarian rule have left their mark on the East German political psyche. Recent studies have found that East Germans are more authoritarian and alienated than West Germans. They are more supportive of the "old" German values of discipline, order, and hard work than the "new values" of individualism, self-realization, and tolerance. They have less trust in the institutions of liberal democracy such as the parliament and courts than West Germans. Their acceptance of foreign residents is also lower than that of West Germans. East Germans also have a more simplistic, either/or conception of democracy than do West Germans. They see democracy either as a very elitist system, that is, the Chancellor or state must take care of them, or as a very participatory system, that is, we must demonstrate to secure our demands. Democracy as a system in which intermediate organizations such as parties, interest groups, and parliament play key roles of channeling citizen demands into policies is still poorly understood in the former East Germany.[9]

These findings are not surprising. While they have been able to watch democracy in the West through television, East Germans are new at participation in democratic politics. As in West Germany during the 1950s and 1960s, the *performance* of the democratic order will be a key factor in the political integration of East Germany.

The stability and performance of German democracy during the past forty years do not mean that the Federal Republic is a political system without problems or that it has become an ideal democracy. As we discuss later, Germany is a society with many problems; they include the massive challenge of rebuilding East Germany's society and economy, that is, putting the country "back together again," discrimination against both political and social minorities as well as a myriad of economic and social problems—energy, the environment, housing, health care costs, unemployment—shared by other advanced industrial societies. Germany must still deal with the legacy of its Nazi past, its national identity, and its new role in international politics. It also does not mean that there are no individuals and groups calling for basic changes in the country's social, economic, and political structures. There is a segment of politically involved citizens, including numerous intellectuals, who regard the postwar system as a reactionary capitalist society that is hardly better than the fascist system it replaced. Indeed, these critics treat the Federal Republic as a country in which the capitalist system, which they argue was directly responsible for Hitler and the Third Reich, was "restored." What the data signify, however, is that these problems will be debated within a consensual framework. In short, the question is no longer whether Germany will remain a liberal democracy, but what kind of and how much democracy the country will have. This is a question that other West European societies also face.

Notes

1. Most respondents over age 45 in 1951 considered the imperial years, 1900–14, to be the best Germany had experienced in this century. Institut für Demoskopie Survey No. 0044, October 1951.

2. Helmut Schmidt, "Erklärung der Bundesregierung zur Lage der Nation vor dem deutschen Bundestag," 17 May 1979, printed in *Bulletin*, no. 64 (Bonn, 18 May 1979): 596.

3. About 40,000 Jews live in the Federal Republic. Seventy-three Jewish congregations receive state financial support. The largest (over 5,000 members) Jewish communities are in West Berlin and Frankfurt. Since the collapse of the Soviet Union, almost 10,000 Jews from Eastern Europe have settled in Germany, mainly in Berlin.

4. *Der Spiegel*, Spezial, no. 1 (1991): 73–74.

5. Cited in Russell J. Dalton, *Politics in West Germany* (Glenview, Ill.: Scott, Foresman, 1989), 138.

6. *Der Spiegel*, no. 37 (9 September 1991): 119.

7. Max Kaase, "Bewusstseinslagen und Leitbilder in der Bundesrepublik Deutschland," in *Deutschland-Handbuch. Eine doppelte Bilanz, 1949–1989,* ed. Werner Weidenfeld and Hartmut Zimmermann (Bonn: Bundeszentrale für politische Bildung, 1989), 205.

8. For an analysis of these changes, see David P. Conradt, "Changing German Political Culture," in *The Civic Culture Revisited,* ed. Gabriel Almond and Sidney Verba (Boston: Little, Brown, 1980), 312–72.

9. Ursula Feist, "Zur politischen Akkulturation der vereinten Deutschen. Eine Analyse aus Anlaß der ersten gesamtdeutschen Bundestagswahl," *Aus Politik und Zeitgeschichte,* nos. 11–12 (March 1991): 21–32.

12

Where Is the Power?

Policy-Making Institutions

Political power in the Federal Republic is fragmented and dispersed among a wide variety of institutions and elites. There is no single locus of power. At the national level, there are three major decision-making structures: (1) the Bundestag, the lower house of parliament; (2) the Bundesrat, or Federal Council, which represents the states and is the German equivalent of an upper house; and (3) the federal government, or executive (the chancellor and cabinet). In addition, the sixteen states that constitute the Federal Republic play important roles, especially in the areas of education and internal security. These states also have a direct influence on national policy making through the Bundesrat, which is composed of delegates from each of the states. The Federal Constitutional Court, which has the power of judicial review, has also become an increasingly powerful institution. Finally, a federal president, indirectly elected but with little independent responsibility for policy, serves as the ceremonial head of state and is expected to be a unifying or integrating figure, above the partisan political struggle.

Formal power is vested in these institutions, but their integration and effectiveness is also very much a function of the new party system that has emerged in the postwar period and the well-organized, concentrated system of interest groups.

The Bundestag

Constitutionally, the center of the policy-making process is the Bundestag, a legislative assembly consisting of about 660 deputies who are elected at least every four years. They are the only political officials in the constitutional structure who are directly elected by the people. The constitution assigns to the Bundestag the primary responsibility for (1) legislation, (2) the election and control of the government, (3) the supervision of the bureaucracy and military, and (4) the selection of judges to the Federal Constitutional Court.

Parliamentary government has a weak tradition and a poor record of performance in German political history. During the empire (1871–1918), effective control over important areas such as defense and foreign affairs and the supervision of the civil service was in the hands of a chancellor appointed by the monarch. In addition, Prussian control of the upper house meant that important legislative proposals of the parliament could be blocked at the will of the Prussian ruling elite. Parliament did have the power of the purse as a source of influence, but it could not initiate any major policy programs. Its position toward the executive, bureaucracy, and military was defensive and reactive. While parliament "debated," the government "acted."

Under the Weimar constitution, the powers of parliament were expanded. The chancellor and his cabinet were directly responsible to it and could be removed by a vote of no confidence. But the framers of the constitution made a major error when they also provided for a strong, directly elected president independent of parliament, who could, in "emergency situations" (i.e., when the government lost its parliamentary majority), rule by decree. The Weimar parliament, especially in its later years, was also fragmented into many different, ideologically oriented parties, which made effective legislation difficult. The institution was immobilized—there were frequent majorities *against* governments, but rarely majorities in favor of new governments. At the last elections under the Weimar constitution, most voters elected parties (Nazi, Nationalist, Communist) that were in one way or another committed to the abolition of parliament. It had become identified in the public mind as weak and ineffective. By approving the Nazi Enabling Act in 1933, parliament ceased to function as a legislative institution.

In the postwar parliament, this pattern of legislative immobility has not been repeated. While important initiatives remain the province of the restructured executive, the parliament's status as an instrument of supervision and control has grown.

The Bundestag, similar to other parliaments, has the responsibility to elect and control the government. After each national election a new parliament is convened, with its first order of business the election of the federal chancellor. The control function is, of course, much more complex and occupies a larger share of the chamber's time. Through the procedure of the question hour, adopted from English parliamentary practice, a member may make direct inquiries of the government either orally or in writing about a particular problem. A further control procedure is the parliament's right to investigate governmental activities and to demand the appearance of any cabinet or state official.

The key organizational unit of the Bundestag is the *Fraktion*, the parliamentary caucus of each political party. Committee assignments, debating time, and even office space and clerical assistance are allocated to the *Fraktionen* and not directly to individual deputies. The leadership of these parliamentary parties effectively controls the work of the Bundestag. The freshman deputy soon discovers that a successful and influential parliamentary career is largely dependent on the support of the leadership of his or her parliamentary *Fraktion*.

The parliament has a committee system that is more important than those in Britain and France yet less powerful than the committees in the American Congress. The twenty-one standing committees, like their American counterparts, mirror the partisan composition of the whole parliament; but committee chairmanships are allotted proportionately according to party strength. Thus the minority opposition party or parties will chair several of the standing committees. These committees have become more significant in recent years due to the introduction of American-style "hearings" and the greater use of committee meetings as forums by the opposition. But German committees, like those in other unitary systems, are still reluctant to engage in full-blown criticism of the executive of the sort associated with presidential systems. This reflects the generally higher level of party discipline and the dependence of the government for continuance on having a parliamentary majority. Committee criticism, if comprehensive enough, could be interpreted as an attempt to bring the chancellor down. This is a major problem with strong committee systems in parliamentary governments.

There is also considerable specialization among committee members, and thus the day-to-day sessions tend to concentrate on details of proposed legislation and rarely produce any major news. Committees cannot pigeonhole bills; all must be reported out. About four of every five bills submitted by the government will be reported out with a favorable recommendation, albeit with a variety of suggested revisions and amendments. Outright rejections are rare. When the government discovers that a bill is in trouble, it is usually withdrawn for "further study" before a formal committee vote.

The Bundesrat (Federal Council)

The Bundesrat represents the interests of the states in the national policy-making process. It is composed of sixty-eight members drawn from the sixteen state governments. Each state, depending on its population, is entitled to three to six members. Most Bundesrat sessions are attended by delegates from the state governments and not by the actual formal members, the state-level cabinet ministers.

Throughout most of its history, the Bundesrat concentrated on the administrative aspects of policy making and has rarely initiated legislative proposals. Since the states implement most national legislation, the Bundesrat tended to examine proposed programs from the standpoint of how they can be best administered at the state level. The Bundesrat thus was not an institution in the partisan political spotlight.

In recent years, this focus has changed. While they were in opposition in the Bundestag from 1969 to 1982, the Christian Democrats were the majority party in the Bundesrat. Thus Germany experienced a form of divided government. Between 1972 and 1982, the frequency of Bundesrat objections to government legislation increased to the point where the leaders of the government accused it of becoming the "extended arm" of the parliamentary opposition. It was suggested that the CDU/CSU was seeking to obstruct the government's electoral majority by turning its majority in the Bundesrat into a politicized counter-government. Thus the Bundesrat blocked or forced compromises on the government on issues such as divorce law reform, speed limits on autobahns, higher education reform, tax policy, the controversial "radicals" in public employment law, and the 1976 treaty with Poland.

In 1991 the Social Democrats, after a series of victories in state elections, gained control of the Bundesrat. The party promptly used its majority to force the government to change some provisions of a new tax law designed to finance the costs of unification. The Social Democratic party's majority also insures that it will have major input into any programs proposed by the government.

To become a genuine second chamber, however, the Bundesrat's delegations, still controlled by state leaders, must also be willing to accept direction from the opposition party's national leadership in the lower house. Thus far, this has happened on only some issues. Generally, the more remote the issue from the concerns of state leaders, the more likely they are to go along with the national opposition leadership in the lower house and try to block the bill in the Bundesrat.

The veto of a proposed bill by a two-thirds majority of the Federal Council can be overridden in the Bundestag only by a two-thirds majority of the *members present and voting*. But a party controlling forty-six or more delegates in the Bundesrat, though in a minority in the Bundestag, can nonetheless bring the legislative process to a halt and force new elections. Such a development would run counter to the intentions of the framers of the Basic Law, who did not envision the Bundesrat as such a politically partisan body. Since the composition of the Bundesrat is determined by the respective state governments, political and electoral developments at the state level can have direct national political consequences. A victory by the Social Democrats at a state election in June 1986, for example, would probably have brought down the Kohl government in Bonn. State elections have become Germany's version of "midterm" elections at which national issues and personalities dominate the campaign.

The Chancellor and Cabinet

The chief executive in the Federal Republic is the chancellor. The powers of this office place it somewhere between those of a strong president in the United States and the prime minister in the British parliamentary system. Constitutionally, the German chancellor is less powerful than an American president, yet a chancellor has more authority and is more difficult to remove than a prime minister on the British model.

The Weimar constitution provided for a dual executive: a directly elected president and a chancellor chosen by the parliament. The president was chief of state and commander in chief of the armed forces; he could in an emergency dismiss the chancellor and his cabinet and rule by decree. The president during the final years of the Weimar Republic, former Field Marshal von Hindenburg, misused especially this latter power and helped undermine public support for democratic institutions. During 1932, for example, the last year before the Nazi seizure of power, the parliament passed only five laws, while the president issued sixty-six decrees. The framers of the Basic Law (the federal constitution adopted in 1949 at the insistence of France, Great Britain, and the United States) sought to avoid a repetition of this problem by concentrating executive authority in the chancellor.

The power of the chancellor derives largely from the constitution, the party system, and the precedent established by the first chancellor under the Basic Law, Konrad Adenauer. The constitution makes the chancellor responsible for determining the "main guidelines" of the government's policies. This places him above his ministers, although they are in turn responsible for policy within their specific area. The chancellor also essentially "hires and fires" cabinet ministers. If the parliament wants the removal of a particular cabinet member, it must vote no confidence in the whole government including the chancellor. Bringing down the government via a vote of no confidence has, in turn, become more difficult in the postwar system because of the *constructive vote of no confidence* provision. This means that a parliamentary majority against an incumbent chancellor does not suffice to bring down the government; the opposition must also have a majority *in favor of a new chancellor* before the chancellor and cabinet are dismissed. The provision was intended to protect the chancellor from the shifting and unstable parliamentary majorities that brought down so many Weimar governments without, however, being able to agree on a replacement.

The constructive vote of no confidence has been tried only twice, in April 1972, when the CDU/CSU opposition attempted (unsuccessfully) to bring down the Brandt government, and in October 1982, when Helmut Schmidt was replaced as chancellor by Helmut Kohl. The rare use of this procedure reflects the strength of the new *party system*. A Bonn chancellor, unlike his Weimar predecessors, can usually count on the firm support of a majority of the parliament throughout the four-year session. Since there are fewer but larger parties in the Federal Republic, the political ties between government and parliament are much stronger. The concentration of electoral support in two large, disciplined parties and a small third party has assured most chancellors of firm parliamentary majorities.

Chancellor Democracy

From Adenauer to Kiesinger

The first chancellor of the Federal Republic, Konrad Adenauer, set the standards by which future chancellors would be evaluated. His performance in the office and the substance he gave to its constitutional provisions have influenced all his successors. Adenauer assumed the office at the remarkable age of seventy-three in 1949 and remained until 1963. Prior to the Third Reich, he had been lord mayor of Cologne, but he had never held any national political office during the Weimar Republic. Shortly after the Nazi seizure of power, he was removed from office and was allowed to retire. Although he had some contact with anti-Nazi resistance groups and was arrested, imprisoned, and nearly executed in 1944, he essentially sat out the Third Reich.

His first government had a majority of only fourteen seats. From the beginning, his chancellorship was characterized by a wide variety of domestic and foreign political successes: the "economic miracle," the integration of 10 million refugees from the Eastern territories, membership in the European Community, and the alliance with the United States.

Adenauer used to the fullest extent the powers inherent in the chancellor's office. In firm control of his party, he was out front on all major foreign and domestic policies and usually presented decisions to his cabinet and the parliament as accomplished facts. Under Adenauer, there was no extensive consultation within either the cabinet or the parliament before important decisions were made. The chancellor *led;* he initiated policy proposals, made the decisions, and then submitted them to the cabinet and parliament essentially for ratification. He did not always succeed in this approach; but on most issues, such as rearmament, membership in NATO, and the Common Market, his views prevailed. During his tenure, the office of the chancellor clearly became the center of the policy-making process. All his successors have benefited from the power Adenauer gave to the office. This presidential-like control over the cabinet, bureaucracy, and even parliament soon became known as "chancellor democracy"—a parliamentary system with a strong, quasi-presidential executive.

Adenauer was pessimistic about the capacities of the average German to measure up to the demands of democratic citizenship. Through his authoritarian-paternalistic style, he encouraged Germans to go about the rebuilding of their private lives and leave the politics to the "old man," as he was often termed. Most people probably agreed with this approach, but it meant that his successors would encounter a host of unfinished business, particularly in the area of citizen involvement in public affairs. In retrospect, Adenauer's major contribution was to demonstrate to many Germans, who were indifferent if not ignorant of democratic norms and values, that a liberal republic could be efficient and successful in Germany.

A glance at table 12.1 shows that, thus far, none of Adenauer's successors has been able to match his thirteen-year tenure in office. His first two CDU/CSU successors, Ludwig Erhard and Kurt-Georg Kiesinger, assumed the office at times when support for the CDU/CSU was on the decline. Erhard, a very successful economics minister, never had control of his party. As long as conditions remained favorable, he could attract voters and was thus tolerated by the Christian Democrats. When the first economic recession came in 1966–67, he was promptly dropped, with his own party taking the lead in urging his departure. Kiesinger became chancellor of the Grand Coalition government with the SPD,

TABLE 12.1

CHANCELLORS AND GOVERNING COALITIONS, 1949–90

Date	Governing parties	Chancellor
1949–53	CDU/CSU[a]–FDP[b]–DP[c]	Adenauer
1953–57	CDU/CSU–FDP–DP–GB/BHE[d]	Adenauer
1957–61	CDU/CSU–DP	Adenauer
1961–63	CDU/CSU–FDP	Adenauer
1963–65	CDU/CSU–FDP	Erhard
1965–66	CDU/CSU–FDP	Erhard
1966–69	CDU/CSU–SPD[e]	Kiesinger
1969–72	SPD–FDP	Brandt
1972–74	SPD–FDP	Brandt
1974–76	SPD–FDP	Schmidt
1976–80	SPD–FDP	Schmidt
1980–82	SPD–FDP	Schmidt
1982–83	CDU/CSU–FDP	Kohl
1983–87	CDU/CSU–FDP	Kohl
1987–90	CDU/CSU–FDP	Kohl
1990–	CDU/CSU–FDP	Kohl

a. Christian Democratic Union (CDU)/Christian Social Union (CSU
b. Free Democratic Party (FDP)
c. German Party (DP)
d. Refugee Party (BHE)
e. Social Democratic Party (SPD)

a novel arrangement that called for a person adept at compromise and mediation with a record of good relations with the Social Democrats. There was no one in Bonn who met these requirements. Kiesinger came from Stuttgart where he had been chief executive of Baden-Württemberg. When the CDU/CSU failed to gain sufficient votes at the 1969 election to form another government, Kiesinger passed from the national scene.

The Social Democratic Chancellors: Brandt and Schmidt

The two Social Democratic chancellors offer a contrast in personality, political style, and policy emphasis. Willy Brandt's two governments, from 1969 to 1974, were characterized by the introduction of a new foreign policy of reconciliation with Germany's eastern neighbors and the acceptance of the permanence of postwar boundaries in Eastern Europe. This *Ostpolitik* (Eastern policy) involved the negotiation and ratification of treaties with the Soviet Union (1970), Poland (1970), East Germany (1972), and Czechoslovakia (1973). This policy put West Germany at the forefront of the worldwide trend toward détente and made Brandt one of the world's most respected political leaders. For this policy of reconciliation he was awarded the Nobel Peace Prize in 1971, only the fourth German ever so honored. For many, he personified the "other Germany," a man of peace and goodwill accepting moral re-

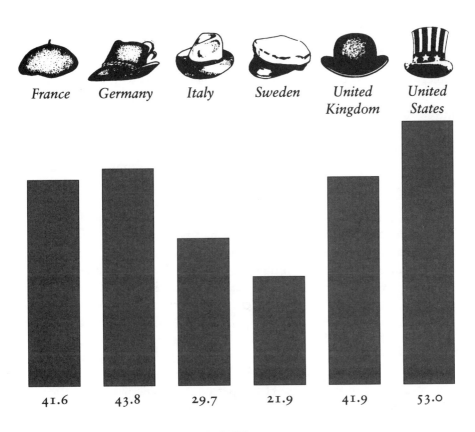

FIGURE 12.1

VOTE FOR CONSERVATIVE PARTIES (IN PERCENT)

NOTE: Most recent elections (U.S.: 1988 presidential election).

sponsibility for the acts committed in Germany's name by the Nazis. As the first chancellor with an impeccable record of uncompromising opposition to Nazism, he contributed greatly to the republic's image abroad as a society that had finally overcome its totalitarian past. For many Germans, especially the young, he became a symbol of a political system that was now democratic in content as well as form.

These foreign policy successes and his great international prestige could not in the long run compensate for Brandt's ineffective leadership in most domestic political matters. During his first government, his inability to institute a wide variety of promised domestic reforms—codetermination in industry (worker representation on a firm's board of control), profit-sharing, tax, and educational programs—could be attributed to the government's small (twelve-seat) majority. But after 1972 his second government held a comfortable majority of fifty seats. Yet his domestic legislative program stalled again. Brandt had little interest in many internal policy areas and little knowledge of economics and finance. He was also unwilling to resolve the conflicts within the cabinet and the SPD, which flared up after 1972. The very weak response of his government to the 1973 Arab oil embargo and the subsequent economic recession prompted suggestions even from within his own cabinet that he step down. Finally, when an East German spy was discovered on his personal staff in April 1974, Brandt assumed full responsibility and resigned.

The fifth chancellor, Helmut Schmidt, assumed the office with more successful national-level experience than any of his four predecessors. An academically trained economist, he had been the leader of the SPD parliamentary party (1966–69), defense minister (1969–72), and finance minister (1972–74). In these posts Schmidt acquired a reputation for being a very capable political decision maker. He was also criticized for what some regarded as an overbearing, arrogant, "cold" personal style. He clearly lacked the emotional, "warm" image of Brandt, yet he is given higher marks for his concrete performance.

Schmidt became chancellor in the midst of the worldwide economic recession that followed the 1973 Arab oil embargo and subsequent astronomical rise in oil prices. His expertise and experience in national and international economic affairs and his ability to take charge in crisis situations (e.g., a 1977 terrorist hijacking and commando raid) soon became apparent. Within two years, inflation was brought under control and unemployment reduced, although it would remain well above pre-1973 figures. In addition, the Schmidt governments continued, albeit at a lower key, the *Ostpolitik* of their predecessors. A 1976 treaty with Poland extended the 1970 pact and provided for the resettlement of German nationals living in Poland but desiring to move to the Federal Republic.

Unlike Brandt, Schmidt had little patience with the SPD's left. He was a strong supporter of the mixed economy and maintained a close relationship with the Federal Republic's economic and industrial elite. Indeed, he was seen even by many CDU voters as more capable than their own party's candidates. Schmidt's policy successes, however, were not matched by his performance as the leader of the Social Democrats. He was unable to overcome and integrate the opposition of the SPD left to many of his policies, especially the 1979 NATO decision, which Schmidt initiated, to station a new generation of midrange nuclear missiles in the Federal Republic should negotiations with the Soviet Union fail. He also underestimated the intensity of opposition within his own party and in the country as a whole to nuclear power as an energy source. Convinced that there was no alternative to nuclear reactors if the Federal Republic were to remain viable in the international marketplace, Schmidt sought allies outside the SPD in his struggle with party critics. While there was some closing of the ranks for the 1980 election, the chancellor's relationship to his party remained a problem throughout his tenure in office.

Germany was unable to avoid the worldwide recession that followed the second oil price shock in 1979. By 1981, unemployment had increased to 7.5 percent, up from less than 4 percent in 1979. The worsening economy coupled with increasing conflict within the Schmidt government over cuts in the budgets for social programs took their toll, and in September 1982 Helmut Schmidt lost his parliamentary majority as the Free Democrats, the junior partner in the coalition with the SPD, abandoned the government. Shortly thereafter, the leader of the CDU, Helmut Kohl, became the republic's sixth chancellor, heading a new coalition comprised of the Christian Democratic Union and the Free Democrats. At the March 1983 national election, the voters endorsed these parliamentary changes by giving Kohl and his coalition a solid majority in the parliament.

Helmut Kohl and German Unity

Helmut Kohl has been a significant figure on the West German political scene since 1969 when he became chief-executive of the state of Rhineland-Palatinate (Rheinland-Pfalz). His successes at the state level coincided with the decline of his party, the CDU, in national politics. After CDU/CSU defeats in 1969 and 1972, Kohl moved out from his provincial power base and in 1973 assumed the leadership of a badly divided and weakened CDU. He is credited with initiating a thorough modernization and revitalization of the party's organization. In 1976, as the chancellor candidate, he conducted a well-planned and executed campaign, which almost toppled the coalition SPD and Free Democrats (FDP) government.

Kohl is a political pragmatist, but he does not have the reputation as a crisis manager or bold decision maker. In domestic politics he comes from a Catholic labor tradition that generally supports Germany's extensive social welfare state. In his first term, however, he cut back many social programs in an effort to reduce government deficits. The market economy is an article of his faith, as is firm support for the Atlantic Alliance. He has been the most pro-American chancellor since Adenauer. But this did not prevent his government in 1989 from open conflict with the United States over the question of when and if a new generation of short-range nuclear missiles should be developed and stationed in the Federal Republic.

More than any of his predecessors, Helmut Kohl, as the first chancellor who did not experience the Third Reich as an adult, has attempted to appeal to patriotic symbols and national pride. The evocation of national themes remains a very sensitive topic in German political culture. Terms such as *Vaterland* (fatherland) and "nation" and an emphasis upon the past forty years of German history as an object of pride have been a frequent theme in Kohl's speeches. He has pushed plans for the construction of two large museums, in Bonn and Berlin, dealing with German history. While not denying the country's responsibility for the Third Reich and World War II, Kohl, together with some conservative intellectuals, has urged that Germans in general and postwar generations in particular develop a positive sense of German history. Germany, Kohl believes, has earned the right to be accepted as an equal in the Western community; the past should no longer limit the capability of the Federal Republic to act.

The collapse of the East German communist regime in 1989–90 and the desire of most East Germans for unity with West Germany provided Kohl with the greatest opportunity and challenge of his political career. Seizing the initiative in late November 1989, just weeks after the opening of the Berlin Wall, Kohl outlined a ten-point plan for unity within five years. The continuing exodus of East Germans to the West, however, caused the government to accelerate this timetable. His personal intervention in East Germany's first free election in March 1990 was a major factor in the victory of the "Alliance for Germany," a coalition of three center-right parties put together by Kohl only a month earlier. Two months after this vote, the two states completed a treaty that unified their currencies, economies, and social welfare systems. Kohl's "rush to unity" was criticized by the opposition parties and some foreign governments, but he continued to press for the complete unification of the two states, including all-German elections and the end of all four-power (United States, Great Britain, France, the Soviet Union) rights in Germany and Berlin, by the end of 1990. The victory of his governing coalition at the December 1990 election, the first free vote in all of Germany since 1932, made him the "Unity chancellor."

The breakneck pace of the unification process was prompted by both political and policy factors. Kohl was in fact more popular among East German voters than those in the West. His promises of rapid economic prosperity corresponded to East German desires to catch up with their cousins as soon as possible. The drive for unification was, however, also due to the fear that any delay could prompt a massive exodus to the West by millions of East Germans with the resultant collapse of the East German state and an unbearable burden for the West German political, economic, and social system.

Formal Policy-Making Procedures

Legislation

Most legislation is drafted in the ministries of the national government and submitted to the parliament for action. Two additional but relatively minor sources of legislative proposals are the state governments and the parliament itself. State governments may submit national legislation via the Bundesrat, but at least nine states (a majority) must support the bill. If at least 5 percent (about 35) of the Bundestag deputies cosponsor a bill, it also enters the legislative process.

Administrative regulations and legal ordinances that deal largely with the technical, procedural aspects of existing programs are introduced and enacted by the government and do not require the consent of parliament. If regulations and ordinances affect the states, however, they must be approved by the Bundesrat. They can also be challenged in the courts. The president can in some cases refuse to sign the regulation or ordinance.

Before a draft bill is submitted to parliament, it is discussed and approved by the cabinet (government). If the legislation affects several ministers, the chancellor's office will coordinate the drafting process and attempt to resolve any interministerial conflicts. At the cabinet level, the states, through the Bundesrat, will be asked to submit their reaction to the legislation. Since cabinet approval is necessary for all draft legislation coming out of the ministries, a minister will usually have the legislation put on the cabinet agenda only if approval is very likely. Indeed, since the chancellor quarterbacks this entire process, most cabinet meetings dealing with legislation already in draft tend largely to formalize decisions already taken informally between the chancellor and the relevant ministers.

After governmental approval, the proposed bill is presented to the Bundesrat for its first reading. The Bundesrat usually assigns it to a committee, which issues a report and recommends the acceptance, rejection, or (in most cases) the amendment of the legislation. Since the Bundestag can override a Bundesrat veto, it considers the bill regardless of Bundesrat action.

In parliament, the bill is given a first reading and assigned to the relevant committee. Since the government has a majority in each committee, a bill will rarely be returned to the floor with a negative report. The committee report before the whole chamber is the occasion for the second reading, at which time amendments to the proposed legislation can be considered. If after debate on the second reading the bill is approved without amendment, the third and final reading follows immediately.

After adoption by the Bundestag, the bill goes back to the Bundesrat for a second reading. If it is approved there without amendment, the legislation goes directly to the president for his signature and promulgation. If the policy area requires Bundesrat approval and it vetoes the bill, it is dead. In some cases, the Bundesrat proposes amendments to the lower-house version, and the two houses form a conference committee to resolve the differences.

The Judiciary

Germany is a law- and court-minded society. In addition to local, regional, and state courts for civil and criminal cases, corresponding court systems specialize in labor, administrative, tax, and social security cases. On a per capita basis, there are about nine times as many judges in the Federal Republic as in the United States. The legal system, like that of most of its West European neighbors, is based on code law rather than case, judge-made, or common law. These German legal codes, influenced by the original Roman codes and the French Napoleonic Code, were reorganized and in some cases rewritten after the founding of the empire in 1871.

In a codified legal system, the judge only administers and applies the codes, fitting the particular cases to the existing body of law. A judge, in theory at least, may not set precedents and thus make law, but must be a neutral administrator of these codes. Counsel for the plaintiff and defendant assist the judge in this search for justice. The assumption behind this system, which is common to other West European societies, is that a right and just answer exists for every case. The problem is to find it in the codes. The judge is expected to take an active role in this process and not be merely a disinterested referee or umpire of court proceedings. Court observers accustomed to the Anglo-American system would be surprised by the active, inquisitorial posture assumed by the judge. At times, both the judge and prosecution seem to be working against the defendant. Unlike the Anglo-American system, the process is not one of *advocacy,* with both sides presenting their positions as forcefully and persuasively as possible and with the judge or jury making the final decision; it is more *inquisitorial,* with all participants—defense, prosecution, and judge—expected to join together in a search for the "truth."

This approach to law has been termed "legal positivism" or "analytical jurisprudence." Some critics of the legal system consider positivism as a basic cause for the scandalous behavior of German judges during the Third Reich, when most judges disclaimed any responsibility for judging the contents of laws they were to administer.

The independence of judges, protected by law, is limited by their status as civil servants. All judges, with the exception of those at the Federal Constitutional Court, are under the supervision of state or national ministers of justice. To move up the judicial hierarchy obviously requires that they perform their duties in a manner consistent with the standards set by their superiors. This bureaucratization of the judiciary, common to all continental West European societies, discourages the type of independence associated with judges in Anglo-American systems.

Judges in Germany are also a tightly knit, largely middle- and upper-class group. While hardly radicals, their attitudes and values (as determined in a number of studies) are quite conventional and conservative. Some critics have charged that many judges dispense "class justice" because they know little about the problems or life-style of the working-class and lower-middle-class defendants who come before them.

Justice in East Germany

During the forty-year reign of the Communist party in East Germany, the rule of law was generally subordinate to the ideological demands of the party. All judges were either members of the Communist party or the puppet parties associated with it in a pseudo-democratic "National Front." They were instructed to consider, above all, the interests of the "working class" and its party, the Communists. Once again, Germany must deal with judges who administered political justice for offenses such as "fleeing the republic" and "behavior damaging to the state," which resulted in numerous political prisoners and questionable legal judgments. The reform of the East German judiciary is an important task now facing the unified country.

The Federal Constitutional Court

The practice of judicial review—the right of courts to examine and strike down legislation if it is considered contrary to the constitution —is alien to a codified legal system. Nonetheless, under the influence of especially American Occupation authorities and the tragic record of the courts during the Third Reich, the framers of the Bonn constitution created a Federal Constitutional Court and empowered it to consider any alleged violations of the constitution, including legislative acts. Similar courts were also established at the state level.

This new court, located in the southwestern city of Karlsruhe, has in its first forty years built an impressive record of constitutional interpretation. In doing so it has also become an increasingly powerful political institution. Unlike other courts, it is independent of any justice ministry. Its members are selected by both houses of parliament, and its budget and other administrative matters are dealt with in direct negotiations with parliament's judiciary committees. It took several years for the Court to achieve this independence, but such independence was recognized as indispensable for the performance of its constitutional responsibilities.

In recent years, the Court has rendered decisions on such controversial political cases as the *Ostpolitik* treaties, abortion reform, university governance, the powers of the Bundesrat, the employment of "radicals" in the civil service, codetermination in industry, and the 1983 census law. Like the U.S. Supreme Court, the Federal Constitutional Court has also been criticized for becoming "too political," for usurping the legislative and policy-making prerogatives of parliament and government, and for not exercising sufficient "judicial restraint." To students of judicial review, this is a familiar charge and reflects the extent to which the Court since its founding has become a legitimate component of the political system. Most important, both winners and losers in these various cases have accepted and complied with the Court's decisions.

13

Who Has the Power and How Did They Get It?

Political Parties

The dispersion of power in the Federal Republic creates a need for its integration and aggregation if there is to be any coherence in the policy process. The key agencies performing these functions of integration and aggregation in the postwar period are the political parties. One of the most striking changes in postwar Germany has been the emergence of a system of political parties that has effectively organized and controlled the political process. Traditionally, parties were marginal factors in German political life. Their home was the legislature, but the executive and the bureaucracy dominated politics; the parties had little influence in these institutions. This pattern was also dominant during most of the Weimar Republic when the party system was fragmented and stable parliamentary majorities became impossible to form. By the late 1920s, effective political power, in spite of the democratic structure of the state, had passed once again into the hands of the executive and the state bureaucracy.

This system of weak, unstable, and fragmented parties did not re-emerge after 1949. Indeed, democratic political parties began to assert themselves early in the Occupation period, and they assumed major leadership roles in the parliamentary council that drafted the Basic Law establishing the West German state. Never before in German history have democratic political parties been as important and powerful as they are in the Federal Republic today.

Related to the increased power of political parties is the sharp decrease over the past forty years in the number of parties seriously contending for power. During the Weimar Republic, up to 100 parties contested elections, and as many as 25 gained parliamentary representation—with no single party able to secure a majority of seats. Coalition governments consisting of several parties were the rule. These were, for the most part, unstable; this meant governments had to expend their resources on surviving instead of planning and implementing policy programs. During the thirteen-year Weimar Republic, there were twenty different governments.

In contrast, the postwar party system has been characterized by a concentration of electoral support in two large parties, the Christian Democratic Union (Christlich Demokratische Union—CDU) and the Social Democratic party of Germany (Sozialdemokratische Partei Deutschlands—SPD), together with a much smaller third party, the Free Democrats (Freie Demokratische Partei—FDP). Since 1983, a new political party, the Greens (die Grünen), has entered parliament, but it has yet to participate in any government at the national level. In 1949, seventeen different parties contested the first national election, and fourteen succeeded in entering the first parliament. By 1961, this had dropped to three parties, and they have carried the Federal Republic. They have dominated the selection and control of governmental personnel and have had major influence in the setting of the policy agenda.

The postwar democratic parties had several advantages over their Weimar predecessors. First, their competitors in previous regimes—the state bureaucracy, the army, the landed nobility, and even big business—were discredited through their association with the Third Reich. Second, the parties from the outset enjoyed the support of the Occupation powers. This gave the parties numerous material and political benefits and put them in a strong starting position when the decision was made (by the Allies) in 1948 to launch a West German state. Third, the parties largely organized and controlled the proceedings of the parliamentary council. The constitution made the parties quasi-state institutions by assigning them fundamental responsibility for "shaping the political will of the people." This provision has also been used to justify the extensive public financing of the parties both for their normal day-to-day activities and during election campaigns. Fourth, these same parties, exploiting their strong constitutional and political position, ensured that the local, state, and national postwar bureaucracies were staffed, at least at the upper levels, by their supporters. In contrast to the Weimar bureaucracy, the civil service in the Federal Republic has not been a center of antirepublican sentiment but has been firmly integrated into the republican consensus.

The Christian Democrats

The Christian Democratic Union (CDU) together with its Bavarian partner, the Christian Social Union (Christlich Soziale Union—CSU), is a postwar political movement. Like the Gaullists in France, the CDU/CSU developed largely as a vehicle to facilitate the election and re-election of a single political personality, Konrad Adenauer. The Union did not even have its first national convention until after it became the major governing party in 1949. From the outset in 1945, the CDU was a broadly based movement that sought to unite both Protestants and Catholics in a political organization that would apply the general principles and values of Christianity to politics. The religious division between Protestants and Catholics was regarded as one factor for the rise of Nazism. But the Union also stressed that it was open to all social classes and regions. The CDU/CSU became a prototype for the new "catchall" parties that emerged in postwar Europe: parties that sought through a pragmatic, nonideological image to appeal to as broad an electoral base as possible. The CDU wanted to attract voters, not necessarily believers, and it refused to place itself in one of the traditional liberal, conservative, socialist, or communist ideological categories. To the more traditionally minded politicians and some intellectuals, this was nothing more than opportunism. How could one have a party without a clearly articulated ideology and program? The CDU/CSU represented a new development in politics.

In the 1950s, the remarkable success of Chancellor Adenauer in foreign policy and the free-market policies of his economics minister, Ludwig Erhard, made the Union Germany's dominant party. At the 1957 election, it became the first democratic party in German history to secure an absolute majority of the popular vote. The CDU/CSU's program was very general: free-market economic policies at home, alliance with the United States and other NATO countries, and a staunch anticommunism abroad; otherwise, "no experiments" (the party's main slogan at the 1957 election).

This approach worked well throughout the 1950s, but the Berlin Wall in 1961 and the 1966–67 economic recession showed the weaknesses in the CDU/CSU's policies. Anticommunism and a refusal to recognize the legitimacy of postwar boundaries in Eastern Europe had not brought Germany any closer to unification. Moreover, the weak American response to the Wall was for many a sign that the Federal Republic could not rely entirely on the United States to run its foreign policy. The 1966–67 recession, although mild in comparison with past economic declines and in comparison with those experienced by other industrial societies, indicated that the postwar boom was over and that the economy was in need of more management and planning. Almost two decades of governing had taken their toll on the leadership of the party. Adenauer's successor, Ludwig Erhard, lacked the political skill of the "old man." Also the Social Democrats, as we discuss below, had since the late 1950s begun to revamp their program, organization, and leadership. The collapse of the Erhard government in 1966 was followed by a Grand Coalition with the Social Democrats. By sharing power with its chief adversary, the Union enabled the SPD to show Germany's middle-class voters that it could indeed be entrusted with national political responsibility.

After the 1969 election, the SPD and FDP formed a coalition that ended twenty-years of CDU/CSU government in Bonn. Lacking a programmatic focus, the party went through four different chancellor candidates in search of a winner who could bring it back to power. In opposition it expended much of its time in internal conflicts revolving around this leadership question.

In 1982, after thirteen years in opposition, the Christian Democrats returned to power. While the party did not receive any direct electoral mandate in 1982, both state elections and national public opinion polls showed that the CDU/CSU enjoyed a sizable advantage over the Social Democrats. This was confirmed at the March 1983 election when the Union scored a solid victory over the SPD.

The party's most difficult task following its return to power in 1983 was to deliver on its promise of economic recovery. In other policy areas it has pursued its traditional pragmatic course: The innovations of the Socialist-Liberal years in foreign policy have been consolidated and even extended; the commitment of the previous government to deploy new missiles was carried out; cuts in social programs were limited.

At the 1987 election, the CDU campaigned on the record of the Kohl government. The party emphasized that it had brought Germany back to economic prosperity, reduced the federal deficit, cut taxes, and restored the Federal Republic's status as a dependable ally of the United States and a major force in the European Community. But with 44.3 percent of the vote, the Christian Democrats declined to their lowest level since 1949. Intracoalition switching to the FDP, low turnout among farmers protesting the government's agricultural policies, and overconfidence among its activists were the major factors cited by the party's leadership in explaining the outcome. The CDU also lost votes to the SPD because of the still high unemployment level among manual workers.

The Christian Democrats and Unification

Prior to the opening of the Berlin Wall and the collapse of the East German regime, the fortunes of the Christian Democrats were at a low ebb. In public opinion polls throughout the first ten months of 1989 the party's level of support ranged from 33 percent to 38 percent. In June Chancellor Kohl's leadership of the party was challenged by several intraparty dissidents. The prospects for the CDU at the upcoming national election were not good. The unity issue clearly gave the party new political life. Led by Chancellor Kohl the CDU in the December, 1990 all-German election received 43.8 percent of the vote and together with the Free Democrats enjoyed a commanding majority of 134 seats in the parliament.

But while the CDU in 1989–90 benefited from the unification issue, in 1991 higher taxes in the West and the continued decline of the economy in the former East Germany hurt the party in several state elections. Voter backlash over Kohl's new taxes and lackluster leadership at the state level were the major factors in the party's postunification decline. Like the SPD in the 1980s under Helmut Schmidt, the CDU in the 1990s under Kohl suffers from a lack of popular leaders in state governments or the cabinet.

The Social Democrats

The SPD is Germany's oldest political party and the only one to emerge virtually intact following the collapse of the Third Reich. The heir to Germany's rich Marxist tradition, the SPD was outlawed and persecuted during the nineteenth century by Bismarck and the kaiser, and by the Nazis in the twentieth century. In 1945 it appeared that the SPD's hour had finally come. Unlike other Weimar parties, its record of opposition to Nazism was uncompromising. In 1933 it was the only political party to vote against Hitler's Enabling Act. Its commitment to socialism had long been tempered by an even greater support for the principles and values of political democracy. Even during the Weimar Republic, the party's interest in the class struggle and the realization of the revolutionary vision had given way to a policy of reformist gradualism designed to change the society and economy by peaceful, political means.

During the Third Reich, the SPD retained a skeletal organization in exile and a small underground movement in Germany. While many Socialists did not survive the war and the concentration camps, the party was still able to regroup in a relatively short time after 1945—its loyal members emerged literally from the ruins of Germany's cities to begin the task of reconstruction. Yet the SPD at the first parliamentary election in 1949 did not become the largest party and found itself in opposition. After the landslide CDU/CSU victories of 1953 and 1957, it could claim the support of only about 30 percent of the electorate.

The SPD's first postwar leader, Kurt Schumacher, was unable to convert the party's opposition to Nazism and its resultant moral authority into electoral success. While he made a substantial contribution to the Bonn democracy by preventing a fusion between the SPD and the communists and shaping the SPD into a viable opposition party, his overall political strategy was unsuccessful. Specifically, Schumacher failed to recognize that the post-1948 success of free-market (capitalist) economic policies left the bulk of the nation's electorate with little interest in socialism, with its connotation of government ownership of the means of production, centralized economic planning, and the class struggle. He also overestimated the interests of the average citizen in an independent "nationalist" foreign policy designed to secure the reunification of the country. Most West Germans, at least by the early 1950s, were willing to accept the division of the old Reich in exchange for the economic prosperity, individual freedom, and security they received from German integration into the American-led Atlantic Alliance. Finally, Schumacher's political style, with its emphasis on conflict, polarization, and ideology, simply reminded too many voters of the Weimar Republic. Postwar Germany and Western Europe had tired of this approach to politics—this was the heyday of the "end of ideology," and most voters were supporting consensual, middle-of-the-road parties and leaders.[1]

During the 1950s, however, an increasing number of SPD leaders in states such as Hamburg, Frankfurt, and West Berlin began to advocate major changes in the party's program, organization, and leadership. The reformers wanted the party to accept the pro-Western foreign policy course of Adenauer and abandon its opposition to the free-market economic policies of the CDU/CSU.

This reform movement culminated in the party's 1959 program that was adopted at its convention in Bad Godesberg. In the Bad Godesberg program the SPD abandoned its advocacy of the nationalization of the means of production and of compulsory economic planning. It stressed its opposition to communism and its support of NATO and the Western alliance. Shortly thereafter, the party sought to broaden its membership base to include more white-collar employees and even independent businessmen. It also made the young, politically attractive mayor of Berlin, Willy Brandt, its national chairman and 1961 candidate for chancellor.

National political responsibility also brought new problems, especially from the SPD's old and new left. The old left, composed of socialists who had always opposed the Bad Godesberg reforms, and the new left, mainly in the party's youth organization, argued that the party had sold out its ideological and revolutionary heritage and its commitment to social and economic change for political power. It had become as opportunistic as the CDU/CSU and in reality was a tool of the "ruling capitalist elite."

Conflicts within the party peaked during the latter years of Helmut Schmidt's chancellorship and were a major factor in the party's return to the opposition after the 1983 election. In opposition, the party was unable to make significant progress toward resolving its internal divisions until 1985 when it won decisive victories in two state elections. But in the 1987 national election, the question of how to deal with the Greens again divided the party, and its vote dropped to 37 percent, its lowest level since 1961.

The Social Democrats and Unification

The 1989–90 unification both surprised and divided the SPD. For years the party had sought to improve the concrete living conditions of East Germans by negotiating with the Communist regime. This contact with the GDR leadership, however, also gave the Communists a certain legitimacy and status in the view of many Germans. When the revolution began, the SPD was ill-prepared. While the party had good contacts with the now beleaguered GDR "elite," it had few if any with the "street," that is the fledgling democratic opposition including the churches. The "rush to unity" that followed the opening of the Wall also divided the party. Many members under the age of forty-five had no living memories of a united country. They had accepted at least tacitly the permanence of Germany's division, or believed that it could only be overcome within a united East and Western Europe.

In the 1990 election, these SPD activists, including the party's 1990 chancellor candidate Oskar Lafontaine, were unable to recognize the broad appeal that unity had in the West and its fundamental importance for the new voters in the East. Older Social Democrats, such as the former Chancellors Willy Brandt and Helmut Schmidt, enthusiastically supported unification and had few problems with the euphoria this issue generated. Lafontaine's lukewarm approach to this issue hurt the SPD at the 1990 election, especially in the East, where the SPD received only 24.5 percent of the vote. Overall, its total of 33.5 percent represented the party's worst performance since 1957.

But while the SPD was hurt in 1989–90 by the "upside" of the unification issue, by mid-1991 it was benefiting from its "downside," that is, voter discontent in the West with the tax increases needed to finance unification and voter unhappiness in the East with the slow pace of economic reconstruction. In both parts of the country the party's fortunes have improved. With four straight victories in state elections in 1991, it gained control of the Bundesrat. Currently, it is the major governing party in a record nine of sixteen states. More importantly perhaps, it now has a group of young, dynamic leaders in most of these states that the Christian Democrats cannot match. If the party can unite behind a strong candidate and minimize intra-party differences, it has a good chance of once again becoming competitive with the Christian Democrats.

The Free Democrats

The Free Democratic party (FDP) is the only small party to survive the postwar emergence of a concentrated and simplified party system. Ideologically and programmatically, it is somewhere between the two large parties. On economic issues it is closer to the CDU/CSU than the SPD; but on matters such as education, civil liberties, and foreign and defense policies, the FDP has had more in common with the Social Democrats.

The FDP owes its continued existence and relative success to the electoral system, which gives the party a proportional share of the parliamentary mandates as long as it secures at least 5 percent of the vote. The FDP has held the balance of power in most national elections. Both major parties have tended to prefer coming to terms with the Free Democrats in a small coalition to forming a Grand Coalition with the other major party. Between 1949 and 1957, and again from 1961 to 1965, the Free Democrats were the junior coalition partner in CDU/CSU governments. From 1969 to 1982, it was in coalition with the Social Democrats. In 1982, the FDP changed partners once again and returned to the Christian Democrats. This last move sharply divided the party, but it was still able to surmount the 5 percent barrier at the 1983 and 1987 elections.

With 11 percent of the vote at the 1990 all-German election the FDP achieved the third best result in its history. This success was largely a tribute to the role the party's titular leader, the long-time (since 1974) Foreign Minister and Vice-Chancellor, Hans-Dietrich Genscher, played in the unification process. As FDP campaign speakers never tired of reminding the voters: "Bismarck unified Germany with blood and iron. Helmut Kohl did it with Hans-Dietrich Genscher!" The FDP also benefited from its "no new taxes" pledge and did especially well in East Germany, from which Genscher fled in the 1950s. Although together with the CDU it did renege on its promise of no new taxes to finance unification, thus far voters have focused their wrath on Chancellor Kohl and the Christian Democrats rather than on the FDP. Nonetheless, there are signs that the Free Democrats view the Kohl government as a sinking ship and are once again considering an alliance with the Social Democrats.

The Greens

In the late 1970s, a variety of environmentalist groups with a common opposition to the government's plans for the expansion of nuclear energy plants banded together into a Federal League of Citizen Groups for the Protection of the Environment, or simply, the "Environmentalists," or "Greens." The Greens were a new face on the political scene. Their antiestablishment, grass-roots, idealistic image had an appeal that was especially strong among younger citizens. In October 1979 a Green party gained entrance into the parliament of the city-state of Bremen, and in March 1980 they surmounted the 5 percent hurdle in the relatively large state of Baden-Württemberg. After a poor showing at the 1980 national election, the environmentalists rebounded by gaining representation in the state parliaments in Berlin, Lower Saxony, Hamburg, and Hesse.

In the early 1980s, the Greens were above all a protest movement with a single issue—the environment. Their opposition to placing American middle-range missiles in West Germany gave them the additional issue they needed to gain representation in the Bundestag in 1983, the first new party to enter the parliament since the 1950s.

The party's string of successes was snapped in 1985 when it fell below the 5 percent minimum in two state elections. The internal divisions within the movement had become an issue. The critical problem was the party's relationship to the Social Democrats. Should the Greens seek power through a coalition with the SPD, or should they remain a protest movement unsullied by any association with the established parties? Most Green voters preferred the former alternative (i.e., an alignment with the SPD). The party's activists and leaders were divided. One group, the Fundamentalists, rejects any cooperation with the SPD, whereas a second wing, the Realists, are willing to form coalitions with the Social Democrats at state and national levels in order to achieve Green goals, if only in piecemeal fashion.

The 1986 nuclear accident at Chernobyl in Ukraine brought the

Fundamentalists back into control of the party. At their convention that year, the Greens passed resolutions calling for West Germany's immediate withdrawal from NATO, unilateral demilitarization, and the dismantling of all nuclear power stations in the country. The Greens also refused to distance themselves from the violent demonstrations that took place at nuclear power plants and reprocessing facilities following the accident.

In the wake of the Chernobyl disaster, support for the party in public opinion polls doubled to over 12 percent. For a time it appeared that if the Greens decided to coalesce with the SPD, the two parties would have an absolute majority after the 1987 election. By mid-1986, however, the effects of Chernobyl began to wane, and the potential Green-SPD vote dropped from 53 percent to 43 percent. Although the Greens clearly gained support because of the accident in Ukraine, they also lost voters because of their radical positions on foreign policy, defense, and domestic issues.

In spite of these problems, the party was able to increase its share of the vote at the 1987 elections from 5.6 percent to 8.3 percent. The proportion of voters who think that it is good that the Greens are in parliament rose from 28 percent in 1983 to 54 percent at the time of the 1987 election. Thus most Germans now seem to accept the party as a legitimate political force.

The Greens were ill-prepared for the unification issue. Their predominantly young electorate had little interest in a unified nation having known only the reality of two German states throughout their lifetime. Most Greens wanted the indigenous East German revolutionary groups to have more time to find a "third way" between the Stalinism of the old GDR regime and what they considered the antienvironmentalist capitalism of the West. With only 3.9 percent of the vote nationwide, down from 8.3 percent in 1987, the party failed to return to parliament. Low turnout among Green voters and losses to the Social Democrats were the major factors in the party's poor performance. The Greens in the former East Germany, however, did surmount the 5 percent barrier in their region and entered the parliament.

Following the 1990 election the Greens rebounded in public opinion polls and in state elections. Currently, the party is governing in coalitions mainly with the Social Democrats in a record four states, Hesse, Bremen, Lower Saxony, and Brandenburg. With the euphoria over unification passed and the Realists firmly in control of the party, the Greens have a good chance of returning to the national parliament after the next election.

Other Parties

Since 1961, a variety of parties besides the Greens have attempted to break the monopoly of the three system parties. Thus far, all of them have failed to surmount the 5 percent mark, but one of them came fairly close. In the mid-1960s, the radical right (if not neo-Nazi) NPD won seats in several state parliaments and seemed to have good chance to enter the national parliament at the 1969 election. The party secured 4.5 percent and thus failed to win any seats. Following this near miss, the NPD faded quickly and by 1972 was no longer represented even at state levels.

In 1989, a new radical-right party, the Republicans (die Republikaner), burst on the political scene at state elections in Berlin, a local election in Frankfurt, and the election of deputies to the European parliament. Led by a former member of the Waffen-SS, the party attracted enormous media attention. Its success was due largely to its strong antiforeigner theme (i.e., its hostility to foreign workers, residents, and even ethnic Germans who since 1988 have been allowed to emigrate from the Soviet Union, Poland, and other Eastern European countries). Voter interest in the Republicans, however, dropped quickly in the wake of the unification movement during 1989–90. After losses in several state elections the party at the 1990 election received only 2.2 percent of the vote. After the national election, however, the continued influx of economic refugees into the Federal Republic and the high costs of unification gave the Republicans new life. In April 1992 the party secured almost 11 percent of the vote at a state election in Baden-Württemberg. In the northern state of Schleswig-Holstein, a sister party of the Republicans, the German Peoples Union, entered the parliament with almost 7 percent. Whether the Republicans can enter the national parliament will depend largely on the ability of the government to deal with the asylum issue and economic reconstruction in the former East Germany.

The East German Party Alignment

The opening of the Berlin Wall and the subsequent collapse of the Communist regime led to rapid changes in the political party spectrum in the GDR. The once subservient "bloc parties"—the Christian Democrats, Liberals, National Democrats, and Farmers' parties—replaced their leaders and began to distance themselves from the Communist Socialist Unity Party (SED). At the same time the various dissident groups who played a crucial role in East Germany's gentle revolution regrouped, with some difficulty, into party-like organizations for the March 1990 parliamentary elections. East German versions of West German parties not previously present in the GDR—the Social Democrats, Free Democrats, and Greens—were also formed. Even an East German CSU (DSU, or German Social Union) emerged in the state of Saxony, with the help of the Bavarians. Finally, the deposed communists replaced their leadership and changed their name to the Party of Democratic Socialism (Partei des Demokratischen Sozialismus—PDS). A few months after the election most parties merged with their West German equivalents in preparation for the December, 1990 all-German election. The only indigenous East German parties now in the national parliament are the old communist party, the PDS, and the Alliance 90/Greens, a group composed of former revolutionaries and environmentalists. But both parties owe their presence largely to the special one-time only provision of the electoral law in effect for the 1990 election (see p. 250). Nationally, the PDS received only 2.4 percent of the vote in 1990 and the Alliance 90/Greens only 1.2 percent. To remain in parliament after the next election they must receive at least 5 percent nationwide. In 1992 the Alliance/Green party merged with the West German Greens, thereby increasing substantially its prospects at the next national election.

Interest Groups

As in other Western European societies, in the Federal Republic a wide variety of groups, associations, and movements play significant political roles. The major interest groups—business, labor, agriculture, the churches, professional organizations—are well organized at local, state, and national levels and work closely with the political parties and state bureaucracy. They have been joined in the past two decades by less structured but widely based "new social movements"—environmentalists, peace and disarmament activists, women's rights groups, as well as other movements for various social minorities. Less established than the traditional interest alignments, the new social movements have nonetheless had a growing influence in the political process.

The hierarchical organizational structure of the established interest associations means that their top officials can speak authoritatively for the membership and ensures them access to state and party elites. Indeed, the rules of procedure in German ministries require officials to consult with the leading representatives of interest groups when drafting legislation that relates to a group's area of concern. Unlike the United States, where the terms "interest" or "pressure" groups and "lobbyists" have negative connotations, Germany treats their counterparts as legitimate and necessary participants in the policy process.

Each major interest-group alignment also maintains contact, although not to the same extent, with all major parties. Labor unions, for example, have closer ties to the Social Democratic party than to the Christian Democrats or the Free Democrats. Yet there is also a labor wing within the CDU; and the FDP, at least while it was in coalition with the Social Democrats, maintained contacts with trade union leaders. Business and industrial interests enjoy a warmer relationship with the center-right CDU/CSU than the SPD, but again, there are supporters of the SPD among the ranks of the country's business-industrial elite. This pattern of strong government interest-group/political party integration

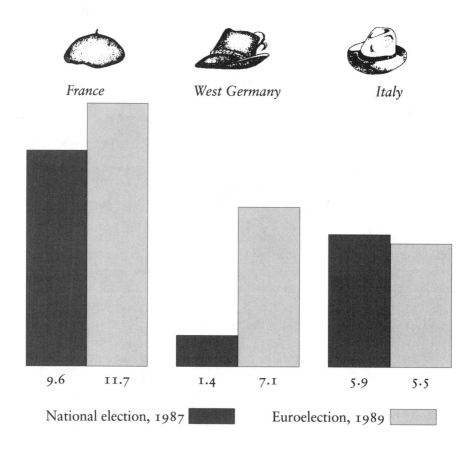

FIGURE 13.1
VOTE FOR RADICAL RIGHT (IN PERCENT)

became somewhat institutionalized during the late 1960s when the top representatives of each area met in a Concerted Action, a regular conference at which general economic conditions were discussed and guidelines for wages, prices, and economic growth were set. At these meetings business, labor, and the national government sought to reach a consensus on (1) what a "reasonable" wage increase would be for various industrial workers, (2) the "acceptable" level of price increases, and (3) the amount of government spending and taxation necessary to ensure stable economic conditions and moderate (i.e., noninflationary) economic growth. Although the Concerted Action disbanded in the late 1970s as labor interests became dissatisfied with what they considered the unreasonable sacrifices they were called on to make, informal labor-business contacts have continued.

Concerted Action and the other less formal interest-group government contracts have prompted some analysts to term Bonn a "neocorporatist" state.[2] *Corporatism* is an old term in social and political thought; it refers to the organization of interests into a limited number of compulsory, hierarchically structured associations recognized by the state and given a monopoly of representation within their respective areas. These associations become in effect quasigovernmental groups: with state approval, training, licensing, and even exercising discipline over the members. The power of these associations is not determined by a group's numerical size alone but also by the importance of its function for the state and community.

Business and Industrial Interests

Three organizations speak for business and industry in the Federal Republic: the League of German Industry, which represents large industrial and business interests; the National Association of German Employers, which represents essentially small and medium-sized firms, and the German Industrial and Trade Chamber, composed of smaller, independent businesses (shopkeepers, artisans).

The impressive accomplishments of the economy and the importance of economic conditions for the political health of any government assure these associations of easy access to the political elite. Recently they have been most concerned with opposing union plans for a shortening of the work week to thirty-five hours with no reduction in wages. Business interests also advocate cuts in government spending and business contributions for social programs, usually citing their negative effect on Germany's competitive position in the world market.

The ability of business interests to influence government policy even under the Social-Liberal coalition that governed from 1969 to 1982 is seen in the relatively weak Codetermination Law passed in 1976, under which the representatives of capital and management still retained a majority on a firm's supervisory board, and in the Apprentice Education Bill of 1976, which continued to assign fundamental responsibility for the training and control of young apprentices, who still account for about 40 percent of the sixteen-to-nineteen-year-old age group, to employers and not to the school or the state. Government efforts to institute a more progressive tax structure in the late 1970s were also, for the most part, successfully opposed by business interests.

Business interests generally supported the return to power of the Christian Democrats in 1982, and the Kohl government has responded with a strong pro business orientation. In addition to cuts in social programs, which reduced or froze the costs of many fringe benefits paid by employers, the government in 1986 passed legislation that weakened the trade unions' capacity to strike. The law, which was widely interpreted as a concession to business shortly before the 1987 elections, changed the provision under which striking workers would receive unemployment compensation. Workers idled by strikes at other plants in the same industry no longer receive state unemployment benefits, which would amount to about two-thirds of their wages. The trade unions bitterly opposed the legislation, claiming it could reduce their power in collective bargaining.

Labor

The German labor movement, like the German political parties, has changed extensively in the postwar period. During the Weimar Republic, labor was divided along politico-ideological lines into socialist, communist, Catholic, and even liberal trade unions. These unions, especially the socialist and communist groups, were concerned with more than wages, hours, and working conditions. They sought to mobilize their members to support and to implement a comprehensive ideology of social, economic, cultural, and political change. Many of their resources were spent on developing and refining this ideology and the accompanying tactics that included confronting fellow workers in competing unions. The labor movement was thus fragmented and relatively ineffectual in securing solid economic gains for its members or, of course, in preventing the Nazi seizure of power.

The postwar Western Occupation authorities and many prewar German trade union leaders sought to restructure and reform the unions. The result of their work is the German Trade Union Federation

(Deutscher Gewerkschaftsbund—DGB), an organization composed of sixteen different unions with a total membership of over 8 million in West Germany and 3.6 million in the former East Germany.[3]

The DGB has become labor's chief political spokesperson and has pursued essentially a policy of "business unionism" concentrating on wages and working conditions. Labor leaders as well as economic policy makers within the Social Democratic party advocate a pragmatic position toward the market economy best summed up by the adage "Do not kill the cow we want to milk."

The trade unions have been successful in securing steady and solid economic gains for German workers. The unions have also shared in this prosperity. One factor in the low strike rate is the economic strength of organized labor, which induces business to take union proposals seriously and seek compromises. Business knows that labor has the financial resources to sustain an extensive strike action. The unions' ties to all parties, especially to the Social Democrats give them direct access to the government. This political power is an additional factor that produces close worker-management cooperation.

Nonetheless, the DGB's pragmatic, nonideological approach has drawn extensive criticism from Germany's new left. The unions are charged with having done little or nothing to change the basic distribution of power in society. In spite of widespread prosperity, there are few signs of any redistribution of economic wealth or of a democratization of economic decision making. While German workers have color television sets, comfortable apartments, automobiles, and month-long vacations in Spain, they have little or no control over the fundamental economic decisions (investment, prices) that affect their lives. Moreover, the working class's share of the nation's capital resources (land, securities, stocks, savings) has not risen significantly during the past forty years. The economic gains of workers, critics charge, have come as a result of the "economic pie" becoming larger, not because of a bigger slice of that pie going to manual workers. For many of the country's young, critical intellectuals, the trade union movement has simply sold out to the existing capitalist system. It is, in their view, conservative, status-quo oriented, and incapable of leading any movement for real economic and social reform.[4]

Unification and Labor

The communist-controlled trade unions in the former East Germany collapsed with the communist state and party. Union membership was compulsory in the old GDR, but the unions were under the control of the party. Collective bargaining, the right to strike and the free election of union officials were unknown. Since unification, the West German DGB has organized about 3.6 million East German workers, or about 38 percent of the membership of the old communist trade unions.[5]

Thus the total membership of the DGB has grown by almost 50 percent since unification. The new unions in the East, however, are in a dilemma. In order to satisfy their new members they must push for higher wages and salaries. Currently, wages in the East are only about 50 to 60 percent of those in the West. But wage gains, without corresponding increases in productivity, would price East German products out of the market and lead, of course, to a further loss of jobs. The present wage differential between East and West in the manufacturing sector corresponds roughly to the difference in productivity, that is, West German workers largely because of their more modern plants and equipment are about twice as productive as their East colleagues. Labor unrest, especially in the service sector where the productivity differences are not as great, has increased in the former GDR in recent months. If the unions are to retain the allegiance of their new members, they must address these problems.

Agriculture

Few interest groups in the Federal Republic have been as successful in securing governmental policies beneficial to their members as have the various organizations representing German farmers. Farmers constitute less than 5 percent of the work force, and agriculture's contribution to the gross national product is less than 3 percent. Yet no occupational group is as protected and as well subsidized by the government as are farmers. They receive guaranteed prices for most of their products; they are given subsidies and tax benefits for new equipment, construction, and the modernization of their holdings. And the increase in the value of farm land has led some observers to term them Germany's "secret rich."[6] While they may be "land rich" but "cash poor," it is difficult to consider them an impoverished or disadvantaged minority in society.

A succession of "green plans" has consolidated many small farms into larger, more efficient units, but German agriculture still could not compete with other Western societies were it not for the strong Common Market protective tariff system for farm products and additional subsidies from Bonn. These benefits to farmers have been estimated to have added an additional 10 to 15 percent to the food bill of consumers; but all governments since 1949, regardless of their party configuration, have essentially continued these policies. Indeed, farmers never fared as well as they did during the years of the Social-Liberal coalition (1969–82).

Agriculture in the former GDR is in a state of transition. Under the communists, almost all farmers were forced to join collective farms. Since the revolution some have reclaimed their land and are attempting to become independent while others are reorganizing the former collectives into cooperatives. East Germany contains some of the country's richest soil and it could become a productive and profitable agricultural region.

Elections

Elections in the Federal Republic offer citizens their chief opportunity to influence the political process. Convinced that the German common man had been supportive of Adolf Hitler and the Nazi regime during most of the Third Reich, the Federal Republic's founders essentially limited popular involvement at the national level to participation in periodic elections.[7] There are thus no provisions for the direct election of the president or the chancellor, referenda, the recall of public officials, or direct primaries to ensure more popular involvement at the national level.[8]

As in other Western European parliamentary systems, national elections do not directly determine the chief personnel of government. The chancellor and cabinet are elected by parliament after parliament has been elected by the voters. Elections must be held at least once every four years, but can take place more frequently if a government loses its majority and parliament is dissolved. The Federal Republic has automatic registration and universal adult suffrage for all citizens over eighteen years of age.

Electoral System

Generally, there are two basic procedures in Western democracies for converting votes into legislative seats: a proportional system in which a party's share of legislative mandates is proportional to its popular vote, and a plurality, or "winner-take-all" system, under which "losing" parties and candidates (and their voters) receive no representation. Proportional systems are usually favored by smaller parties because under "pure" proportionality, a party with even a fraction of a percent of the vote would receive some parliamentary representation.

Conversely, plurality systems are usually favored by the large parties, which have both the resources and candidates to secure pluralities

TABLE 13.1

SEAT DISTRIBUTION IN THE 1990 ELECTION

Party	Percent first ballot	Percent second ballot	Seats entitled to[a]	District contests won[b]	List candidates elected[c]
CDU/CSU	45.7	43.8	287	235	84
SPD	35.2	33.5	220	91	148
FPD	7.8	11.0	72	1	78
Greens	4.4	3.9	26	0	0
PDS	2.3	2.4	16	1	17
Alliance 90/ East Greens	1.2	1.2	8	0	8
Minor parties	3.4	4.2	27	0	0
Total	100.0	100.0	656	328	335[d]

a. Number of seats entitled to under "pure" proportional representation.
b. Number of district contests won on first ballot.
c. Number of list candidates elected.
d. The CDU received six extra deputies because of its "excess" victories in the new East German states.

in electoral districts. Some political scientists have hypothesized that there is a causal relationship between the electoral law and the number of political parties with a proportional law causing a multiparty pattern and a plurality system producing a concentration of electoral support in two parties.

The German electoral law has elements of both plurality and proportionality, but is essentially a proportional system. One-half of the delegates to parliament are elected on a plurality basis from 328 districts; the other half are chosen on the proportional principle from state lists. The voter thus receives two ballots—one for a district candidate, the other for a party. But the second ballot is by far the more important. The proportion of the vote a party receives on the second ballot determines ultimately how many seats it will have in parliament because the district contests won by the party's candidates are deducted from the total due it on the basis of the second ballot vote.

An example from the 1990 election should illustrate this procedure (see table 13.1). In 1990, the SPD won 33.5 percent of the second ballot vote and was thus entitled to 220 mandates. Since it had already won 91 contests at the district level, however, these were deducted from the total due it on the basis of the second ballot vote. Thus its total of 239 was composed of 91 direct district victories plus 148 from the second ballot party lists. Similarly, the CDU/CSU with 235 district victories received an additional 84 from the second ballot to bring its total to 319. Note that the FDP won only one direct victory (its first since 1957) as did the PDS in the former East Germany. The Greens won no direct district contests. Thus all but one of the FDP's 79 seats and the 17 received by the PDS came from the party list part of the ballot.

Since the West German Greens and other smaller parties failed to surmount the 5 percent hurdle, the 8 percent of the vote and approximately 53 seats they would have received under "pure" proportionality were awarded to the parties that did secure representation. Thus the final total for the SPD, for example, was 239 seats, 19 more than the party actually "earned." These additional seats came from the 53 that the smaller parties would have been awarded in the absence of the 5 percent clause.

There are two further exceptions to pure proportionality. If a party secures more district mandates than it would be entitled to on the basis of the second ballot vote, it is allowed to keep these excess mandates and the parliament is enlarged accordingly. In 1990 there were a record 6 of these seats, all won by the CDU/CSU. The final total for this party was thus 319 seats, 235 direct victories, 52 from the list and an additional 32 from its share of the seats forfeited by the small parties who did not receive the 5 percent minimum. Finally, if a party wins three direct district victories, it need not meet the 5 percent minimum on the second ballot. In 1990 no party entered the Bundestag through this provision.

Two additional changes in the law were in effect for only the 1990 election, the first free all-German vote since 1932. First, largely as a concession to the East German parties, a party in the 1990 election was required to secure the 5 percent minimum in *either* the former West or East Germany. Hence the PDS, the former communist party and the East German Greens, now allied with the East German citizen democracy movement, Alliance/90, are both in the parliament even though they only received 2.4 percent and 1.2 percent respectively of the national vote. In the former GDR they met the 5 percent minimum. Secondly, parties were allowed to combine their electoral lists, that is, form alliances in the various states. This was also designed to help the new East German parties. Ironically, had the West German Greens formed such an alliance with their East German counterparts they would have returned to parliament with about 26 seats.

This complicated electoral law, which most German voters do not fully understand, was intended to combine the best features of the plurality and proportional systems. The district contests were to introduce a "personalized" component into elections and give voters a means of identification with "their" parliamentary deputy; the party list allocations were meant to ensure that a programmatic or policy dimension to elections would be present. The 5 percent clause was designed to prevent small, antisystem splinter parties from gaining representation and making coalition building in parliament difficult. In spite of its basically proportional character, the party system has become more concentrated over the past forty years. The two small parties, the Free Democrats and the Greens, owe their existence to this system. They are both, of course, opposed to any change in the direction of an Anglo-American plurality system.

Candidate Selection

Candidates for the party lists are selected at state-level conventions held several months before the general election. The composition of a list involves considerable bargaining within the party and between it and its major interest clientele. Generally, the very top positions are reserved for the party's notables in the state, followed by representatives of factions and interest groups. In some cases, a candidate assigned a relatively weak district will be compensated by a promising list position. All participants in this procedure have a rough idea of how many list positions will be allotted to the party; that is, how many candidates will actually be elected. As the assumed cutoff point is approached, the intensity of the bargaining increases.

District candidates are nominated at local meetings of party organizations. These meetings are intended to provide an opportunity for all party members to screen prospective candidates. In fact, the district leadership of the party dominates the proceedings. Nonetheless, state and national party leaders have relatively little influence in the district-level nominating process, and there have been cases where prominent legislators have had difficulty because they had paid insufficient attention to the grass-roots membership.

Because most candidates are incumbents, the most obvious qualification for nomination to the parliament is previous experience in the job. A successful local- or state-level legislative background, long service in a local party organization, and close association with an interest group important to the party are other major qualifications. For a list nomination, expertise in a particular policy area can also be significant.

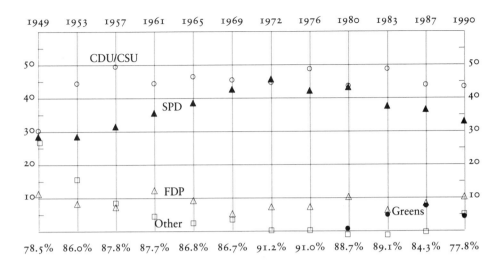

FIGURE 13.2

VOTER TURNOUT AND RESULTS OF FEDERAL ELECTIONS, 1949–90

NOTE: CDU/CSU = ∘ ; SPD = ▲; regional special interest parties = □; FDP = △; Greens = • .
Percentage of voter turnout found at foot of each column.

The German Voter, 1949–90

The results of the twelve national elections held since 1949, presented in
Figure 13.1, reveal several major trends in German elections:

1. A generally high rate of turnout, which by the 1970s exceeded
   90 percent, the highest proportion of any major Western democracy without legal penalties for nonvoting. This high turnout
   reflects the strong emphasis in the political culture placed on voting as a duty, but it also indicates a tendency to perceive elections as ways for citizens to influence policy making.
2. The increasing concentration of support in two large parties
   from 1949 to 1972, and between 1983 and 1990 two small but
   strategically important third parties, all of which support the basic democratic structure of the system.
3. The dominant position of the CDU/CSU between 1953 and
   1969. During this period, the Union was the largest political
   party and the major partner in all coalition governments.
4. The steady rise of the SPD between 1953 and 1972 from the "30
   percent ghetto" to relative parity with the Christian Democrats.

5. A decline in turnout and support for the two major parties since the mid-1980s. At the 1990 election, the CDU/CSU-SPD share of the vote, which has been as high as 93 percent, dropped to 77 percent. Long-term trends, such as the steady gains of the Social Democrats, have been replaced by short-term oscillations from election to election.

In 1949, fourteen political parties entered the parliament. Most of them were absorbed by 1957 into the Christian Democrats led by Konrad Adenauer. Extremist parties such as the Communists and several radical right-wing groups also disappeared by 1957, rejected by the electorate. Campaigns of the 1950s focused on the performance of Adenauer's governments. CDU gains during this period came largely from the ranks of the smaller parties. Most SPD advances between 1957 and 1972 were from CDU/CSU voters and new voters, not from those of the minor parties. The Free Democrats, depending on their coalition partner, attempt to appeal to CDU/CSU and SPD voters dissatisfied with their "normal" party. The FDP projects itself as a "liberal" corrective to the major parties: less conservative and clerical than the CDU/CSU, but not as "radical" or "socialist" as the SPD. In election campaigns, the FDP must to an extent campaign against its coalition partner.

At the 1983 election, the voters solidly endorsed the CDU/CSU-FDP government of Helmut Kohl, which had governed since October 1982. The Christian Democrats, with 48.8 percent of the vote, achieved their best result since 1957. The CDU/CSU gains came largely at the expense of the Social Democrats, and almost 2 million 1980 SPD voters switched to the Union. The major issues of the campaign were unemployment, the security of the pension system, the reduction of deficit spending, and price stability. In all these areas the CDU/CSU was regarded as better qualified to deal with current problems than the SPD. The Social Democrats' campaign focused on the missile question, which was not nearly as important to the majority of voters as the bread-and-butter economic problems. The Free Democrats, with 7 percent of the vote, were able to gain the support of voters who were dissatisfied with the Christian Democrats but who also wanted the coalition to remain in power. Nonetheless, the party's performance was its worst since 1969.

In the 1987 election, voters returned the ruling Christian Democratic–Free Democratic coalition, but with a reduced majority. For the first time in postwar electoral history, both major parties lost support at the same election. The combined CDU/CSU (44.3 percent)–Social

Democratic (37 percent) share of the vote dropped to 81 percent, the lowest level since 1953. The Free Democrats increased their vote to 9.1 percent while the Greens' proportion of the party vote rose to 8.3 percent. Voting turnout dropped to 84.4 percent the lowest since the first federal election in 1949.

In the 1990 all-German election, the Kohl-led coalition was returned for the third straight time. In the current parliament (1990–94), which has about 160 additional seats because of unification, the government enjoys a solid majority of 134 mandates. Within the governing coalition, the big winner was the Free Democratic party, which achieved the third best result (11 percent) in its history. This vote was largely a personal tribute to Foreign Minister Genscher for his achievements in the unification process.

The parties on the left of the German political spectrum were the major losers in the 1990 election. The Social Democrats, garnering only 33.5 percent of the vote, dropped to their lowest level since 1957. In the new East German states the party received less than one-quarter of the vote. The big surprise of the 1990 election was the failure of the West German Greens to return to parliament.

Voting Behavior

The votes of most Germans can be explained by: (1) demographic characteristics of voters, especially social class and religion; (2) voter attitudes toward major candidates; (3) the policies and images of the political parties; and (4) voter attitudes about important policy issues facing the country.

Demographics. Manual workers still form the core of the Social Democratic electorate, while the Christian Democrats and the FDP do well in middle-class or nonmanual occupations. In 1990, manual workers in West Germany preferred the SPD over the other parties by about a 60:40 ratio. Among middle-class voters, Christian Democratic and Free Democratic support is about as high. The religious factor also structures the party vote. Most Catholics who regularly attend church are staunch supporters of the Christian Democrats. But the party preference of Catholics varies significantly by their attachment to the church (as measured by church attendance). Catholic voters who seldom or never go to church are far less likely to support the Christian Democrats than those who regularly attend services. For nominal Catholics, social class rather than religion is a more important determinant of voting behavior. The SPD and FDP and the Greens receive disproportional support from Protestants, especially those with a weak attachment to their church. The Greens also do very well among voters who report no religious affiliation.

While social class and religion remain important factors in voting behavior, their impact relative to other factors has declined over the past forty years. The proportion of citizens in manual occupations has dropped from 51 percent in 1950 to 38 percent in 1990. Thus there is less of a "proletariat" for the Social Democrats to draw on. Similarly, the "old" middle-class component of the electorate—the small shop-keepers, farmers, self-employed doctors and lawyers—has declined from 28 percent in 1950 to only 12 percent by the end of the 1980s. This reservoir of Christian Democratic–Free Democratic strength has become smaller.

The erosion of the social-class cleavage is also evident for the religious division. A generation ago, conservative German politicians characterized elections as a competition between Christian good and atheist evil, and such rhetoric succeeded in polarizing many voters along religious lines. But social change in the Federal Republic includes a strong secular trend. In the 1950s, over 40 percent of voters reported going to church on a weekly basis; by the 1990 election, barely 25 percent attended church this regularly. Among Catholics, regular church attendance has declined from 54 percent in 1953 to 30 percent in 1987. While church-going Catholics were about as likely to vote for the CDU/CSU in 1990 as they were in the 1950s, their numbers and hence the aggregate impact of religion on the vote have declined.[9]

These social changes have an especially strong impact among young voters. They are the least likely to be tied to the old class and religious networks and hence the most likely to seek out new alternatives. Age, in short, is one demographic factor whose importance has increased. Age is of particular importance in explaining support for the Greens. In 1987, for example, almost two of every three Green votes came from voters under thirty-five years of age. While about 16 percent of voters under age twenty-five supported the Greens, double their national average in 1987, only about 1 percent of citizens over age sixty voted for this party. As Green voters age, this polarization should decline, but in the near future the generation gap will remain an important factor in voting behavior. The Social Democrats in 1990 under Oskar Lafontaine made a strong appeal to younger age groups and among those voters under thirty-five years of age the SPD was indeed the strongest party.

Attitudes toward Candidates. Voters' perceptions of major candidates, especially party leaders and those slated for the chancellorship or cabinet membership, are important influences on voting behavior. The incumbent chancellor, for example, generally has an advantage, or "bonus," over the challenger. As in other Western societies, the chief executive can to an extent influence the news—announce new programs such as tax reductions, increased spending for social programs, and subsidies to various groups, all timed to the election.

A major factor in the landslide CDU/CSU victories in 1953 and 1957 was the personal popularity of Adenauer. More voters liked Adenauer than liked his party, and the SPD's chancellor candidates were less popular than their party. The low popularity of the Christian Democratic candidate in 1980, Franz Josef Strauss, was an important factor in the victory of the SPD-FDP coalition. In 1990 Chancellor Kohl following unification became more popular than his party.

Party Policies and Strategies. Through their policies and strategies the parties have also played an independent role in shaping electoral outcomes. The SPD's decision, for example, in 1983 to all but ignore the unemployment issue and emphasize noneconomic issues such as the NATO missile decision cost the party sizable blue-collar support. In 1987 the Christian Democrats underestimated the extent of discontent among farmers, many of whom stayed home. The Social Democrats' decision to seek an absolute majority with its chancellor candidate conducting an "American style" campaign lacked credibility in the view of most voters. By bringing down the Schmidt government in 1982, the Free Democrats lost many voters and were able to return to the parliament in 1983 only with the support of some CDU/CSU supporters who split their ballots. The party narrowly escaped political extinction. In 1990 the Social Democrats' division over the unification question was an important factor in the party's poor performance.

Issues. In most elections, the issues of prime concern to German voters revolve around the economy and social stability: inflation, unemployment, law and order (terrorism), and the viability of the social welfare system. "Security" is a word often used by all major parties in their electoral appeals; the bulk of the electorate does not want any major political or socioeconomic changes. Nonetheless, other specific issues, while not of concern to a great majority of the electorate, can be important in effecting the small voting shifts that can be decisive in an election. In 1972, for example, the SPD-FDP coalition was clearly helped by the issue of *Ostpolitik,* the government's policy of improving relations with the Soviet Union and Eastern Europe. Some voters, normally CDU/CSU, supported the Brandt government because of this issue; they saw the policy as a step toward a more lasting peace in Europe.

Since the early 1980s noneconomic or "new politics" issues have increased in importance. Chief among them was the protection of the environment and specifically the problem of nuclear power plants. By 1990, almost 75 percent of voters considered the environment to be a "very important" issue, second only to unemployment. The 1986 nuclear disaster at Chernobyl struck Germany with a special force, as citizens were told not to eat certain foods and to keep their children indoors. This crisis was soon followed by a series of chemical spills into the Rhine. The ecological cries of the Greens were now taken seriously by supporters of all political colors, and support for the Greens in public opinion polls soared. Over 40 percent of all voters considered the Greens to be the "most competent" party to deal with the nuclear power issue; this is almost five times greater than the party's vote at the 1983 election. Other noneconomic issues whose importance increased in the 1980s were women's rights, peace and disarmament, and the treatment of foreign minorities.

Notes

1. For a discussion of this point, see Gordon Smith, *Democracy in Western Germany* (New York: Holmes and Meier, 1979), 96 ff.

2. Gerhard Lehmbruch, "Liberal Corporatism and Party Government," in *Trends toward Corporatist Intermediation,* ed. Philippe Schmitter and Gerhard Lehmbruch (Beverly Hills: Sage 1979), 147–88.

3. There is a union for white-collar employees (*Angestellten*) with about a half million members that is not affiliated with the DGB. This is the only non-DGB union of any significant size in the private sector.

4. Andrei S. Markovits and Christopher S. Allen, "Power and Dissent: Trade Unions in the Federal Republic of Germany Re-Examined," Council of European Studies, Washington, D.C., March 1979. See also Andrei S. Markovits, *The Politics of the West German Trade Unions* (Cambridge: Cambridge University Press 1986).

5. Michael Fichter, "From Transmission Belt to Social Partnership? The Case of Organized Labor in Eastern Germany," *German Politics and Society,* no. 23 (Summer, 1991): 10.

6. Michael Jungblut, "Die heimlichen Reichen," *Die Zeit,* no. 46 (10 November 1978): 25.

7. Kurt Sontheimer, "Die Bundesrepublik und ihre Bürger," in *Nach dreißig Jahren,* ed. Walter Scheel (Stuttgart: Klett-Cotta, 1979), 175–86.

8. Referenda are constitutionally possible in most states, and a little-known provision of the Basic Law allows local communities to be governed by citizen assemblies. Thus far, no locality has employed this form of governance.

9. David P. Conradt and Russell J. Dalton, "The West German Electorate and the Party System: Continuity and Change in the 1980s," *Review of Politics* 50, no. 1 (January 1988): 3–29. For the 1990 election: Rainer-Olaf Schultze, "Bekannte Konturen im Westen—ungewisse Zukunft in Osten," in *Wahlverhalten* ed. Hans-Georg Wehling (Stuttgart: Verlag W. Kohlhammer, 1991), 78.

14

How Is Power Used?

The Federal Republic is a complex political system characterized by the presence of several power centers. Although the national executive with its control over the civil service initiates the broad outlines of policy, it cannot secure the approval of its policy proposals or their implementation without at least the tacit prior approval of other actors in the political system: major interest groups, extraparliamentary organizations of the governing parties, key members of parliament, the states, the courts, semipublic institutions such as the Federal Bank, the health and social security system leadership, the Federal Employment Service administration, and even the opposition parties through their chairmanship of several parliamentary committees and their delegates in the Bundesrat. Strong opposition by any of these actors will hinder the efforts of the government and chancellor to determine the "main guidelines" of policy.

Successful policy making must be accomplished within the framework of the politicoeconomic consensus that has developed since 1949. This means that the system resists any efforts at introducing major innovations within a relatively short time frame. Change tends to be gradual and incremental, and rarely will it have a redistributive effect. The issue of codetermination, for example, has been a policy problem throughout most of the republic's history. Codetermination—the right of workers and other employees to share in a firm's decision-making process through representation on its supervisory board—was a key element in the SPD program in 1969 when it became the major partner in a coalition with the FDP and again in 1972 when this coalition secured a comfortable parliamentary majority. Yet in spite of these very favorable political conditions, the new Co-Determination Law, which finally went into effect in 1976, did not give a firm's workers parity with capital and management. Attempts to change the tax system in the direction of more progressive rates have been stymied partly by the opposition of the small coalition partner, the Free Democrats, but also through the efforts of well-organized interest groups that have extensive contacts with governmental ministries.

／ The federal structure of the republic, which gives the states extensive responsibilities in implementing national legislation, represents a further dispersion of political power and is thus another factor inhibiting major policy innovation.[1] The importance of the constituent states in the policy process has increased as the scope of their veto power in the Bundesrat has expanded. At present, almost two-thirds of all legislation is subject to a Bundesrat veto.

In addition, between 1972 and 1982 the combination of a CDU/CSU majority in the Bundesrat and a Social Democratic–Free Democratic majority in the Bundestag reduced the chances of the national government using its power without extensive bargaining with the states. Thus the 1976 treaty with Poland, although negotiated by the national government, was ratified only after a variety of changes and concessions were made at the insistence of the CDU/CSU majority in the Bundesrat. Planned changes in education policy and the liberalization of regulations governing the employment of "radicals" in the public service were also thwarted by state opposition. But even friendly states (those governed by the same coalition that rules in Bonn) can and indeed have opposed national policy initiatives when they perceive a threat to state interests. Thus the national government had to struggle for decades to change significantly the distribution of taxes between the national and state governments, or to expand its influence in higher education, urban planning, and environmental protection legislation. In these areas, all the states have guarded their prerogatives.

In 1991 this condition of divided government returned as the Social Democrats acquired a majority in the Bundesrat while the Christian Democrats and Free Democrats held a solid majority in the Bundestag. The Social Democrats used this new influence to force changes in the government's tax program to finance unification. Because of the SPD majority any change in the provisions for granting asylum to foreigners (see chapter 15) will require the consent of the opposition party.

Semipublic Institutions

The use of political power in the Federal Republic is not restricted to the formal governmental institutions. Germany has an extensive network of semipublic institutions that play major roles in determining how power is to be used and how policy is to be implemented. Among the semipublic institutions, the social security and health systems, like the bureaucracy and courts, have survived the frequent and sudden regime changes of the past century. Both were established in the 1880s by the conservative Chancellor Otto von Bismarck, who sought to ensure that the growing working class would support the existing monarchical regime and not the Socialists. Through these social welfare programs, Bismarck in effect tried to buy the workers' political support. The Federal Labor Institute (Bundesanstalt für Arbeit), located in Nürnberg, which administers a nationwide network of employment offices, was established during the Weimar Republic and reemerged relatively intact after 1949. The Federal Bank in Frankfurt, which is primarily responsible for monetary policy, is a postwar creation, although it can trace its origins to the Reichsbank of the empire. These institutions assume functions performed by national governments in centralized systems such as Britain and France. In Germany, they lessen the total political load carried by the national government, but they also reduce its strength. Their distance from the national and state governments has also generally shielded them from the conflicts of partisan politics.[2]

The Social Security and Health Systems

The German welfare state is one of the most generous and comprehensive in the world. Expenditures of the health, pension, industrial accident, child support, public housing, and veterans' programs account for about 30 percent of the national government's budget and provide citizens with over a fourth of their disposable income. The pension and health care programs are financed largely through equal employer and employee contributions. The state does pay for civil servant pensions and about 80 percent of the pension costs for farmers. The costs of other programs, such as child support, housing and rent subsidies, and welfare, are taken from general tax revenue. Employers must pay the costs of the accident insurance program.

Yet the administration of these huge programs is not carried out by either the national or state governments but by more than eighteen hundred social security and health funds located throughout the country. The health, or "sickness," funds cover about 90 percent of the population. They are organized by economic sector (business, agriculture, professions), occupational group, and geographic area. The social security (pension and accident) programs insure about 39 million adults.

Although dating from the late nineteenth century, these social insurance programs have undergone extensive changes since the founding of the Federal Republic. The governing boards of all the funds are now based on the principle of parity representation for the various business, professional, and labor interests most concerned with the programs. After 1949, the left or labor wing of the ruling Christian Democratic Union, working with the trade unions and the opposition Social Democrats and enjoying the support of Chancellor Adenauer, was able to convince business interests that the confrontational class politics of the Weimar Republic should be replaced with an emphasis on "social partnership." This required concessions from both business and labor. The trade unions gave up their majority control of the health funds, while employers did the same for the pension and accident insurance programs.

The administrative independence of the funds is limited by federal law. The size of pension payments and the taxes to pay for them, for example, are determined by the parliament. But they do have considerable power to set the fee structure for physicians, the construction and management of hospitals, and the investment of pension fund capital. The concept of social partnership thus extends to the state as well.

The health and pension system funds, according to one authority, are "political shock absorbers," connecting "state with society because they leave it to the major economic interest groups to mediate the state's administration of major social welfare programs."[3]

The postwar emphasis on consensus and social partnership is seen most clearly in the 1957 reform of the pension system. Previous pension legislation based the size of payments largely on the individual's contributions. The 1957 law, while retaining some elements of individual insurance, linked increases in pension payments, with some time lag, to increases in the overall national wage level. This dynamic feature enabled all pensioners, regardless of their individual contribution, to share directly in the expanding national economy. The 1957 law was a political compromise. Conservative business interests and the Christian Democrats accepted its dynamic provisions, that is, indexing pensions to the national economy, while the labor unions and the Social Democrats abandoned their preference for a more uniform, egalitarian pension scheme. The system now combines elements of individual insurance with collective welfare. In recent years, however, this postwar consensus on the pension and health systems has been strained by budgetary cutbacks, rising unemployment, and slower economic growth.

The Federal Labor Institute

The Federal Labor Institute is another semipublic institution and is assigned primary responsibility for organizing the labor market (i.e., bringing jobs and job seekers together) and administering the system of unemployment insurance. The institute also administers programs, financed from unemployment insurance revenues, that retrain workers and supplements the income of those put on short time. In its programs, the institute must give special attention to the elderly, women, the handicapped, long-term unemployed, and other special groups such as seasonal workers. The institute, which was established in 1952, is lo-

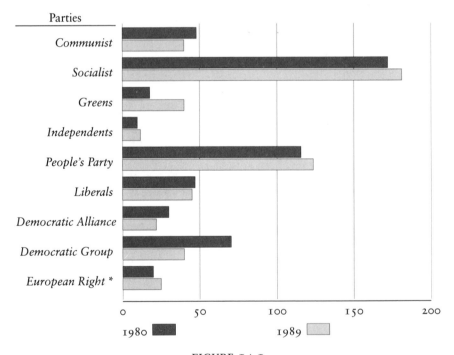

FIGURE 14.1
EUROPEAN PARLIAMENTARY ELECTIONS
(NUMBER OF DEPUTIES)

NOTE: * = radical right.

cated in Nürnberg and is under the supervision, but not the direct control, of the Labor Ministry in Bonn. It is governed by a president, an executive committee, and a supervisory board; the board includes representatives from trade unions, employers, and federal and state officials. The major guidelines determining labor policy are developed in Nürnberg and administered in hundreds of branch, local, and regional offices. Most of the unemployment compensation program is financed by equal employer and employee contributions, which amount to about 3 percent of a worker's gross income. If the unemployment level is high, however, the federal government must subsidize the institute. Thus in certain circumstances it can be financially dependent on the federal government.

But, as in the case of the pension and health systems, business and labor representatives are closely involved in the work of the institute's employment offices through their membership on its local, regional, and national administrative committees. The members of these committees are proposed by the trade unions, business associations, the federal government and local government authorities.

The power of the institute was also enhanced during the twenty-year tenure of its former president, Josef Stingl. Although a member of the conservative Christian Social Union (CSU), Stingl enjoyed the support of the trade unions and remained in office during the Social-Liberal era in Bonn. Through skillful use of the media he established himself in the view of many Germans as the preeminent authority on the unemployment problem and was relatively immune from criticism from Bonn. His stature also had a positive impact on the institute's budget.

The Bundesbank

The Bundesbank is the German national bank roughly equivalent to the Federal Reserve Bank in the United States or the Bank of England. It is the institution chiefly responsible for monetary policy and hence price stability. Indeed, some observers consider its chief mission to be the "guarding of West Germany's Holy Grail, a low inflation rate."[4] It is largely independent from the federal government, the states, and private interest groups. Its autonomy is in fact greater than that of its counterparts in Britain, France, Japan, Sweden, and even the United States. Since 1982, the bank has also been directly involved in reducing the national government's deficits by transferring a portion of its profits from foreign exchange transactions to the federal government. These transfers, which since 1982 have amounted to over $40 billion, have enabled the Kohl government to reduce borrowing and cut taxes.

The power and independence of the bank reflect the strong concern about inflation held by all Germans. Twice in this century, following the two world wars, Germany experienced disastrous inflations that wiped out the savings of millions of citizens. Determined to keep monetary policy out of the reach of politicians, West Germany's constitution did not make the Bundesbank subject to any national government ministry, nor to the general supervision of the chancellor under his guideline power. While the bank, according to its constitution, is obligated to support the government's overall economic policy, this applies only as long as government policy, in the judgment of the bank's leadership, does not conflict with its prime mission, the safeguarding of the currency. If a bank decision is opposed by the federal government, it can only delay its implementation for two weeks.

The Bundesbank is governed by two executive bodies: a Directorate and a Central Bank Council. Members of the Directorate are appointed to eight-year terms by the federal president upon the recommendation of the federal government. The Central Bank Council represents mainly the interests of the regional branches of the bank. It is largely controlled by the regional bank presidents appointed by the Bundesrat upon the recommendation of the various state governments. Thus the Directorate has a more national perspective, while the Central Bank Council tends to reflect state or regional interests.

In spite of its power and influence on national economic policy, the Bundesbank has not become a partisan political institution. Although the CDU has been in power in Bonn since 1982, there is only one CDU supporter among the Directorate's six members. The current chief executive officer is an independent. In recommending appointments to the Directorate, the national government has usually selected individuals who are acceptable to the banking community and generally in agreement with the main economic policy objectives of the government. Once appointed for eight-year terms, however, the directors have tended to be independent. After a careful analysis of central bank policy in West Germany, France, and Italy from 1973 to 1985, John Goodman found no evidence that the Bundesbank, in contrast to its counterparts in France and Italy, had manipulated monetary policy for electoral purposes.[5]

Major disagreements between the Bundesbank and the government have been rare but by no means unknown. In the late 1970s, the bank initially opposed Chancellor Schmidt's plan to create a European Monetary System (EMS), which linked the Deutsch Mark (DM) to the currencies of several other European Community nations. The bank feared for the stability of the mark in a system where it was tied to the weaker currencies of such high-inflation countries such as France and Italy. Chancellor Helmut Schmidt, however, was able to convince the bank that the advantages of the EMS, such as decoupling European currencies from the unstable dollar, outweighed the possible disadvantages of rising inflation. In practice, the EMS did not restrict German monetary policy or the bank's independence. On the contrary, in the view of many of West Germany's neighbors, the EMS imposed German anti-inflationary discipline on its participants and promoted German trade.

The Bundesbank has also been wary of plans for a European Central Bank. German political leaders have generally been enthusiastic about a common European bank and currency as part of the European Community's drive toward the elimination of all economic barriers before the end of 1992. As in the case of the EMS, the Bundesbank fears that the more free-spending French and Italians will undermine the stability of its monetary policy. The bank's objections became more muted, however, when its directors were assured a major role in the planning and eventual operation of the new European bank.

In 1987 the Bundesbank became a major actor in the conflict between the United States and West Germany over international economic policy. The Reagan administration urged the Germans, as one of the world's leading trading nations, to speed up their economy in order to increase the demand for American goods in Germany and thus reduce the huge U.S. trade deficit. While the Kohl government could and did cut taxes and increase spending, it had little control over interest rates, which fell largely within the domain of the Bundesbank. The bank downplayed Germany's economic influence and pointed instead to the U.S. budget deficit as the primary cause of the American trade imbalance and falling dollar.

This German-American impasse became an important factor in the international financial crisis that began with the plunge of the New York stock market in October 1987. When the Bundesbank in the week preceding the October crash actually increased one of its key interest rates, U.S. Treasury Secretary James Baker warned the Germans that unless they stopped raising interest rates and restraining their economy, the United States would take no steps to prevent a drastic decline in the value of the dollar.

Responding to pressure from the Kohl government, the international financial community and major German business interests, the Bundesbank within six weeks after the New York stock market crisis, finally lowered rates on several types of loans. Until the stock market drop, however, the bank's Central Council was divided over the question of whether to give first priority to keeping inflation low or stimulating the economy. The council's low inflation faction, composed largely of regional bankers less concerned about international factors and more about the effects of inflation on their institutions, held the upper hand. But the sharp drop in the dollar and stock prices increased the influence of the bank's growth faction.

In 1990 the Bank strongly opposed the monetary union between the two German states in which the West German Deutsch Mark became the sole currency for both states. The union gave East Germans a very generous exchange rate for their "East Marks" and resulted in a 20 percent increase in the money supply without a corresponding increase in productivity. Less than a year later, inflation reached a nine-year high. The Bank finally accepted the union as a political necessity. The Kohl government argued that it had little choice. Unless the fabled Deutsch Mark was brought to East Germans, they would come to the Mark, that is, emigrate in increasing numbers to the West. Nonetheless, the Bank's outgoing president in 1991 still referred to the currency union as a disaster which was largely responsible for the slow pace of economic reconstruction in the former East Germany.

Use of Power in the Social-Liberal Era, 1969–82

The basic pattern of incrementalism, a problem-solving bargaining orientation to politics, continued unchanged under the Social-Liberal coalition that governed in Bonn from 1969 to 1982. Indeed, the SPD since 1959 was committed not to change the rules of the game if it did achieve national political responsibility. Most Social Democrats do not propose any basic changes in the structure of the economy or polity. In economic policy they have advocated only gradual changes in capitalism German style. Capital and labor are viewed as "partners" rather than opponents, with government mediating any major differences. This basic orientation means, of course, that governmental power will be used cautiously and above all in a manner that will not disrupt consensus. The thirteen years (sixteen including the 1966–69 Grand Coalition) of Social Democratic rule did not produce any basic changes in this pattern. What the SPD effected was a gradual shift in distributive policies in the direction of greater benefits for lower- and lower-middle-status groups (tax, welfare, education policies) and the beginnings of a possible shift in the distribution of power and influence within the industrial enterprise (codetermination). The other major change associated with SPD rule from 1969 to 1982—Ostpolitik, the normalization of relations between Eastern Europe and the Soviet Union—did not in fact represent any major challenge to the consensus but drew on previous initiatives made during the mid- and late 1960s when the Christian Democrats were still the dominant party. Thus there was considerable support for the "new policy" within the parliamentary opposition.

Conflicts between the two coalition partners were more frequent in socioeconomic policy and especially over questions of the organization of the economy, the reform of vocational (apprenticeship) training, land-use laws, the inequality of capital resources (compulsory profit sharing), and tax reform. The Free Democrats generally are opposed to increased state intervention in the economy and the extension of worker participation in a firm's decision-making process at the expense of capital and management. The leveling implied in the profit-sharing plans supported by the Social Democrats and their plans for increasingly progressive taxation were also opposed by the FDP. In short, when the issue involved the *redistribution* of economic resources and power, that is, increasing the resources of one group (workers) at the expense of another (the middle and upper classes), there was extensive conflict within the coalition. The Free Democrats were usually able to force a compromise that benefited its largely upper- and middle-class clientele. The Social Democrats, in this area, probably gave up more than their numerical strength required; also, the Free Democrats exerted more influence than their size would have entitled them to.[6]

The coalition was more harmonious when problems were largely regulative and distributive in character. There was essentially little difference between the Social Democrats and Liberals in the areas of civil liberties, education, internal security, defense, and foreign policies. These latter problems dominated the legislative program of the first SPD-FDP government led by Willy Brandt (1969–72).

How Power Was Used after the Wende, 1982–89

The Christian Democrats returned to power in 1982 promising a fundamental change (Wende) in the republic's policies and its "moral-cultural" climate. The era of free-spending, permissive socialism had, in the view of the Christian Democrats, a corrupting effect on the West German community. Kohl promised a return to traditional values: thrift, hard work, and discipline, and an end to the entitlement mentality of the Social-Liberal years. The victory of his government in the 1983 election, however, was due primarily to the recession of 1981–83, Germany's worst since the Great Depression of the 1930s. Many voters associated this economic slump with the policies of the previous government. The Christian Democrats promised an economic upturn through a German version of supply-side economics: cuts in government spending including most social programs, investment incentives for business, lower taxes, and reduced state deficits. While these policies, when finally implemented, did not produce changes as drastic as those associated in the early 1980s with "Reaganomics" or "Thatcherism," they did represent a departure from the generous support given to social welfare programs during the SPD-FDP governments.

But the welfare state was by no means drastically cut during these years. Indeed, most analysts argue that many of the cutbacks in education, health, and pension spending lasted only until early 1984.[7] And by 1985 the Kohl government suffered sharp losses in state elections to the Social Democrats that were related to public opposition to any further reductions in the welfare state. Numerous surveys over the past twenty years have consistently shown that while Germans are willing to accept marginal reductions during difficult economic times, they still firmly support welfare programs and expect the state to assume fundamental responsibility for the health and well-being of the population. Thus spending for social programs dropped only from 32.3 percent of GNP in 1983 to 30 percent in 1986. While budget deficits dropped from $30 billion in 1982 to $8 billion in 1987, by 1989 they had risen again to about $20 billion. At the 1987 election there was little talk of a Wende, or of any further reductions in social programs by the Christian Democrats.

Policy Implementation

The process of implementing national legislation takes place largely through the administrative structures of the state governments. The national government is thus dependent, in many cases, on the states if legislation is to have its intended effect. At first glance, this system would seem to allow the sixteen states, especially those governed by parties not in power in Bonn, to sabotage or undermine national legislation they oppose on ideological or partisan political grounds. In practice, this has not taken place.

German federalism has a number of unifying or centralizing characteristics that make this implementation phase function remarkably well. First, as we have discussed, state governments and their bureaucracies have extensive input into the national-level legislative process through their membership in the Bundesrat. They are well aware of what the legislation will entail in terms of administrative machinery and resources. Second, the laws and rules of procedure for state bureaucracies are unified. Unlike American federalism, constituent states do not have different laws for divorces, bankruptcy, or criminal offenses. Also, the rules by which the civil service operates are the same for all states and the national government. Third, the constitution requires that there be a "unity of living standards" throughout the republic. In practice, this has meant that richer states, such as North Rhine-Westphalia and Hamburg, must pay via grants and tax transfers to bring the poorer states up to their level of government services and standards. Thus the expenditures of poorer states for public works or welfare are not drastically different from those of more prosperous states. Differences between resources and expenditures are made up by this system of tax redistribution, or revenue sharing.

Differences between states do exist in policy areas where the states have sole or major responsibilities—mainly education (especially primary and secondary) and internal security (police and law enforcement). Educational reform, for example, has proceeded differently in the various states, although the CDU/CSU governs seven of the sixteen states, only one of every ten comprehensive schools is in a CDU state. Procedures for the screening of candidates for public employment have also varied, with CDU/CSU states taking a more hard-line position on this issue. There have been cases of prospective schoolteachers whose applications were rejected in CDU/CSU governed states such as Bavaria and Baden-Württemberg for alleged "radical" political activity securing positions in SPD states.

Until 1992 the abortion issue divided the West German states and the five new East German regions. The former German Democratic Republic allowed abortion "on demand" during the first trimester of pregnancy. West German law permitted abortions only under certain conditions usually connected with the physical or psychological health of the woman. The 1990 unification treaties allowed each region to retain its own law until 1992. In June 1992 the Bundestag in a dramatic vote approved a new law, which was much closer to the old East German statute than the West German law. The government of Chancellor Kohl, however, with the support of Bavaria, is contesting the constitutionality of the new "pro-choice" legislation in the Constitutional Court.

Notes

1. Although Berlin is now the official political capital and will be the seat of the parliament and central government, not all major administrative units of the federal government will have their central offices there. The current practice of dispersing national offices throughout the country will continue. For example, none of the major federal courts are in the current capital, Bonn; they are scattered about in Karlsruhe, Kassel, Berlin, and elsewhere. The federal railways and federal bank are in Frankfurt, the airline has its administrative center in Cologne, the national archive is in Koblenz, the Federal Criminal Office (the German version of the FBI) is in Wiesbaden. This dispersion of administrative offices reflects the decentralized character of the Federal Republic and, perhaps more important, the fact that the states preceded the federal government after 1945. Indeed many of these offices were the product of the Occupation period. The five new East German states will eventually receive their "share" of national offices. The Bundesrat will remain in Bonn.

2. Peter J. Katzenstein, *Policy and Politics in West Germany* (Philadelphia: Temple University Press, 1987), 90–95.

3. Katzenstein, 58.

4. Katzenstein, 60.

5. John B. Goodman, "Monetary Politics in France, Italy, and Germany: 1973–1985," unpublished paper, Graduate School of Business Administration, Harvard University, 1988, 23.

6. Manfred G. Schmidt, "The Politics of Domestic Reform in the Federal Republic of Germany," *Politics and Society* 8, no. 2 (1979): 165–200.

7. Jens Alber, "Der Wohlfahrtstaat in der Wirtschaftskrise—Eine Bilanz der Sozialpolitik in der Bundesrepublik seit den frühen siebziger Jahren," *Politische Vierteljahresschrift* 27, no. 1 (March 1986): 28–60.

15

What Is the Future of German Politics?

As the Federal Republic begins its fifth decade, it is faced with a variety of domestic and foreign political problems, many of which are common to other advanced industrial democracies: unemployment, environmental protection, crime, drug abuse, urban development, energy, the financing of the extensive social welfare system, European integration, economic growth, and East-West relations in a post-Cold-War world. All of these issues are dwarfed, however, by the challenge of unification. The Federal Republic in the 1990s is attempting to integrate 16 million East Germans into its Western-style society, economy, and polity. Most of these new citizens have lived either under the Nazi or Communist dictatorships. Their experience with Western democracy is limited to the short period since November 1989 and to knowledge gained from West German media and, for some, visits to the West. Unified Germany must also define its role in the international arena and especially its relationship to the postcommunist societies of the former Soviet Union and Eastern Europe. This chapter will examine these issues.

None of the republic's current tasks, however, should obscure its fundamental accomplishments since 1949. A consensus on liberal democracy has finally been achieved in a German political order. The Federal Republic has become an effective and legitimate democratic political system. Indeed, for some it has become a model of an advanced industrial society.[1] Its critics—those who view it as a "republic in suspense," very vulnerable to a major economic crisis, and those who regard it as a neofascist "restoration"—are simply mistaken. That these clichés endure testifies to the power of stereotypes and not to any actual political developments in the past forty years.

This process of consensus building and legitimation has taken most of the postwar period to develop. As a result, many institutional and policy changes have been slower to emerge in the Federal Republic than in other Western democracies. Thus there is no lack of problems for Germany. Nevertheless, few modern industrial democracies have more resources to deal with these issues than the Federal Republic.

Putting Germany Back Together Again: The Rebuilding and Integration of the East

The October 1990 unification of the two German states ended a legal and international political process that began less than a year earlier with the breaching of the Berlin Wall. Germany was formally united, but two societies divided for forty years cannot simply be brought together by the signing of a few agreements and treaties. The unification and integration of the two states will take at least a generation to complete.

This process has political, economic, social, and psychological dimensions. What happened on 3 October 3 1990? Was West Germany simply enlarged by the addition of 16 million new citizens, about a fourth of the population of the "old" Federal Republic? Or was a new state created from the merger of two independent states? Or was the Germany which was defeated and divided in 1945 *reunified* in 1990? Will the addition of 16 million East Germans produce a new political cultural mix? Will Germany now look more to the East and reassert its historic economic and political role in this region? These are the questions that Germans themselves are now posing. Discussion and debate over these issues and related problems will constitute much of the substance of politics in the years ahead.

The 1990 unification was not a merger of two independent sovereign states but rather a friendly takeover. East Germany was practically bankrupt, the communist regime discredited, and the great majority of Easterners wanted unification—the security, prosperity, and freedom they associated with the West—as soon as possible. After the disappearance of their own state, however, East Germans discovered that many West Germans considered them an economic and political burden. Over 70 percent of East Germans, according to surveys conducted throughout 1990 and 1991, feel that they are second-rate citizens. They resent the arrogance of some West Germans, the *Besserwessis* ("know it all" Westerners), who treat them like colonial subjects. East Germans also see the Westerners as too materialistic and manipulative. Many East Germans feel that their condition was just an accident of history. They do not have a sense of responsibility for the forty years of Communist dictatorship. By 1991 West Germans realized that stiff tax increases and large deficits would be the price for real unity and many wondered why they should sacrifice. Some Westerners see the *Ossies* (Easterners) as lazy, always expecting a handout: "They think they can live like we do without working for it." German political leadership is now attempting to deal with this "Wall in people's heads" or "inner" unification.

The June 1991 decision to move the government and parliament to Berlin was in part an attempt to demonstrate to East Germans that unified Germany was more than a simple enlargement of the old Federal Republic. The narrow vote in parliament was preceded by a nationwide debate. Supporters and opponents of Berlin and Bonn were found in all the political parties.

The 1990 unification treaty stated that Berlin was the capital but left open the question of whether the government and parliament would remain in Bonn or move to Berlin. Supporters of Bonn contended that the postwar federal system would be weakened by moving the government. Bonn is associated with West Germany's postwar transformation into a stable democracy and a model member of the Western community of nations. For some Berlin is a symbol of Germany's militaristic, authoritarian, and totalitarian past—the Prussian kaisers and Hitler all waged war from Berlin. The city's supporters counter that it is unfair to blame an entire city for the acts of a few individuals many years ago. They pointed to Berlin's steadfast commitment to Western values during the darkest days of the Cold War.

The controversial vote expressed the conviction of at least a narrow majority of political leaders that the country had to integrate its new eastern regions into the larger political community as quickly as possible. Unified Germany will be a more eastern, northern, and secular society than the "old" Federal Republic.

A New Constitution?

One means for furthering the political integration of the two former states would be through a new constitution. The Bonn Constitution or Basic Law of 1949 contains two provisions that were relevant to the unification process. The first is found in Article 23, which allows for new states to petition the parliament for admission to the federation, much as territories once joined the United States as new states. This was the procedure used in 1957 when the Saar joined the Federal Republic. It was the one favored by the Kohl government and finally adopted in the August, 1990 unification treaty. West Germany was thus simply enlarged by the addition of the East German states.

The Constitution also includes a second provision, Article 146, which nullifies the Basic Law when "a constitution adopted by a free decision of the German people comes into force." This would have required the election of a constituent assembly in which both nations would have been represented as equals. The new constitution would have created an entirely new entity. This approach was favored by the East German dissidents and elements of the West German Greens and Social Democrats. They had hoped for a gradual unification process with East Germany, retaining some of what they considered the positive aspects of the country's forty-year history: women's rights, full employment, low cost housing, and day care. The Kohl government, however, rejected using Article 146 as too time-consuming and cumbersome. It wanted unification as quickly as possible. Using Article 146 would have meant that unification was more of a merger than a takeover.

In the final unification treaty in August, 1990 there is a provision (Article 5) for the parliament to examine whether constitutional changes dealing with "the federal structure and the goals of the state" are necessary. Thus the door was left open for a new constitution in which some of the specific concerns of East Germans could be addressed.

In May 1991 the Bundestag took up this question for the first time. Not surprisingly the government and opposition differ on whether and how much the existing document should be changed. The current governing coalition of Christian and Free Democrats supports only a "constitutional committee," which would "modernize" the current Basic Law by making changes; those changes would, however, stop short of a new constitution. The government wants this constitutional committee to consider questions such as the right of foreigners to vote in local elections, the rights of the Länder in the European Community and German military participation in United Nations operations. Current law does not give the franchise to foreign residents, nor does it allow, in the opinion of most constitutional experts, for military forces to be active outside of NATO territory.

The Social Democrats and elements of the Greens, however, want a "constitutional council," which would develop the current Basic Law into a permanent constitution for the unified country. This council would have 120 members, who would be equally divided by gender and elected by the Federal Assembly, the same body that elects the Federal president.[2]

In addition to the members elected by the Assembly, the SPD wants to have representatives of the former East German opposition and "leading personalities" from all areas of public life. In essence the Social Democrats advocate a new constitution, based on the Basic Law, that would contain provisions making environmental protection, the right to a job, decent housing, equal rights for women, a prohibition against the export of arms, and the rejection of atomic, biological, and chemical weapons for the armed forces formal goals of the state, thus obligating all governments, regardless of party composition, to support them. The completed constitution would then be presented to the people via a referendum, and, if approved, it would replace the present Basic Law as called for in Article 146.

Some compromise must be found between these two positions since any change in the Basic Law requires a two-thirds majority in both parliamentary bodies, the Bundestag and the Bundesrat. Consequently, both large parties have the votes to veto any proposed changes. Regardless of the final institutional form, it is expected that either a revised Basic Law or a new constitution will be presented to the electorate for its approval.

Public support for a referendum on a new constitution is indeed stronger in the former East Germany than in the "old" Federal Republic. Only about 30 percent of the adult population in the West think it is necessary to vote on a new document as compared to 57 percent in the East. About half of West German respondents think that such a vote is not necessary in contrast to only 16 percent in the former GDR. A new constitution, approved in a referendum, would legitimate the unification process for many East Germans.[3]

The Economic and Environmental Reconstruction of the East

Unification has revealed the full extent of the former East Germany's economic problems. Its economy was characterized by an outmoded, overstaffed industrial sector, an underdeveloped service sector, and a dilapidated infrastructure. Many of the region's industrial enterprises were largely incapable of competing in a market economy. East German products were antiquated and of poor quality; now, priced in "hard" currency, they are more expensive than those of Germany's Western competitors. East Germany's largest customers, Eastern Europe and the Soviet Union, could not afford to pay for imports in the Western currencies demanded after the July 1990 unification treaty. East Germans themselves also stopped buying the products from their own region. Many East Germans were also underemployed; featherbedding was widespread. By 1989 the average West German worker produced almost four times as many goods and services as his or her East German counterpart, that is, the Gross National Product produced by East Germany's 9.2 million workers only equaled the GNP of 2.4 million West Germans.

Following unification the country's economy went into a free fall; hundreds of plants were closed, some for environmental reasons, and unemployment soared. Production in some areas dropped by 50 to 70 percent. By the end of 1991 the region's work force had declined by about 25 percent from 9.2 million in October 1990 to 6.75 million. One million were unemployed, an additional million were on subsidized short-time, and over a half million had moved to the West. The great majority of short-time workers will be laid off in the near future.

The rebuilding of this economy will require massive infusions of capital investment from the West. A fundamental prerequisite to economic development is a modern infrastructure: communication systems, transportation networks, water and waste treatment facilities. The former GDR's infrastructure is in a desolate condition. Much of the telephone system is pre-World War II in origin, roads and highways have not been properly maintained and are inadequate for the new traffic flows, less than a third of the country's rail lines are electrified. In the former GDR's cities there is an acute shortage of space for commercial enterprises. Modern hotels and restaurants are rarities. The country's service sector is at least three decades behind that of West Germany. The modernization of this infrastructure has been a top priority in the government's plans. By the end of 1991 almost $50 billion had been invested or allocated to give the region a modern phone system, railways, roads, and highways.

The formerly state-owned economic enterprises—over 8,000 companies, 22,000 small businesses (restaurants, shops), 30 percent of the farmland, and 60 percent of the forests—have been put under the ownership and control of a Trusteeship Authority (*Treuhand*). The Authority, which is the world's largest holding company, has the task of selling those enterprises that are competitive, modernizing those that have a chance to compete in a free market, and closing the firms that cannot survive. By the end of 1991 it had disposed of about 4,600 enterprises, but the toughest part of its mission, the closing of hopeless companies, is yet to come. The Authority's operations ran a deficit of about $13 billion in 1991, largely due to its assumption of the firms' old debts and to the costs of closing outmoded companies. In 1992 this deficit will increase to about $17 billion. The Treuhand, which now employs over

3,000 administrators, is expected to remain in operation until at least the end of the century.

A major problem in the economic reconstruction of the East is the question of disputed property ownership. Should people who fled East Germany before the building of the Wall be entitled to reclaim their property? What about the rights of East Germans who have been living in homes for decades and who now discover that the original owners had these homes taken from them by the communists or, in some cases, even the Nazis? In the final unification treaty, the principle of "restitution before monetary compensation" was agreed upon, albeit with some reluctance by the East Germans. This provision opened the door to over one million claims for restitution, which are now working their

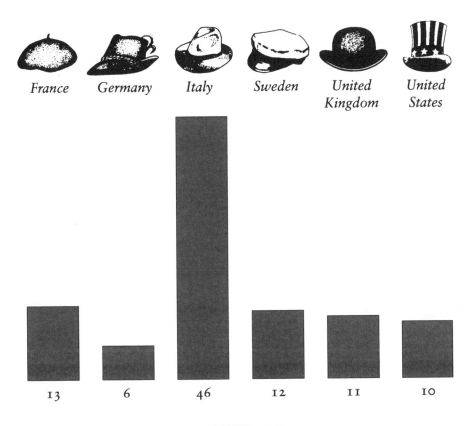

France	Germany	Italy	Sweden	United Kingdom	United States
13	6	46	12	11	10

FIGURE 15.1
NUMBER OF POST-1945 CABINETS

NOTE: For France, Fifth Republic only.

way at a very slow pace through the courts. Apart from the personal loss and tragedy, this problem is holding up an estimated $65 billion of planned investment in the East. Many West Germans now agree that the "restitution before compensation" principle was probably a mistake and should have been reversed.

By 1992 assistance from the West will account for about 60 percent of the gross national product (GNP) in the former East Germany. In 1991 the costs of unification increased the indebtedness of the public sector to over 6 percent of its GNP, or $850 billion, the highest level in the history of the Federal Republic. In 1992 total public debt will increase still more to an estimated $1 trillion. While this is still below the level of other Western societies, most notably the United States, it is a cause of growing concern for economists and some political leaders.

Eventually, of course, these investments in the East will begin to pay dividends. This region will have one of the most modern infrastructures and industrial plants in Europe. It should benefit from the growing market in Eastern Europe. Indeed, by the end of 1991 the massive infusions of capital were beginning to show results. The construction industry, small business, and the service sector were clearly expanding even as the overall employment picture continued to worsen.

The Environmental Crisis

Cleaning up the environment in the East will probably be a harder task than rebuilding its economy. Water, ground, and air pollution levels are among the highest in Europe. Since unification, the closing down of some of the worst polluters, largely for economic reasons, has already produced some marginal improvement in air and water quality, but the monumental clean-up job will last well into the next century.

Only 3 percent of the region's rivers and streams are ecologically intact, and only 1 percent of its lakes are free from pollution. Almost 80 percent of the area's water sources are either biologically dead or heavily polluted. The remainder are only "moderately" poisoned. The most important waterway in the East, the Elbe, is the most polluted river in Europe.

Pollution is most severe in the industrialized south and southwest parts of the region. Outmoded industrial plants, many built before World War II, dumped millions of pounds of untreated industrial and chemical wastes into waterways or huge pits each year. The area's major source of energy, lignite or brown coal, was the chief cause of air pollution including virtually nonstop smog during the fall and winter months.

The sulfur dioxide emitted when lignite is burned affects the nose, throat, and lungs. Skin cancers and respiratory ailments are two to three times higher in this area than in the rest of the former East Germany.

Soil pollution is most extensive in the uranium mine areas in the states of Saxony and Thuringia. From 1946 until 1990 over 200,000 tons of uranium were shipped to weapons factories and power stations in the Soviet Union. Whole villages were evacuated and destroyed during the mining operations. The clean up of this area will take at least 12 to 15 years.

Minorities— Foreign Residents, Refugees, and Resettlers

After unification, the most difficult social problem confronting the Federal Republic is the condition of its almost 6 million foreign residents. The economic miracle of the 1950s transformed Germany from an economy with a surplus of labor to one with an acute labor shortage. There were simply too many jobs available for the native work force, especially in menial, low-paying positions. To remedy this problem and maintain economic growth, the government, working closely with employers, recruited workers from Italy, Greece, Spain, Turkey, and other less-developed countries. By 1973 there were almost 2.6 million foreign workers in the Federal Republic; the 1974–76 recession reduced this to the present 1.9 million. Foreign workers usually occupy the lowest rung on the occupational ladder: unskilled manual positions, sanitary and sewage workers, custodial and janitorial staff. They tend to be concentrated in large cities: Berlin, for example, is the city with the third-largest Turkish population in the world. They have been subjected to discrimination in housing. Apart from their jobs, many foreign workers have little or no social contact with the native German population.

The dependents of foreign workers, especially their children, make this a potentially explosive issue. Many of these children have spent most or all of their lives in Germany. Yet their parents cling to the goal of someday returning to their home country and thus want the children to retain its language and values. The result is that children grow up in a sort of twilight zone—they master neither their parents' language nor German. They invariably drop out of school and, urged on by the parents, attempt to secure employment to augment the family's finances and hasten its "return" to the homeland. But in recent years the tightened job market has made it difficult for young, half-literate, untrained foreign people to find work. The result is a growing body of unemployed adolescents, especially in the large cities, involved in petty crime, and increasingly, the drug trade.

Discrimination, a lack of social mobility, and poor educational and job opportunities for their children are the result, in part, of the workers' lack of political influence. As non-Germans they cannot vote, and the acquisition of citizenship is a difficult process even for those foreign residents who want to be naturalized. The political system has simply not responded to the needs of an unorganized, politically powerless minority, and as long as foreign workers do not have the vote, it is difficult to envision any major changes. In fact, new restrictions on residency for foreign workers imposed by some local governments hinder their freedom of movement and hence decrease their prospects for upward social mobility.

The problem is compounded by the ambiguity of the foreign workers' future plans. Many still insist that their goal is to return to their home country. They are in Germany just to earn as much money in as short a period of time as they can and are thus not interested in becoming politically involved. For some, this "return to the homeland" has become a myth or illusion that enables them to endure the discrimination and deprivation they experience. By the second and third generation, however, it becomes less viable, and the frustration of their children increases.

Several proposals have been made to improve the status of guest workers and their families. One involves giving the franchise to foreign workers for local elections. One state, Schleswig-Holstein, passed such legislation in 1989. This would, it is argued, make local officials more responsive to their needs, especially in housing and education. In 1990, however, the Federal Constitutional Court declared the law unconstitutional. Some students of the problem have advocated that all children of foreign workers, born in the Federal Republic, automatically become German citizens when they reach the age of eighteen. It would thus become easier for the second and third generation to identify with the Federal Republic and reject the "return-to-the-homeland" myth. Finally, it has been suggested that the naturalization laws be liberalized so that foreign workers could have a viable option to their present condition. Thus far, however, there is little significant support for any of these proposed changes. In a practical sense, the churches, labor unions (by requiring equal pay for equal work) and charitable organizations have done more than the government.

By the late 1980s, the problem of foreign workers was compounded by the arrival of hundreds of thousands of "political" refugees from various Third World countries and ethnic German resettlers from the Soviet Union and Eastern Europe. A strong antiforeigner backlash also developed among native Germans in some cities and was related to the successes of the radical right-wing Republican party. Germany has the most liberal political asylum law in Western Europe, which is due in part to the fact that many of the founding fathers of the Federal Republic were themselves political refugees during the Third Reich. But, in recent years, a flood of asylum seekers has prompted the government to seek to change the existing laws. The German government contends that many asylum seekers are not victims of political persecution, but rather want access to the Federal Republic's prosperous economy and generous welfare state. In 1991 groups of skin heads and young neo-Nazis attacked some of the hostels and dormitories where many asylum seekers are housed. Resentment towards foreigners is also strong in the former East Germany. While political leaders and the great majority of the public condemned the violence, there is growing support in the nation for reducing the influx of foreigners. Germany in 1991 was the target country for almost 250,000 refugees, three times the number in any other European nation.

Beginning in 1988, hundreds of thousands of ethnic Germans began to resettle in the Federal Republic. For decades, the government had attempted to persuade the Soviet Union, Poland, and other Eastern European countries to allow their nationals, who by virtue of their language, ancestry, or education profess to be German, to resettle in the country. To the surprise of many German leaders, the countries of the former Soviet bloc relented; it is now estimated that a total of about two million ethnic Germans will eventually settle in the Federal Republic.

The constitution makes these settlers, many of whom do not speak German, eligible for immediate full citizenship. Thus the descendants of eighteenth- and nineteenth-century Germans can appear in the Federal Republic and become citizens. Many of them, however, have suffered persecution and discrimination as the price for maintaining their German heritage. With a shortage of affordable housing and unemployment still high, the arrival of these distant cousins has evoked some resentment among native residents. But others, pointing to the Federal Republic's low birthrate and aging population, welcome them as a positive demographic development. Their strongest champion has been Chancellor Kohl, who contends that the country has a moral obligation to let these people, after so many years, finally experience the "sunny side" of being German.

Civil Liberties—
Terrorism and the Computerized Police

A small remnant of the extraparliamentary opposition of the 1960s turned to political violence in the 1970s. Organized into a variety of "urban guerrilla" factions, the most notable being the Baader-Meinhof band, they committed bombings, kidnapings, and murders in the name of the revolution. Terrorist activity reached its zenith in 1977 when the chief federal prosecutor, the head of one of the largest banks, and a major industrialist were murdered. Links between German and Palestinian terrorist groups also became dramatically apparent in 1977 when a German commercial aircraft was hijacked by Arab terrorists who demanded the release of their German comrades. The dramatic rescue of the passengers at Mogadischu (Somalia) by special German commando units dealt a severe blow to the terrorist movement.

In 1985–86, however, terrorist activity increased once again. Two leading executives of companies involved in nuclear power plants and arms manufacturing were murdered. In October 1986 a senior official of the Foreign Ministry was shot and killed after he emerged from a taxi outside his home in Bonn. In addition, there were about forty bombings and fires at NATO and American military installations, most of which were attributed to the Red Army Faction (RAF), the successor to the Baader-Meinhof gang. While the extent of terrorist activities in the 1980s had declined from the 1970s, there remain about twenty to forty hard-core terrorists at large in the Federal Republic supported by about 500 to 700 sympathizers, who distribute propaganda and provide logistical support.

The end of the communist regime in East Germany revealed another dimension of the terrorist scene in West Germany. The East German secret police, the Stasi, had sheltered, trained, and supported the Red Army Faction for almost fifteen years. At least two attacks during the 1980s were led by terrorists who had been trained for the operations in East Germany. Some of the participants in terrorist acts during the 1970s also escaped to the East, where they were given new identities by the Stasi.

The RAF stepped up its activity during the unification process. In 1989 Germany's leading banker, Alfred Herrhausen of the Deutsche Bank, was murdered by an RAF car bomb. In 1991 the head of the agency charged with privatizing East Germany's formerly state-run economy, Detlev Karsten Rohwedder, was shot and killed at his home in West Germany.

In response to the terrorist problem, police and internal security agencies have established one of the most sophisticated systems of computerized and electronic eavesdropping in the world. Huge collections of personal and political data on hundreds of thousands of citizens, most of them with no connection to terrorists or the radical "scene," are stored in the computers of the Federal Criminal Office (BKA, the German version of the FBI). An increasing number of civil libertarians and some political leaders are concerned about the possible abuse of these data by law enforcement officials. Some cases of excessive police zeal have taken place. Given the memory of the Third Reich and its Gestapo and of East Germany's Stasi, this issue has become one of the most sensitive on the current political agenda.

Germany's International Role

Like Japan, Germany since the end of World War II has maintained a low profile in the international political arena. While an economic powerhouse, it has been content, indeed has encouraged, other Western nations, especially the United States, Britain, and France, to take the lead in dealing with international issues. During the 1991 Gulf War, for example, it sent no combat troops to the Middle East but did make a multibillion dollar financial contribution to the effort. But because of its size and strength, Germany's allies and neighbors expect it be a more important player in international politics in the future.

Germany has been reluctant to assume a leadership role for a variety of reasons. First, its leaders and most of its citizens know that many of the country's neighbors still remember the Third Reich and what the Nazis did to Europe and the world. There is still a residual distrust of Germany stemming from this experience. Second, this low political profile approach has been successful. Never before in its history have so many Germans had so much peace, prosperity, and freedom as they have had since 1945.

Thirdly, Germans fear that increased international leadership will eventually bring the country into a military conflict somewhere in the world. The memories of the death and destruction caused by the world wars of this century are still very alive; they have been passed down from generation to generation. There is a latent, yet pervasive pacifism in the country that inhibits the actions of its political leadership. Fourth, Germany will be preoccupied with unification for at least the next decade. Any international initiatives would be premature and not supported by public opinion. Finally, the Federal Republic hopes that its international responsibilities can be accommodated through its membership in the European Community. It wants the Community to assume a stronger role and it wants to act only with and through a united Europe.

It is doubtful that these factors will be as important in Germany's future foreign policy as they have been in the past. With the collapse of the Soviet empire in Eastern Europe and of the Soviet Union itself a vacuum has developed. Germany has little choice but to assume a leading economic and political position in this region. Hopes that this can be accomplished through the European Community have thus far been unfulfilled. The Community, for example, failed its first foreign policy test when it was unable to stop the civil war in Yugoslavia.

The Federal Republic's size and economic resources make it a key participant in the political, social and economic reconstruction of Eastern Europe and the former Soviet Union. From 1989 to the end of 1991 Germany had committed over $40 billion in loans and grants to the region, far more than any other country. It must attempt to convert this economic influence into the promotion of democratic stability.

Yet its involvement in the East must not come at the expense of the requirements of West European integration. As one authority has observed, "German leaders know that a race is currently being waged between integration in Western Europe and disintegration in Eastern Europe; hence they also know that they must forge a set of policies that facilitate the deepening of the European Community while simultaneously keeping it open as a safety net to deal with the problems produced by the collapse of communism in Eastern Europe and the disintegration of the Soviet Union."[4]

From 1945 to 1990 as a divided country protected against Soviet power by the nuclear shield of the Western Alliance, Germany led a sheltered existence. Unification and the collapse of the Soviet empire will increase its influence, but they will also impose new responsibilities and challenges on the Federal Republic.

Notes

1. M. Donald Hancock, *West Germany: The Politics of Democratic Corporatism* (Chatham, N.J.: Chatham House, 1988), 143–51.

2. The Federal Assembly is composed of the members of the national parliament together with representatives from the sixteen state parliaments.

3. INFAS, "Deutschland—Politogramm," no. 38 (1990): 3.

4. Ronald D. Asmus, "A Unified Germany," in *Transition and Turmoil in the Atlantic Alliance,* ed. Robert A. Levine (New York: Crane Russak, 1992), 84.

For Further Reading

ABENHEIM, DONALD. *Reforging the Iron Cross. The Search for Tradition in the West German Armed Forces.* Princeton: Princeton University Press, 1988.

ARDAGH, JOHN. *Germany and the Germans.* New York: Harper and Row, 1987.

BAKER, KENDALL L.; DALTON, RUSSELL J.; AND HILDEBRANDT, KAI. *Germany Transformed.* Cambridge, Mass.: Harvard University Press, 1981.

BECKER, JILLIAN. *Hitler's Children: The Story of the Baader-Meinhof Terrorist Gang.* Philadelphia: Lippincott, 1977.

BLAIR, J.M. *Federalism and Judicial Review in West Germany.* London: Oxford University Press, 1981.

BOTTING, DOUGLAS. *From the Ruins of the Reich. Germany, 1945–1949.* New York: Crown, 1985.

BRACHER, KARL DIETRICH. *The German Dictatorship.* New York: Praeger, 1970.

CONRADT, DAVID P. *The German Polity,* 5th ed. New York: Longman, 1992.

CRAIG, GORDON A. *The Germans.* New York: Putnam, 1982.

DALTON, RUSSELL J. *Politics in West Germany.* New York: Scott, Foresman, 1989.

GUNLICKS, ARTHUR B. *Local Government in the German Federal System.* Durham, N.C.: Duke University Press, 1986.

HAMILTON, RICHARD. *Who Voted for Hitler?* Princeton: Princeton University Press, 1982.

HANCOCK, M. DONALD. *West Germany: The Politics of Democratic Corporatism.* Chatham, N.J.: Chatham House, 1988.

KATZENSTEIN, PETER J. *Policy and Politics in West Germany.* Philadelphia: Temple University Press, 1987.

KITSCHELT, HERBERT. *The Logic of Party Formation: The Structure and Strategy of the Belgian and West German Ecology Parties.* Ithaca: Cornell University Press, 1989.

KOMMERS, DONALD. *Constitutional Jurisprudence in the Federal Republic of Germany.* Durham, N.C.: Duke University Press, 1989.

MAIER, CHARLES S. *The Unmasterable Past.* Cambridge, Mass.: Harvard University Press, 1988.

MARKOVITS, ANDREI. *The Politics of the West German Trade Unions: Strategies of Class and Interest Representation in Growth and Crisis.* Cambridge: Cambridge University Press, 1986.

NOELLE-NEUMANN, ELISABETH. *The Germans: Public Opinion Polls, 1967–1980.* Westport, Conn.: Greenwood Press, 1981.

POND, ELIZABETH. *After the Wall: American Policy Toward Germany.* Washington, D.C.: Brookings Institution, 1990.

ROCHON, THOMAS. *Mobilizing for Peace: Antinuclear Movements in Western Europe.* Princeton: Princeton University Press, 1988.

SCHWEIGLER, GEBHARD. *West German Foreign Policy: The Domestic Setting.* New York: Praeger, 1984.

TURNER, HENRY ASHBY, JR. *The Two Germanies since 1945.* New Haven: Yale University Press, 1987.

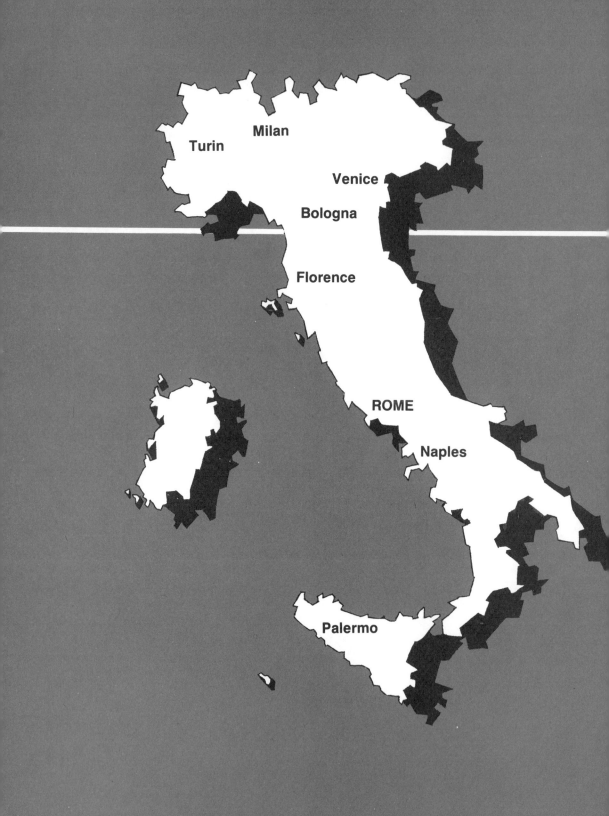

Part Four

Italy

Raphael Zariski

16

The Context of Italian Politics

Among the larger industrial states of Western Europe, Italy possesses certain unique characteristics. It has become one of the world's ten leading industrial powers, yet the southern half of Italy is relatively underdeveloped and lags far behind the rest of the country—to say nothing of Western Europe—in per capita income. It has achieved spectacular social and economic progress since World War II, yet the Italian Communist party (which in 1991 adopted the name "Democratic party of the Left" [Partito Democratico di Sinistra—PDS]) is the strongest Communist party in Western Europe, stronger in electoral terms now than it was in 1946 and relatively more powerful than Communist parties in such less prosperous societies as Spain, Portugal, and Greece. Italy has attained a high degree of modernization in its economic structures, yet it is burdened with an antiquated, inefficient bureaucratic apparatus. In short, Italy presents a dramatic contrast between rapid economic and social change on the one hand and the survival of anachronistic regional imbalances, political cleavages, and administrative deficiencies on the other. This political lag characterizes a dangerous transitional period, which Italy is now traversing on the road to becoming a stable and modern democracy.

Italy covers an area of only 301,200 square kilometers, compared to the 547,000 square kilometers that make up the domestic territory of the French Republic. Italy's population, however, is slightly larger than that of France: 57.6 million compared to France's 56.2 million.[1] Italian population density should not be overstressed, however. Impressive by American standards, it is actually lower than that of Great Britain, pre-1991 West Germany, and the Netherlands. Moreover, the Italian birthrate is lower than that of the United States, Great Britain, or

France. The historic Italian predicament of too many people on too little land no longer seems to be as acute or as difficult to resolve as was true in the late nineteenth and early twentieth centuries.

Thanks to its mountainous Alpine frontier, which makes for clearly defined boundaries, Italy has an overwhelmingly Italian-speaking population. Ethnic minorities are relatively insignificant: 250,000 to 300,000 German-speaking people in Bolzano Province, less than 100,000 French-speaking people in the Val d'Aosta, and a few thousand Slovenians near the Yugoslav border. The religious composition of Italy's population is also quite homogeneous. There are only about 75,000 Protestants and 30,000 Jews, with the rest of the population being at least nominally Catholic. To be sure, a very significant number of nominal Catholics are also confirmed anticlericals, especially in north-central Italy, who resist the Catholic church whenever it attempts to exercise influence or obtain special privileges from the government.

While the people of Italy are almost entirely of Italian nationality, they are divided by significant regional differences. These differences may be attributed partly to Italy's mountainous terrain. The Apennine mountain range divides central and southern Italy from the Po Valley in the north and impedes transportation between the major cities of the south. Regional differences are also the result of the many waves of invaders that have swept across the Italian Peninsula, Sicily, and Sardinia. Latins, Greeks, Etruscans, Gauls, Germans, Moors, and Normans have settled and intermingled in various parts of Italy, producing a great variety of regional customs and dialects. Although the Italian language and its dialects are based on Latin, the transformations Latin has undergone reflect the ethnic background and composition of each region. For example, the dialect of Piedmont in the northwest bears some resemblance to French. To be sure, standard Italian prevails in the schools and in the political and commercial life of the country; dialect usage is usually confined to the family and other face-to-face groups.

Historical Context

Like Germany, Italy did not attain national unification until the latter half of the nineteenth century.[2] There were a number of reasons for this long delay in the nation-building process. For several centuries after the fall of the Roman Empire, the north of Italy was under Germanic political domination while most of the south was under Byzantine or Moorish rule. Later, the south came under the control of the centralized and autocratic, but largely inefficient, Kingdom of the Two Sicilies, while northern and central Italy were divided into a number of prosperous but mutually antagonistic city-states. This internal division permitted foreign powers such as Spain and, later, Austria to dominate large portions of Italy. Not until the French Revolution of 1789–93 and Napoleon's subsequent invasion of Italy did a sense of Italian nationality begin to gain ground among Italy's educated elites. Even so, after Napoleon's defeat in 1814–15, Italy was still split into eight territorial units: the Kingdom of Sardinia (Piedmont) in the northwest; the Lombard and Venetian possessions of the Hapsburg Empire in the north and northeast; the duchies of Parma and Modena in north-central Italy; the duchy of Lucca, the Grand Duchy of Tuscany, and the Papal States in central Italy; and the Kingdom of the Two Sicilies in the south.

Nationalist agitation in the nineteenth century culminated in 1848–70 in a resurgence of nationalistic sentiment known as the Risorgimento. During that period, the Kingdom of Sardinia (Piedmont) led the drive for Italian unification after a republican movement headed by Giuseppe Mazzini and Giuseppe Garibaldi had launched several unsuccessful uprisings against Austrian and papal rule. Receiving military support first from France (1859) and later from Prussia (1866), exploiting and taking over control of Garibaldi's unexpectedly successful invasion and occupation of the Kingdom of the Two Sicilies, the Kingdom of Sardinia occupied the entire Italian peninsula by 1870. Backed mostly by a town-dwelling educated minority, the Risorgimento resulted in the creation of a unified Kingdom of Italy. In most of Italy, the process of unification consisted partly of a military occupation by Piedmont and partly of a revolution from above, viewed with hostility or apathy by the peasantry. Moreover, foreign intervention played a key role in ensuring the success of this process.

The newly established Kingdom of Italy was a constitutional democracy with a parliamentary form of government, but it faced a severe problem of legitimacy because of the way in which it had been founded and consolidated. First, Italy had been unified by a series of military conquests, involving the elimination of several existing Italian states and their simple annexation by the Kingdom of Sardinia. Second, the *fait accompli* was ratified by obviously rigged plebiscites in the various Italian regions. Third, a rigidly centralized unitary system was set up, with no political or institutional concessions being made to the autonomist aspirations of the several regions. This extreme centralization followed the French model of a prefectoral unitary system, while the German Second Reich was to move instead toward a federal system. And finally, by annexing the Papal States and storming Rome, the Kingdom of Italy provoked a conflict with the Catholic church. As a result, devout Catholics abstained for almost half a century from playing an active role in Italian politics. They, and many other Italians as well, did not feel a moral obligation to obey the commands of the Italian government. When obedience is based mainly on expediency, a political system lacks full legitimacy.

In addition to its problem of legitimacy, the Kingdom of Italy faced the difficult task of achieving national integration, of creating a sense of nationhood among Italians with diverse regional allegiances and ethnic origins. The elitist character of the Risorgimento had failed to give the peasant masses a feeling of participation in the nation-building process. It also had tended to create a certain contempt for majority rule among many Italian intellectuals, who were fully aware of the fact that the Risorgimento had been the work of an active minority. There was also a feeling among Italian elites that only new foreign conquests and foreign wars could create a sense of national allegiance among the common people of Italy. This sense of incomplete integration helps explain why the right to vote was withheld from most industrial workers and peasants until 1912. It also helps explain why Italy embarked on a series of colonial adventures in East Africa and Libya and why Italy intervened in World War I on the Allied side against the wishes of a neutralist parliamentary majority.

The Italian constitutional monarchy lasted barely half a century. Italy's costly participation in World War I, in which over 600,000 Italian soldiers died, brought the crises of legitimacy and integration to a head. The Italian masses—workers and peasants barred from the polls until 1912—voted mainly for the Socialist and Popular (Christian Democratic) parties, both of which threatened to encroach on the rights of private property. Also, these parties had shown a marked reluctance to support Italy's entry into World War I in 1915. After the war, the rise of Benito Mussolini's Fascist party represented, to a considerable degree, a middle-class backlash against the redistributive and pacifist implications of the entry of the Italian masses into politics. With the aid of an armed militia, which was financed by industrialists and large landowners, the Fascist party between 1920 and 1922 unleashed a reign of terror against the Socialist and Popular parties in local communities all over Italy. The army and police, like the Italian government itself, were unable or unwilling to intervene effectively against Fascist violence. Finally, in October 1922, Mussolini's blackshirt militiamen marched on Rome, the king refused to sign a government decree to declare a state of emergency, the government resigned, and the king appointed Mussolini to be the next prime minister. Mussolini soon took advantage of his executive powers to establish a Fascist dictatorship, a regime that was to last until 1943.

The Italian Fascist regime differed in a number of ways from Adolf Hitler's Nazi dictatorship. Italian Fascism was far less totalitarian. Controls over Italian business and agriculture were nowhere near as thoroughgoing as in Germany, though labor unions were suppressed and replaced by Fascist-sponsored organizations. Italian Fascism was much more closely identified with propertied interests than was Nazism. It did a much less effective job of mobilizing the economy for total war. Corruption and inefficiency plumbed almost incredible depths. It never laid primary stress on doctrines of racial supremacy, and the means it employed to suppress political opposition were less radical than those employed in Germany. And it retained the king as nominal constitutional monarch (whereas Hitler assumed the position of chief of state as well as head of government after President Hindenburg's death in 1934). By so doing, Italian Fascism paved the way for its own legal demise. In July 1943, with the Western Allied armies newly landed in Sicily and Italian forces in full retreat, the king was persuaded by a number of military and civilian notables to exercise his rarely used constitutional prerogative, remove Mussolini as prime minister, and appoint Marshal Badoglio in his place. The Badoglio government signed an armistice with the Allies on 8 September 1943. This was followed by a rapid German occupation of continental Italy. Until May 1945, which marked the Allied victory over Nazi Germany, the Italian government exercised some limited authority only over the Allied-occupied areas of central and southern Italy.

The democratic parties, which had emerged in the liberated zones of Italy under the protection of the Western Allies, had not forgotten the failure of the monarchy to support the legally elected government of Italy in 1922 during the march on Rome. After considerable discussion, it was decided to hold an institutional referendum on the question whether the monarchy was to be retained. The referendum was duly held on 2 June 1946, and about 12 million Italians voted for a republic; about 10 million voted to keep the monarchy. As a result of the referendum, the royal family went into exile and Italy became a republic. An elected Constituent Assembly then drew up and ratified a constitution, which went into effect in 1948.

The constitution of the Italian Republic provided for a parliamentary system but with some deviations from the classic parliamentary model. To be sure, it included the customary provisions for an elected Parliament, a prime minister and cabinet responsible to that Parliament, and an indirectly elected, largely ceremonial president. It also possessed features that differentiated it from most other parliamentary systems. First, both houses of the Italian Parliament were to be popularly elected and were to be roughly equal in power, in contrast to the weaker, less representative upper houses in Great Britain, France, and West Germany. Second, a constitutional court was to exercise the function of judicial review over parliamentary legislation. This was consistent with constitutional innovations in West Germany, but not with the British parliamentary system, characterized by parliamentary sovereignty, as well as with other pre-World War II parliamentary systems. Third, there was an element of direct democracy in the form of provisions for the initiative and referendum. Finally, certain specified powers were entrusted to semiautonomous regions listed in the constitution. These regions were not to have as much power as states or provinces in a federal system, but they would enjoy a much higher status than did the subnational units of government in a unitary system such as the British or French. In short, the Italian constitution established neither a unitary nor a federal system, but an intermediate form: regional devolution.

One flaw in the Italian constitution was the failure of postwar Italian governments to implement the provisions cited above with a reasonable degree of dispatch.[3] The Constitutional Court was not set up until 1955 and did not begin to function until 1956. Legislation to implement the referendum was not passed until 1970. As for the regions promised by the constitution, four "special regions" with special ethnic or separatist problems—Sicily, Sardinia, Val d'Aosta, and Trentino–Alto Adige —were created shortly after World War II; the fifth special region, Friuli–Venezia Giulia, was established by Parliament in 1963. But the fifteen "ordinary regions" listed in the constitution were not instituted until 1970.

These delays in implementing the constitution could be attributed to the unwillingness of the ruling Christian Democratic party to share power with the opposition or to tolerate potentially crippling restraints on its power to govern Italy. Before 1948, when Communists, Socialists, and Christian Democrats had governed together in a tripartite cabinet, the Christian Democrats had been staunch advocates of decentralization, judicial independence, and other checks on the executive. The Communists and Socialists, in contrast, had favored a strong Parliament and cabinet and had opposed any checks on absolute majority rule, since they expected that a leftist government was just around the corner. After the 1948 parliamentary elections, which gave the Christian Democrats an absolute majority and made it clear that they would be the dominant force in Italian politics for many years to come, the roles were reversed. Now the Communists and Socialists demanded regional autonomy, judicial review, and similar checks on the government indicated by the constitution; the Christian Democrats dragged their feet on implementing such measures.

The political history of postwar Italy may be divided into phases corresponding to the type of government formula that usually, but not invariably, prevailed. Between 1945 and 1947, the three major Italian parties—the Christian Democrats, the Communists, and the Socialists—collaborated in cabinet coalitions, with the help of several minor parties of the center. This was the period of so-called tripartite rule, which ended in 1947 when the Communists and their Socialist allies were ousted from the cabinet. From 1947 through 1962, Italy was usually governed by centrist coalitions, which were always dominated by the Christian Democratic party. The minor center parties (the Social Democrats, the Republicans, and the business-oriented Liberals) played the role of junior partners in these coalitions. Then, in 1962, the first center-left government was formed: The Christian Democrats and the minor center parties formed a cabinet with the favorable abstention of the Italian Socialist party, which had gradually drifted away from its former close alliance with the Communists. After abstaining on confidence votes for a year, the Socialist party finally entered the cabinet in December 1963 after sixteen years in opposition. The center-left formula simply subtracted the Liberals from, and added the Socialists to, the center coalitions of the 1947–62 period.

From 1962 until 1982, the center-left coalition was the dominant combination in Italian politics, though developments in the 1970s and early 1980s eroded this dominance. One development was the increasing moderation and consequently enhanced respectability of the Communist party. The Communists were actually treated as part of the parliamentary majority between 1976 and 1979 (although they were not granted any cabinet posts), and Italy seemed for a time to be on the verge of being governed by a grand coalition of all non-Fascist parties. A second development was the declining strength of the Christian Democratic party. This trend compelled the party to make greater concessions to its allies as the price for preserving the center-left formula. One concession was a willingness to relinquish the party's monopolistic stranglehold on the position of prime minister. Thus, in 1981, Italy had its first non-Christian Democratic prime minister in thirty-five years: Giovanni Spadolini, leader of the Republican party. And in 1983, the Socialist leader, Bettino Craxi, was able to form a cabinet.

A third trend also must be noted. Since 1982, the moderate rightist Liberal party had been asked to share cabinet office with the four left-center parties. Thus, since 1982, the left-center formula has been replaced by an oversized five-party coalition ranging from the moderate left through the moderate right. In 1991, however, the Republican party (PRI) withdrew temporarily from the center coalition.

Socioeconomic Context

Before World War I, the Italian economy was only partly industrialized, with most heavy industry concentrated in the Milan-Genoa-Turin industrial triangle; total Italian industrial production lagged far behind that of France, West Germany, and Great Britain. The Fascist era was marked by a sluggish, stagnant economy, held back by the rigorously deflationary policies of the Fascist regime. World War II brought devastation to Italian industry and transportation facilities alike.

After an arduous period of postwar reconstruction, Italy managed to bring about an economic takeoff that has been generally described as an "economic miracle." During the 1950s, per capita income in Italy rose more than it had during the ninety-year span from 1861 to 1950.[4] The occupational composition of the labor force also underwent a remarkable transformation that both fueled and reflected economic expansion. At Liberation in 1945, over 40 percent of the Italian labor force was employed in agriculture; by 1978, only 11.2 percent was so employed, compared to 33.6 percent in industry and 55.2 percent in the service sector.[5]

Growth in per capita income and growth in industrialization and services at the expense of agriculture were accomplished by massive movements of population. People migrated from rural areas to cities, from southern Italy, Sicily, and Sardinia to the northwest industrial triangle, and from southern Italy to northern Europe. These migrations had far-reaching implications for the Italian economy and Italian society. Overloaded social services in the cities, soil erosion and eventual flooding in depopulated mountainous rural areas, rising expectations, and a general loosening of social bonds and restraints—these were some of the less desirable side effects of the "economic miracle." Nevertheless, the 1950s and 1960s were times of great economic progress and expanding horizons for most Italians.

The spectacular economic growth depended on a number of favorable conditions. A war-shattered economy cried out for reconstruction and provided entrepreneurs with many investment opportunities. Marshall Plan aid from the United States furnished the necessary capital. A divided and weak labor movement was in no position to make major demands on Italian employers. Foreign raw material prices were conveniently low. And vigorous economic leadership was furnished by a free-spending public sector headed by giant public corporations that formed part of two industrial empires, the Institute for Industrial Reconstruction (Istituto per Ricostruzione Industriale—IRI) and National Hydrocarburants Corporation (Ente Nazionale Idrocarburi—ENI). The bold entrepreneurs who managed Italy's public corporations helped create the climate of optimism and adventure that pervaded the growth-oriented Italian economy.

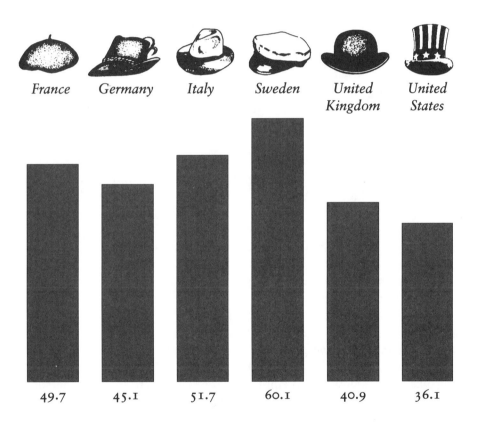

France	Germany	Italy	Sweden	United Kingdom	United States
49.7	45.1	51.7	60.1	40.9	36.1

FIGURE 16.1

TOTAL GOVERNMENT EXPENDITURES AS A PERCENTAGE OF
GROSS DOMESTIC PRODUCT

SOURCE: OECD, 1991.

By the late 1960s, however, these favorable conditions were beginning to fade, and the 1970s brought a rude awakening to the Italian economy. A wave of unprecedented labor unrest during the "Hot Autumn" of 1969 gave a clear signal that Italian employers could no longer expect to deal with a docile, self-denying labor force. Far-reaching wage concessions had to be granted; indexation arrangements had to be accepted tying wages more closely to the cost of living; and discipline in the factories had to be greatly relaxed. Moreover, Parliament passed legislation consolidating and extending the gains labor had achieved through collective bargaining. Italy's three labor confederations were impelled by these developments to work more closely together and to adopt a more militant posture. As a result, Italian labor costs rose sharply, not only in terms of wages but also in terms of social security benefits. The competitive advantage formerly enjoyed by Italian manufactured products was a thing of the past.

In the 1970s, further misfortunes befell the Italian economy. The rise in raw material prices, particularly the price of oil, did serious damage to the balance of trade by raising the prices of imports and making Italian exports more expensive. Public corporations were increasingly involved in financial speculation, empire building, currying favor with the major political parties, and allowing political considerations to influence their hiring and personnel policies. As a result, the public sector was running large deficits, keeping sick industries alive, and creating grave problems for the Italian economy. The decade was marked by declining economic growth, a high rate of inflation combined with rising unemployment, and serious deficits in the balance of trade. The larger corporations, burdened with onerous health insurance and pension costs imposed by the unions as part of the wage package, were especially affected by this situation.

As a result of the hard times of the 1970s and 1980s, some entirely new problems have come to the fore. One has been the issue of unemployment among young people seeking their first job. Facing oppressive wage and social security costs, and restricted in their ability to discharge surplus labor, many Italian employers are reluctant to hire new personnel. This creates a bulge of unemployment among psychologically vulnerable high school and university graduates, with frightening implications for the future of Italian society. A second problem has been the emergence and proliferation of a "submerged economy" consisting of a multitude of small employers who pay their workers substandard wages, fail to pay payroll or social security taxes for their employees, and keep their economic operations a well-guarded secret from the prying eyes of the government. Such clandestine employers provide second jobs for moonlighting civil servants, low but untaxed wages for migrants or part-time workers, and part-time employment for housewives or pensioners. A third and basic issue is excessive government spending, which drags down the Italian economy, builds large deficits, and perpetuates inflation. And finally, one should cite the growing gap between the relatively prosperous employed worker, protected by indexation against economic vicissitudes, and the various "marginals"—workers in the submerged economy, the unemployed, students facing a precarious future, and others who have been left behind by economic progress.

Religion

The Catholic church has traditionally played a major role in Italian politics. During the Middle Ages and the Renaissance, the Papal States, the temporal domain of the pope, resisted numerous attempts by the Germanic Holy Roman Empire to unite Italy. In the nineteenth century, the Papal States opposed Piedmont's bid to unify the Italian peninsula; and in fact the final event of the Risorgimento was the forcible seizure of Rome by Italian troops in 1870. From 1870 to 1913, the church hierarchy advised religious Italians to abstain from voting in Italian national elections. This boycott of the Italian state was brought to an end by the Gentiloni Agreement of 1913, under which Italian Catholics began to give large-scale electoral support to candidates for Parliament. In 1919, a Christian Democratic party—the Popular party led by Don Sturzo —entered Italian national elections and openly campaigned for the support of religious voters. After Mussolini's coming to power, the Popular party was disbanded and the church eventually (in 1929) signed the Lateran Agreements with the Fascist state, signaling a complete reconciliation between church and state. One of these agreements, the Concordat of 1929, recognized the sovereignty of the pope over Vatican City, guaranteed religious education in Italian public schools, and declared Catholicism to be the official religion of the Italian state. The church was granted a number of far-reaching privileges with regard to the holding of property, jurisdiction over divorce, and so on.

After the defeat of Fascism, the church was able to strike a favorable bargain with the new Italian Republic. The Lateran Agreements of 1929 were actually incorporated into the new constitution. Article 7 provided that the agreements could be modified only by mutual consent of both parties or by a constitutional amendment. It is interesting to note that the Communist delegates to the Constituent Assembly actually voted for Article 7 in 1947, possibly in an effort to conciliate their Christian Democratic coalition partners and avert the impending expulsion of the Communist party from the Italian cabinet.

During the 1940s and 1950s, political Catholicism was an aggressive and pervasive force in Italian politics. With the Christian Democratic party playing a dominant role in the Italian political system, the church and its lay organizations enjoyed privileged access to the national centers of decision making. Priests and bishops openly took sides in election campaigns, urging the faithful to support candidates sympathetic to the Catholic church. Catholic Action, a church-sponsored lay organization, set up a network of civic committees to conduct canvassing and propaganda activities on behalf of the Christian Democratic party. A number of Catholic interest groups representing labor, peasants, teachers, and others were directly affiliated with the Christian Democratic party, with which they enjoyed a *parentela* relationship. Such groups had the right, as "members of the family," to be consulted on appointments to cabinet positions, nominations of candidates for Parliament, and policy questions affecting their interests.[6] In short, the Italian Catholic church was much more prominent on the political scene than its French counterpart.

Since the early 1960s, the political aggressiveness of Italian Catholicism has waned. Under Popes John XXIII and Paul VI, the church assumed a lower profile in Italian politics and displayed much less hostility toward leftist parties. To be sure, the church was by no means united. Some bishops continued to maintain a politically active stance and to oppose any alliances with leftist forces. Nevertheless, as the papacy in the early 1960s abandoned its hostility to the idea of a center-left coalition government, most bishops reluctantly followed suit. Later, even the partial collaboration between Christian Democrats and Communists at the national level in 1976–79 did not call down the anathema of the church.

What underlay the more cautious line followed by the church was the growing secularization of Italian society. Church attendance declined in the 1960s and 1970s. An increasing number of Catholics, especially Catholic intellectuals, displayed independent attitudes in direct conflict with the dictates of the church hierarchy. Some Catholic associations loosened their ties with the Christian Democratic party. And the exodus from Catholic rural strongholds to the big cities, from agricultural occupations to industrial and service jobs, seriously undermined the influence of religious tradition.

Clear evidence of the weakening of religiosity in Italy was the passage of a divorce bill in 1970 despite the strong resistance of the Christian Democratic party and the Vatican. More striking still was the aftermath of the bill's passage. When militant Catholics pushed the issue to a referendum in an effort to get the divorce law repealed, the result was a clear-cut victory for secularism. A 1974 referendum upheld the divorce law, with only 41 percent of the voters casting their ballots for its repeal. Forces favoring divorce carried most of Italy with the exception of the Catholic northeast and the continental south. Even Sicily, Sardinia, and Latium (the region that includes Rome!) voted to retain divorce. During the campaign, a number of priests and Catholic laymen spoke out against repeal. Moreover, the size of the vote against repeal clearly indicated that it had the support of a considerable number of Christian Democratic voters.

The receding influence of the Catholic church in Italy is in line with a tendency toward secularization that is affecting all of Europe. This tendency is reflected not only in declining Christian Democratic voting strength but also in the increasingly secular attitudes of voters who (often for socioeconomic reasons) continue to support Italian Christian Democracy. That secular attitudes are spreading and intensifying is evident when we observe the results of a referendum held in 1981 to decide whether a rather liberal abortion law should be repealed. Sixty-eight percent of Italians who took part in the balloting voted against repeal—a bigger majority than the pro-divorce majority of 1974. It is probably in recognition of its waning strength that the Catholic church agreed in 1984 to accept a revision of the Concordat.

Education

The Italian educational system has undergone a major transformation since World War II. In the 1950s, 90 percent of the population had not attended school more than five years. Moreover, at the end of fifth grade, the child was assigned either to an academic junior high school or a terminal vocational school. This was more or less standard European practice at the time; yet to assign a child to a secondary school on the basis of aptitude at such an early age meant that "aptitude" was all too frequently determined on the basis of family background and social class.

In the 1960s, with the entry of the Socialist party into center-left cabinets, educational opportunities were broadened. A unified junior high school was established to replace the earlier two-track system. The decision regarding eligibility for eventual university entrance was thus postponed several years to the time when the student was admitted to one of several types of senior high school. Even in the senior high schools, transfers from one type of school to another were permissible during the first two years. Comprehensive schools have thus come to Italy, but so far only at the junior high school level (as in France) rather than at the senior high school level (as in Britain and Sweden).

The educational changes of the 1960s led to a great increase in high school enrollment. They also led, naturally enough, to the lowering of standards to accommodate the incoming masses. Moreover, pressure for further democratization led to the adoption in 1970 of an open admissions policy for the universities. Thus the universities, too, became overcrowded and lost much of their usefulness, performing neither their traditional function of training an elite nor their supposed new function of facilitating social mobility.

Initial results of these reforms have been somewhat disappointing, producing unforeseen side effects. The great wave of student unrest that submerged Italian universities in the late 1960s and early 1970s, and brought chronic indiscipline and frequent violence in its wake, was a direct outcome of the skyrocketing enrollments. The depressing working conditions that prevailed, the frustrated expectations of the students, and the example of what was happening in American and French universities combined to foment student unrest. Many a young terrorist spent his formative years in the chaotic milieu of Italian higher education. Even today, when the more obvious and blatant disorders of 1968–70 appear to have abated, there is a residual climate of laxity and indiscipline. For this reason, perhaps, the Conference of University Rectors recommended in 1979 that Italian universities be permitted to restore a selective admissions policy.

Political Culture

What we have seen thus far in the Italian political context is a pattern of drastic change—a remolding of the Italian political, social, economic, religious, and educational landscapes. In the four decades since liberation, Italians have seen their country transformed. Inevitably, this metamorphosis has had a notable impact on political attitudes.

The most significant attitudes that have traditionally characterized Italian political culture may be summed up briefly before we examine changes that have taken place since the early 1960s.[7] First, Italians have ranked rather low in social trust. They have appeared to lack faith in the motives and actions of their fellow citizens. Second, Italians have had a low degree of political trust; that is, they have had little confidence in the efficiency and integrity of government institutions and officials. Both elected officials and bureaucrats are distrusted. Third, Italians have had a tendency to seek protection against a potentially hostile environment by joining informal but hierarchical groupings (cliques and clienteles) where they can enjoy the protection of a powerful patron. Fourth, Italians have finally acquired a sense of national identity after two world wars and a period of partisan resistance against German occupation forces in 1943–45. Fifth, Italians have had a low sense of political competence (they have felt unable to influence the formation of public policy) and a low sense of administrative competence (they have not believed they could obtain fair treatment from government agencies). Sixth, many Italians have been politically alienated. They have felt very little pride in and much suspicion toward the political system; their alienation has frequently expressed itself in riots, demonstrations, and, more recently, kneecappings and assassinations.

The most important feature of Italian political culture has been its heterogeneity and fragmentation. The above attitudes have not been universally shared; instead, there have been competing sets of values and attitudes—competing subcultures, in other words. These divergent subcultures—elite and mass, northern and southern, liberal or clerical or Marxist—have helped shape Italy's party system and the tendency of Italian voters to think in left-right, clerical-anticlerical terms. They also account for the stability of partisan preferences (voters frequently continue supporting the same parties election after election) and the high degree of hostility that some parties arouse among voters at the other end of the political spectrum.

During the past twenty years, this set of attitudes has undergone some significant changes. The balance of forces among competing subcultures seems to have changed, with Catholic (clerical) traditions losing popular support and suffering from a weakened organizational network. Partisan hostility has diminished a great deal, especially with regard to the Communist party, which has gained considerable acceptance as a legitimate political force among Italian political elites. Among more educated, influential Italians, there seems to be a pronounced movement toward bridging the cleavages that have divided the respective subcultures.

At the level of mass culture much has remained the same. Voters still tend to place themselves along a left-right spectrum, identifying themselves as left, center, or right. While the Catholic tradition has declined, about 40 percent of Italian voters still support repeal of the divorce law. Distrust of the political system is still very pronounced despite the improvement in socioeconomic conditions experienced by most Italians. Actually, evaluations of the political system have been more negative in the recent decades than they were in the 1960s. The sense of political competence has also dropped considerably since the 1960s. Widespread political alienation and political distrust still exist. This would help explain the frequent occurrence of direct confrontations between demonstrators—using a variety of provocative strategies—and public authorities. It also helps explain the tendency of disaffected fringe groups to resort to acts of terrorism. Nevertheless, some scholars have come to the conclusion that alienation and distrust do not represent a passionate rejection of the Italian style of democracy but a sober and realistic recognition of the limited potentialities of *any* political system.[8]

In general, it would seem that although Italian political elites are conducting their quarrels with more moderation and mutual forbearance, the potential for unrest and violent upheaval is alive and well among noninfluentials. Italian mass culture poses a major threat to Italian democracy should the political system fail to perform more effectively in the years ahead than it has in the past.

Yet the Italian political system has a record of great resiliency. Some very promising elements in the current picture offset the negative features we have described. For instance, the growing convergence among Italian elites may eventually have an impact on the residual cleavages in the mass culture. Voters seem to be giving somewhat greater support than in the past to middle-of-the-road minor parties. Secularization is visible in both Catholic and Marxist camps, as Italian voters appear to reject extremist tendencies. In short, the Italian polity may survive the dangers we have outlined, as it has done so often in the past.

Notes

1. See "OECD Member Countries," 1987 ed., 22d year, *OECD Observer*, no. 121 (April-May 1987): 17.

2. For the period before 1970, see Raphael Zariski, *Italy: The Politics of Uneven Development* (Hinsdale, Ill.: Dryden Press, 1972), chap. 1.

3. See Norman Kogan, *A Political History of Italy: The Postwar Years* (New York: Praeger, 1983), 104–6, 255–56.

4. See Rosario Romeo, *Breve storia della grande industria in Italia* (Bologna: Cappelli, 1967), 113–14.

5. See "OECD Member Countries," 21.

6. See Joseph La Palombara, *Interest Groups in Italian Politics* (Princeton, N.J.: Princeton University Press, 1964), chap. 9.

7. On the traditional features of Italian political culture, see, for example, Zariski, *Italy,* chap. 3; and Gabriel A. Almond and Sidney Verba, *The Civic Culture: Political Attitudes and Democracy in Five Nations* (Princeton, N.J.: Princeton University Press, 1963). On recent changes in Italian political culture, see Giacomo Sani, "The Political Culture of Italy: Continuity and Change," in *The Civic Culture Revisited,* ed. Gabriel A. Almond and Sidney Verba (Boston: Little, Brown, 1980), chap. 8.

8. See Joseph La Palombara, *Democracy Italian Style* (New Haven: Yale University Press, 1987), 152–55, 263–64.

17

Where Is the Power?

Italy, like Britain and Germany, has a parliamentary system. There has been some discussion in recent years about setting up a quasi-presidential system on the French model; but such institutional reform at the national level has thus far not generated much support. There are some additional similarities with Germany. First, Italy is a parliamentary republic with a weak, indirectly elected president. Also, Italy is far more decentralized than most parliamentary systems. It does not actually have a federal system like that of the German Federal Republic, but it has a form of regional devolution that differentiates it quite clearly from unitary systems such as Great Britain and France.

The President: Ceremonial Chief of State

Unlike the hegemonic French president, the Italian president resembles the ceremonial chief of state in other parliamentary republics (e.g., Germany). Most of his formal executive powers—the promulgation of laws, signing of treaties, making of executive appointments, command of the armed forces—require the prior initiative of a member of the cabinet before the president can act and ministerial countersignature before the president's action can have legal effect. Like other ceremonial chief executives, Italy's president is expected to greet visiting dignitaries, dedicate major public projects, visit disaster zones in order to comfort the populace, and perform other purely formal duties as the symbolic head of the Italian state.

To be sure, his position is a bit more powerful than that of a British monarch. First, a strong, ambitious president may hold press conferences and discuss current issues or may include controversial statements about public policy matters in a public address. Second, he may deliver a message to Parliament and comment critically on the state of the nation. Third, he may return a bill to Parliament for reconsideration, along with a message stating his reasons for doing so. Such a suspensive veto may be overridden by a simple majority of those voting in each house in Parliament. Fourth, given the complex nature of Italy's multiparty system, the president's formal function of appointing the prime minister provides him with a great deal of potential influence. For no one party has a majority in Parliament, and the appointment of a new prime minister is therefore preceded by intricate negotiations among various parties and factions. In the course of those negotiations, the president could seek to promote a candidate of his own, as President Gronchi did in 1960 when he put forward the name of Fernando Tambroni. Or he could ask a resigning prime minister to reconsider his resignation. Fifth, the president appoints five of the fifteen judges of the Constitutional Court and has the power to dissolve Parliament on the prime minister's request.

Apart from the constitutional and customary restraints cited above, the power of an Italian president is limited mainly by the manner of his selection. He is elected indirectly by an Electoral Assembly composed of the members of the Chamber of Deputies (630), the members of the Senate (320), a delegate from the Val d'Aosta, and three delegates from each of Italy's other nineteen regions. Election is by secret ballot. On the first three ballots, a two-thirds majority of the members of the Electoral Assembly is necessary to elect a president; from the fourth ballot on, a simple majority suffices. The secret ballot makes party cohesion and party discipline impossible. A party cannot really compel its members to support its officially designated candidate. The nominee who emerges from this long drawn-out procedure lacks the mandate to act as a popular tribune, to speak for the Italian nation over the head of its government. He is also apt to be partly dependent on the extreme left or the extreme right for his election, since the Christian Democrats invariably split their votes among two or more candidates.

This system of election, with its clandestine procedures and resulting breakdowns in party discipline, often produces unforeseen results. It can turn out factional bosses capable of unpredictable adventures rather than men of broad vision. Some presidents have been quite distinguished: Luigi Einaudi (1948–55), a prominent Liberal economist; Giuseppe Saragat (1964–71), leader of the Social Democratic party; Sandro Pertini (1978–85), a venerable and respected Socialist factional leader with a slight tendency to outspokenness. Others have been Christian Democratic factional chieftains who have reflected little credit on the office: Giovanni Gronchi (1955–62), who appointed the notorious Tambroni to head a cabinet that brought Italy to the brink of civil conflict; Antonio Segni (1962–64), who was suspected by some journalists of having been involved in the preliminary planning for an abortive military coup; and Giovanni Leone (1971–78), who was forced to resign six months before his term expired because of alleged complicity in several cases of tax fraud and bribery.

The Italian president from 1985 to 1992, Francesco Cossiga, was also a Christian Democrat. During the first five years of his term, he maintained a relatively low profile. After 1990, however, he became extremely outspoken, making numerous controversial and often intemperate statements on public issues and delivering blistering personal attacks on the competence and integrity of a number of Italian political leaders, even demanding the resignation of the chief justice of the Italian Constitutional Court. He was one of the chief advocates of a stronger presidency and, on one occasion, claimed he might have the right to dissolve the Parliament on his own, without the prime minister's consent. A number of Italian commentators expressed grave doubts about his emotional balance. Be that as it may, he indubitably overstepped the boundaries of his ceremonial functions.

In a break with precedent and with the letter of the Constitution, Cossiga dissolved Parliament during his last six months in office—the so-called blank semester when a president is constitutionally barred from dissolving Parliament. (This action was apparently taken at the behest of the leaders of the various parties, since Parliament's term had only two more months to run.) In May of 1992, in a surprise move, Cossiga resigned, two months before his own term was due to expire. The new president, Oscar Luigi Scalfaro, is also a Christian Democrat, but he is likely to be more stable and less controversial than his mercurial predecessor.

The Prime Minister and the Cabinet

The Italian cabinet (officially labeled the Council of Ministers) and the prime minister (whose official title is president of the Council of Ministers) constitute the political wing of Italy's dual executive. They resemble the classic model of the political executive in a continental European parliamentary system. The prime minister is asked by the president to form a cabinet, after the president has first engaged in a series of consultations with the leaders of the various parties in Parliament. The newly designated prime minister selects a cabinet—usually a coalition cabinet, composed of members of several parties—from among the members of Parliament. Then, on the prime minister's recommendation, the president proceeds to appoint the cabinet.

The Italian cabinet is considerably larger than the British one, for it includes all the ministers in the government, including the ministers without portfolio. Its size may be attributed in large part to the representative function it must perform. Since Italy has a much more complex party system than France or Germany, to say nothing of Britain, it is necessary to provide each party in the governing coalition with adequate representation in the cabinet. In most cabinets, at least two parties are involved and have a right to their share of cabinet posts. Moreover, each Italian party contains within its ranks a number of highly organized factions; these, too, demand representation in the cabinet. A disgruntled intraparty faction is just as capable as a disaffected party of withdrawing its support from a coalition cabinet, thereby causing that cabinet to fall.

Since the cabinet usually consists of several parties, and since even one-party cabinets are usually torn by interfactional strife, the cabinet cannot and does not function as a united team. Its members, even when they belong to the same party, regard one another as political rivals. Consequently, they often fail to consult one another before initiating new legislation and frequently leak information to the press regarding what took place in cabinet meetings. It should also be noted that the prime minister does not really enjoy freedom of choice in selecting his cabinet. Before nominating members for appointment by the president, he must consult the leaders of the various parties in his coalition, as well as a number of leaders of intraparty factions. Since he is more or less obligated to accept the recommendations of these party and factional leaders, his power of appointment is severely restricted. At the same time, he cannot dismiss cabinet members. (To be sure, even if he had the power to force them to resign, he would still be running the risk of alienating the parties or factions that had sponsored them.)

In addition to its heterogeneous partisan and factional character, the cabinet is split by some major functional cleavages. Most notably, financial and economic policy is divided among three separate ministries with overlapping functions: the Ministry of the Treasury, the Ministry of the Budget and Economic Planning, and the Ministry of Finance. The Ministry of the Treasury, primarily interested in a stable economy, has usually prevailed over the expansion-minded Ministry of the Budget.

Unlike the French cabinet, the Italian cabinet has no residual or re-served powers to govern by decree in areas from which Parliament has actually been excluded by the constitution. In this respect, it is again in line with the classic parliamentary model in which legal sovereignty is vested in Parliament, as opposed to the French quasi-presidential system. The Italian cabinet can issue decrees under only two types of conditions. *Legislative decrees* may be enacted if Parliament first passes an enabling act, with a time limit attached, authorizing the cabinet to legislate on a specified subject matter in accordance with certain guidelines. *Decree-laws* may be promulgated by the cabinet in case of emergency: they expire within sixty days of their publication unless converted into statutory law by Parliament. In addition to these two types of decrees, the cabinet and individual ministries may issue administrative orders ("regulations") without prior authorization by Parliament. These regulations are presumably more specialized in content and inferior in legal status to decrees.

Italian cabinets do not normally enjoy a long or peaceful existence. Their average life span is slightly less than a year, though some manage to survive for eighteen or even twenty-four months. Cabinets can be forced to resign in a variety of ways by either house of Parliament. The legal procedure prescribed by the constitution stipulates that if 10 per-cent of the members of either of the two houses of Parliament sign a motion of no confidence, and if a majority of those voting in that house support the motion at least three days after it has been presented, then the cabinet must resign. But numerous cabinets have resigned without waiting for this procedure to be employed. Cabinets have resigned after having suffered a defeat on a government bill or after a party or faction has announced that it no longer intends to support the cabinet. Even a hostile statement by a party secretary outside of Parliament or an adverse resolution by a party congress or executive committee may precipitate a cabinet's resignation.

Yet what appears on the surface to be extreme cabinet instability in Italy is accompanied by some features of continuity. With only two exceptions (Giovanni Spadolini of the Republican party in 1981–82 and Bettino Craxi of the Socialist party in 1983–87), all prime ministers since June 1946 have been Christian Democrats. A number of Christian Democratic leaders have headed not one but several cabinets: There have been seven De Gasperi cabinets, five Moro cabinets, five Rumor cabinets, and five Fanfani cabinets. Some cabinet positions—the Ministry of the Interior and the Ministry of the Treasury, for example—have been continually or almost continually under the control of the same party since 1946. Some cabinet ministers hold the same position year after year, in successive cabinets. For example, Emilio Colombo was treasury minister in no less than eleven cabinets.

What usually happens after a cabinet falls is not a complete turnover but a slight shift in the balance of power within the majority coalition. Since 1946 it has been an unwritten rule of Italian parliamentary politics that the Christian Democratic party *must* form part of any majority coalition in order for the coalition to have sufficient votes to survive in Parliament. The only two questions left open have been which allies the Christian Democratic party will select and how cabinet posts will be allocated among the various Christian Democratic factions and among the other parties in the cabinet.

Since 1946 there have been relatively few general formulas available for forming a cabinet. They are summarized briefly here:[1]

1. *The tripartite formula.* Communists, Socialists, and Christian Democrats all serve together in the cabinet. One or more of the minor center parties (the Social Democrats, Republicans, or Liberals) may also be represented. This formula was employed roughly from July 1946 through June 1947 in the second and third De Gasperi cabinets.

2. *The center coalition.* The Christian Democrats govern in coalition with one or more of the three minor center parties. About a dozen Italian cabinets have been organized on the basis of this formula for a collective but discontinuous duration of almost fourteen years. This formula was used most frequently from 1947 to 1962, before the "opening to the left" that brought the Socialist party into the cabinet.

3. *The monocolor cabinet.* An all-Christian Democratic minority cabinet is formed, relying on the external ad hoc support of other parties. This formula has been used often—there have been eleven monocolor cabinets since 1946 with a combined duration of about ten years—and is employed to buy time for the formation of a coalition cabinet. Its incidence has been pretty evenly distributed over the past forty years, without the pre-1962 bunching effect noted in the center coalition.

4. *The right-center coalition.* A cabinet composed of Christian Democrats and Liberals (a moderate right-center party), possibly including monarchists and receiving the support of the extreme right. This formula has been used only once, in late 1947, during the fourth De Gasperi cabinet, for about six months. Some

monocolor cabinets, like the Tambroni cabinet in 1960, have been right-center in their orientation. Ever since Tambroni's resignation, this formula has ceased to be considered a credible alternative.

5. *The left-center coalition.* Christian Democrats and Socialists govern together with the possible participation of Social Democrats and/ or Republicans. This formula has been used only since 1962, but it has tended to play a dominant role ever since then. There have been about a dozen left-center cabinets since 1962, with a combined duration of almost twelve years. From 1963 to 1980, the number of months during which Italy was governed by left-

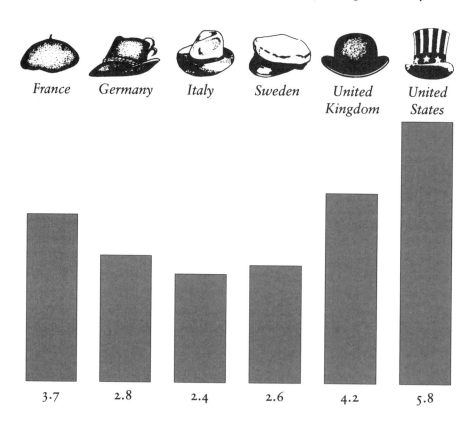

France   Germany   Italy   Sweden   United   United
                                       Kingdom   States

3.7   2.8   2.4   2.6   4.2   5.8

FIGURE 17.1
DEFENSE EXPENDITURES AS A PERCENTAGE OF
GROSS DOMESTIC PRODUCT

SOURCE: U.S. Arms Control and Disarmament Agency, 1991.

center cabinets exceeded the combined total duration of centrist coalition cabinets and monocolor cabinets.

6. *A broadened center coalition embracing five parties.* During most of the period since 1980, Italian cabinets have included not only the parties of the left-center coalition but also the moderately right Liberals. Since the Liberals can hardly be called a left-center party, this new approach appears to involve a broadening of the centrist formula to include the Socialist party, whose leader, Bettino Craxi, has been increasingly preoccupied with the nonideological goal of ensuring the "governability" of Italy.

Some additional formulas have been advocated in recent years but have yet to be employed at the national level.

1. *The left alternative.* A Communist-Socialist-Social Democratic-Republican coalition cabinet, seeking the support of left-wing Christian Democrats. Advocated by the Communist party.

2. *The historic compromise.* A cabinet including Communists, Christian Democrats, Socialists, and all or almost all non-Fascist parties. Major emphasis is placed on the Communist-Catholic alliance. This formula was advocated by Communist party leaders between 1976 and 1979, but it has been temporarily dropped in favor of the left alternative. It bears some resemblance to the tripartite formula of 1945–47 and to the Grand Coalition that has been tried out in West Germany and Austria.

While the cabinet is a loose-jointed and motley body with a great number of uncoordinated ministries often operating at cross purposes, there has been a growing trend in the direction of a dominant position for the prime minister. The prime minister is increasing his influence by virtue of his ability to mediate differences among various power centers within and outside the cabinet and to give some measure of central direction to the government. He has been able to assume this key role with the help of the Office of the Prime Minister, a staff agency that has grown remarkably in the past forty years and now employs about 800 people. In the last few years, the Office of the Prime Minister has acquired control over government spending, over the expenditures of public corporations, over supervising relations with the regions, and over some aspects of security and public order. This increase in the prime minister's influence has depended less on his formal powers than on his strategic location and his possession of a growing and skilled staff.[2]

The Parliament

In its structure and mode of operation, the Italian Parliament differs in some significant ways from most other West European parliamentary bodies. First, it is truly bicameral. A bill *must* pass both houses —the Chamber of Deputies and the Senate—in order to become law. Moreover, the cabinet is equally responsible to both houses. This legal equality is reinforced by the fact that both houses are elected by popular vote. The differences between the two elections are these: (1) the minimum voting age for senatorial elections is twenty-five, whereas the minimum voting age for elections to the Chamber of Deputies is eighteen; (2) senators are elected from the regions, with each region entitled to one senator per 200,000 population and no region (with three exceptions) to have fewer than six senators, a formula that results in the slight overrepresentation of several smaller regions; on the other hand, lists of candidates for the Chamber of Deputies compete against each other in multimember districts called electoral circumscriptions, each of which (with the exception of the tiny Val d'Aosta) comprises two to five provinces. Because there are anywhere from two to nine provinces in a region, each region will contain one or more (usually more) electoral circumscriptions. Since these differences are not very striking, the Senate can rightfully claim that it is hardly less representative than the Chamber of Deputies and is therefore entitled to equal legislative power.

Representing roughly similar electorates, the two houses do not differ sharply in their political makeup—the respective strength of the various parties is roughly the same in both chambers. Moreover, they tend to represent the Italian electorate at the same point in time. Although the Chamber of Deputies originally had a five-year term and the Senate a six-year term, in practice the Senate was always dissolved simultaneously with the Chamber of Deputies. Finally, in 1963, the constitution was amended to establish a five-year term for both houses. Thus, given the similarity of composition of the two houses, the Senate fails to give special representation or protection to any specific minority interest (as do the French Senate and the German Bundesrat). Bicameralism becomes little more than a device for delaying the passage of legislation.

A second, rather distinctive feature of the Italian Parliament is the power possessed by its standing committees. They receive a bill just after first reading and may subject it to drastic changes before reporting it to the floor. The chairperson of a standing committee appears to be master of the committee's timetable and can expedite or slow down the progress of a bill without having to worry about pressure from the presiding officer (president) of the chamber. Most important, committees have the power to pass certain bills. When the president of the chamber refers a bill to a standing committee, he or she decides whether the committee is to act *in sede referente* (report the bill back to the chamber with proposed amendments) or *in sede deliberante* (take final action on the bill: pass it and send it on to the president of the Republic, or defeat it once and for all). Thus, Italian standing committees literally act as miniature legislatures. Most bills approved by the Italian Parliament are enacted through this unique *in sede deliberante* procedure. There are only two limitations on its use. First, certain kinds of important legislative proposals (constitutional amendments, electoral laws, delegations of legislative power, treaties, budgetary and spending bills) *must* be discussed on the floor after being considered in committee. Second, a bill being considered *in sede deliberante* must be brought to the floor of the chamber if so requested by the cabinet or by ten percent of the members of the chamber or by 20 percent of the members of the standing committee.

The procedures of the Italian Parliament include several atypical usages, which help to differentiate it from the parliaments of other West European democracies. First, there is no effective limit on the number of private-member bills that may be introduced; the cabinet has far less control over the agenda than is the case in Britain and Germany. Second, there is no conference committee to iron out differences between Senate and Chamber of Deputies versions of a bill. Consequently, many bills shuttle between the two houses for years without ever achieving passage. Finally, there was until recently a requirement in the rules of the Chamber of Deputies that the final vote on a bill be taken by secret ballot. Such a procedure permitted recalcitrant Christian Democratic deputies ("snipers") to vote against measures supported by their party leadership. Of course, when a bill was defeated in a secret ballot, the cabinet could ask for a formal vote of confidence, which required a roll call. But sniping was an embarrassing event that lowered the prestige of cabinet members and might impel them to resign. The parliamentary secret ballot has recently been abolished.

In other respects, the Italian Parliament is much more in line with other West European parliamentary systems (excluding France, which possesses both presidential and parliamentary features). It can pass any law that does not violate a provision of the constitution, and it can manage its own procedures without being subject to external interference. Its powers are fairly conventional. It can pass laws, delegate rule-making power to the cabinet, ratify treaties, approve the budget, and conduct investigations. It meets in joint session to elect the president of Italy, to impeach the president for high treason or offenses against the constitution, and to elect one-third of the members of the Constitutional Court. It may also amend the constitution. An amendment has to be passed twice by each chamber with the two votes at least three months apart. The second vote requires an absolute majority of each house. Unless at least two-thirds of the members of each house support the amendment on the second vote, it may have to be submitted to a popular referendum on the demand of one-third of the members of each house, or of 500,000 voters, or of five regional councils (legislatures).

The organization of the Italian Parliament is also fairly orthodox. Two presiding officers, the president of the Senate and the president of the Chamber of Deputies, have partial control over the order of business, which they must share with the Conference of Presidents (heads of various standing committees and parliamentary groups). They have the power, subject to appeal, to assign bills to standing committees, to determine whether a bill should be passed in the committee itself *in sede deliberante* or reported to the floor *in sede referente*. And they appoint the members of select committees. Unlike the Speaker of the House of Commons, they tend to be prominent partisans with ambitious plans for future advancement (e.g., to president or prime minister). But given the loose power structure of the Italian Parliament, the two presiding officers are very limited in the power they can exercise.

In addition to a presiding officer who resembles the continental European model of an avowedly partisan Speaker and who has political clout and ambitions of his own, each house of the Italian Parliament possesses another characteristic trait of a continental European parliamentary system. It is divided into parliamentary groups that are essentially cohesive and disciplined caucuses of the respective parties. These groups are responsible for assigning members to standing committee positions that have been allocated to each group; they also advise the president of the chamber on the appointment of investigating committees and on filling vacancies on select committees.

The president of each parliamentary party group represents the group on the Conference of Presidents, which is supposed to reach agreement on the order of business for the chamber. The parliamentary group leaders are also consulted by the president of the Republic during a cabinet crisis, when a prime minister has resigned and a successor must be appointed. The parliamentary group reaches binding decisions as to how its members are to vote on pending legislation. Finally, the parliamentary group is itself subject to pressure from the party organization outside Parliament. Some parliamentary groups are more successful than others in maintaining a certain degree of autonomy against directives issued by extraparliamentary party organs. Overall, however, the party outside Parliament exercises more influence over legislative affairs in Italy than is the case in Britain or Germany.

In 1971, both houses of the Italian Parliament adopted some major changes in their rules and procedures. One of the most ambitious of these changes gave formal recognition to the Conference of Presidents and assigned it the task of setting the legislative agenda, by unanimous agreement, for periods of from two to three months. The pious hope that long-term legislative planning by unanimous consent would somehow be possible has proved to be unjustified. What was supposed to be an organic plan for a long-term legislative program has turned out to be either an incoherent shopping list based on log rolling or a series of brief one- or two-week calendars for which unanimity is not required.[3]

In 1976, when the Communist party was unofficially admitted to the governing majority without actually being granted cabinet positions, some changes took place in the leadership structure of Parliament. These changes were designed to offer some concessions to the Communist party in exchange for the benevolent abstention or external support it was offering to a center-left cabinet. Leonilde Iotti, a prominent Communist leader, was elected president of the Chamber of Deputies with Christian Democratic support, and seven out of twenty-five committee chairships in the Senate and Chamber of Deputies were allotted to the Communists. This cooptation of the Communist party into positions of parliamentary leadership seems to reflect a shift in the partisan balance of power rather than any real consensus among the two major forces in Italian politics.

It is evident, from what we have observed so far, that the sort of executive domination of Parliament that exists in Britain and France is not really present in the Italian parliamentary system. The multiparty, multifactional system that prevails in Italy makes the Italian Parliament almost unmanageable, despite the existence of party cohesion (generally solid bloc voting by each parliamentary group) and party discipline (sanctions against individual legislators who stray from the party line). The power of dissolution, which the president of the Republic can exercise on the recommendation of the prime minister, is rather ineffective, since elections rarely can be counted on to improve the government's mandate. What is the use of dissolving Parliament when the percentage of the total vote polled by each party is subject only to relatively minor changes and proportional representation minimizes the impact of these changes? As a result, between 1948 and 1968, Parliament was always allowed to serve out its full five-year term. Shorter intervals (usually four years, except in 1976–79) occurred between elections in 1972, 1976, 1979, 1983, and 1987.

Some of the structural characteristics and procedures of the Italian Parliament tend to protect it further against executive dominance. These include the absence of any limit on private-member bills; the lack of tight cabinet control over the agenda; the power of Italian standing committees to enact laws *in sede deliberante* and the presence of a powerful, popularly elected second chamber. And of course, lacking a secure majority, cabinets come and go; Parliament is protected against dissolution by the party system and the electoral law.

One other basic characteristic of the Italian Parliament should be noted in closing: its hybrid nature. On the one hand, it has cohesive, disciplined parties acting through parliamentary groups in the tradition of European parliamentary systems. On the other, it has a fragmentation of decision making among the presidents of the two chambers, the standing committees and their chairs, and even private members, who play a far larger role than elsewhere in Europe. In these respects, the Italian Parliament bears some vague resemblance to the U.S. Congress. This curious combination of "a fragmented but mostly stable and internally cohesive structure of parliamentary groups with parliamentary rules protecting individual and minority prerogatives"[4] makes it difficult to fit the Italian Parliament into a neat category for classification purposes.

The Bureaucracy

It is estimated that there are about 2 million state employees in Italy at present. But if one subtracts over a million employed in the schools and in the armed forces, the number of regular civil servants is approximately 600,000, about 40,000 of whom are higher civil servants with policy-making duties. In addition to this vast army of state employees, there are approximately 2.33 million employed by the *para-statale* (state-controlled) sector. These people work for local and regional governments, public corporations, service agencies, and the like.[5]

The Italian higher civil service (*carriera direttiva*) is staffed mostly on the basis of merit, though there are a certain number of patronage appointments and a fairly sizable minority of positions are filled without competitive examination by temporary appointees who eventually acquire permanent status. For those recruited by competitive examinations, either by direct entry from the universities or by promotion, the examinations tend to stress legal training rather than the broad social science background emphasized in France.

This recruitment system results in an overrepresentation of the south in the higher civil service because the south, like other developing and economically backward areas, has a higher percentage of its university population attracted to traditional professions like law and medicine. Moreover, southerners are more apt to be attracted to the secure if rather humdrum career provided by the bureaucracy; young people from economically stagnant regions often lack the contacts and know-how to embark on a business career. Many southern recruits are apt to be of lower-middle-class origin, in sharp contrast to the upper-middle-class Parisians recruited into the French higher civil service. Thus, Italian higher civil servants are drawn disproportionately from the most underdeveloped, tradition-bound regions of Italy. This bureaucracy, which also receives a brief period of in-service training, tends to be cautious and negative in its attitude toward policy innovations. Moreover, its members are obsessed with the need to find a legal justification for every action, and this obsessive legalism makes for a certain reluctance to take any action if it can possibly be avoided. Finally, it should be mentioned that the Italian bureaucracy—unlike the British, French, and German bureaucracies—is regarded by many Italians as corrupt. This reputation is probably based on somewhat exaggerated perceptions stemming from a low level of political trust. Still, perceptions count heavily in shaping public attitudes.

Public Corporations and Semi-Independent Agencies

Another major source of policy making in Italy is the so-called para-state sector: public corporations and the semi-independent agencies that preside over the Italian public sector and a variety of regulatory and welfare functions. These include such holding companies as the Institute for Industrial Reconstruction (IRI) and the National Hydrocarburants Corporation (ENI), each of which supervises a number of subsidiary companies that hold controlling stock in a broad assortment of enterprises ranging from steel mills to oil refineries to motels. Also in the para-state sector are ENEL, the public corporation that runs the electric power industry (nationalized in 1962); and EFIM and GEPI, two financial agencies set up to help businesses in distress. A number of social welfare and social insurance funds and a hodgepodge of miscellaneous agencies and companies are also part of the heterogeneous para-state sector.

State control over the public sector has been uncoordinated and therefore ineffective. Both IRI and ENI were placed under the Ministry of State Share Holdings, but this cabinet department was unable to check the expansionist policies pursued by these giant holding companies and their subsidiaries. More recently, the Office of the Prime Minister has gradually extended its sphere of influence to encompass many of the public corporations. Other para-state agencies are under the Ministry of Industry (ENEL, for instance) or under one of the ministries concerned with social welfare. So, supervisory responsibility has been divided among a number of ministries. This situation, along with interparty, interfactional division within the Italian cabinet, seems to have made it virtually impossible for the executive to impose a measure of coherence and discipline on the para-state sector.

In the 1950s and early 1960s, numerous observers regarded the public corporations, headed by adventurous entrepreneurs like Enrico Mattei of ENI, as a major constructive force in Italy's economic recovery. By the 1970s, however, it had become all too evident that the public enterprises had contracted some serious economic maladies and had developed some deplorable managerial and fiscal habits. Employing about 25 percent of the Italian labor force and producing about 25 percent of Italy's gross domestic product, the Italian public sector became a serious drain on the country's economy.

The defects of the public enterprises have often been recited. Their executives and managers have engaged in reckless speculation and unscrupulous empire building. Gains in productivity have slackened or disappeared altogether; large sums have been squandered on mergers and takeovers. Executive positions at the helm of these public-sector enterprises have become political patronage plums to be divided among members of various parties or even warring factions within a party. Such patronage appointments have certainly bolstered the political influence of the public sector, but at the price of efficiency. Finally, the state holding companies have sheltered their weaker, less viable enterprises, thus encouraging the unfit to survive. As one caustic comment put it, the state holding companies have become "paddle ponds for lame ducks."[6]

The new financial and managerial elite that has emerged in the public sector has come to be regarded as a new parasitical class—a "state bourgeoisie." Obsessed with patronage and with financial manipulations, members of this new class were responsible for overstaffing Italian factories, permitting labor discipline to deteriorate, and piling up enormous debts. Placing increasing reliance on state grants and on loans from public credit institutions, the public holding companies have contributed heavily to the rising tide of inflation and to the alarming budget deficits that have resulted from excessive public spending.

In the past few years, there have been some heartening signs that the Italian government may be addressing itself seriously to the problem of limiting the excesses of the public sector. The fifth Fanfani cabinet (1982–83) named two highly respected economic managers—Franco Reviglio and Romano Prodi—to head ENI and IRI respectively. Both were committed to reducing deficits and to weeding out firms that were losing money, by reducing the amount of government subsidies and privatizing unsuccessful or superfluous firms. These objectives had to be pursued in the face of political interference (by the patronage-addicted party machines) and working-class resistance to industrial layoffs. Entrenched habits die hard. Nevertheless, progress has been made; by 1987, the large public-sector holding companies were no longer running massive deficits. IRI, in fact, was actually in the black with a sizable profit.[7] Moreover, there is now a general consensus, which includes the Italian Communist party, that the public sector should not be expanded further. Unlike their French comrades, Italian Communists put little stock in nationalization.

The Judiciary

Like France and Germany, Italy has a legal system in the civil-law tradition, which stems originally from Roman law. The judge is simply supposed to apply the law as stated in the relevant provisions of the legal code, not to analyze the facts of the case and explore the applicability of past judicial decisions. Law is not determined primarily by an accumulation of judicial opinions but is to be found in statutes, executive decrees, legal codes, and accepted interpretations of legal scholars. In short, the concept of judge-made law is foreign to the civil-law tradition. The judge's function appears to be viewed as somewhat mechanical, and there is little room for judicial discretion. To be sure, there are inevitable departures in any civil-law country from this model of the civil-law tradition.

The Italian judicial system has some features in common with that of France. There are two parallel judicial hierarchies: five tiers of ordinary law courts, culminating in the Court of Cassation, and a system of administrative courts. As in France, judges are recruited into a judicial career service after graduation from law school and work their way up the judicial ladder in a series of promotions and transfers.

There are some significant differences between the two systems.

First, Italian judges at the lowest rung of the hierarchy receive much lower salaries than their French and German counterparts. Second, there is nothing corresponding to the National Center of Judicial Studies in France, which provides modern training for future magistrates; Italian judges enter the judicial corps with only the formalistic legal training they received in law school. Third, promotion in Italy is less dependent on executive fiat than it is in France. While it is generally agreed that the French executive branch has come to dominate the promotion process, in Italy a Superior Council of the Judiciary has effective control over appointments, transfers, and promotions. From its inception, this council has been dominated by senior judges of the higher courts, who tend to be somewhat conservative. Thus, Italian judicial independence has been threatened less by executive encroachment than by the financial penury that younger judges have to endure and the domination that senior judges of the higher courts have exercised over the promotion process. Nevertheless, the hegemony of the senior judges has been eroded by recent reform measures, which have made some promotions virtually automatic.

The administrative court system deviates from the French model to a still greater degree than the ordinary judicial system. There are two separate hierarchies of administrative court, one headed by the Court of Accounts and the other by the Council of State. Italian administrative courts are less prestigious and self-assertive than the French, since at the lower levels they are staffed by civil servants rather than full-time judges. Unlike the French administrative courts, which can hear both suits by private citizens for damages against the state and suits challenging the legality of executive decrees, Italian administrative courts can consider only the question of legality. Damage suits must be introduced in the ordinary law courts. Finally, the Italian Council of State has been much more cautious in challenging the executive than has the French Conseil d'Etat.

We have noted how both the Italian cabinet and the public corporations have been permeated by partisan and factional conflicts. The same phenomenon is to be found in the Italian judiciary. A split has developed among Italian judges between the older and more senior judges associated with the Court of Cassation and the younger, more interventionist judges who seek a more active, socially conscious judiciary. As a result, two competing judicial associations have been formed, and they compete for control of the High Council of the Judiciary.

In one important respect, the Italian judicial system bears a strong resemblance to that of Germany. There is a Constitutional Court with powers of judicial review. Established by the constitution, this court was not actually set up by parliamentary law until 1956. It had taken almost a decade to overcome the foot-dragging of the Christian Democratic party, which saw the court as a threat to majority (i.e. Christian Democratic) rule.

The Constitutional Court has fifteen members, five selected by the president of Italy, five elected by a three-fifths vote of a joint session of Parliament, five elected by judges of the highest Italian courts (the Court of Cassation, the Council of State, and the Court of Accounts). The members serve a twelve-year term, which is not immediately renewable. The Constitutional Court has the power to determine the constitutionality of national and regional laws. Any case may be brought before the Constitutional Court on the appeal of an individual, a group, or a region. There is one serious obstacle to utilization of the appellate procedure. The judge of the lower court from which an appeal to the Constitutional Court is being sought may block the appeal by issuing an interlocutory judgment to the effect that the appeal is patently unfounded. Since many Italian judges (especially in the Court of Cassation) resented the establishment of the Constitutional Court as a departure from the traditions of the Italian legal system and could not accept the concept of judicial review, such interlocutory judgments were not uncommon during the first years of the Court's existence.

The Constitutional Court has had a major impact on the Italian political system. It has struck down numerous provisions of the penal code adopted during the Fascist regime. In 1961, for example, it declared the unconstitutionality of an old law that forbade an individual from moving from one locality to another unless he first had a guarantee of a job in his new locality. A number of laws restricting freedom of expression have also been invalidated. In recent controversies over divorce and abortion, the court has strengthened the cause of secularism. In 1970, it decided that a pending divorce bill would not require an amendment of the constitution despite the fact that Article 7 of the constitution incorporated the Concordat of 1929. Also in 1970, the court declared the Italian law forbidding adultery to be unconstitutionally discriminatory against women. In 1971, a law prohibiting the publication of birth control information and the sale of contraceptives was struck down. In 1975 the court declared unconstitutional some provisions of an antiabortion law of long standing. Many restrictions on civil liberties are still on the books. But the Constitutional Court has done a great deal to extend individual freedom, while avoiding any major clash with the executive branch.

Subnational Governments

The three main tiers of governmental authority below the national level are the regions, the provinces, and the communes. The regions—five "special regions" and fifteen "ordinary regions"—correspond in size to the French regions and the German *Länder.* The provinces, ninety-four in number, are comparable to French *départements.* And the 8,000-odd communes are counterparts of the French communes, although they are far less numerous and fragmented than the French.

There have traditionally been some strong similarities between French and Italian patterns of local government. Both have been characterized by elected local and departmental/provincial councils, which in turn elected executive committees or juntas from their ranks. Both had a system of appointed central officials—the prefects—named by the minister of interior to supervise closely the departments/provinces and communes. There was a prefect for each department/province, and he had the power to annul the decisions of communal or departmental/provincial councils and to suspend local officials who were derelict in their duties. At the communal level, the executive committee or junta was headed by a mayor whose job was to supervise the executive organs of the commune and negotiate both with central government agencies and with the prefect. Finally, before World War II, both systems were highly centralized (the central government had direct control over the schools, the prefect had authority over local police functions) and unitary (the departments/provinces and communes possessed only such legal powers as the central government chose to grant them). There were no regional units of government in either country before World War II.

The main difference between the two systems lay in the role of the prefect. While the French prefect also acted as coordinator and supervisor of central government field agencies, the Italian prefect was confined to controlling local government. Moreover, unlike the French prefect, he had to share this power of control with a number of central government field services. In short, while France had an integrated prefectoral system, the Italian prefectoral system was unintegrated.[8]

In 1948, with the ratification of the constitution of the Italian Republic, Italy adopted a system that is neither unitary nor federal but possesses some quasi-federal features. Under a form of regional devolution, the Italian regions have been granted extensive concurrent powers to share with the national government in a number of fields. As in a federal system, the powers of regional governments are specified in the Italian constitution and may be formally repealed only by constitutional amendment, although of course the Constitutional Court may restrict or dilute those powers by judicial interpretation. Moreover, the regions are specifically named in the constitution, thus protecting them against any ordinary parliamentary statute or executive decree reorganizing the boundaries and powers of subnational governments.

But the Italian system of regional devolution contains some definitely nonfederal restrictions on regional autonomy. First, the regions cannot exercise their concurrent powers until central government organs have issued the necessary enabling statutes and decrees. Second, the regions have no original taxing power of their own and have to depend on central legislation to authorize such taxes as they are permitted to impose. Third, an appointed central government commissioner in each region has a suspensive veto over bills passed by the regional councils (legislatures). Finally, a bill passed once again by a regional council after such a veto can be blocked either by the Constitutional Court (which can rule on its constitutionality before it goes into effect) or by the Italian Parliament (which can declare that a bill is contrary to the national interest). Thus, not only is national law supreme over regional law, but regional law must give way to the national interest as defined by Parliament.

Before 1970, the regional autonomy provided by the 1948 constitution remained largely a dead letter. Five "special regions" had been created because they contained special ethnic minorities or displayed marked separatist tendencies. These regions comprised three ethnic border zones—French-speaking Val d'Aosta, partly German-speaking Trentino–Alto Adige, and partly Slovenian Friuli–Venezia Giulia—and the two big islands of Sicily and Sardinia. The other fifteen regions —the "ordinary regions"—remained only on paper, since no enabling legislation was passed. Once again, as in the case of the Constitutional Court, the fault lay with the dominant Christian Democratic party, which did not want to establish any institutional checks on majority rule. By the late 1960s, however, the situation had become ripe for change. The centrist coalition cabinets of the 1950s had given way to a series of center-left cabinets that included the Italian Socialist party; and the Socialists wanted to see the regions established at long last. There was also a great deal of support for the regions among a number of more progressive factions in the Christian Democratic party; and the Communist party was favorably inclined, since it expected to control several regional governments. Moreover, after the strikes and demonstrations of the Hot Autumn of 1969, it seemed advisable to deflect some popular grievances to lower levels of government. Accordingly, enabling legislation was passed, and regional councils were elected in the "ordinary regions" in 1970.

Even then, the position of the regions was still quite precarious. While regional councils existed and regional juntas were assuming their executive duties, very few decision-making powers had been transferred to the regions. Not until 1975, when the left and particularly the Communists made remarkable gains in the second set of regional elections, was Parliament induced to authorize real progress toward regional devolution. In 1975, a law was passed directing the government to complete the transfer to the regions of all powers assigned to them by the constitution. And in 1977, a set of decrees was issued carrying out many but by no means all of the transfers envisioned by the 1975 law and turning over to the regions approximately 25 percent of the national budget. With Law No. 382 (1975) and D.P.R. 616 (1977), the regions were finally in business.[9]

Since 1978, the regions have been engaged in a continuing contest with the central government to defend and, if possible, extend the powers they have been granted, to obtain an adequate share of national revenues, to protect their turf against encroachment by the central government, and to clarify their role vis-à-vis central and local authorities. Their status leaves much to be desired from the regional point of view.[10] First, the process of transferring the constitutionally defined regional powers from the central to the regional governments is far from completion. There are still areas where delegation of powers to the regions has *not* taken place. Second, the Parliament and the ministries often take it upon themselves to saddle the regions with the task of enforcing certain national laws, thus reducing the resources and options available to regional governments. Third, the central government still decides what revenues will be assigned to each regional government. Fourth, the central government has tended to develop direct ties with local authorities, bypassing the regions; and central government proposals for a prospective new local government reorganization law have tended to downplay the supervisory role of the regions in relation to local governments. Fifth, the Constitutional Court has generally ruled against the regions in cases involving conflict between national and regional powers. Finally, consultation between the central government and the regions has been sporadic and unsystematic at best.

The situation of Italian local governments is even less satisfactory. Despite the repeated introduction of abortive bills and numerous debates, it was not until the late spring of 1991 that the Italian Parliament finally got around to passing a new law redefining the structure and powers of local governments and their relationship to the regions and the central government. Until such a law was passed, everything was provisional at the subnational level. And even now, it must be borne in mind that it may take several years for the Italian bureaucracy to churn out the executive decrees putting the law into actual practice.

In the meantime, some trends are discernible. The prefect has been stripped of most of his supervisory powers over local government, especially those involving prior surveillance of local government decisions. That function is now performed by a regional Control Committee, a majority of whose members are elected by the regional council. A second development has been a delegation of certain powers to the local governments on the part of both the national government and the regions. But it should be noted that the regions have shown a marked tendency to procrastinate in delegating functions to local authorities, or to delegate only minor functions, or to attempt to exercise rigid controls over how those functions are carried out. This points to a third tendency in Italian local government: Regions seem to be pushing for a centralized relationship with the local authorities. And by way of reaction, local governments are sometimes seeking a closer link with the central government, which is seen as a protector against regional domination. The future of both regional and local autonomy in Italy is, for now, uncertain.

Notes

1. On Italian cabinet formulas since 1946, see Alberto Marradi, "Italy: From 'Centrism' to Crisis of the Center-Left Coalitions," in *Government Coalitions in Western Democracies,* ed. Eric C. Browne and John Dreijmanis (New York: Longman, 1982), chap. 2, esp. 48–56.

2. See Sabino Cassese, "Is There a Government in Italy? Politics and Administration at the Top," in *Presidents and Prime Ministers,* ed. Richard Rose and Ezra N. Suleiman (Washington, D.C.: American Enterprise Institute, 1980), 171–202.

3. See Giuseppe Di Palma, "The Available State: Problems of Reform," in *Italy in Transition: Conflict and Consensus,* ed. Peter Lange and Sidney Tarrow (London: Frank Cass, 1980), 162–63; and Giuseppe Di Palma, "Risposte parlamentari alla crisi del regime," in *La crisi italiana,* ed. Luigi Graziano and Sidney Tarrow (Torino: Einaudi, 1979), 2:404, 410.

4. See Giuseppe Di Palma, *Surviving without Governing: The Italian Parties in Parliament* (Berkeley: University of California Press, 1977), 190.

5. See Cassese, "Is There a Government in Italy?" 179; and Carlo Donolo, "Social Change and Transformation of the State in Italy," in *The State in Western Europe,* ed. Richard Scase (London: Croom Helm, 1980), 170.

6. "A Survey of Italy," *Economist,* 23 July 1983, 37.

7. "The Flawed Renaissance: A Survey of the Italian Economy," *Economist,* 27 February 1988, 3, 28.

8. See Robert C. Fried, *The Italian Prefects: A Study in Administrative Politics* (New Haven: Yale University Press, 1963), 116–18, 249–95, 303–8.

9. Robert Leonardi, Raffaella Y. Nanetti, and Robert D. Putnam, "Devolution as a Political Process: The Case of Italy," *Publius* 11 (Winter 1981): 95–117.

10. See "Editoriale," *Le regioni* 11 (January-April 1983): 1–4.

18

Who Has the Power and How Did They Get It?

The Italian multiparty system is much more complex than that of France or Germany.[1] No fewer than nine national parties (parties that presented lists of candidates in all or most constituencies) are represented in the Italian Parliament.

1. *The Democratic Party of the Left* (PDS), known until 1991 as the Italian Communist party, the strongest Communist party in Western Europe
2. *Communist Refoundation,* a party of orthodox Communists who objected to the moderate course and symbolic change of label adopted by the PDS
3. *The Green party,* which tends to focus its efforts on environmental questions
4. *The Italian Socialist party* (PSI), once allied with the Communists but now somewhat closer to the left-center of the political spectrum
5. *The Italian Social Democratic party* (PSDI), more cautious and moderate than its Socialist cousin
6. *The Italian Republican party* (PRI), moderately left-of-center and increasingly prestigious
7. *The Christian Democratic party* (DC), which has played a dominant and usually hegemonic role in Italian politics since 1946
8. *The Italian Liberal party* (PLI), actually a moderately conservative party of the right-center

9. *The Italian Social Movement* (MSI), a neo-Fascist party that is
   something of an outcast among the national political movements

In addition to these national parties, there are a number of
regional, ethnic, or splinter parties: the Northern League; the Liga
Veneta; the Südtiroler Volkspartei, a German-speaking party in Bolzano
Province; the Val d'Aosta List; the Network, representing an anti-Mafia
movement in Sicily; the Pannella Lists, an assortment of former
Radicals concerned with postmaterialist life-style issues; and the Party
of Pensioners.

Some of the traditional characteristics of the post-World War II
Italian party system should be duly noted in order that the significance
of recent trends may be assessed. One set of characteristic features has
to do with the strength of the parties in the system. There is a dominant
party—the Christian Democratic party—which headed every Italian
cabinet between 1946 and 1981. The second-ranking party—the Communist party (now the PDS)—is the strongest Communist party in
Western Europe. The Italian Socialist movement has been split ever
since 1947, with the exception of a brief interval from 1966 to 1969,
and consequently the position of Italian Socialism is much weaker than
in most other West European countries. And nowhere else in Western
Europe except in France is there a neo-Fascist movement whose strength
even remotely approaches that of the Italian Social Movement.

Some authors have stressed the polarization of the Italian party system, which includes powerful extremist parties (the Communists and
the neo-Fascists) at its left and right poles. Others refer to its remarkable stability. Parties make only minor gains or suffer only minor losses
in general elections, and voters rarely shift far along the political spectrum but move, say, from extreme left to moderate left or from center
to center-right. This stability has been attributed partly to the very high
degree of party identification, partly to the existence of one-party
regions like the Catholic Veneto, and partly to the remarkably large
turnout that reduces the number of undecided voters to be mobilized.
Finally, it has been pointed out that *two* of the parties in Italy's multiparty system tend to corner the lion's share of the vote. Between them,
the Communists and the Christian Democrats have polled between 60
and 70 percent of the votes in every election from 1953 through 1972,
and rose to 73.1 percent in 1976 before ebbing to a very respectable
68.7 percent in 1979 (see table 18.1, page 336).[2] (The outcomes for
party representation in the Chamber of Deputies are given in table 18.2,
page 338).[3] This has led to the conclusion that Italy has an "imperfect

two-party system," with one of the two major parties permanently in the cabinet and the other permanently in the opposition.[4] Recent events have cast considerable doubt on this thesis, however. The combined vote of the Communists and Christian Democrats dropped to 62.8 percent in 1983, 60.9 percent in 1987, and a startling 51.4 percent (counting the votes of both Communist parties) in 1992.

Italian parties also possess some organizational traits that endow them with a distinctive character. They are highly centralized, and the central party organization does not hesitate to intervene in nominations at the local level. They are cohesive; members of the party in Parliament generally vote together as a solid bloc, though there *are* deviations. And they are disciplined; legislators who fail to follow the instructions of their party leaders and whips may be courting severe disciplinary sanctions, not excluding expulsion from the parliamentary party group. Another point to be stressed is the important role played by the party outside of Parliament in its relationship with the parliamentary party. Many cabinet crises originate outside Parliament with decisions reached by party secretaries or party directorates (executive committees). To be sure, there is much overlap between the parliamentary and extraparliamentary party organizations. The secretaries and members of party directorates are frequently themselves simultaneously members of Parliament.

Perhaps the most interesting property of Italian political parties is the presence within their ranks of highly organized competing factions. These intraparty groupings reflect more than mere tendencies or currents of opinion. They have, in many cases, a well-defined organizational structure, press and research organs to formulate and disseminate their views, their own sources of financing independent of the party organization, and their own leadership hierarchy. Factions vie with one another for control over the party organization and over patronage appointments, and they demand appropriate representation when cabinets and regional and local juntas are being formed. On numerous occasions, the formation of a cabinet or a regional or municipal junta is held up while negotiations proceed to determine which Christian Democratic or Socialist factions are to be assigned which executive posts.

The Elections of 1983, 1987, and 1992

With the Italian parliamentary elections of 1983 and 1987, some of the traditional features of the Italian party system seemed to be undergoing major and perhaps permanent alterations. For one thing, the Christian Democratic party (DC) appears to be in serious danger of losing its he-

TABLE 18.1

PERCENTAGES OF THE TOTAL VOTE POLLED BY ITALIAN PARTIES IN ELECTIONS FOR THE CONSTITUENT ASSEMBLY IN 1946 AND FOR THE CHAMBER OF DEPUTIES, 1948–92

	1946	1948	1953	1958	1963	1968	1972	1976	1979	1983	1987	1992
Proletarian Democrats	—	—	—	—	—	4.5	1.9	1.5[a]	2.3	1.5	1.7	—
Radicals	—	—	—	—	—	—	—	1.1	3.5	2.2	2.6	—[b]
Greens	—	—	—	—	—	—	—	—	—	—	2.5	2.8
Communists	19.0	31.0[b]	22.6	22.7	25.3	26.9	27.1	34.4	30.4	29.9	26.6	21.7[i]
Socialists	20.7[c]		12.7	14.2	13.8	14.5[d]	9.6	9.6	9.8	11.4	14.3	13.6
Social Democrats	—	7.1	4.5	4.5	6.1		5.1	3.4	3.8	4.1	3.0	2.7
Republicans	4.4	2.5	1.6	1.4	1.4	2.0	2.8	3.1	3.0	5.1	3.7	4.4
Christian Democrats	35.2	48.5	40.0	42.4	38.3	39.1	38.7	38.7	38.3	32.9	34.3	29.7
Liberals	6.8	3.8	3.6	3.5	7.6	5.8	3.9	1.3	1.9	2.9	2.1	2.8
Qualunquists (extreme right)	5.3	—	—	—	—	—	—	—	—	—	—	—
Monarchists	2.8	2.8	6.8	4.8[e]	1.7	1.3	—	—	—	—	—	—
Neo-Fascists	—	2.0	5.9	4.8	5.1	4.5	8.7	6.1[f]	5.3	6.8	5.9	5.4
Others	5.8[g]	2.3	2.9	1.7	1.3	1.4	2.1	0.7	1.7	3.2	3.3	16.9[j]

a. The PDUP (Democratic party of Proletarian Unity) was the successor of the Italian Socialist party of Proletarian Unity (PSIUP), which ran in 1968 and 1972 and then merged with the Communists. In 1979, the PDUP polled 1.4 percent of the votes and the DP (Proletarian Democrats) polled .9 percent for a total of 2.3 percent. By 1983, the PDUP had merged with the Communists.

b. In 1948, the Communists and Socialists formed a single electoral bloc, the People's Democratic Front (FDP). The experiment was not repeated.

c. In 1946, the Socialists and Social Democrats were united in a single party. The Social Democrats broke away in 1947.

d. In 1968, the Socialists and Social Democrats ran together as a single unified party: the Unified Socialist party (PSU). The party split up in 1969.

e. There were two Monarchist parties in 1958, polling 2.2 percent and 2.6 percent of the votes, respectively.

f. In December of 1976, the MSI split, with about half of its deputies joining a new right-wing party: the National Democrats (DN). DN failed to gain any representation in 1979.

g. In 1946, this category included the short-lived Action party, many of whose members joined the Socialists or the Republicans in 1946, 1947, or 1948.

h. The Radical party has split into warring factions since 1987. Seven deputies were elected in 1992 as candidates on the "Pannella Lists" sponsored by the former leader of the Radical party, Marco Pannella. These lists garnered about 1.2 percent of the vote.

i. There were two Communist parties on the ballot in 1992: Occhetto's Democratic Party of the Left (PDS) and a party of orthodox Communists (Communist Refoundation), who rejected Occhetto's reformist ideas. The PDS polled 16.1 percent of the vote, whereas Communist Refoundation received 5.6 percent.

j. The "Others" included the Northern League with 8.7 percent of the votes; an anti-Mafia party, the Network (La Rete), with 1.9 percent of the votes; the Pannella Lists with about 1.2 percent of the votes; the South Tyrol People's Party and the Liga Veneta, each with less than 1 percent.

TABLE 18.2

SEATS WON BY THE VARIOUS ITALIAN PARTIES IN THE ITALIAN CONSTITUENT ASSEMBLY IN 1946 AND IN THE ITALIAN CHAMBER OF DEPUTIES FROM 1948 THROUGH 1992

	1946	1948	1953	1958	1963	1968	1972	1976	1979	1983	1987	1992
Proletarian Democrats	—	—	—	—	—	23	0	6[a]	6	7	8	—
Radicals	—	—	—	—	—	—	—	4	18	11	13	—[h]
Greens	—	—	—	—	—	—	—	—	—	—	13	16
Communists	104	183[b]	143	140	166	171	179	228	201	198	177	142[i]
Socialists	115[c]		75	84	87	91[d]	61	58	62	73	94	92
Social Democrats	—	33	19	22	33		29	15	20	23	17	16
Republicans	23	9	5	6	6	9	15	14	16	29	21	27
Christian Democrats	207	305	262	273	260	265	266	262	262	225	234	206
Liberals	41	19	14	17	39	31	20	5	9	16	11	17
Qualunquists (extreme right)	30	—	—	—	—	—	—	—	—	—	—	—
Monarchists	0	14	40	25[e]	8	6	—	—	—	—	—	—
Neo-Fascists	—	6	29	15	27	24	56	35[f]	30	42	35	34
Others	35[g]	5	3	5	4	3	4	3	6	6	7	80[j]

a–g. See table 18.1, explanatory notes a through g.

h. See note h, table 18.1. The Pannella Lists obtained 7 seats.

i. See note i, table 18.1. The PDS won 107 seats, while the Communist diehards of the Communist Refoundation obtained 35.

j. See note j, table 18.1. Fifty-five seats were won by the Northern League, 7 by the Pannella Lists, 12 by the Network, 3 by the South Tyrol People's party, one by the Liga Veneta, one by the Union Valdôtaine, and one by the Party of Pensioners.

gemony over the Italian party system. The DC polled only 32.9 percent of the votes in 1983, a drop of 5.4 percentage points from its showing in 1979 and the lowest percentage it has polled in the history of the Italian Republic. By 1987, it had increased its percentages to 34.3, but this slight gain still left it below the 35.2 percent it had polled in 1946, which had previously been the DC's poorest performance. The 1992 election results were disastrous for the DC; with 29.7 percent of the total vote, it plumbed new depths of electoral failure, 3.2 percentage points below its 1983 low.

The PDS (formerly the Italian Communist party or PCI) is still the second-ranking party on the Italian political scene. But the hitherto consistent forward progress of Italian Communism was halted as early as 1979, when the PCI captured only 30.4 percent of the votes as compared to its 1976 high-water mark of 34.4 percent. This retrogression continued in the 1983 elections (29.9 percent) and, more sharply, in 1987, when the Communist party received only 26.6 percent of the votes, its weakest showing since 1968. This setback was the "second most serious defeat in its history [as of that time]."[5] But the worst was yet to come.

In 1991, the PCI split into the Democratic Party of the Left (PDS) and Communist Refoundation—the former representing the bulk of the former PCI and committed to a moderate leftist posture, the latter a party of diehards rebelling against the triumph of reformist tendencies in Italian Communism. In 1992, the PDS received 16.1 percent of the votes, whereas Communist Refoundation mustered only 5.6 percent. The combined total of 21.7 percent was 4.9 points below the already deplorable 1987 mark of 26.6 percent.

The Socialist movement is still divided between Socialists (PSI) and Social Democrats (PSDI). In 1983, both parties made heartening gains: the PSI rose from 9.8 percent in 1979 to 11.4 percent in 1983 (its best showing in twenty years); the PSDI increased its voting percentages from 3.8 percent in 1979 to 4.1 percent in 1983. In the 1987 elections, after four years of relative stability under the commanding leadership of Socialist Prime Minister Bettino Craxi, the Italian electorate rewarded the PSI with 14.3 percent of the total vote—its highest percentage, as an independent and distinctive party, since 1947. However, in 1992, the PSI dropped back to 13.6 percent, undergoing its first slump in twenty years. As for the PSDI, it steadily lost ground, receiving 3 percent in 1987 and 2.7 percent in 1992.

The other two minor center parties (the Republicans—PRI, and the Liberals—PLI) have chalked up very modest achievements. Both had gained heavily in 1983. The PRI rose from 3 percent in 1979 to 5.1 percent and the PLI from 1.9 percent to 2.9 percent. In 1987, however, they lost most of the ground they had captured. Recent gains in 1992, when the PRI rose to 4.4 percent and the PLI rose to 2.8 percent, still fell short of the 1983 performance. As for the neo-Fascists of the MSI, they have steadily lost ground since 1983: 5.3 percent in 1979, 6.8 percent in 1983, 5.9 percent in 1987, and—despite the presence of Mussolini's granddaughter on their ticket—only 5.4 percent in 1992. For these two minor center parties and for the MSI, the promising future which the 1983 results seemed to portend has never come to pass.

Italy's "imperfect two-party system" seems to be in critical condition in light of the results of the past three elections. The combined DC and PCI vote dropped from 73.1 percent in 1976 and 68.7 percent in 1979 to 62.8 percent in 1983 and 60.9 percent in 1987. This last figure represented the poorest showing for the two parties combined since the first postwar election in 1946, when they totaled only 54.2 percent. But 1992 broke even the 1946 record: The DC and the PDS together polled only 45.8 percent of the total vote. By contrast, if one adds the PSI vote to that of the three minor center parties (PSDI, PRI, PLI), the "laic bloc" (the bloc of secular democratic parties) won 23.5 percent of the votes in 1983, 23.1 percent in 1987, and 23.5 percent in 1992, compared to 18.5 percent in 1979 and 17.4 percent in 1976. Thus the "imperfect two-party system" is showing signs of unraveling, and the laic bloc is emerging as a potent third force in Italian electoral politics. It also appears that the 8.7 percent garnered by the regionalist League of the North (dominated by the Lombard League) in 1992, as well as the 5.6 percent captured by Communist Refoundation, have been won at the expense of the DC and the PDS, not the laic bloc.

The 1983, 1987, and 1992 elections also call into question the stability so often ascribed to the Italian party system. Both of the factors that have contributed to this stability in the past—strong party identification and high voter turnout—seem to be declining. Voter turnout dipped below 90 percent for the first time in 1979 and has never regained that level. Moreover, more voters are casting blank and invalid ballots. As we see later, Italian voting traditions seem to be eroding under the impact of the social and cultural changes we observed in chapter 16. The result has been a remarkable downward dip in the Christian Democratic vote.

The Christian Democratic decline was already foreshadowed in 1981 when the Christian Democratic grip on the office of prime minister was finally broken. In that year, the Republican leader Giovanni

Spadolini became prime minister. A number of factors facilitated Spadolini's takeover: a referendum vote to retain the relatively liberal abortion law, Christian Democratic implication in a scandal involving the political influence of a secret Masonic lodge, Christian Democratic losses in local elections that year, and Socialist demands that the office of prime minister be given to a Socialist or at least to a leading member of one of the left-center parties. Spadolini emerged as a compromise candidate because the Christian Democrats were not yet ready to let the Socialist leader, Craxi, become prime minister. The visibility and credibility bestowed on the Republican party by Spadolini's sixteen-month tenure as prime minister probably help to explain Republican gains and Christian Democratic losses in 1983.

The Main Political Parties

The Communists (PCI, now PDS)

The Italian Communist party was founded in 1921 at Leghorn. During the Fascist regime, it was outlawed (like all other non-Fascist parties) and had to operate as an underground organization. Its leader, Antonio Gramsci, was arrested in 1927 and died shortly after his release from prison a decade later. Gramsci's successor as party leader, Palmiro Togliatti, lived in exile in the Soviet Union until 1944 when the Allies liberated most of southern Italy. On his return to Italy, Togliatti took over the leadership of the party cadres on Italian soil and declared that the PCI should cooperate with all anti-Fascist forces until the Germans had been driven from Italy.

During the underground struggle against the German occupation forces in northern Italy, the PCI played a leading role in the Resistance, thus attracting many idealistic intellectuals to its ranks. After the war, the PCI emerged as the third-ranking party in the elections to the Constituent Assembly in June 1946. It polled 19 percent of the total vote, compared to 20.7 percent for the Socialist party. The following year, the Socialist party split in two, with about a third of the party breaking away to form the Social Democratic party. As a result, the Communist party became the leading leftist party and has gradually increased its margin over the Italian Socialist party, polling at least twice and frequently three times as many votes as the Socialists.

The Italian Communist party adopted a number of strategies after Togliatti's return to Italy in 1944, but the general trend, with occasional changes of pace, was in the direction of greater moderation.[6] From 1944 through 1948, the Communist party participated in alliances and coalitions with the other anti-Fascist parties, particularly with the Socialists and Christian Democrats. After the Communists were ousted from the Christian Democratic-led coalition cabinet in the spring of 1947, they and the Socialists adopted a posture of all-out opposition to the center coalition that was governing Italy. During this period, which lasted roughly from 1948 to 1956, the Communists and Socialists were closely allied under the auspices of a Unity of Action Pact. This shift to a policy of bitter confrontation with the Christian Democratic regime and the Atlantic Alliance was virtually forced on the Communist party by the coming of the Cold War and the jelling of intransigent attitudes in both Washington and Moscow. Then came Stalin's death in 1953, Khrushchev's speech in 1956 denouncing the crimes of the Stalin era, and the invasion of Hungary by Soviet troops in 1956. These events undermined the old Stalinist myths and made uncompromising opposition by the PCI harder to justify. At the same time, the exclusive alliance with the Socialists was showing some signs of erosion, and the PCI was losing ground in the labor movement and losing membership as well. In 1956, therefore, the PCI adopted a strategy of constructive opposition within the system.

By the early 1970s, the rightist coup against the Allende leftist coalition government in Chile and the apparent danger of an ultraconservative backlash against the excesses of the student riots of 1968 and the labor unrest of 1969 combined to push the PCI leaders still further in the direction of moderation and broader alliances. From 1973 to 1979, they pressed for a "historic compromise" that would include all Italian parties that were willing to uphold the constitution, but that would emphasize an alliance between the Communists and the Christian Democrats. During the latter part of this period, the PCI gave external support in Parliament to Christian Democratic monocolor cabinets and external support in some regional councils to left-center juntas. By 1979, however, the PCI was ready to table its demand for a "historic compromise." Its relatively loyal support of Christian Democratic cabinets had aroused much discontent among its own rank and file and had failed to induce the Christian Democrats to admit the PCI to a share of cabinet posts. Denied entry into the cabinet, the PCI returned to its opposition role in 1979 and called for a "left alternative" formula for future cabinets. This would include Communists, Socialists, Social Democrats, Republicans, and progressive elements in Christian Democracy.

The PCI's domestic and foreign policies tended to deviate ever more sharply, not only from the position of the Communist party of the Soviet Union but even from the orthodox Marxism and egalitarian extremism of the French Communist party. The PCI pledged itself to come to power though free elections, to maintain a multiparty system, and to allow itself to be voted out of office. It pressed for enforcement of the provisions of the constitution. With regard to nationalization, which the French Communists want to extend still further, the Italian Communist party actually suggested that the public sector was large enough for the present and that additional expansion of nationalized industries would be inadvisable. It favored all the pet projects of reformist Socialism: tightening of the tax loopholes, aid to small business, greater financial autonomy for local authorities, government spending for full employment and social welfare, and honesty in government. Its attitude toward both right-wing and left-wing terrorism was stern and uncompromising, far more so than that of the Socialist party. In fact, the PCI urged the passage of legislation giving special powers to the police to deal with terrorist violence, and it rejected the notion of negotiating with the terrorists over release of a hostage. Finally, it should be noted that in the late 1970s the PCI frequently advocated that labor accept some degree of wage restraint, and PCI leaders spoke out for austerity. On this last point, however, rank-and-file protests compelled PCI leaders to retreat on what many workers consider to be a vital bread-and-butter issue.

In the field of foreign affairs, the PCI clearly asserted its independence of Soviet influence. As early as 1956, Togliatti proclaimed the "Italian road to Socialism" as a separate path to be followed by the PCI and defended the concept of "polycentrism"—of numerous centers of policy initiative in the communist world. In 1968, the PCI emphatically condemned the Soviet invasion of Czechoslovakia. By 1969, the PCI had abandoned its hostility to an Italian role in the European Community; and by 1974, it had dropped its objections to Italy's continued membership in NATO. In 1975, the PCI denounced attempts being made by the Portuguese communists to come to power by force. And finally, the PCI sharply criticized both the Soviet invasion of Afghanistan in 1979 and the military coup in Poland in late 1981. In fact, Berlinguer (leader of the PCI until his death in 1984) publicly stated in late 1981 that Eastern European communism was no longer capable of generating creative contributions to Marxist theory and practice.

The PCI's stance could not really be described as pro-Western, however. It denounced U.S. policy in Latin America, clearly sympathized with revolutionary movements in the Third World, and tended to accept the Soviet view that American medium-range missiles should not be installed on European soil. It seemed willing to accept NATO protection, but it was not at all clear whether it believed that Italy should make a positive contribution to NATO.

The PCI's independent and moderate stance paid off in electoral terms. Practicing Gramsci's "politics of presence," offering sensible pragmatic solutions to concrete problems in every area of Italian life, the PCI won many positions in local, provincial, and regional governments. There were Communist mayors in some of Italy's biggest cities. In national elections, the Communist voting percentages peaked in 1976, but the Communists still commanded 26.6 percent of Italian voters in 1987.

The PCI faced increasingly serious difficulties—the price of its success. Its moderate policies had somewhat dissipated the feelings of distrust that animated many Italians when they considered the prospect of Communist entry into the cabinet, but only at the cost of arousing rank-and-file discontent with its lack of militancy. Its collaboration with the Christian Democrats in 1976–79 laid it open to charges that it had joined the establishment and saddled it with part of the blame for hard times. Its reputation for excellent municipal administration, based partly on its long and successful governance of Bologna, was tarnished by a failure to solve the unsolvable problems of Naples and by a municipal scandal in Turin, reminiscent of the bad old days of Christian Democracy. And if it tried to halt the desertion of marginals and students on its left by making militant noises, it then proceeded to lose moderate votes on its right—as was apparently the case in 1983 and 1987. In short, the period of cheap and easy progress was over.

When the PDS was founded in 1991, at the behest of PCI Secretary Achille Occhetto, it did not escape the difficulties that the old PCI had encountered. Quite the contrary, in fact. Veteran PCI diehards split off to form a separate Communist grouping called Communist Refoundation, which received 5.6 percent of the votes in 1992, as compared to 16.1 percent for the PDS. This secession further weakened the already dwindling forces of Italian Communism.

The Socialists (PSI)

The Italian Socialist party was founded in 1892 and has faced internal schisms ever since. One of the most dramatic of these splits occurred in 1947 when the Social Democrats broke away from the Italian Socialist party. The rump PSI then proceeded to tighten its alliance with the Communists. Not until 1956 did the PSI begin the process of gradually loosening its ties with the Communist party. This process—marked by much internal dissension and acute factional conflict—was completed by 1963 when the Socialists entered a Christian Democratic–led cabinet (they had already given external support to a Christian Democratic–led cabinet from 1962 until 1963).

This "opening to the left," as it was called, had a disillusioning outcome. For the next eleven years, the Socialist party was a captive junior partner in Christian Democratic–dominated left-center cabinets. It proved unable to have much impact on government policy or to spur the Christian Democrats into speeding up progress toward social re-

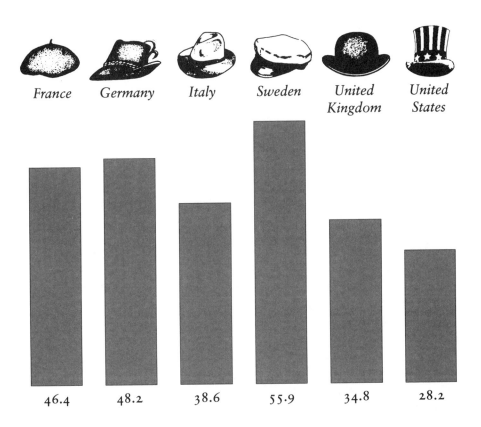

France	Germany	Italy	Sweden	United Kingdom	United States
46.4	48.2	38.6	55.9	34.8	28.2

FIGURE 18.1

SOCIAL WELFARE AS A PERCENTAGE OF
CENTRAL GOVERNMENT EXPENDITURES

SOURCE: World Bank, 1992.

form. Instead, it proved adept in obtaining its share of patronage. Just as the PSI's reputation had been seriously damaged by its earlier dependence on the Communist party, similarly its post-1963 alliance with the ruling Christian Democrats had overtones of dependency and opportunism. The result was electoral decline, a decline that an abortive reunification with the Social Democrats between 1966 and 1969 did nothing to arrest. By 1972, the PSI was down to 9.6 percent of the vote, its lowest percentage in a quarter century.

In the 1970s, the PSI abandoned the left-center formula and sought to establish a separate identity. Its efforts had a forced, reactive quality to them. Sometimes it seemed to be trying to outflank the Communist party on its left. When the Communists advocated the historic compromise, the PSI demanded a left alternative, excluding the Christian Democrats. When the Communists rejected negotiations with leftist terrorists who kidnapped (and who would eventually murder) former Christian Democratic Prime Minister Aldo Moro, the Socialists, in a transparent pitch for extreme leftist votes, urged that some symbolic concessions be made to the kidnappers. And when Communist leaders preached austerity, the Socialists defended free collective bargaining. It almost seemed as if the Socialist leaders of the 1970s were more interested in distinguishing the party from its giant neighbors on the political spectrum than in developing a coherent policy line of its own.

Despite all this, there has been an unexpected upswing in Socialist fortunes since 1976, the year that Bettino Craxi took over the party leadership. Under Craxi, the PSI began to adopt the posture of unpredictable pragmatism to which we have referred. By 1979, Craxi indicated that the left alternative would have to be postponed, presumably until the PSI had become stronger and until the Communist party had further established its democratic credentials. In 1980, the PSI once again embraced the left-center formula and signed an agreement with the Social Democrats providing for future collaboration. Meanwhile, the PSI was still collaborating with the Communists in a number of regional juntas. With this bewildering series of tactical shifts, Craxi was attempting to establish the PSI as the fulcrum of future coalition cabinets. His ultimate goal was to obtain the position of prime minister for himself, thus breaking the Christian Democratic monopoly of that office.

In 1981, under the pressure of defeats in local elections, the Christian Democrats agreed to surrender the office of prime minister—but not to Craxi. In a time-purchasing compromise between the Christian Democrats and the PSI, the job of forming a cabinet was entrusted to the Republican leader Giovanni Spadolini. Two years later, after the disastrous Christian Democratic setback in the parliamentary elections, Craxi could no longer be denied. His party had made some electoral progress, increasing its percentage of the total vote from 9.8 percent in 1979 to 11.4 percent in 1983. It was stronger than any of the minor center parties, it occupied the pivotal position in the political spectrum, and the weakened Christian Democrats lacked the bargaining power to raise serious objections.

As party leader, Craxi has established his definite supremacy in the PSI, replacing many party officials belonging to leftist factions with his own reformist followers. As prime minister, he adhered to the cautious and pragmatic line pursued by his Socialist counterparts elsewhere in southern Europe: Gonzalez in Spain, Soares in Portugal, Mitterrand in France after 1982. He worked hard to reduce government spending and budget deficits, and while his ultimate goal was to reduce unemployment, he gave top priority to cutting inflation.[7] In foreign affairs, he supported the installation of the U.S. cruise and Pershing missiles in Italy, while pushing for greater U.S. moderation in arms control negotiations and in the Caribbean.

The future of the PSI is uncertain at this point. Presumably, Craxi hoped that the prestige of the prime minister's office and his own record of innovative moderation would help the PSI close the big gap that divides its voting percentages from those of the Communists. He hoped, in other words, to duplicate the great leap forward achieved by the French Socialists. But the office of the prime minister in Italy lacks the prestige and clout of the elective French presidency, and Italian proportional representation dilutes the effects of electoral gains. Also, the Italian Communist leadership is much more flexible and imaginative than the French in appealing to all areas of the political spectrum. Finally, the Socialists, too, have been tarred by scandal, more than the Communists. Yet, as we have seen, the PSI made substantial gains in the parliamentary elections of 1987. Craxi's four years as prime minister apparently yielded a goodly electoral harvest. Given the PSI's steady progress since 1979, the slight repulse it encountered in the 1992 elections (it dipped from 14.3 percent to 13.6 percent of the votes cast) was somewhat discouraging.

It is probably because of the slow electoral progress of the PSI that Craxi has become a leading proponent of the adoption of a quasi-presidential system on the French model. Such a system, with a strong elected president, might enable Craxi to duplicate Mitterrand's achievement: to attain the presidency through his own personal charisma and then use his coattails to bring in a Socialist majority or near-majority in Parliament. Since ex-President Cossiga also favors a strong presidency, as do the neo-Fascists of the MSI, Craxi seems to have acquired some strange allies in his struggle for the so-called Second Republic.

The Christian Democrats (DC)

The Italian Christian Democratic party (DC) was founded in September 1943. It is a direct descendant of another Catholic party, the Popular party of Don Sturzo, which was founded in 1919 and dissolved under Fascist pressure in 1926. During the Fascist regime, Catholic Action was allowed to survive under the terms of the Concordat of 1929. Its leaders and cadres were prominent among the early founders of the DC, but the DC also attracted the allegiance of many middle-class Italians with secular leanings, who regarded it as the most reliable bulwark against a possible Communist victory. The Liberal party, which had governed Italy before 1922 and which most middle-class Italians would normally have supported, had been discredited by its collaboration with the Fascists in the years before and shortly following the march on Rome. With both the traditional Catholic vote and the support of middle-class people and peasant proprietors of conservative leanings, the DC emerged as Italy's largest party.

Since 1946, the DC has been the leading party in Italy. From 1946 to 1981, every Italian prime minister was a Christian Democrat. So, unlike the Communists and the Socialists, the Christian Democrats formed the major part of every cabinet. The party has had to resolve two chief questions: what alliances it should form and what the political coloration of a cabinet should be (monocolor, left-center, center, or right-center). As said in an earlier chapter, the main trend of coalition formation has moved from center to left-center, with frequent monocolor interludes. But the question of coalition formation, a perpetual bone of contention, has helped keep the DC divided into warring factions.

The characteristics of the DC as a party include, first and foremost, its heterogeneous catchall nature. It ranges across a large part of the Italian political spectrum, from moderate left to moderate right, and includes in its ranks supporters of virtually every type of alliance or cabinet combination. Among those who vote for the DC are industrialists, Catholic workers, small farmers, housewives, pensioners, and shopkeepers—a mixed bag indeed.

Not only is the DC faction-ridden but the factions are bewilderingly volatile. A given faction may, within the space of one or two years, completely reverse its position on an issue involving party policies or party alliances. Frequently, a faction that professes to be left, right, or center will turn out to be little more than the personal following of one or more prominent DC leaders. And personal rivalries among the leaders may outweigh policy considerations. Finally, an issue may cut across factional lines, splitting virtually every faction in two. This was the case with the question whether the DC should seek an eventual understanding with the Communists or should stress its relationship with the Socialists, to the exclusion of the Communists.

The DC is also internally divided on policy matters, more so than other Italian parties. It contains strong supporters of private enterprise and champions of the state sector (which helps finance the party), representatives of management and spokesmen for organized labor, die-hard opponents of divorce, and advocates of a more liberal set of moral codes for Italian society. The party is essentially all things to all men. As Aldo Moro once put it, in a revealing slip of the tongue, "The DC emphasizes everything."[8] Perhaps the one common denominator that may be discerned throughout the DC is a distributive approach to public policy. The party has built its strength, especially in the formerly Liberal south, by judiciously allocating contracts, jobs, and public money. Patronage, however, has become more than a means to an end; it has become an end in itself.

The ambiguity and ambivalence of the DC have taken their toll in elections. Even before the electoral debacles of 1983 and 1992, the DC had been unable, all through the 1960s and 1970s, to regain the 40 percent level it had once attained. In addition to voter reaction against its lack of a clear sense of purpose and against its image of patronage and corruption, the DC has suffered the inevitable erosion that affects any dominant party after an extended period in power. The previous party secretary, Ciriaco De Mita, attempted to commit the party to a program of economic austerity, to an abandonment of excessive reliance on the spoils system, to an emphasis on productivity gains rather than purely distributive policies. This new rigor may actually have contributed to the DC's losses over the short run. Its long-range effects may be more positive, assuming, of course, that De Mita's successors continue in his footsteps and succeed in regenerating the DC.

The Minor Center Parties—Social Democrats (PSDI), Republicans (PRI), and Liberals (PLI)

The minor center parties include (1) the Social Democrats, whose commitment to social democracy appears to focus on public works, social welfare measures, and a preoccupation with the interests of pensioners; (2) the Republicans, a moderately left-of-center party committed to fiscal austerity and honesty in government, which has been helped by the fact that its leader, Giovanni Spadolini, was the first non-Christian Democratic prime minister since 1945; and (3) the Liberals, a party of the moderate right, competing with the Christian Democrats for the votes of businessmen and large landowners. The one common strand connecting these three parties has been their commitment to democracy and to a secular society. They have tended to side with the DC on many issues but not on matters having to do with church-state relations.

In the years since 1946, the minor center parties have registered very modest electoral performances, with their combined share of the total vote fluctuating between 7.8 percent in 1976 (their postwar low point) and a high-water mark of 14.5 percent in 1963. Viewed from this perspective, their performance in 1983—12.1 percent of the vote— looks less dramatic. It would appear to be a modest comeback from their decline in the 1970s and was followed in 1987 and 1992 by less auspicious showings: 8.8 and 9.9 percent, respectively. Some observers have suggested that occasional good centrist showings have been largely achieved at the expense of the Christian Democrats, who gain votes from the centrists when the Communist threat appears to be acute (1972 and 1976) and lose votes to the centrists as soon as the extremist tide recedes (1963, 1983, and 1987). Be that as it may, centrist gains have sometimes been moderately significant; but it is still far too early to speak of a new third force in Italian politics unless one includes the PSI in that third force. Much will depend on the degree to which the minor center parties and the Socialists can collaborate effectively in the future.

Other Parties

The only other parties worth dwelling on in the Italian political spectrum are Proletarian Democracy, the Radical party, the Green party, the Italian Social Movement (the neo-Fascists of the MSI), and the recently formed Lombard League. Proletarian Democracy, the Radical party, and the Greens are parties of the extreme left. They belong to two different leftist traditions: intransigent Marxism in the case of the Demo-Proletarians, postmaterialist libertarian socialism and populist democracy in the case of the Radicals and the Greens. The Demo-Proletarians, the Radicals, and the Greens have criticized the Communist party for being too close to the establishment and have nibbled away at the PCI's left flank. In 1979, the extreme left gained heavily at the expense of the

Communists, reaching a total of almost 6 percent of the votes. In 1983, the Radicals and Demo-Proletarians polled less than 4 percent. In 1987, however, these two parties, plus the newly formed Greens, once again scored impressive gains, scoring a combined total of 6.8 percent. The existence of these forces, and their potential attractiveness for alienated students and other fringe voters, compels the Communist leaders not to carry their moderating tendencies to immoderate extremes.

As for the neo-Fascists of the MSI, they are little more than a minor irritant on the right flank of Christian Democracy. Their gains in the 1983 elections were substantial—they polled 6.8 percent of the votes as compared to 5.3 percent in 1979—but did not reach the 8.7 percent peak attained in 1972. And, as we saw, they dropped to 5.9 percent in 1987 and 5.4 percent in 1992. Their positions on public issues seem conventionally ultraconservative. They oppose national economic planning and restrictions on free enterprise, they favored repeal of the divorce law in the 1974 referendum campaign, and they advocate heavy defense spending. Nevertheless, their commitment to a corporate state based on functional representation, and the undercurrent of violence that seems to lurk behind their speeches and their party rituals places them under suspicion. They are generally treated as untouchables by the other Italian parties, and their external backing for a coalition cabinet is considered tainted and unacceptable.

A relative newcomer on the Italian political scene is the Lombard League, which polled 19 percent of the votes in Lombardy (equivalent to 4.8 percent of the votes in Italy) in local and regional elections in 1990. Far outnumbering similar regional leagues in other regions of Northern Italy, the Lombard League stands for a much greater measure of regional autonomy, restrictions on immigration from foreign countries, and an end to the colonization of the bureaucratic field services in Northern Italy on the part of southern Italians. It also demands that the northern regions should have much greater control over their own revenue base, instead of being taxed heavily by the central government to finance allegedly unproductive public investments in the South. In the elections of 1992, the Lombard League formed an electoral bloc —the League of the North, in which it was the preponderant element— with several other regional leagues. Its showing in the elections was little sort of spectacular. With 8.7 percent of the votes in Italy, the League of the North received over 30 percent of the votes in Lombardy, replacing the DC as the leading party in a number of provinces. And it won no less that 55 seats in the Chamber of Deputies. In short it has become the fourth largest party in Italian electoral politics.

The Electoral System and Voting Behavior

In electing members of the lower house of Parliament, the Chamber of Deputies, Italy employs a list system of proportional representation.[9] The country is divided into thirty-two electoral circumscriptions. One (the Val d'Aosta) is a single-member district because of its very small population; the rest are multimember districts and consist—in almost all cases—of two to five provinces. In every circumscription except the Val d'Aosta, each party has a list of candidates on the ballot. The voter is voting not for a single candidate but for one of several competing party lists. Each party list is the product of a long process of interfactional consultation and bargaining at the provincial, regional, and national levels.

The number of seats from an electoral circumscription awarded to a party is arrived at by dividing that party's total vote in the circumscription by an electoral quotient. The electoral quotient is equal to the total number of valid votes cast in the circumscription divided by two plus the number of seats to be assigned in it. To cite a hypothetical example, if 850,000 valid votes were cast in the three-province circumscription Cuneo-Asti-Alessandria, and sixteen seats were at stake in that circumscription, the electoral quotient would be 850,000 divided by 18 (16+2) or 47,222. If the total of votes cast for the Christian Democrats in the circumscription was 300,000, the seats to be allotted to the Christian Democrats would be determined by dividing the electoral quotient of 47,222 into the Christian Democratic vote of 300,000. The result would be six seats plus an unutilized remainder of 16,668. The electoral quotient of 47,222 would also be divided into the total number of votes cast for each of the other parties running lists of candidates in that circumscription. Under this procedure, each party would be left with an unutilized remainder (if a party polled less than 47,222 votes, its entire vote would be treated as a remainder), and one or two seats in the circumscription might remain unassigned.

The remainders and unassigned seats from each circumscription are then sent to Rome to be added up and pooled in a Single National College. A procedure very similar to the one described above is then followed, employing the pooled unutilized remainders to award several dozen unassigned seats to the various competing party lists in that College. As a result of this electoral system, each party obtains a share of parliamentary seats roughly proportional to its share of the total votes. Moreover, under the distribution of remainders by the Single National College, even a party with between 1 and 2 percent of the vote should be able to win a few seats.

In addition to voting for a party list, each voter is permitted to express a preference vote for one name from that list (prior to 1991, when the results of a popular referendum provided for limiting each voter's preference to one name, the voter was permitted to express from three to five preference votes). The preference votes are then used to determine who shall represent the party in the Chamber of Deputies. If a party list is entitled to, say, five seats, the five persons on that list who have polled the most preference votes are elected to the Chamber. If no preference votes have been cast, then the first five names on the list are designated for election to the lower house. This is, of course, a far cry from the Anglo-American system of single-member districts.

In electing senators, each of the twenty regions is divided into single-member districts (one of these regions, the Val d'Aosta, is small enough in population not to require such a procedure). A candidate receiving 65 percent of the votes in his or her district is declared elected; but 65 percent is rarely attained by a senatorial candidate. If no one receives 65 percent of the vote, each party's vote in that district is sent to the regional capital to be pooled with all the other votes received by that party in districts where the 65 percent threshold was not reached. The remaining seats—usually all but one or two seats in the region—are then distributed among the parties on the basis of proportional representation. After it has been determined that a party in a given region shall be entitled to, say, three senators, the three candidates polling the highest percentages of the total vote in their respective single-member districts will be elected. Thus, in a given region, Socialist candidate X with 25,000 votes (50 percent of the votes cast in his or her district) would go to the Senate rather than Socialist candidate Y with 35,000 votes (only 45 percent of the votes cast in his or her district).

The Italian electoral system has some important consequences for the party system. First, as we have seen, it favors the proliferation and survival of splinter parties with as little as 1 to 2 percent of the vote, since even such tiny parties are enabled to win a few seats. Nor is there anything like the German 5 percent rule to block splinter parties from entering Parliament. Second, the Italian electoral system prevents any landslide in parliamentary elections and consequently makes it all but impossible for one party to get a majority in Parliament. Under proportional representation, small shifts in voting behavior only result in equally small shifts in legislative representation. Third, the system of preferential voting encourages factionalism by giving minority factions in a party a chance to appeal to party voters over the heads of party leaders.

Voting patterns in Italy have been based, to a considerable degree, on traditional cleavages of a social, economic, or religious nature. The prime example of a socioeconomic cleavage is, of course, the ever present factor of social class. The Communists have had a plurality of the working-class vote, with substantial minorities being polled by the Socialists and Christian Democrats. Among middle-class voters, the Christian Democrats have had a majority of the votes cast by shopkeepers and artisans, and at least a plurality among business and professional people, with the Liberals and neo-Fascists being their chief competitors. The Communists and Socialists have had substantial success in penetrating one stratum of middle-class voters: white-collar workers and lower-level civil servants. Social class has also served to divide the agricultural electorate, with large landowners supporting Liberals and neo-Fascists, for the most part; medium and small landowners voting overwhelmingly for the Christian Democrats; and sharecroppers and farm laborers backing the Communists and Socialists.

Other lines of cleavage have reduced the impact of social class. One such source of division has been religious practice as opposed to anticlericalism. The Christian Democrats have polled a substantial share of the working-class vote, especially in devoutly Catholic areas in the northeast. Communist and Socialist successes among a substantial minority of middle-class voters in north-central Italy may be explained partly in terms of the anticlericalism of regions like Emilia-Romagna. Region has been another line of demarcation. Regional voting traditions have cut across class lines in influencing voting behavior. As we saw, however, such regional traditions may have simply been expressing or reinforcing religious cleavages. Finally, union membership may have been a more reliable factor than mere social class in predisposing voters to cast their ballots for leftist parties.

The traditional patterns of the 1950s and 1960s are undergoing some major changes. For one thing the rural exodus has uprooted great numbers of small landowners, sharecroppers, and farm laborers from their traditional political and social networks and often from their home regions. Second, the rise of the service sector has injected a new element of ambiguity into the Italian class structure. Third, families and social networks such as the church and its lay organizations seem to be losing their ability to socialize young voters into traditional patterns of voting behavior. As a result, more and more voters are making their choices less on the basis of traditional party identification (vote of *appartenenza* or belonging) and more on the basis of the parties' positions on the issues (vote of opinion). At the same time, the number and variety of voters who cast ballots on the basis of satisfaction or frustration of their personal needs by the incumbents (vote of exchange) is growing as the Christian Democrats lose their monopoly over sources of patronage. While the urban middle classes are most likely to cast a "vote of opinion," the "vote of exchange" characterizes the precariously employed service workers of the urban subproletariat.[10]

Pressure Groups

The Italian interest-group system has both traditional and modern features. An example of the kind of interest group that one finds quite frequently in developing countries is the anomic group in the form of more or less spontaneous violent demonstrations. The 1970–71 riots in Reggio Calabria, to protest the designation of Catanzaro to be the capital of the region of Calabria, are a case in point. Also, nonassociational groups—groups that articulate their demands on an ad hoc basis without setting up a formal public organization—are quite common in Italy. Examples would be the various informal patron-client networks. At the same time, like other West European countries, Italy has a system of well-organized associational interest groups—labor confederations, farm organizations, employees' associations, and so on—that operate continuously with the aid of professional staffs.

The Italian interest-group system since World War II has borne some similarity to the French system, while differing in some significant ways. Like France, Italy has had an ideologically divided labor movement: there is a Communist-dominated labor confederation (the CGIL), which contains some Socialist members; a labor confederation (the UIL) in which Socialists and Republicans are the prevalent element; and a Catholic-dominated labor confederation (the CISL). In both countries, too, anomic group behavior (riots and demonstrations) has been somewhat more acceptable in the eyes of public opinion than it has been in northern Europe. (To be sure, anomic group behavior is beginning to flourish also in Britain and Germany.)

There have also been some notable contrasts. Since the Italian Parliament has so much more influence on policy making than does the Parliament of the Fifth Republic, Italian interest groups have expended much more effort in the legislative arena. They have found the powerful standing committees, with their ability to enact minor bills directly into law, a most rewarding site for their endeavors. Many interest groups have gone beyond mere lobbying and have tried to get their officials elected to Parliament on some party's list. These are the so-called *parentela* groups, which have very close official ties with a political party and may openly act as organized factions within that party in Parliament. They can be contrasted to the *clientela* groups, which are regarded by government agencies as sole official representatives of a given set of interests. An example of a *clientela* group would be the Italian General Confederation of Industry (Confindustria); an example of a *parentela* groups would be Catholic Action in the Christian Democratic party. As we shall see, some *parentela* groups have begun to loosen their linkages with political parties.

Agricultural Interest Groups

Because Italian family farms have tended to be much smaller on the average than French or German family farms, the Italian farm organization that speaks for medium and large landowners—the Italian General Confederation of Agriculture (Confagricoltura)—has represented only a minority of Italian agricultural proprietors. A much more powerful farm organization has been the National Confederation of Direct Cultivators (Coldiretti), whose members mostly live on smaller farms. Coldiretti has been a *parentela* group directly affiliated with the Christian Democrats, while a much smaller rival organization, the National Peasants' Alliance (ANC), is sponsored by the Communist party. By virtue of its control over the Federation of Agricultural Consortiums (Federconsorzi), a quasi-public organization that furnishes credits, subsidies, storage facilities, and other services to farmers, Coldiretti has been one of Italy's most powerful pressure groups.

In addition to organizations speaking for landowners and peasant proprietors, there are three separate federations of farm laborers, associated with the three major labor confederations. Similarly, there are several competing associations of agricultural cooperatives. Most of these farm organizations are under either Communist or Christian Democratic leadership.

What appears to have taken place in the past twenty years has been a remarkable debilitation of Italian agricultural pressure groups. This trend is comprehensible, given the steady movement of agricultural emigrants to cities and towns. With the farm population rapidly diminishing, groups like Coldiretti have suffered a severe loss of clout. Farm organizations are still powerful, but the curve plotting their influence definitely slopes downward. Among other manifestations of relative weakness has been the inability of southern citrus growers to get the kind of protection from the European Community that is liberally accorded north European (and north Italian) producers of grain, beef, and dairy products.

Labor Interest Groups

Italian organized labor has been weakened in the past by its division into the Italian General Confederation of Labor (CGIL, Communist-dominated), the Italian Confederation of Workers' Unions (the Catholic CISL), and the Italian Union of Labor (UIL, Socialists and Republicans). Also, Italian unions have been chronically weak in membership recruitment, dues collections, and economic resources to support possible strikes. Lack of leadership at the plant level has been another disability. Heavy unemployment in the post-World War II era weakened the bargaining power of Italian unions and resulted in persistently low wages for Italian workers. It also resulted, it must be admitted, in lower prices and other competitive advantages for Italian exports, thus encouraging the expansion of the Italian economy.

Since 1968, new tendencies have developed within the Italian labor movement. First, the three labor confederations have manifested increasing independence from their respective parties. Second, the three labor confederations have shown a marked tendency to cooperate on many issues, though in the past few years cooperation has diminished considerably. Third, the unions no longer allow their officials to hold a parliamentary seat and a trade union office simultaneously. Fourth, labor became temporarily much more powerful in the 1970s and the CGIL, CISL, and UIL confederations were much more militant in pushing their demands. In fact, at times, particularly in 1976–79 when the Communist party was supporting austerity, the Catholic unions made more far-reaching demands than the Communist unions. Labor's increased intransigence reflected pressure from newly employed southern migrants and semiskilled workers, who demanded more rapid progress to make up for past privations.

Developments in the trade union field have by no means been marked by linear progression, however. After greater expansion, intransigence, and decentralization of authority to the plant level in 1968–72, there has been a movement toward decline of trade union membership, recentralization of union authority at the national level, and a more cooperative relationship with employers and with the state during the 1980s. Selling Italian products in increasingly competitive export markets, the impact of free collective bargaining in improving the lot of skilled workers while raising economic hurdles against the employment of marginal workers, and the rising burden of inflation have greatly weakened unions and have induced union leaders to moderate their demands. The January 1983 agreement by the noncommunist unions to accept a slight downward modification of the system of wage indexation (the so-called *scala mobile,* or escalator, that ties wages to the price index) was a straw in the wind. The failure of a Communist attempt to challenge the government's settlement with the noncommunist unions by appealing to the voters in a referendum was a clear indication of labor's diminished influence.

Business Interest Groups

In the first few decades after World War II, Italian business had several leading characteristics. There was a higher degree of concentration and less distrust of big business than in France. Also, small business lacked the autonomy and self-assertiveness of the big firms of the Genoa-Milan-Turin industrial triangle. Confindustria, representing the great majority of industrial firms, tended to speak for big-business interests.

Confindustria had a classic lobbying relationship with the Christian Democratic party. Its efforts to transform this *clientela* relationship into a *parentela* bond, however, were not successful. It was also unsuccessful in preserving a united front among Italian employers. Some industrial giants (e.g., Fiat) preferred to pursue their own policies independently of Confindustria guidance. Far more important was the position taken by the public corporations, which had their own employers' association, Intersind. While Confindustria tended to be allied with the Liberals and with the right wing of the Christian Democracy, Intersind seemed more inclined toward a kind of Italian New Deal, based on welfare capitalism and social reforms. In this, it had much in common with the Socialists and with the left-wing Christian Democrats.

Recent developments have changed the above picture. First of all, the public-sector enterprises have been pretty thoroughly discredited by their partisan connections and by the gross inefficiency that increasingly reigned in their factories. By the 1970s they had lost the aura of infallibility they had acquired in the 1960s. Second, Confindustria staged something of a comeback in Italian public opinion in the 1970s, profiting from the backlash against the Hot Autumn of 1968–1969. Finally, small businessmen are playing a much more decisive role in Confindustria. This reflects the economic slump that has hit the traditional heavy industry of the northwest triangle, while medium and small enterprises have brought great prosperity to the central Italian regions of Emilia-Romagna, Tuscany, Umbria, and Latium.

Catholic Interest Groups: The Church and Its Lay Organizations

The Catholic church and various associations of Catholic laymen have played a very active part in Italy's interest-group system. As we saw, the Concordat of 1929 had constitutional status and could be altered only by bilateral agreement between church and state or by a formal constitutional amendment; and religion was part of the public educational curriculum. Heavily influential throughout Italian public life, the church intervened openly in Italian domestic politics in the first two decades after World War II. But its intervention tended to diminish in intensity in the 1960s and 1970s under Popes John XXIII and Paul VI. It should also be borne in mind that there have always been factional disputes within the church regarding the scope and purpose of political intervention.

The principal church-sponsored lay organization is Catholic Action, which at its peak had 3 million members and contains a number of separate groups or branches, such as the Union of Men, the Union of Women, Italian Catholic Action Youth (GIAC), and the Federation of Italian Catholic University Students (FUCI). The president of Catholic Action and the presidents of its component branches are appointed by individual bishops at the diocesan level. In addition to organizations like Catholic Action, which are directly controlled by the hierarchy, there are Catholic associations set up to pursue specialized nonreligious goals and not under the tutelage of the hierarchy. These include Coldiretti, the Italian Association of Catholic Schoolteachers (AIMC), and the Christian Association of Italian Workers (ACLI). These organizations have acted as economic and social pressure groups and have not behaved primarily as spokespersons for the church.

Since the late 1960s, the influence of the church and its lay organizations has greatly diminished. The failure of a referendum campaign to repeal the divorce law (1974), the more recent failure of a referendum campaign to repeal an abortion law (1981), and the revision of the Concordat are all indicative of waning clerical influence. It should be noted that some Catholic lay organizations (e.g., the Confederation of Catholic University Students) actually came out in favor of the divorce law. It should also be noted that such associations as ACLI have been steering a more autonomous course: ACLI has cut its formal ties with both Catholic Action and the Christian Democratic party, though it still maintains a dialogue with the church.

Perhaps one reason for the increasingly independent stance adopted by Catholic organizations is their greatly reduced strength, which is itself a symptom of the growing secularization of Italian society. Catholic Action, which had 3 million members in the 1950s, was down to 600,000 by the late 1970s. ACLI, which had a million members in the 1950s, had only 400,000 in the late 1970s.[11] Clearly, Catholic organizations are no longer the dominant, hegemonic force they were in the immediate postwar decades.

Notes

1. See Raphael Zariski, "Italy," in *Western European Party Systems: Trends and Prospects,* ed. Peter R. Merkl (New York: Free Press, 1980), 122–52.

2. Ibid., 130; and "The New Parliament," *News from Italy* (published by the Fondazione Giovanni Agnelli), no. 10 (July 1983): 11. See also Robert H. Evans, "The Italian Election of June 1987," *Italian Journal* 1, nos. 2 and 3 (1987): 15.

3. See Zariski, "Italy," 131; and "New Parliament," 11. See also "A Comprehensive Report on the 1987 Political Elections: Nine Tables of Statistical Data," *Italian Journal* 1, nos. 2 and 3 (1987): 24.

4. See Giorgio Galli, *Il bipartitismo imperfetto* (Bologna: Il Mulino, 1966).

5. See Evans, "Italian Election," 12.

6. See Donald L.M. Blackmer, "Continuity and Change in Postwar Italian Communism," in *Communism in Italy and France,* ed. Donald L.M. Blackmer and Sidney Tarrow (Princeton, N.J.: Princeton University Press, 1975): 21–68.

7. See Joseph La Palombara, "Letter from Italy," *Italy* 1 (September 1983): 6–7.

8. See "Centro sinistra e politica locale," *Il Mulino* 12, no. 3 (March 1963): 240.

9. For a fuller discussion of the Italian electoral system, see Raphael Zariski, *Italy: The Politics of Uneven Development* (Hinsdale, Ill.: Dryden Press, 1972).

10. See Arturo Parisi and Gianfranco Pasquino, "Changes in Italian Electoral Behaviour: The Relationship between Parties and Voters," in *Italy in Transition: Conflict and Consensus,* ed. Peter Lange and Sidney Tarrow (London: Frank Cass, 1980), 6–30.

11. See Gianfranco Pasquino, "Italian Christian Democracy: A Party for All Seasons?" in *Italy in Transition: Conflict and Consensus,* ed. Peter Lange and Sidney Tarrow, 92–93.

19

How Is Power Used?

We have observed the sharp divisions of power that exist within the Italian decision-making system: the coalition cabinets that are split, not only by competing parties, but by competing intraparty factions as well; the Parliament that is not really under the unifying tutelage of any cohesive leadership structure or ruling committee; the public corporations that enjoy a high degree of de facto autonomy. These cleavages within the decision-making apparatus make it difficult to ascertain who, if anyone, is in charge. Reflecting these internal divisions, the policy-making process is itself fragmented and incoherent. Although we have become increasingly aware of the inefficiency and lack of central direction that exist in any policy-making system—including the much touted British and American models—Italy seems, on the surface, to constitute a particularly acute case of poor coordination and lack of harmony.

Policy Formulation

The process of policy formulation begins with the initiation of proposals. In any democratic country, proposals are brought to the attention of policy makers by parties, pressure groups, higher civil servants in the bureaucracy, and individual legislators. In Italy, the individual member of Parliament is given a comparatively large voice in the process of policy initiation. Italy, in fact, is one of the few Western democracies that places no restrictions on the introduction of private-member bills in Parliament. Nevertheless, even though a majority of the bills *introduced* in Parliament are private-member bills, only a minority of bills *passed* by Parliament have been initiated by individual deputies and senators without some sort of executive sponsorship. So, once the phase of proposal initiation is completed, the executive still emerges as wielding more weight than the legislature in the process of policy formulation.

While most bills originate in the ministries, there is strong reason to suspect that parties and pressure groups play a much more important part in initiating legislation than does the bureaucracy per se. It is a well-known fact that Italy lacks a strong bureaucratic tradition, that Italian civil servants tend to be conservative and legalistic in their attitudes and to show little interest in policy innovations. Unlike French higher civil servants, they are unlikely to search for new and controversial solutions to socioeconomic problems.

The political parties affect the initiation of policy proposals in a number of ways. While they do not bother with the great number of *leggine* ("little laws," that is, private or minor bills) initiated by government agencies and individual members of Parliament, they do stimulate the introduction of broader bills of general application. And they have other ways of exercising influence. In a broad sense, they have on occasion replaced the cabinet as the source of general policy decisions. Between 1976 and 1979, when the Communist party was part of the ruling coalition without actually holding ministerial positions, the cabinet was committed to applying a program agreed upon by the parties that supported the ruling coalition. Since these parties included some (like the Communist party) that were not represented in the cabinet, a particular procedure was followed. The government program was drawn up outside Parliament by leaders of the parties committed to supporting the cabinet. It was then adopted by the cabinet. In effect, the cabinet was simply ratifying decisions adopted by an extraparliamentary conference of party leaders.[1]

Parties also have a major impact on detailed and specific policy initiatives, even if they do not *as parties* introduce vast numbers of proposed *leggine* in Parliament. There has developed, especially since the opening to the left in the early 1960s, a tendency to allocate policy-making positions on various executive and administrative agencies to the various political parties supporting the cabinet. Before the 1960s, it was almost invariably the Christian Democrats who received patronage in the form of such decisional posts. Since the opening to the left, the Socialists and the other allies of Christian Democracy have been increasingly successful in obtaining a significant share of strategic jobs. The distributive spending decisions made by such government agencies are in effect made by the political parties that participate in managing the agencies. What has changed since the 1960s is that a Christian

Democratic-dominated spoils system has been broadened to include other parties, with pieces of the action distributed on a quota basis.[2]

In addition to political parties, Italian pressure groups are responsible for initiating many proposals that ministries adopt as their own. One reason for the accentuated role of pressure groups is that the Italian bureaucracy is neither willing nor able to generate many proposals on its own. This is partly due to the inadequacy of the research facilities available to the bureaucracy and to Parliament. Both the bureaucracy and Parliament are unusually dependent on pressure groups for information and expertise.

Once a proposal has been initiated, the ministry involved engages in a long process of consultation with affected interests. Each ministry has an advisory council representing the various *clientela* groups with which that ministry deals. Moreover, an intricate system of cabinet committees is supposed to keep ministers informed about what their colleagues are doing or planning to do. But there are gaps in this consultation process, and very often interested groups and agencies are not kept informed.

The complaint is often voiced that there is no adequate coordination of the various policy proposals initiated by government agencies. The great number of cabinet committees makes for a functional decentralization of policy. Each cabinet committee has its own restricted sphere of public policy, in which it all too often acts as final arbiter; the cabinet, supposedly the supreme organ of policy coordination, is too large and too internally divided to perform this function. As a result, many bills come before the cabinet without adequate notice and catch ministers by surprise; meetings are called suddenly with much the same effect; minutes are sketchy and incomplete; and there is no regular exchange of information among cabinet members. In short, the cabinet does not maintain adequate control over policy formulation.[3]

In the absence of effective cabinet surveillance, there are few real limitations on the activities of Italy's various executive agencies and public corporations. Many of their decisions involve the awarding of grants or contracts or loans, and require no action by the legislature. The Office of the Prime Minister exercises some oversight over policy formulation but is in no position routinely to block initiatives of which it disapproves. Some checks on excessive spending can be imposed by the Ministry of the Treasury and the governor of the Bank of Italy by regulating the cash reserves required of Italian banks, thus encouraging or curtailing borrowing or lending.

But the Bank of Italy, for all the technocratic expertise of its governor, is not as independent as many observers assume. The Administrative Council of the Bank, which chooses the new governor, is made up of the present governor and fifteen members, of whom twelve are nominated by an assembly of banks and credit agencies that hold Bank of Italy stock. The governor is responsible, then, to Italian banking interests, but these interests in turn are partly under the influence of Christian Democratic-controlled public corporations like the Institute of Industrial Reconstruction (IRI).[4] The policies pursued by the Bank of Italy in the 1940s and 1950s had the effect of favoring business and simultaneously strengthening the position of Christian Democracy. With the opening to the left in the 1960s, the Bank of Italy loosened controls to a degree that encouraged large-scale wage increases—a policy designed to retain Socialist support for the new left-center cabinet formula. This was in accordance with the views of Christian Democratic factions committed to the opening to the left—factions powerfully entrenched in the public corporations that exercise a significant influence on the Italian banking sector and consequently on the Bank of Italy.

Apart from the credit and monetary restraints imposed by the Ministry of the Treasury and the Bank of Italy, there is no effective check within the executive branch on the process of policy formulation. The cabinet does not serve as a reliable gatekeeper preventing the introduction of bills that do not enjoy the support of the executive branch, because the executive branch does not speak with one voice. In its divisiveness and lack of coherence, it bears more resemblance to the U.S. executive branch than to the executive branch of a model parliamentary system. Some executive and administrative agencies have more clout than others (just as a feudal system has greater and lesser feudal lords), but no single committee or institution is clearly in charge.[5]

As we have seen, numerous policy proposals—such as those involving investments, grants, and loans undertaken by the public corporations and other government agencies—do not need approval by Parliament. It is sufficient for them to secure the approval of the relevant supervisory ministry (often the Ministry of State Holdings) or of the entire cabinet—approval that is usually forthcoming. Policy proposals that do go the parliamentary route in the form of bills are assigned to a standing committee by the president of the Chamber of Deputies or the president of the Senate. He or she will instruct the committee to report the bill back to the floor *in sede referente* with its recommendations, or to enact the bill into law *in sede deliberante*. Whichever path is chosen, the committee stage is the crucial stage in the life of a bill. Many controversial bills never emerge from committee. In fact, the standing committees, by preventing bills from reaching the floor for a vote, spare the executive branch much embarrassment by sidetracking measures the executive organs do not support wholeheartedly but are afraid not to sponsor.

If the *in sede referente* procedure is followed and if the bill is reported to the floor, the Conference of Presidents (heads of parliamentary party groups) decides the bill's place on the legislative calendar.

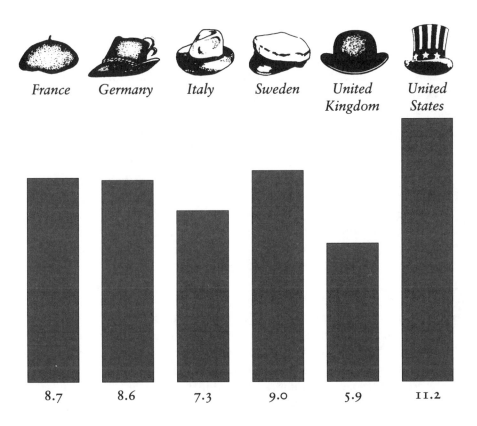

France	Germany	Italy	Sweden	United Kingdom	United States
8.7	8.6	7.3	9.0	5.9	11.2

FIGURE 19.1
HEALTH EXPENDITURES AS A PERCENTAGE OF
GROSS DOMESTIC PRODUCT

SOURCE: *Statistical Abstract of the United States, 1991.*

The bill is then discussed in the chamber, first on a general motion for approval and then article by article. In this second and more detailed discussion, amendments may be introduced and voted on. The final version of the bill after the amendment stage is then voted on by the entire house. If it passes, it goes on to the other chamber, where the same lengthy and cumbersome procedure is followed. It must pass both chambers in the same form to become law, and this means it may have to shuttle between the chambers for discrepancies to be ironed out.

Most laws are adopted in committee through the *in sede delibe-rante* procedure. This procedure is used mostly for *leggine*—incremental bills of minor importance that affect relatively small segments of society. Such bills are often introduced by the government as an alternative to an executive decree, which might be blocked by the Court of Accounts, or they originate with private members seeking to curry favor with some constituents. It should be remembered that, under the *in sede deli-berante* procedure, 10 percent of the members of Parliament or 20 percent of the members of a standing committee can prevent a bill from being passed by insisting it be brought to the floor for plenary debate. This means that the Communist party always has enough votes to prevent the procedure from being used. Yet it has usually not employed this power to obstruct legislation, even in the 1950s and 1960s when it was still considered an antisystem party. Evidently some behind-the-scenes compromises with the Christian Democratic regime took place even before the 1970s.

In the case of executive orders (legislative decrees, decree laws, and regulations), numerous consultations are required by law or by administrative practice. If a cabinet measure is involved, not just a minor regulation of interest to only a single ministry, the measure must be considered by a cabinet committee before obtaining the consent of the cabinet as a whole. The cabinet committee stage is crucial in most cases. Also, the Council of State must be consulted in its advisory capacity, and the Court of Accounts may refuse to register the executive order. Finally, the president of Italy has the right (he exercises it only occasionally) to refuse to authorize the issuance of a cabinet decree or the introduction of a government bill in Parliament.

One device for redressing the apparent weakness of the executive branch vis-à-vis Parliament, the parties, and the pressure groups has been a tendency to resort more and more to decree laws as a way of proposing legislation. They have been used as a means of obtaining quick, temporary action and bypassing normal legislative procedures. To be sure, decree laws expire within sixty days unless approved by

Parliament, but meanwhile an accomplished fact has been created. Moreover, if Parliament, during the sixty days, rejects or drastically modifies a decree law, the cabinet does not feel obligated to resign.[6]

Policy Implementation

The responsibility for implementing policies that have emerged from the policy-formulation process lies with the Italian bureaucracy. Italian civil servants tend to be obsessed with the primacy of the law and the need to find a legal justification for every action. This attitude—laudable enough under normal circumstances and when balanced against other considerations—is carried to ridiculous extremes in Italy because of the predominantly legal training and traditionalist orientation of most Italian civil servants.

Policy implementation proceeds with agonizing slowness and indecision. Each step in the implementation of a law or decree must be subjected to a series of controls and procedures: approval by a subsidiary branch of the General Accounting Office, registration by the Court of Accounts, consultation with the Council of State for all contracts above a certain sum, and so on. At any one of numerous way stations a file may be sent back to the point of origin because of some minor irregularity or may even be mislaid. Cases may literally take years to resolve, even when no particularly controversial problem is involved.

Overcentralization also slows down the policy-implementation process. Local authorities and regional authorities are subject to a variety of central controls. National field services of ministries in Rome are compelled to refer a great number of relatively minor decisions to the capital for the signature of the director general of a bureau. In fact, even when the rules do not so specify, minor officials prefer to pass the buck to their superiors in the hierarchy. This centralizing tendency has deep roots in Italian political culture. It should be noted that since the regions were created in 1970, the new regional governments have employed the same techniques of overcentralization in their relations with local authorities.

Other factors impeding effective policy implementation are overstaffing and corruption. The expansion of the bureaucracy since World War II has contributed to the sluggishness of bureaucratic procedures. The introduction of more modern methods would mean a reduction in staff; on the other hand, the imposition of an additional set of checks or controls may serve to justify an individual's salary. As for corruption, it is probably not as prevalent as people assume; but cases of favoritism, often based on family or friendship ties, are constantly discussed in the media, to a greater degree than in other Western democracies. In a civil service recruited from a traditionalist region like the Italian south, family loyalty is bound to have a serious impact on behavior.

One glaring example of the inefficiency of the policy-implementation process is the growing importance of so-called *residui passivi* (residual liabilities) in Italy. These are funds that have been allocated to an agency in a given budgetary period but have remained unspent. Residual liabilities have been increasing in size; this helps explain why so many reform measures represent only paper promises, given the bureaucratic controls that stand in the way of transforming words into deeds.[7]

On the surface, Italian decision making appears cumbersome, rather chaotic, and grossly inefficient. Yet, as some observers have pointed out,[8] behind this disorderly façade of conflict and resulting sclerosis is an underlying process of compromise and collaboration among leaders —national, regional, and local—of the various parties. This process, characterized by hard-headed pragmatism, mutual tolerance, and distributive incrementalism, makes it possible from time to time to overcome the institutional obstacles. Necessary deals are hammered out by the parties, which share a stake in keeping the consensual system going despite its obvious imperfections. Thus, while policy procedures and outputs leave very much to be desired, Italy is unquestionably a going concern and has yet to encounter the system breakdown that so many prophets of doom have predicted.

Notes

1. See Stefano Bartolini, "The Politics of Institutional Reform in Italy," *West European Politics* 5 (July 1982): 207–8.

2. See Carlo Donolo, "Social Change and Transformation of the State in Italy," in *The State in Western Europe,* ed. Richard Scase (London: Croom Helm, 1980), 195–96; and Giuseppe Di Palma, "The Available State: Problems of Reform," in *Italy in Transition: Conflict and Consensus,* ed. Peter Lange and Sidney Tarrow (London: Frank Cass, 1980), 153–57.

3. See Sabino Cassese, "Is There a Government in Italy? Politics and Administration at the Top," in *Presidents and Prime Ministers,* ed. Richard Rose and Ezra N. Suleiman (Washington: American Enterprise Institute, 1980), 175, 201–2.

4. See Alan R. Posner, "Italy: Dependence and Political Fragmentation," in *Between Power and Plenty: Foreign Economic Policies of Ad-*

vanced Industrial States, ed. Peter J. Katzenstein (Madison: University of Wisconsin Press, 1978), 234–35.

5. See Donolo, "Social Change and Transformation of the State in Italy," 172–75.

6. See Bartolini, "The Politics of Institutional Reform in Italy," 208.

7. See Donolo, "Social Change and Transformation of the State in Italy," 182.

8. See Joseph La Palombara, *Democracy Italian Style* (New Haven: Yale University Press, 1987).

20

What Is the Future of Italian Politics?

Our treatment of the Italian political system has focused on its weaknesses and imperfections. We have seen the serious problems facing the Italian economy and Italian society; the disruptive effects of rapid modernization; the survival of widespread political alienation at the level of the mass culture; the lack of unified, coherent political leadership; and the absence of effective coordination over the institutions responsible for policy formulation and policy implementation. It would be tempting, at this point, to add another voice to the chorus that proclaims the Italian polity to be hovering on the brink of the precipice.

Instead, we begin this final appraisal with a brief discussion of the positive features of the Italian political system. After all, the system has survived for four decades and has weathered a number of crises. Only after dealing with the more hopeful aspects of the Italian scenario will we turn to some of the critical problems Italy must overcome.

Elements of Strength in the Italian Political System

Some contemporary observers of Italian politics have pointed to some of the possible reasons why the Italian Republic has endured despite all its travails.[1] We deal first with the political factors. As we have seen, Italy lacks a strong party of the extreme right. The Communist party —representing the extreme left over most of the past four decades —has generally been a moderate and constructive force. There have been no protracted foreign wars or colonial adventures to politicize the Italian armed forces. And, thus far, no ethnic minority has called into question the continued existence of the Italian state. In short, there have been no irreconcilable conflicts to overload the Italian polity.

Other political factors have been identified as contributing to system survival. First, the Christian Democratic party, with all its faults, has managed to bridge the divisions among social classes by virtue of its catchall nature, has strengthened small and medium industry and given invaluable transfusions to backward regions, and has kept the Catholic middle class committed to democratic institutions and democratic methods. Second, the Italian political elites—with all their inefficiency and seemingly unprincipled opportunism—have shown resourcefulness, imagination, and an ability to rise to the occasion in a crisis. They are also far more united and willing to cooperate than they appear. Third, subcultural differences have been narrowing as the secularization of Italian society and the increasing moderation of the Communist party bring the Catholic and Marxist subcultures closer together. The rising generation of party activists seem less ideologically committed than were their fathers. Fourth, the parties of the left—including the Communists—have acquired a stake in the system. They have by no means been excluded from the politics of patronage practiced by the Christian Democratic–dominated regime. Quite the contrary, their share of the action has been increasing.

Certain socioeconomic factors are also contributing to the resilience and underlying strength of Italian democracy. Living standards have risen enormously since the late 1940s when movies like *Bitter Rice* and *Bicycle Thief* dramatized the plight of the Italian masses. Indicators of this trend include the decline in both the birth rate and the death rate, the growing per capita consumption of meat and dairy products, and the increasing acquisition of automobiles and household appliances by the masses.[2] Urbanization, too, has undermined the traditional allegiances that divided Italy into regions committed to different political families. Although the regional differences in voting behavior remain, they no longer seem to reflect fundamental cleavages in values and political orientations. Also, the rise of the service sector is doing much to reduce the intensity of class conflict. And the advent of mass education has fostered national integration, reduced the differences among regional subcultures, and perhaps contributed to the more pragmatic attitudes displayed by Italian voters (e.g., the "vote of *appartenenza*" —based on pure party identification—is to some degree being replaced by the "vote of opinion" and the "vote of exchange"). It is no longer possible to dismiss Italy as the sick man of Western Europe; this would be true even if Ireland, Spain, Portugal, and Greece had not joined the West European club.

The Italian Economy: The Endangered Miracle

One of the chief problems facing Italy is the same one that confronts every modern industrial society: how to maintain an expanding economy with a low rate of unemployment while avoiding excessive inflation and keeping exports competitive in world markets. This problem became acute in the Hot Autumn of 1969, when Italian labor abandoned its postwar behavior pattern of relatively docile industriousness, and in the fall of 1973, when skyrocketing oil prices began to affect the economy. Since that time, the Italian economic miracle has lost much of its magic.[3] Inflation, unemployment (particularly among young people), and a balance of payments deficit are chronic threats. And government spending has grown by leaps and bounds, producing massive deficits. Italy has had occasional spurts of growth since 1973—the economy expanded by 12 percent between 1977 and 1980—but the unbroken linear progression of the 1950s and early 1960s is a thing of the past. In fact, a further increase in oil prices in 1980 led to a trade deficit of $22 billion and an inflation rate of 21 percent. The Bank of Italy had to impose a squeeze on credit that promptly reduced growth and pushed up unemployment.

Heroic measures taken by the Craxi government (1983–87) were successful in lowering the inflation rate to 5 percent; unemployment and interest rates remained high, however, and the budget deficit approached American levels (despite the fact that Italy has a much smaller economy than the United States). By the end of 1987, the Italian annual deficit was 11.5 percent of gross domestic product (GDP), and Italy's public-sector debt was a staggering 93 percent of GDP. By way of contrast, the much touted U.S. deficit was only 3 percent of GDP, and the public-sector debt was only 35 percent of GDP.[4]

Is there an alternative to this stop-go process marked by frequent administration of debilitating financial castor oil by the Bank of Italy? The answers seems to be: Reduce government spending and establish some control over wage increases. In a word, a policy of austerity. This would involve checking the impact of the escalator (*scala mobile*) system of wage indexation, under which wages rise every three months to conform to upward movements in the price index. And it would require either reducing the vast amounts disbursed by the public corporations and various public services (especially in the social welfare area) or increasing taxes and users' fees.

The trouble with austerity is that it is a politically unpalatable solution in any democracy, and it runs counter to several basic characteristics of the Italian political and social system. For example, it directly repudiates the distributive policy that was followed by the Christian Democratic regime as a means of building electoral support and that was later adopted by the Socialists when they entered the cabinet in 1963. It would require hard choices—as opposed to the blurred alternatives of the grand coalition toward which all Italian parties (except for the neo-Fascists) seem to be groping. And it might well restore the class conflict and general alienation that are playing a diminishing role in Italian politics today.

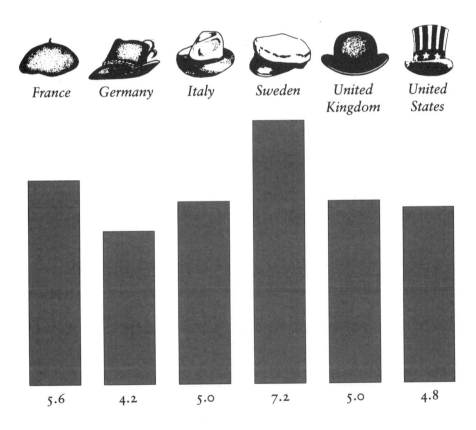

France	Germany	Italy	Sweden	United Kingdom	United States
5.6	4.2	5.0	7.2	5.0	4.8

FIGURE 20.1

EXPENDITURES ON PUBLIC EDUCATION AS A PERCENTAGE OF
GROSS DOMESTIC PRODUCT

SOURCE: OECD, 1991.

Worse, austerity bears an electoral price tag, at least in the short run. In 1976–78 the Communist party supported some measure of wage restraint in exchange for a greater voice for labor in management decisions; and in 1979, many young voters (in the labor force but still looking for their first job) and marginal workers (lacking modern skills required by today's labor market) voted for minor parties of the extreme left (the Radicals and Demo-Proletarians) rather than for the Communist party. By the same token, the Christian Democratic leader Ciriaco de Mita advocated austerity in 1983; that same year, the Christian Democratic party suffered heavily at the polls. Yet the Republican party, which also supported austerity, gained heavily in 1983. And Prime Minister Craxi's policy of retrenchment did not bring about severe electoral repercussions for the PSI. Nevertheless, widespread fear remains that a policy of austerity would result in drastic reprisals at the polls. It remains to be seen whether political elites—in Italy and elsewhere—will be able to cope successfully with the hardships austerity would bring in its wake.

The Question of Institutional Reform

Some Italian politicians have raised the question whether Italy's political institutions should be altered to enable the government to develop a more coherent set of policies based on a firm mandate.

One such proposal, favored by Craxi and the PSI, as well as by a strange rightist coalition ranging from former President Cossiga to the neo-Fascists, would be to emulate the French quasi-presidential system. A popularly elected chief executive might be better able to dominate Parliament and coordinate his own cabinet. An electoral law based on single-member districts with election by absolute majority, or a runoff election if the threshold was not reached, might force the major parties to combine (as in France) and might bring about firm parliamentary majorities like those attained by the Gaullists in the 1960s or by the Socialists in 1981. This set of proposals has aroused a great deal of opposition. For one thing, given Italian political traditions, the system might produce an Italian reincarnation of Mussolini rather than an Italian de Gaulle or an Italian Mitterrand. Moreover, before 1991 and the growing malaise of Italian communism, which was symbolized by the foundation of the PDS to replace the PCI, it was feared that alliances promoted by a French-type runoff system might be dominated by Communists rather than Socialists. (The Italian Communist party enjoyed more widespread support and more general public acceptance than did the French Communist party). There is no assurance, then, that the adoption of certain French constitutional procedures would result in a duplication of the coup achieved in France: the rejuvenation and rise to power of the Socialist party. And, even if such an assurance could somehow be given, the Christian Democrats could hardly be expected to collaborate in bringing their own hegemony to an end.

Others, especially a sizable bloc of Christian Democratic politicians (many of whom regard former President Cossiga as a dangerous maverick) and a major proportion of the Communist party, want to reform the present parliamentary system by bolstering the power of the prime minister and the cabinet. Supporters of this goal are often attracted by the features of the German system that would strengthen the prime minister and his cabinet and also reinforce the dominant party at the expense of the smaller parties in the system. Some would like to adopt the German constructive vote of no confidence, which would make it impossible for Parliament to overthrow a cabinet except by a resolution approved by an absolute majority of the members of either chamber—a resolution which would specifically designate the outgoing prime minister's successor. Some have also suggested reducing the number of parties in the Italian Parliament by adopting the German 5 percent rule, which permits a party to benefit from proportional representation in Bundestag elections only if it carries three single-member districts or polls 5 percent of the total vote. Such a rule, applied in Italy, would not have barred either the Communists or the neo-Fascists from Parliament but would have banished the minor center parties, unless they agreed to merge their forces under a single electoral rubric. For example, Spadolini's Republicans obtained over 5 percent of the vote in 1983 but would have been shut out in all previous elections. Thus a German-style system would result in fewer parties in the Italian Parliament but might also eliminate the small centrist parties that moderate and check the Christian Democratic giant. Since these proposals would serve to entrench the Christian Democratic party's hegemony, the Socialists and the minor center parties have expressed their opposition. However, it is important to bear in mind the fact that each Italian party is internally divided to some degree on the question of institutional reform.

As matters stand today, neither a presidential nor a strengthened parliamentary model has enough support in Parliament to guarantee its adoption in the face of sharp partisan opposition. Adoption would be rendered doubly arduous by the fact that most reform proposals would need to be passed as constitutional amendments. Furthermore, a recent Christian Democratic attempt to revive the "swindle law" of 1953, and provide a coalition of parties that receives a bare plurality of the votes with two-thirds of the seats in the Chamber of Deputies, has also encountered a very cold reception, in view of the fact that it—like the reform proposals based on the German model—would tend to strengthen the Christian Democratic party.

The creation of the Italian regions has been an institutional reform of major importance. But it is a reform that is far from complete; it was supposed to be followed by a delegation of national and regional powers to local governments and by a complete revamping of the structure and powers of local governments. These supplementary reforms have been only partially adopted. Some delegation of powers has taken place; but until the late spring of 1991, Parliament was unable to agree on a law restructuring and reorganizing local and provincial governments. Even after the passage of this law, it will take several years for the executive branch to issue the necessary executive decrees to put the law into effect. Thus the ultimate outcome of regional reform remains in some doubt.

Urbanization, Violence, and Terrorism

The shift of population from the countryside to the cities has done a great deal to loosen the social restraints that made Italians law-abiding and tradition-minded. The big cities of northern and central Italy have had difficulty coping with the hordes of urbanized peasants they were called on to absorb. Similarly, many of these newcomers (or their children) could not adapt to big-city life. One result has been an upsurge of crime and violence in many Italian cities.

Violence has also manifested itself in the activities of a number of extreme leftist terrorist groups—among them Front Line and the Red Brigades, groups that are in no way related to the Italian Communist party. Composed of disgruntled intellectuals (particularly ex-students) and common criminals recruited by members of the intelligentsia, these organizations have operated with the help of several thousand sympathizers who provide them with shelter and encouragement. From 1968 to 1983, 296 civilians and 92 policemen were killed by terrorist groups, 44 members of which were killed by police bullets. The Red Brigades kidnapped and eventually murdered Aldo Moro, a prominent Christian-Democratic leader and former prime minister. Terrorists also shot in the legs or badly beat numbers of middle-echelon people (labor union officials, professors, engineers) for the alleged crime of having accepted positions of responsibility in a sick and degenerate capitalist society.

The Italian government has gradually prevailed against the left-wing terrorists. After 1979, Minister of the Interior Virginio Rognoni built a system of elite counterterrorist units, obtained legislation to reduce the sentences of terrorists who inform on their colleagues, and strengthened the powers of the police to hold suspects without charges for fairly lengthy periods (the latter measure was eventually repealed). Thanks to informers and police raids, the number of terrorist attacks has sharply diminished.

Italy has also had to cope with other terrorism. Fascist terrorists have been fewer in number than left-wing terrorists but have been lethal in their activities. Their specialty is setting off bombs in public places; one of their most notorious exploits was the 1980 bombing of the Bologna railroad station, resulting in several dozen deaths. A much older brand of terrorism is the activity of a number of criminal secret societies devoted to the acquisition of power through such illicit activities as racketeering, drug dealing, union busting, and the forcible acquisition of control over wholesale and retail facilities. These organizations include the Mafia in Sicily, the 'Ndrangheta in Calabria, and the Camorra in Naples. Gang wars have resulted in hundreds of deaths in Sicily, Calabria, and Naples. One of the most noted victims was a top police official, General Dalla Chiesa, who was responsible for the successful campaigns against the Red Brigades. Dalla Chiesa was shot by the Mafia shortly after being assigned to Palermo to organize a campaign against that organization in Sicily.

The outbreak of terrorism in Italy may be attributed partly to urbanization, partly to the spread of mass education. Many students and junior faculty, disillusioned by overcrowded and poorly equipped universities, and aware of the uncertain future that awaits young intellectuals, have turned to terrorism. The chaotic state of many Italian cities creates conditions under which some young people suffer mental or emotional breakdowns. One outlet for such pressures is terrorism.

The Problem of Defense

The Italian position on defense has not given rise to the controversy that developed in Britain and West Germany during the years before 1990. This was partly due to the fact that the Italian Socialist party, under Craxi's leadership, was not as vulnerable to neutralist appeals as were the Labour and Socialist parties of Northern Europe. When the Italian Parliament in December 1979 decided to approve the government's plan to accept the placement of cruise missiles on Italian soil, the Christian Democrats and the bulk of the Socialists voted for the proposal. Even the Communist party was moderate in its opposition to the installation of the missiles, urging a bilateral freeze and further negotiations instead of simply denouncing American imperialism. The Communist party took the line that the balance of military power in Europe had to be preserved and that the new missiles would upset that balance. Shrill denunciations of the United States came from the forces to the left of the PCI: the green-tinged Radicals and the Demo-Proletarians.

To be sure, the Italian position, while clearly pro-Western, has not been one of unconditional support for U.S. policy. Italian defense spending has been well below the actual amounts, as well as the proportions of Gross Domestic Product, disbursed by major NATO partners such as France and West Germany, although recent defense ministers have reversed the downward trend in defense spending. Italian politicians have strongly criticized American policies in Central America. And Italy's relations with the Arab world are colored to some degree by a Mediterranean outlook and by heavy dependence on Libyan oil. While recognizing Israel's right to exist, Italy has taken a generally pro-Arab stance in matters relating to the Arab-Israeli conflict. Also, Italy refrained from criticizing Colonel Quaddafi's adventures in Chad. Yet, even with Libya, Italy did not follow a line of supine submission. For example, in 1981, Italy signed a treaty with Malta guaranteeing Malta's defenses in exchange for an implied understanding that the Soviet Union would not be allowed to use Maltese naval bases. The treaty with Malta clearly undercut Colonel Quaddafi's efforts to establish a Libyan presence on the island.

Thus, Italy's foreign policy posture might be defined as following the American lead but with certain deviations and nuances, and occasional questions or even mildly critical comments regarding American policies, especially in the Mediterranean and the Middle East. This approach was certainly clearly visible during the Gulf crisis. Virtually every Italian party, not excluding the Communists, was divided on the policy to be followed by Italy with regard to the impending war against Iraq. At first, this division was reflected by calls for a negotiated settlement or for a West European effort to seize the initiative and manage the crisis. When it became evident in late 1990 that war was all but inevitable and that Britain and France would back up the Bush Administration, Socialist Foreign Minister de Micheli's interventionist views prevailed over the more cautious and ambiguous course pursued by Prime Minister Andreotti (DC). Italy then fell into line with the U.S.-led coalition and dispatched Italian forces to the Gulf. But the Italian military effort was half-hearted and largely symbolic: three small warships, eight Tornado aircraft, and one Italian pilot shot down and captured during the war. Still, when the chips were down, Italy had clearly sided with Washington.

Italy's relatively pro-U.S. stance, despite its occasional differences with the Americans, may be explained in terms of Italy's economic and military vulnerability. The Germans and the French may envision an autonomous or even an independent political role for their respective countries; Italians can harbor no such illusions about their country's ability to go it alone. Even the Communist party has shown an awareness of the importance of NATO in safeguarding Italian security. Only a continued association with a strong and cohesive West can permit Italy to lay the foundations for a more secure and stable democracy in the years ahead. Thus, whatever state assumes the mantle of Western leadership can eventually count on Italian support.

Notes

1. See, for example, Sidney Tarrow, "Italy: Crisis, Crises, or Transition?" in *Italy in Transition: Conflict and Consensus,* ed. Peter Lange and Sidney Tarrow (London: Frank Cass, 1980), 166–85. See also Norman Kogan, *A Political History of Italy: The Postwar Years* (New York: Praeger, 1983), chap. 22.

2. See Kogan, *A Political History of Italy,* 329. By 1979, there was one automobile in Italy for every 3.4 people.

3. See "The Flawed Renaissance: A Survey of the Italian Economy," *Economist,* 27 February 1988, special insert, 3–34.

4. Ibid., 3, 10.

For Further Reading

ABERBACH, JOEL D.; PUTNAM, ROBERT D.; AND ROCKMAN, BERT A. *Bureaucrats and Politicians in Western Democracies*. Cambridge, Mass.: Harvard University Press, 1981.

ALLUM, P.A. *Italy: Republic without Government?* New York: Norton, 1973.

———. *Politics and Society in Postwar Naples*. Cambridge: Cambridge University Press, 1973.

BARNES, SAMUEL H. *Party Democracy: Politics in an Italian Socialist Federation*. New Haven: Yale University Press, 1967.

———. *Representation in Italy: Institutionalized Tradition and Electoral Choice*. Chicago: University of Chicago Press, 1977.

BARZINI, LUIGI. *The Italians*. New York: Bantam, 1964.

BELLONI, FRANK P., AND BELLER, DENNIS C., eds. *Faction Politics: Political Parties in Comparative Perspective*. Santa Barbara: ABC-Clio Press, 1978.

BLACKMER, DONALD L.M., AND TARROW, SIDNEY G., eds. *Communism in Italy and France*. Princeton, N.J.: Princeton University Press, 1975.

CASSESE, SABINO. "Is There a Government in Italy? Politics and Administration at the Top," 171–202. In *Presidents and Prime Ministers*, edited by Richard Rose and Ezra N. Suleiman. Washington, D.C.: American Enterprise Institute for Public Policy Research, 1980.

DI PALMA, GIUSEPPE. *Surviving without Governing: The Italian Parties in Parliament*. Berkeley: University of California Press, 1976.

EVANS, ROBERT H. *A Venetian Community, an Italian Village*. Notre Dame: University of Notre Dame Press, 1976.

———. "Regionalism and the Italian City," 212–31. In *Western European Cities in Crisis*, edited by Michael C. Romanos. Lexington, Mass.: Lexington Books, 1979.

FRIED, ROBERT C. *Planning the Eternal City*. New Haven: Yale University Press, 1973.

———. *The Italian Prefects: A Study in Administrative Politics*. New Haven: Yale University Press, 1963.

GALLI, GIORGIO, AND PRANDI, ALFONSO. *Patterns of Political Participation in Italy*. New Haven: Yale University Press, 1970.

GREW, RAYMOND. "Italy." In *Crises of Political Development in Europe and the United States*, edited by Raymond Grew. Princeton, N.J.: Princeton University Press, 1978.

KOGAN, NORMAN. *A Political History of Italy: The Postwar Years.* New York: Praeger, 1983.

LANGE, PETER, AND TARROW, SIDNEY, eds. *Italy in Transition: Conflict and Consensus.* London: Frank Cass, 1980.

LA PALOMBARA, JOSEPH. *Democracy Italian Style.* New Haven: Yale University Press, 1987.

———. *Interest Groups in Italian Politics.* Princeton, N.J.: Princeton University Press, 1964.

LOW-BEER, JOHN R. *Protest and Participation: The New Working Class in Italy.* Cambridge: Cambridge University Press, 1978.

PENNIMAN, HOWARD R., ed. *Italy at the Polls: The Parliamentary Elections of 1976.* Washington, D.C.: American Enterprise Institute for Public Policy Research, 1977.

———. *Italy at the Polls, 1979: A Study of the Parliamentary Elections.* Washington, D.C.: American Enterprise Institute for Public Policy Research, 1981.

———. *Italy at the Polls, 1983: A Study of the National Elections.* Durham, N.C.: Duke University Press, 1987.

PUTNAM, ROBERT D. *The Beliefs of Politicians: Ideology, Conflict and Democracy in Britain and Italy.* New Haven: Yale University Press, 1973.

RANNEY, AUSTIN, AND SARTORI, GIOVANNI, eds. *Eurocommunism: The Italian Case.* Washington, D.C.: American Enterprise Institute for Public Policy Research, 1978.

SANI, GIACOMO. "The Political Culture of Italy: Continuity and Change," 273–324. In *The Civic Culture Revisited,* edited by Gabriel A. Almond and Sidney Verba. Boston: Little, Brown, 1980.

TARROW, SIDNEY. *Between Center and Periphery: Grassroots Politicians in Italy and France.* New Haven: Yale University Press, 1977.

———. *Peasant Communism in Southern Italy.* New Haven: Yale University Press, 1967.

VANNICELLI, PRIMO. *Italy, NATO and the European Community.* Cambridge, Mass.: Center for International Affairs, Harvard University, 1974.

WILLIS, F. ROY. *Italy Chooses Europe.* New York: Oxford University Press, 1971.

ZARISKI, RAPHAEL. *Italy: The Politics of Uneven Development.* Hinsdale, Ill.: Dryden Press, 1972.

ZUCKERMAN, ALAN S. *The Politics of Faction: Christian Democratic Rule in Italy.* New Haven: Yale University Press, 1979.

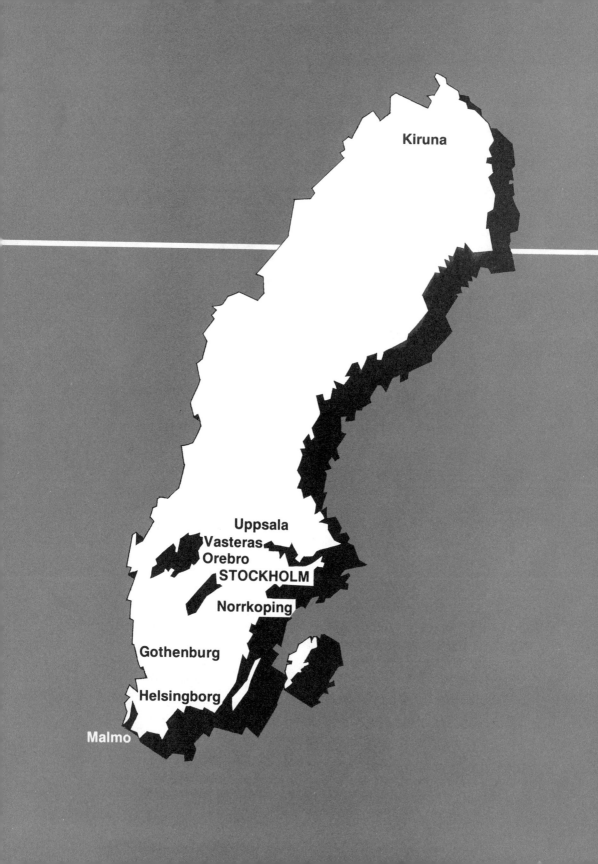

Part Five

Sweden

M. Donald Hancock

21

The Context of Swedish Politics

Since at least the mid-1930s, Sweden has fascinated many outside observers. Some commentators have praised Sweden's economic and social achievements as a "middle way" between competitive capitalism and state socialism and as a "model for the world."[1] Others, ranging from skeptical conservatives to radical socialists, have criticized the centralization of political and economic power in the hands of public officials, unions, and/or an alleged governing class made up of a small group of wealthy capitalists.[2] These diametrically opposed assessments underscore Sweden's singularity in comparison with more familiar capitalist democracies such as Britain, France, Germany, and the United States.

Sweden has undeniably attained one of the world's highest standards of living and most fully developed welfare systems. At the same time, twentieth-century economic and social reforms have resulted in an extraordinarily high rate of taxation and pervasive tendencies toward bureaucratization. Sweden's political parties and organized interest groups have responded with different strategies of policy modification and system change. The result is an ongoing struggle to redefine fundamental tenets of the "Swedish model" of advanced industrial society.

In this and following chapters, I describe basic historical, contextual, institutional, party, and group characteristics of modern Sweden. Analytically, my principal objective is to assess Sweden's status with respect to the distinction that Lawrence D. Brown draws between "breakthrough politics" and a more restrictive form of "rationalizing politics." By the term *breakthrough politics*, Brown means government initiatives to expand the scope of public commitment in response to socioeconomic need. By the term *rationalizing politics,* in contrast, he means the attempts by public officials "to solve evident problems of existing government programs." Thus, breakthrough politics embraces a strategy of ongoing system reform, whereas rationalizing politics settles for less ambitious government measures to make public policies "more rational, that is, problem free."[3] The latter approach, Brown contends, characterizes contemporary American politics and, by implication, policy choices by Thatcherites in the United Kingdom and the Kohl government in Germany as well.

The empirical test of these contrasting approaches to economic and social management in contemporary Sweden involves opposing efforts to reconstitute the Swedish model in response to domestic and international changes. Can the Social Democrats and their trade union allies realize their long-term ideological aspirations to achieve an unprecedented form of economic democracy? Or will key features of the Swedish model be modified or even abandoned as political and economic elites seek to "rationalize" political power and public policy?

Geography, Resources, Population

Located on approximately the same latitude as Alaska and northern Siberia, Sweden is geographically part of the northwestern European land mass known as Scandinavia (or Norden). The other Nordic states include neighboring Denmark, Norway, and Finland, as well as more remote Iceland in the North Atlantic.[4] Sweden is the largest of the Scandinavian countries, having an area somewhat greater than California. It shares a long, largely mountainous boundary with Norway to the west and a considerably shorter border with Finland to the northeast. The rest of Sweden is surrounded by water: the Gulf of Bothnia to the east, the Baltic Sea to the east and south, and to the southwest a narrow passageway known as the Kattegat, which separates Sweden from Denmark.

Sweden is a land of rugged beauty. Much of the country is covered by forests and lakes, with the hills of central and northern Sweden yielding gradually to majestic peaks along the northwestern border. Approximately 10 percent of the land is arable. The richest soil is located in the southernmost province of Skåne, although highly productive farms also surround lakes Vättern and Vänern in the south-central lowlands. A relatively mild climate, attributable to warming winds from the Atlantic and the indirect effects of the Gulf Stream, permits good harvests despite a short growing season. Rivers crisscross the country, providing transportation links and indispensable sources of natural energy. Two large islands guard the Baltic approaches to Sweden: Gotland, with its ancient fortress city of Visby, and Öland, now connected by a modern causeway to the mainland.

Various natural resources serve as the mainstay of Sweden's economy. Among them are large deposits of some of the world's highest-grade iron ore, timber and timber by-products, and abundant fish in the coastal waters. Partially compensating for the absence of domestic supplies of coal and oil are numerous rivers and waterfalls that provide a plentiful and cheap source of hydroelectric power. The principal other sources of energy are imported oil and twelve nuclear energy plants.

Sweden's population of 8.5 million inhabitants is unevenly distributed. Fully 85 percent of the Swedes live in the southern half of the country, where most industry, services, and agriculture are concentrated. The remainder of the populace is scattered throughout the various provinces that make up the forested and mining regions of Norrland. Stockholm, Sweden's capital, is the largest city, with a population of 1.5 million. Göteborg, on the west coast, is second with 726,000. Third is Malmö, which is located in Skåne directly across the Sound from Copenhagen, with 471,000 inhabitants. Other important cities include Uppsala, the site of Scandinavia's oldest university (founded in 1477); Västerås, Örebro, Norrköping, and Helsingborg, all of which are centers of industry, shipping, or both; and the mining town of Kiruna in the far north.

Similar to the other Scandinavian countries but in contrast to the United Kingdom and most of continental Europe, Sweden is a highly homogeneous nation. Ethnically, most Swedes are descendants of the ancient Germanic tribes that settled the region beginning about 7000–5000 B.C. The native exceptions are some 40,000 Finnish-speaking Swedes who live along the Finnish border and approximately 10,000 Lapps in the northern provinces. Traditionally, many of the latter were nomads, moving with their herds of reindeer across northern Scandinavia in search of pasture with the annual change of seasons. In recent decades, however, more and more Lapps have settled in permanent residences.

Like Britain, Germany, and France, Sweden claims a sizable contingent of immigrants. They number approximately 400,000 and make up nearly 5 percent of the total population. Most of the immigrants occupy lower-paid jobs in industry and services. By far the largest group are Finns (who constitute 43 percent of the immigrants), followed in descending order by Yugoslavs, Danes, Norwegians, Turks, and Iranians.

Because of their close linguistic, ethnic, and other affinities with the Swedes, the Danes and the Norwegians are virtually invisible within the majority culture. In contrast, many Finns and, even more so, the southern European and Asian workers are not well integrated. Most of these ethnic minority workers live in semisegregated housing in working-class neighborhoods and suburbs and interact socially far more with members of their own subculture than with the majority Swedes. Nonetheless, government efforts to provide quality housing for the immigrants and facilitate instruction in Swedish for the adults during working hours and bilingual education for their children at school have lessened the degree of social alienation that many guest workers experience in Britain and elsewhere on the Continent.

Religion and language reinforce national cohesiveness. An overwhelming majority of Swedes (94 percent) belong to the state Lutheran church. The remainder are either members of dissenting Protestant sects, Catholic, or non-Christian. In addition, virtually all citizens speak Swedish as their common language, albeit with regional variations in pronunciation (especially among Finno-Swedes and in Skåne, which until the seventeenth century belonged to Denmark).

Although Sweden's ethnic and cultural homogeneity strikes some foreign observers as monotonous in comparison with more colorfully diverse societies elsewhere in Europe, the absence of significant social cleavages has proved an important factor contributing to distinctive national political traits. Among them is Sweden's largely peaceful transition from an agrarian society governed by a traditional monarchy to today's advanced industrial democracy.

Early Political Development

Swedish political development is a product of both regional and domestic factors of system change. From the appearance of the first hunters and fishermen in prehistoric times until the beginning of the Viking era in the ninth century A.D., Swedish history was virtually indistinguishable from that of the Scandinavian region as a whole. Gradually, however, separate Danish, Norwegian, and Swedish kingdoms began to evolve on the basis of rudimentary legal codes, recognized political authority in the form of elected monarchs, a sense of national identity shaped by language and an oral tradition of heroic sagas, and warfare with other Europeans. The advent of Christianity in the ninth century helped domesticate Viking impulses to pillage and conquer and facilitated the incorporation of the Scandinavian kingdoms into the larger fabric of Western civilization. Christianization also encouraged incipient processes of modernization within the region as members of the clergy introduced literacy and codified the legal basis of state authority.

Through conquest Sweden absorbed present-day Finland in the thirteenth century. Domestically, feudal estates similar to those elsewhere in Europe, which consisted of a landed aristocracy, the clergy, and farmers, gradually evolved. By the fifteenth century, a fourth estate of urban "burghers" (*borgare*) had emerged as well. Unlike later developments in Russia and even neighboring Denmark, however, the independence of the farmers, which was rooted in their ownership of land, prevented the emergence of serfdom in Sweden. Thus, each estate retained its corporate autonomy.

The three Scandinavian kingdoms were united temporarily under Danish dominance in 1397. In subsequent decades, the more numerous Swedes became increasingly resentful of their Danish rulers. Representatives of the nobility and the *borgare* undertook an early move toward Swedish independence when they convened Sweden's first parliament (Riksdag) in 1435 to select a military commander. Full rebellion ensued in 1521 when peasants, miners, and nobles joined in an armed uprising in response to a number of punitive acts by the Danes. Their efforts succeeded, and in 1523 the Riksdag unanimously elected the leader of the rebellion, Gustav Vasa, Sweden's king. As Gustavus I, the youthful monarch centralized political and administrative authority in Stockholm and proclaimed Sweden's break with Catholicism in support of the Protestant Reformation in 1540.

During the sixteenth and seventeenth centuries, successive kings and their armies wrested sovereignty over Skåne and other southwestern provinces from Denmark and established a formidable Baltic empire. The most important of Sweden's heroic monarchs was Gustavus II Adolphus, who reigned from 1611 to 1632. Under his energetic leadership, Sweden extended its boundaries eastward and southward at the expense of both Russia and Poland and intervened decisively in the Thirty Years War (1618–48). To pursue Sweden's wartime exploits more effectively, Gustavus Adolphus and his advisers further centralized state authority by reorganizing the Riksdag as a four-estate parliament formally representing the nobility, clergy, *borgare,* and farmers. Through a series of taxation and financial reforms, the government also encouraged economic development and the growth of Stockholm, Göteborg, and other urban centers.

Defeat at the hands of Russia in 1709 marked the beginning of an extended period of territorial retrenchment that culminated in Russia's annexation of Finland in 1808–9. The victorious anti-Napoleonic coalition sought to compensate Sweden for the loss of Finland by transferring control over Norway from Denmark to Swedish authorities in 1814. Norway's peaceful bid for independence in 1905 reduced Sweden to its present boundaries.

Democratization and Industrialization

From independence through the Napoleonic wars, Sweden experienced successive constitutional cycles that oscillated between extremes of monarchical and parliamentary supremacy. Defeat by Russia prompted a palace coup against the last of the despotic monarchs in 1809, resulting in the adoption of a new constitution that institutionalized shared authority between the king and the four-estate Riksdag. The outcome was a broadly based elite consensus on constitutional arrangements comparable to the Glorious Revolution in England in 1688. Members of parliament elected Jean-Baptiste Bernadotte, a French marshal, regent in 1810. He served as king from 1818 until his death in 1844.

The diffusion of liberal political doctrines during the first half of the nineteenth century, coupled with the spread of industry and the advent of social democracy during the second half, brought about Sweden's piecemeal democratization. Liberal demands to transform the archaic four-estate parliament into a more modern representative body resulted in the introduction of a bicameral Riksdag in 1865–66. Popular agitation for more sweeping political reforms followed in the wake of industrialization, which began in the 1850s and reached "takeoff" proportions in the 1890s.

Out of industrialization arose in the 1880s an organized labor movement and the Social Democratic Workers' party (SAP), founded in 1889. Together, the Liberals and the Social Democrats advocated an extension of the right to vote and the introduction of a parliamentary form of government. Conservative and centrist leaders at first resisted, but, acknowledging the inevitable, they conceded manhood suffrage in exchange for the introduction of proportional representation in the "Great Compromise" of 1907–9.[5]

The Liberals and the Social Democrats established a parliamentary form of government, modeled on the British pattern, when they formed a majority coalition in 1917. The coalition partners proceeded to introduce universal suffrage in 1918, which was ratified by constitutional amendments in 1919–21, as the final major step in Sweden's democratization. Subsequent constitutional revisions have refined but not substantially modified the historic achievements of 1907–21.

Political Culture: Constants and Change

Sweden's evolutionary process of system change during the nineteenth and twentieth centuries is both cause and effect of a political culture that affirms traditional values and simultaneously endorses efforts at political creativity. Linking these attributes is a willingness among political actors to seek compromise solutions to partisan disagreements.

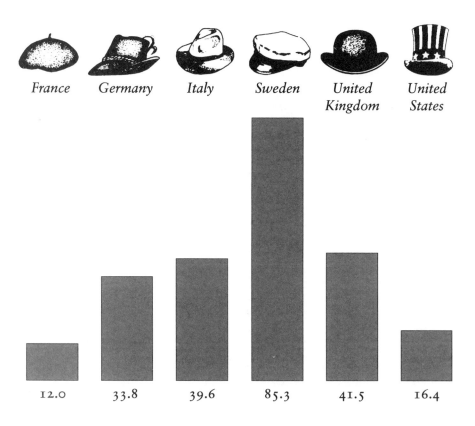

France	Germany	Italy	Sweden	United Kingdom	United States
12.0	33.8	39.6	85.3	41.5	16.4

FIGURE 21.1
TRADE UNION MEMBERSHIP (PERCENTAGE OF WORKFORCE)

SOURCE: OECD, 1991.

The most important traditional element inherent in Swedish political culture is a deeply ingrained respect for constitutionalism and law. Among Sweden's oldest historical documents are legal codes that served to limit kingly power and prescribe procedures for settling private disputes. Indeed, as Dankwart Rustow observes, an ancient Swedish adage proclaims: *Land skall med lag byggas* ("The country shall be built with law").[6] Shared respect for orderly legal procedures among legislative, administrative, and military officials underlay the restoration of constitutional government in 1809 and has served as a powerful stimulus for regulating conflict within the political system and in the labor market in the intervening years.

Associated with diffuse support for government by law is broad-based veneration of established political institutions. The Riksdag dates from the fifteenth century and a national monarchy from the sixteenth. As they do in British custom, important monarchical occasions serve as unifying symbols of national identity and pride. These range from ceremonies opening the Riksdag and honoring Nobel Prize recipients to intermittent royal marriages, births, and funerals. Other institutions that have proven their worth over time are similarly valued, including the office of the parliamentary ombudsman (a form of legislative watchdog) and Sweden's decentralized form of public administration (both of which are discussed in the next chapter).

Respect for law and traditional institutions by no means translates into resistance to system change. On the contrary, receptivity to institutional reform and policy innovation stands out as a third basic tenet of Swedish political culture. Legal codes have been continually revised to meet changing political, economic, and social conditions, just as both the Riksdag and the monarchy have undergone profound transformation in the course of democratization. In each instance, reforms were the products of group demands to revise existing structures and government policies advanced variously by Liberals, Conservatives, farmers, Social Democrats, and others.

That reform aspirations did not spark violent social confrontations comparable to events in France, Germany, and Russia reflects, finally, shared values of moderation and pragmatism. These attributes of Sweden's acclaimed "politics of compromise" are rooted in diverse factors. Among them are cultural-ethnic homogeneity; a historical pattern of collaboration among members of the medieval estates; the absence of oppressive government measures directed against the advocates of reform; and responsible behavior on the part of Liberal, Social Democratic, and trade union officials. A willingness among key political and economic actors to seek compromise or pragmatic solutions to partisan disputes significantly facilitated the constitutional settlements of 1809, 1865–66, and 1907–9, as recounted above. In more recent decades, party and interest-group leaders have similarly acted on traditional values of moderation and pragmatism to achieve consensus on successive economic, social, and constitutional initiatives, as is explained below.

Sweden's compromising style of politics has not precluded recurrent class or political conflict. Employers and public officials linked forces to suppress striking workers in a major local dispute in 1879 and on a national scale in 1909. Also, nonsocialist spokesmen have vehemently opposed Social Democratic initiatives since World War II to establish supplementary pensions, extend worker rights, and introduce a compulsory system of wage-earner funds, as is discussed below. Nonetheless, a willingness among political and economic elites to accept reforms (at least ultimately) rather than sabotage them through obstructionist tactics remains a central hallmark of Swedish political culture.

Nor have prevailing traditions of moderation and restraint precluded individual acts of violence, as tragically demonstrated by the assassination on 28 February 1986 of Prime Minister Olof Palme. Chairman of the Social Democratic party and head of government from 1969 to 1976 and after September 1982 (see below), Palme was gunned down by an assailant late one evening on a street in Stockholm as he and his wife were walking home from a movie. In late 1988, the police arrested a native Swede previously convicted of murder as a suspect in the slaying. He was later tried and acquitted for lack of evidence.

Neutrality and Internationalism

A key instance of political consensus in Sweden is popular endorsement of the country's foreign policy of neutrality. Since 1814, Sweden has successfully avoided involvement in successive European wars. National attempts to escape invasion during World War II failed in Denmark, Norway, and Finland, but not in Sweden. As a result, Swedish leaders resolved to maintain a voluntary policy of nonalignment during the postwar period despite decisions by Iceland, Norway, and Denmark to join the North Atlantic Treaty Organization (NATO). Finland, too, remains nonaligned within the Nordic region, albeit on the basis of a state treaty with the Soviet Union that binds the country not to undertake measures detrimental to the Soviets.

Sweden enforces its neutrality by maintaining a strong national defense. In 1989 the government spent 2.6 percent of Sweden's gross national product on military expenditures, with principal emphasis on air and naval defense. This percentage was significantly lower than that in the United States (5.9 percent) and the United Kingdom (4.2 percent), but it was approximately equal to that in most other advanced industrial democracies. Sweden's per capita defense expenditures that same year were $536 compared to $1,186 in the United States, $606 in the United Kingdom, $655 in France, $571 in West Germany, and $363 in Italy.[7]

Government officials further underscored Sweden's neutrality in an important foreign policy move in 1971 by deciding not to join Britain, Ireland, Denmark, and Norway in applying for membership in the European Economic Community (EC).[8] However attractive the economic advantages of free access to the European Community for the country's industrial and agricultural exporters, cabinet spokesmen declared that membership in the EC would undermine the international credibility of Sweden's policy of neutrality by potentially restricting the government's freedom of action in the event of war. Hence, Sweden negotiated a more restricted industrial free-trade agreement that does not formally bind the nation to EC political or economic decisions.[9]

The subsequent demise of Communism in Eastern and Central Europe and the virtual end of the cold war prompted Swedish leaders to reconsider their position on EC membership. After a majority of the members of parliament voted in December 1990 to endorse full membership, the cabinet submitted Sweden's application in 1991. Leaders of the principal parties have declared, however, that Sweden will maintain its established policy of neutrality even if it joins the Community.

Sweden couples its policy of nonalignment with strong support for the United Nations and other international organizations, such as the International Monetary Fund (IMF), the Organization for Economic Cooperation and Development (OECD), and the General Agreement on Tariffs and Trade (GATT). Sweden's internationalism is rooted in a blend of economic self-interest and political idealism. Economically, Sweden is highly dependent on trade with other industrial nations and Third World countries for continued growth and affluence. In 1989, for instance, exports accounted for fully 29 percent of the nation's gross domestic product.[10] Politically, the Swedes and other Scandinavians have affirmed collective security and principles of international economic and social cooperation since the founding of the League of Nations in the 1920s. In the post–World War II period, all the Scandinavian states have contributed men and materiel to a variety of UN peacekeeping operations in Africa and the Middle East. Dag Hammarskjöld, a distinguished civil servant whose father was Swedish prime minister during World War I, served as secretary-general of the United Nations from 1953 until his untimely death in a plane crash in Africa in 1961.

Development of the Welfare State

An object of both widespread support and partisan dissent in Sweden is the nation's array of welfare services. The development of the Swedish welfare state is primarily associated with the Social Democrats. With the support of the Agrarians and occasionally the Liberals, they sponsored legislation from the mid-1930s onward that provided for a voluntary program of unemployment insurance, an improved national pension system, school lunch subsidies, and public assistance to individuals and families in need. World War II interrupted the social reform movement, but by the late 1940s the Social Democrats resumed their efforts to provide minimum standards of collective social security. Postwar legislation included the introduction of compulsory sickness insurance (1947), improved basic retirement benefits (1948), a new system of supplementary pensions based on individual earnings (1959), and a Law on Social Help (1956) that consolidated and extended a variety of welfare benefits. Among the latter are government-financed maternity care, quarterly cash allowances to single parents or families with children, and rent subsidies to those in need.

The cumulative effect of these measures is that all citizens and registered aliens (including guest workers) experience an extraordinary degree of social security. They pay relatively little "out of pocket" for health care and education, and are guaranteed generous pensions on retirement. Since workers and families whose income falls below minimum standards receive a variety of government payments to help defray rent and other expenses, a strikingly visible consequence of Sweden's comprehensive welfare system is the virtual absence of urban slums comparable to those in most metropolitan areas in North America and elsewhere in Western Europe.

To finance their extensive welfare provisions, the Swedes pay one of the highest levels of taxes in the world. As indicated in table 21.1, the per capita tax contribution in 1987 in Sweden was the equivalent of $10,707. This amount corresponds approximately to tax levels in the neighboring Scandinavian countries (which are also noted for their comprehensive welfare benefits) but is significantly higher on a per capita basis than in the United Kingdom, Germany, Italy, and the United States.

TABLE 21.1

COMPARATIVE TAX PAYMENTS, 1987

(IN U.S. DOLLARS)

Country	Annual per capita tax pay-ment	As percentage of gross domestic product
Sweden	$10,707	53.5
Denmark	10,257	52.0
Norway	9,546	48.3
Finland	6,515	35.9
France	7,099	44.8
Germany	6,880	37.6
Italy	4,778	36.2
United Kingdom	4,451	37.5
Canada	5,710	34.5
United States	5,396	30.0

SOURCE: Sweden, Statistiska centralbyrån, *Statistisk årsbok 1991* (Stockholm, 1991), 494.

A majority of the electorate has repeatedly honored the Social Democrats for their social policy achievements. As indicated in table 23.1, the Socialists steadily increased their share of the popular vote during the 1930s and 1940s and have achieved an absolute majority on three occasions. Since the end of World War II, their electoral strength has fluctuated between a high of 50.1 percent in 1968 and a low of 37.6 percent in 1991, for a postwar average of 45 percent. Because of their majority status in parliament, the Social Democrats were able to retain control of the national executive from 1932 to 1976 with virtually no interruption.

Yet the welfare state is not without its critics. Conservatives and other nonsocialists have continually attacked both the nation's high rate of taxation and bureaucratizing tendencies within the public sector. On the left, radical socialists have broadened the bourgeois critique of bureaucratization to include centralizing tendencies within the trade unions and simultaneously have condemned the Social Democrats for their failure to achieve a socialist economy. These opposing views, combined with an offensive initiated by the Social Democrats in the 1970s to extend worker and union rights, thus define the substance of

Sweden's ongoing public debate concerning its political and economic future.

Notes

1. See, for example, Marquis W. Childs, *Sweden: The Middle Way,* rev. ed. (New Haven: Yale University Press, 1947); and Hudson Strode, *Sweden: Model for a World* (New York: Harcourt, Brace, 1949). Childs has updated and marginally revised his optimistic assessment in *Sweden: The Middle Way on Trial* (New Haven: Yale University Press, 1980).

2. For contrasting right vs. left critiques, see Roland Huntford, *Sweden: The New Totalitarians* (New York: Stein & Day, 1972); and Jan Myrdal, *Confessions of a Disloyal European* (New York: Pantheon, 1968).

3. Lawrence D. Brown, *New Policies, New Politics: Government's Response to Government's Growth* (Washington, D.C.: Brookings Institution, 1983), 7.

4. Greenland, an autonomous province of Denmark located off the North Atlantic coast of Canada, is also culturally and politically a part of Scandinavia.

5. The "Great Compromise" sanctioned a new elite consensus on fundamental constitutional principles comparable to the settlement of 1809.

6. Dankwart A. Rustow, *The Politics of Compromise* (New Haven: Yale University Press, 1957), 236–37.

7. Sveriges officiella statistik, *Statistisk årsbok för Sverige 1991* (Stockholm, 1991), 400.

8. Sweden has been a member of the more loosely organized European Free Trade Association (EFTA) since its creation in 1960. EFTA was established to facilitate the abolition of industrial tariffs among its members but lacks supranational decision-making structures and a common agricultural market comparable to the more ambitious EC. Its founding members included, besides Sweden, the United Kingdom, Denmark, Norway, Ireland, Austria, and Switzerland. As early as 1963 British officials resolved to abandon EFTA in favor of the EC because the latter promised greater economic benefits. Because of the importance of their trade links with both Britain and the EC countries, Denmark and Norway also sought membership in the EC when negotiations began in earnest in 1971.

9. Britain, Ireland, and Denmark proceeded to join the EC in 1973, while a narrow majority of Norwegian voters rejected a membership treaty in a national referendum in 1972. As a result, Norway joined Sweden (as well as Finland) in negotiating a free-trade agreement instead.

10. Sveriges officiella statistik, *Statistisk årsbok för Sverige 1991* (Stockholm, 1991), 133.

22

Where Is the Power?

Sweden's contemporary institutional arrangements are the product of a century and a half of evolutionary political and constitutional change. Whereas the constitution of 1809 provided for a division of power between the king and parliament, the Riksdag gradually acquired increased competence in the course of the nineteenth century as various categories of law became subject to joint jurisdiction rather than royal jurisdiction alone. In parallel fashion, members of the king's advisory council (the cabinet) gradually displaced the monarch as the effective center of executive authority. The prime minister and members of the cabinet subsequently became politically accountable to the Riksdag in the course of Sweden's democratization between 1907 and 1921. Sweden's contemporary status as a parliamentary democracy was formally ratified with the adoption of a series of constitutional amendments in 1968–69 and a wholly new constitution in 1973–74.

The cabinet and the Riksdag are thus the principal sites of policy initiative and ratification, with the role of the monarch reduced to ceremonial and symbolic functions. Since Sweden is a unitary rather than a federal state, other political functions are exercised by national and local institutions that are constitutionally subordinate to parliament and the central government.

The Riksdag

From 1866 until 1970, the Riksdag consisted of two houses: a popularly elected "second chamber" equivalent to the British House of Commons and a smaller, indirectly elected "first chamber" whose members were chosen by Sweden's twenty-four provincial assemblies. Constitutional reforms ratified in 1968–69 and implemented in 1970 abolished the bicameral system, establishing in its place a unicameral parliament similar to the national legislatures in Denmark and Finland. Further changes were incorporated with the adoption of a new Instrument of Government and Act of Parliament in 1973–74, which went into effect in 1975. These documents, which are of equal constitutional weight, define executive and legislative functions and the organization of the Riksdag, respectively. The two acts can be amended only by majority vote by two successive sessions of parliament with an intervening election.[1] The preamble to the Instrument of Government defines the principles of Swedish parliamentary democracy as follows:

> All public power in Sweden emanates from the people. The Swedish democracy is founded on freedom of opinion and on universal and equal suffrage and shall be realized through a representative and parliamentary polity and through local self-government. Public power shall be exercised under the laws.

The first of these principles is institutionalized in the form of free, competitive elections to the Riksdag and to the nation's city and county representative assemblies. Full rights of suffrage are accorded citizens eighteen years of age and older. Registered aliens also have the right to vote, but only in local elections. Elections to parliament and local government units are held simultaneously at three-year intervals on the third Sunday in September unless a dissolution election intervenes. If a dissolution election intervenes, Riksdag deputies merely serve out the remainder of the legislative term (rather than constitute a new parliament as is the practice elsewhere in Europe). The result is that dissolution elections are extremely rare in Sweden; since the advent of parliamentarianism, the Riksdag has been dissolved only once (in 1958, as recounted below).

Sweden employs a proportional electoral system, dating from the constitutional reforms of 1907–9, that utilizes a modified version of the Sainte-Laguë method for distributing seats among contending parties.[2] The nation's twenty-four provinces serve as regional constituencies for the election of the Riksdag's 349 deputies. Most of the seats (310) are allocated among the constituencies on the basis of the number of eligible voters and the relative strength of the parties competing for support in each of them. The remaining 39 seats are distributed among the parties according to their aggregate percentage of votes within the country as a whole. The purpose of the latter provision is to compensate the largest party or parties for the possible loss of seats in individual constituencies and thereby ensure strict proportionality. To be represented in the Riksdag a party must receive a minimum of either 4 percent of the national vote or 12 percent of the vote in a single constituency.

The Riksdag provides the legislative basis for cabinet formation and tenure and serves as Sweden's principal lawmaking body. In the former capacity, the Riksdag elects the prime minister (*statsminister*) following each general election. After interparty consultation, the speaker nominates a candidate, and the Riksdag votes for or against the candidate. If a government resigns, as happened in 1978 and 1981, the Riksdag elects a successor prime minister. The Instrument of Government does not require that a candidate receive an absolute majority (as is true under normal circumstances in Germany). Instead, a prime minister is elected if not more than half of the members of the Riksdag vote against him. This feature of Swedish constitutionalism makes possible the formation of minority governments in the absence of a majority by a single party or coalition of parties.

Since 1970, the Riksdag has also been empowered to move a vote of no confidence against an incumbent prime minister and individual cabinet officials. Such a motion must be signed by a tenth of the deputies and approved by an absolute majority.[3] In such an event, a prime minister or cabinet member would be compelled to resign his or her ministerial post.

As in other parliamentary systems, one of the most important functions of the Riksdag is to hold the government accountable for its actions and omissions on a day-to-day basis. For this purpose, Riksdag deputies utilize both written and oral questions, which are addressed to cabinet ministers, and the right of general debate. Although party discipline has thus far ensured the survival even of minority cabinets in the face of parliamentary queries and criticism, the various control devices usefully serve to extract information and official justifications concerning government policy. The number of written questions (known as interpellations) averaged 190 per year between 1978 and 1990, while the annual number of oral questions averaged 694 during the same period.[4]

The Riksdag's legislative powers include the exclusive right of taxation and appropriation. In addition, parliament shares authority with the cabinet to propose constitutional amendments, initiate changes in civil and criminal law, and schedule advisory referenda on major political issues.[5]

For deliberative purposes, the Riksdag is divided into sixteen standing committees whose powers of scrutiny and amendment are broadly comparable to those of committees in the U.S. Congress and the German Bundestag. They include committees on finance, taxation, justice, laws, foreign affairs, defense, social insurance, social welfare, cultural affairs, education, agriculture, economic affairs, communications, the labor market, local government, and the constitution. A principal purpose of the committee on the constitution is to examine the minutes of cabinet meetings to determine whether any member of the government has violated the law. If such proves the case, the committee on the constitution is authorized to bring legal charges against the offending official before a special court of impeachment.[6]

All bills, whether submitted by the cabinet or backbench members of the parliament, are referred to the relevant committee for deliberation. Unlike the American congressional practice, Swedish committees may not pigeonhole (and thereby kill) legislation but must report all bills back to parliament. Their recommendations almost invariably serve as the basis of legislative enactment.

Riksdag officers include a Speaker and three vice-Speakers, all of whom are elected by majority vote. (In practice, the positions are distributed among the major parties represented in parliament.) The Speaker and vice-Speakers play a key legislative role by presiding over parliamentary deliberations and determining, in consultation with the chairmen of the standing committees and four other elected members of parliament, the order in which bills and committee reports are considered on the floor of the Riksdag. In addition, the Speaker is empowered under the 1975 constitution to nominate the prime minister prior to his election by parliament.

The Prime Minister and the Cabinet

The relative significance of the Riksdag and the cabinet in Sweden's policy-making process varies in relation to the strength of the government's parliamentary backing. During the 1920s, when no party or coalition commanded a stable majority, the Riksdag was the dominant partner. The advent of "majority parliamentarianism" under Social Democratic–Agrarian aegis in 1932–33 marked the beginning of a long-term shift in the balance of power in favor of the prime minister and his cabinet. More recently, periods of minority rule under the Social Democrats and later the nonsocialists resulted in the reassertion of parliamentary influence during the 1970s and early 1980s. Because of its direct access to administrative structures and organized interest groups, however, the cabinet remains the central source of policy initiative and coordination.

Since 1932, most Swedish prime ministers have been selected because of their status as chairman of either the largest party in parliament (the Social Democrats) or the largest party within a nonsocialist coalition (as was true in 1976–78, 1980–81, and 1991–   ). Recent exceptions include nonsocialist leaders who held office as prime ministers in minority cabinets in 1978–79 and 1981–83. Until the constitutional reforms of 1973–74, the king appointed the prime minister on the advice of party leaders in parliament. Since 1975, as previously noted, the prime minister has been elected by the Riksdag.

The prime minister is *primus inter pares* the seventeen or so persons who make up the cabinet. (The actual number varies from government to government.) The prime minister chairs cabinet sessions and is primarily responsible for determining the broad outlines of government policy. He is also the chief spokesman for cabinet policy both within and outside parliament. The prime minister is assisted by a deputy with cabinet rank, whose task is to coordinate and plan government activities, and a staff of political advisers and professional civil servants who make up the royal chancery.

Members of the cabinet are selected by the prime minister. They may be dismissed by him or through a vote of no confidence by parliament, as described above. Ministerial positions, which correspond in most cases to the standing committees in the Riksdag, include finance, budgetary affairs, foreign policy, defense, justice, social policy, communications, education, agriculture, interior, labor market, housing, industry, and interior. The deputy prime minister and three to five ministers without portfolio serve as policy generalists with rotating responsibilities.

Each of the designated ministers heads an administrative "department" that is responsible primarily for policy formation (including the preparation of the annual budget). Unlike the national ministries in other Western democracies, Swedish departments are quite limited in size. Typically, they consist of an administrative assistant to the minister (a "state secretary," who in most cases is a high-level civil servant rather than a political appointee), an office manager, a legal adviser, and a relatively small number of civil servants who handle departmental planning, budgetary proposals, and policy coordination. The actual implementation of policy is delegated to a decentralized network of administrative agencies (see below).

Thanks in large measure to its executive authority over the various departments and administrative agencies, the cabinet plays the central role in Sweden's formal policy-making process. Members of the Riksdag are by no means negligent in proposing legislation. During the 1980–81 parliamentary session, for example, they submitted no fewer than 2,218 private members' bills.[7] In contrast, the cabinet initiated fully 26,220 executive actions during the same period. They included 203 government bills (most of which were duly enacted), 4,434 budgetary and other decrees, 8,690 appeals, and 7,560 miscellaneous measures (including administrative appointments). The remaining executive acts in-

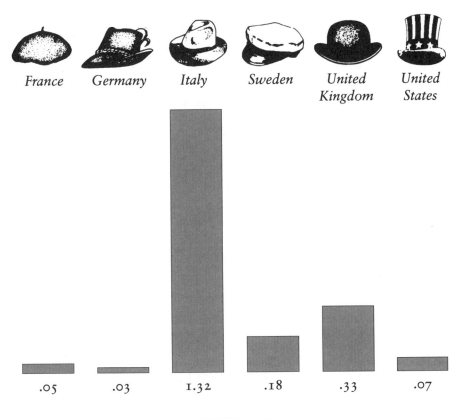

France	Germany	Italy	Sweden	United Kingdom	United States
.05	.03	1.32	.18	.33	.07

FIGURE 22.1
STRIKE ACTIVITY (1980–87)
WORKING DAYS LOST PER WORKER PER YEAR

volved responses by cabinet members to interpellations and single-member questions raised in parliament.[8]

The cabinet's policy-making role is further enhanced by its authority to mobilize the resources of Sweden's powerful organized interest groups in the prelegislative stage of parliamentary decisions. Since the nineteenth century, Swedish cabinets have regularly appointed "state commissions" (*statsutredningar,* commonly translated as "Royal Commissions") to gather facts and advise the government on pending legislation. On major questions, such commissions characteristically consist of experts representing the important interest groups, political parties, and relevant administrative agencies. Commission members are usually very thorough in their work, with their final recommendations frequently serving as the basis of the cabinet's legislative proposal concerning the issue.

Interest-group viewpoints are also solicited through a consultative process known as *remiss.* Under this procedure, ministerial departments invite organized groups and administrative agencies to comment on pending legislation. A government proposal to the Riksdag contains a summary of the state commission's report and *remiss* replies along with the government's own recommendation for action.

Together, the state commissions and the *remiss* procedures constitute the formal core of Sweden's version of democratic corporatism as defined in the introduction to this volume: namely, institutionalized consultative arrangements that permit public officials and representatives of the nation's principal interest associations to confer jointly about pending policy issues. By serving as channels for initiating and/or reviewing important legislative initiatives, the commissions and the *remiss* procedure accord organized interest groups a more direct means to influence policy outcomes than is true of most Western democracies.

The Monarch

The reigning monarch in Sweden is Carl XVI Gustav, who was crowned king in September 1973 following the death of his grandfather, King Gustaf VI Adolf. The latter performed residual executive functions dating from the nineteenth century in his constitutional role as chairman of formal cabinet sessions, but even this monarchical prerogative was deleted with the adoption of the present constitution in 1973–74. A key reason was lingering Social Democratic resentment of efforts by King Gustaf V Adolf, who had reigned from 1907 to 1950, to influence cabinet policy in Germany's favor during both world wars. Thus, since

1975, the monarch's role has been restricted largely to ceremonial acts, such as presiding over the annual opening of parliament and conferring Nobel prizes on academic and literary dignitaries.

King Carl XVI helped ensure the survival of the monarchy through his marriage in 1976 to an attractive West German "commoner" from Bavaria, who as Queen Sylvia has charmed even many erstwhile republicans within Social Democratic ranks. Two daughters and a son have been born to the royal couple. First in line of succession is the eldest, Princess Viktoria Ingrid Alice Desiree, born in 1978. The constitution was amended in 1979–81 to permit Viktoria, as the first born, to succeed her father as future Swedish monarch. Previously, the constitution had permitted succession only by male offspring.

Other Institutional Actors

While policy-making authority is concentrated in the hands of the cabinet and parliament, powers of implementation and enforcement are functionally dispersed among a variety of institutions. They include public administrative bodies, county and local government units, state-owned enterprises, the court system, and four ombudsmen.

The Public Administration

Responsible for most policy implementation in Sweden is a decentralized network of central administrative boards (*centrala ämbetsverk*) and a dual system of county and municipal government. On the national level, the administrative boards number approximately eighty. Among the most significant are the National Board of Health and Welfare, the National Industrial Board, the Labor Market Board, the National Nuclear Energy Inspection Board, and the Central Office of Statistics. Other important administrative agencies include the national railways, the postal service, telecommunications, civil defense, and the court system (see below). Many administrative agencies, especially those dealing with economic and social policy, maintain regional offices on the level of county government.[9]

Alongside the central administrative boards are several legislative agencies that perform important policy tasks as well. They include the Bank of Sweden, which issues currency and controls the nation's supply of money, and the National Debt Office, which is empowered to borrow money in the name of the government and is responsible for administering the national debt.

In contrast to the hierarchical structure of public administration in Britain and elsewhere on the Continent, Sweden's administrative boards and agencies are legally autonomous from the cabinet and parliament. The present system, dating from the seventeenth century, was established to maximize the rational implementation of public policy. As Thomas Anton observes: "Administrative power was ... a function of Swedish insistence that 'political' and 'administrative' decisions were clearly distinct and that the latter could be made simply by applying law to the facts of a particular case. The administrative boards ... were designed to provide such legal judgments, and officials were assigned full authority to make those judgments, free from 'political interference.' "[10]

Despite their legal autonomy, Sweden's administrative agencies are nonetheless subordinate to the central government and the Riksdag for authoritative policy directives. Moreover, cabinet officials have increasingly relied in recent decades on detailed budgetary guidelines as a means to oversee and coordinate day-to-day administration.

Regional and Local Governments

Regional and local governments consist of partially overlapping structures made up of appointive state county administrative boards and elected county and municipal councils. Heading the former in each of Sweden's twenty-four counties is a provincial governor appointed by, and therefore responsible to, the cabinet. The fourteen other members of the administrative boards are designated by the elected members of the parallel county councils. The appointive boards supervise regional planning, county employment offices, worker retraining programs, environmental protection, and the administration of justice.

Sweden's 24 elected provincial councils and 284 subordinate rural and municipal assemblies are responsible for implementing medical and health care; social welfare; education; housing policy; land use; ambulance service; fire protection; and cultural, youth, and athletic policies. The regional administrative agencies, appointive county boards, and elective councils work closely together in coordinating and implementing their designated policy assignments.

Growth of the Public Sector

Sweden's public sector has grown significantly in both size and economic importance in recent decades. From fewer than 45,000 civil servants at the turn of the century, the number of public officials has increased to approximately 1.6 million out of the country's work force of 4.4 million (nearly 40 percent of the total). Private consumption accounts for the lion's share of the gross national product (59 percent in 1988), while public consumption comprises 31 percent of the total. County and local government expenditures account for 22 percent of total public consumption compared to 8 percent on the part of the central government and its administrative agencies.[11]

Fifty-nine public enterprises and financial institutions make up an important component of the public sector. Although state-owned firms comprise only about 10 percent of Sweden's overwhelmingly private economy, they accord the national government varying degrees of control over investments, production, and sales in designated economic sectors. Among the major enterprises in which the government is sole owner or majority shareholder are LKAB, Sweden's largest iron ore mining company; Swedish Petroleum; Swedish Steel; *Systembolaget,* a state-owned monopoly controlling the distribution and sale of wine, liquor, and strong beer; the Swedish Pharmaceutical Corporation; much of the forestry industry; and various banks and insurance companies.[12]

Courts and the Administration of Justice

The Swedish court system dates from legislation originally passed in 1734. Three levels define its basic structural hierarchy: some ninety-seven district courts of first instance (*tingsrätter*), six intermediate courts of appeal (*hovrätter*), and a Supreme Court (högsta domstolen). Jurisdiction extends in each case to both civil and criminal law.

By far the largest number of cases are settled in the courts of first instance. In 1988, for example, the district courts heard nearly 65,000 civil disputes and 71,000 criminal cases. The courts of appeal, in contrast, reviewed 3,294 civil appeals and 7,745 criminal cases. That same year, only 590 civil disputes and 1,190 criminal appeals reached the Supreme Court.[13]

Judges must have a university degree in legal studies and are appointed by the cabinet. They are assisted in all criminal and most civil cases on the local level by panels (*nämnd*) of lay judges, who are elected for six-year terms by the county assemblies. Unlike Anglo-American juries, the *nämnd* not only hear evidence and help reach a verdict but also confer with the judge concerning points of law.

The Riksdag has also established various specialized courts to deal with conflicts that arise outside normal civil and criminal jurisdiction. They include the fiscal courts of appeal, the supreme administrative court, the labor court, and a market court. The purpose of the latter is to help enforce the Competition Act of 1982, which the Riksdag implemented to prohibit restrictive business practices.

The Ombudsmen

A distinctive Swedish institution that serves as an important legislative control device over administrative behavior is the parliamentary ombudsman (*justitieombudsman,* or JO for short). The office was created under the constitution of 1809 as a means to prevent the potential abuse of executive-administrative power. Elected for a four-year term by the Riksdag, the *justitieombudsman* is accorded legal autonomy to investigate internal records of all state agencies (including the central administrative boards, courts, the military, and county and local governments) in an effort to determine whether public officials are guilty of violating constitutional or statutory law. A JO may undertake such investigations either on his own initiative or in response to complaints by individual citizens.

Through the years, the JO's caseload has increased so substantially that the office has been steadily expanded. In 1915 a military ombudsman was added. In 1968 the two offices were merged and three ombudsmen were established in their place, each with equal legal competence. A fourth ombudsman was added in 1976.

The ombudsmen review approximately 3,500 cases a year, most of which are filed by private citizens. Only a handful ultimately result in a formal reprimand or prosecution through the courts. In 1979–80, for instance, the ombudsmen initiated disciplinary action against offending officials in only six cases. Nonetheless, 417 milder rebukes and 13 public pronouncements served as a sobering reminder to all public officials that scrupulous obedience of the law remains a fundamental principle of Swedish political life.[14]

Corporatism and Swedish Democracy

The distribution of political power in Sweden thus corresponds to Stein Rokkan's concept of a "two-tiered system of decision-making," which he used in the mid-1960s to describe neighboring Norway.[15] The first tier consists of popularly elected members of the parliament and the county and municipal assemblies, which are responsible for formulating and ratifying government policy. The second tier of decision makers encompasses representatives of the principal organized interest groups and the public administration, who are accorded a recognized policy role through their participation in state commissions and the *remiss* consultative procedure.

The sum of these arrangements is a form of democratic corporatism characterized by institutional openness and broad group participation in the policy process. Coupled with the strength of the Social Democratic party and organized labor (described in the following chapter), democratic corporatism facilitated efforts by political and group leaders to sustain a pattern of active system change throughout much of the postwar era.

Notes

1. Four documents constitute the composite Swedish constitution. They include the aforementioned Instrument of Government and the Riksdag Act, as well as the Act of Succession and the Freedom of the Press Act. They are compiled in English translation in the Swedish Riksdag, *Constitutional Documents of Sweden* (Stockholm: Norstedts Tryckeri, 1975).

2. Under the Sainte-Laguë method of proportional representation, which was adopted in 1952, the total of the votes for each party in a given electoral district is divided by a succession of uneven numbers, and seats are awarded to the highest quotients obtained among the various parties. For a detailed discussion of Swedish electoral law, see Dankwart A. Rustow, *The Politics of Compromise* (Princeton, N.J.: Princeton University Press, 1955), 123–28.

3. To date, no votes of no confidence have been held.

4. Statistiska centralbyrån, *Statistisk årsbok för Sverige 1991* (Stockholm, 1991), 404.

5. National referenda have been conducted on four policy issues: prohibition (in 1922, which failed), a switch from left- to right-hand traffic (in 1955, which also failed but was nonetheless implemented by the Riksdag in 1977), supplementary pensions (1957), and nuclear energy (1980). The latter two measures are discussed below. A national referendum is likely to be held during the mid-1990s on prospective Swedish membership in the European Community.

6. In practice, the committee has not initiated formal charges against a cabinet member since 1854. Statistiska centralbyrån, *Statistisk årsbok för Sverige 1981* (Stockholm, 1981), 429.

7. Bengt Owe Birgersson and Jörgen Westerståhl, *Den svenska folkstyrelsen,* (Stockholm: Liber Förlag, 1982), 171. Recent trends include a gradual reduction in the number of bills submitted to parliament by the government (which declined from 225 in 1984–85 to 159 in 1989–90) and an increase in the number of private members' bills (which rose from 3,245 to 4,849 during the same period). The Riksdag endorses nearly all cabinet proposals, while most private members' bills are dismissed in committee.

8. Statistiska centralbyrån, *Statistisk årsbok för Sverige 1991* (Stockholm, 1991), 404.

9. Birgerson and Westerståhl, *Den svenska folkstryrelsen*, 171.

10. Thomas J. Anton, *Administered Politics: Elite Political Culture in Sweden* (Boston: Martinus Nijhoff, 1980), 5.

11. Statistiska centralbyrån, *Statistisk årsbok för Sverige 1990* (Stockholm, 1990), 231.

12. Contrary to the practice of the British Labour party and the French Socialists, Sweden's Social Democrats have nationalized very little industry. Instead, the SAP has relied much more on a combination of fiscal, monetary, and active labor-market policies to achieve its economic objectives of continued growth and full employment. In ironic contrast, the non-socialist parties nationalized the shipbuilding industry while they were in office from 1976 to 1982 in an attempt to salvage the branch in the face of increased international competition. See chapter 24.

13. *Statistisk årsbok för Sverige 1990*, 338–40.

14. The annual statistical yearbook no longer contains detailed summaries of JO activities. In 1991, the Statistical Office reported only that 3,054 cases were entered in 1988–89. Of these, individual citizens initiated 2,855 and the various ombudsmen instigated 163. *Statistisk årsbok för Sverige 1991*, 343.

15. Stein Rokkan, "Norway: Numerical Democracy and Corporate Pluralism," in *Political Oppositions in Western Democracies*, ed. Robert Dahl (New Haven: Yale University Press, 1966), 107.

23

Who Has the Power and How Did They Get It?

The capacity to participate in policy decisions in Sweden is shared by political parties, organized interest groups, and administrative elites. Of these diverse political actors, parties and interest groups have played the key role in initiating systemic reforms as well as basic policy decisions, including political democratization, the rise of the welfare state, the extension of worker rights, and ongoing changes in the political management of the economy. Administrative elites, in contrast, are significant with respect to policy refinement, continuity, and implementation.

Political Parties

From the early part of the twentieth century through most of the 1980s, Sweden sustained a multiparty system consisting of five major parties: a small Left party (formerly the Communists), the far larger Social Democrats, the Liberals, the agrarian-based Center party, and the Moderates (Conservatives). A sixth political movement, known as the "Environmentalist party–the Greens," became in September 1988 the first new party to enter the Riksdag in seventy years. In the September 1991 election the Greens lost their parliamentary mandate, but two other minor parties succeeded in gaining representation in the Riksdag: the conservative Christian Democratic Union and a "new-right" movement, New Democracy, which advocated substantial tax cuts and other radical reforms. Hence, Sweden's party system has begun in recent years to resemble the more complex multiparty systems of neighboring Denmark, Norway, and Finland.

Party fragmentation in Sweden has not meant political stalemate or parliamentary immobilism, as was true in the final years of the Weimar Republic of Germany and frequently in postwar Italy and the Third and Fourth republics of France. Instead, Sweden's multiparty system has proved capable of sustaining stable governments and adapting to changing economic and social conditions. The principal explanation lies in the persistence of loosely united socialist and nonsocialist blocs that partially blunt the parliamentary effects of party fragmentation. The Social Democrats and Left party are popularly identified as the socialist bloc because they usually vote together on most legislative matters, while the Liberals, the Center, the Moderates, and the Christian Democrats constitute the nonsocialist bloc. During the 1989–91 legislative session, the Greens were officially unaligned but generally sided with the Social Democrats, just as New Democracy tacitly supports the other nonsocialist parties in the Riksdag elected in September 1991. The existence of opposing socialist and nonsocialist alignments thus partially blunts the parliamentary effects of structural fragmentation by facilitating legislation and the formation of majority-backed governments.

The Social Democrats

The Swedish Social Democratic Workers' party (Socialdemokraterna—SAP) is both Sweden's oldest political party (founded in 1889) and, since 1917, its largest. The party was initially established to represent working-class political and economic interests with respect to suffrage reform, the introduction of parliamentarianism, and improved working conditions and social services. With time, the party extended its appeal to middle-class voters as well. Thanks to the success of its economic and social policies after 1932, the SAP increased its popular support from 38 percent in the 1920s to an average of nearly 47 percent during the 1930s and 1940s. From 1948 through 1991, the party has averaged 45 percent of the popular vote in successive national elections. Its postwar peak came in 1968 when the SAP received 50.1 percent; in the September 1991 election the party received 37.6 percent to plummet to its lowest level of support since 1928 (see table 23.1, page 413).

The SAP's principal ideological commitment comparable to that of other West European democratic socialist parties is to collective measures designed to enhance individual economic and social security and the equality of opportunity. Social Democratic leaders have pursued these objectives through economic policies designed to promote material growth and full employment, parliamentary action (e.g., in the form of welfare legislation, educational reforms, and the extension of worker

TABLE 23.1

ELECTION RESULTS, 1914–91[a]

Year	Type[b]	VP	MP	SAP	FP	C	M[b]	KDS	NYD
1914	R			36.4	26.9	.2	36.5		
1917	R			39.2	27.6	8.5	24.7		
1919	C			36.3	25.4	13.2	24.9		
1920	R			36.1	21.8	14.2	27.9		
1921	R	4.6		39.4	19.1	11.1	25.8		
1922	C	4.5		34.7	17.1	11.9	31.8		
1924	R	5.1		41.1	16.9	10.8	26.1		
1926	C	4.1		39.0	16.1	11.7	28.9		
1928	R	6.4		37.0	15.9	11.2	29.4		
1930	C	4.0		41.4	13.5	12.5	28.4		
1932	R	8.3		41.7	11.7	14.1	23.5		
1934	C	6.8		42.1	12.5	13.3	24.2		
1936	R	7.7		45.9	12.9	14.3	17.6		
1938	C	5.7		50.4	12.2	12.6	17.8		
1940	R	4.2		53.8	12.0	12.0	18.0		
1942	C	5.9		50.3	12.4	13.2	17.6		
1944	R	10.3		46.7	12.9	13.6	15.9		
1946	C	11.2		44.4	15.6	13.6	14.9		
1948	R	6.3		46.2	22.8	12.4	12.3		
1950	C	4.9		48.6	21.7	12.3	12.3		
1952	R	4.3		46.1	24.4	10.7	14.4		
1954	C	4.8		47.4	21.7	10.3	15.7		
1956	R	5.0		44.6	23.8	9.4	17.1		
1958	R	3.4		46.2	18.2	12.7	19.5		
1958	C	4.0		46.8	15.6	13.1	20.4		
1960	R	4.5		47.8	17.5	13.6	16.5		
1962	C	3.8		50.5	17.1	13.1	15.5		
1964	R	5.2		47.3	17.0	13.2	13.7		
1966	C	6.4		42.2	16.7	13.7	14.7		
1968	R	3.0		50.1	14.3	15.7	12.9		
1970	R	4.8		45.3	16.2	19.9	11.5		
1973	R	5.3		43.6	9.4	25.1	14.3		
1976	R	4.8		42.7	11.1	24.1	15.6	1.4	
1979	R	5.6		43.2	10.6	18.1	20.3	1.4	
1982	R	5.6		45.6	5.9	15.5	23.6	1.9	
1985	R	5.4		44.7	14.2	12.4	21.3		
1988	R	5.7	5.5	43.9	12.0	11.9	17.9	2.9	
1991	R	4.5	3.4	37.6	9.2	8.4	21.9	7.0	6.7

a. Party abbreviations: VP = Left party (Communists); MP = Greens; SAP = Social Democratic party; FP = Liberals; C = Center; M = Moderates (Conservatives); KDS = Christian Democrats; NYD = New Democracy.

b. Type of election: R refers to Riksdag (parliamentary) elections; C refers to communal (county and municipal) elections.

rights), and trade union negotiations with employer associations on the labor market (see below).

A distinctive feature of Swedish social democracy is that the movement emerged simultaneously with organized liberalism during the latter part of the nineteenth century. Because both parties were intent on achieving similar political objectives, they were able to cooperate during the formative decades of industrialization and democratization rather than engage in fratricidal conflict (as was the case with competing Liberal and Social Democratic parties in much of continental Europe). This historical legacy has contributed to the emergence of Sweden's largely consensual political culture.

The SAP is also distinguished by a tradition of stable leadership. Since the party was founded, only five men have served as chairman: Hjalmar Branting (1889–1926), Per Albin Hansson (1926–46), Tage Erlander (1946–69), Olof Palme (1969–86), and Ingvar Carlsson (1986–   ). Each leader has been an able parliamentarian and adept at forging unity among diverse party factions, thereby enhancing the party's claim to long-term executive competence.

A major strength of the Social Democratic party is its close organizational link with the Swedish Federation of Trade Unions (Landsorganisationen—LO). Through a combination of overlapping leadership on the party's Executive Committee and rank-and-file membership between the unions and the party, the LO contributes important policy initiatives as well as the bulk of the SAP's electoral support. Unions also provide a major share of SAP financial contributions.

The Left Party

Similar to other European communist movements, the Swedish Communist party was formed in the aftermath of the Bolshevik revolution in 1917 as a leftist offshoot of the Social Democrats. Unlike most of their continental counterparts, Sweden's Communists have maintained a tradition of ideological independence of the Soviet Union rooted in their country's historical antipathy toward Russia and prevailing political cultural values of moderation and pragmatism. A Stalinist faction exists within the party, but it is eclipsed by a revisionist (Eurocommunist) majority that affirms Western-style parliamentary democracy and individual civil liberties. A small group of hard-core Stalinists broke with the party to form a separate Swedish Communist party in 1977, but thus far they have failed to attract appreciable electoral support.

Party leaders adopted the name of Left party–Communists (Vänsterpartiet-kommunisterna) and a new party program in 1967 in an effort to affirm their allegiance to democratic norms. Left party activists define themselves as a radical alternative to Social Democracy through their ideological critique of capitalism and their advocacy of state ownership of key industries, banks, and insurance companies. In 1990 party leaders dropped the designation "Communist" altogether and shortened the official party name to Left party (Vänsterpartiet—VP) in an effort to distance themselves from discredited Marxist-Leninist regimes in Eastern and Central Europe. The VP draws most of its electoral support from among industrial workers and intellectuals. Since World War II, the Left's share of the popular vote has fluctuated between a high of 6.3 percent (1948) to a low of 3.4 percent (1958), for a postwar average of 4.9 percent.

Given its minuscule size, the VP's only hope of affecting policy outcomes is through a tactical alliance with the Social Democrats in the Riksdag. Thus, party deputies have usually supported SAP parliamentary initiatives (or at least have abstained in crucial votes) and thereby have helped ensure the continuance of Social Democratic governance throughout most of the postwar era.

The Environmentalist Party—the Greens

Also identified as a "left" party but with a much less clearly defined ideological profile than either the VP or the Social Democrats are the Greens. Officially, the movement calls itself the Environmentalist party —the Greens (Milj partiet De Gröna, abbreviated MP). The movement was founded during the early 1980s in emulation of similar parties in Germany and neighboring Finland and Denmark. By mid-decade the Greens had succeeded in winning seats on more than half of Sweden's city and county councils, and in September 1988 they made their first entrance into parliament with 5.5 percent of the popular vote.

Similar to their counterparts in other West European countries, the Greens stress measures to protect the natural environment and promote the socioeconomic interests of less privileged groups. Accordingly, during the 1988 campaign they advocated an end to the use of nuclear energy, the introduction of new taxes on energy use and factory and automobile emissions, and tax cuts for lower-income workers. They also urged a ban on new highway construction in favor of increased reliance on the nation's extensive railway system.

The Greens are a highly heterogeneous movement. They attract most of their members and voters from among younger, better-educated, and urban citizens. They are led by a committee made up of rotating members, with no spokesperson standing out as a discernible leader. Twenty MP deputies served in the Riksdag from September 1988 until the September 1991 election, when the Greens received only 3.4 percent of the popular vote and thereby failed to win sufficient support to remain in parliament.

The Nonsocialist Bloc

The fragmentation of Sweden's nonsocialist forces has inhibited the emergence of a cohesive alternative to Social Democracy comparable to the Conservative party in Britain or the Christian Democrats in Germany and Italy. Nonetheless, leaders of the Liberal, Center, and Moderate parties forged a limited form of bourgeois unity that enabled them to displace the Social Democrats in executive office from 1976 to 1982. The nonsocialist parties once again won a majority in the September 1991 election and formed a new governing coalition.

The Liberals

The Liberals were the smallest bourgeois party from 1968 until the parliamentary election of September 1985, when they scored a substantial advance to become the second largest nonsocialist party. In subsequent elections the Liberals have lost electoral support but remain second in size to the Moderates within the nonsocialist bloc (see table 23.1, page 413).

Their literal name, Folkpartiet (People's party), suggests the Liberals' simultaneous strength and weakness. As a broadly based movement appealing variously to businessmen, workers, intellectuals, prohibitionists, and free thinkers, the Liberals have at times been Sweden's largest nonsocialist party. They peaked at 40 percent of the popular vote in 1911, fell below Conservative strength during the 1930s and early 1940s, and then resumed their dominant status among the nonsocialist parties from 1948 until 1958. At the same time, the very diversity of the Liberals' popular support makes them highly vulnerable to electoral shifts within the nonsocialist bloc. Thus, from 1958 through the mid-1980s, the Liberals lost votes to both the Center and the Moderates, declining to a historical low of 5.9 percent in 1982. Their resurgence in 1985 was, in turn, primarily at the expense of the other two nonsocialist parties.

The Liberals' support of suffrage reform and parliamentarianism enabled them to play an important role, through cooperation with the Social Democrats, in achieving Sweden's democratization. They lost votes to the left during the 1920s and 1930s because of their opposition to an active government role in the economy and society. Under new leadership, the Liberals dramatically increased their electoral support in the late 1940s by endorsing the Social Democrats' social program while simultaneously advocating greater individual economic freedom. Their recovery was halted in 1958 when they proposed a compromise solution to a controversy over supplementary pensions that failed to satisfy either the left or right (see below).

Liberal spokesmen have contributed significantly to the nonsocialist critique of centralizing tendencies within government and the economy, even though the party itself has suffered recurrent electoral losses in recent decades. In an attempt to assure the party's survival in the light of the 4 percent minimum threshold for parliamentary representation, Liberal deputies elected a new chairman in October 1983: Bengt Westerberg, a former state secretary in the Department of Finance and an acknowledged party moderate. Westerberg's factual and pragmatic style of leadership contributed to the Liberals' advance during the mid-1980s.

The Center Party

The Center party (Centerpartiet) is more solidly anchored than the Liberals in terms of socioeconomic support. Yet, like the Folkpartiet, the Center is vulnerable to recurrent electoral shifts. Founded in 1921 as the Farmers' party (a successor organization to several nineteenth-century ruralist movements), the Center adopted its present name in 1959 along with a more broadly based program emphasizing the need for economic decentralization and a more humane urban environment. The party's transformation coincided with increased public concern about ecological issues as symbolically expressed by the advent of a popularly based *gröna vågen* (green wave). The result was an increase in electoral support, primarily at the expense of the Liberals. Center strength rose from 9.4 percent in 1956 to an average of 14 percent during the 1960s and a peak of 25 percent in 1973. Most of the increase was due to the party's strategic success in expanding its appeal from farmers (who still contribute a quarter of the party's support) to include blue- and white-collar workers (who together make up 42 percent of Center voters). Like the Liberals, the Center has subsequently lost support to the Moderates. Party strength began to decline in 1976 and in 1991 fell to 8.4 percent.

Recent fluctuations in the Center's electoral fortunes reflect the party's stand on policy issues. Increased Center support in the 1976 election, for example, was attributed primarily to Chairman Thorbjörn Fälldin's opposition to an expansion of Sweden's nuclear energy program as a central plank in the party's pro-ecological stance. Conversely, the party's electoral declines in 1979 and 1982 were related to an interim resolution of the nuclear energy conflict in 1980 (see below) and the Center's subsequent failure to identify new policy issues as a basis for mobilizing continued popular support.

Largely in response to the party's recent electoral decline, Fälldin resigned under pressure as Center chairman in 1986. He was succeeded by Karin Söder, former foreign minister and the first woman to head a major Swedish political party. Söder subsequently stepped down a year later because of ill health; she was succeeded by Olof Johansson, party secretary and a specialist in economics.

The Moderates

Since 1979 the largest of Sweden's nonsocialist parties, the Moderates (Moderaterna) have consistently offered policies clearly alternatives to those of the Social Democrats. Among their chief demands are tax reductions, deregulation of private enterprise, and the partial privatization of education and childcare services. The Moderates also strongly oppose measures undertaken by the LO and the SAP during the 1970s and 1980s to extend the collective economic influence of organized labor (see below).

The Moderates are linear descendants of nineteenth-century bureaucratic-economic conservatives, who initially opposed democratization. Their ideological forebears nonetheless, to ensure the political survival of Swedish Conservatism, endorsed the introduction of manhood suffrage in the Great Compromise of 1907–9 in exchange for proportional representation. Separate party organizations were established in the former upper and lower houses of parliament in 1912; they were known as the National party and the Ruralist and Citizens' party, respectively. The two factions merged in 1935 as "the Right" (Högern), a term utilized throughout Scandinavia from the mid-nineteenth century onward to designate Conservatives.

From the 1930s through the 1950s, the Right distinguished itself primarily by its opposition to the Social Democrats' activist economic and social policies. As a consequence, the party steadily lost popular support. Its share of the national vote fell from 29.4 percent in 1928 to an average of 20.6 percent during the 1930s and 15.4 percent in the 1940s.

Conservative strength rose marginally during the 1950s (to 17.3 percent) under the articulate leadership of a new chairman, Gunnar Heckscher, a political scientist at the University of Stockholm, who sought to establish a more positive party profile. His successors have pursued a similar strategy, with the adoption of the party's present name and a progressive program in 1969 signaling a determined effort by Conservative spokesmen to adjust the party's image and ideology to changing economic and social conditions. Thus, the Moderates have embraced a more positive view toward government intervention in the economy and society while defending principles of private ownership and political decentralization.

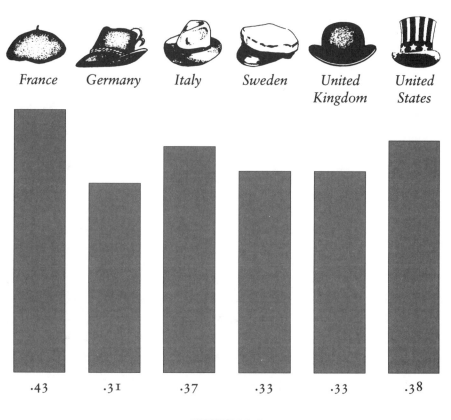

FIGURE 23.1

INEQUALITY INDEX

NOTE: A measure of the extent to which the income distribution departs from perfect equality. The higher the number, the more unequal the distribution.

The Moderates' dual emphasis on economic individualism and the government's responsibility to enable "all persons, to the greatest possible extent, to live well both physically and psychologically under socially equitable conditions"[1] has facilitated the party's recent electoral recovery. Its strength increased from 11.5 percent in 1970 to 14.3 percent in 1973 and continued to climb through the 1982 election. The party lost support in 1985 and 1988 but regained strength in September 1991 when it received 21.9 percent of the popular vote. The Moderates displaced the Center as the largest nonsocialist party in 1979.

The chairman of the Moderates is Carl Bildt, who was elected in 1986 on the basis of his experience as a former political secretary and coordinator for nonsocialist governmental cooperation in 1979–81. In October 1991 Bildt became Sweden's first conservative prime minister in sixty years when the nonsocialists formed a four-party coalition following the September election (see below).

Christian Democrats and New Democracy

Sweden's newest political parties in parliament are the Christian Democratic Union (Kristlig demokratisk samling—KDS) and New Democracy (Ny Demokrati). Both are more conservative on social and economic issues than the three older nonsocialist parties, with the Christian Democrats resolutely affirming traditional values of family and Christian morality and New Democracy advocating deep tax cuts and a sweeping reduction in the size of the public sector.

The Christian Democrats established themselves as a national political party in the 1960s on the model of Christian Peoples' parties in neighboring Denmark and Norway. Its programmatic sobriety appealed to fundamentalist voters, but its organizational weakness and lack of a solid socioeconomic base restricted its initial electoral advances to local and provincial assemblies. The party sought to legitimize its claim to national office through a tactical electoral alliance in 1985 and 1988 with the Center, and in September 1991 finally managed to surpass the minimum threshold for representation in the Riksdag when it won 4.1 percent of the vote. Contributing to its electoral success was widespread public confidence in the party chair, Alf Svensson.

New Democracy is a self-proclaimed maverick in Swedish politics. The party was founded in late 1990 by two antiestablishment cultural figures: Bert Karlsson, an amusement park owner and publisher of popular music, and Ian Wachtmeister, a satirist and industrialist who is a member of Sweden's minuscule aristocracy. Both leaders claim to speak for an emergent "new populism" that reflects a growing popular distrust of state bureaucrats and the high cost of government. In addition to its attacks on the state, New Democracy demands stiffer penalties for criminals and restrictions on rights of immigration. Ideologically, the party thus corresponds closely to other "new right" parties elsewhere in Europe including the Progress parties in Denmark and Norway, the National Front in France, and the Republikaner in Germany. New Democracy scored an overnight success in the September 1991 election by attracting the support of 6.7 percent of the electorate.

Interest Groups

Alongside Sweden's national parties, three organized interest associations stand out as major centers of political power: the National Federation of Trade Unions (LO), the Swedish Association of Employers (Svenska Arbetsgivareföreningen—SAF), and the Central Organization of Salaried Employees (Tjänstemännens Centralorganisation—TCO). Also important, though less influential than the preceding groups, are the Swedish Central Organization of University Graduates (SACO-SR), the National Association of Farmers (LRF), and the Swedish Cooperative Association (KF).[2]

The political significance of Sweden's principal organized interest groups lies foremost in their affiliation or alignment with important political parties and their participation in state commissions and the *remiss* consultative procedure, as described in the preceding chapter. In addition, the LO, the SAF, and their constituent organizations play an important role in economic and social outcomes through their direct negotiations with each other on the labor market. Employer groups and organized labor also participate in the formation and implementation of labor-market policy through their membership (along with government officials) in the National Labor Market Board (Arbetsmarknadsstyrelsen—AMS), which is discussed in the next chapter.

National Federation of Trade Unions (LO)

The most important labor association is the LO, which was founded in 1898 as a federation of local and regional craft (later, industrial) unions. Since then, the federation has grown to encompass twenty-three national trade unions that together claim as members 54 percent of Sweden's total labor force (2.3 million workers out of 4.5 million in 1989). The LO's largest constituent units are the Association of Local Government Workers with 634,000 members and the Metal Workers' Union with 466,000 (1986).[3]

As previously noted, the LO is closely linked with the SAP through a combination of overlapping leadership and the collective membership of most rank-and-file union members in the party. Its affiliation with the Social Democratic party has enabled LO leaders to initiate a number of significant legislative measures in recent decades. As discussed below, these have primarily involved extensions in the rights of individual workers and unions at the workplace.

In its simultaneous role as Sweden's principal bargaining agent on behalf of higher wages and improved working conditions, the LO until recently negotiated directly with the Association of Employers (SAF) to establish annual framework agreements covering all its member unions. This practice, which was inaugurated in the 1950s, was abandoned in 1983 when the Metal Workers' Union negotiated its own wage pact. The LO remains responsible for coordinating the overall negotiation process, but actual agreements now tend to be reached on an industry-by-industry basis. Both union leaders and employers have welcomed the return to a more decentralized system of wage negotiations on the grounds that it permits greater flexibility.

Throughout the postwar period, the LO and its member unions have pursued a largely cooperative strategy in their relations with the SAF. As a result, Sweden has sustained one of the world's lowest levels of industrial conflicts. A major exception was a protracted dispute over wages in 1980 that resulted in a national lockout by the SAF and a retaliatory strike by the LO affecting nearly a million workers. The country was virtually paralyzed for three days before the two labor-market partners agreed on a compromise solution.[4] Since then, organized labor and employers have succeeded in reaching wage agreements with a minimum of open strife.

The pattern of peaceful labor relations is rooted in two important historical accords: (1) the Collective Agreements Act of 1928, which prohibited strikes and lockouts over the interpretation of wage contracts and required that they be settled instead by a newly created Labor Court; and (2) the "Saltsjöbaden Agreement" of 1938, which was negotiated by the SAF and the LO and established a consensual framework governing wage negotiation and grievance procedures.

The Central Organization of Salaried Employees (TCO)

Sweden's second most important labor organization is the TCO (Tjänstemännens Centralorganisation). Representing primarily white-collar workers, the TCO consists of twenty-one national unions that together claim nearly 1.3 million members (1989). Slightly more than half of its membership is employed in the public sector on either the national or regional/local levels of government; the remainder work for private firms.[5]

The TCO comprises a more heterogeneous clientele than the LO. As a result, its leaders studiously pursue an official strategy of "neutrality" in their relations with the principal political parties rather than one of alignment or affiliation. In practice, however, the TCO cooperates closely with the LO in promoting bread-and-butter economic issues such as annual wage increments on behalf of its members. As a result, the TCO leadership is inclined, on balance, to endorse SAP legislative initiatives more than those of the nonsocialist parties. One consequence is that the Social Democrats tapped the TCO chairman, Lennart Broström, to become foreign minister after their electoral victory in September 1982. Broström later shifted cabinet seats to assume duties as minister of education in 1988.

Association of Employers (SAF)

The SAF (Svenska Arbetsgivareföreningen) was founded in 1902 as a counterpart employer organization to the LO. Similar to both the LO and the TCO, the SAF is a national federation made up of constituent parts (in its case, branch associations of industrial and service firms). Its membership in 1989 consisted of 46,000 companies represented in the national organization through thirty-two branch associations. The largest corporate members are those involved in manufacturing, commerce, and forestry.[6]

Like the LO, the SAF has a dual identity. On the labor market, the SAF and its branch associations are responsible for negotiating wage and related agreements with organized labor as described above. Politically, the SAF is closely aligned with the nonsocialist bloc, especially the Moderates. Through a combination of research and publication activities, publicity campaigns, its participation in government commissions and the *remiss* procedure, and lobbying efforts vis-à-vis the cabinet and parliament, the SAF seeks to maximize employer influence in policy outcomes. In recent years, the SAF has concentrated on tax reform, wage restraint, and a largely unsuccessful campaign to impede Social Democratic–LO initiatives to extend the formal power of unions in economic decisions.

Overlapping in large part with the SAF is a second employer association: the Swedish Federation of Industry (Svenska Indistriförbundet

—SIF). The SIF concentrates on promoting economic, trade, and environmental policies favorable to business interests.

Administrative Elites

High-level civil servants (i.e., the administrative elites who manage the planning and budgetary processes within the various cabinet-level departments) are also instrumental actors in Sweden's policy process. Unlike leaders of the various parties and interest groups, they are not politically accountable to the public at large or organizational members. Instead, they exercise power on the basis of their academic qualifications, institutional status, and bureaucratic skills. As such, Sweden's departmental bureaucrats are a principal source of empirical information, technical expertise, and long-range reform perspectives.

As Thomas Anton observes in his assessment of elite political culture in Sweden, the administrative elites who constitute the ministerial departments in Stockholm are distinctive in comparative perspective primarily because of their close personal interaction "in a world that is small, comfortable, well-understood, and highly specialized;" their social skills, coupled with a pragmatic orientation toward people and problem solving; and their formal participation alongside politicians and interest-group representatives on Sweden's myriad state commissions.[7] Together, these personal and institutional attributes of the administrative elites contribute significantly to Sweden's highly deliberative and rational mode of policy making.

Elections

Electoral outcomes determine whether the socialist or nonsocialist bloc—and therefore indirectly which organized interest groups—dominates the legislative agenda. Between elections, the composition of the cabinet and interparty as well as intergroup bargaining determine the specific content of policy choice.

Sweden is the only country among the five nations presented in this volume that has held competitive elections on schedule throughout the twentieth century. Even the onset of World Wars I and II did not cause political leaders to postpone national elections. From democratization through 1968, Riksdag elections were held every four years (except for a special dissolution election in 1958). Elections to county and city assemblies were also conducted at four-year intervals, albeit midway through each legislative session. Thus the Swedes voted every two years, alternating between Riksdag and county/local elections. The election dates were merged through the constitutional reforms of 1968–69 (effective in 1970) that reduced the terms of national and regional office from four to three years.

Electoral outcomes are associated with three distinctive stages in Swedish parliamentary development. The first was one of "minority parliamentarianism," which spanned the years from 1920 to 1932 and was characterized by the absence of stable legislative majorities by a single party or governing coalition. The Social Democrats' advance in the 1932 election inaugurated a shift toward "majority parliamentarianism," which involved forty-four years of informal and formal coalitions between the SAP and other parties alternating with periods of a Social Democratic legislative majority. Since 1976, Sweden has experienced more indeterminate electoral results resulting in the formation of successive majority and minority cabinets and an alteration of executive power between the Social Democrats and the nonsocialists.

The Social Democrats have consistently remained Sweden's largest political party since 1917 (see table 23.1, page 413). Their strength has peaked during two electoral cycles: in the late 1930s–early 1940s and briefly in the 1960s. Within the nonsocialist bloc considerable electoral fluctuations have occurred over time. The Liberals relinquished their dominant status to the Conservatives in the aftermath of World War II but regained it from the mid-1940s through the mid-1960s. From then through the early 1980s the Center and the Moderates vied for leadership among the nonsocialist forces; subsequently, the Liberals displaced the Center as the second largest nonsocialist party.

The emergence of a shared sense of nonsocialist identity among the Liberal, Center, and Moderate parties during the 1960s effectively transformed the conditions of electoral competition. Henceforth, bloc rather than merely party outcomes became decisive for determining government formation and the thrust of policy decisions. An increase in aggregate nonsocialist strength from the communal election of 1966 onward, as indicated in table 23.2 (page 426), thus enhanced bloc competitiveness between the socialist and nonsocialist parties and presaged later shifts in executive leadership. Recent electoral advances by the Christian Democrats and New Democracy contributed to a discernible increase in aggregate nonsocialist strength in 1991.

Continuity and change characterize recent electoral behavior. Each party retains an identifiable core of supporters, as noted in table 23.3 (page 427). Both the Social Democrats and the Left party draw most of their support from among workers and lower-level salaried employees; the Liberals recruit broadly among all major occupational groups; the

TABLE 23.2

BLOC ALIGNMENTS, 1966–91

Year	Type of election[a]	Socialist parties[b]	Nonsocialist parties[c]
1958	C	50.8	49.1
1960	C	52.3	47.6
1962	C	54.3	45.7
1964	R	52.5	43.9
1966	C	48.6	45.1
1968	R	53.1	42.9
1970	R	50.1	47.6
1973	R	48.9	48.8
1976	R	47.5	50.8
1979	R	48.8	49.0
1982	R	51.2	45.0
1985	R	50.1	47.9
1988	R	49.6	41.8
1991	R	42.1	55.5

a. Type of election: R = Riksdag; C = Communal.

b. Combined support for the VP and the SAP; excludes the MP.

c. Excludes support for the KDS except for 1985 and 1988 when the Center and the KDS formed an electoral alliance.

Center draws most of its support from among farmers, workers, and civil servants; and the Moderates attract the bulk of their voters among businessmen and higher- and medium-level civil servants.

At the same time, new political issues have motivated many voters (especially younger ones) to abandon their occupational or class identities to vote across party or bloc lines. Among such issues are nuclear energy, environmental concerns, and both economic and social policy. Increased electoral volatility has contributed in turn to discontinuities in executive leadership from the mid-1970s onward.

Governments and Opposition

From 1932 into the 1991–94 legislative session, thirteen distinct coalitions or single-party governments have held executive office (see table 23.4, page 427). The Social Democrats controlled the cabinet, either

TABLE 23.3

DISTRIBUTION OF ELECTORAL SUPPORT
BY OCCUPATION, IN PERCENT

Occupational group	VP	SAP	FP	C	M	Others
Industrial workers	5	71	5	12	5	2
Other workers	5	62	8	15	8	2
Lower-level white-collar workers	3	42	16	12	24	3
Middle-level white-collar workers	8	36	14	15	25	2
Higher-level white-collar workers	3	20	20	10	46	1
Businessmen	5	20	14	19	40	2
Farmers	0	7	5	65	23	0
Students	19	25	7	21	22	6

SOURCE: Adapted from Søren Holmberg, *Svenska väljare* (Stockholm: Liber Förlag, 1981), 300.

TABLE 23.4

GOVERNMENT FORMATION, 1932–91

Years	Composition[a]	Prime minister and party
1932–36	SAP	Hansson (SAP)
1936	C	Pehrsson i Bramstorp (C)
1936–39	SAP-C	Hansson (SAP)
1939–45	SAP-C-FP-M	Hansson (SAP)
1945–51	SAP	Hansson/Erlander (SAP)
1951–57	SAP-C	Erlander (SAP)
1957–76	SAP	Erlander/Palme (SAP)
1976–78	C-FP-M	Fälldin (C)
1978–79	FP	Ullsten (FP)
1979–81	C-FP-M	Fälldin (C)
1981–82	C-FP	Fälldin (C)
1982–91	SAP	Palme/Carlsson (SAP)
1991–	M-FP-C-KDS	Bildt (M)

a. Party abbreviations: SAP = Social Democratic party; FP = Liberals; C = Center party; M = Moderates ; KDS = Christian Democrats alone or in coalition with one or more of the nonsocialist parties, between 1932 and 1976. A succession of nonsocialist cabinets governed from 1976 to 1982: first, a three-party coalition led by the Center, then a Liberal minority cabinet, next a restored three-party coalition, and finally a Center-Liberal minority coalition. The Social Democrats resumed executive leadership following the 1982 parliamentary election. They lacked an absolute majority but could rely, depending on the policy issue at stake, on either the VP, the Greens (after 1988), and/or one or more of the nonsocialist parties to enact their legislative agenda. In October 1991 a four-party coalition was formed consisting of the Moderates, the Liberals, the Center, and the Christian Democrats that is tacitly supported by New Democracy.

Long-term Social Democratic governance, interrupted by the nonsocialist interregnum from 1976 to 1982 and the formation of a four-party nonsocialist government in 1991, thus distinguishes Swedish politics from that of other advanced industrial democracies. The SAP has utilized its executive status to pursue a succession of transforming and often controversial policy initiatives that constitute a long-term pattern of breakthrough politics. Perceived shortcomings of this strategy have prompted growing citizen dissatisfaction and increased electoral support for nonsocialist alternatives.

Notes

1. Moderata samlingsparti, "Program," Stockholm, 1969, 12.

2. The latter organizations are discussed more fully in Nils Elvander, *Intresseorganisationerna i dagens Sverige,* 2d ed. (Lund: CWK Gleerup Bokförlag, 1969).

3. Statistiska centralbyrån, *Statistisk årsbok för Sverige 1991* (Stockholm, 1991), 200.

4. The best summary and analysis of the conflict is Anders Broström, ed., *Storkonflikten 1980* (Stockholm: Arbetslivscentrum, 1981).

5. *Statistisk årsbok för Sverige 1991,* 200.

6. Ibid.

7. Thomas J. Anton, *Administered Politics: Elite Political Culture in Sweden* (Boston: Martinus Nijhoff, 1980), esp. 129–57.

24

How Is Power Used?

Qualities of pragmatism and a willingness to seek compromise solutions to partisan differences coupled with Sweden's highly institutionalized system of democratic corporatism have facilitated a consensual approach to many aspects of both domestic and foreign policy. Thus, leaders of the major political parties, SAF, the LO, and other organized interest groups have jointly affirmed the constitutional reforms that modernized Swedish parliamentarianism in the 1970s, the need to sustain material growth on the basis of SAF-LO-TCO cooperation, an active labor-market policy, and neutrality. Within this broad consensus on fundamental principles of Swedish politics and economics, however, the socialist and nonsocialist blocs have simultaneously promoted competing ideological visions of system change. In short, power is used by political parties and organized interest groups on behalf of both shared and divergent socioeconomic objectives.

Among Sweden's key political actors, the Social Democrats and the LO have decisively influenced policy outcomes because of their numerical and organizational strength, the SAP's long-term parliamentary majority, and the fragmentation of the nonsocialist opposition. During their five decades of executive leadership (1932–76, 1982–91), the Social Democrats undertook major policy initiatives and systemic reforms that culminated in today's comprehensive welfare state. Many of the attributes associated with the Swedish model are products of the SAP-LO's strategic commitment to active system change, including the "historic compromise" between private capital and organized labor codified in the Saltsjöbaden agreement of 1938 and an overarching commitment to full employment and equality of opportunity for all citizens.

The nonsocialist parties, the SAF, and other organized groups have endorsed many of the SAP-LO innovations, but on important occasions they also resisted Social Democratic initiatives. With the maturation of the Swedish model during the 1960s and 1970s, the result has been a mixed record of economic and social performance accompanied by recurrent political conflict.

Economic Performance

Economic factors significantly enhanced the SAP's long-term claim to cabinet office. By introducing expansionist fiscal policies along Keynesian lines when they first came to power in the early 1930s, the Social Democrats helped engineer Sweden's recovery from the devastating effects of the prevailing international economic crisis. The advent of World War II led to a sharp reduction in trade and the introduction of rationing, as well as numerous economic controls that resulted in a temporary decline in the nation's standard of living. But from the late 1940s onward, Sweden, like most of Western Europe, North America, and Japan, experienced an unprecedented rate of economic growth and national prosperity. The upshot, as indicated in table 24.1, is that today Sweden claims a per capita income that is one of the highest among the world's industrial democracies.

TABLE 24.1

PER CAPITA GROSS NATIONAL PRODUCT, 1988
(AT CURRENT PRICES USING CURRENT
PURCHASING POWER PARITIES)

Country	Amount
Canada	$18,413
France	$13,577
Germany	$14,134
Italy	$12,960
Japan	$14,285
Sweden	$14,743
Switzerland	$16,641
United Kingdom	$13,402
United States	$19,558

SOURCE: OECD, *Economic Surveys 1991* (Paris, 1991).

Much of Sweden's postwar economic expansion is the result of external factors. Among them are American loans and grants to Sweden and other West European countries under the Marshall Plan (initiated in 1947), a rapid expansion of world trade from the early 1950s onward, and the success of the European Coal and Steel Community (founded in 1952) and the European Economic Community (established in 1957) in stimulating growth throughout Western Europe as a whole. Yet international economic trends alone do not account for other, more distinctive Swedish patterns of economic performance. Among them are one of the lowest unemployment rates among the industrial democracies and a long-term pattern of labor peace.

As seen in table 24.2 (page 432), Sweden's unemployment rate has fluctuated in recent years between a high of 3.5 percent in 1983 and a low of 1.4 percent in 1989, the former at a time when unemployment climbed to record postwar levels in Britain, France, Germany, Italy, and North America. Equally noteworthy, Sweden has experienced a comparatively low level of labor-management conflict. During the 1960s, workers went on strike an average of only 18 times a year, compared to an annual average of 166 times in Germany, 1,943 in France, 2,446 in Britain, and 4,107 in the United States. The number of strikes in Sweden increased during the 1970s to an annual average of 87. Yet even this figure is significantly lower than the annual averages during the same decade in other industrial democracies: 2,604 in Britain, 3,258 in France, and 5,249 in the United States.[1] During the 1980s, only Germany among the countries surveyed in this volume has maintained a record of less industrial conflict.[2]

Sweden's low levels of unemployment and industrial conflict have not been accidental. First, the SAP's largely sustained executive leadership from 1932 to 1976 and again from 1982 to 1991 facilitated long-term efforts to fine-tune the nation's economic performance through a combination of indicative economic planning (as opposed to command planning), short-term adjustments in fiscal and monetary policies, and government measures designed to encourage economic rationalization.[3] As a result, Sweden was spared abrupt changes in macroeconomic policy making associated with periodic shifts in power between conservative and socialist parties in postwar Britain and during the 1980s in France.

Second, the Social Democrats have utilized their executive status to promote an active labor-market policy in collaboration with their LO allies and the SAF. The concept of an active labor-market policy was originally formulated by several prominent LO economists during the 1950s and formally implemented by the Social Democrats in response

TABLE 24.2

UNEMPLOYMENT RATES, 1972–90

(STANDARDIZED RATES AS A PERCENTAGE OF TOTAL LABOR FORCE)

	1972	1975	1980	1981	1982	1983	1984	1985	1986	1987	1988	1989	1990
Canada	6.2	6.9	7.4	7.5	10.9	11.8	11.2	10.4	9.5	8.8	7.7	7.5	8.1
France	2.8	4.0	6.3	7.4	8.1	8.3	9.7	10.2	10.4	10.5	10.0	9.4	9.0
Germany	8.0	3.6	2.9	4.2	5.9	7.7	7.1	7.2	6.4	6.2	6.2	5.6	5.1
Italy	6.3	5.8	7.5	7.8	8.4	8.8	9.4	9.6	10.5	10.9	11.0	10.9	9.9
Japan	1.4	1.9	2.0	2.2	2.4	2.6	2.7	2.6	2.8	2.8	2.5	2.3	2.1
Sweden	2.7	1.6	2.0	2.5	3.2	2.5	3.1	2.8	2.7	1.9	1.6	1.4	1.5
United Kingdom	4.0	4.3	6.4	9.8	11.3	12.4	11.7	11.2	11.2	10.3	8.5	7.1	6.9
United States	5.5	8.3	7.0	7.5	9.5	9.5	7.4	7.1	6.9	6.1	5.4	5.2	5.4

SOURCE: OECD, *Economic Outlook July 1990* (Paris, 1990), 192.

to an economic slowdown during the late 1960s. In contrast to Keynesian theory and practice, which emphasize reliance on fiscal measures to combat unemployment, advocates of an active labor-market policy urged collaborative actions by administrative officials, unions, and employers to maintain or create jobs on the level of individual firms. A basic instrument for this purpose is the National Labor Market Board (AMS), which is composed of government, union, and employer representatives. The AMS coordinates public and private efforts to promote employment through a combination of training and retraining programs, the relocation of workers displaced when companies are forced to shut down, and temporary relief work. The government supplements the activities of the AMS and its decentralized network of county and local employment agencies by providing cash subsidies to companies willing to hire workers who might otherwise not be able to find a job, among them many young people and the handicapped. An important consequence of the active labor-market policy is that Sweden has far fewer people "on welfare" than is the case in the United States.

Augmenting Sweden's active labor-market policy are other political factors that have contributed specifically to labor peace. One is the numerical strength of the LO and its member unions, which has permitted organized labor to bargain effectively with employer groups on behalf of higher wages and improved working conditions, thereby lessening potential causes of employee dissatisfaction. A second is the pattern of institutionalized collaboration between employers and unions that has governed SAF-LO relations since their Saltsjöbaden agreement of 1938. The joint resolve by leaders of both associations to resolve differences with minimum government interference and, during the 1960s and 1970s, to negotiate nation-wide collective wage agreements, significantly facilitated labor-management cooperation. This does not mean that labor disputes do not occur in Sweden. As previously noted, a major wave of strikes and a national lockout by employers took place in May 1980, but the conflict proved shorter and less disruptive than comparable labor-management confrontations in most other industrial democracies.

The Welfare State: Achievements and Dissent

A crucial adjunct of the Social Democrats' emphasis on active economic management is their successive extension of welfare services, as recounted in chapter 21. Postwar SAP reform initiatives have included improved unemployment and retirement benefits, a national health insurance program, and a variety of individual and family cash allowances. As a prominent LO economist observes, the result of these measures is that "public services and payments are provided, under specific rules, to everyone who is entitled to them, regardless of means-tested need. Good examples are children's allowances and pensions, which are sent automatically to millionaires and the unemployed alike."[4]

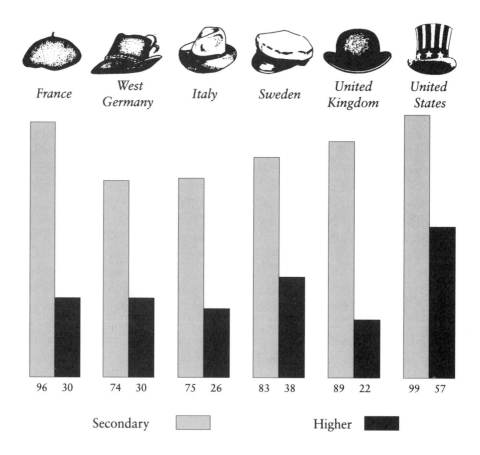

France	West Germany	Italy	Sweden	United Kingdom	United States
96 30	74 30	75 26	83 38	89 22	99 57

Secondary   Higher

FIGURE 24.1

SCHOOL AGE POPULATION IN SECONDARY AND HIGHER EDUCATION
(IN PERCENT)

SOURCE: Wallerstein (1989: 482)

With varying degrees of enthusiasm, nonsocialist leaders endorsed most of the SAP's early postwar reform initiatives. A dramatic exception occurred in the mid-1950s, however, when the LO and the Social Democrats moved to introduce a new system of supplementary pensions (ATP). The basic purpose of the ATP was to accord individual workers additional retirement benefits amounting to an average of 60 percent of their taxable income during their fifteen best-paid years of employment. In addition, the Social Democrats viewed the reform as a means to generate collective savings that could be used for government-sponsored economic objectives (such as the construction of new apartments to relieve recurrent housing shortages). All three nonsocialist parties, as well as the SAF, opposed the compulsory features of the SAP-LO proposal. Dissent was so intense that the Center party withdrew from the government coalition with the Social Democrats in 1957. A national referendum, held that same year, and a dissolution election, conducted in 1958, were required to settle the issue.

The Social Democrats obtained a relative majority of votes in both the referendum and the dissolution election. The Center and the Moderates, both of which rejected mandatory legislation, gained in electoral support, while the Liberals, who advocated a "positive compromise solution" that would enable individual workers to contract out of a collective system of supplementary pensions, lost heavily (see table 23.1). The Social Democrats interpreted their electoral advance as a mandate to proceed with implementing their version of supplementary benefits. The ATP proposal was endorsed by a narrow parliamentary majority in May 1959.

In subsequent decades, Swedish welfare provisions have become among the most comprehensive in the world. Sweden's current government disbursements (including the purchase of goods and services as well as transfer payments) are among the highest in the world, while its annual rate of infant mortality is one of the lowest. In parallel fashion, postwar Social Democratic legislative initiatives to enhance educational opportunities for lower-middle-class and working-class youth have led to a greater public investment in education than in most other advanced democracies (see table 24.3, page 436). The largest expenditures in Sweden's annual welfare budget are for retirement-disability benefits and health care, with each constituting approximately 38 percent of the total, followed by family welfare as a distant third (13 percent).[5]

As noted in chapter 21, the Social Democrats have implemented a correspondingly high rate of taxation to finance Sweden's extensive social programs ($10,707 per capita in 1987). By 1989, central govern-

TABLE 24.3

MEASURES OF COMMITMENT TO PUBLIC WELFARE

	General government disbursements as a percentage of GDP 1989[a]	*Public spending on education as a percentage of GNP* 1988[b]	*Infant mortality per thousand live births* 1989[c]
Canada	41.6	7.1	7
France	46.2	5.4	7
Germany	41.6	4.4	8
Italy	47.1	5.0	9
Sweden	57.3	6.7	6
United Kingdom	47.6	5.0	9
United States	34.6	6.8[d]	10

SOURCE: Based on Francis C. Castles, *The Social Democratic Image of Society* (Boston: Routledge & Kegan Paul, 1978), 68.

a. OECD, *Economic Surveys 1991* (Paris, 1991).

b. United Nations Educational, Scientific and Cultural Organization, *Statistical Yearbook 1990* (Paris, 1990), 4–10, 4–12, 4–17, 4–19.

c. World Bank, *World Development Report 1991* (New York: Oxford University Press, 1991), 225.

d. Percentage is for 1987.

ment expenditures accounted for 41 percent of the gross domestic product, compared to 48 percent in Italy, 43 percent in France, 35 percent in the United Kingdom, 29 percent in Germany, and only 23 percent in the United States.[6]

Critics on the right and left have joined in attacking the concentration of power and the high cost of welfare government in Sweden while advocating specific partisan remedies. Nonsocialist leaders have criticized bureaucratization in both government and private organizations and repeatedly denounced Sweden's high tax rate as a disincentive to private initiative and savings. From the opposite end of the political spectrum, the VP and other left socialists attacked the Social Democrats for their failure to socialize industry and thereby mitigate the concentration of private economic power in the hands of wealthy shareholders. The cumulative effect of left and right criticisms of Social Democratic governance was the onset of a continuing pattern of dealignment in electoral behavior and the gradual erosion of central tenets of the Swedish model.

The Nonsocialist Interlude

Joint left-right criticism of Social Democracy resulted in a sharp decline in SAP electoral strength in the 1966 county and municipal elections.[7] The SAP recovered in the 1968 parliamentary election but gradually lost support during the 1970s as the nonsocialist parties succeeded in projecting an image of bloc unity on behalf of an alternative program of government decentralization and tax reduction. The outcome was a nonsocialist electoral victory in 1976 and the formation of a Center-Liberal-Moderate coalition that displaced the Social Democrats from cabinet office after forty-four years in power (see tables 23.1 and 23.4).

Once in power, however, the Center, the Liberals, and the Moderates proved incapable of maintaining interparty unity on important policy issues. The first partisan conflict involved nuclear energy. During the 1976 campaign, Center party leaders had strenuously opposed SAP plans to increase the number of Sweden's nuclear energy plants from six to thirteen by the mid-1980s. Liberal and Moderate officials, in contrast, endorsed the measure. Following the election, the latter compelled Prime Minister Fälldin to reverse his party's campaign stance and agree that a seventh plant could begin operations.

The Center party subsequently held firm in its resolve to oppose any further development of nuclear energy. A government crisis ensued in October 1978 when the Moderates and Liberals endorsed a recommendation of the National Nuclear Energy Inspection Board to activate two additional nuclear energy plants. Fälldin and his fellow Centrists promptly resigned from the cabinet to protest this action. The Liberals formed a minority government in place of the previous three-party coalition.

The nuclear energy impasse was resolved in March 1980 when a majority of the Swedish electorate voted in favor of a temporary expansion of the country's nuclear energy program to include a maximum of twelve plants. The Liberals and the Social Democrats concurred on a joint government-opposition decision to phase out all twelve plants by the early part of the twenty-first century in tandem with a policy of stringent conservation and the development of alternative sources of energy such as solar and fusion.

Despite their interbloc disagreement on the nuclear energy issue, the nonsocialist parties won a one-seat majority in the September 1979 Riksdag election (see tables 23.1 and 23.2). Accordingly, they reconstituted a three-party coalition government under Center leadership.

Ultimately, the nonsocialists failed once again to sustain executive unity. Ironically, the second divisive issue proved to be taxation policy. Center and Liberal spokesmen acted in the spring of 1981 to honor an earlier agreement with the Social Democrats to reduce marginal tax rates in exchange for a simultaneous cut in the amount of deductions allowable for interest paid on home mortgages. In response, Moderate spokesmen, who were opposed to the tradeoff on ideological grounds, angrily withdrew from the government coalition. As a result, the Center and the Liberals formed a minority government in May 1981. They governed jointly until September 1982 when the Social Democrats resumed power with the indirect support of the Left party.

The Quest for Economic Democracy

Intense partisan disagreements over nuclear energy and tax policy during the late 1970s and early 1980s revealed a deepening conflict between nonsocialist forces and the Social Democrats over long-term economic policy and strategies of system change. Similar to other advanced industrial nations, Sweden has experienced a slowdown in economic growth since the mid-1970s. The causes are rooted primarily in global factors, including successive oil price increases in 1973–74 and 1978–79 and increased international trade competition from Asia in such industries as steel production and shipbuilding.

The onset of "stagflation" as an international phenomenon meant that Sweden's average annual growth rate fell from 4.4 percent during the 1960s to 2 percent or less from 1970 through the early 1980s. Accompanying the decline in economic growth were increases in the rate of inflation, which jumped from an annual average of 4.3 percent during the 1960s to 9.3 percent in the 1970s, and unemployment, which rose from an annual average of 1.8 percent in 1956–78 to more than 3 percent by the summer of 1982. A spiraling budgetary deficit and a negative trade balance further exacerbated Sweden's bleak economic situation.

During their time in office, nonsocialist leaders sought to restore domestic growth through a combination of measures. Among them were the Liberal-Center-SAP accord in 1981 to reduce marginal taxes, the introduction of tax-sheltered savings and equity programs designed to stimulate the growth of investment capital, the socialization of Sweden's ailing shipbuilding industry, and government subsidies to encourage increased employment among younger persons. To pay for these expansionary measures, the nonsocialists resorted to heavy borrowing from international capital markets and raised the value-added tax (VAT), which is a form of national sales tax, from 17.65 to 23.46 percent. In addition, the Center-Liberal minority government reduced health-care benefits marginally in 1982 in an effort to decrease public expenditures and thereby restrict the growing budgetary deficit.

The Social Democrats attacked the nonsocialists' economic strategy from both an immediate and a longer-term perspective. In the short run, the SAP and the LO criticized the nonsocialists on the grounds that their fiscal policies were inadequate to achieve the economic recovery that presumably all Swedes desired. Above all, the SAP cited the unprecedented postwar jump in the unemployment rate after 1976 as evidence of the inadequacy of the nonsocialist response to prevailing international conditions of stagflation. As an alternative approach, the Social Democrats called for even greater government economic activism to be financed by yet another increase in the VAT.

Far more controversial was the SAP-LO's ideological commitment to a "breakthrough" strategy of industrial and economic democracy. LO and SAP leaders had jointly launched a series of important legislative reforms during the mid-1970s that considerably strengthened the status of individual workers and unions vis-à-vis private management. The bills included the Employment Security Act of 1974, which restricted the right of employers to dismiss workers; the Work Environment Act of 1974, which accorded floor-level safety stewards sweeping powers to enforce strict health and safety standards; and the Employee Participation Act of 1976, which transformed the traditional right of managers to "direct and allocate work" into an object of collective bargaining.[8] 1976, LO spokesmen formally urged that these increments in the collective power of organized labor be augmented through the introduction of a national system of wage-earner funds.

The LO proposal evolved from a resolution at the federation's 1971 congress calling for a study group. The group was to investigate steps to implement some form of profit-sharing arrangement that would tap so-called excess profits in private industry to the collective advantage of organized labor.[9] Five years later, the study group, which was headed by Rudolf Meidner, a leading LO economist, submitted a report recommending the creation of a collective system of employee funds that would be financed through a tax on company profits. The funds would be empowered to purchase company shares on the domestic stock market. Thus, in time the funds could acquire majority ownership of individual companies. Precisely that prospect outraged employer groups and the nonsocialist parties, and caused even many rank-and-file Social Democrats to question the wisdom of the Meidner plan. The resulting controversy over the LO proposal proved a major factor in the SAP's electoral defeat in 1976.

While in opposition, the LO and the SAP refined the original Meidner concept to include provisions for a decentralized system of funds and the transfer of dividend income into the ATP system as a means of safeguarding future individual retirement benefits. From 1977 onward, the Social Democrats also stressed the importance of the wage-earner funds as a source of domestic investment capital. These revisions were endorsed by overwhelming majorities at LO and SAP congresses held during the early fall of 1981.

The Social Democrats thus conducted their 1982 campaign against the Moderates, the Center, and the Liberals on the dual basis of short-term charges of economic mismanagement and their longer-term advocacy of enhanced economic democracy. The SAP victory in September 1982 enabled the Social Democrats to proceed with new initiatives on both fronts.

Both the nonsocialist interlude and the Social Democratic resumption of power revealed underlying factors of political, economic, and social change that point toward a redefinition of the Swedish model in the 1990s and beyond. At stake is the confrontation between opposing strategies of continued reform ("breakthrough politics") and retrenchment ("rationalizing politics").

Notes

1. The averages are tabulated on the basis of annual data published in International Labour Office, *Year Book of Labour Statistics* (Geneva: ILO, 1950 to the present).

2. During the 1980s the number of working days lost in Sweden as a result of strikes and lockouts has ranged from none in 1982 to 1.06 days per civilian worker in 1980. In Germany the only statistically relevant year of conflict during the decade was 1984 when 21 working days were lost per worker, but this was an exceptionally high figure for Germany.

3. A useful though decidedly apolitical account of postwar Swedish fiscal and monetary policy is Assar Lindbeck's *Swedish Economic Policy* (Berkeley: University of California Press, 1974). A central component of

the government's effort to facilitate structural and technological modernization on the part of Swedish industry and services has been increased public expenditures on research and development as part of an active industrial policy. See M. Donald Hancock, "Industrial Policies in the United Kingdom, Sweden, and Germany: A Study in Contrasts and Convergence," in *Managing Modern Capitalism: Industrial Renewal and Workplace Reform in the United States and Western Europe,* ed. M. Donald Hancock, John Logue, and Bernt Schiller (Westport, Conn.: Greenwood, 1991).

4. Gösta Rehn, "The Wages of Success," *Daedalus,* Spring 1984, 142.

5. Statistiska centralbyrån, *Statistisk årsbok för Sverige 1980* (Stockholm, 1981), 282–83.

6. World Bank, *World Development Report 1991* (New York: Oxford University Press, 1991), 225.

7. SAP strength dropped from 47.3 percent in the 1964 Riksdag election to 44.2 percent in the communal election of 1966, which was the party's lowest point since 1934.

8. These reforms are described and assessed in greater detail in M. Donald Hancock and John Logue, "Sweden: The Quest for Economic Democracy," *Polity,* Fall/Winter 1984. See also Bernt Schiller's chapter, "The Swedish Model Reconstituted," in *Managing Modern Capitalism.*

9. "Excess profits" refer, in the eyes of the LO, to those additional profits gained by individual firms attributable to wage restraint exercised by the trade unions.

25

What Is the Future of Swedish Politics?

Political and economic trends during the 1980s revealed that Sweden, perhaps more than any other advanced industrial democracy, stands at an important systemic crossroad. The central issue is whether the Social Democratic model of welfare Sweden will endure and conceivably be transformed in the direction of further industrial and economic democracy or whether the nonsocialists and other critics of the established system can manage to reconstitute the Swedish model in response to a combination of domestic and international challenges to its continued viability.

The Social Democrats Back in Office

In empirical response to these opposing choices, Prime Minister Palme and members of his cabinet proceeded cautiously but with a clear sense of direction when they resumed office in 1982. As initial steps, they honored the SAP's campaign promises to restore nonsocialist-sponsored reductions in health care and increase government expenditures on behalf of job creation (both of which were financed by a higher VAT rate). They also moved to stimulate renewed economic growth by devaluing the Swedish *krona* (crown) by 16 percent in an effort to reduce the cost of Swedish exports and thereby encourage an export-led recovery from the economic doldrums of the early 1980s.[1] The cabinet simultaneously enacted an austere budgetary policy designed to reduce the government's deficit below levels projected by the previous Center-Liberal coalition.[2] In the process, Social Democratic leaders incurred the temporary wrath of some trade unionists and rank-and-file activists who demanded a more expansionist economic policy even at the cost of a greater budget deficit.

Early in their renewed term of office, the Social Democrats also acted to implement the controversial system of wage-earner funds. Despite nonsocialist criticism and the absence of a popular majority in support of the concept (as measured by successive public opinion surveys), the SAP formally proposed during the summer of 1983 the creation of five regional funds to be financed through a combination of a 20 percent tax on company profits and a 0.2 percent increase in employee contributions to the ATP retirement system. They would be governed by appointive boards dominated by trade union officials. The government sought to diffuse nonsocialist fears that the wage-earner funds could eventually acquire majority ownership of specific companies by restricting both their total capitalization (a maximum of 17.5 billion Swedish crowns by 1990) and the percentage of shares that each of the funds can purchase in a single enterprise (8 percent per fund for a hypothetical total of 40 percent shared by the five funds). Moreover, the Social Democrats stipulated that the wage-earner funds would remain in place only through 1990.[3] This seven-year period would suffice, in the view of the cabinet, to facilitate the necessary structural transformation of the Swedish economy with the assistance of the additional investment capital generated by the five funds.[4]

The Riksdag endorsed the government's proposal in December 1983. The Social Democrats voted solidly in favor, the VP abstained to ensure the bill's passage, and the three nonsocialist parties voted against. The bill went into effect on 1 January 1984.

Tactically, the SAP legislative initiative on the wage-earner fund issue was dictated by both the timing of parliamentary elections and the party's calculation of foreseeable international economic trends. The Riksdag's approval of the government's proposal in late 1983 ensured that the funds would be operative prior to the September 1985 election. If the domestic economy noticeably improved by then, the Social Democrats could reasonably expect an electoral plurality and thus a renewed parliamentary mandate. To help ensure the latter outcome, the LO and its constituent unions negotiated as an explicit tradeoff for the introduction of the wage-earner fund system wage settlements averaging a modest 5 percent or less in both 1982–83 and 1983–84. The intent of the LO's policy of wage restraint was to curtail domestic inflationary pressures and thus facilitate Sweden's economic recovery from the doldrums that prevailed at the beginning of the decade.

The full implementation of the wage-earner fund system promised a partial transformation of authority relations in the Swedish economy. The diluted version of the wage-earner fund system enacted in 1983 was not designed to achieve outright nationalization or "trade unionization" of industry (to the consternation of some left Social Democrats), since the legislation explicitly restricted the total percentage of company shares that the regional funds were permitted to purchase. Nonetheless, SAP and LO leaders had originally anticipated that the extension of collective ownership of company stock in combination with the various workplace reforms implemented during the 1970s and sketched above would inevitably induce managers to be more responsive to union demands concerning employment, investments, and production. The minimum result of the funds would thus be to increase managerial awareness of the social consequences of microeconomic decisions and thereby indirectly strengthen workplace democracy.

Precisely because the wage-earner fund system involved central issues of share ownership and managerial prerogatives, the nonsocialist parties, the SAF, and other private interests remained adamant in their opposition to the concept of collective ownership and control of the funds as a potentially important source of investment capital. Accordingly, nonsocialist leaders repeatedly announced their determination to abolish the funds when they returned to power.

Economically, Social Democratic policies met with greater interim success. The SAP's return to power coincided with the beginning of a general improvement in international economic conditions. Renewed growth of world trade and a decline in the world price of oil by the mid-1980s helped stimulate renewed domestic growth. From a negative rate of −0.3 percent in 1981, Sweden experienced a steady expansion of its real gross national product through 1984 when the rate peaked at 4.0 percent.[5] Accompanying the restoration of growth was a decline in the unemployment rate, which fell from 3.5 percent in 1983 to less than 2 percent by the end of the decade (see table 24.2, page 432). Other positive signs included a substantial increase in exports and the attainment of a slight budget surplus in 1987. These solid achievements contributed to a Social Democratic victory in the September 1985 election and the extension of the SAP's executive mandate into the early 1990s.

In a major departure from its ideological principles, however, the Social Democrats signalled through their actions that the era of social reform was at an end. They were determined to maintain the existing welfare state; but because of severe budgetary constraints, they in effect announced that no additional benefits would be forthcoming. In addition, party leaders yielded to long-standing nonsocialist claims that

Sweden's taxation rate was too high. In 1988 the SAP initiated negotiations with the Liberals and other opposition parties to reduce taxes and thereby bring them closer in line with prevailing rates in their principal trading partners. The declared purpose of tax reform was to encourage greater private investment at home and, in the process, discourage a damaging drain of investment capital abroad (primarily to EC countries and the United States).

The principal architect of Sweden's new "politics of austerity" was Kjell-Olof Feldt, a moderate Social Democrat whom Prime Minister Palme appointed minister of finance when the SAP resumed power in 1982. Economically conservative and distrustful of LO demands to transform property relations via the wage-earner fund system, Feldt sought to impose financial discipline on the nation by urging unions to practice self-restraint in their negotiations with employers over annual wage increases. His most compelling argument was that wage increases in excess of government guidelines of 3 percent or less contributed to a higher inflation rate during the 1980s in Sweden than in other industrial democracies.[6] When union leaders balked at his demands, Feldt induced the cabinet to adopt a stringent anti-inflationary program in February 1990 that prescribed a freeze on prices, wages, and rents and prohibited strikes by unions.

The cabinet's restrictive economic proposals and attempt to curtail trade union activity sparked immediate outrage on the part of organized labor, the Left party, many rank-and-file Social Democrats, and the non-socialist parties. After a heated debate, an overwhelming majority of Riksdag deputies rejected the government package in February 1990. The cabinet temporarily resigned as a result, but Prime Minister Ingvar Carlsson, who had succeeded Palme following the latter's assassination in February 1986, formed a new Social Democratic government when nonsocialist leaders rejected an offer from the speaker of the Riksdag to form a minority coalition. Feldt thereupon resigned from the cabinet.

Although the Social Democrats survived the government crisis of February 1990, they remained henceforth on the political defensive. They clearly confronted a policy and ideological crisis from which they could not readily recover.

The Swedish Model Transformed

Events during the 1980s indicated a gradual erosion of the Swedish model as a consequence of a combination of domestic and international factors. Sweden experienced recurrent fluctuations in its economic performance, accompanied by inflationary surges and an average annual growth rate of only 2.9 percent (compared to an annual average of 3.7 percent within the Organization for Economic Cooperation and Development as a whole).[7] These trends were by no means unique to Sweden, as all industrial democracies were similarly affected by an international crisis of stagflation at the beginning of the decade.[8] Complicating attempts by Swedish officials to sustain stable growth, however, were the country's high rate of taxation and the costly size and rigidity of its public sector. Efforts by Social Democratic leaders to maintain a "coordinated market" strategy characterized by active government economic intervention and continued support for comprehensive social services became out of step with more restrictive macroeconomic policies pursued by Thatcherites in the United Kingdom and the Reagan-Bush administrations in the United States.[9] This became increasingly apparent by the end of the decade when inflation resumed its upward spiral, in part as a result of substantial wage increases conceded to unions in the aftermath of a wave of strike activity beginning in 1985. As indicated in table 25.1, Sweden's annual rate of inflation in 1989 was second only to that of the United Kingdom among its principal trading partners. By the end of 1990 the rate had soared to 11.4 percent. Strikes on behalf of higher wages, meanwhile, resulted in an uncharacteristically high number of working days lost per worker (12 in 1985, 16 in 1986, and 18 in 1988).[10]

TABLE 25.1

ANNUAL PERCENTAGE INCREASE IN CONSUMER PRICES,
1989–91

	1989	*1990*	*1991*[a]
Canada	5.1	5.0	5.8
France	3.6	3.6	3.4
Germany	3.2	2.7	4.1
Italy	6.5	6.5	6.3
Sweden	6.6	11.4	8.2
United Kingdom	7.7	9.7	4.7
United States	4.6	6.3	2.8

SOURCE: *The Economist,* 27 January–2 February, 1990, 109; 5–11 January 1991, 81; 21–27 September 1991, 123.
    a. Rates are for the 12-month period ending during the summer of 1991.

The difficulty cabinet officials experienced in implementing a traditional Social Democratic approach to economic management was exacerbated by another important international constraint on domestic policy discretion: Sweden's increasingly close economic ties with the European Community. Recognizing that the country's future economic fortunes were inextricably linked with the EC by virtue of expanding trade and investment with its continental neighbors, the cabinet issued a policy paper in December 1987 outlining a strategy to promote intensified cooperation between Sweden (as well as other members of the European Free Trade Association) and the EC.[11] The proposal entailed extensive coordination of Swedish monetary, fiscal, and industrial policies with those of the EC, the elimination of existing restrictions on the free flow of investment capital, and deregulation of agriculture (including a gradual reduction in government subsidies to farmers). The government hoped thereby to encourage the "increased movement of goods, services, people, and capital in Western Europe as well as the maintenance of full employment and social security."[12] The fall of the Berlin Wall less than two years later, symbolizing the collapse of Soviet-style communism in Eastern and Central Europe, subsequently induced Swedish leaders to conclude that neutrality no longer precluded much more extensive collaboration with the EC. Accordingly, Prime Minister Carlsson submitted a formal bid for membership in June 1991.[13]

While EC membership indeed promises to encourage long-term Swedish material growth through trade expansion, the necessity to adapt Swedish structures and policies to accord more closely with Community norms sets discernible limits to distinctive economic dimensions of the Swedish model. As a result, future leaders, Social Democratic as well as nonsocialist, are no longer as free as they have been in the past to pursue an autonomous approach to economic management. Sweden's active labor-market policy, in contrast, is likely to remain largely intact because of its demonstrated effectiveness and widespread endorsement among key economic elites and rank-and-file workers. Far more problematic for Sweden's future are domestic factors of political change. The first involves the abandonment of centralized wage negotiations between the LO and SAF on the labor market. Simultaneous pressure on the part of both individual trade unions (notably in the engineering industries) and employer associations within SAF to pursue direct bargaining over wages and other terms of employment yielded during the 1980s a more decentralized mode of industrial relations. While direct negotiations have facilitated more flexible responses to changing labor-market conditions (including labor shortages in manufacturing and construction), an unintended consequence has been to undermine worker solidarity. The result has been increased trade union "egoism" and heightened discord between public-sector and private-sector employees. Empirical measures of lessened solidarity among LO and TCO members include an increase in strike activity during the latter part of the decade, noted above, and the resistance by unions to Feldt's ill-fated attempt to impose greater trade union discipline through legislation in February 1990. Thus, Sweden's pattern of labor peace has already proved an early victim of the gradual erosion of the Swedish model. Accompany-

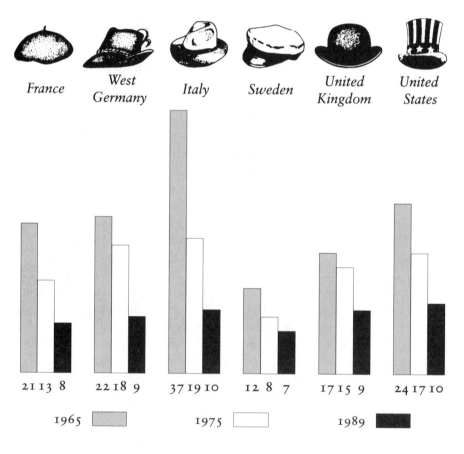

France	West Germany	Italy	Sweden	United Kingdom	United States
21 13 8	22 18 9	37 19 10	12 8 7	17 15 9	24 17 10

1965   1975   1989

FIGURE 25.1
INFANT MORTALITY RATE PER 1,000 LIVE BIRTHS

ing new strains on the labor market is discernible conflict between the LO and the SAP over key political issues. Incipient discord was already apparent during the 1970s when the LO promoted, much more aggressively than the party itself, the introduction of wage-earner funds. LO leaders were partially mollified when the Social Democrats proceeded to introduce a version of the system in 1983, but the fact that the regional wage-earner funds were restricted in their capitalization and capacity to purchase majority shares in individual firms curtailed their effectiveness as a direct instrument of economic democratization. Instead, with the maturation of the wage-earner funds in 1990, the Social Democrats proposed that they be merged with existing national pension funds to create a series of five "superfunds" with capital assets totaling 430,000 million *kronor* that would be used for investment purposes. Tensions heightened between the two branches of Swedish Social Democracy during the latter part of the decade over the government's austere budgetary policies and its agreement with the nonsocialist parties in 1988 to proceed with an overhaul of the tax system designed to benefit middle- and upper-income citizens. LO leaders promptly charged that the reform would prove disadvantageous to lower-income workers and successfully pressed the SAP into granting marginal concessions. The tax reform was implemented despite LO misgivings on 1 January 1990.

Growing LO and rank-and-file worker dissatisfaction with SAP economic and financial policies coincided with an incipient electoral dealignment. During the late 1940s and 1950s the Social Democrats had confronted a decline in support as the number of industrial workers (who constituted their traditional core of supporters) dwindled in the wake of postindustrialization, but they managed to recoup their losses during the 1960s by extending their appeal among members of the new middle class of salaried employees in the public and private sectors. Beginning in the early 1970s, however, the party experienced a renewed erosion of support (except for periodic fluctuations during the early 1980s) as more and more citizens switched partisan allegiances or abstained from voting altogether. By the spring and summer of 1991, opinion polls indicated a decisive realignment in favor of the nonsocialist bloc, with the Christian Democrats and New Democracy emerging as the principal beneficiaries of dealignment at the expense of the Social Democrats. Explanations for the electoral shift include voter protests against short-term Social Democratic economic policies, disappointment on both the left and right concerning tax reform, discontent among women over wage inequalities, and the diffusion of "postmaterialist" values among many younger citizens who are critical of conformist norms and bureaucratic constraints associated with the established welfare state.[14]

Thus, diverse international and domestic factors converged in the September 1991 election to spell an end to Social Democratic governance for at least the immediate future. As indicated in tables 23.1 and 23.2, the SAP lost heavily, falling to its lowest point since the early 1930s, while the nonsocialist bloc garnered fully 55.5 percent of the popular vote. Contributing significantly to the latter outcome was the success of the Christian Democrats and New Democracy in together capturing 13.7 percent. Prime Minister Carlsson promptly resigned, and in early October Carl Bildt formed a four-party nonsocialist cabinet pledged to bring an end to Sweden's "age of collectivism."[15]

"Breakthrough" vs. "Rationalizing" Politics

Whether the 1991 election marks the beginning of an enduring realignment of the Swedish electorate in favor of the nonsocialist bloc or will prove only a temporary setback for the Social Democrats remains to be seen. In the immediate aftermath of the election, one prominent analyst interpreted the outcome as a definitive closure to long-term "Social Democratic hegemony in Swedish politics,"[16] while others anticipate that the SAP will inevitably recover a substantial share of its former support as the new nonsocialist coalition implements unpopular policies of its own. Buttressing the latter view is the fact that protest votes have proved fleeting elsewhere, as was the case with short-lived support in state elections for the right-wing National Democratic party during the 1960s in Germany and a temporary resurgence of Liberal strength during the 1980s in Britain.

At a minimum, the election reveals at least two significant features of contemporary Swedish politics. First, it provided additional evidence of increased electoral volatility, accompanied by a decline in the importance of party as a determinant of voter choice.[17] Electoral participation declined for the second time in a row, falling to 85.3 percent (compared to 86 percent in 1988 and 89.3 percent in 1985). At the same time, the number of voters who did not know which party they would support a week prior to the election has steadily risen from 6.0 percent in 1985 to 9.1 percent in 1988 to 13.4 percent in 1991. Whereas only 7 percent of Swedish voters switched party allegiances between elections during the late 1950s, fully 20.2 percent changed loyalties in 1988. In the September 1991 election voters deserted not only the Social Democrats but also the Liberals, the Center, and the Greens. New Democracy benefited most dramatically from the decline of voter loyalty, drawing support from both the traditional nonsocialist parties and especially the Social Democrats. Indeed, exit polls revealed that a majority of New Democracy adherents were trade unionists.[18]

Although the nonsocialist parties as a whole obtained a clear mandate to form an alternative government, the pattern of increased electoral volatility suggests that Swedish politics will become more unstable and certainly less predictable in the future. The Moderate-led cabinet announced in its first policy statement in October 1991 that the four parties jointly affirmed a number of shared objectives. Among them are partial deregulation of the economy, additional tax reforms designed to encourage private savings and strengthen small business firms, the dismantling of the controversial wage-earner fund system, the partial privatization of education and social services, and membership in the European Community.[19] Yet the Moderates, Center, Liberals, and Christian Democrats are divided among themselves on important details of policy formulation, especially concerning taxes and the terms on which Sweden would join the EC. Moreover, the fact that the coalition is technically a minority government commanding 170 out of 349 seats in the Riksdag, or 9 short of a majority, means that it is indirectly dependent on the support of New Democracy's 25 deputies to remain in office. This dependency may well intensify policy tensions within the coalition because of strong antipathy among traditional nonsocialist forces, especially the Liberals, toward New Democracy's ideological demands for radical structural and policy change.

A second feature of the election outcome was that it confirmed a retreat from what Lawrence Brown depicts as reformist "breakthrough politics" toward a more restrictive style of "rationalizing politics."[20] From their rise to power in 1932 through most of the postwar period, the Social Democrats sponsored successive policy initiatives that had the cumulative effect of transforming modern Swedish society: the implementation of a coordinated approach to economic management, the extension of welfare benefits, the introduction of a supplementary pension system (which not only provided individualized retirement benefits but also accorded the state significant sources of investment capital), legislation during the 1970s that significantly enhanced worker rights, and the creation of the wage-earner fund system. By the early 1980s, however, the Social Democrats embarked on a strategy of ideological retrenchment when they began to embrace a market approach to economic management and suspended further social reforms. The welfare state remained intact, but in practice the Social Democrats increasingly sought under the leadership of Prime Minister Carlsson and Finance Minister Feldt to harmonize Swedish policies with those of its principal trading partners as they struggled to cope with erratic patterns of economic performance. In the process the SAP shifted course toward a "rationalizing" approach to public policy.

The nonsocialist victory in September 1991 will intensify the new direction in Swedish politics for the foreseeable future. The nonsocialists may well succeed, at least in part, in creating the material and institutional conditions for greater individual choice and initiative. Whether Sweden's contemporary era of rationalizing politics will necessarily make politics "more trouble free," as Brown suggests, is another question.

Notes

1. Organization for Economic Cooperation and Development, *Economic Surveys: Sweden 1983–84* (Paris: OECD, 1982), 35.

2. "Så här skall vi spara 7 miljarder kronor," *Från Riksdag & Departementet,* 4 November 1983, 6–7.

3. Regeringens proposition 1983/84:50, *Löntagarfonder* (Stockholm: Norstedts Trykeri, 1983).

4. Quoted in "Löntagarfonder," in *Frän Riksdag & Departementet,* 18 November 1983, 3.

5. OECD, *Economic Outlook July 1990* (Paris, 1990), 192.

6. The annual rate of increase in consumer prices had declined substantially from 13.7 percent in 1980 to 8.0 percent by mid-decade but was nonetheless higher than than the OECD average of 5.2 percent (1985).

7. OECD, *Economic Outlook Historical Statistics 1960–1989* (Paris, 1991), 3.1.

8. An earlier crisis of international stagflation in 1973–74 had yielded similar results, albeit less immediately in Sweden because the Social Democratic government stockpiled industrial production to ensure full employment.

9. Contrasting approaches to economic management include Germany's "social market" economic system and a "regulated market" approach associated with Thatcherism and Reaganism. These distinctions are explored in greater detail in Hancock, "Contrasting Approaches to Economic Management and Industrial Policy," in *Managing Modern Capitalism: Industrial Renewal and Workplace Reform in the United States and Western Europe,* ed. M. Donald Hancock, John Logue, and Bernt Schiller (Westport, Conn.: Greenwood, 1991).

10. See Appendix, table A.11, p. 549.

11. European Community officials declared their intention to elimi-

nate remaining restrictions on free trade and the movement of capital and labor within the EC with the adoption of the "Solemn Declaration on European Union" in 1983 and the "Single European Act" in 1986. The Swedish cabinet coupled Sweden's affirmation of closer ties with the EC with a renewed declaration that prospective membership in the Community would be incompatible with the nation's traditional foreign policy of neutrality.

12. "Ökat samarbete utan medlemskap år Sveriges linje mot EG," *Från Riksdag & Departementet,* 15 January 1988, 13.

13. As a prelude to full membership, Sweden took an important step toward closer ties with the EC when the EFTA nations and the European Community concluded a treaty on 22 October 1991 to establish a common market linking the two regional associations in the form of a new European Economic Area. The EEA will constitute the world's largest trading bloc. See *New York Times,* 23 October 1991.

14. An excellent assessment of citizen demands for new forms of political participation in Sweden is Olof Petersson's "Democracy and Power in Sweden," *Scandinavian Political Studies* 14 (1991): 173–91. Diane Sainsbury discusses efforts by the Social Democrats to respond to domestic economic and social change in "Swedish Social Democracy in Transition: The Party's Record in the 1980s and the Challenge of the 1990s," *West European Politics* 14 (1991): 32–57. The diffusion of postmaterialist values in Western democracies is explored in Ronald Inglehart, *The Silent Revolution: Changing Values and Political Styles among Western Publics* (Princeton, N.J.: Princeton University Press, 1990); and Inglehart, *Culture Shift in Advanced Industrial Democracies* (Princeton, N.J.: Princeton University Press, 1977).

15. Quoted in *New York Times,* 6 October 1991.

16. Olof Petersson, a political scientist at the University of Uppsala, quoted in "Borgerlig salseger—protest mot etablissemanget," *Från Riksdag & Departementet,* 27 September 1991, 3.

17. These trends have also been apparent for some time in other Western democracies. See Russell Dalton, et al., *Electoral Change in Advanced Industrial Democracies: Alignment or Realignment?* (Princeton, N.J.: Princeton University Press, 1984); and Dalton, *Citizen Politics: Public Opinion and Political Parties in the United States, United Kingdom, France, and West Germany* (Chatham, N.J.: Chatham House, 1988).

18. Ibid, 2.

19. Swedish Information Service, "Four Parties to Govern Sweden," *Swedish News,* 4 October 1991. See also "Swedish Coalition Plans Overhaul of Policies," *New York Times,* 6 September 1991.

20. Lawrence D. Brown, *New Policies, New Politics: Government's Response to Government's Growth* (Washington, D.C.: Brookings Institution, 1983).

For Further Reading

ADLER-KARLSON, G. *Functional Socialism. A Swedish Theory for Democratic Socialism.* Stockholm: Prisma, 1969.

ANDRÉN, NILS. *Modern Swedish Government.* 2d ed. Stockholm: Almqvist and Wiksell, 1964.

ANTON, THOMAS J. *Administered Politics: Elite Political Culture in Sweden.* Boston: Martinus Nijhoff, 1980.

ÅSTRÖM, SVERKER. *Sweden's Policy of Neutrality.* Stockholm: Swedish Institute, 1983.

BERGSTRÖM, HANS. "Sweden's Politics and Party System at the Crossroads." *West European Politics* 14 (1991): 8-29.

BOARD, JOSEPH. *Government and Politics of Sweden.* Boston: Houghton Mifflin, 1970.

BOSWORTH, BARRY P., AND RIVLIN, ALICE M. eds. *The Swedish Economy.* Washington, D.C.: Brookings, 1987.

CASTLES, FRANCIS. *The Social Democratic Image of Society: A Study of the Achievements and Origins of Scandinavian Social Democracy in a Comparative Perspective.* Boston: Routledge & Kegan Paul, 1978.

CERNY, KARL H., ed. *Scandinavia at the Polls.* Washington, D.C.: American Enterprise Institute, 1977.

CHILDS, MARQUIS W. *Sweden: The Middle Way on Trial.* New Haven: Yale University Press, 1980.

Daedalus, "Nordic Voices," Spring 1984, and "The Nordic Enigma," Winter 1984.

EINHORN, ERIC S. "Employment Policies in Scandinavia." *Scandinavian Review* 72 (1984): 75–83.

EINHORN, ERIC S., AND LOGUE, JOHN. *Modern Welfare States: Politics and Policy in Social Democratic Scandinavia.* New York: Praeger, 1989.

———. *Welfare States in Hard Times: Denmark and Sweden.* Rev. ed. Kent, Ohio: Kent Popular Press, 1982.

ESPING-ANDERSEN, GØSTA. *Politics Against Markets: The Social Democratic Road to Power.* Princeton, N.J.: Princeton University Press, 1985.

FURNISS, NORMAN, ed. *Futures for the Welfare State.* Bloomington: Indiana University Press, 1986.

FURNISS, NORMAN, AND TILTON, TIMOTHY. *The Case for the Welfare State.* Bloomington: Indiana University Press, 1977.

HANCOCK, M. DONALD. *Sweden: The Politics of Postindustrial Change.* Hinsdale, Ill.: Dryden Press, 1972.

HANCOCK, M. DONALD, AND LOGUE, JOHN. "Sweden: The Quest for Economic Democracy." *Polity* 17 (Winter 1984): 248–70.

HECKSCHER, GUNNAR. *The Welfare State and Beyond: Success and Problems in Scandinavia.* Minneapolis: University of Minnesota Press, 1984.

HECLO, HUGH. *Modern Social Politics in Britain and Sweden.* New Haven: Yale University Press, 1974.

HEIDENHEIMER, ARNOLD J.; HECLO, HUGH; AND ADAMS, CAROLYN TEICH. *Comparative Public Policy: The Politics of Social Choice in Europe and America.* 3d ed. New York: St. Martin's Press, 1990.

HUNTFORD, ROLAND. *The New Totalitarians.* New York: Stein and Day, 1972.

KATZENSTEIN, PETER. *Small States in World Markets.* Ithaca, N.Y.: Cornell University Press, 1985.

KOBLIK, STEVEN, ed. *Sweden's Development from Poverty to Affluence, 1750–1970.* Minneapolis: University of Minnesota Press, 1975.

KORPI, WALTER. *The Democratic Class Struggle.* London: Routledge & Kegan Paul, 1983.

———. *The Working Class in Welfare Capitalism: Work, Unions and Politics in Sweden.* London: Routledge & Kegan Paul, 1981.

LEWIN, LEIF. *Governing Trade Unions in Sweden.* Cambridge, Mass.: Harvard University Press, 1980.

LINDBECK, ASSAR. *Swedish Economic Policy.* Berkeley: University of California Press, 1974.

MEIDNER, RUDOLF. *Employee Investment Funds: An Approach to Collective Capital Formation.* London: Allen & Unwin, 1978.

MILNER, HENRY. *Sweden: Social Democracy in Practice.* New York: Oxford University Press, 1989.

PETERSSON, OLOF. "Democracy and Power in Sweden." *Scandinavian Political Studies* 14 (1991): 173–91.

RIKSDAG. *Constitutional Documents of Sweden: The Instrument of Government, the Riksdag Act, the Act of Succession, the Freedom of the Press Act.* Stockholm: Norstedts tryckeri, 1975.

ROSENTHAL, ALBERT H. *The Social Programs of Sweden: A Search for Security in a Free Society.* Minneapolis: University of Minnesota Press, 1967.

RUSTOW, DANKWART A. *The Politics of Compromise: A Study of Parties and Cabinet Government in Sweden.* Princeton, N.J.: Princeton University Press, 1955.

Rydén, Bengt, and Bergström, Villy, eds. *Sweden: Choices for Economic and Social Policy in the 1980s*. London: Allen & Unwin, 1982.

Sahr, Robert C. *The Politics of Energy Policy Change in Sweden*. Ann Arbor: University of Michigan Press, 1985.

Sainsbury, Diane. "Swedish Social Democracy in Transition: The Party's Record in the 1980s and the Challenge of the 1990s." *West European Politics* 14 (1991): 31–57.

Scott, Franklin D. *Sweden: The Nation's History*. Minneapolis: University of Minnesota Press, 1977.

Sundelius, Bengt, ed. *Foreign Policies of Northern Europe*. Boulder, Colo.: Westview Press, 1982.

Tomasson, Richard F. *Sweden: Prototype of Modern Society*. New York: Random House, 1970.

Wheeler, Christopher. *White-Collar Power*. Chicago: University of Illinois Press, 1975.

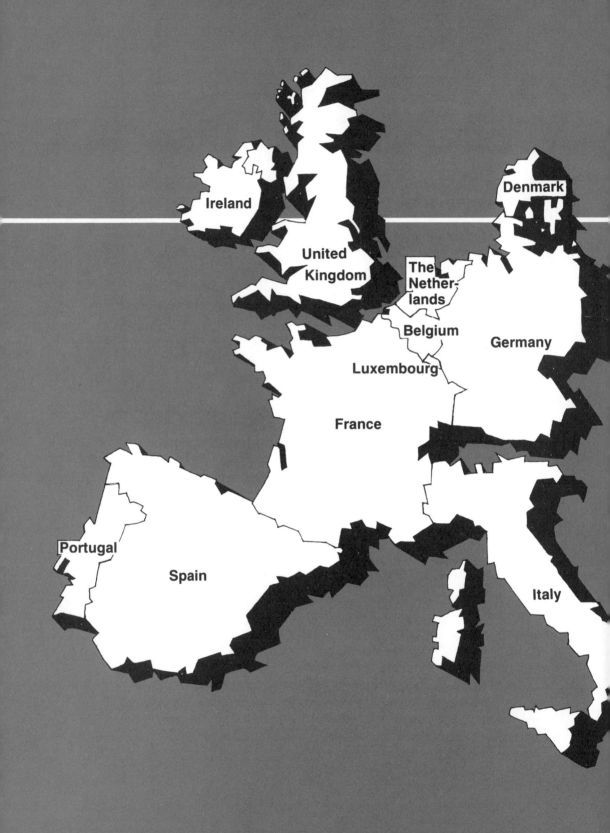

Part Six

The European Community

M. Donald Hancock
and
B. Guy Peters

Greece

26

The European Community: Development
and the Primacy of Bureaucratic Politics

Alongside national governments in Britain, France, Germany, and other West European countries, the European Community (EC) constitutes a crucial organization for the coordination and implementation of economic, social, and foreign policies on the regional level of governance. The significance of the EC lies not only in its economic status as the world's largest trading bloc but also in the declared intentions of political leaders in both the EC and its member countries to achieve an integrated regional market by the end of 1992 and economic, monetary, and political union by the end of the decade. Implementing these objectives will entail the further transfer of significant degrees of national decision-making authority to supranational institutions,[1] a process that began when the European integration movement was launched during the early 1950s. Once economic, monetary, and political union are fully attained, the European Community will be firmly established as a powerful governmental system in its own right.

From the ECSC to the EC

In its present form the European Community is the institutional culmination of political initiatives by West European governments dating from the early postwar years—which were inspired by a combination of idealism, national self-interest, and pragmatism—to transcend historical factors of national rivalry that had contributed to the outbreak of World Wars I and II.[2] Political leaders from France, Germany, Italy, Belgium, the Netherlands, and Luxembourg established the European Coal and Steel Community (ECSC) in 1951 as a practical first step toward regional economic and political integration. The purpose of the ECSC was to eliminate custom duties on iron, coal, and steel products among the six member countries while simultaneously erecting a common external tariff, thereby creating a limited customs union. Executive and legislative powers of the new organization were divided between a Council of Ministers, representing the six governments, and an appointive High Authority with supranational authority to initiate common decisions and oversee their execution. Largely symbolic consultative authority was vested in a European Assembly, whose deputies were appointed by the national parliaments of the six member states. In addition, a European Court of Justice was established to adjudicate disputes over the interpretation and implementation of the ECSC treaty. That court has played an active role in removing artificial barriers to trade and has had its decisions accepted by national governments. The signatories agreed that the Council of Ministers and High Authority would meet in Brussels, the Assembly would conduct its plenary sessions in Strasbourg, and the Court of Justice would hear its cases in Luxembourg.

The success of the ECSC in promoting regional economic growth encouraged the same six nations to create a significantly more comprehensive European Economic Community (EEC) in 1957. "Determined to lay the foundations of an ever closer union among the peoples of Europe [and] resolved to ensure the economic and social progress of their countries by common action to eliminate the barriers which divide Europe,"[3] France, Germany, Italy, and the Benelux countries pledged to achieve economic integration as a crucial step toward ultimate political union. Alongside the ECSC and the EEC, the six signatories also established a third regional organization known as Euratom, which was designed to promote intergovernmental cooperation in the development of peaceful uses of nuclear energy.[4] The Treaty of Rome, which provided the legal foundations for the new European Economic Community, called for the gradual elimination of customs duties on all industrial and agricultural products, the establishment of a common external tariff, the free movement of labor and capital, and the implementation of common policies in such areas as agriculture, transport, and competition. Parallel executive-legislative structures to those of the ECSC were established in the form of an intergovernmental Council of Ministers and a supranational European Commission. Serving both regional organizations were the European Assembly and the Court of Justice.

The United Kingdom, which had refused to join in the negotiations leading to the creation of the ECSC and the EEC because British officials and most citizens objected to relinquishing national sovereignty to supranational bodies such as the High Authority and the European Commission, led a regional counteroffensive to establish a strictly intergovernmental economic organization that would restrict itself to the elimination of tariffs on industrial products among its members. British efforts resulted in the creation of the European Free Trade Association (EFTA) in 1960. In addition to Britain, EFTA members included Austria, Denmark, Norway, Portugal, Sweden, and Switzerland. Institutional authority was vested in an EFTA Council, where each member country was represented by a single delegate with the power to veto any collective decision.

Rapid economic expansion within the EEC during the 1950s and early 1960s prompted Britain to abandon its commitment to EFTA and apply instead for membership in the EEC in 1961. French President Charles de Gaulle publicly vetoed the British initiative at a press conference in January 1963, but his successors proved much more responsive to expanding the boundaries of the EEC to include Britain and other European democracies. Thus, the United Kingdom, Denmark, and Ireland joined the Community in 1973;[5] they were followed in 1981 by Greece and in 1986 by Spain and Portugal. Austria in 1990 and Sweden in 1991 submitted applications for membership that are under review for possible action by mid-decade. Pending a further enlargement of the Community, its present twelve members negotiated an agreement with the remaining EFTA nations in October 1991 to establish a common European Economic Area (EEA) for the free flow of capital, goods, services, and people among the nineteen countries that make up the two regional blocs.[6]

The demonstrated advantages of regional economic integration, as measured by a steady expansion of the EEC countries' industrial and agricultural production and foreign trade, inspired French, German, Italian, and other European leaders to broaden the Community's policy responsibilities and accord it greater institutional autonomy. In 1962 they voted on the implementation of a common agricultural policy designed to stabilize prices and guarantee a higher standard of living for farmers through a system of subsidies, achieved the completion of a customs union in 1968 (eighteen months ahead of the original schedule), and accorded the Community financial autonomy in 1970 by agreeing to allocate to it all custom duties on imported industrial and agricultural goods and a percentage of the value-added tax collected by each of the member countries. Simultaneously, the EEC members acted to strengthen the EEC's institutions. In 1965 they concluded a treaty to combine the ECSC, the EEC, and Euratom to form the present-day European Community (effective 1967). Accordingly, the two Councils became a single Council, and the High Authority and the European Commission merged to form a single Commission. A decade later, in 1974–75, the Council of Ministers agreed to allow the direct election of delegates to the European Assembly (which was renamed the European Parliament). This move, which was accompanied by an enlargement of the Parliament and an increase in its budgetary powers, significantly enhanced the authority of the Parliament vis-à-vis other European Community institutions by according it greater legitimacy in the eyes of national electorates. The first direct elections to the European Parliament were held in 1979; subsequent elections occurred in 1983 and 1989.

The integration movement experienced a serious setback in December 1965. The Treaty of Rome stipulated that majority voting in the Council of Ministers was to take effect in 1966. Fearing a reduction in France's influence in the Council of Ministers and encroachments on French national sovereignty, President de Gaulle ordered French officials to boycott European Community activities in protest against the scheduled introduction of majority voting.[7] Seven months later, in June 1966, Community officials resolved the crisis by negotiating an agreement known as the "Luxembourg compromise," which in effect retained the original rule of unanimity in Council decisions in issues deemed of "vital interest" to an individual member.[8] Mollified, de Gaulle ordered a resumption of French participation in Community affairs.

Toward Monetary and Economic Union

Under de Gaulle, the French had been consistently mistrustful of the value of European integration for the French economy. Official French skepticism about the scope and pace of European integration abated, however, following de Gaulle's resignation from the presidency in 1969. Under Presidents Georges Pompidou, Valéry Giscard d'Estaing, and François Mitterrand, France linked forces above all with Germany in promoting not only a territorial enlargement of the Community during the 1970s and 1980s but also an expansion of the EC's policy responsibilities. In successive moves, the EC implemented common measures regarding regional policy, research and development, the free movement of labor, worker rights, vocational training, the environment, energy, and fisheries. In 1978–79, the Community took an important qualitative step beyond functional integration when its members agreed to establish a common European Monetary System (EMS) as a means to promote economic stability and growth in response to the international crisis of "stagflation" during the early 1970s. Key components of the EMS included a new European Currency Unit (the ECU) for accounting and budgetary purposes, provisions for informational exchange about economic conditions, stable currency exchange rates via an Exchange Rate Mechanism (ERM), and greater convergence of economic policies among the member countries.[9]

To improve high-level policy consultation and coordination, the Council inaugurated regular meetings of the foreign ministers of the member states in 1970. At a summit meeting in 1974 in Paris, the heads of government and the French head of state concurred that they, too, should personally convene several times a year as the European Council. Together, these moves created highly visible and effective mechanisms for the Community to extend its role from regional economic and social policy to foreign policy as well.

A Conservative electoral victory in 1979 and the formation of an assertive new government under Margaret Thatcher set the stage for an incipient cleavage between Britain and other members of the EC concerning the pace and scope of European integration. Voicing reservations about the expansion of EC's policy responsibilities and concern about the costs of membership, Prime Minister Thatcher and her ministers strenuously advocated changes in the common agricultural policy and a reduction in British contributions to the annual EC budget. The other EC countries reluctantly acceded to both demands, agreeing at successive Council meetings in 1984 to curb agricultural surpluses and grant the United Kingdom monetary compensation for what the British considered to be excessive budgetary payments to the Community (which the Thatcher cabinet depicted as subsidies to less-efficient agricultural markets on the Continent). Prime Minister Thatcher criticized Community aspirations to achieve economic and political unity in a widely publicized speech in Bruges, Belgium, in September 1988, and adamantly refused at a meeting of the European Council in 1989 to join the other eleven members of the EC in affirming a common "social charter" designed to protect workers' rights. Mrs. Thatcher and her partisan supporters viewed her actions not as a repudiation of the European idea but instead as an affirmation of legitimate national self-interests and a commitment to a form of internationalism that includes but is not restricted to the European Community.[10]

Several factors converged during the 1980s to add momentum to the integration movement despite British misgivings. First was a second international economic crisis in 1979–80, which had prolonged effects. That crisis compelled European leaders to intensify their efforts to coordinate policies in an effort to combat inflation and revive growth. Second was the appointment of Jacques Delors as president of the Commission in 1985. Delors, a former minister of finance in the French government, proved a determined policy activist. He has repeatedly utilized his institutional position to mobilize support in favor of expanding the responsibilities and authority of the Community. Third, influential members of the elective European Parliament demanded a renewed commitment to European political integration. Their demands culminated in the adoption by the Parliament in 1984 of a draft treaty on European union.

Under Delors' leadership, the Commission in June 1985 submitted to the Council a White Paper outlining a comprehensive strategy for transforming the EC from a customs union and free trade area into a fully integrated regional market. As the Commission declared: "Europe stands at the crossroads. We either go ahead—with resolution and determination—or we drop back into mediocrity."[11] Emphatically favoring the former approach as consistent with the Treaty of Rome's vision of eventual European union, the Commission recommended nearly 300 measures to eliminate technical and other barriers to the attainment of an integrated regional market by the end of 1992. The measures, which require the approval of the member countries to be fully implemented, ranged from the abolition of frontier controls and technical restraints on the free movement of goods to technological standardization, the mutual recognition of professional qualifications, the attainment of a common market for services, and the harmonization of financial and fiscal policies within the Community.[12]

The initiatives of the European Parliament and the Commission resulted in the formation of an intergovernmental conference that drafted a treaty entitled the Single European Act, which members of the European Council signed in Luxembourg on 17 February 1986. The agreement endorsed the goal of economic and monetary union envisioned in the Commission's White Paper of 1985 (including the free movement of goods, services, people, and capital) and called on the member countries to cooperate to ensure policy convergence in these important areas. To facilitate this process, the Single European Act substituted the earlier unanimity rule with a new "qualified majority voting"[13] procedure with regard to Council decisions governing the implementation of the internal market, research and development, economic and social cohesion, and improved working conditions. In addition, regarding decisions subject to qualified majority voting, the Single European Act established a new "cooperation procedure" that compels the Council to consider parliamentary opinions on proposed legislation (including possible amendments and rejection) in a second reading. The agreement also granted Parliament the right of joint decision making with respect to the accession of new members and agreements of association and cooperation with nonmember countries. The Single European Act was merged into the Treaty of Rome in the form of amended and new articles of the original treaty.

In a crucial summit meeting held in Hanover, Germany, in June 1988, the European Council appointed a committee headed by Commission President Delors and composed primarily of the governors of the central banks in the twelve member countries to study and propose concrete stages that would lead to economic and monetary union (EMU). The Delors committee published its report in June 1989. Its central provisions called for progress toward EMU through successive stages of implementation: first, the attainment of monetary union, characterized by ever closer cooperation among the central banks, the attainment of permanently fixed exchange rates, and the creation of a "European System of Central Banks" (ESCB); and, second, the realization of regional economic union, characterized more vaguely by "effective competition policy, common policies for structural change, and macroeconomic policy coordination."[14] The European Council endorsed the Delors report at its session that same month in Madrid and declared that the first stage leading to monetary and economic union would begin on 1 July 1990.

At a summit meeting in Dublin in June 1990, members of the European Council resolved to formulate a concrete integration agenda by convening intergovernmental conferences on economic, monetary, and political union. Members of the Commission and high-level diplomats labored for the next eighteen months to produce successive drafts of such a treaty. During the deliberations, all but the United Kingdom agreed on most principles of closer union. Thatcher and John Major, her successor as (Conservative) Prime Minister, restated British opposition to key elements of a common economic policy. The consultations culminated in a historic accord at a European Council meeting in early December 1991 in Maastricht, the Netherlands, in which the EC heads of government, foreign ministers, and finance ministers concurred on separate draft treaties on political union and economic and monetary union that provide the legal basis for an enhanced role of the European Parliament in Community decisions, a common foreign and security policy, and the creation of a joint currency and a European bank by 1997 (or, at the latest, by 1999).[15] Britain joined the other eleven members of the Community in endorsing the agreement to establish "an ever closer union of the peoples of Europe,"[16] but reserved the right to "opt out" of the decision to establish a common currency. The two treaties on political union and economic and monetary union were combined in the Treaty on European Union signed at Maastricht in February 1992. If ratified by the parliaments of the twelve EC members, the treaty would be scheduled to go into effect by the end of that year.

In the months following the Maastricht summit, the ratification process became highly politicized in some of the member countries. A narrow majority of 50.7 percent of the Danish electorate rejected the Treaty on European Union in a national referendum on 2 June 1992, primarily on the grounds that many Danes feared the potential dominance of the larger EC states within the proposed union. The Danish vote raised a number of important legal and political issues for the future of the Community. Among them were the question of whether the Maastricht accord would be amended to allow for its implementation with the approval of the remaining EC members, Denmark's status as a member of the European Community but not of the envisaged political union, possible changes in the treaty, and the possibility of a second Danish referendum. In the immediate aftermath of the Danish decision, President Mitterrand hastily announced that he would schedule a national referendum during the fall in France as well. In Ireland, a domestic dispute involving a conflict between the Republic of Ireland's constitutional ban on abortions and Community law permitting the free movement of persons (e.g., to EC countries where abortions are permitted) initially clouded the prospective outcome of an Irish referendum on the Maastricht treaty. When the vote was held on 18 June, however, 69 percent of the electorate endorsed the accord. Germany's governing Christian Democrats and Free Democrats also faced mounting public criticism "that the [Maastricht] treaty might not provide adequate safeguards for future monetary and price stability."[17] Despite the Danish vote and various reservations about the treaty, most public officials throughout the Community anticipated that the Maastricht amendments of the Treaty of Rome would be implemented on schedule.

Challenges to Community Institutions

The prospective attainment of economic, monetary, and political union presents numerous interrelated challenges to individuals and organizations in Western Europe. Many of the immediate challenges are economic and managerial and have been forced upon firms that want to do business within the more closely integrated Community. Some member governments are challenged to adjust their own policies and modes of governing to correspond to the reality of an enhanced role for the Community in economic and foreign policy decisions. The most severe challenge, however, will confront the institutions of the EC themselves. This will be the challenge of becoming the governing bodies for an immense and exceedingly complex economic unit composed of a number of political units with varying degrees of commitment to the new political center. These European institutions are to serve as both the governing bodies for an enhanced, if not exactly new, autonomous political entity and the locus of international diplomacy, negotiation, and even confrontation over the character of that emerging entity. Given the rapidly changing nature of Western Europe in the late 1980s and early 1990s, the institutions of the European Community have at times appeared to be in a desperate race to stay abreast of events and in coordination with each other. The institutions have different amounts of sail and anchor for integration so that coordination among them can be difficult. They must find a means to supply that scarce commodity of "governance" to the Community during and after the attainment of a single market and closer economic, monetary, and political union.

Bureaucratic Politics

Our objective in this and the following chapters is to provide a means to understand decision-making structures and processes within the EC as a political system. Our basic argument is that knowledge about conventional models of governing in both an international organization and a European parliamentary democracy is inadequate for understanding the nature and functions of the institutions designed to govern the European Community. Instead, we need to understand governing as occurring on two levels. One is that of highly visible sessions of the European Council when political leaders of the member nations meet to negotiate among themselves concerning the future shape of Europe. At these discussions, the Community itself (usually represented by Commission President Delors) plays an increasingly important role. The momentous decisions that have moved Europe from "Eurosclerosis" to "Europhoria" have been announced from these meetings, occurring at least semiannually. Political outcomes emerging from these meetings have at times appeared to be almost counter to the interests of the participants, given that their own powers may be reduced, but participants have made such decisions notwithstanding.

The second level of policy making involves the bureaucracy within the European Commission. This level of activity is less visible to the average observer, but it has nonetheless been important for promoting policy integration within the Community. With enhanced policy integration has come an increased need for political integration. The bureaucratic level of policy making—and therefore of politics—is characterized by a gradual accretion of common policies and standards through the European bureaucracy (and its masters within the Commission) and through its contacts with national bureaucracies and with national and transnational interest groups.

Policy making at the bureaucratic level appears fragmented into relatively narrow, specialized fields of competence. This apparent fragmentation and increased linkages between the components of the Commission and components of national bureaucracies constitute the crucial aspects of decision making within the EC. Accordingly, the politics of the European Community can best be understood as bureaucratic politics.[18] Moreover, the tendency of bureaucratic decision making to occur within policy communities (especially those of a technical nature) has been to depoliticize what could have been highly divisive issues. As a result, the less overt politics of the EC has been able to force, or perhaps cajole, integration along. The process of bureaucratic rule making is facilitated by the powers given the Commission to initiate rules and the regulatory nature of much of the emerging European political system.

In the following chapters, we utilize the concept of bureaucratic politics to analyze decision-making structures and processes within the European Community. Chapter 27 briefly describes the EC's principal institutions (except for the Court of Justice). We do not describe in detail the various institutions but focus instead on the factors crucial for our argument about the importance of bureaucratic politics within the Community. Chapter 28 describes some of the fundamental political processes involving these institutions—including budgeting and rule making. Again, we concentrate on the role of the European bureaucracy within the system of policy making and the complex linkages it has to national governments and interest groups. In addition, we emphasize the importance of regulation and lawmaking, as opposed to large taxation and spending programs, in the progress of the Community toward integration. A regulative style of intervention can be less divisive than taxing and spending, and winners and losers in policy can be less easily identified. Our evaluation will clearly differ from most descriptions of how parliamentary democracies operate, but these differences are crucial for understanding the present functioning of the European Community.

In the final chapter, we will discuss in greater detail analytical models for understanding institutional decision making within the EC that may be more appropriate than either international organization or parliamentary government models. This chapter emphasizes the bureaucratic politics model and the importance of policy-making fragmentation within the Community. The implicit question in chapter 29 can be stated as follows: What are the "end-states" toward which the EC may now be evolving, and are existing institutions appropriate for the governance needs of the emerging political and economic system? An answer to this question involves an assessment of the ability of the EC's institutions to make appropriate policies while simultaneously achieving democratic accountability to its member states and citizens.

Notes

1. Supranational institutions are decision-making structures in international organizations that possess legal authority to make rules that are binding on the member nation-states. Supranational laws and policies thereby transcend national policy-making autonomy to a greater degree than intergovernmental treaties or agreements whose enforcement is contingent on the willingness of individual countries to comply with their terms. The European Community combines supranational and intergovernmental features in its institutional arrangements and decision-making powers, as explained in this and following chapters.

2. The concept of European regional integration has deep philosophical and historical roots, but it did not began to take concrete form until shortly after the end of World War II. Important milestone events included a widely publicized speech by wartime British Prime Minister Winston Churchill in Zürich in 1946 in which he advocated the creation of a United States of Europe, the formation of a privately supported "European Movement" later that same year, American encouragement of European economic cooperation with the proclamation of the Marshall Plan aid program in 1947, the formation of the Organization for European Economic Cooperation in 1948 to promote the reduction of financial and tariff barriers to

free trade throughout the region, and the creation of the Council of Europe in 1949. These initiatives, which many idealistic adherents hoped would culminate in a federal political system, coincided with the formation of partially overlapping military security systems in the form of the Western European Union (1948) and the North Atlantic Treaty Organization (NATO) in 1949. A comprehensive account of postwar integration efforts is Derek W. Urwin, *The Community of Europe: A History of European Integration since 1945* (New York: Longman, 1991).

3. Quoted from the preamble to the Treaty of Rome, published by the Office for Official Publications of the European Communities, *Treaties Establishing the European Communities* (Brussels and Luxembourg: ECSC-EEC-EAEC, 1987), 217.

4. In contrast to the ECSC and the EEC, Euratom proved relatively moribund as a regional organization.

5. Norway negotiated a membership treaty with the EEC in 1972, but a narrow majority of Norwegian voters rejected it in a national referendum held in September of that year. Subsequently, Norway along with Sweden, Finland, Austria, and Switzerland concluded industrial free-trade agreements with the Community in 1973.

6. The European Court of Justice dealt the accord an interim setback in December 1991 when it declared that the EEA treaty would impinge on EC autonomy. The EEA treaty provided for the creation of a new regional court that would consist of five judges from the Court of Justice and three from the EFTA countries. The judges' task would be to settle disputes between the EC, EFTA, and its member nations. The European Court, in ruling that these provisions would infringe on the original Treaty of Rome, in effect declared that the judicial provisions of the EEA treaty would have to be renegotiated.

7. Prior to this scheduled change in voting procedures, all Council decisions required unanimous consent among the member countries. De Gaulle was also strongly opposed to efforts by the other member countries to grant the EEC financial autonomy.

8. The agreement is named after the city where it was reached.

9. The ECU serves as a unit for calculating Community revenues and expenditures and in accounting for intergovernmental transactions among member states. Its value "derives from a weighted average of the value of the different Community currencies, with each currency given an influence to reflect its relative economic importance" (House of Lords, Select Committee on the European Communities, *The Delors Report: With Evidence* [London: Her Majesty's Stationery Office, 1989], 5). So far, the ECU does not physically exist in the form of bank notes and coins, but it is slated to become the basis for a common EC currency by the end of the 1990s. The ERM, meanwhile, promotes exchange rate stability within the Community by establishing a central parity for each national currency against "the currencies of the other

Member States involved. The currencies can fluctuate to either side of this figure within an agreed band. Beyond these limits, the stability of the currencies must be defended by foreign exchange intervention or by tools of economic policy such as interest rates. The central parities can be adjusted from time to time by mutual consent of ERM members" (ibid).

10. Such commitments include British membership in NATO and the United Nations and its leadership role in the Commonwealth of Nations. See Stephen George, *Britain and European Integration since 1945* (Oxford: Blackwell, 1991).

11. Commission of the European Communities, "Completing the Internal Market," *White Paper from the Commission to the European Council* (Brussels: June 1955), 55.

12. Ibid.

13. Under the new procedure, France, Germany, Italy, and the United Kingdom are each accorded ten votes; Spain has eight; Belgium, Greece, the Netherlands, and Portugal each have five; Denmark and Ireland have three votes; and Luxembourg two. Fifty-four votes constitute a "qualified majority," which means that at least seven states must concur in a Council decision. Neither the large countries as a bloc nor a coalition of small ones can prevail over each other, which places a premium on compromise and joint decisions in Council deliberations.

14. *The Delors Committee Report,* 7.

15. The Treaty on European Union provides that if at least seven of the twelve members of the EC meet stringent requirements for monetary union by 1997, the Community can proceed by a two-thirds vote of the members of the Council to create the common currency and European Bank. If no such "critical mass" of qualified nations exists by then, the Community will be required to implement both objectives by 1 January 1999.

16. Office for Official Publications of the European Communities, *Treaty on European Union* (Brussels and Luxembourg: ECSE-EEC-EAEC, 1992), 7.

17. *Financial Times,* 7, 8 March 1992.

18. Jerel Rosati, "Developing a Systematic Decision-Making Framework: Bureaucratic Politics in Perspective," *World Politics* 10 (1981): 234–52.

27

The Institutions of European Government

The European Community is simultaneously an international organization and the protogovernment for a regional political system, the parameters of which are not yet completely defined. As such, EC institutions as they were originally designed have some of the characteristics of an international organization, but they have also always had a more governmental nature than most international organizations. Further, the institutions have evolved over time and, in the process, have come to resemble those of a parliamentary government, although the similarities with national legislatures and executives are not at all exact. Understanding the European institutions, therefore, requires understanding that these institutions perform several types of tasks and that both legislative and executive functions are divided between two structures. It also requires understanding the evolutionary path upon which the institutions are embarked. Finally, it requires understanding the importance of the executive, and especially the fragmented nature of the executive, in segmenting conflict and allowing decision making in what might otherwise be difficult political circumstances.

Council of Ministers

Among the various EC decision-making structures, the Council of Ministers is the most similar to an institution that might be found in a conventional international organization. According to the Treaty on European Union, the Council consists "of a representative of each Member State at ministerial level, authorized to commit the government of that Member State."[1] Thus, the Council directly represents the nation-states that comprise the European Community, and its mode of interactions are to a great extent diplomacy and bargaining among sovereign powers rather than the more collegial interactions that might be expected within an organization pushing toward full economic integration in a relatively short period of time. As a result, the Council of Ministers often operates as the brake on movement toward a Single Europe or toward further economic and especially political integration. Yet, at the same time, the movement toward fuller economic integration could not have occurred unless the Council had made decisions to proceed. It is at this level, and especially in the European Council (which, as previously noted, is composed of the heads-of-government of the member countries), that the most visible decisions about integration are processed. Moreover, individual members of the Council of Ministers have been instrumental in the process of integration, so that individuals as well as institutions have been consequential at this level of executive-legislative decisions.

As its name implies, the Council of Ministers is composed of cabinet ministers who are appointed (one each) by the twelve member governments. In addition, the Commission appoints one representative to the Council to propose and defend policies and represent the interests of the Community as a whole. Assisting the Council of Ministers is a Committee of Permanent Representatives (COREPER), which is made up of senior civil servants from the member countries. Its task is to help on a day-to-day basis in the preparation and management of the work of the Council. The Council is also served by a secretary-general, who heads a General Secretariat made up of professional civil servants recruited from the member countries.

Members of the Council of Ministers are elective politicians from the member countries; they are rotated according to the issue being debated. For example, if agriculture is on the agenda, ministers of agriculture will represent each country during that particular session of the Council. Similarly, if financial matters are to be discussed, the ministers of finance from the member countries serve as the Council. When particularly important matters are debated, the foreign ministers or even the prime ministers of each country (the president in the case of France) will attend the Council sessions. The presidency of the Council of Ministers rotates among the member countries every six months; toward the end of each presidency, the European Council convenes in the host country. These meetings have been a major source of movement toward greater economic and especially political integration.

Because the ministers who participate in the Council of Ministers are major political figures in their own countries, considerations of na-

475

tional politics characteristically motivate their behavior. This means that the ministers must be concerned about the impact of any decisions made in Brussels on the population back home and about the effects of those decisions on any upcoming elections (and there is almost always an election of some sort looming somewhere in the twelve countries). As the populations of the member countries become increasingly cognizant of the importance of the EC for their economic and political futures, it has become more difficult for politicians to escape repercussions for decisions they may take within the European framework. For example, a loss of popular support for the Conservative party in Britain in both local elections and the European election in 1989 was attributed in part to the anti-European attitudes of Mrs. Thatcher and her willingness to broadcast those views in official venues.

The Council of Ministers functions through a number of component councils. A relatively sparse policy agenda during the early years of the Community meant that the work of the Council could be processed by the general Council of Ministers, which was usually attended by the foreign ministers of the member countries. As the workload became more extensive and had more policy foci, however, the need arose for more specialized councils. The most important of those is the General Affairs Council, which is composed of the foreign ministers or their deputies. Several other long-standing councils have also been established. Paramount among them is the Council of Finance Ministers, which is responsible for coordinating and harmonizing monetary and fiscal policy among the member countries. It is also responsible for monitoring the European Monetary System (EMS) and the place of the European Currency Unit (ECU) in international financial markets. The Agriculture Council, composed of the twelve agricultural ministers, is another well-established and important council. Since the largest proportion of the EC budget is allocated to agricultural programs, the importance of agricultural constituencies and the central place of the agricultural program in EC politics have made the Agriculture Council a central locus of policy making.[2]

As the EC's policy concerns have expanded, the number of other specialized councils functioning under the umbrella of the Council of Ministers has gradually increased. They include councils dealing with fisheries, budgets, the nonfinancial aspects of the internal market, foreign aid, social affairs, environment, and science and technology. Each council involves the relevant ministers from the member countries and establishes a basis for ongoing personal cooperation and negotiation among executives specializing in a given policy area. Since the completion of the internal market by the end of 1992 will involve greater harmonization of all of these activities, the work of these specialized councils will inevitably increase.

The functional differentiation of the councils is an important element of EC governance. It contributes to the complexity of governance, and beneath a proliferation of professional and expert language it tends to mask many potentially divisive issues. Furthermore, because these councils are linked directly to experts at the national level, interest groups such as farmers, unions, and employer associations lobby at both national and European levels of governance. Specialization and differentiation make EC policy making resemble policy making in the U.S. federal government, with the numerous Community policy communities or networks appearing to exert significant influence (if not control) over public policy to a greater degree than in most national governments in Europe.

One of the most important functions of the COREPER and the Council of Ministers is monitoring the numerous decisions taken within the Commission in the name of the EC and analyzing draft legislation emanating from the Commission. This constitutes, in essence, one executive institution exercising oversight over another (even though, as previously noted, the Council embodies features of a legislative body as well). The Commission is the principal source of the large volume of rules and regulations required to implement the Treaty of Rome and other agreements having the force of law in the EC. Although the Commission has the authority to act independently in making some rules, the Council is organized for oversight of these decisions through a large number of working groups. The working groups are composed of members of the permanent missions of the member states as well as numerous national civil servants, who fly back and forth between their national capitals and Brussels. As with the full Council of Ministers, its component councils, and COREPER, the Commission has a representative on each working group to defend the position of the Commission, present draft texts, and thereby advance the cause of integration. The Commission representatives are often unsuccessful in preventing national interests from being voiced in opposition to specific Commission proposals, but they do have an opportunity to defend such proposals.

The Council remains the locus of most parochialism in the European Community. Indeed, it was conceived from the outset as an institution that would permit member nations to express national views about regional policy. There are, however, supranational checks on nationalism. First, a member of the Commission is present at every level of the Council's operations to represent the "European" perspective and to prevent any manifestation of nationalism from remaining unchallenged. This means that the style of Council deliberations is usually more like a discussion within a partnership than a debate between adversaries, although there will always be debate. Second, with at least two levels of officials always functioning beneath the more manifestly political level of activity within the Council, much of the Council's work can be performed with less regard to domestic political considerations. Likewise, the involvement of professional civil servants from the EC nations means that decisions at the official level often are made in conformity with the technical standards prevailing in a given policy area rather than along national lines. (Again, a bureaucratic or "policy community" perspective is more apt for understanding policy in the EC than strictly partisan or nationalist perspectives.)

It is especially important that the agenda and draft decisions are prepared for the Council of Ministers by COREPER and other permanent officials (e.g., members of the Council's Secretariat). If issues can be kept off the Council's agenda or defused before they reach it, then parochial conflict can be minimized. This is one indication of the importance of bureaucratic processes for understanding politics in the European Community. This will be even more evident when we look at the role of the Commission in fostering integration and at the role of national bureaucracies in implementing European policy. The cause of movement toward a single market and greater economic and political union is perhaps better served by nonpolitical processes (political here meaning partisan and national). Progress toward supranationalism appears possible when manifestly political institutions are confined to the mere "enregisterment of decisions made elsewhere,"[3] a point that was raised in much of the functionalist and neofunctionalist literature during the initial phase of the integration movement.[4] The institutions of the European Community have not achieved that bureaucratized state perfectly, but they do permit substantial policy-making activity by bureaucracies before political officials ever see the prospective decisions.

Qualified Majority Voting

The adoption of "qualified majority voting" through the Single European Act of 1986 has begun to alter the role of the Council and, to some extent, to change the entire Community. Since the Council of Ministers was designed as a venue where national representatives could defend their national interests, voting rules prior to the acceptance of the Single European Act required unanimity on most issues. The rules have now been changed so that, except for actions that clearly involve constitutional issues or new competences for the EC or areas of important national interest, qualified majority voting is sufficient to enact policies.[5] The change of rules to allow qualified majority voting thus moves policy making in the Community away from what might be expected in an international organization and toward what might be expected regarding policy making and coalition formation in a parliamentary democracy.

Although the larger members of the Community are clearly more powerful than the smaller countries, the requirement that a qualified majority must consist of fifty-four votes prevents the former from dictating policy to the latter. The same decision-making rule simultaneously protects the larger countries from attempts by the smaller countries to impose policies they oppose or that may require them to make greater economic contributions to the Community budget. Decision making within the Community, therefore, involves more of an emphasis on coalition-building than reliance on national vetoes for protection.

More subtle procedural changes have also influenced the manner in which the Council of Ministers functions. Following the adoption of the Luxembourg compromise in 1966, package deals analogous to American legislative "logrolling," which benefits all parties involved, have become a common means to generate policy consensus, albeit sometimes an expensive one. Although these changes in decision-making procedures have not silenced opposition by Britain or other EC countries to particular Council decisions, many politicians and informed citizens in the member countries increasingly perceive national isolation as a real danger. For example, many Conservative politicians viewed official British reservations about movement toward monetary union during the summer and fall of 1990 as a major threat to Britain's role in the EC; their growing unease helped intensify internal party opposition to Mrs. Thatcher's leadership and contributed to her decision to resign as prime minister in late November.[6]

Greater use of qualified majority voting in the Council also may alter policy-making dynamics among the member countries. If countries see a risk of becoming isolated by bargaining too hard on an issue, they may become more compromising and willing to accept some short-term losses to perceived national interests in preference to losing a vote publicly. Furthermore, if one country were to lose frequently in Council decisions, it would risk becoming a pariah within the Community and losing even more power and influence with respect to other countries.

Isolation would be a much greater danger for smaller countries, but the established pattern of decision making, in which playing the game is as important as winning all the time, is a more familiar pattern of politics in those countries than in the larger European democracies.[7] The Netherlands, in particular, has managed a political pattern of inclusion and accommodation that has been beneficial in preserving the democratic stability and effective decision making that will be crucial for the future success of the EC once the euphoria over 1992 wanes.

The European Commission

The Commission is the more permanent executive of the European Community and has been the source of much of the movement toward greater unification. With the accession of new EC members during the 1970s and 1980s, the Commission was expanded to include seventeen members who are appointed for four-year terms by the Council from member countries in consultation with the other countries. France, Germany, Italy, Spain, and the United Kingdom have two commissioners each; the other countries have one each. Once the Treaty on European Union is implemented by the end of 1992, the size of the Commission will be reduced to the number of member countries belonging to the EC (presently twelve but likely to increase by mid-decade as other countries such as Austria and Sweden join). Simultaneously, the commissioners' term of office will be lengthened to five years.

Once appointed to office, commissioners take an oath of loyalty to the European Community and pledge to accept no national instructions on policy. Members of the Commission are often individuals who have been politically active but who have decided, for personal or ideological reasons, to leave the fray of national politics and work on the European stage. Perhaps less generously, the Commission has become a place where national governments can "exile" politicians too difficult to have at home or who need to be retired with an honorable (and remunerative) position. This pattern has begun to change, however, with the appointment in recent years of younger and more "technocratic" commissioners. What is most interesting is that politicians who have been deeply involved in national affairs (including Roy Jenkins of Britain and Jacques Delors of France) honor their oath of office and become rather quickly active in, and committed to, broader European issues. Some commissioners, on the other hand, have been criticized for being too nationally oriented, too eager to obtain positions in order to further the interests of their home countries. The Council, in close consultation with the member countries, appoints one commission member to be president of the Commission and thereby *primus inter pares*. The president of the Commission serves a two-year renewable term. The operating understanding has been that the presidency will alternate between larger and smaller member countries. To date, two presidents have been from France, one each from the other founding nations, and one from the United Kingdom. The member countries tend to nominate their commissioners to reflect in part national political pressures. The Federal Republic of Germany, for example, has tended to have one commissioner from the major government party and the second commissioner from the opposition. Clearly, then, although the Commission is a European and supranational institution, it also has direct and important links to national politics and national policy considerations.

In addition to meaning the commissioners themselves, the term *Commission* is also applied to all the permanent staff of the Community, namely, the "Eurocrats."[8] At present, the Commission employs approximately 2,500 senior civil servants plus well over 10,000 additional staff members. Some of these employees are on secondment from their national governments, although an overwhelming majority are direct employees of the European Community. While certainly smaller than the bureaucracies of any of the member nations, this is still a sizable staff with impressive professional capabilities for rule making and rule enforcement.

As previously noted, the Commission has been the locus of much of the movement toward greater economic and political integration. A great deal of this movement has resulted from gradual bureaucratic pressure rather than from more dramatic political decisions. Political decisions by the Council may receive greater media attention, as was the case with the passage of the Single European Act in 1986 and agreement on the draft treaties on economic, monetary, and political union at Maastricht in 1991, but day-by-day activities by the Commission and its Eurocrats—in the form of regulation after regulation—have established the public policy foundation for integration envisaged by such political acts. Likewise, their seemingly incremental and "bureaucratic" activities interpret and extend the meanings of political actions and may at times push integration even further than the more politicized Council intends or considers politically possible.

The European Community bureaucracy is divided into twenty-three directorates-general (DGs), usually referred to by number, e.g. DG XII. The directorates-general are assigned specific functional tasks, but the evolving character of their work means that it is easier to use simple numerical designations to distinguish among them. New tasks can be added to one or another DG, although not without debate. The organizational location of important new functions may be the subject of intense bureaucratic infighting among the DGs, but that can be managed without having to alter titles and the organization chart. The internal structure of the directorates varies. Generally it is hierarchical. At the apex is a member of the Commission who is shadowed by a European civil servant (the director-general); both are served by a small cabinet that coordinates the work of a number of subordinate directorates and sections. Some DGs, with more complex policy responsibilities, have more than one commissioner. For example, DG XV, which is responsible for financial institutions and company law, currently has three. Given the sensitivity of the Commission's role and the possibility of trampling on national sensibilities, component sections of the DGs tend to work on a somewhat shorter leash from their political leaders than might be true in many national bureaucracies.

The activity of the Commission is analogous to that of a public bureaucracy in a nation-state except for one important factor. The European bureaucracy is concerned less than its national counterparts are with the direct implementation of laws. In most instances, they must depend upon national bureaucracies (including national police forces) to implement Community law.[9] The principal task of the Commission, therefore, is to generate rules, specifically *European* rules. Much as a national bureaucracy issues secondary legislation (comparable to American "regulations") to supplement any primary legislation passed by the legislature, the Commission generates rules and regulations in pursuit of the Treaty of Rome, the Single European Act, and other primary agreements governing the Community. These rules are monitored by working groups within the Council, as well as by committees in national governments, and most must be approved by the Council. The initiative for rule making, however, lies in the hands of the Commission, which accords its members considerable influence over the final shape of Community policy.

As well as having the capacity to generate a few rules on its own, the Commission has the exclusive right and the duty to introduce legislation to the Council. The Council may accept a proposal or not, but it cannot act without prior initiation by the Commission. Few items ever come to the Council without previous widespread discussion within its working groups, COREPER, and to some extent with the national governments, but the Commission sets the Council's agenda. This right of initiation gives the Commission the ability to speed up the pace of integration, or at least the capacity to *attempt* to speed up the pace. At times, it may be able to accelerate the pace simply by the volume of its activity. With hundreds of employees and highly specialized personnel in the DGs, the Commission may be able to overwhelm the more political bodies of the Community by sheer volume and speed of action. Again, this may be analogous to the central position that permanent bureaucracies have achieved by virtue of their size and technical capacity in most national political systems.[10] One consequence is that the Commission has provoked reactions similar to those in national political systems. An example is a recent decision by the Council to expand its Secretariat as a means to ensure that the overtly political institutions of the EC government have the ability to make their voices heard effectively.

The position of the Commission constitutes something of a dilemma for both the Commission and its leadership. On the one hand, the Commission is recognized as the "conscience" of the Community and the most powerful force for a more integrated Europe. On the other hand, the Commission embodies a substantial "democratic deficit" in that its appointive and bureaucratic nature makes its members appear remote and intrusive to many actors in national governments, if not to the average citizen in Europe. Thus, the Commission must at once be active in advocating its own agenda while it remains cognizant of the needs of individual member countries and their political leaders. This dilemma encourages the Commission to utilize bureaucratic politics as a means of preserving its position within the Community. That is, individual commissioners are conscious of the need to build coalitions around specific proposals with members of affected interests and relevant national actors political as well as bureaucratic. This is not democracy in the usual sense, but does constitute a means of responding to functional and national demands.

The European Parliament

The third major political institution of the European Community is the European Parliament, which consists of 518 members who are directly elected by citizens in the member countries according to national electoral laws.[11] Both its size and electoral provisions are likely to change by mid-decade as a result of the Maastricht summit in December 1991. The European Council agreed to consider treaty provisions governing the number of parliamentary deputies prior to the next election in 1994, and the Treaty on European Union stipulates that the "European Parliament shall draw up proposals for elections by direct universal suf-frage in accordance with a uniform procedure in all Member States."[12]

An assessment of the evolution of the European Parliament reveals a great deal about the development of the European Community.[13] The Parliament began as an institution in which the national governments were in reality the dominant players; the "Euro MPs" were initially ap-pointed by their national parliaments and therefore behaved somewhat like ambassadors from their national governments as representatives of the general public. Since the advent of direct elections in 1979, however, the European Parliament has evolved to the point that it can fill some of the "democratic deficit" that afflicts the Community as a whole since citizens now have a direct electoral relationship with their Euro MPs. In addition, the European Parliament has begun to assert its prerogatives as it attempts to play a role similar to that expected of a legislature in a conventional parliamentary democracy. The European Parliament must evolve a good bit further before it achieves a degree of power equivalent to that of national parliaments, but progress has been steady and sub-stantial.

The Community's need to achieve greater legitimation in response to the inevitable strains that will accompany the achievement of a single market and movement toward economic, monetary, and political union accords Parliament a crucial opportunity to assert further its power and importance. The Commission and the Council of Ministers will contin-ue to possess greater decision-making authority under the Treaty on Eu-ropean Union, but a pending expansion of the supervisory and legisla-tive roles of the European Parliament will help make the actions of the former institutions appear legitimate to populations accustomed to be-ing governed by legislative bodies and cabinet governments. Specifically, the Treaty on European Union accords Parliament the future right to approve the Council's nominations of the president and other members of the Commission, authorizes Parliament (at the request of a quarter of its members) to appoint a temporary Committee of Inquiry "to investi-gate ... alleged contraventions or maladministration in the implemen-tation of Community law," creates a new office of an appointive om-budsman "empowered to receive complaints from any citizen of the Union," and significantly extends Parliament's right of co-decision mak-ing in the EC's legislative process (see details below and in chapter 28).[14]

Among the most important features of the European Parliament is that it now has a partisan rather than national basis. Euro MPs are nominated by political parties that are organized on a Europewide basis or that campaign in at least several countries.[15] Once elected, Euro MPs sit by party, not by nation, with nine party groups presently represented (see table 27.1). National party caucuses are sometimes (if rarely) convened, but the basic organization of the European Parliament is partisan and supranational. This does not mean that the issues on which candidates are elected to the EP are necessarily European; many campaigns are concerned with the relationship of the nation-state to Europe, as electoral difficulties experienced by the British Conservatives during the summer campaign of 1989 indicated.[16] Still, Europewide issues (including progress toward the single market and the attainment of monetary and economic union) are also a component of electoral campaigns.

One important organizational feature enhancing the decision-making powers of the European Parliament is its well-developed committee structure. Unlike many national parliaments, the Parliament has developed an elaborate structure consisting of eighteen permanent committees specialized by policy area. Members are assigned to a committee at the beginning of a five-year term of office (roughly according to the partisan distribution of seats) and can therefore serve long enough to develop substantial policy expertise. Furthermore, the committees meet in Brussels (unlike the European Parliament itself, which conducts its ple-

TABLE 27.1

ELECTIONS TO THE EUROPEAN PARLIAMENT, 1979–89
(NUMBER OF SEATS)

Party	1979	1984	1989
European left	44	41	42
Rainbow Group[a]	—	20	42
Socialists	113	130	180
Independents	20	7	12
European People's Party[b]	107	110	128
Liberals	40	31	45
European Democratic Alliance[c]	22	29	21
European Democracy Group[d]	64	50	34
European right[e]	—	16	14
Total	410	434	518

a. The Greens plus various nationalist and ethnic minority parties.
b. Primarily Christian Democrats.
c. Primarily French Gaullists and Irish Fianna Fail.
d. Dominated by British Conservatives.
e. Various Republican and non-Christian Democratic parties.

nary sessions in Strasbourg) and hence have the capacity to oversee closely the work of the Commission and Council. Because these committees review, at least informally, most draft legislation by the Commission and Council, they have a substantial influence on the shape of the final rules.

The differentiation of the European Parliament into functional committees facilitates cooperation between Euro MPs and Commission bureaucrats in the equally differentiated DG structure. The predictable outcome is policy segmentation, much as in the United States. The resultant symbiotic relationship that is emerging between the committees and the DGs whose work the committees oversee appears heightened by informal linkages between both of these institutional actors and European and national interest groups, and policy communities are emerging around each of the major issue areas within which the Community has competence.[17]

The Single European Act substantially enhanced the powers of the European Parliament in a variety of ways. The act requires that the Parliament approve all accession and association agreements with other states before they are considered by the Council. It also introduced a new cooperation procedure affecting qualified majority decisions that concern the internal market, social policy, regional policy, and research. Prior to the adoption of the act, Parliament would render an opinion on legislation proposed by the Commission before the Council took final action, but that opinion had little real impact. Now, the European Parliament has the right to review the Council's "common position" before the Council can make a final decision. Parliament has three options under the new legislative procedures: (1) The position can be approved or simply not disapproved within three months; (2) the position can be rejected, in which case the legislation fails unless the Council acts unanimously (with approval of the Commission) within three months to endorse it; or (3) the European Parliament may propose amendments which, if they are supported by the Commission, require unanimity on the part of the Council to overturn. (A qualified majority suffices for the Council to accept proposed amendments.). Amendments that are rejected by the Commission require unanimity on the Council for passage. Rejection and amendment of Council positions require a simple majority of Parliament. These powers have provided the European Parliament with the basis of becoming a real force in decision making within the Community. The interactions among the Commission, the European Parliament, and the Council in the Community's decision-making process are depicted in figure 27.1.

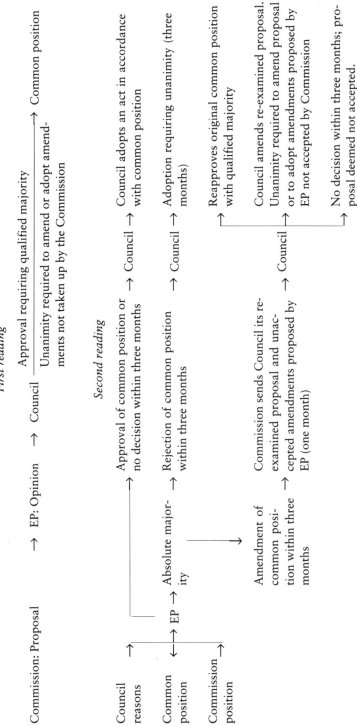

FIGURE 27.1
DECISION-MAKING PROCEDURES IN THE EUROPEAN COMMUNITY

The decision-making authority of the European Parliament will be enhanced under terms of the Treaty on European Union. As under present arrangements, the Parliament will have the right to approve or not make a decision on a common position by the Council, in which case the Council shall "definitively enact" the proposal and it becomes law. Alternatively, an absolute majority of the members of the European Parliament may decide to reject or amend a common position. In the case of rejection, the Council may decide to convene a Conciliation Committee composed of a representative of the Commission and an equal number of Council members or their deputies and members of the European Parliament in an effort to reconcile the differences. Following such deliberations, the Parliament will have the option of once again rejecting the proposal by an absolute majority (in which case it fails) or of proposing amendments to the act in question. In the case of proposed amendments, both the Council and the Commission will be required to state their opinions. The Council may decide within three months to accept such amendments, either by a qualified majority, if the Commission concurs in them, or unanimously, if the Commission rejects the amendments. In either event, the proposal becomes law. If, however, the Council does not approve the proposed amendments, the presidents of the Council and of Parliament are required to convene a meeting of the Conciliation Committee. If the Conciliation Committee approves a joint text of the law within a six-week period, the Council and the European Parliament may decide by qualified and absolute majorities, respectively, to enact the proposal. The failure of either institution to approve the text, however, means that it will not be enacted. Conversely, if members of the Conciliation Committee are unable to reach a compromise agreement, the proposal automatically fails unless the Council reaffirms its original position on the proposal by a qualified majority. In such an event, the act is adopted unless Parliament rejects it by an absolute majority.[18]

Pending changes in the composition of the Commission, the political powers of Parliament, and decision-making procedures underscore the continuing evolution of European institutions as Europe moves toward closer economic, monetary, and political union. The Treaty on European Union establishes the outlines of an emerging regional political system in which the Council, the Commission, and the European Parliament will play the manifest political game of influencing the policies of the Community as distinctive yet more equal partners.

Notes

1. Article 146, *Treaty on European Union,* 64.

2. See Joan Pearce, "The Common Agricultural Policy: The Accumulation of Special Interests," in Helen Wallace, William Wallace, and Carole Webb, eds., *Policy-Making in the European Community,* 2d ed. (Chichester: Wiley, 1983).

3. Alfred Grosser, cited in Mattei Dogan, "The Political Power of the Western Mandarin," in *The Mandarins of Western Europe,* ed. Mattei Dogan (New York: Halsted, 1975).

4. In a classic review and critique of the functionalist concept in international relations theory, Ernst B. Haas asserts that functionalism refers to the potential emergence of international organizations (such as the World Health Organization) that are based on "shared human needs and desires that exist and clamor for attention outside the realm of the political. [Functionalists] believe in the possibility of specifying technical and 'noncontroversial' aspects of governmental conduct, and of weaving an ever-spreading web of international institutional relationships on the basis of meeting such needs. They would concentrate on commonly experienced needs initially, expecting the circle of the noncontroversial to expand at the expense of the political, as practical cooperation became coterminous with the totality of interstate relations. At that point a true world community will have arisen." Neofunctionalists, such as Haas himself, concur with functionalists in anticipating prospective institutional "spillover" from one sphere of international cooperation to another as such cooperation proves mutually beneficial to the actors concerned, but they argue that such spillover is driven less by altruism or voluntarism than by "an institutionalized pattern of interest politics, played out within existing international organizations." That is, institutionalized cooperation—such as the European integration movement—does not simply "happen" but, instead, is the product of overt political choices and pressure. See Ernst Haas, *Beyond the Nation State: Functionalism and International Organization* (Stanford, Calif.: Stanford University Press, 1964), 6, 35.

5. For example, of the eighty-five issues that were under active consideration in October 1989, only eleven (among them, tax harmonization) were deemed to require unanimity.

6. "The Fall of Thatcher: Was It, or Was It Not, a Plot?" *The Economist* (9 March 1991): 21–24.

7. Martin O. Heisler, with Robert Kvavik, "Patterns of European Politics: The European Polity Model," in Heisler, ed., *Politics in Europe* (New York: David McKay, 1974).

8. The term comes from Altiero Spinelli, a leading Italian advocate of European federalism.

9. Heinrich Seidentopf and Jacques Ziller, *Making European Policies Work: The Implementation of Community Legislation in the Member States* (London: Sage, 1987).

10. See Joel D. Aberbach, Robert D. Putnam, and Bert A. Rockman, *Politicians and Bureaucrats in Western Democracies* (Cambridge, Mass.: Harvard University Press, 1981).

11. Members of the Community are accorded different numbers of seats according to differences in the size of the population. Hence, Britain, France, Germany, and Italy each have eighty-one deputies; Spain has sixty; the Netherlands has twenty-five; Belgium, Greece, and Portugal each have twenty-four; Denmark has sixteen; Ireland has fifteen; and Luxembourg has six. Deputies are elected in the Continental members of the Community according to national varieties of proportional representation, whereas delegates from the United Kingdom are chosen according to that country's plurality electoral system. These differences are explained in the country chapters of this volume.

12. Article 137, *Treaty on European Union*, G 2.

13. Michael Palmer, "The Development of the European Parliament's Institutional Role Within the European Community, 1974–83," *Journal of European Integration* (1983): 183–202.

14. Articles 138c, 138e, 158, 189, 189a, 189b, and 189c of the *Treaty on European Union*, 63–64, 75–79.

15. Geoffrey Pridham and Pippa Pridham, *Towards Transnational Parties in the European Community* (London: Policy Studies Institute, 1979), and Roswitha Bourguignon-Wittke, et al., "Five Years of the Directly Elected European Parliament," *Journal of Common Market Studies* 23 (1985): 31–53.

16. Conservative strength fell from 43.3 percent of the popular vote in the 1987 election to 34.7 percent in the European election two years later (a loss of 8.6 percent). In contrast, the opposition Labour party advanced from 31.5 percent in 1987 to 40.1 percent in 1989.

17. See Peter M. Haas, "Do Regimes Matter? Epistemic Communities and Mediterranean Pollution Control," *International Organization* 43 (1989): 377–403. The concept of "epistemic communities" is similar to "policy communities" used elsewhere, but it depends more upon the existence of a common professional or scientific basis for the formation of a particular community of shared interests.

18. Articles 189b–c, *Treaty on European Union*, 76–79.

28

Political Processes in the European Community

As the preceding assessment of institutional actors indicates, the European Community is characterized by distinctive features of decision making and implementation. One is the dichotomy between national interests and supranational interests and the dynamic interplay among individuals and institutions representing these often divergent interests. A second distinctive feature is the importance of bureaucratic decision making within the EC. Even if the Community is not wholly dominated by permanent bureaucrats in the Commission, it is certainly heavily influenced by them and their interactions with the bureaucrats of member states. Finally, a problem of "democratic deficit" persists within the Community. Despite direct elections to the European Parliament, the EC still lacks a strong direct relationship with its citizens and has a considerable distance to go before the Community will resemble a conventional parliamentary democracy.

The comparison between West European parliamentary democracies and Community institutions should not be extended too far. For example, public revenue and expenditure issues, while important for the EC, are not as central as they are for most national governments. The major impact of the European Community on its constituent nations is increasingly felt through law and regulation rather than through spending programs. Reliance on regulatory instruments as mechanisms for integration may be a wise choice: It is a characteristic of regulative instruments that they tend to mask the effects of policies and to make winners and losers less visible than expenditure programs commonly do. This characteristic of regulatory policy may minimize (although not eliminate) national, regional, and class conflicts over EC policy. The choice of this policy instrument, however, also enhances the relative powers of the Commission and the bureaucracy.

The Budgetary Process

The budgetary process is crucial in any political system, even one emphasizing primarily laws and regulations. The question of who gets what remains a central political issue, and the budgetary process is where that question is answered most explicitly. The obverse question of who pays what is equally important, especially when it has national-level as well as individual-level answers. For example, countries that have efficient agricultural sectors (the United Kingdom, for one) have expressed reservations about subsidizing less efficient agriculture elsewhere. We need to understand, therefore, where the money to run the European Community comes from, where it goes, and who makes the decisions about these flows of funds. The adequacy of the funding arrangements for any movement toward greater integration, especially greater political integration, should also be understood as a way of understanding the likelihood of greater integration.

The Revenue Process

Where does the money come from? Compared to most international organizations, the European Community is in an extremely advantageous position in raising money. It has four designated revenue sources, three of which it can claim as its own. Therefore, the EC generally does not have to beg member countries for funds. In contrast to the United Nations, the EC is reasonably sure of receiving its rightful revenues. On the other hand, the revenues the Community does receive are still conceptualized somewhat in national terms—who is "contributing" how much. As a result, arguments about fiscal equity and fairness revolve more around national considerations than around socioeconomic class, progressivity, or even the horizontal neutrality of the revenue structure. The Community does not yet have a mechanism for taxing citizens directly; the tax revenues it enjoys are indirectly collected for it by national governments. Consequently, the national governments continue to play an obvious and significant role in the revenue process.[1]

The EC's first two revenue sources are comparable to a national government's taxes on goods and services. One is the common levy on industrial imports from outside the EC. This is derived from virtually the same revenue process as national governments' tariff collections on imports except that national customs agents hand the money directly over to the EC. The other is the common levy applied to all relevant agricultural products imported from outside the Community, which is collected in much the same way as the common industrial tariff.

The EC's third source of revenue is tied to the nationally assessed value-added tax (VAT), which is an excise or sales tax paid by consumers at the time of purchase on incremental increases in the value of goods during their production. The EC is entitled to 1.4 percent of the base rate used for calculating the VAT in each country. The member states are largely free to make their own regulations establishing that base and to extract their VAT in their own manner; hence, the tax rates vary from country to country, although harmonization in this area has begun.[2] Thus, the third source of EC revenue is *not* a flat 1.4 percent of national VAT but rather 1.4 percent of the arithmetic base that each country uses to calculate the national VAT obligations of businesses and services.

The EC's fourth revenue source, recently added and still controversial, grew out of a Community financial crises during the mid-1980s that was resolved in the form of the "Brussels agreements" of 1988. The Brussels agreements established a negotiated level of resource availability for the EC based upon a percentage of the combined gross national products (GNP) of the member countries.[3] If Community revenues from the first three sources just described do not provide sufficient resources to meet this GNP ceiling in a given year, then special levies can be imposed on the member countries. In 1989, for example, a deficit of 3.9 billion ECUs was covered by a levy of approximately one-tenth of one percent of each member's GNP.

This fourth source of revenue has strengthened the financial basis of the Community, but it also raises doubts about the Community's financial future. This new source of funds permits Community resources to keep up with expenditure demands. Furthermore, the agreement acknowledges that the Community must have sufficient money to implement its programs and that, to some extent, expenditure commitments will determine the size of the annual EC budget. Furthermore, this source of additional funds is flexible and can be used to meet the financial needs of the Community without regard to revenue generated by the volume of international trade or other uncontrollable economic aggregates. On the other hand, this additional source of revenue represents a departure from the principle of EC fiscal independence and places the Community more at the mercy of the member countries, since it is dependent on the ability of each member state to pay.[4] This move toward potentially greater dependence occurred at precisely the same time that the EC was seeking a more independent role through the adoption of the Single European Act.

Of these four sources of revenue, the EC's share of national VATs generates the largest source of Community income. Custom duties are second, followed in descending order by GNP resources and agricultural levies (see table 28.1).

Revenue policy in the EC is an administratively driven and virtualy automatic process even more than are equivalent processes within single countries. Two of the four revenue sources function automatically; they depend more upon trade and implementation by national tax collectors than on decisions made in Brussels. The third source of revenue (the percentage of the VAT base) is also beyond the control of Community policymakers because it is automatically linked to the tax systems of the member countries. Admittedly, the Community must decide through meetings of the European Council or the Council of Ministers what the EC percentage of the national tax base will be; but once those decisions are made, the process becomes automatic and wholly dependent upon economic activity. Likewise, after the initial agreement on the fourth source of revenue (including the provision that it could be levied on national governments), the process itself appears largely statistical; the real decisions concerning whether member states will use their financial

TABLE 28.1

GENERAL COMMUNITY BUDGET: SOURCES OF REVENUE
IN 1989

Revenue source	ECUs (in millions)	Percent of total
Customs duties	9,954	22.20
Agricultural levies	2,462	5.49
VAT	26,219	58.47
GNP resource	3,907	8.71
Miscellaneous	274	0.61
Balance from previous financial year	2,025	4.52
Total	44,841	100.00

SOURCE: Commission of the European Communities, *The European Community Budget* (Luxembourg: Office for Official Publications of the European Communities, August-September 1989), 5.

obligations to the EC to exert leverage over the Community devolve onto the national governments. Although the collection and remittance of the EC's revenue from these four sources are nearly automatic, government officials are fully aware of the magnitude and costs of their countries' contributions to the Community. Hence, revenue questions remain important political issues, both for the Community and the member states.

Expenditures

The EC budgetary process is now largely driven by expenditure commitments. The budgetary agreements of the 1980s established a ceiling, linked to the total GNP of EC members, above which expenditures should not rise; beneath that ceiling, expenditure commitments determine how much money will pass through the Community budget.[5] The Community now spends money for a wide variety of purposes. The EC's expenditures, unlike those of other international organizations, often have a direct impact on citizens of the member countries. Spending arising from agricultural policy currently accounts for approximately 53 percent of total EC expenditures. Other important kinds of expenditures are payments for regional development, spending designed to promote economies of scale (e.g., research) and the harmonization of social policies, and spending on external affairs (including an increasing amount of foreign aid) (see table 28.2).

Like that of national governments, a great deal of EC spending is mandatory and largely uncontrollable. Agricultural expenditures are obligatory under the Treaty of Rome and the agreements arising out of it, so that any Community budget will contain forecasts of expenditures in this area rather than impose ceilings on the amount that can legally be spent. In 1984, the Council issued a decree that the rate of increase of agricultural spending should not exceed the rate of increase in its own source revenues. That was an admirable guideline, but in practice it is useful primarily for determining how much excess spending has occurred. Subsequent changes in agricultural policies, such as a reduction in levels of support for cereals after 160 million tons of production, have introduced some degree of control over agricultural expenditures in the Community. Recent Commission decisions have further tended to reduce agricultural expenditures. Agriculture is forecast to be a declining component of EC expenditure in future years, and even greater overall budgetary control may be obtainable.

Although there is a substantial uncontrollable element of expenditures determined by the Treaty and other agreements, the process for determining EC expenditures is broadly similar to revenue processes on the national level. The European Parliament has a greater role in expenditures than it does with respect to revenues. It can, as it did in both 1979 and 1984, reject the budget presented by the Commission. Moreover, the Parliament can affect the amount and purpose of expenditures that do not result directly from treaty provisions (which are called "noncompulsory expenditures"). Perhaps most important is the dual fact that the overall level of expenditures has not kept pace with ceilings established in the Brussels agreements and that, unlike most legislatures in national democratic systems, the European Parliament has some flexibility with which it can agree to finance policy initiatives. Such decisions will not occur without politics, however, as the poorer members of the EC (notably Spain, Portugal, and Greece) press for full use of the GNP ceilings to fund development programs for themselves. In contrast, the more affluent countries urge financial restraint and advocate the expansion of high-tech research and development projects that are likely to benefit their own citizens. Further, the increased need to finance economic development in Central and Eastern Europe in the aftermath of Communism's demise has placed substantial additional strains on the Community budget.

TABLE 28.2
COMMUNITY EXPENDITURES, 1991 AND 1992
(IN ECUS)

Budget category	1991 (000 omitted)	1992 (000 omitted)
Common agricultural policy	31,516,000	34,660,000
Regional development	14,804,000	17,965,255
Research and development	2,465,800	2,700,047
Political expenditures (energy, fisheries, transport, environment, youth)	2,473,490	2,633,442
Foreign assistance	2,400,940	2,414,338
Administration	3,911,751	3,823,834
Monetary reserve	1,000,000	1,000,000
Total	58,571,981	65,196,916

SOURCE: European Commission, *Preliminary Draft Budget for 1992* (press release) (Brussels: 1991). The figures for 1992 are the Commission's proposed budget. In 1992, one ECU was approximately the equivalent of $1.40.

Assessment

The budget has been one means through which central governments in newly formed federations have expanded their influence and power over their component units. The evidence to date about the success of European institutions in using the budget for similar purposes is mixed. On the one hand, the European budget remains a relatively small component: approximately 3 percent of total public expenditures in the twelve member nations. Even with GNP ceilings to provide greater latitude for European spending, the EC operates with greater budget constraint than does any member nation. If for no other reason, the EC is forbidden by Article 199 of the Treaty of Rome from running a deficit.[6] Finally, most Community spending has been on a single program—agriculture—and that program has become highly controversial in some of the member countries as well as for many individual Europeans. Thus, the EC has gained somewhat less public support (except among farmers and agricultural interest groups) through public expenditure than its adherents might have hoped.

On the other hand, the budgetary base of the European Community has expanded. The GNP ceiling has provided substantial latitude for decision makers to utilize expanded revenues to undertake new policy initiatives. In addition, the European Parliament is becoming a more central actor in setting expenditure priorities and promoting nonmandatory expenditure programs such as research and development, regional development, and aid to Eastern Europe. Now that these programs are in place, it will be difficult for the Community to withdraw from such activities, and public expenditures are therefore likely to increase. Furthermore, some of the most effective instruments for integration are regulatory in nature and may not require great financial resources to implement. The Community's institutions now have a stronger financial base and a stronger budgetary process and thus appear to have the capacity to achieve continued increases in supranational policy-making activity.

Executive Accountability

The European Community has an executive and a parliament. What it still lacks is a clear, democratic means of linking the one with the other. The members of the Council of Ministers are accountable to their national governments and will remain thereby constrained in the foreseeable future. Therefore, it remains for the Commission to be held accountable to the European Parliament. As presently constituted, the

Commission is a responsible body but not an accountable or responsive institution in the usual meanings of these terms. The commissioners are responsible primarily to their own consciences to act in a European manner and to defend the Treaty of Rome. This does not yet constitute a conventional democratic government, and there are few means available for directly enforcing responsibility or accountability on the members of the Commission or even the bureaucrats employed by the Commission. The only real check available to the European Parliament is to dismiss the entire Commission through a vote of no confidence, which thus far has never occurred. The potential disruption from such a dramatic action would produce great upheaval and serve little purpose, and such a move is unlikely until Community institutions are better entrenched and legitimated. Moreover, in such an event nothing would prevent national governments from simply reappointing the same commissioners, thereby provoking an even greater political crisis within the Community. Until the implementation of the pending Treaty on European Union, which allows a vote of approval of the commissioners by the European Parliament, the Commission must therefore remain accountable to the commissioners themselves, their own consciences, and only in the most extreme cases to the European Parliament.

Thus far, the established system of responsible government has worked. The commissioners have been deeply committed to the Community and its goals, and most of them have played their roles responsibly. Indeed, most members and especially the presidents of the Commission have promoted supranational values and have been driving forces in developing greater Community powers over policy. Still there is a need, if the EC is to become a genuine political entity, for better articulated mechanisms of popular and political accountability on the part of the Commission. Until the European Parliament achieves greater influence over the appointment of commissioners, the Community must depend upon the good will and competence of national governments to send the correct people to Brussels. The national governments have thus far acted very responsibly, but few political systems can afford to rely too long on the good will of others and survive.

Some changes have made EC institutions more closely approximate the governments of European nations. One important move is that budgetary accountability to Parliament has now been institutionalized and, as noted, Parliament has twice rejected budgets submitted by the Commission. Historically, the power of the purse has been the central lever for legislative acquisition of power, and it appears that the development of legislative-executive relationships in the EC will be little different. In addition, a "question hour" has been institutionalized in Parliament, with members of the Commission required to attend when issues under their purview within the various DGs are discussed. Likewise, members of the Commission increasingly are expected to attend committee meetings in the European Parliament and may have to respond to questions advanced there.

What is missing in these existing processes is a clear conception of cabinet government and ministerial responsibility. First, if the president of the Commission is to become the analogue of a prime minister, he or she should be able to select the other members of the "cabinet." At present, however, all commissioners are appointed by the member states. The Dooge Commission, which submitted a comprehensive report on the functioning of Community institutions in 1985, suggested that the president should be empowered to select the other commissioners, subject to review by the national governments.[7] This suggestion has been provisionally adopted in the proposed Treaty of Political Union, which stipulates that the "governments of the Member States shall, *in consultation with the nominee for President,* nominate the other persons whom they intend to appoint as members of the Commission."[8] A persisting problem, which the treaty revisions do not address, concerns the inability of either the president or Parliament to dismiss individual commissions once they are appointed. The president and the Council have the power of assigning portfolios and can bury a less competent or cooperative commissioner in a minor position, but such an individual remains a commissioner until his or her normal replacement, voluntary retirement, or "compulsory retirement" by a member government. If the European Parliament is to achieve more complete control over the Commission as the equivalent of its own government, it would have to be able to dismiss individual commissioners rather than resort to the draconian treaty provision for dismissing the Commission as a whole. Given the delicate balance that exists between national interests and the role of the Commission, this would be a difficult reform for many governments to accept. Such a change, however, is almost inevitable if governance as understood in European democracies is to be fully achieved within the EC.

Policy Making

Policy making in the Community involves processes by which Community institutions decide what proposals to accept as authoritative and therefore which proposed laws they should attempt to implement. A decision at the Community level, more than at a national level, involves strategic choices in addition to the usual questions concerning the desirability and feasibility of a given policy. Leaders of Community institutions must decide not only what they want to do substantively but also how fast and how far they can push member governments and citizens of member countries. Some dedicated Europeanists are willing to push very hard and very far, but they risk creating manifest opposition to economic and political union and the EC more generally. If the European Community and its integration can be compared to a "bicycle" that remains upright only so long as it is going forward, then creating manifest (and needless) opposition is dangerous.[9] Feasibility is used too facilely as a constraint on policy making at the national level, but it becomes a crucial consideration at this level.[10] The regulatory issues central to the Community generate sufficient controversy, but in general not as much as fiscal issues in which the winners and losers are more visible.

In accordance with the initial formulation of decision making in the Treaty of Rome, the Commission prepared draft legislation and the Council of Ministers made the principal decisions. For a few issues, the Commission could issue laws and engage in quasi-legislative activities; this was closely analogous to secondary legislation by national bureaucracies. In this arrangement, the European Parliament was largely excluded. It might debate the merits of legislation, but it had little impact on final decisions. The Single European Act changed the relative powers of institutions by introducing a "cooperation procedure," the second reading described above that accords Parliament powers of co-decision with the Council over a substantial range of policy issues. In addition to the formal changes brought about through this procedure, there is now substantially more consultation and indirect contact between the Parliament and the other institutions.[11] With these changes in the decision-making process, the European Parliament became for the first time a significant legislative body. This is important for reasons other than simply constituting an increase in the relative institutional power of the European Parliament. The most important secondary feature of enhanced powers for the Parliament is that, like the Commission, it appears to have a more European perspective than does the Council of Ministers. This perspective is demonstrated in the workings of unofficial components of the Parliament as well as the official support of the Parliament for federalist solutions to European political relations such as those contained in the Treaty on European Union, which (as previously noted) will accord Parliament even greater authority in joint decision making with the Council. As Parliament assumes an enhanced role in European legislation in years ahead, it appears that the rider on the bicycle may have to pedal very fast to keep up with the changes in the political system.

In fairness, it would be easy to exaggerate the importance of the "cooperation procedure" established by the Single European Act. The ultimate powers of decision making remain in the Council so long as it can achieve unanimity. The Parliament has to date rejected outright several "common positions" from the Council. For one on occupational health, there was no chance of unanimity and a compromise emerged. On others, the Council achieved unanimity.[12] This pattern of rule making makes the interactions between these institutions somewhat analogous to the separation of powers in the United States, except that the executive has the right to overturn the veto and therefore to make the final decision, rather than vice versa. Further, the unanimity rule is a much tougher standard—even if the Council has worked with such a rule when not technically required—than is the two-thirds requirement for Congress to overturn a presidential veto.

As important as the Council and parliamentary levels of decision making are for the EC, the impetus for most European rule making occurs at a lower level. The impetus typically comes from the the Commission and its component units. In addition to broad legislative statements, rule making in the Community comes in three forms. The simplest and most compelling rules are called *regulations*, which must be put into effect automatically by national governments. Such rules are directly binding on national governments and other actors (including corporations and individuals) and pass into national law without additional action. Regulations may be made by a simplified written procedure rather than the more complex oral procedure required for most rule making.

At the second level, rules made through this process are *directives*. The goals expressed in a directive are also binding, but the actual content remains open to some variation and interpretation by the member nations. National governments can decide how they put a directive into effect, which gives them the opportunity for delay, bargaining with the Commission, and bargaining with interests within their own borders. To become effective, directives must be incorporated in some manner into national law. As a result, directives provide substantial latitude to national governments to impose their own priorities.

Finally, the Community also issues *decisions* which are very specific and apply only to the individuals or governments to which they are addressed. They are, however, binding on the target of the action.

Since 1970, as table 28.3 indicates, the number of each of these outcomes has increased dramatically. Greatest in frequency are regulations, followed by "decisions" and—in distant third place— directives.

TABLE 28.3

COUNCIL OUTCOMES, 1970–90

	Percent		
Type of outcome	*1970*	*1980*	*1990*
Regulations	43	92	479
Decisions	14	92	330
Directives	18	38	54
Other acts	2	18	8

SOURCE: *Official Journal of the European Communities. Directory of Community Legislation in Force and Other Acts of the Community Institutions*, vol. 2, Chronological Index. Alphabetical Index, 18th ed. (Brussels: European Communities, 1991). The annual totals do not include amended versions of the various acts in question.

Although the Council has preponderant authority in making Community decisions, the Commission is not without some direct and indirect powers of its own. For administrative matters, it can make binding declarations; it issues several thousand rules of its own each year. As the experience with secondary legislation at the national level indicates, administrative discretion can include a wide variety of issues with significant policy consequences. At least twice, for example, the Commission has had to decide on the amount of price supports in the Common Agricultural Program because the Council was deadlocked.[13] In addition, the Commission decides what cases should be submitted to the European Court of Justice and can, in essence, use the Court (if successful) to make rules on its own behalf. Finally, simply by announcing its opinion on an issue, the Commission (and especially its president) has been able at times to gain compliance without resort to formal rule making. Some of that power may be a function of the personal influence of Delors himself rather than a function of his office, but in the short run the Commission does have this kind of informal influence.

The Role of Implementation

A realistic assessment of rule making in the Community must take into account the substantial powers exercised by national bureaucracies in the implementation of EC regulations, directives, and decisions. What does it mean, for example, that a government must "automatically" enforce the regulations made by the Commission and Council? Numerous studies of national policy making indicate that a purely legalistic conception of the performance of administrative systems in implementation is at best self-delusory on the part of politicians.[14] In fact, a great deal of interpretation and even redefinition of policy occurs during implementation. Unless that influence of administration on policy intentions is understood adequately, analysts risk making errors in assigning responsibility for policy failures or even policy successes.[15]

Implementation in the European Community is no less subject to the impact of implementing agents. The process within the EC is analogous to implementation of policies in a federal regime such as the Federal Republic of Germany, in which policies are made centrally and implemented by subnational governments. Thus, even if policy emanates from Brussels, the national governments are by no means impotent.[16] They have the opportunity to bargain over policy and its meaning with their counterparts in Brussels, and they can then attempt to interpret policy in their own terms. The existing evidence on implementation of EC directives and regulations is that there is still substantial room for national action and that such actions can substantially alter the meaning of regulations in practice.[17] These findings further reinforce multilevel "interlocking" interpretations of the Community, with winning and losing the game being defined differently at different levels and at different stages of the rule-making process. Losing at the policy-making stage in Brussels may not be so important if there is a second round at the implementation stage at which time the national government, through its bureaucracy, has an opportunity to determine what will actually happen in the policy area in that country.

The Special Case of Foreign Policy

In addition to their primary preoccupation with "domestic" economic and social issues, Community leaders have also begun the arduous process of establishing a common foreign policy. This has become a compelling necessity as the Community increasingly emerges as a political entity in international politics. Yet the quest for Community consensus on foreign policy and regional security represents a more difficult challenge than even the thorniest economic and institutional issues in that foreign policy has traditionally been the reserve of national governments.

European politicians and Community officials are fully cognizant of the EC's dependence on the international economy, which underscores the necessity to link economic and foreign policy concerns. Moreover, the dramatic political and economic changes in Central and Eastern Europe and the virtual end of the Cold War have accelerated the movement toward a common foreign policy during the 1990s. The reactions of the EC and its leaders to these extraordinary events have brought the Community closer to a common policy toward foreign events, including such matters as foreign aid to the former Soviet Union and the various East European countries. Nonetheless, the special problems of forming a common foreign policy within the EC should be understood separately from other policy areas.

The member governments established a preliminary framework for forming a common foreign policy when they launched a consultative procedure known as European Political Cooperation (EPC) in 1969 and agreed to convene regular meetings of the European Council, beginning in 1974. This framework for foreign policy consultations has been partially institutionalized in the form of a Political Committee, which serves common administrative purposes, and a Group of Correspondents in the member countries, which monitors EPC activities. The linkage between the EC and EPC was deepened when the European Council adopted the "Solemn Declaration on European Union" in Stuttgart in June 1983, which bound Community members to "intensified consultations with a view to permitting timely joint action on all major foreign policies."[18] The relationship between the Community and EPC became more formalized through the Single European Act with its requirements for consultation and policy consistency between the two organizations.

Economic globalization and increased international political fluidity in the wake of the collapse of Communist regimes in Central and Eastern Europe have intensified pressures for greater economic and foreign policy coordination among EC members. The need for the Community to serve as a unitary actor in international affairs will be true regardless of whether its partners in economic and political negotiations are nation-states such as the United States and Japan or regional blocs such as EFTA. Coping with the admission of new members or forging closer economic ties with European countries that are not presently members of the EC through the proposed creation of a joint European Economic Area will also have substantial political implications in addition to the economic ones over which the EC already has competence. In short, movement toward a single European market will necessarily be matched by continuing efforts to forge a common European foreign policy. Tentative steps in that direction began with an attempt by EC members to negotiate a peaceful settlement to the Gulf crisis in January 1991 and gathered momentum later in the year when the Community's foreign ministers sought, with mixed results, to mediate a cease-fire among warring nationalist factions in the Yugoslav civil war.

The Treaty on European Union establishes a comprehensive legal basis for a common foreign and security policy in the future. Affirming a collective commitment to safeguarding "the common values, fundamental interests and independence of the European Union" and strengthening "the security of the Union and its Member States in all ways," the twelve EC countries agreed to establish joint cooperative procedures for "gradually implementing ... joint action in the areas in which the Member States have interests in common." They pledged that a joint Council (presumably made up of the foreign ministers) shall define a common position on foreign and security policy "[w]henever it deems it necessary" and that "Member States shall ensure that their national policies conform to the common position." The European Council will be responsible for defining general guidelines for determining whether "a matter should be of joint action."[19] Detailed decisions concerning policy implementation are to be made by qualified majority voting.

Treaty provisions largely skirt the thorny issue of how the member states will actually institutionalize collective military security. Key national players are profoundly divided on this central question, with the British favoring close cooperation between the Community and NATO while the French prefer an autonomous European defense pillar that would be anchored in the Western European Union (WEU).[20] These differences were reflected in alternative proposals that surfaced during the fall of 1991 when the British and the Italians suggested incremental steps toward creating an independent European force as part of NATO and French and German leaders proposed a joint military command within the framework of the EC.[21] These competing concepts were superficially merged in the Maastricht accord when the signatories agreed that the Community "shall request the Western European Union ... to elaborate and implement decisions and actions of the Union which have defence implications" and, simultaneously, that future foreign and security policies "shall respect the obligations of certain Member States under the North Atlantic Treaty and be compatible with the common security and defence policy established within that framework."[22] These potentially contradictory demands will inevitably provoke continued controversy among EC members, particularly between Britain and the Franco-German coalition, and it is by no means certain whether a joint European military command will in fact be established. Nor are the institutional procedures for joint decision making in the area of foreign and security policy, including the roles to be performed by the Commission and the European Parliament, entirely clear in the Treaty on European Union. Nonetheless, the Community's demonstrated resolve to proceed beyond the attainment of a regional market and economic union to external political cooperation points toward greater European detachment from the United States as an important consequence of an increasingly integrated European polity.

Notes

1. Citizens are not totally unaware that some portion of their taxes help fund the European Community, but the process remains less visible than direct EC taxation would be.

2. This base is to be calculated on a harmonized basis and bargaining over tax harmonization is one of the most difficult issues in moving toward a single market. See Lucy Kellaway, "Commission to Study Tax 'Threat' to Single Market," *Financial Times*, 28 February 1990.

3. The percentage of GNP available to the EC was to increase gradually from 1.15 percent in 1988 to 1.2 percent in 1992. The original Commission target had been 1.4 percent.

4. When, however, member countries have withheld revenue collected for the EC (as Britain did in 1983), the European Court has ruled that they were, in essence, *ultra vires* and required them to pay interest.

5. Michael Shackleton, *The Budget of the European Community* (London: Pinter, 1990).

6. There are, however, a variety of borrowing arrangements financed by the Community, although these activities are "off-budget" and are not figured as a part of the official Community budget.

7. *Report of the Ad Hoc Committee on Institutional Affairs (the Dooge Report)* (Brussels: The European Commission, 1985).

8. Article 158, *Treaty on European Union*, 67. Italics added for emphasis.

9. Michael Emerson, "1992 and After: The Bicycle Theory Rides Again," *Political Quarterly* 59 (1988): 289–99.

10. Giandomenico Majone, "The Feasibility of Social Policy," *Policy Sciences* 6 (1975): 49–69.

11. John Fitzmaurice, "An Analysis of the European Community's Co-operation Procedures," *Journal of Common Market Studies* 26 (1988): 389–400.

12. Richard Corbett, "Testing the New Procedures: The European Parliament's First Experiences with Its New 'Single Act' Powers," *Journal of Common Market Studies* 27, no. 4 (June 1989): 364.

13. Alan Swinbank, "The Common Agricultural Policy and the Politics of European Decision Making," *Journal of Common Market Studies* 27, no. 4 (June 1989): 303–21.

14. The classic study is Jeffrey L. Pressman and Aaron Wildavsky, *Implementation* (Berkeley: University of California Press, 1973).

15. For discussions of these contrasting outcomes, see William S. Pierce, *Bureaucratic Failures* (New York: Humanities Press, 1981); Nelson Polsby, *Political Innovation in America* (New Haven, Conn.: Yale University Press, 1984); and John Schwartz, *America's Hidden Policy Successes* (New York: Norton, 1985).

16. Werner Feld and John Wildgen, "National Administrative Elites and European Integration: Saboteurs at Work?" *Journal of Common Market Studies* 13 (1975): 244–65.

17. Heinrich Siedentopf and Jacques Ziller, *Making European Politics Work: The Implementation of Community Legislation in the Community States* (London: Sage, 1979).

18. Federal Republic of Germany, *European Political Co-operation (EPC)* 5th ed. (Bonn: Press and Information Office, 1988), 75–76.

19. Articles J.1, J.2, J.3, "Provisions on a Common Foreign and Security Policy," *Treaty on European Union*, 123–24.

20. "In the beginning was the word, and the word was defence," *The Economist*, 18 May 1991, 55. The Western European Union, as noted in Chapter 26, was established in 1948 as a European military alliance one year prior to the creation of the more encompassing North Atlantic Treaty Organization. The WEU was vastly overshadowed by NATO throughout the years of the Cold War, but it retains a separate organizational structure that permits policy consultation and coordination among its nine members (Britain, France, Germany, Italy, the Benelux countries, Spain, and Portugal). France, which withdrew from military cooperation with NATO under President de Gaulle in 1966, views the WEU with special favor.

21. "France, Germany Initiate EC Plan for Defense Role," *Wall Street Journal*, 17 October 1991, A18.

22. Article J.4, "Provisions on a Common Foreign and Security Policy," *Treaty on Political Union*, 126.

29

Institutional Analysis

This chapter focuses on contrasting theoretical approaches to understanding the European Community and the movement toward economic
and political union. As the assessment of European institutions and political processes in the Community in chapters 27 and 28 suggests, institutional analysis constitutes a useful means to explain changes that have
already occurred within the EC and to anticipate future changes. Although much of the day-to-day movement toward a single market might
be explained through functionalist and neofunctionalist logic,[1] the major transformations of the EC have taken place as a result of political
acts. Some of these have been individual acts of leadership, such as political initiatives by former Commission President Roy Jenkins in relation to monetary and fiscal policy and current President Delors in advocating the Single European Act and the target date for completing the
internal market by the end of 1992. Individual actions, however, must
be translated into an institutional framework if they are to persist and
produce the intended policy outcomes. These outcomes can be explained and interpreted in different ways, each of which provides particular utility for understanding highly complex problems of analysis. We
will conclude with some thoughts of our own about an explanation that
draws on both the "new institutionalism" advanced by some political
scientists and the old bureaucratic politics characteristic of the "real
world" model of politics.[2]

An institutional analysis of the European Community must, first of
all, take into account multiple interconnected "games" being played simultaneously within that Community. The idea of a two-stage game or
decision-making process, in which actors first negotiate "the best possible terms for agreeing to pursue another's preferences ..." and then
"execute the contracts,"[3] is much too simplistic to capture the com-

plexity of motives and interactions occurring within the EC. Instead, one game is the national game, in which individual nations attempt to extract as much from the EC as possible while relinquishing as little as possible. Phrased differently, this is a game of coping with interdependence. A second game is played by the institutions themselves, with each seeking to gain powers vis-à-vis other institutions. This game may be played for all the right reasons (e.g., the Commission believes that it is the protector of the Treaty of Rome while the Council considers itself the protector of national interests), but it is a complex, multifaceted game nonetheless. This second game is, of course, intimately linked with the first.

Finally, there is a bureaucratic game that appears to be becoming an important determinant for everything else that is occurring within the EC. The twenty-three directorates-general within the Commission appear to be developing their own organizational cultures and approaches to policy. As in most governmental structures, the boundaries among different policy competences are not entirely clear, and the DGs may therefore compete for policy space. Where, for example, is the boundary between research and development on the one hand and the telecommunications industry or science policy on the other? Even within a single DG, conflicts may occur over policy definitions. For example, is vocational education a concern of education policy or of labor-market policy? The components of the European bureaucracy also appear to be developing their own working relationships with national governments, or at least with relevant components of national governments. Likewise, individuals and organizations in the national bureaucracies are promoting their own relationships and their own policy goals with organizations in Brussels. At times, policies with little support within a nation (such as environmental protection in Britain) may have a great deal of support in Brussels. While these developments in the EC may lead to the diminution of national dominance over policy, they also raise the prospect that the European government may have to fight the "government against sub-government" battle familiar at the national level.[4] It will be important to remember throughout this discussion that all these games are occurring simultaneously, and that strategies adopted in one may have real consequences for outcomes in another.[5]

The National Basis

It would be misleading to analyze institutional and policy-making changes in Europe solely from the perspective of the European Community and its institutions. We must remain aware of the role that the member states have played and will continue to play in the integration movement. Furthermore, policy choices made by the member states are, to some extent, conditioned by events in their own international economic and political environments. Hence, it would also be incorrect to assess regional change without considering what has been occurring outside of Western Europe. The European Community is becoming a major actor on the international stage, but it has yet to supplant fully the nation-states that belong to it or to achieve its own capacity to steer the international political economy.[6] One of the most significant developments for the European Community, which is rooted in domestic politics and policy management, has been a tendency for many regimes to minimize the role performed by central governments in delivering government services and even policy making. At the least extreme level, this has involved decentralizing many policy-making and implementation activities to subnational governments, even in states such as France and Spain that historically have been highly centralized.[7] At a more extreme level, a number of governments have undertaken to supply public services through paragovernmental or "third party" organizations.[8] At the most extreme level, many European governments have privatized a number of public corporations and public services.[9] Such privatization has been carried out by governments with traditions of étatist management of their economies and societies as well as those with histories of laissez-faire policies toward the economy.

The principal question that the above changes have generated is whether the nation-state remains of central importance. Numerous governments, and a particularly large number of politicians, have opted for a governing style that permits the private sector to make an increasing number of decisions that once would have been made by government. If government is not the best way to make policy decisions—especially about the economy—then does it perhaps not matter so much who constitutes the government? Devaluing the role of national governments, in that case, may make the creation of a more powerful "European government" of some sort more palatable to politicians and citizens alike.

It may be that governing in the early 1990s is not so much undesirable as it is impossible or at least difficult. Interdependence has become a buzz word to describe ongoing changes in the international political economy, and it contains a considerable element of truth. National governments, or even large blocs like the EC, are increasingly incapable of determining their own economic futures. As a consequence, being compelled to take responsibility as a national government is often like being handed a poisoned chalice; taking credit for the good times in the 1950s, 1960s, and 1970s makes it difficult not to be blamed for the economic slowdown of the 1980s and early 1990s. Adopting a more cooperative attitude toward Europe and permitting more economic decisions to be made in Brussels is a means of avoiding blame for anything that goes wrong and perhaps making a few things go right. Indeed, politics in this era has been described as "blame avoidance" rather than credit claiming.[10]

Federalism

We can begin a discussion of institutional politics in the European Community with the institutional option that most clearly addresses the issue of the national game. To many adherents of European integration, the political situation of the EC appears ripe for a federal solution. Federalists such as the Italian politician Altiero Spinelli are not content with maintaining a regional system whose political foundations remain a number of independent states. Instead, they advocate the transformation of the European Community into a full political union as a means to transcend nationalism and achieve a common European identity.[11] To such activists, a federal arrangement appears to be a natural mechanism for accommodating the existing nation-states while still providing a superordinate government for the entire aggregation.

If there is indeed to be a federal solution to the European political question, an immediate question arises concerning what type of federalism is meant. For Anglo-Saxons, the contractual and constitutional model of federalism appears to be the most logical answer. According to this approach, the component governments, acting as independent and autonomous units, initially agree to establish a new level of government and grant certain specified powers to that new, superordinate entity. The granting of those powers is never sufficiently clear to prevent a need for future elaboration and interpretation, but some attempt would be made to allocate powers and to form a binding and enduring contract. Where such federal arrangements have been established, as in the United States and Australia, political power has tended to gravitate toward the highest level of government, in part because of the availability of financial resources and in part because of "spillover" effects. These national outcomes are analogous to the same effects deemed important by functionalist and neofunctionalist theorists of supranational integration.[12] That is, in most federal systems, it quickly becomes apparent that only the higher level of government is capable of regulating the numerous interactions and externalities that result from the independent actions of individuals and subnational governments.

For many Continental Europeans, in contrast, federalism may have a very different connotation, based on the concept of "subsidiarity" in Roman Catholic social thought. This term first appeared in Pope Pius XI's Encyclical Letter *Quadragesimo Anno* (1931) and means, according to the *Oxford English Dictionary,* "the principle that a central authority should have a subsidiary function, performing only those tasks which cannot be performed effectively at a more immediate or local level."[13] In other words, all actions in social and political life should be performed by the smallest possible unit of government. The subsidiarity principle implies a more organic view of society and political life than does the more mechanistic and legalistic approach of Anglo-Saxon federalism. A leading European advocate of subsidiarity is Commission President Delors.

The subsidiarity principle is likely to serve as the basis for a European federation. Commission documents repeatedly cite the term, and the Treaty on European Union explicitly affirms that the proposed union "shall respect the principle of subsidiarity."[14] As a logic of federal structures and political processes, subsidiarity implies that a regional EC government would do as little as possible, leaving most functions to the national and perhaps especially subnational governments. It may even imply that as many things as possible would be done by private and voluntary organizations rather than *any* level of government. This approach would appear to give the subnational governments an important place in European government, even though the European Court has ruled that it is the responsibility of national governments to make subnational governments conform to European policy. The concept of subsidiarity also leaves a great deal of room for interpretation, most obviously with respect to the "lowest possible" unit of government that should perform a given function.

From the perspective of the national game being played in Europe, these alternative visions of federalism have rather different implications. The Anglo-Saxon version would place the nation-state in the central position in bargaining over the shape of a future political entity in Europe. In essence, the nation-states would bargain over how much of their "sovereignty" they would be willing to grant to the European Community in exchange for how much benefit they would derive from the coordination of policies, reduced trade barriers, and perhaps direct subsidies for some sectors (e.g., agriculture and less developed regions). In the Continental conception of federalism with its emphasis on subsidiarity, the nation-states are important but are only one among many sets of institutions that have a right to participate in the bargaining process. The subsidiarity approach, therefore, may permit the EC to deal directly with subnational governments, interest groups, and citizens without having to be overly concerned with the rights of nation-states. Of course, the EC is already involved with relationships circumventing national governments, so the acceptance of subsidiarity as the defining principle of federalism might only institutionalize and legitimize current practices.

Although federalism and other ideas about intergovernmental relations are usually discussed in terms of the political relationships among the political units, we should also note that these alternatives may have consequences for the other games being played within the EC. In particular, the acceptance of the Continental version of federalism might encourage the development of "picket fence federalism" and intergovernmental relations similar to established practices in the United States.[15] These patterns could develop under other more formal models of federalism (as indeed they have), but they appear more likely with the Continental version. If a nation-state comparable to the federal system in the United States has no special claims to bargaining on behalf of its constituent units, it would be easy for a government in Brussels to seek out smaller units where policy can be made and implemented. Those units could be political (e.g., local governments) or functional (e.g., interest groups, businesses, etc.). In any case, policy making would be likely to develop along functional lines, with important linkages forged between Brussels and the smaller units. This would, in turn, enhance the powers of the DGs within the Commission or any other bureaucratic structures that manage interactions with the public and private entities that actually deliver services.

If the pattern of intergovernmental relations within the EC assumes a functional style in which the intermediate political institutions (in this case nations) can be virtually bypassed, then most vertical constitutional models of federalism would appear to be inapplicable. In their place, something more like the "policy community" approach would seem to make greater sense for understanding policy-making relationships. This suggests that any "top-down" conception of intergovernmental relations dominated by the center and involving the equivalent of diplomatic relations between the levels of government would not be an appropriate analytical approach. Instead, the problems demanding consideration would appear to "bubble up" more than trickle down, and multilateral negotiations involving all or several nation-states would be an appropriate means of problem solving. Moreover, the shift in the general approach to European policy making from harmonization to mutual recognition means that there would be less need for close coordination and control from the center. So long as the constituent units act as they are expected to act (comparable to the practice of "full faith and credit" in the United States), the center would have less need to impose Community rules and standards from above.

The European Polity

In a European community requiring unanimity among the members on almost all issues, all countries could expect to be heard and to have a substantial influence over policies. They could therefore also afford to bargain very hard for their national interests, with only good will and the rather intangible commodity "political influence" as the possible costs. Such a political phase of European integration occurred from the late 1950s through the early 1970s, which was a period of largely sustained affluence. Affluence meant that countries could extract substantial "side-payments" if they conceded on a point that other members of the Community (and perhaps most of all the Commission itself) wanted to have approved. After the adoption of the Single European Act in 1986, however, the advent of qualified majority voting in most Council decisions initiated a different political dynamic that may enable the Community to alleviate some of the decision-making problems apparent on the national level of decision making in some of the larger member countries. This dynamic appears similar to the politics of smaller European democracies that seek to accommodate a wide range of interests within potentially fragile political systems; Heisler and Kvavik referred to this pattern as "the European polity."[16]

The fundamental dynamic of the European polity is that the members must adopt more constrained strategies to remain active and effective participants in the political process. In this model of a political system, continuing to play the game is just as important a component of politics as winning or losing any single decision. Nation-states within the EC almost certainly would never be excluded from participation in the same way that interest groups might be in a single nation, but they can be isolated and excluded from the informal stages of policy making. Participation in bargaining and coalition formation have become crucial now that unanimity is no longer required in Council decisions, and a number of possible winning coalitions exist concerning any policy under deliberation. In a policy-making setting such as this, nations may be willing to accommodate the interests of others to ensure both their continued access to the early and often determinative stages of negotiations and their right to be consulted throughout the policy-making process. Bargaining too implacably for national interest under majority rule ultimately may produce formal inclusion for a nation in less important decisions but exclusion when it counts the most. Unanimity is still required in some instances, especially in responding to amendments by the European Parliament to common positions adopted by the Council, but the changes in the rules are sufficient to produce some rethinking of the policy-making dynamics within Europe.

It could be argued that the events surrounding the European Council meeting in Milan in 1985 constituted a first step toward instituting a European polity type of system within the EC. During the summit, which addressed proposals for European political union, Britain isolated itself by resisting a decision to convene an intergovernmental conference to deliberate appropriate measures. Britain's isolation was especially pronounced because of close political cooperation between France and Germany in Community affairs.[17] In response, Prime Minister Thatcher begin to modify her more extreme stances and play a somewhat more positive and conciliatory role. Similarly, Greece has also modified some of its reservations about the completion of the internal market to minimize the risk of isolation. Such evidence is far from conclusive, but it does point to the potential for an evolutionary new political dynamic within the Community.

In particular, if the European polity model is appropriate for the EC, it would feed back into at least one of the institutional decision-making processes discussed above by making coalition formation within the Community appear a great deal more like coalition politics in a nation-state. As Heisler and Kvavik argue, a central dynamic component of the European polity model is that political actors have more to gain by being coopted into the encompassing system than by going it alone.[18] This utilitarian balance is almost always in favor of participation in the decision-making process by interest groups within nations, and the same would be true for national actors within the EC if membership is perceived to create benefits greater than the costs imposed. Thus, participation in the EC can be analyzed in terms of the costs and benefits of national involvement, with an increasing number of decision-making situations within the Community becoming positive-sum games. Likewise, some of the pressures in favor of economic and monetary union have come from widely publicized reports of projected large-scale economic benefits arising from full integration.[19] The country that has questioned this positive balance most often is Britain, but events since the Milan summit and the Conservatives' loss in the European election of 1989 have tended to make British opposition less vigorous. Finally, another component of the dynamic of the European polity model is that actors, once they are involved in joint decision making, must bear some responsibility for the actions taken by the political unit. In other words, participation is traded for complicity in decisions. This complicity means that national governments, to be credible, will have few opportunities of returning home and blaming Brussels. They are now a part of Brussels even more than perhaps in the past.

The European polity model appears to some extent contrary to the bureaucratic politics model described below. In particular, the European polity model depends more on the individual nation-states deciding that the benefits of participation in the system are greater than the costs of membership. This requires them to make overt choices about continued involvement in, and acceptance of, policy decisions made within the EC. While the bureaucratic politics style of governing, and the regulatory policies associated with it, seek to disguise decisions and obfuscate the values involved in choices, the European politics model is a more political model that emphasizes understanding on the part of policy makers and their necessity to make a choice about participation and acquiescence. It may be that policy making in the EC oscillates between large-scale politics and small-scale increments of regulation, and that no single model is able to capture the totality of motives and processes involved in building Europe.

Bureaucratic Politics

A third, and very promising, approach to understanding policy-making dynamics within the institutions of the European Community would be bureaucratic politics. This approach is closely linked with many ideas such as "picket fence federalism" mentioned above, but it considers the linkages existing within a policy area from the perspective of the bureaucratic organizations involved rather than from the perspective of the national or subnational governments.[20] According to the politics of bureaucracy approach, the component units of a government administrative apparatus are assumed to be quasi-autonomous actors pursuing their own goals through the policy-making process. Many or most of those goals may be held in common with other organizations in government, but some are confined to each particular organization. All, or virtually all, of the organizations will assume that they are indeed serving the public interest by promoting their more individualized goals. Further, some organizations goals are *purposive,* being concerned with achieving policy goals (including in this case greater integration within the EC), while other goals may be *reflexive,* having to do primarily with enhancing the power and prestige (or at a minimum survival) of the organization itself.[21] In the case of reflexive goals, it may be difficult to distinguish the individual goals of key members from the collective goals of their organizations.

Bureaucratic politics may be occurring within the European Community on two levels at once. The first is on the level of the major institutions: the Council, the Commission, and the European Parliament taken as a whole. The goals pursued by some of these institutions may be attainable only if certain changes occur in the overall structure of the European Community. If the European Parliament is to achieve greater power, for instance, it may be successful only if the EC itself obtains greater power vis-à-vis the national governments. Similarly, the Commission may perceive the Council as its natural rival for power and authority within the Community in the sense that both are playing a "zero-sum" bureaucratic game in a competitive quest for greater or lesser European integration. In short, if the bureaucratic politics model is to be applied to interorganizational interactions and change, then the analyst must be clear when purposive and reflexive goals are being pursued (if the two types can be separated) and what the principal actors are attempting to gain through their interactions with other institutions.

The president of the Commission has also become a central player in EC decision making and the process of institutional change. The president's potential role as a political catalyst has become highly visible during Delors's tenure in office, but previous presidents also played major roles in defining the nature and speed of progress toward European solutions to policy problems.[22] From the perspective of bureaucratic politics, the question arises about whether the institutional goals of the presidency are compatible with specific policy goals. By attempting to focus attention on himself, the power of the Commission, and very broad goals of supranationalism, the president may be able to minimize potential national opposition to specific policy initiatives within the Council. Likewise, focusing on the presidency may help reduce fragmentation within the Commission itself. Delors appears to have accepted this role at times to the exclusion of other members of the Commission. For example, he has issued some Commission papers virtually without prior consultation with other commissioners, and he has made some of the most important economic policy issues his personal concern rather than that of the commissioner nominally in charge of economic affairs.

The president of the Commission is far from the only actor in the game of bureaucratic politics. Another principal aspect of the game involves coalition formation over specific issues and agendas. At this level, we move into the second level of bureaucratic politics in the EC: the politics of functional policy areas. In organizational terms, each policy area is populated with its allotment of organizations—including DGs and their commissioners, committees in the European Parliament, and representatives of affected interests. As we discussed in chapter 28, the formation of coalitions is crucial for determining the final shape of European policies. Given the decentralized structure of policy making in Europe, with multiple actors involved at the European stage and even more involved at the national level, it should not be surprising if policies were the product of loosely organized and flexible policy communities. Once a coalition is formed within a particular policy area, another coalition must be constructed across the institutions of the Community as well as with the relevant actors in national governments.

Several important features of the fragmentation of policy making and politics in Community affairs stand out. First, coalition formation and bargaining occur at several points throughout the policy process. This process involves interest groups and functional ministries on the national level of politics, European-wide interest groups, and relevant directorates-general in Brussels. Extensive discussions occur within the Commission itself concerning, first, the allocation of a policy among relevant commissioners and DGs and, second, policy coordination. Often, consultations are required with the advisory committees organized by the Commission for various policy areas as well. Then, at both the national and supranational levels, negotiations necessarily involve functional government organizations (such as ministries) and other government institutions (such as the Commission). Moreover, discussions can take place between the national government and the EC at either the functional and/or general political level. Thus, EC policy making is highly interactive, with preliminary decisions, bargaining over policy ideas, and so forth, constantly flowing throughout the system. Such a fragmented arrangement for policy making provides multiple points of access and may make coherent policy making difficult.

Whether the European or the national bureaucracy proves to be the dominant actor, the policy-making process manifests characteristics of decentralization and outcomes beneficial to interest groups typical of bureaucratic politics. Institutionally, the actors involved will strive to preserve their own powers, perhaps even in the face of a reduction in the capacity of the resulting arrangements to make "good" policy for the Community as a whole.

The fragmentation of policy making may be further increased through the increased powers of the European Parliament, which are scheduled to expand still further under the Treaty on European Union. First, the addition of the second reading provisions and "cooperation" provisions discussed in chapter 27 have already transformed the Parliament into an actor that must be reckoned with in almost all policy decisions. If nothing else, a parliamentary majority is theoretically able to form blocking coalitions with other actors such as single nation-states in cases when unanimity is required to override parliamentary wishes. This makes decision making more difficult while simultaneously providing additional incentives for a national actor to pursue action through bureaucratic channels (perhaps at home) rather than through more overtly politicized Community institutions. Of course, this option is not available for all issues but it may be for many; and a seemingly slower accretion of decisions may prove faster for a member country in the long run than attempting more dramatic action through the Council.

The Council retains, after consultation with Parliament, the final powers of decision within the Community, but the Commission has an increasing number of weapons at its disposal and apparently increasing influence. This is in part a function of the sheer volume of decisions that must be processed, especially in preparation for the completion of a regional market and progress thereafter toward economic, monetary, and political union. The Council is a well-articulated structure, and with the assistance of its working groups it can monitor the activities of the Commission. But the Council still cannot compete with the expertise available to the Commission and its DGs. Moreover, the Commission sets the agenda for decisions, albeit after extensive discussion with the relevant national and European actors. The linkages between the DGs and various components of national governments tend to be functionally specific, so that professional and technical criteria often guide decisions more than national concerns that may arise in the Council. Finally, the Commission can claim the moral high ground of being the defenders of Europe and standing above national concerns.

The emphasis on bureaucratic politics and policy making in the Community also has important implications for the character of future European policies. Decision making in the Commission is a crucially important element of policy making in the EC, and its increasing importance makes the transition to a single market that much easier. In essence, a shift has occurred from the Council's earlier preoccupation with large-scale issues such as budgetary disputes to greater attention to regulatory directives and indirect intervention by the Community in national markets. Commission regulations over competition policy as well as recent court cases involving a variety of topics have supplanted the budget, at least for now, as the most visible actions emanating from Brussels. As previously noted, regulatory policy making has the advantage of obscuring who wins and who loses in the policies; the outcomes are uncertain and widely variable within individual countries. Issues of revenue collection and spending, however, make redistributive issues readily apparent to national participants. Therefore, reliance on bureaucratic decision making and regulative rule making should, everything else being equal, make the transition to economic (though not necessarily monetary and political) union less divisive.

Although less divisive, bureaucratic rule making may not necessarily produce the "best" objective policy decisions for Europe or the Europeans. If the preceding description of fragmented policy making is accurate, policy making in the EC is beginning to bear a substantial resemblance to policy making in the American government. The traditional characterization of "iron triangles" (three-way coalitions embracing a Congressional committee, an executive agency, and an affected interest group) in American politics may have been replaced by "big sloppy hexagons" and a wider range of interests participating in decisions, but the tendency to divide and subdivide policy domains persists.[23] In the European context, this fragmentation is heightened by an ongoing shift from harmonization to mutual recognition of policies and standards as the measure of successful integration. No longer will a common standard necessarily prevail if all member countries can acknowledge one another's laws and standards. In addition, qualified majority voting in the Council gives member countries less incentive to package decisions together to produce agreement. As a result, an important control over policy decisions may well be undermined. Finally, policy making is further fragmented among policy communities within both the EC itself and in the national policy-making systems. As a result, policy making may have become somewhat easier but relatively ineffective in producing coherence and uniformity. The political question that immediately arises involves appropriate trade-offs between the value of making decisions that are simply "European" versus the value of making the best possible decisions in the name of Europe.

Fritz Scharpf has characterized the problem of coherence in decision making in Europe in terms of a "joint decision trap."[24] His argument is that policy making in the Federal Republic of Germany and other federal systems requires the need to obtain agreement between at least two levels of government and therefore tends to produce suboptimal decisions. This problem is exacerbated in the context of European policy making when unanimity is required among the constituent units before a decision can be reached. Scharpf argues further that this pattern of joint decision making enables the constituent units to extract resources from the center, resulting in a high level of cost relative to output in the system as a whole and incoherent outputs, since policies are adopted to satisfy particular constituent units. Partially offsetting such dangers in the European Community are several crucial features of central policy making, including the capacity of the Commission and its component units to structure the decision-making agenda and the move to qualified majority voting in the Council. Scharpf's analytic perspective, however, does raise interesting and important questions about the institutional dynamics of European policy making.

Finally, if we return to the "games" metaphor we used earlier, we can see a number of games nested within the overall process of decision making. National games are played at the highest level of Community politics by member countries seeking to gain as much as possible, in both financial and policy terms, and European institutions attempting to press their common agendas against those of the individual nation-states. Games are simultaneously played within each of the European institutions, with functional differentiation encouraging contests over the allocation of money and policy-making attention. Fragmentation may result in policy patterns that are not well coordinated unless the Commission president or the Commission as a whole can intervene. After decisions are made at the European Community level, political games continue in the form of interactions among EC institutions, member states, and interest groups as various players develop strategies for policy implementation. In short, it makes sense to think of policy making within Europe as highly differentiated and functionally specific. The great decisions about Europe may be made at the level of heads of government and foreign ministers, but much of what happens after a European summit concludes depends upon less glamorous bureaucratic interaction and bargaining.

Conclusion

Two observations summarize our analysis of the European Community. The first is that institutions matter. The formal institutions established by the Treaty of Rome and other basic agreements, and the rules governing the relationships of those institutions, have established the parameters of Community action. The complexity built into institutional relationships has been increased by the structural elaboration that they all have undergone in response to the pressure of increased workloads and the increased pace of movement toward a single market. These institutions may also help define pending movement toward economic and political union that may ultimately result in federalism. More than theoretical concepts such as functionalism or neofunctionalism, institutional relationships within the EC have defined the pace of integration and the character of the emerging European political and economic system. It is especially important to understand that the institutions are not static structures that simply process external policy demands but, instead, constitute a dynamic factor of change in their own right.

Yet European Community institutions are not the only things that matter. The Council, Commission, and European Parliament only establish the parameters within which individuals and groups function. Changes in the institutional rules of the game, such as the transition from unanimity to qualified majority voting in most Council decisions, will matter to the extent that the actors permit them to matter. If preexisting patterns of decision making persist, as was the case with the Luxembourg compromise of 1966, then formal changes in rule making will make little difference. In particular, there is no institutional basis for predicting the influence of individual leaders in moving the process of integration forward or retarding it. The use of qualified majority voting appears to have had the desired effect, and perhaps an even greater impact than was anticipated. Furthermore, the complex patterns of consultation and bureaucratic involvement in policy making that have been created could not have been predicted adequately from formal institutional patterns. Institutions do matter, but individual policy makers and informal understandings among the inhabitants of the institutions matter as well.

The dynamic interplay among multiple institutional, individual, and group actors will continue to characterize the emerging European Union. Especially in a more fully integrated and expanded Community, politics will remain a multiplayer game with uncertain outcomes.

Notes

1. For an analytical overview of functionalism, neofunctionalism, and other theoretical perspectives on integration, see Charles Pentland, *International Theory and Economic Integration* (New York: Free Press, 1972).

2. Paul Taylor, "The New Dynamics of EC Integration in the 1980s," in *The European Community and the Challenge of the Future,* ed. Juliet Lodge (London: Pinter, 1989), and Richard Corbett, "The Intergovernmental Conference and the Single Europe Act," in *The Dynamics of European Union,* ed. Roy Price (London: Croom Helm, 1987).

3. James G. March and Johan P. Olsen, *Rediscovering Institutions: The Organizational Basis of Politics* (New York: Free Press, 1989).

4. George Tsebelis, *Nested Games: Rational Choice in Comparative Politics* (Berkeley: University of California Press, 1990).

5. Other games may also be played simultaneously. The member countries themselves are not homogeneous actors, and subnational components both public and private may be using the EC as an arena to advance their own purposes. Firms, for instance, may believe that greater European control of environmental policy would mean a less restrictive regulatory environment than national standards. Likewise, interest groups that have been relatively unsuccessful at home may find the European arena more congenial promoting their policy objectives.

6. John Fitzmaurice, "European Community Decisionmaking: The National Dimension," in *Institutions and Policies of the European Community,* ed. J. Lodge (London: Pinter, 1983). Some scholars argue that the integration process has actually strengthened the nation-states. See Stanley Hoffman, "Reflections on the National State in Western Europe Today," *Journal of Common Market Studies* 21 (1982): 21–37.

7. Michael Keating, "Does Regional Government Work? The Experience of Italy, France and Spain," *Governance* 1 (1988): 184–204.

8. Christopher Hood and Gunnar Folke Schuppert, *Delivering Public Services in Western Europe* (London: Weidenfeld and Nicolson, 1987).

9. C. de Croisset, *Denationalisations* (Paris: Economica, 1986); and Cento Veljanovski, *Selling the State* (London: Weidenfeld and Nicolson, 1987).

10. R. Kent Weaver, "The Politics of Blame Avoidance," *Journal of Public Policy* 6 (1986): 371–98.

11. See Michael Burgess, *Federalism and European Union* (London: Routledge, 1989).

12. Robert E. Riggs and I. Jostein Mykletun, *Beyond Functionalism* (Oslo: Universitetsforlaget, 1979).

13. Select Committee on the European Committees, House of Lords, *Economic and Monetary Union and Political Union. Volume I: Report*

(London: HMSO, 1990), 14. The Select Committee's report notes that subsidiarity "has frequently been used in 'federal' Member States, notably with reference to the relationship between the Länder and the federal government in Germany." Its first application in an EC document occurred in the preamble to the European Parliament's Draft Treaty Establishing the European Union in 1984, which states that the parties were "Intending to entrust common institutions, in accordance with the principle of subsidiarity, only those powers required to complete successfully the tasks they may carry out more satisfactorily than the States acting independently." Ibid.

14. Article B, *Treaty on European Union*, 8.

15. See Deil S. Wright, *Understanding Intergovernmental Relations*, 3d ed. (Pacific Grove, Calif.: Brooks/Cole, 1988). "Picket fence federalism" refers to the tendency of interactions to develop among experts and administrators along functional lines (e.g., health, education, etc.) rather than between political actors such as presidents and state governors.

16. Martin O. Heisler with Robert B. Kvavik, "Patterns of European Politics: The 'European Polity' Model," in *Politics in Europe: Structures and Processes in Some Postindustrial Democracies* (New York: David McKay, 1974).

17. Haig Simonian, *The Privileged Partnership: Franco-German Relations in the European Community, 1969–1984* (Oxford: Clarendon Press, 1985).

18. Heisler with Kvavik, *Politics in Europe*.

19. Paolo Cechini, et al., *The European Challenge 1992: The Benefits of a Single Market* (Aldershot: Wildwood House for the European Commission, 1988).

20. The bureaucratic politics approach has been used to analyze both international and domestic politics. Important examples include Graham Allison, *The Essence of Decision* (Boston: Little, Brown, 1971) and Anthony Downs, *Inside Bureaucracy* (Boston: Little, Brown, 1967).

21. Lawrence B. Mohr, "The Concept of Organizational Goal," *American Political Science Review* 67 (1973): 470–81.

22. Guy de Bassompierre, *Changing the Guard in Brussels: An Insider's View of the EC Presidency* (New York: Praeger, 1988).

23. Charles O. Jones, *The United States Congress* (Homewood, Ill.: Dorsey, 1982).

24. Fritz W. Scharpf, "The Joint Decision Trap: Lessons from German Federalism and European Integration," *Public Administration* 66 (1988): 239–78.

For Further Reading

DALTROP, ANNE. *Politics and the European Community.* 2d ed. New York: Longman, 1986.

BURGESS, MICHAEL. *Federalism and European Union.* London: Routledge, 1989.

CECHINI, PAOLO, ET AL. *The European Challenge 1992: The Benefits of a Single Market.* Aldershot: Wildwood House for the European Commission, 1988.

EL-AGRAA, A.M., ed. *The Economics of the European Community.* 2d ed. Oxford: Philip Alan, 1985.

HAAS, ERNST B. *Beyond the Nation State: Functionalism and International Organization.* Stanford, Calif.: Stanford University Press, 1964.

HAAS, ERNST B. *The Uniting of Europe: Political, Social, and Economic Forces, 1950–1957.* Stanford, Calif.: Stanford University Press, 1958.

IFESTOS, P. *European Political Cooperation: Towards a Framework of Supranational Diplomacy.* Aldershot: Avebury, 1987.

KERR, ANTHONY J.C. *The Common Market and How it Works.* 3d ed. Oxford: Pergamon Press, 1986.

LODGE, JULIET, ed. *The European Community and the Challenge of the Future.* London: Pinter, 1989.

MORGAN, R., AND BRAY, C. *Partners and Rivals: Britain, France and Germany.* Aldershot: Gower.

NUGENT, NEILL. *The Government and Politics of the European Community.* Durham, N.C.: Duke University Press, 1989.

PENTLAND, CHARLES. *International Theory and European Integration.* New York: Free Press, 1973.

PRIDHAM, GEOFFREY, AND PRIDHAM, PIPPA. *Towards Transnational Parties in the European Community.* London: Policy Studies Institute, 1979.

SBRAGIA, ALBERTA M., ed. *Euro-Politics: Institutions in the 'New' European Community.* Washington, D.C.: Brookings Institution, 1992.

SEIDENTOPF, HEINRICH, AND ZILLER, JACQUES. *Making European Policies Work: The Implementation of Community Legislation in the Member States.* London: Sage, 1987.

SELECT COMMITTEE ON THE EUROPEAN COMMUNITIES (HOUSE OF LORDS). *A Community Social Charter. With Evidence.* London, 1989.

————. *The Delors Committee Report. With Evidence.* London, 1989.

————. *Economic and Monetary Union and Political Union,* Volume 1—*Report,* Volume 2—*Evidence.* London, 1990.

————. *European Union. With Minutes of Evidence.* London, 1985.

————. *Political Union: Law-Making Powers and Procedures. With Evidence.* London, 1991.

SHACKLETON, MICHAEL. *The Budget of the European Community.* London: Pinter, 1990.

SIMONIAN, HAIG. *The Privileged Partnership: Franco-German Relations in the European Community, 1969–1984.* Oxford: Clarendon Press, 1985.

SPRINGER, BEVERLY. *The Social Dimension of 1992: Europe Faces a New EC.* New York: Praeger, 1992.

URWIN, DEREK W. *The Community of Europe: A History of European Integration since 1945.* New York: Longman, 1991.

WALLACE, HELEN; WALLACE, WILLIAM; AND WEBB, CAROLE, eds. *Policy-Making in the European Community.* 2d ed. Chichester: Wiley, 1983.

Appendix

NATIONAL ELECTION OUTCOMES: PERCENTAGE OF POPULAR SUPPORT

FRANCE, 1962–88 (NATIONAL ASSEMBLY, FIRST BALLOT)

Year	PCF	Ecologists/ Greens	PS	UDF, other centrists	RPR	FN	Other
1962	21.9		12.4	21.6	33.7	–	10.3
1967	22.5		18.9	22.9	33.0	–	2.8
1968	20.0		16.5	20.8	38.0	–	4.6
1973	21.4		19.1	29.4	26.0	–	5.8
1978	20.6	2.0	22.8	26.1	22.8	0.3	9.7
1981	16.1	1.1	36.6	23.1	21.2	0.2	4.2
1986	9.7	1.2	31.3	18.8	26.8	9.8	4.5
1988	11.2	0.4	36.6	22.5	19.1	9.8	2.2
1993	9.2	7.6	20.3	24.1	20.4	12.4	6.0

NOTE: Abbreviations of party names: PCF = Community party of France; PS = Socialist party; UDF = Union for French Democracy (moderate liberals); RPR = Rally for the Republic (Gaullists; moderate right); FN = National Front (radical right).

FEDERAL REPUBLIC OF GERMANY, 1949–90

Year	Participation	KPD/PDS	Greens	SPD	FDP	CDU/CSU	Radical Right	Other
1949	78.5	5.7		29.2	11.9	31.0	1.8	20.3
1953	86.0	2.3		28.8	9.5	45.2	1.1	13.1

Year							
1957	87.8			31.8	7.7	50.2	1.0	10.3
1961	87.7			36.2	12.8	45.3	0.8	5.7
1965	86.8			39.3	9.5	47.6	2.0	3.6
1969	86.7	0.6		42.7	5.8	46.1	4.3	0.5
1972	91.1	0.3		45.8	8.4	44.9	0.6	0.1
1976	90.7	0.4		42.6	7.9	48.6	0.3	0.2
1980	88.6	0.2	1.5	42.9	10.6	44.5	0.2	0.1
1983	89.1		5.6	38.2	7.0	48.8		0.5
1987	84.3		8.4	37.0	9.1	44.3		1.4
1990	77.8	2.4	5.1	33.5	11.0	43.8	2.1	0.2

ELECTION RESULTS BY TERRITORY (DECEMBER 1990)

Western Germany	0.3	4.7	35.9	10.6	44.1	2.3	1.0
Eastern Germany	9.9	5.9	23.6	13.4	43.4	1.3	

NOTE: Abbreviations of party names: KPD/PDS: Communist party of Germany/Party of Democratic Socialism; SPD = Social Democratic party of Germany; FDP = Free Democratic party (moderate liberals); CDU/CSU = Christian Democratic Union/Christian Social Union; the radical right includes the NPD (National Democratic party of Germany) and the Republikaner (Republicans).

Continued ....

TABLE A.1 — *Continued*

ITALY, 1949–1992

Year	PCI/PDS	PSI/PSU	PSDI	Green List	PLI	PRI	DC	Northern League	MSI-DN	Other
1948	31.0				3.8	2.5	48.5		2.0	12.8
1953	28.6	12.7	4.5		3.0	1.6	41.2		5.8	9.9
1958	22.7	14.2	4.6		3.5	1.4	43.0		4.7	5.9
1963	25.3	13.8	6.1		7.0	1.4	38.3		5.1	3.0
1968	26.9	14.5			5.8	2.0	39.1		4.5	7.2
1972	27.2	9.6	6.1		3.9	2.9	38.8		8.7	2.8
1976	34.4	9.6	3.4		1.3	3.1	38.7		6.1	3.6
1979	30.4	9.8	3.8		1.9	3.0	38.3		5.9	6.9
1983	29.9	11.1	4.1		2.9	5.1	32.9		6.8	5.4
1987	26.6	14.3	3.0	2.5	2.1	3.7	34.3	0.5	5.9	7.1
1992	16.1	3.6	2.7	2.8	2.8	4.4	29.7	8.7	5.4	6.3

NOTE: Abbreviations of party names: PCI = Communist party of Italy; PDS = Party of Democratic Socialism; PSI = Socialist party of Italy; PSU = Unified Socialist party; PSDI = Social Democratic party of Italy; PLI = Liberal party of Italy; PRI = Republican party of Italy; DC = Christian Democratic party; MSI–DN = Italian Social Movement–National Right (neofascist).

SWEDEN, 1944–91

Year	Type[a]	VP	SAP	MP	FP	C	M	KDS	NYD
1944	R	10.3	46.7		12.9	13.6	15.9		

Year	Type[a]	VP	SAP	FP	C	M	KDS	MP	NYD
1946	C	11.2	44.4	14.9	15.6	13.6			
1948	R	6.3	46.2	22.8	12.4	12.3			
1950	C	4.9	48.6	21.7	12.3	12.3			
1952	R	4.3	46.1	24.4	10.7	14.4			
1954	C	4.8	47.4	21.7	10.3	15.7			
1956	R	5.0	44.6	23.8	9.4	17.1			
1958	R	3.4	46.2	18.2	12.7	19.5			
1958	C	4.0	46.8	15.6	13.1	20.4			
1960	R	4.5	47.8	17.5	13.6	16.5			
1962	C	3.8	50.5	17.1	13.1	15.5			
1964	R	5.2	47.3	17.0	13.2	13.7			
1966	C	6.4	42.2	16.7	13.7	14.7			
1968	R	3.0	50.1	14.3	15.7	12.9			
1970	R	4.8	45.3	16.2	19.9	11.5			
1973	R	5.3	43.6	9.4	25.1	14.3			
1976	R	4.8	42.7	11.1	24.1	15.6	1.4		
1979	R	5.6	43.2	10.6	18.1	20.3	1.4		
1982	R	5.6	45.6	5.9	15.5	23.6	1.9		
1985	R	5.4	44.7	14.2	12.4	21.3			
1988	R	5.7	43.9	12.0	11.9	17.9	2.9	5.5	
1991	R	4.5	37.6	9.2	8.4	21.9	7.0	3.4	6.7

NOTE: Abbreviations of party names: VP = Left party (Communists); MP = Greens; SAP = Social Democratic party; FP = People's party (Liberals); C = Center; M = Moderates (Conservatives); KDS = Christian Democrats; NYD = New Democracy.
a. Type of election: R = Riksdag (parliamentary) elections; C = communal (county and municipal) elections.

Continued ....

UNITED KINGDOM, 1945–92

	Participation	Labour	Liberals/SDP Liberal Democrats	Conservatives/SDP	Other
1945		61.4	1.9	31.1	5.6
1950	83.6	46.1	9.1	43.4	1.4
1951	81.9	48.8	2.6	48.0	0.6
1959	78.7	43.8	5.9	49.4	0.9
1964	77.1	44.1	11.2	43.4	1.1
1966	75.8	42.9	7.5	41.9	1.7
1970	72.0	42.9	7.5	46.4	3.2
1974					
February	78.2	37.2	19.3	38.1	6.6
October	72.8	39.3	18.3	35.8	5.5
1979	76.0	36.9	13.8	43.9	5.5
1983	71.8	27.6	25.4	42.4	4.6
1987	73.2	30.8	22.6	42.2	4.4
1992	77.7	34.4	17.9	41.9	5.7

NOTE: Abbreviations of party names: SDP = Social Democratic party. The Liberals and a majority of Social Democrats merged in 1989 to form the Social Liberal party.

TABLE A.2
DISTRIBUTION OF SEATS IN NATIONAL LEGISLATURES

FRANCE, 1962– (NATIONAL ASSEMBLY)

Year	PCF	PS	Radicals	MRP	Dem-Cen/ UDF	RPR	Cons	FN	Other	Total
1962	41	64	41	32	18	230	32			465
1967	72	118		7	52	191	7			470
1968	33	57		8	90	282	8			470
1973	73	89		15	75	178	15		11	473
1978	86	102		10	124	142	10		10	474
1981	43	268		10	59	80	10		14	474
1986	32	198		4	128	146	4	35	13	556
1988	24	260		8	130	123	8	1	9	555
1993	23	70			213	247	24			577

FEDERAL REPUBLIC OF GERMANY, 1949– (BUNDESTAG)

Year	KPD/PDS	Greens	SPD	FDP	CDU/CSU	Other	Total
1949	15		131	52	139	65	402
1953			151	48	244	44	487
1957			169	41	270	17	497
1961			190	67	247		499
1965			202	49	245		496
1969			224	30	242		496

	KPD/PDS	Greens	SPD	FDP	CDU/CSU	Other	Total
1972			230	41	225		496
1976			214	39	243		496
1980			218	53	226		497
1983		27	193	34	244		498
1987		42	186	46	223		497
1990	17	8	239	79	319		662

ITALY, 1949–   (CHAMBER OF DEPUTIES)

	PCI/PDS	PSI/PSU	PSDI	Green List	PLI	PRI	DC	Northern League	MSI-DN	Other	Total
1948	183		33		19	9	305		6	19	574
1953	143	75	19		13	5	263		29	43	590
1958	140	84	22		17	6	273		24	30	596
1963	166	87	32		40	6	260		27	12	630
1968	177	91			31	9	266		24	32	630
1972	179	61	29		21	14	267		56	3	630
1976	228	57	15		5	14	262		35	14	630
1979	201	62	20		9	16	262		30	30	630
1983	198	73	23		16	29	225		42	24	630
1987	177	94	17	13	11	21	234	1	35	27	630
1992	107	92	16	16	17	27	206	55	34	60	630

SWEDEN, 1944– (RIKSDAG)[a]

	VP	MP	SAP	FP	C	M	KDS	NYD	Other	Total
1944	15		115	26	35	39				230
1946	8		112	57	30	23				230
1952	5		110	58	26	31				230
1956	6		106	58	19	42				231
1958	5		111	38	32	45				231
1960	5		114	40	34	39				232
1964	8		113	42	33	32			5	233
1968	3		125	32	37	29			7	233
1970	17		163	58	71	41				350
1973	19		156	34	90	51				350
1976	17		152	39	86	55				349
1979	20		154	38	64	73				349
1982	20		166	21	56	86				349
1985	19		159	51	44[b]	76				349
1988	21	20	156	44	42	66				349
1991	16		138	33	31	80	26	25		349

a. Through 1968, the distribution of seats is shown for the lower house (Second Chamber). Elections from 1970 onward are to the unicameral Riksdag.

b. Includes one seat for the KDS.

UNITED KINGDOM, 1945– (HOUSE OF COMMONS)

	Labour	Liberals/SDP Liberal Democrats	Conservatives	Other	Total
1945	393	12	199	39	640
1950	315	9	298	3	625
1951	295	6	321	3	625
1955	277	6	344	3	630
1959	258	6	365	1	630
1964	317	9	304	0	630
1970	288	6	330	4	630
1974					
February	301	14	297	23	635
October	319	13	277	16	635
1979	269	11	339	16	635
1983	209	23	397	45	633
1987	229	22	375	24	650
1992	271	20	336	24	651

TABLE A.3

POSTWAR EXECUTIVE LEADERSHIP

FRANCE, 1958–

Years	Governing party, coalition	President/Premier
President		
1958–1969	Gaullist	De Gaulle
1969–1974	Gaullist	Pompidou
1974–1981	Independent Republican	Giscard d'Estaing
1981–	Socialist	Mitterrand
Parliament		
1958–1981	RPR + UDF + other centrists	Debré, Pompidou, Couve de Murville, Chabas-Delmas, Messmer, Chirac, Barre
1981–1984	PS-PCF	Mauroy
1984–1986	PS	Fabius
1986–1988	RPR + UDF	Chirac
1988–1993	PS	Rocard, Cresson, Bérégovoy
1993–	RPR + UDF	Edouard Balladur

FEDERAL REPUBLIC OF GERMANY, 1949–

Years	Governing coalition	Federal chancellor
1949–1966	CDU/CSU + FDP + smaller nonsocialist parties	Adenauer, Erhard
1966–1969	CDU/CSU + SPD	Kiesinger
1969–1982	SPD + FDP	Brandt, Schmidt
1982–	CDU/CSU + FDP	Kohl

ITALY, 1948–

Years	Governing party, coalition	Prime minister
May 1948–Jan. 1950	DC + PSDI + PRI + PLI	DeGasperi
Jan. 1950–July 1951	DC + PSDI + PRI	DeGasperi
July 1951–July 1953	DC + PRI	DeGasperi
July 1953–Aug. 1953	DC	DeGasperi
Aug. 1953–Jan. 1954	DC	Pella
Jan. 1954–Feb. 1954	DC	Fanfani
Feb. 1954–July 1955	DC + PLI + PSDI	Scelba
July 1955–May 1957	DC + PSDI + PLI	Segni
May 1957–July 1958	DC	Zoli
July 1958–Feb. 1959	DC + PSI	Fanfani
Feb. 1959–Mar. 1960	DC	Segni
Mar. 1960–July 1960	DC	Tambroni
July 1960–Feb. 1962	DC	Fanfani
Feb. 1962–June 1963	DC + PSDI + PRI	Fanfani
June 1963–Dec. 1963	DC	Leone
Dec. 1963–June 1964	DC + PSI + PSDI + PRI	Moro
July 1964–Feb. 1966	DC + PSI + PSDI + PRI	Moro
Feb. 1966–June 1968	DC + PSI + PSDI + PRI	Moro
June 1968–Dec. 1968	DC	Leone
Dec. 1968–Aug. 1969	DC + PSI + PRI	Rumor
Aug. 1969–Feb. 1970	DC	Rumor
Mar. 1970–Aug. 1970	DC + PSDI + PSI + PRI	Rumor
Aug. 1970–Feb. 1972	DC + PSDI + PSI + PRI	Colombo
Feb. 1972–June 1972	DC	Andreotti
June 1972–June 1973	DC + PLI + PSDI	Andreotti
June 1973–Mar. 1974	DC + PSDI + PRI	Rumor
Mar. 1974–June 1974	DC + PSI + PSDI	Rumor
June 1974–Oct. 1974	DC + PSI + PSDI	Rumor
Nov. 1974–Jan. 1976	DC + PRI	Moro
Feb. 1976–July 1976	DC	Moro
July 1976–Mar. 1978	DC	Andreotti
Mar. 1978–Jan. 1979	DC	Andreotti
Jan. 1979–Mar. 1979	DC + PSDI + PRI	Andreotti
Aug. 1979–April 1980	DC + PSDI + PLI	Cossiga
April 1980–Sept. 1980	DC + PSI + PRI	Forlani
Oct. 1980–May 1981	DC + PSI + PSDI + PRI	Forlani
July 1981–Aug. 1982	PRI + DC + PSI + PSDI +PLI	Spadolini
Aug. 1982–Nov. 1982	PRI + DC + PSI + PSDI +PLI	Spadolini

ITALY, 1948–   *(Continued)*

Years	Governing coalition	Prime minister
Nov. 1982–Aug. 1983	DC + PSI + PSDI + PLI	Fanfani
Aug. 1983–Mar. 1987	PSI + DC + PRI + PSDI + PLI	Craxi
April 1987–June 1987	DC (minority government)	Fanfani
July 1987–Mar. 1988	DC + PSI + PSDI + PRI +PLI	Goria
April 1988–May 1989	DC + PSI + PSDI + PRI + PLI	DeMita
July 1989–Mar. 1991	DC + PSI + PSDI + PLI	Andreotti
April 1991–June 1992	DC + PSI + PSDI + PLI	Andreotti
July 1992–April 1993	PSI + DC + PSDI + PLI	Amato
April 1993–	Nonpartisan technocrats	Ciampi

SWEDEN, 1944–

Years	Governing party, coalition	Prime minister
1944–1951	SAP	Hansson, Erlander
1951–1957	SAP + C	Erlander
1957–1976	SAP	Erlander, Palme
1976–1978	C + FP + M	Fälldin
1978–1979	FP	Ullsten
1979–1981	C + FP + M	Fälldin
1981–1982	C + FP	Fälldin
1982–1991	SAP	Palme, Carlsson
1991–	M + C + FP + KDS	Bildt

UNITED KINGDOM, 1945–

Years	Governing party	Prime minister
1945–1951	Labour	Attlee
1951–1964	Conservatives	Churchill, Eden, Macmillan, Douglas-Home
1964–1970	Labour	Wilson
1970–1974	Conservatives	Heath
1974–1979	Labour	Wilson, Callaghan
1979–	Conservatives	Thatcher, Major

TABLE A.4

PER CAPITA GROSS DOMESTIC PRODUCT, 1960–88

(IN U.S. DOLLARS)

	France	Germany	Italy	Sweden	United Kingdom	United States
1960	5344	6038	4375	6483	6370	9983
1961	5578	6256	4732	6808	6507	10035
1962	4861	6422	5018	7044	6504	10418
1963	6103	6518	5299	7349	6739	10697
1964	6447	6927	5292	7832	7074	11135
1965	6676	7246	5315	8057	7174	11670
1966	7003	7340	5585	3124	7275	12186
1967	7292	7258	5991	8326	7438	12381
1968	7605	7714	6302	8586	7712	12801
1969	8128	8250	6663	8953	7778	13047
1970	8536	8664	6937	9279	8006	12923
1971	8848	8808	7005	9254	8078	13161
1972	9177	9095	7182	9451	8388	13645
1973	9626	9441	7690	9868	8981	14194
1974	9853	9462	8050	10161	8785	13936
1975	9745	9267	7775	10307	8727	13531
1976	10118	9861	8328	10255	8995	14174
1977	10411	10140	8600	10096	9227	14677
1978	10711	10472	8934	10410	9605	15315
1979	11019	10850	9518	10778	9893	15532
1980	11148	10993	9986	10910	9680	15310
1981	11200	11034	10061	11035	8567	15510
1982	11366	10903	10070	11175	9737	14968
1983	11280	11130	10130	11424	10092	15441
1984	11300	11501	10440	11884	10309	16464
1985	11376	11646	10584	12382	10679	16779
1986	11662	11958	10955	12398	11000	17251
1987	11831	12124	11310	12702	11495	17735
1988	12190	12604	11741	12991	11982	18339

SOURCE: Adapted from Robert Summers and Alan Heston, "The Penn World Table. An Expanded Set of International Comparisons, 1950–1988," *Quarterly Journal of Economics*, May 1991, 327–68.

TABLE A.5
GROWTH OF REAL GROSS NATIONAL PRODUCT/GROSS DOMESTIC PRODUCT (GNP/GDP), 1978–90
(PERCENTAGE CHANGES FROM PREVIOUS YEAR)

	1978	1979	1980	1981	1982	1983	1984	1985	1986	1987	1988	1989	1990
France	3.4	3.2	1.6	1.2	2.5	0.7	1.3	1.9	2.5	2.3	4.2	3.9	2.8
Germany	3.4	4.0	1.0	0.1	-1.1	1.9	3.1	1.8	2.2	1.5	3.7	3.8	4.5
Italy	3.7	6.0	4.2	1.0	0.3	1.1	3.0	2.6	2.5	3.0	4.1	3.0	2.0
Sweden	2.0	4.0	1.4	0.0	1.1	1.8	4.0	2.2	2.2	2.8	2.3	2.1	0.3
U.K.	3.5	2.8	-1.7	-1.0	1.5	3.5	2.1	3.6	3.8	4.6	4.2	1.9	0.6
U.S.	5.3	2.5	-0.2	1.9	-2.5	3.6	6.8	3.4	2.7	3.4	4.5	2.5	0.9

SOURCE: OECD, *Economic Outlook*, 49 (July 1991): 175.

TABLE A.6
CONSUMER PRICES, 1978–89 (PERCENTAGE CHANGES FROM PREVIOUS YEAR)

	1978	1979	1980	1981	1982	1983	1984	1985	1986	1987	1988	1989	Average 1979–89
France	9.5	11.3	15.1	13.0	11.4	9.4	7.4	6.1	2.1	3.4	2.8	3.2	7.3
Germany	3.2	5.0	6.0	6.8	5.0	3.5	2.7	2.7	-.3	0.1	2.0	2.9	3.1
Italy	11.7	15.2	23.9	18.5	17.0	15.9	11.4	9.3	6.0	5.1	5.6	6.3	11.7
Sweden	10.2	8.0	14.0	11.3	7.5	8.1	6.9	7.9	3.5	4.5	5.9	6.6	7.6
United Kingdom	8.4	13.7	19.6	12.9	8.9	4.9	4.7	6.7	3.3	4.3	5.2	8.3	7.8
United States	7.2	11.4	14.6	10.9	6.6	3.5	4.3	3.9	1.6	3.5	4.1	4.6	5.7
OECD average	8.4	11.2	15.4	11.3	8.3	6.0	5.6	5.5	3.2	4.0	5.1	5.6	6.9

SOURCE: OECD, *Economic Outlook. Historical Statistics, 1960–1989* (Paris, 1991): 87.

TABLE A.7

AVERAGE UNEMPLOYMENT RATES, 1960–89

	1960–67	*1968–73*	*1974–79*	*1980–89*	*1960–89*
France	1.5	n/a	4.5	9.0	n/a
Germany	0.8	0.8	3.5	6.8	–
Italy	4.9	5.7	6.6	9.9	7.1
Sweden	1.6	2.2	1.9	2.5	2.1
United Kingdom	1.5	2.4	4.2	9.5	4.9
United States	5.0	4.6	6.7	7.2	6.0
OECD average	3.1	3.4	5.1	7.4	5.0

SOURCE: OECD, *Economic Outlook. Historical Statistics 1960–1989* (Paris, 1991).

TABLE A.8
ANNUAL UNEMPLOYMENT RATES, 1972–90

	1970	1980	1981	1982	1983	1984	1985	1986	1987	1988	1989	1990	Average 1980–89
France	2.8	6.3	7.4	8.1	8.3	9.7	10.2	10.4	10.5	10.0	9.4	9.0	6.8
Germany	0.8	2.9	4.2	5.9	7.7	7.1	7.2	6.4	6.2	6.2	5.6	5.1	6.8
Italy	6.3	7.5	7.8	8.4	8.8	9.4	9.6	10.5	10.9	11.0	10.9	9.9	7.1
Sweden	2.7	2.0	2.5	3.2	3.5	3.1	2.8	2.7	1.9	1.6	1.4	1.5	2.5
United Kingdom	4.0	6.4	9.8	11.3	12.4	11.7	11.2	11.2	10.3	8.5	7.1	6.9	9.5
United States	5.5	7.0	7.5	9.5	9.5	7.4	7.1	6.9	6.1	5.4	5.2	5.4	7.2

SOURCE: OECD, *Economic Outlook July 1990* (Paris, 1990), 192, and OECD, *Economic Outlook. Historical Statistics 1960–1989* (Paris, 1991).

TABLE A.9

TOTAL GOVERNMENT EXPENDITURES

AS PERCENTAGE OF GDP, 1978–89

	1978	1979	1980	1981	1982	1983	1984	1985	1986	1987	1988	1989
France	44.6	45.0	46.1	48.7	50.4	51.4	52.0	52.2	51.4	51.1	50.4	49.7
Germany	47.8	47.6	48.3	49.2	49.4	48.3	48.0	47.5	46.9	47.0	46.6	45.1
Italy	46.1	45.5	41.7	45.8	47.4	48.6	49.3	50.8	50.9	50.5	50.8	51.7
Sweden	59.2	60.7	61.6	64.2	66.3	66.0	63.5	64.7	63.0	59.2	59.5	60.1
United Kindgom	43.1	42.5	44.7	47.5	46.9	46.7	47.2	46.1	45.1	43.0	41.1	40.9
United States	31.6	31.7	33.7	34.1	36.5	36.9	35.8	36.7	37.1	36.8	36.1	36.1

SOURCE: OECD, *Economic Outlook*, 49 (July 1991): 189.

TABLE A.10
CURRENT RECEIPTS OF GOVERNMENT
AS PERCENTAGE OF GDP, 1978–89

	1978	1979	1980	1981	1982	1983	1984	1985	1986	1987	1988	1989
France	41.1	42.7	44.5	45.1	45.9	46.6	47.5	47.6	46.9	47.4	46.8	46.5
Germany	44.7	44.4	44.7	44.8	45.4	45.1	45.3	45.6	44.9	44.4	43.8	44.6
Italy	36.0	35.7	33.0	34.1	35.9	37.7	37.4	38.0	39.0	39.2	39.6	41.1
Sweden	57.5	56.4	56.3	57.6	58.0	59.6	59.2	59.5	60.4	62.3	61.8	64.1
United Kingdom	37.5	38.0	39.9	42.1	42.8	42.1	42.1	42.2	41.2	40.6	40.2	39.7
United States	29.9	30.5	30.8	31.6	31.1	30.7	30.7	31.3	31.4	32.0	31.5	31.8

SOURCE: OECD, *Economic Outlook*, 49 (July 1991): 190.

TABLE A.11

INDUSTRIAL CONFLICT: PER CAPITA WORKING DAYS LOST
BASED ON TOTAL CIVILIAN EMPLOYMENT, 1960–89

	France	Germany	Italy	Sweden	United Kingdom	United States[a]
1960	.06	.00	.29	.00	.13	.29
1961	.14	.00	.49	.00	.13	.25
1962	.10	.02	1.14	.00	.23	.28
1963	.31	.07	.58	.01	.07	.24
1964	.13	.00	.67	.01	.09	.33
1965	.05	.00	.37	.00	.12	.33
1966	.13	.00	.78	.09	.09	.35
1967	.21	.02	.45	.00	.11	.58
1968	n/a	.00	.49	.00	.19	.65
1969	.11	.01	2.03	.03	.28	.55
1970	.09	.00	1.12	.04	.45	.94
1971	.21	.17	.79	.22	.56	.67
1972	1.00	.18	.00	1.06	.00	.37
1973	.19	.02	1.28	.02	.29	.36
1974	.16	.04	1.04	.01	.60	.61
1975	.19	.00	1.45	.00	.24	.41
1976	.24	.02	1.34	.01	.13	.48
1977	.17	.00	.83	.02	.41	.44
1978	.10	.17	.51	.01	.38	.43
1979	.17	.02	1.36	.01	1.19	.40
1980	.07	.00	.80	1.06	.47	.00
1981	.07	.00	.51	.05	.18	.00
1982	.10	.00	.90	.00	.22	.09
1983	.06	.00	.68	.01	.16	.17
1984	1.13	.06	.21	2.93	.01	.08
1985	.03	.00	1.28	.12	.26	.07
1986	.03	.00	1.88	.16	.05	.11
1987	.02	.00	1.54	.00	.14	.04
1988	.05	.00	n/a	.18	n/a	.04
1989	.04	.00	n/a	.09	n/a	.14

SOURCE: Calculated from International Labour Office, *Year Book of Labour Statistics 1970, 1980, 1988, 1989–90* (Geneva: ILO).

a. From 1980 onward, U.S. statistics include only strikes involving more than 1,000 workers.

TABLE A.12

INFANT MORTALITY RATE (PER 1,000 LIVE BIRTHS)

1960–88

Year	France	Germany	Italy	Sweden	United Kingdom	United States
1960	27.4	33.8	43.9	16.6	22.5	26.0
1965	21.9	23.9	36.0	13.3	19.0	24.7
1970	18.2	23.6	29.6	11.0	18.1	20.0
1975	13.8	19.8	21.2	8.6	15.7	16.1
1980	10.0	12.6	14.6	6.9	12.1	12.6
1988	7.7	8.3	9.5	5.8	8.8	9.9

SOURCE: United Nations, *United Nations Demographic Yearbook* (New York, 1978, 1982, 1984, 1990).

TABLE A.13

LIFE EXPECTANCY AT BIRTH, 1960–85

Year	France	Germany	Italy	Sweden	United Kingdom	United States
1960–65						
Male	67.6	67.2	67.4	71.6	67.9	66.7
Female	74.5	72.9	72.6	75.6	73.8	73.4
1970–75						
Male	68.6	67.6	69.2	72.1	69.0	67.5
Female	76.2	73.7	75.2	77.5	75.2	75.3
1980–85						
Male	70.5	70.4	71.2	73.4	70.7	70.6
Female	78.7	77.2	78.0	79.4	76.9	78.1

SOURCE: United Nations, *United Nations Demographic Yearbook* (New York, 1978, 1982, 1984, 1986).

TABLE A.14

PERCENTAGE OF AGE GROUPS ENROLLED IN EDUCATION,
1965 AND 1988

	Primary		*Secondary*		*Tertiary*	
	1965	*1988*	*1965*	*1988*	*1965*	*1988*
France	134	114	56	94	18	35
Germany	n/a	105	n/a	94	11	32
Italy	112	95	47	76	11	26
Sweden	95	101	62	90	13	31
United Kingdom	92	107	66	83	12	23
United States	100	100	n/a	98	40	60

SOURCE: World Bank, *World Development Report 1991. The Challenge of Development* (New York: Oxford University Press, 1991): 261.

TABLE A.15

RELIGIOUS ADHERENTS BY DENOMINATION
(MID-1980S)

	France	*West* Germany	*East* Germany	*Italy*	Sweden	*United* Kingdom
Catholic	76.4	43.8	5.8	83.2	1.4	13.3
Anglican	0.0	0.0	0.0	0.1	0.0	56.8
Protestant	2.0	46.7	43.0	0.4	67.6	15
Jewish	1.1	0.0	0.0	0.1	0.2	0.8
Muslim	3.0	3.7	0.0	0.1	0.1	1.4
Nonreligious	12.2	3.7	11.4	13.6	17.0	8.8
Other	1.9	1.1	0.0	0.0	2.0	8.2

SOURCE: David B. Barrett, ed., *World Christian Encyclopedia: A Comparative Study of Churches and Religions in the Modern World A.D. 1900–2000* (New York: Oxford University Press, 1982).

Indexes

Index of Names

NOTE: The abbreviations in parentheses—EC, E. Ger, Fr, Ger, It, Sc, Sw, UK, and U.S.—stand for European Community, East Germany, France, Germany, Italy, Scotland, Sweden, United Kingdom, and United States respectively.

Index of Subjects